WA 1252761 0

# The Global Transf' tions Reader

D0993780

# Visit the Global Transformations website for a whole range of globalization resources

The Global Transformations website has been specially designed to complement this Reader and the textbook, featuring a comprehensive range of resources and features for both lecturers and students. At the site, you will find:

- Articles on what globalization means and how to research it

- An executive summary of the key features of globalization

- A debate on realism vs cosmopolitanism

- A comprehensive set of globalization links to sites of related interest, including governments, regional bodies, research institutions and international organizations

- More information on the ground-breaking textbook, Global Transformations, and this accompanying Reader

**The complete globalization resource package!**
This is a completely free resource
for users of this book. Simply log on at:

## www.polity.co.uk/global

www.polity.co.uk/global

# The Global Transformations Reader

An Introduction to the Globalization Debate

Second edition

Edited by

David Held and Anthony McGrew

polity

Copyright © editorial matter and organization David Held and Anthony McGrew 2003

First edition published 2000
Reprinted 2000, 2001, 2002

This edition published 2003 by Polity Press in association with Blackwell Publishing Ltd

*Editorial office*:
Polity Press
65 Bridge Street
Cambridge CB2 1UR, UK

*Marketing and production*:
Blackwell Publishing Ltd
108 Cowley Road
Oxford OX4 1JF, UK

Distributed in the USA by
Blackwell Publishing Inc.
350 Main Street
Malden, MA 02148, USA

Learning Resources
Centre

12527610

All rights reserved. Except for the quotation of short passages for the purposes of criticism and review, no part of this publication may be reproduced, stored in a retrieval system, or transmitted, in any form or by any means, electronic, mechanical, photocopying, recording or otherwise, without the prior permission of the publisher.

A catalogue record for this book is available from the British Library.

**Library of Congress Cataloging-in-Publication Data**

The global transformations reader : an introduction to the globalization debate / edited by David Held and Anthony McGrew.—2nd ed.
    p. cm.
  Includes bibliographical references and index.
  ISBN 0-7456-3134-7 — ISBN 0-7456-3135-5
    1. Globalization.  2. International relations.  I. Held, David.  II. McGrew, Anthony G.
JZ1318 .G56 2003
303.48′2—dc21
                                                2002152351

Typeset in 10 on 12 pt Times Ten
by Graphicraft Limited, Hong Kong
Printed and bound in Great Britain by TJ International, Padstow, Cornwall

For further information on Polity, visit our website: www.polity.co.uk

# Contents

*Preface to the Second Edition*                                              ix
*Preface to the First Edition*                                                x
*Sources and Acknowledgements*                                              xi
*Acronyms*                                                                 xvi

The Great Globalization Debate: An Introduction                              1
*David Held and Anthony McGrew*

## Part I   Understanding Globalization

Introduction                                                                51

1   Globalization
    *George Modelski*                                                       55

2   The Globalizing of Modernity
    *Anthony Giddens*                                                       60

3   Rethinking Globalization
    *David Held and Anthony McGrew, David Goldblatt and*
    *Jonathan Perraton*                                                     67

4   Globalization: What's New? What's Not? (And So What?)
    *Robert O. Keohane and Joseph S. Nye Jr.*                               75

5   What is 'Global' about Globalization?
    *Jan Aart Scholte*                                                      84

6   The Problem of Globalisation Theory
    *Justin Rosenberg*                                                      92

7   Globalization – A Necessary Myth?
    *Paul Hirst and Grahame Thompson*                                       98

8   Clash of Globalizations
    *Stanley Hoffmann*                                                     106

9   Globalization and American Power
    *Joseph S. Nye Jr.*                                                    112

10  Globalization as Empire
    *Michael Hardt and Antonio Negri*                                      116

# Contents

## Part II  Political Power and Civil Society: A Reconfiguration?

Introduction                                                                121

11  The Declining Authority of States
    *Susan Strange*                                                         127

12  Has Globalization Ended the Rise and Rise of the Nation-State?
    *Michael Mann*                                                         135

13  Sovereignty in International Society
    *Robert O. Keohane*                                                    147

14  The Changing Structure of International Law: Sovereignty Transformed?
    *David Held*                                                           162

15  The Security State
    *Ian Clark*                                                            177

16  Governing the Global Economy Through Government Networks
    *Anne-Marie Slaughter*                                                 189

17  Power Shift
    *Jessica T. Mathews*                                                   204

18  Globalization and Modes of Regionalist Governance
    *Anthony Payne*                                                        213

19  Governance in a New Global Order
    *James N. Rosenau*                                                     223

## Part III  The Fate of National Culture in an Age of Global Communication

Introduction                                                                235

20  Encountering Globalization
    *Kevin Robins*                                                         239

21  The Globalization of Communication
    *John B. Thompson*                                                     246

22  The New Global Media
    *Robert W. McChesney*                                                  260

23  Globalization and Cultural Identity
    *John Tomlinson*                                                       269

24  Towards a Global Culture?
    *Anthony D. Smith*                                                     278

25  Global Governance and Cosmopolitan Citizens
    *Pippa Norris*                                                         287

# Part IV   A Global Economy?

Introduction                                                         299

26   A New Geo-economy
     *Peter Dicken*                                                   303

27   Global Informational Capitalism
     *Manuel Castells*                                                311

28   The Limits to Economic Globalization
     *Paul Hirst and Grahame Thompson*                               335

29   The Nation-State in the Global Economy
     *Robert Gilpin*                                                 349

30   Global Market versus the New Regionalism
     *Björn Hettne*                                                  359

31   Globalization and the Political Economy of Capitalist Democracies
     *Fritz Scharpf*                                                 370

32   Has Globalization Gone Too Far?
     *Dani Rodrik*                                                   379

33   Global Markets and National Politics
     *Geoffrey Garrett*                                              384

34   The Effect of Globalization on Taxation, Institutions, and Control of
     the Macroeconomy
     *Duane Swank*                                                   403

# Part V   Divided World, Divided Nations?

Introduction                                                         421

35   Patterns of Global Inequality
     *UNDP Report 1999*                                              423

36   The Rise of the Fourth World
     *Manuel Castells*                                               430

37   Are Global Poverty and Inequality Getting Worse?
     *Robert Wade/Martin Wolf*                                       440

38   Spreading the Wealth
     *David Dollar and Aart Kraay*                                   447

39   Globalization and Gendered Inequality
     *Jill Steans*                                                   455

40   Order, Globalization and Inequality in World Politics
     *Ngaire Woods*                                                  463

41   The Promise of Global Institutions
     *Joseph Stiglitz*                                               477

# Part VI  World Orders, Normative Choices

Introduction 483

42  Global Governance: Prospects and Problems
    *Fred Halliday* 489

43  Models of Transnational Democracy
    *Anthony McGrew* 500

44  Cosmopolitanism: Taming Globalization
    *David Held* 514

45  Can International Organizations be Democratic? A Skeptic's View
    *Robert A. Dahl* 530

46  The Postnational Constellation
    *Jürgen Habermas* 542

47  Priorities of Global Justice
    *Thomas W. Pogge* 548

48  Global Civil Society
    *Mary Kaldor* 559

49  A World Gone Wrong?
    *Chris Brown* 564

50  Beyond the States System?
    *Hedley Bull* 577

*Index* 583

# Preface to the Second Edition

In preparing the second edition of this Reader, we have sought to bring together many of the most significant contributions to the globalization debate published in recent years. Much of this new scholarship has added important theoretical, empirical or normative insights that have in their different ways altered the terms of the globalization debate. In selecting the contributions, itself a mammoth task, we have sought to identify what, in our judgement, have been the key interventions in that debate. As with the previous edition, the choices have been guided by a desire to make available the most salient contributions from within the globalist and sceptical camps.

This second edition is the product of our continuing and highly fruitful collaboration, which began many years ago. It also builds upon our experience of designing and teaching courses on globalization, to graduates and undergraduates, at our respective institutions – the LSE and Southampton University. We are grateful to our past and present students for their input, which has been significant in improving the design and contents of this new edition. The result is a Reader which, we believe, brings clarity to the 'great globalization debate', whilst also consolidating in one place extracts from many of the most important recent works on globalization. As well as being comprehensive, the Reader is designed to be accessible. To this end, we have composed much more substantial Part Introductions, contextualizing and summarizing each extract, as well as developing and extending the main Introduction.

As with the previous edition, it has been necessary to edit many extracts. However, following useful feedback on the first edition we have kept this to a minimum to ensure, as much as possible, that the substantive argument of the originals is not over-simplified. Where we have excised material, we have followed the convention of the first edition, annotating in the following way: cuts are marked by [ . . . ], and where more than a single paragraph has been omitted, the ellipses appear on a line of their own; editorial insertions or alterations are indicated by [insertion or alteration]. Beyond that, we have left the original texts unaltered. In exercising our editorial judgement, it is our intention that students should return to the original text to follow up specific points, arguments or matters of evidence.

In preparing this volume, we have benefited greatly from the advice and assistance of many individuals. Andrew Harmer and Alison Waller provided invaluable editorial assistance; Sandra Byatt, Sue Pope and Pam Thomas ensured the smooth processing of the entire manuscript; Louise Spencely dealt speedily with all the necessary copyright clearances; Sarah Dancy copy-edited the manuscript to exacting standards; and Ali Wyke helped at decisive stages of the production process. We are, in addition, indebted to the many contributors who commented on our proposed editorial changes and who approved the inclusion of their work in this second volume.

David Held
Tony McGrew

# Preface to the First Edition

Few contemporary phenomena elicit such political and academic controversy as globalization. Some consider it the fundamental dynamic of our epoch, a process of change which is to be promoted, managed or resisted; by contrast, others consider it the great myth of our times, a notion which misrepresents and misconstrues the real forces which shape our lives. In the public sphere especially, the idea of globalization is creating a new political faultline around which politicians and political parties of all persuasions seek to mobilize public opinion. From the 'globaphobia' of the radical right to the more adaptive strategies found in Third Way politics, globalization has become the rationale for diverse political projects. In the process, the idea of globalization has often become debased and confused.

In constructing this Reader, our central aim has been to bring clarity and enlightenment to the terms of the globalization debate. Because it is so important, it demands nothing less. The Introduction develops an intellectual framework for making sense of the controversy. It pursues an extended discussion between the sceptical account of globalization and those that defend its significance – the globalist position. In doing so, it identifies and examines the core areas of disagreement and convergence. Subsequent parts build on this by introducing the reader to the work of the main protagonists in the globalization discussion.

This Reader developed out of our earlier collaboration on *Global Transformations: Politics, Economics and Culture* (1999). As we contemplated designing and teaching courses on globalization, it readily became apparent that for most students the vast and diverse literature on globalization was an excessively daunting prospect. What was needed, we believed, was a collection which brought together the essential interventions in the globalization debate, from across the social sciences. The result is a Reader which, we hope, is the most comprehensive and up to date available.

David Held
Tony McGrew

# Sources and Acknowledgements

Chapter 1 from *Principles of World Politics*, by George Modelski (1972). Reprinted with the permission of The Free Press, a Division of Simon & Schuster Adult Publishing Group, from *Principles of World Politics* by George Modelski. Copyright © 1972 by The Free Press.

Chapter 2 from *The Consequences of Modernity*, by Anthony Giddens, 1990. Reproduced by permission of Polity Press.

Chapter 3 from *Global Transformations: Politics, Economics and Culture*, by David Held and Anthony McGrew, David Goldblatt and Jonathan Perraton, 1999. Reproduced by permission of Polity Press and Stanford University Press.

Chapter 4: Robert O. Keohane and Joseph S. Nye Jr., 'Globalization: What's New? What's Not? (And So What?)', from *Foreign Policy*, Spring 2000 issue, pp. 104–19. Reproduced by permission of the authors.

Chapter 5: Jan Aart Scholte, 'What is "Global" about Globalization?' from *Globalization – A Critical Introduction*, 2000. Reproduced with permission of Palgrave Macmillan.

Chapter 6 from *The Follies of Globalization Theory*, by Justin Rosenberg, 2000. Reproduced by permission of Verso.

Chapter 7 from *Globalization in Question*, second edition, by Paul Hirst and Grahame Thompson, 1999. Reproduced by permission of Polity Press.

Chapter 8: Stanley Hoffmann, 'Clash of Globalizations', from *Foreign Affairs*, vol. 81, no. 4, 2002, pp. 104–15. Copyright © 2002 by the Council on Foreign Relations Inc. Reproduced by permission of *Foreign Affairs*.

Chapter 9 from *The Paradox of American Power*, by Joseph S. Nye Jr. Copyright © 2002 by Joseph S. Nye Jr. Used by permission of Oxford University Press Inc.

Chapter 10: Reprinted by permission of the publisher from *Empire*, by Michael Hardt and Antonio Negri, pp. xi–xvi, Cambridge, Mass.: Harvard University Press. Copyright © 2000 by the President and Fellows of Harvard College.

Chapter 11 from Susan Strange, *The Retreat of the State: The Diffusion of Power in the World Economy*, 1996. Reproduced by permission of Cambridge University Press and the author's estate.

Chapter 12: Michael Mann, 'Has Globalization Ended the Rise and Rise of the Nation-state?' from *Review of International Political Economy*, vol. 4, no. 3 (Autumn 1997), pp. 472–96. Reproduced by permission of Taylor & Francis Ltd, http://www.tandf.co.uk/journals.

Chapter 13: Robert O. Keohane, 'Hobbes's Dilemma and Institutional Change in World Politics: Sovereignty in International Society', from Hans-Henrik Holm and Georg Sørensen (eds), *Whose World Order? Uneven Globalization and the End of the Cold War*. Copyright © 1995 by Westview Press Inc. Reproduced by permission of Westview Press, a member of Perseus Books, L.L.C.

Chapter 14: David Held, 'Law of States, Law of Peoples', from *Legal Theory*, 8 (2002), 1–44. Reproduced by permission of Cambridge University Press.

Chapter 15: Ian Clark, 'The Security State', from *Globalization and International Relations Theory*, 1999. Reproduced by permission of Oxford University Press.

Chapter 16: Anne-Marie Slaughter, 'Governing the Global Economy through Government Networks', from M. Byers (ed.), *The Role of Law in International Politics*, 2000. Reproduced by permission of Oxford University Press.

Chapter 17: Jessica T. Mathews, 'Power Shift', from *Foreign Affairs*, Jan/Feb 1997. Copyright © 1997 by the Council on Foreign Relations Inc. Reproduced by permission of *Foreign Affairs*.

Chapter 18: Anthony Payne, 'Globalization and Modes of Regionalist Governance', from J. Pierre (ed.), *Debating Governance Authority, Steering and Democracy*, 2000. Reproduced by permission of Oxford University Press.

Chapter 19: James N. Rosenau, 'Governance in a New Global Order', from David Held and Anthony McGrew, *Governing Globalization*. Reproduced by permission of Polity Press.

Chapter 20: Kevin Robins, 'What in the World's Going On?' from Paul du Gay (ed.), *Production of Culture/Cultures of Production*, 1997. Reproduced by permission of Sage Publications.

Chapter 21 from *The Media and Modernity*, by John B. Thompson, 1995. Reproduced by permission of Polity Press and Stanford University Press, www.sup.org.

Chapter 22: Robert W. McChesney, 'The New Global Media', from *The Nation*, November 29, 1999. Reproduced by permission of Illinois University Press.

Chapter 23: John Tomlinson, 'Globalization and Cultural Identity'. Reproduced by permission of the author.

Chapter 24: Anthony D. Smith, 'Towards a Global Culture?' from *Theory, Culture and Society*, vol. 7 (1990), pp. 171–91. Reproduced by permission of Sage Publications.

Chapter 25: Pippa Norris, 'Global Governance and Cosmopolitan Citizens', from Joseph S. Nye and John D. Donahue, *Governance in a Globalizing World*, 2000. Reproduced by permission of Brookings Institution Press.

Chapter 26 from *Global Shift: Transforming the World Economy*, third edition, by Peter Dicken, 1998. Reproduced by permission of Paul Chapman Publishing.

Chapter 27 from *The Rise of the Network Society*, by Manuel Castells, 2000. Reproduced by permission of Blackwell Publishing and the author.

Chapter 28 from *Globalization in Question*, second edition, by Paul Hirst and Grahame Thompson, 1999. Reproduced by permission of Polity Press and Blackwell Publishing.

Chapter 29 from *Global Political Economy*, by Robert Gilpin, 2001. Reproduced by permission of Princeton University Press.

Chapter 30: Björn Hettne, 'The Double Movement: Global Market versus Regionalism', from R. W. Cox (ed.), *The New Realism: Perspectives on Multilateralism and World Order*, 1998. Reproduced by permission of the United Nations University Press.

Chapter 31 from *Governing in Europe*, by Fritz Scharpf, 1999. Reproduced by permission of Oxford University Press.

Chapter 32 from *Has Globalization Gone Too Far?* by Dani Rodrik, 1997. Copyright © 1997 Institute of International Economics, Washington DC. All rights reserved. Reproduced by permission of the International Institute of Economics.

Chapter 33: Geoffrey Garrett, 'Global Markets and National Politics: Collision Course or Virtuous Circle?' from *International Organization*, vol. 52, no. 4 (Autumn 1998), pp. 787–824. Reproduced by permission of MIT Press Journals.

Chapter 34 from *Global Capital, Political Institutions and Policy Change in Developed Welfare States*, by Duane Swank, 2002. Reproduced by permission of Cambridge University Press and the author.

Chapter 35 from *Human Development Report 1999*, by United Nations Development Programme. Copyright © by the United Nations Development Programme. Used by permission of Oxford University Press Inc.

Chapter 36 from *End of Millennium*, by Manuel Castells, 2000. Reproduced by permission of Blackwell Publishing and the author.

Chapter 37: Robert Wade and Martin Wolf, 'Prospect Debate, Robert Wade and Martin Wolf: Are Global Poverty and Inequality Getting Worse?' from *Prospect*, March 2002. This is an edited version of an article published in the March 2002 edition of *Prospect*, www.prospect-magazine.co.uk. Reproduced by permission of *Prospect*.

Chapter 38: David Dollar and Aart Kraay, 'Spreading the Wealth', from *Foreign Affairs*, vol. 81, no. 1, 2002, pp. 120–33. Copyright © 2002 by the Council on Foreign Relations Inc. Reproduced by permission of *Foreign Affairs*.

Chapter 39: Jill Steans, 'The Gender Dimension of Global Political Economy and Development', from *Gender and International Relations*. Copyright © 1998 by Jill Steans. Reproduced by permission of Polity Press, Rutgers University Press and the author.

Chapter 40: Ngaire Woods, 'Order, Globalization and Inequality in World Politics', from Andrew Hurrell and Ngaire Woods (eds), *Inequality, Globalization and World Politics*, 1999. Reprinted by permission of Oxford University Press.

Chapter 41 from *Globalization and Its Discontents*, by Joseph Stiglitz, 2002. Reproduced by permission of Penguin Books Ltd.

Chapter 42: Fred Halliday, 'Global Governance: Prospects and Problems', from *Citizenship Studies,* vol. 4, no. 1 (2000). Reproduced by permission of Taylor & Francis Ltd. http://www.tandf.co.uk/journals

Chapter 43: Anthony McGrew, 'Models of Transnational Democracy', from A. Carter and G. Stokes (eds), *Democratic Theory Today*, 2002. Reproduced by permission of Polity Press and the author.

Chapter 44: David Held, 'Law of States, Law of Peoples', from *Legal Theory*, 8 (2002). Reproduced by permission of Cambridge University Press and the author.

Chapter 45: Robert A. Dahl, 'Can International Organizations be Democratic: A Sceptic's View', from Ian Shapiro and Casiano Hacker-Cordon (eds), *Democracy's Edges*, 1999. Reproduced by permission of Cambridge University Press and the author.

Chapter 46 from *The Postnational Constellation*, by Jürgen Habermas, 2001. Reproduced by permission of Polity Press.

Chapter 47: Thomas W. Pogge, 'Priorities of Global Justice', abbreviated and updated from Thomas W. Pogge (ed.), *Global Justice*, 2001. Reproduced by permission of Blackwell Publishing.

Chapter 48: Mary Kaldor 'Civilizing Globalization: The Implication of the Battle in Seattle', from *Millennium: Journal of International Studies*. This article first appeared in *Millennium* 2000, vol. 29, no. 1, pp. 105–14 and is reproduced by permission of the publisher.

Chapter 49 from *Sovereignty, Rights and Justice*, by Chris Brown, 2002. Reproduced by permission of Polity Press.

Chapter 50 from *The Anarchical Society: A Study of Order in World Politics*, by Hedley Bull, 1977. Reproduced with permission of Palgrave Macmillan and the Columbia University Press.

# Acronyms

| | |
|---|---|
| **AFP** | Agence France-Presse |
| **AIDS** | acquired immune deficiency syndrome |
| **AP** | Associated Press |
| **APEC** | Asia-Pacific Economic Cooperation |
| **ARF** | ASEAN Regional Forum |
| **ASEAN** | Association of South East Asian Nations |
| **BIS** | Bank for International Settlements |
| **CCTV** | Central China Television |
| **CENTO** | Central Treaty Organization |
| **CEO** | chief executive officer |
| **CFCs** | chlorofluorocarbons |
| **CIS** | Commonwealth of Independent States |
| **CNN** | Cable News Network (US) |
| **CNRS** | Centre national de la recherche scientifique (National Centre for Scientific Research – France) |
| **COMECON** | Council for Mutual Economic Assistance |
| **CSCE** | Conference on Security and Cooperation in Europe (Helsinki) |
| **DARPA** | Defense Advanced Research and Projects Agency (USA) |
| **DBS** | direct broadcast satellite |
| **DFID** | Department for International Development |
| **EAEC** | East Asian Economic Caucus |
| **EC** | European Community |
| **ECE** | Economic Commission for Europe (UN) |
| **ECOSOC** | Economic and Social Council (UN) |
| **ECOWAS** | Economic Organization of West African States |
| **EEZ** | Exclusive Economic Zone (for oceans) |
| **EFTA** | European Free Trade Association |
| **EMS** | European Monetary System |
| **EMU** | Economic and Monetary Union (EU) |
| **ERM** | exchange rate mechanism (Europe) |
| **EU** | European Union |
| **FAO** | Food and Agriculture Organization |
| **FDI** | foreign direct investment |
| **FLSAW** | Forward Looking Strategies for the Advancement of Women to the Year 2000 |
| **FTA** | free trade area |
| **G3** | triad of Europe, Japan and North America |
| **G5** | Group of Five: France, Germany, Japan, UK, US |

| | |
|---|---|
| **G7** | Group of Seven: G5 plus Canada and Italy |
| **G22** | Finance Ministers of G7 states, plus emerging market economies |
| **GAD** | Gender and Development |
| **GATT** | General Agreement on Tariffs and Trade |
| **GDP** | gross domestic product |
| **GE** | General Electric |
| **GNP** | gross national product |
| **GONGOs** | government-controlled NGOs |
| **IBRD** | International Bank for Reconstruction and Development (World Bank) |
| **ICRC** | International Committee of the Red Cross |
| **IGO** | intergovernmental organization |
| **ILE** | interlinked economy |
| **ILO** | International Labour Organization |
| **IMF** | International Monetary Fund |
| **INCOTERMS** | International Chamber of Commerce glossary defining terms used in international trade |
| **INGO** | international non-governmental organization |
| **INSTRAW** | International Institute for Training and Research for the Advancement of Women (UN) |
| **IO** | international organization |
| **IPCC** | Intergovernmental Panel on Climate Change |
| **IPE** | international political economy |
| **IR** | international relations |
| **ISI** | import substitution industrialization |
| **ISSP** | International Social Security Program |
| **ITU** | International Telecommunication Union |
| **LDC** | less developed country |
| **MARPOL** | International Convention for the Prevention of Pollution from Ships, 1973, as modified by the Protocol of 1978 relating thereto (MARPOL 73/78) |
| **MERCOSUR** | Southern Cone Common Market (Latin America) |
| **MITI** | Ministry of International Trade and Industry (Japan) |
| **MNC** | multinational corporation/company |
| **MOU** | memoranda of understanding |
| **NAFTA** | North American Free Trade Agreement |
| **NATO** | North Atlantic Treaty Organization |
| **NBC** | National Broadcasting Company (US) |
| **NGO** | non-governmental organization |
| **NIC** | newly industrializing country |
| **NIE** | newly industrializing economy |
| **NWICO** | New World Information and Communication Order |
| **OAS** | Organization of American States |
| **OAU** | Organization of African Unity |
| **ODA** | official development assistance |
| **OECD** | Organization for Economic Cooperation and Development |
| **OSCE** | Organization for Security and Cooperation in Europe |
| **PBEC** | Pacific Basin Economic Council |

| | |
|---|---|
| **PPP** | purchasing power parity |
| **PUMA** | public management section of the OECD |
| **R&D** | research and development |
| **RMA** | revolution in military affairs |
| **SAARC** | South Asian Association for Regional Cooperation |
| **SADC** | Southern African Development Community |
| **SADCC** | Southern Africa Development Coordinating Conference/Committee |
| **SAP** | structural adjustment programme |
| **SDR** | Special Drawing Right |
| **SEATO** | South East Asia Treaty Organization |
| **SEC** | Securities and Exchange Commission (USA) |
| **SOA** | sphere of authority |
| **TNC** | transnational corporation/company |
| **TRIPS** | trade in intellectual property rights |
| **TRO** | transgovernmental regulatory organization |
| **UN** | United Nations |
| **UNCITRAL** | United Nations Commission on International Trade Law |
| **UNCTAD** | United Nations Conference on Trade and Development |
| **UNDP** | United Nations Development Programme |
| **UNEP** | United Nations Environment Programme |
| **UNESCO** | United Nations Educational, Scientific and Cultural Organization |
| **UNICEF** | United Nations Children's Fund |
| **UNIFEM** | Voluntary Fund for the UN Decade for Women |
| **UPA** | United Press Association |
| **UPI** | United Press International |
| **USAID** | United States Agency for International Development |
| **USDA** | United States Department of Agriculture |
| **WARC** | World Administrative Radio Conference |
| **WID** | Women in Development |
| **WMD** | weapons of mass destruction |
| **WTO** | World Trade Organization |

# The Great Globalization Debate: An Introduction

## David Held and Anthony McGrew

Much has been made of the consequences for globalization of the cataclysmic events of 11 September 2001. Some observers have proclaimed the events mark the end of globalization, while others suggest they symbolize the beginning of the post-globalization era. As the reassertion of geopolitics and state power has come to dominate international responses to 11 September, it is tempting to conclude that globalization has now reached its historical limits. Such a conclusion, however, over-looks the manifold ways in which the very responses to the events are themselves products of, and conditional upon, a globalizing world. As Stanley Hoffmann has phrased it, the world after 11 September confronts not so much the end of globalization as a growing 'clash of globalizations' (Hoffmann 2002). Although the war on terrorism may have displaced it from the media spotlight, the great globalization debate continues apace, no longer just on the streets and in the academy but increasingly within the citadels of global power. Paradoxically, in the aftermath of the terrorist attacks on the United States – the principal architect and icon of a globalizing world – making sense of globalization, and its implications for the twenty-first-century world order, has become a more, rather than less, urgent intellectual and political task.

Although public references to globalization have become increasingly common over the last two decades, the concept itself can be traced back to a much earlier period. Its origins lie in the work of many nineteenth- and early twentieth-century intellectuals, from Saint-Simon and Karl Marx to students of geopolitics such as MacKinder, who recognized how modernity was integrating the world. But it was not until the 1960s and early 1970s that the term 'globalization' was actually used. This 'golden age' of rapidly expanding political and economic interdependence – most especially between Western states – generated much reflection on the inadequacies of orthodox approaches to thinking about politics, economics and culture which presumed a strict separation between internal and external affairs, the domestic and international arenas, and the local and the global. For in a more interdependent world events abroad readily acquired impacts at home, while developments at home had consequences abroad. In the context of a debate about the growing interconnectedness of human affairs, world systems theory, theories of complex interdependence and the notion of globalization itself emerged as largely rival accounts of the processes through which the fate of states and peoples was becoming more intertwined (Modelski 1972; Wallerstein 1974; Keohane and Nye 1977). Following the collapse of state socialism and the consolidation of capitalism worldwide, academic and public discussion of globalization intensified dramatically. Coinciding with the rapid spread of the information revolution, these developments appeared to confirm the belief that the world was fast becoming a shared social and economic space – at least for its most affluent inhabitants. However, whether the notion of globalization ultimately helps or hinders our understanding of the contemporary human condition, and strategies to improve it, is now a matter of intense intellectual and public controversy. In short, the great globalization debate has been joined.

Trying to make sense of this debate presents some difficulties, since there are no definitive or fixed lines of contestation. Instead, multiple conversations coexist (although few real dialogues), which do not readily afford a coherent or definitive characterization. Within shared traditions of social enquiry, whether neoclassical economics or world systems theory, no singular account of globalization has acquired the status of orthodoxy. On the contrary, competing assessments continue to frame the discussion. Nor do the dominant ideological traditions of conservatism, liberalism or socialism offer coherent readings of, or responses to, a globalizing era. Just as some conservatives and socialists find common ground in dismissing the significance of globalization, others of similar political persuasion view it as a dramatic new threat to cherished values, whether the nation or social democracy. Indeed, the very idea of globalization appears to disrupt established paradigms and political orthodoxies.

Accepting this heterogeneity, it is, nevertheless, feasible to identify a clustering of arguments around an emerging fissure between those who consider that contemporary globalization is a real and significant historical development – the *globalists* – and those who conceive it as a primarily ideological or social construction which has marginal explanatory value – the *sceptics*. Of course, as used here, the labels – globalists and sceptics – refer to ideal-type constructions. Ideal-types are heuristic devices which help order a field of enquiry and identify the primary areas of consensus as well as dispute. They assist in identifying the principal areas of contention and, thus, in establishing the fundamental points of disagreement. They provide an accessible way into the mêlée of voices – rooted in the globalization literature but by definition corresponding to no single work, author or ideological position.

Neither the sceptical nor the globalist thesis, of course, exhausts the complexity or the subtleties of the interpretations of globalization to be found in the existing literature. Even within each position, considerable differences of emphasis exist with respect to matters of historical interpretation as well as normative commitments. Such differences will become apparent throughout the volume. For in selecting the contributions, we have sought to represent fairly both positions in the debate, and also the diversity of views within these dominant schools. A further editorial principle has been the desire to reflect the richness of the different disciplinary contributions of social science in order that the essential interdisciplinarity of the debate is given proper exposure. Accordingly, each of the subsequent parts reflects a representative set of major contributions to the literatures on globalization, while further embellishing, as well as carefully qualifying, the characterization of the globalization debate described below.

In organizing the contributions to the debate, we have constructed the volume around the critical themes which are addressed in the globalist and sceptical literatures alike. Part I (Understanding Globalization) commences with an overview of the historical and conceptual debates surrounding the idea of globalization. Part II (Political Power and Civil Society: A Reconfiguration?) focuses on the controversy concerning the modern nation-state: its continued primacy versus its transformation. Building on this discussion, Part III (The Fate of National Culture in an Age of Global Communication) illuminates the debate about the cultural ramifications of globalization, particularly in respect of the question of national culture and identity. Parts IV (A Global Economy?) and V (Divided World, Divided Nations?) introduce the major contributions to the discussion concerning the nature of the contemporary global economy and its consequences for patterns of global inequality. Finally, with critical issues of social justice and world order to the fore, Part VI (World Orders, Normative Choices) considers the normative considerations raised in the globalization debate.

# I  Understanding Globalization

Globalization has been variously conceived as action at a distance (whereby the actions of social agents in one locale can come to have significant consequences for 'distant others'); time–space compression (referring to the way in which instantaneous electronic communication erodes the constraints of distance and time on social organization and interaction); accelerating interdependence (understood as the intensification of enmeshment among national economies and societies such that events in one country impact directly on others); a shrinking world (the erosion of borders and geographical barriers to socio-economic activity); and, among other concepts, global integration, the reordering of interregional power relations, consciousness of the global condition and the intensification of interregional interconnectedness (Harvey 1989; Giddens 1990; Rosenau 1990; Jameson 1991; Robertson 1992; Scholte 1993; Nierop 1994; Geyer and Bright 1995; Johnston et al. 1995; Zürn 1995; Albrow 1996; Kofman and Youngs 1996; Held et al. 1999). What distinguishes these definitions is the differential emphasis given to the material, spatio-temporal and cognitive aspects of globalization. It is worth dwelling initially on this tripartite cluster of characteristics as the first stage in clarifying the concept of globalization.

# Defining globalization

Globalization has an undeniably material aspect in so far as it is possible to identify, for instance, flows of trade, capital and people across the globe. These are facilitated by different kinds of infrastructure – physical (such as transport or banking systems), normative (such as trade rules) and symbolic (such as English as a lingua franca) – which establish the preconditions for regularized and relatively enduring forms of global interconnectedness. Rather than mere random encounters, globalization refers to these entrenched and enduring patterns of worldwide interconnectedness. But the concept of globalization denotes much more than a stretching of social relations and activities across regions and frontiers. For it suggests a growing magnitude or intensity of global flows such that states and societies become increasingly enmeshed in worldwide systems and networks of interaction. As a consequence, distant occurrences and developments can come to have serious domestic impacts while local happenings can engender significant global repercussions. In other words, globalization represents a significant shift in the spatial reach of social relations and organization towards the interregional or intercontinental scale. This does not mean that the global necessarily displaces or takes precedence over local, national or regional orders of social life. Rather, the point is that the local becomes embedded within more expansive sets of interregional relations and networks of power. Thus, the constraints of social time and geographical space, vital coordinates of modern social life, no longer appear to impose insuperable barriers to many forms of social interaction or organization, as the existence of the World Wide Web and round-the-clock trading in global financial markets attests. As distance 'shrinks', the relative speed of social interaction increases too, such that crises and events in distant parts of the globe, exemplified by the events of 11 September 2001, come to have an immediate worldwide impact involving diminishing response times for decision-makers. Globalization thereby engenders a cognitive shift expressed both in a growing public awareness of the ways in which distant events can affect local fortunes (and vice versa) as well as in public perceptions of shrinking time and geographical space.

Simply put, globalization denotes the expanding scale, growing magnitude, speeding up and deepening impact of interregional flows and patterns of social interaction. It refers to a shift or transformation in the scale of human social organization that links distant communities and expands the reach of power relations across the world's major regions and continents. However, as the rise of the anti-globalization protests demonstrates, it should not be read as prefiguring the emergence of a harmonious world society or as a universal process of global integration in which there is a growing convergence of cultures and civilizations. Not only does the awareness of growing interconnectedness create new animosities and conflicts, it can fuel reactionary politics and deep-seated xenophobia. Since a significant segment of the world's population is either untouched directly by globalization or remains largely excluded from its benefits, it is arguably a deeply divisive and, consequently, vigorously contested process.

## The myth of globalization

For the sceptics, the very concept is suspect: what, they ask, is the 'global' in globalization (Hirst 1997)? If the global cannot be interpreted literally, as a universal phenomenon, then the concept of globalization lacks specificity. With no identifiable geographical referents, how is it possible to distinguish the international or the transnational from the global, or, for that matter, processes of regionalization from processes of globalization? It is precisely because much of the literature on globalization fails to specify the spatial referents for the global that, so the sceptics argue, the concept becomes so broad as to become impossible to operationalize empirically and, therefore, misleading as a vehicle for understanding the contemporary world.

In interrogating the concept of globalization, sceptics generally seek to establish a conclusive test of the globalization thesis. For the most part this involves constructing an abstract or a priori model of a global economy, global culture or world society and assessing how far contemporary trends match up to it (Sterling 1974; Perlmutter 1991; Dore 1995; Boyer and Drache 1996; Hirst and Thompson 1996). Embedded in many such models is a conception of a globalized economy or global society as akin to a national economy or society writ large. Others critical of the globalist thesis seek to assess how far contemporary trends compare with what several economic historians have argued was the *belle époque* of globalization, namely the period from 1890 to 1914 (Gordon 1988; Jones 1995; Hirst 1997). In both cases, there is a strong presumption that the statistical evidence by itself can establish the 'truth' about globalization. In this regard, the sceptical analysis is decidedly dismissive of the descriptive or explanatory value of the concept of globalization. Rather than globalization, the sceptics conclude that a more valid conceptualization of current trends is captured by the terms 'internationalization' – that is, growing links between essentially discrete national economies or societies – and 'regionalization' or 'triadization' – the geographical clustering of cross-border economic and social exchanges (Ruigrok and Tulder 1995; G. Thompson 1998a; Weiss 1998; Hirst and Thompson 1999). This is an argument for the continuing primacy of territory, borders, place and national governments to the distribution and location of power, production and wealth in the contemporary world order. Yet a puzzle arises: namely, how to explain the disjuncture between the widespread discourse of globalization and the realities of a world in which, for the most part, the routines of everyday lives are still dominated by national and local circumstances?

Instead of providing an insight into the forces shaping the contemporary world, the concept of globalization, argue many sceptics, is primarily an ideological construction; a convenient myth which, in part, helps justify and legitimize the neoliberal global project, that is, the creation of a global free market and the consolidation of Anglo-American capitalism within the world's major economic regions (Callinicos et al. 1994; Gordon 1988; Hirst 1997; Hoogvelt 1997). In this respect, the concept of globalization operates as a 'necessary myth', through which politicians and governments discipline their citizens to meet the requirements of the global marketplace. It is, thus, unsurprising that discussion of globalization became so widespread just at that juncture when the neoliberal project – the Washington consensus of deregulation, privatization, structural adjustment programmes (SAPs) and limited government – consolidated its hold within key Western capitals and global institutions such as the IMF.

Frequently associated with this sceptical position is a strong attachment either to an essentially Marxist or to a realist ontology. Traditional Marxist analysis considers that capitalism, as a social order, has a pathological expansionist logic, since to maintain profits capital constantly has to exploit new markets. To survive, national capitalism must continuously expand the geographical reach of capitalist social relations. The history of the modern world order is the history of Western capitalist powers dividing and redividing the world up into exclusive economic zones. Today, it is argued, imperialism has acquired a new form as formal empires have been replaced by new mechanisms of multilateral control and surveillance, such as the G7 and World Bank. As such, the present epoch is described by many Marxists not in terms of globalization, but instead as a new mode of Western imperialism dominated by the needs and requirements of finance capital within the world's major capitalist states (Van der Pijl 1999).

Realism too presents the existing international order as constituted primarily by and through the actions of the mightiest economically and militarily powerful states (and their agents). Accordingly, the internationalization of economic or social relations is argued to be contingent upon the policies and preferences of the great powers of the day since only they have sufficient military and economic muscle to create and maintain the conditions necessary for an open (liberal) international order (Waltz 1979). Without the exercise of American power, so the argument suggests, the existing liberal world order, which underpins the recent intensification of international interdependence, would eventually collapse (Gilpin 1987). This leads to a further critical point; namely, that liberal orders are historically unlikely to endure, since, in a system in which states constantly struggle for dominance, the power of hegemonic states ultimately has a finite life. As many sceptics are wont to assert, without a hegemon to police a liberal system, as in the period 1919–39, a rush to autarky and the breakdown of world order will ensue (Gilpin 1981). International interdependence, according to this interpretation, is ultimately a temporary and contingent condition.

## The globalist's response

The globalist account rejects the assertion that the concept of globalization can be simply dismissed either as a purely ideological or social construction or as a synonym for Western imperialism. While not denying that the discourse of globalization may well serve the interests of powerful social forces in the West, the globalist account also emphasizes that it reflects real structural changes in the scale of modern social organization. This is evident in, among other developments, the growth of MNCs, world financial markets, the diffusion of popular culture and the salience of global environmental degradation. Rather than conceiving globalization as a solely economic phenomenon, the globalist analysis gives equal status to the other key dimensions of social relations. This attachment to a differentiated or multidimensional conception of globalization reflects a Weberian and/or post-Marxist and post-structuralist understanding of social reality as constituted by a number of distinct institutional orders or networks of power: the economic, technological, political, cultural, natural, etc. (Mann 1986; Giddens 1990). To reduce globalization to a purely economic or technological logic is considered profoundly misleading since it ignores the inherent complexity of the forces that shape modern societies and world order. Thus, the globalist analysis commences from a conception of globalization as a set of interrelated processes operating across all the primary domains of social power, including the military, the political and the cultural. But there is no a priori assumption that the historical or spatial pattern of globalization within each of these domains is identical or even comparable. In this respect, patterns of cultural globalization, for instance, are not presumed necessarily to replicate patterns of economic globalization. The globalist account promotes a conception of globalization which recognizes this differentiation, allowing for the possibility that it proceeds at different tempos, with distinctive geographies, in different domains.

Central to this globalist conception is an emphasis on the particular spatial attributes of globalization. In seeking to differentiate global networks and systems from those operating at other spatial scales, such as the local or the national, the globalist analysis identifies globalization primarily with activities and relations which crystallize on an interregional or intercontinental scale (Geyer and Bright 1995; Castells 1996; Dicken 1998). This involves globalists in attempting to establish more precise analytical distinctions between the concept of globalization and the concepts of regionalization and localization, that is, the nexus of relations between geographically contiguous states, and the clustering of social relations within states, respectively (Dicken 1998).

This attempt to establish a more systematic specification of the concept of globalization is further complemented by the significance attached to its temporal or historical forms. Rather than trying to assess how contemporary global trends measure up to some abstract model of a globalized world, or simply comparing the magnitude of global flows between different epochs, the globalist account draws on established socio-historical modes of analysis. This involves locating contemporary globalization within what the French historian Braudel refers to as the perspective of the 'longue durée' – that is, very long-term patterns of secular historical change (Helleiner 1997).

As the existence of premodern world religions confirms, globalization is not only a phenomenon of the modern age. Making sense of contemporary globalization requires placing it in the context of secular trends of world historical development (Modelski 1972; Hodgson 1993; Mazlish and Buultjens 1993; Bentley 1996; Frank and Gills 1996; Clark 1997; Frank 1998). That development, as the globalist account also recognizes, is punctuated by distinctive phases – from the epoch of world discovery to the *belle époque* or the interwar years – when the pace of globalization appears to intensify or, alternatively, sometimes regress (Fernández-Armesto 1995; Geyer and Bright 1995). To understand contemporary globalization requires investigating what differentiates these discrete phases, including how such systems and patterns of global interconnectedness are organized and reproduced, their different geographies and histories, and the changing configuration of interregional power relations. Accordingly, the globalist account stretches the concept of globalization to embrace the idea of its distinctive historical forms. This requires an examination of how patterns of globalization, both within and between different domains of activity, compare and contrast over time.

This historicized approach encourages a conception of globalization as a somewhat indeterminate process; for globalization is not inscribed with a preordained logic which presumes a singular historical trajectory or end condition, that is, the emergence of a single world society or global civilization. In fact, teleological or determinist thinking is roundly rejected. Globalization, it is argued, is driven by a confluence of forces and embodies dynamic tensions. As noted earlier, the globalist analysis dismisses the presumption that globalization can be explained solely by reference to the imperatives of capitalism or technology (Axford 1995). Nor can it be understood as simply a projection of Western modernity across the globe (Giddens 1990). Rather, it is considered a product of multiple forces, including economic, political and technological imperatives, as well as specific conjunctural factors, such as, for instance, the creation of the ancient Silk Route or the collapse of state socialism. It harbours no fixed or given pattern of historical development. Moreover, since it pulls and pushes societies in different directions it simultaneously engenders cooperation as well as conflict, integration as well as fragmentation, exclusion and inclusion, convergence and divergence, order and disorder (Harvey 1989; Giddens 1990; Robertson 1992; Hurrell and Woods 1995; Rosenau 1997). Rejecting historicist or determinist interpretations of globalization, the globalist account invites an open-ended conception of global change rather than a fixed or singular vision of a globalized world. It is therefore equally valid to talk of a partially globalized world or processes of de-globalization.

Central to this globalist interpretation is, nonetheless, a conception of global change involving a significant reconfiguration of the organizing principles of social life and world order. Three aspects of this are identified in the globalist literature; namely, the transformation of dominant patterns of socio-economic organization, of the territorial principle, and of power. By eroding the constraints of space and time on patterns of social interaction, globalization creates the possibility of new modes of transnational social organization, for instance global production networks and regulatory regimes, while simultaneously making communities in particular locales vulnerable to global conditions or developments, as expressed in the events of 11 September 2001 and the responses to them.

In transforming both the context of, and the conditions for, social interaction and organization, globalization also involves a reordering of the relationship between territory and political space. Put simply, as economic, social and political activities increasingly transcend regions and national frontiers a direct challenge is mounted to the territorial principle of modern social and political organization. That principle presumes a direct correspondence between society, economy and polity within an exclusive and bounded national territory. Globalization disrupts this correspondence in so far as social, economic and political activity can no longer be understood as coterminous with national territorial boundaries. This does not mean that territory and place are becoming irrelevant, but rather that, under conditions of contemporary globalization, they are reinvented and reconstructed, that is, increasingly cast in a global context (Castells 1996; Dicken 1998). The latter point connects with the third and final aspect of the transformations identified in the globalist literature; namely, the transformation of power relations.

At the core of the globalist account lies a concern with power: its instrumentalities, configuration, distribution, and impacts. Globalization is taken to express the expanding scale on which power is organized and exercised. In this respect, it involves a reordering of power relations between and across the world's major regions such that key sites of power and those who are subject to them are literally oceans apart. To paraphrase Jameson, under conditions of contemporary globalization the truth of power no longer resides in the locales in which it is immediately experienced (Jameson 1991). Power relations are deeply inscribed in the dynamics of globalization, as the continuing disquisitions on its implications for the nation-state confirm.

## II  Political Power and Civil Society: A Reconfiguration?

Contemporary social life is associated with the modern state which specifies the proper form of nearly all types of human activity. The state appears to be omnipresent, regulating the conditions of life from birth registration to death certification. From the policing of everyday activities to the provision of education and the promotion of health care, the steady expansion of state power appears beyond question. Quantitatively, the growth of the state, from the size of its budget to the scope of its jurisdiction, is one of the few really uncontested facts of the twentieth century. On many fundamental measures of political power (for example, the capacity to raise taxes and revenues, the ability to hurl concentrated force at enemies) states are, at least throughout most of the OECD world, as powerful as, if not more powerful than, their predecessors (Mann 1997). The sceptics make a great deal of this, as they do of the rise and dominance of the modern state in general. It is useful to rehearse this position and its many implications for the form and distribution of political power, before examining the globalists' alternative account.

### The formation and rule of the modern state

The claim of the modern state to an overarching role is a relatively novel one in human history, even in the place which gave birth to it – Western Europe. A thousand years ago, for example, an inhabitant of an English village knew little of life beyond it; the village was the beginning and practically the end of his or her world. She or he would have visited the nearest market town but would scarcely have ventured further; would have probably recognized the name of the king, although would rarely, if ever, have seen him; and may well have had more contact with representatives of the church than with any 'political' or military leaders (Lacey and Danziger 1999). And while five hundred years later two forms of political regime – absolute and constitutional monarchies – were beginning to crystallize across the European continent, Europe resembled more a mosaic of powers, with overlapping political claims and jurisdictions (Tilly 1975; Poggi 1978). No ruler or state was yet sovereign in the sense of being supreme over a bounded territory and population.

Modern states emerged in Western Europe and its colonial territories in the eighteenth and nineteenth centuries, although their origins date back to the late sixteenth century (Skinner 1978; Held 1995: chs 2–3). They distinguished themselves initially from earlier forms of political rule by claiming a distinctive symmetry and correspondence between sovereignty, territory and legitimacy. The distillation of the concept of sovereignty was pivotal to this development, for it lodged a special claim to the rightful exercise of political power over a circumscribed realm – an entitlement to rule over a bounded territory (see Skinner 1978). Modern states developed as nation-states – political bodies, separate from both ruler and ruled, with supreme jurisdiction over a demarcated territorial area, backed by a claim to a monopoly of coercive power, and enjoying legitimacy as a result of the loyalty or consent of their citizens. The major innovations of the modern nation-state – territoriality that fixes exact borders, monopolistic control of violence, an impersonal structure of political power and a distinctive claim to legitimacy based on representation and accountability – marked out its defining (and sometimes fragile) features. The regulatory power of such states expanded throughout the modern period creating – albeit with significant national differences – systems of unified rule across demarcated territories, centralized administration, concentrated and more effective mechanisms of fiscal management and resource distribution, new types of lawmaking and law enforcement, professional standing armies, a concentrated war-making capacity and, concomitantly, elaborate formal relations among states through the development of diplomacy and diplomatic institutions (P. Anderson 1974; Giddens 1985).

The consolidation of the power of leading European nation-states was part of a process in which an international society of states was created, first in Europe itself, and then, as Europe expanded across the globe, in diverse regions as Europe's demands on its colonies were pressed and resisted (Ferro 1997). This 'society of states' laid down the formal rules which all sovereign and autonomous states would, in principle, have to adopt if they were to become full and equal members of the international order of states. The origins of this order are often traced to the Peace Treaties of Westphalia of 1648, which concluded the Thirty Years' War (see Falk 1969; Krasner 1995; Keohane 1995). But the rule system codified at Westphalia is best understood as having created a *normative trajectory* in international law, which did not receive its fullest articulation until the late eighteenth and early nineteenth century. It was during this time that territorial sovereignty, the formal equality of states, non-intervention in the internal affairs of other recognized states, and state consent as the foundation stone of international legal agreement became the core principles of the modern international order (see Crawford and Marks 1998). Of course, the consolidation of this order across the world would, paradoxically, have to wait until the decline of its earliest protagonists – the European powers – and the formal initiation of decolonization after the Second World War. But it is perhaps fair to say that it was not until the late twentieth century that the modern international order of states became truly global; for it was only with the end of all the great empires – European, American and finally Soviet – that many peoples could finally join the society of states as independent polit-ical communities. The number of internationally recognized states more than doubled between 1945 and the early 1990s (www.state.gov, accessed May 2002). The high point of the modern nation-state system was reached at the end of the twentieth century, buttressed and supported by the spread of new multilateral forms of international co-ordination and cooperation, in international organizations like the UN, and new international regulatory mechanisms, such as the universal human rights regime.

Not only has the modern nation-state become the principal type of political rule across the globe, but it has also increasingly assumed, since decolonization and the collapse of the Soviet empire, a particular political form; that is, it has crystallized as liberal or representative democracy (Potter et al. 1997). Several distinctive waves of democratization have brought particular countries in Europe, such as Portugal and Spain, into the democratic fold, while they have also brought numerous others closer to democracy in Latin America, Asia, Africa and Eastern Europe. Of course, there is no necessary evolutionary path to consolidated liberal democracy; the path is fragile and littered with obstacles – the hold of liberal democracy on diverse political communities is still tentative and open to challenge.

Surveying the political scene at the start of the twenty-first century there are good reasons, argue the sceptics, for thinking of this period as the age of the modern nation-state. For states in many places have increasingly claimed a monopoly of the legitim-ate use of force and judicial regulation, established permanent military forces as a symbol of statehood as well as a means of ensuring national security, consolidated tax raising and redistributive mechanisms, established nation-wide communication infra-structures, sought to systematize a national or official language, raised literacy levels and created a national schooling system, promulgated a national identity, and built up a diverse array of national political, economic and cultural institutions. In addi-tion, many states, west and east, have sought to create elaborate welfare institutions, partly as a means to promote and reinforce national solidarity, involving public health provision and social security (Ashford 1986). Moreover, OECD states have pursued macroeconomic management strategies, shifting from Keynesian demand manage-ment in the 1950s to 1970s to extensive supply-side measures in the 1980s and 1990s, in order to help sustain economic growth and widespread employment. Success in these domains has often remained elusive, but the Western nation-state's array of policy instruments and objectives have been emulated recently in many regions of the world.

It certainly can be argued that much of this 'emulation' has been more the result of necessity than of choice. Decolonization clearly did not create a world of equally free states. The influence of Western commerce, trade and political organization out-lived direct rule. Powerful national economic interests have often been able to sus-tain hegemonic positions over former colonial territories through the replacement of 'a visible presence of rule' with the 'invisible government' of corporations, banks and international organizations (the IMF and the World Bank, for example) (Ferro 1997: 349–50). Furthermore, interlaced with this has been the sedimented interests and machi-nations of the major powers, jostling with each other for advantage, if not hegemonic status (Bull 1977; Buzan et al. 1993). The geopolitical roles of individual states may have changed (for example, the shifts in the relative position of the UK and France during the twentieth century from global empires to middle-ranking powers), but these changes have been accommodated within the prevailing structures of world order – the modern nation-state system and capitalist economic relations – which have governed the strategic choices open to political communities. The restricted nature of these choices has become even clearer with the collapse of Soviet communism and the bipolar division of the world established during the Cold War. Accordingly, the development programmes of states in sub-Saharan Africa, East Asia and Latin America appear to have acquired a uniform shape – market liberalization, welfare cut-backs, minimal regulation of private capital flows, deregulation of labour markets – and to be governed by political necessity rather than publicly sanctioned intervention.

Yet, however limited the actual control most states possess over their territories, they generally fiercely protect their sovereignty – their entitlement to rule – and their autonomy – their capacity to choose appropriate forms of political, economic and social development. The distinctive 'bargains' governments create with their citizens remain fundamental to their legitimacy. The choices, benefits and welfare policies of states vary dramatically according to their location in the hierarchy of states, but, in the age of nation-states, the independence bestowed by sovereignty, in principle, still matters greatly to all states. Modern nation-states are political communities which create the conditions for establishing national communities of fate; and few seem willing to give this up. Although national political choices are constrained, they still count and remain the focus of public deliberation and debate. According to the sceptics, national political traditions are still vibrant, distinctive political bargains can still be struck between governments and electorates, and states continue, given the political will, to rule. The business of national politics is as important as, if not more important than, it was during the period in which modern states were first formed.

## Towards a global politics

Globalists would generally contest many aspects of the above account. Their argument runs as follows. The traditional conception of the state, in which it is posited as the fundamental unit of world order, presupposes its relative homogeneity, that is, that it is a unitary phenomenon with a set of singular purposes (Young 1972: 36). But the growth of international and transnational organizations and collectivities, from the UN and its specialized agencies to international pressure groups and social movements, has altered the form and dynamics of both state and civil society. The state has become a fragmented policy-making arena, permeated by transnational networks (governmental and non-governmental) as well as by domestic agencies and forces. Likewise, the extensive penetration of civil society by transnational forces has altered its form and dynamics.

The exclusive link between territory and political power has been broken. The contemporary era has witnessed layers of governance spreading within and across political boundaries. New international and transnational institutions have both linked sovereign states together and transformed sovereignty into the shared exercise of power. A body of regional and international law has developed which underpins an emerging system of global governance, both formal and informal.

This transformation can be illustrated by a number of developments, including the rapid emergence of international organizations and regimes. New forms of multilateral and global politics have been established involving governments, intergovernmental organizations (IGOs) and a wide variety of transnational pressure groups and inter-national non-governmental organizations (INGOs). In 1909 there were 37 IGOs and 176 INGOs, while in 2000 there were 6,743 IGOs and 47,098 INGOs (Union of International Associations 2001). (The 2000 figure for IGOs and INGOs has to be treated with some caution because it includes some inactive or defunct organizations.) In addition, there has been an explosive development in the number of international treaties in force, as well as in the number of international regimes, such as the nuclear non-proliferation regime.

To this pattern of extensive political interconnectedness can be added the dense web of activity within and among the key international policy-making fora, including the UN, G7, IMF, WTO, EU, APEC, ARF and MERCOSUR summits and many other official and unofficial meetings. In the middle of the nineteenth century there were two or three interstate conferences or congresses per annum; today the number totals over nine thousand annually (Union of International Associations 2001). National gov-ernment is increasingly locked into a multilayered system of governance – local, national, regional and global – and can barely monitor it, let alone stay in command.

At the regional level the EU, in remarkably little time, has taken Europe from the disarray of the post-Second World War era to a supranational polity in which sovereignty is pooled across a growing number of areas of common concern. Despite its contested nature, the EU represents a novel system of governance which institu-tionalizes intergovernmental collaboration to address collective and transborder issues. There has also been an acceleration in regionalization beyond Europe: in the Americas, Asia-Pacific and, to a lesser degree, in Africa. While the form taken by this type of regionalism is very different from the EU model, it has nonetheless had significant consequences for political power, particularly in the Asia-Pacific (ASEAN, APEC, ARF, PBEC and many other groupings). As regionalism has deepened so interregional diplomacy has intensified as old and new regional groupings seek to consolidate their relationships with each other. In this respect, regionalism has not been a barrier to contemporary political globalization – involving the shifting reach of political power, authority and forms of rule – but, on the contrary, has been largely compatible with it.

The momentum for international cooperation shows no sign of slowing, despite the many vociferous complaints often heard about it. The concerns of regional and global politics already go far beyond traditional geopolitics. Drug smugglers, capital flows, acid rain, the activities of paedophiles, terrorists and illegal immigrants do not recog-nize borders; neither can the policies for their effective management and resolution. International cooperation and coordination of national policies have become neces-sary requirements for managing the consequences of a globalizing world.

Fundamental changes have also occurred in the world military order. Few states now consider unilateralism or neutrality as a credible defence strategy. Global and regional security institutions have become more important. Most states today have chosen to sign up to a host of multilateral arrangements and institutions in order to enhance their security. But it is not just the institutions of defence which have become multinational. The way military hardware is manufactured has also changed. The age of 'national champions' has been superseded by a sharp increase in licensing, co-production agreements, joint ventures, corporate alliances and subcontracting. This means that few countries – not even the United States – can claim to have a wholly autonomous military production capacity. The latter can be highlighted also in connection with key civil technologies, such as electronics, which are vital to advanced weapons systems, and which are themselves the products of highly globalized industries.

The paradox and novelty of the globalization of organized violence today is that national security has become a multilateral affair. For the first time in history, the one thing that did most to give modern nation-states a focus and a purpose, and which has always been at the very heart of statehood, can now only be realized effectively if nation-states come together and pool resources, technology, intelligence, power and authority.

With the increase in global interconnectedness, the scope of strategic policy choices available to individual governments and the effectiveness of many traditional policy instruments tends to decline (see Keohane and Nye 1972: 392–5; Cooper 1986: 1–22). This tendency occurs, in the first instance, because of the growing irrelevance of many border controls – whether formal or informal – which traditionally served to restrict transactions in goods and services, production factors and technology, ideas and cultural interchange (see Morse 1976: chs 2–3). The result is a shift in the relative costs and benefits of pursuing different policy options. States suffer a further diminution in power because the expansion of transnational forces reduces the control individual governments can exercise over the activities of their citizens and other peoples. For example, the increased mobility of capital induced by the development of global financial markets shifts the balance of power between markets and states and generates powerful pressures on states to develop market-friendly policies, including low public deficits and expenditure, especially on social goods; internationally competitive (that is, low) levels of direct taxation; privatization and labour market deregulation. The decisions of private investors to move private capital across borders can threaten welfare budgets, taxation levels and other government policies. In effect, the autonomy of states is compromised as governments find it increasingly difficult to pursue their domestic agendas without cooperating with other agencies, political and economic.

In this context, many of the traditional domains of state activity and responsibility (defence, economic management, health and law and order) can no longer be served without institutionalizing multilateral forms of collaboration. As demands on the state have increased in the postwar years, the state has been faced with a whole series of policy problems which cannot be adequately resolved without cooperating with other states and non-state actors (Keohane 1984; McGrew 1992). Accordingly, individual states alone can no longer be conceived of as the appropriate political units for either resolving key policy problems or managing effectively a broad range of public functions.

These arguments suggest that the modern state is increasingly embedded in webs of regional and global interconnectedness permeated by quasi-supranational, intergovernmental and transnational forces, and unable to determine its own fate. Such developments, it is also contended, challenge both the sovereignty and legitimacy of states. Sovereignty is challenged because the political authority of states is displaced and compromised by regional and global power systems, political, economic and cultural. State legitimacy is at issue because with greater regional and global interdependence, states cannot deliver fundamental goods and services to their citizens without international cooperation, and even the latter can be quite inadequate in the face of global problems – from global warming to the volatile movements of the financial markets – which can escape political regulation altogether. To the extent that political legitimacy depends on competence and the ability to 'deliver the goods' to citizens, it is under increasing strain. Globalization, conclude the globalists, is eroding the capacity of nation-states to act independently in the articulation and pursuit of domestic and international policy objectives: the power and role of the territorial nation-state is in decline. Political power is being reconfigured.

## III   The Fate of National Culture

For long periods of human history most people have lived out their lives in a web of local cultures. While the formation and expansion of the great world religions and premodern empires carried ideas and beliefs across frontiers with decisive social impacts, the most important vehicle for this, in the absence of direct military and political intervention, was the development of networks of ruling class culture (Mann 1986). At points these bit deeply into the fragmented mosaic of local cultures, but for most people, most of the time, their daily lives and routines persisted largely unchanged. Prior to the emergence of nations and nation-states, most cultural communication and interaction occurred either between elites or at very local and restricted levels. Little interaction took place between the court and the village. It was not until the eighteenth century that a new form of cultural identity coalesced between these two extremes.

## The story of national culture: the sceptic's resource

The rise of the modern nation-state and nationalist movements altered the landscape of political identity. The conditions involved in the creation of the modern state were often also the conditions which generated a sense of nationhood. As state makers sought to centralize and reorder political power in circumscribed territories, and to secure and strengthen their power base, they came to depend on cooperative forms of social relations with their subjects (Giddens 1985; Mann 1986). The centralization of power spawned the dependence of rulers on the ruled for resources, human and financial. Greater reciprocity was created between governors and governed and the terms of their 'exchange' became contested. In particular, the military and administrative requirements of the modern state 'politicized' social relations and day-to-day activities. Gradually, people became aware of their membership in a shared political community, with a common fate. Although the nature of this emergent identity was often initially vague, it grew more definite and precise over time (Therborn 1977; Turner 1986; Mann 1987).

The consolidation of the ideas and narratives of the nation and nationhood has been linked to many factors, including the attempt by ruling elites and governments to create a new identity that would legitimize the enhancement of state power and the coordination of policy (Breuilly 1992); the creation, via a mass education system, of a common framework of understanding – ideas, meanings, practices – to enhance the process of state-coordinated modernization (Gellner 1983); the emergence of new communication systems – particularly new media (such as printing and the telegraph), independent publishers and a free market for printed material – which facilitated interclass communication and the diffusion of national histories, myths and rituals, that is, a new imagined community (B. Anderson 1983); and, building on a historic sense of homeland and deeply rooted memories, the consolidation of ethnic communities via a common public culture, shared legal rights and duties, and an economy creating mobility for its members within a bounded territory (Smith 1986, 1995).

Even where the establishment of a national identity was an explicit political project pursued by elites, it was rarely their complete invention. That nationalist elites actively sought to generate a sense of nationality and a commitment to the nation – a 'national community of fate' – is well documented. But 'it does not follow', as one observer aptly noted, that such elites 'invented nations where none existed' (Smith 1990: 180–1). The 'nation-to-be' was not any large, social or cultural entity; rather, it was a 'community of history and culture', occupying a particular territory, and often laying claim to a distinctive tradition of common rights and duties for its members. Accordingly, many nations were 'built up on the basis of pre-modern "ethnic cores" whose myths and memories, values and symbols shaped the culture and boundaries of the nation that modern elites managed to forge' (Smith 1990: 180; and see Smith 1986). The identity that nationalists strove to uphold depended, in significant part, on uncovering and exploiting a community's 'ethno-history' and on highlighting its distinctiveness in the world of competing political and cultural values (cf. Hall 1992).

Of course, the construction of nations, national identities and nation-states has always been harshly contested and the conditions for the successful development of each never fully overlapped with that of the others (see Held et al. 1999: 48–9, 336–40). States are, as noted previously, complex webs of institutions, laws and practices, the spatial reach of which has been difficult to secure and stabilize over fixed territories. Nations involve cross-class collectivities which share a sense of identity and collective political fate. Their basis in real and imagined cultural, linguistic and historical commonalities is highly malleable and fluid, often giving rise to diverse expressions and ambiguous relationships to states. Nationalism is the force which links states to nations: it describes both the complex cultural and psychological allegiance of individuals to particular national identities and communities, and the project of establishing a state in which a given nation is dominant. The fixed borders of the modern state have generally embraced a diversity of ethnic, cultural and linguistic groups with mixed leanings and allegiances. The relationships between these groups, and between such groups and states, has been chequered and often a source of bitter conflict. In the late nineteenth and twentieth centuries, nationalism became a force which supported and buttressed state formation in certain places (for example, in France) and challenged or refashioned it elsewhere (for instance, in multi-ethnic states such as Spain or the United Kingdom) (see Held et al. 1999: 337–8).

However, despite the diversity of nationalisms and their political aims, and the fact that most national cultures are less than two hundred years old, these new political forces created fundamentally novel terms of political reference in the modern world – terms of reference which appear so well rooted today that many, if not the overwhelming majority of, peoples take them as given and practically natural (cf. Barry 1998). While earlier epochs witnessed cultural institutions that either stretched across many societies (world religions) or were highly localized in their form, the rise of nations, nationalism and nation-states led to the organization of cultural life along national and territorial lines. In Europe this assisted the consolidation of some older states, the creation of a plethora of new nation-states and, eventually, the fragmentation of multinational empires. The potency of the idea of the 'nation' was not lost on the rest of the world and notions of national culture and nationalism spread – partly as a result of the expansion of European empires themselves – to the Americas, Asia, Africa and the Middle East. This helped fuel independence movements, cementing once again a particular link between culture, geography and political freedom.

The struggle for national identity and nationhood has been so extensive that the sceptics doubt the latter can be eroded by transnational forces and, in particular, by the development of a so-called global mass culture. In fact, advocates of the primacy of national identity emphasize its enduring qualities and the deep appeal of national cultures compared to the ephemeral and ersatz qualities of the products of the trans-national media corporations (see Smith 1990; Brown 1995). Since national cultures have been centrally concerned with consolidating the relationships between political identity, self-determination and the powers of the state, they are, and will remain, the sceptics suggest, formidably important sources of ethical and political direction (see section VI below). Moreover, the new electronic networks of communication and information technology which now straddle the world help intensify and rekindle tra-ditional forms and sources of national life, reinforcing their influence and impact. These networks, it has been aptly noted, 'make possible a denser, more intense interaction between members of communities who share common cultural characteristics, notably language'; and this provides a renewed impetus to the re-emergence of 'ethnic com-munities and their nationalisms' (Smith 1990: 175).

Furthermore, the sceptics argue, while new communication systems can create access to distant others, they also generate an awareness of difference; that is, of the incredible diversity in lifestyles and value orientations (see Gilroy 1987; Robins 1991; Massey and Jess 1995). Although this awareness may enhance cultural understand-ing, it often leads to an accentuation of what is distinctive and idiosyncratic, further fragmenting cultural life. Awareness of 'the other' by no means guarantees intersub-jective agreement, as the Salman Rushdie affair only too clearly showed (see Parekh 1989). Moreover, although the new communication industries may generate a language of their own, a particular set of values and consumption patterns, they confront a mul-tiplicity of languages and discourses through which people make sense of their lives and cultures (J. B. Thompson 1990: 313ff.). The vast majority of the products of the mass-market cultural corporations which flood across borders originate within the US and Western societies. But the available evidence, according to the sceptics, suggests that national (and local) cultures remain robust; national institutions continue in many states to have a central impact on public life; national television and radio broadcasting continues to enjoy substantial audiences; the organization of the press and news cov-erage retains strong national roots; and foreign cultural products are constantly read and reinterpreted in novel ways by national audiences (Miller 1992; Liebes and Katz 1993; J. B. Thompson 1995).

Finally, defenders of national culture point out that there is no common global pool of memories; no common global way of thinking; and no 'universal history' in and through which people can unite. There is only a manifold set of political mean-ings and systems through which any new global awareness must struggle for survival (see Bozeman 1984). Given the deep roots of ethno-histories, and the many ways they are often refashioned, this can hardly be a surprise. Despite the vast flows of information, imagery and people around the world, there are few signs of a universal or global culture in the making, and few signs of a decline in the political salience of nationalism.

## Cultural globalization

Globalists take issue with most of the above, although they by no means dismiss the significance of 'the national question'. Among the points they often stress are the *constructed* nature of nationalist cultures; if these cultures were created more recently than many are willing to recognize, and elaborated for a world in which nation-states were being forged, then they are neither immutable nor inevitable in a global age. Nationalism may have been functional, perhaps even essential, for the consolidation and development of the modern state, but it is today at odds with a world in which economic, social and many political forces escape the jurisdiction of the nation-state.

Given how slow many people's identities often are to change, and the strong desire many people feel to (re)assert control over the forces which shape their lives, the complexities of national identity politics are, globalists concede, likely to persist. But such politics will not deliver political control and accountability over regional and global phenomena unless a distinction is made between cultural nationalism – the conceptual, discursive and symbolic resources which are fundamental to people's lives – and political nationalism – the assertion of the exclusive political priority of national identity and national interests. The latter cannot deliver many sought-after public goods and values without regional and global collaboration. Only a global political outlook can ultimately accommodate itself to the political challenges of a more global era, marked by overlapping communities of fate and multilayered (local, national, regional and global) politics. Is there any reason to believe that such an outlook might emerge? Not only are there many sources for such an outlook in the present period but, globalists would argue, there are precedents to be found in the history of the modern state itself.

While the rise of nation-states and nationalist projects intensified cultural formation and interaction within circumscribed political terrains, the expansion of European powers overseas helped entrench new forms of cultural globalization with innovations in transport and communications, notably regularized mechanical transport and the telegraph. These technological advances helped the West to expand and enabled the secular philosophies which emerged in the late eighteenth and nineteenth centuries – especially science, liberalism and socialism – to diffuse and transform the cultural context of almost every society on the planet.

Contemporary popular cultures may not yet have had a social impact to match this but, globalists argue, the sheer scale, intensity, speed and volume of global cultural communications today is unsurpassed. For instance, the value of cultural exports and imports has increased many times over the last few decades; there has been a huge expansion in the trade of television, film and radio products; national broadcasting systems are subject to intensifying international competition and declining audience shares; and the figures for connections and users of the Internet are growing exponentially as communication patterns increasingly transcend national borders (UNESCO 1950, 1986, 1989; OECD 1997). The accelerating diffusion of radio, television, the Internet, satellite and digital technologies has made instant communication possible. Many national controls over information have become ineffective. People everywhere are exposed to the values of other cultures as never before. Nothing, not even the fact that we all speak different languages, can stop the flow of ideas and cultures. The English language is becoming so dominant that it provides a linguistic infrastructure as powerful as any technological system for transmitting ideas and cultures.

Beyond its scale, what is striking about today's cultural globalization is that it is driven by companies, not countries. Corporations, argue the globalists, have replaced states and theocracies as the central producers and distributors of cultural globalization. Private international institutions are not new but their mass impact is. News agencies and publishing houses in previous eras had a much more limited impact on local and national cultures than the consumer goods and cultural products of today's global corporations.

For the globalists the existence of new global communication systems is transforming relations between physical locales and social circumstances, and altering the 'situational geography' of political and social life (Meyrowitz 1985). In these circumstances, the traditional link between 'physical setting' and 'social situation' is broken. Geographical boundaries are overcome as individuals and collectivities experience events and developments far afield. Moreover, new understandings, commonalities and frames of meaning are elaborated without direct contact between people. As such, they can serve to detach, or disembed, identities from particular times, places and traditions, and can have a 'pluralizing impact' on identity formation, producing a variety of hyphenated identities which are 'less fixed or unified' (Hall 1992: 303, 309). While everyone has a local life, the ways people make sense of the world are now increasingly interpenetrated by developments and processes from diverse settings. Hybrid cultures and transnational media corporations have made significant inroads into national cultures and national identities. The cultural position of the modern state is transformed as a result (cf. McLuhan 1964; Rheingold 1995).

Those states which seek to pursue rigid closed-door policies on information and culture are certainly under threat from these new communication processes and technologies, and it is likely that the conduct of socio-economic life everywhere will be transformed by them as well. Cultural flows are transforming the politics of national identity and the politics of identity more generally. These developments have been interpreted, by some global theorists, as creating a new sense of global belonging and vulnerability which transcends loyalties to the nation-state, that is, to 'my country right or wrong' (see, for instance, Falk 1995b). The warrant for this latter claim can be found, it has been argued, in a number of processes and forces, including the development of transnational social movements with clear regional or global objectives, such as the protection of natural resources and the environment, and the alleviation of disease, ill-health and poverty (Ekins 1992). Groups like Friends of the Earth and Greenpeace have derived some of their success precisely from their ability to show the interconnectedness across nations and regions of the problems they seek to tackle. In addition, the constellation of actors, agencies and institutions – from regional political organizations to the UN – which are oriented towards international and transnational issues is cited as further evidence of a growing global political awareness. Finally, a commitment to human rights as indispensable to the dignity and integrity of all peoples – rights entrenched in international law and championed by transnational groups such as Amnesty International – is held to be additional support of an emerging 'global consciousness'. These factors, it is also maintained, represent the cultural foundations of an incipient 'global civil society' (Falk 1995b; Kaldor 1998).

## IV  A Global Economy?

Assessing competing claims about the fate of national cultures is complicated by the fact that, in part, it involves subjective questions of meaning for which systematic and reliable cross-cultural evidence is difficult to acquire. By contrast the debate about economic globalization suffers from almost the opposite problem: namely, the existence of a multiplicity of data sources on diverse global trends, from merchandise trade and migration to foreign direct investment and child labour. At times, this tends to lend the debate a certain spurious objectivity as appeals to 'hard' evidence seek to establish the basis for conclusive judgements about competing claims. In practice, the discussion revolves as much around conflicting assessments of the validity of existing evidence and the value of different types of data as it does around issues of theoretical interpretation.

Although the debate about economic globalization has produced a voluminous literature, with contributions covering all the main traditions of economic and social analysis, the critical points of contention cluster around four fundamental questions. Put simply, these embrace:

- the extent to which the evidence shows that economic activity is being globalized;
- whether a new form of global capitalism, driven by 'the third industrial revolution', is taking hold across the globe;
- how far economic globalization remains subject to proper and effective national and international governance; and
- whether global competition spells the end of national economic strategy and the welfare state.

These four questions preoccupy both globalists and sceptics. A critical dialogue has opened up concerning the historical evidence about economic globalization; the dominant regime of capitalist accumulation; the modes and effectiveness of contemporary economic governance; and the robustness of national economic autonomy and sovereignty.

## The persistence of national economies

The sceptical position reflects a cautious interpretation of contemporary global economic trends. Rather than a truly global economy the sceptics argue that, judged in historical terms, the present world economy remains far from closely integrated. By comparison with the *belle époque* of 1890–1914 both the magnitude and geographical scale of flows of trade, capital and migrants are currently of a much lower order (Gordon 1988; Weiss 1998; Hirst and Thompson 1999). Although today gross flows of capital between the world's major economies are largely unprecedented, the actual net flows between them are considerably less than at the start of the twentieth century (Zevin 1992). Many of these economies are less open to trade than in the past, and this is also the case for many developing countries (Hoogvelt 1997; Hirst and Thompson 1999). In addition, the scale of nineteenth-century migration across the globe dwarfs that of the present era by a significant magnitude (Hirst and Thompson 1999). In all these respects, the contemporary world economy is significantly less open and globalized than its nineteenth-century counterpart. It is also, argue the sceptics, significantly less integrated.

If economic globalization is associated with the integration of separate national economies, such that the actual organization of economic activity transcends national frontiers, then a global economy might be said to be emerging. Theoretically, in a glob-alized economy world market forces take precedence over national economic condi-tions as the real values of key economic variables (production, prices, wages and interest rates) respond to global competition. Just as local economies are submerged within national markets so, suggests the strong sceptical position, the real test of economic globalization is whether world trends confirm a pattern of global economic integra-tion, that is, the existence of a single global economy (Hirst and Thompson 1999). In this respect the evidence, it is argued, falls far short of the exaggerated claims of many globalists. Even among the OECD states, undoubtedly the most interconnected of any economies, the contemporary trends suggest only a limited degree of economic and financial integration (Feldstein and Horioka 1980; Neal 1985; Zevin 1992; Jones 1995; Garrett 1998). Whether in respect of finance, technology, labour or production the evidence fails to confirm either the existence or the emergence of a single global eco-nomy (Hirst and Thompson 1999). Even multinational corporations, it is concluded, remain predominantly the captives of national or regional markets, contrary to their popular portrayal as 'footloose capital' (Tyson 1991; Ruigrok and Tulder 1995).

In contrast to the globalists, the sceptics interpret current trends as evidence of a significant, but not historically unprecedented, internationalization of economic activity, that is, an intensification of linkages between separate national economies. Internationalization complements, rather than displaces, the predominantly national organization and regulation of contemporary economic and financial activity, conducted by national or local public and private entities. All economics is considered princip-ally national or local. Even the trend towards internationalization repays careful scrutiny; for it betrays a concentration of trade, capital and technological flows between the major OECD states to the exclusion of much of the rest of the world. As Hoogvelt (1997, 2001) notes, in the post-war period (1950–95) developing countries' share of world exports and outward foreign investment declined from 33 per cent to 27.7 per cent and from 50 per cent to 16.5 per cent respectively. The structure of world eco-nomic activity is dominated (and increasingly so) by the OECD economies and the growing links between them (Jones 1995). By far the largest proportion of humanity remains excluded from the so-called global market; there is a growing gap between North and South.

Far from an integrated global economy, the sceptical analysis confirms the increas-ing concentration of world economic activity within three core blocs, each with its own centre and periphery; namely, Europe, Asia-Pacific and the Americas. This triadization of the world economy is associated with a growing tendency towards economic and financial interdependence *within* each of these three zones at the expense of integration between them (Lloyd 1992; Hirst and Thompson 1999). This growing regionalization of economic activity is further evident in the evolution of the formal structures of APEC, NAFTA, MERCOSUR, ASEAN and the EU and in the regional production and marketing strategies of multinational corporations and national firms (G. Thompson 1998a). Far from the present being an era of economic globalization, it is, especially by comparison with the *belle époque*, one defined by the growing segmentation of the world economy into a multiplicity of regional economic zones dominated by powerful mercantilist forces of national economic competition and economic rivalry (Hart 1992; Sandholtz et al. 1992).

If the sceptical argument dismisses evidence of a globalized economy, it is equally critical of the proposition that the current era is defined by the existence of a nascent global capitalism. While not denying that capitalism, following the collapse of state socialism, is the 'only economic game in town' or that capital itself has become significantly more internationally mobile, such developments, it is argued, should not be read as evidence of a new globalized ('turbo') capitalism, transcending and sub-suming national capitalisms (Callinicos et al. 1994; Ruigrok and Tulder 1995; Boyer and Drache 1996; Hirst and Thompson 1999). On the contrary, distinct capitalist social formations continue to flourish on the models of the European social-democratic mixed economy, the American neoliberal project and the developmental state of East Asia (Wade 1990). Despite the aspirations of its most powerful protagonists, the neolib-eral tide of the 1990s has not forced a genuine or substantive convergence between these; nor can it claim a serious victory over its competitors (Scharpf 1991; Hart 1992). The 'end of history', in this respect, has turned out to be short-lived. The idea of global capitalism, personified by the business empires of figures such as George Soros and Bill Gates, may have great popular appeal but it is, ultimately, an unsatisfactory and misleading concept since it ignores the diversity of existing capitalist forms and the rootedness of all capital in discrete national capitalist structures.

Although the images of foreign exchange dealing rooms in New York or London reinforce the idea that capital is essentially 'footloose', the reality, suggest the scep-tics, is that all economic and financial activity, from production, research and devel-opment to trading and consumption, has to take place somewhere. To talk of the 'end of geography' is a serious exaggeration when place and space remain such vital deter-minants of the global distribution of wealth and economic power. Granted that, in a world of almost real-time communication, corporate capital and even small businesses may have the option of greater mobility, the fate of firms, large or small, is still primarily determined by local and national competitive advantages and economic conditions (Porter 1990; Ruigrok and Tulder 1995; G. Thompson 1998b). Even among the most substantial multinationals, competitive advantages are largely rooted in their respective national systems of innovation, while production and sales tend to be strongly regionally concentrated (Ruigrok and Tulder 1995; Thompson and Allen 1997). In effect, multinationals are little more than 'national corporations with international operations' since their home base is such a vital ingredient of their continued success and iden-tity (Hu 1992) – a point British Airways learnt to its cost when its frequent flyers (predominantly of non-British origin) forced the airline to reconsider its policy of repla-cing the Union Jack with global images on its aircraft tailplanes. Furthermore, a brief glance at the Fortune 500 list of the world's largest companies would confirm this since few are headquartered outside the US, UK, Germany or Japan. Indeed, closer inspection of the list would reveal the 'myth' of global capitalism as a convenient cover for the internationalization of American business above all else (Callinicos et al. 1994; Burbach et al. 1997). Governments, or at least the more powerful among them, thus retain considerable bargaining power with MNCs because they control access to vital national economic resources.

In dismissing the idea of 'footloose capital', the sceptical argument undermines the proposition that there is a new pattern of interdependence emerging between North and South. There is, the sceptics acknowledge, a popular belief that the deindustrialization of OECD economies is primarily a consequence of the export of manufacturing business and jobs to emerging economies and less developed economies, where wage rates are lower and regulatory requirements much less stringent. This interdependence between North and South is taken by some to define a new international division of labour in which developing economies are moving away from primary products to manufacturing, while the OECD economies are shifting from manufacturing to services. But the actual evidence, the sceptics suggest, does not bear out such a dramatic shift, while the argument overgeneralizes from the East Asian experience (Callinicos et al. 1994; Hirst and Thompson 1996). The bulk of the world's poorest economies remain reliant on the export of primary products, while the OECD economies continue to dominate trade in manufactured goods (Hirst and Thompson 1999). Deindustrialization cannot be traced to the effects of foreign trade, especially cheap exports from the developing world, but rather is a consequence of technological change and changes in labour market conditions throughout the OECD economies (Rowthorn and Wells 1987; Krugman 1994, 1995). By exaggerating the changes in the international division of labour there is a serious risk of overlooking the deeper continuities in the world economy. Despite internationalization and regionalization, the role and position of most developing countries in the world economy have changed remarkably little over the entire course of the last century (Gordon 1988). The present international division of labour is one Marx would instantly recognize.

If the international division of labour has changed only marginally, so also has the governance of the world economy. Although the post-1945 era witnessed significant institutional innovations in international economic governance, especially with the creation of a multilateral system of economic surveillance and regulation – the Bretton Woods regime – the actions of the US, as the world's largest single economic agent, remain critical to the smooth functioning of the world economy. In effect, the governance of the world economy still remains reliant, especially in times of crisis, on the willingness of the most powerful state(s) to police the system – as the East Asian crash of 1997–8 demonstrated so dramatically. However, even in more stable times, it is the preferences and interests of the most economically powerful states, in practice the G7 governments, that take precedence. Economic multilateralism has not rewritten the basic rules of international economic governance, argue the sceptics, for it remains a realm in which might trumps right: where the clash of competing national interests is resolved ultimately through the exercise of national power and bargaining between governments (Gilpin 1987; Sandholtz et al. 1992; Kapstein 1994). In this respect, multilateral institutions have to be conceived as instruments of states – and the most powerful states at that.

Of course, it is not part of the sceptical argument that the governance of the world economy has not changed at all in response to growing internationalization and, especially, regionalization (Hirst and Thompson 1999). There is, on the contrary, a strong recognition that the most pressing issue confronting the guardians of the world economy, in the aftermath of the East Asian crash, is how to reform and strengthen the Bretton Woods system (Kapstein 1994; Hirst and Thompson 1999). Furthermore, there is an acknowledgement of growing tensions between the rule-making activities of multilateral bodies, such as the WTO, and regional bodies such as the EU. New issues, from the environment to food production, have found their way on to the governance agenda too. Many of these are highly politicized since they bite deep into the sovereign jurisdiction of states – the very core of modern statehood itself.

Nevertheless, national governments, the sceptics hold, remain central to the governance of the world economy, since they alone have the formal political authority to regulate economic activity. As most states today rely, to varying degrees, on international flows of trade and finance to ensure national economic growth, the limits to, and the constraints on, national economic autonomy and sovereignty have become more visible, especially in democratic states. Historically, however, these constraints are no greater than in previous epochs when, as noted previously, international interdependence was much more intense. Paradoxically, the *belle époque* was precisely the era during which nation-states and national economies were being forged (Gilpin 1981; Krasner 1993). Thus, contemporary conditions pose no real threat to national sovereignty or autonomy. Far from economic interdependence necessarily eroding national economic autonomy or sovereignty, it can be argued to have enhanced the national capabilities of many states. Openness to global markets, many economists argue, provides greater opportunities for sustained national economic growth. As the experience of the East Asian 'tigers' highlighted, global markets are entirely compatible with strong states (Weiss 1998). But even in those contexts where state sovereignty appears to be significantly compromised by internationalization, as in the case of the European Union, national governments, according to the sceptical interpretation, effectively pool sovereignty in order to enhance, through collective action, their control over external forces. Rather than conceiving of national governments as simply captives of external economic forces, the sceptical position acknowledges their critical role (especially that of the most powerful) in creating the necessary national and international conditions for global markets to exist in the first place. In this respect, states are both the architects and the subjects of the world economy.

As subjects, however, states do not respond in identical ways to the dynamics of world markets or to external economic shocks. While international financial markets and international competition may well impose similar kinds of economic disciplines on all governments, this does not necessarily prefigure a convergence in national economic strategies or policies. Such pressures are mediated by domestic structures and institutional arrangements which produce enormous variations in the capacity of national governments to respond (Garrett and Lange 1996; Weiss 1998). States can and do make a difference, as the continuing diversity of capitalist forms indicates. This is especially the case in relation to macroeconomic and industrial policy, where significant national differences continue to exist even within the same regions of the world (Dore 1995; Boyer and Drache 1996; Garrett 1998). Nor is there much convincing evidence to suggest that international financial disciplines by themselves either preclude governments from pursuing progressive and redistributive economic strategies or, alternatively, prefigure the demise of the welfare state or robust policies of social protection (Garrett 1996, 1998; Rieger and Liebfried 1998; Hirst and Thompson 1999). The fact that levels of national welfare spending and social protection continue to differ considerably, even within the EU, points to the absurdity of the latter argument. In the judgement of the sceptics, national governments remain, for the most part, the sole source of effective and legitimate authority in the governance of the world economy, while also being the principal agents of international economic coordination and regulation – a condition reinforced by the growing reassertion of state power following the events of 11 September 2001.

## The new global economy

For the globalists this conclusion is hard to credit, for it overlooks the ways in which national governments are having to adjust constantly to the push and pull of global market conditions and forces. Contesting both the sceptics' evidence, and their interpretation of world economic trends, the globalist account points to the historically unprecedented scale and magnitude of contemporary global economic integration (O'Brien 1992; Altvater and Mahnkopf 1997; Greider 1997; Rodrik 1997; Dicken 1998). Daily turnover on the world's foreign exchange markets, for instance, currently exceeds some sixty times the annual level of world exports, while the scale and intensity of world trade far exceeds that of the *belle époque*. Global production by multinational corporations is considerably greater than the level of world exports, and encompasses all the world's major economic regions. Migration, though perhaps slightly smaller in magnitude than in the nineteenth century, nevertheless has become increasingly globalized. National economies, with some exceptions, are presently much more deeply enmeshed in global systems of production and exchange than in previous historical eras, while few states, following the collapse of state socialism, remain excluded from global financial and economic markets. Patterns of contemporary economic globalization have woven strong and enduring webs across the world's major regions such that their economic fates are intimately connected.

Although the global economy, conceived as a singular entity, may not be as highly integrated as the most robust national economies, the trends, argue the globalists, point unambiguously towards intensifying integration within and across regions. The operation of global financial markets, for example, has produced a convergence in interest rates among the major economies (Fukao 1993; Gagnon and Unferth 1995). Financial integration also brings with it a contagion effect in that economic crisis in one region, as the East Asian crash of 1997–8 demonstrated, rapidly acquires global ramifications (Godement 1999). Alongside financial integration the operations of multinational corporations integrate national and local economies into global and regional production networks (Castells 1996; Gereffi and Korzeniewicz 1994; Dicken 1998). Under these conditions, national economies no longer function as autonomous systems of wealth creation since national borders are increasingly marginal to the conduct and organization of economic activity. In this 'borderless economy', as the more radical globalists conceive it, the distinction between domestic economic activity and global economic activity, as the range of products in any superstore will confirm, is becoming increasingly difficult to sustain (Ohmae 1990).

Accordingly, the contemporary phase of economic globalization, the globalists suggest, is distinguished from past phases by the existence of a single global economy transcending and integrating the world's major economic regions (Geyer and Bright 1995; Dickson 1997; Scholte 1997; Dicken 1998; Frank 1998). By comparison with the *belle époque*, an era distinguished by relatively high levels of trade protectionism and imperial economic zones, the present global economy is considerably more open and its operations impact upon all countries, even those nominally 'pariah' states such as Cuba or North Korea (Nierop 1994). Nor has the growth of regionalism produced a sharp division of the world into competing blocs; for the regionalization of economic activity has not been at the expense of economic globalization (Lloyd 1992; Anderson and Blackhurst 1993; Anderson and Norheim 1993). On the contrary, regionalism has largely facilitated and encouraged economic globalization since it offers a mechanism through which national economies can engage more strategically with global markets (Gamble and Payne 1991; Hanson 1998). Furthermore, there is little evidence to suggest, as do many sceptics, that a process of triadization is occurring in so far as economic interdependence between the three major centres of the global economy – the US, Japan and Europe – appears itself to be intensifying (Ohmae 1990; Dunning 1993; Greider 1997; Perraton et al. 1997; Dicken 1998; Haass and Liton 1998). Although the contemporary global economy is structured around three major centres of economic power – unlike the *belle époque* or the early postwar decades of US dominance – it is best described as a post-hegemonic order in so far as no single centre can dictate the rules of global trade and commerce (Gill 1992; Geyer and Bright 1995; Amin 1996). Of course, it remains a highly stratified order in that by far the largest share of global economic flows – such as trade and finance – are concentrated among the major OECD economies. But the dominance of OECD economies is being diluted as economic globalization significantly alters the geography of world economic activity and power.

Over the last few decades developing economies' shares of world exports and foreign investment flows (inwards and outwards) have increased considerably (Castells 1996; Dicken 1998; UNCTAD 1998a, 1998c). In 2000 they accounted for 27 per cent of world manufactured export, by comparison with 17 per cent in 1990; and by 2001 their share of FDI (inflow) was 28 per cent compared to 18 per cent in 1986 (WTO 2002; UNCTAD 2002). The NICs of East Asia and Latin America have become an increasingly important destination for OECD investment and an increasingly significant source of OECD imports – São Paulo, it is sometimes quipped, is Germany's largest industrial city (Dicken 1998). By the late 1990s almost 50 per cent of total world manufacturing jobs were located in developing economies, while over 60 per cent of developing country exports to the industrialized world were manufactured goods, a twelvefold increase in less than four decades (UNDP 1998). Contrary to the sceptical interpretation, contemporary economic globalization is neither solely, nor even primarily, an OECD phenomenon but, rather, embraces all continents and regions (UNCTAD 1998c).

By definition, the global economy is a capitalist global economy in that it is organized on the basis of market principles and production for profit. Historically, apart from the division of the world into capitalist and state socialist camps during the Cold War era, many would argue this has been the case since early modern times, if not since much before that (Wallerstein 1974; Braudel 1984; Fernández-Armesto 1995; Geyer and Bright 1995; Frank and Gills 1996; Frank 1998). However, what distinguishes the present global capitalist economy from that of prior epochs, argue the globalists, is its particular historical form. Over recent decades, the core economies in the global system have undergone a profound economic restructuring. In the process they have been transformed from essentially industrial to post-industrial economies (Piore and Sabel 1984; Castells 1996). Just as the twentieth century witnessed the global diffusion of industrial capitalism, so at the century's end post-industrial capitalism began to take its place.

With this restructuring has come a dramatic alteration in the form and organization of global capitalism. In variously referring to 'global informational capitalism', 'manic capitalism', 'turbo-capitalism', or 'supraterritorial capitalism', commentators seek to capture the qualitative shift occurring in the spatial organization and dynamics of this new global capitalist formation (Castells 1996; Greider 1997; Scholte 1997; Luttwak

1999). In the age of the Internet, to simplify the argument, capital – both productive and financial – has been liberated from national and territorial constraints, while markets have become globalized to the extent that the domestic economy constantly has to adapt to global competitive conditions. In a wired world, software engineers in Hyderabad can do the jobs of software engineers in London for a fraction of the cost. Inscribed in the dynamics of this new global capitalism is a powerful imperative towards the denationalization of strategic economic activities.

Central to the organization of this new global capitalist order is the multinational corporation. In 2001 there were approximately 65,000 MNCs worldwide with 850,000 foreign subsidiaries selling $18.5 trillion of goods and services across the globe (UNCTAD 2002). Today transnational production considerably exceeds the level of global exports ($7.4 trillion) and has become the primary means for selling goods and services abroad. Multinational corporations now account, according to some estimates, for at least 20 per cent of world production, 11 per cent of world GDP (compared to 7 per cent in 1990), 54 million direct jobs and 70 per cent of world trade (Perraton et al. 1997; UNCTAD 2002). They span every sector of the global economy from raw materials, to finance, to manufacturing, integrating and reordering economic activity within and across the world's major economic regions (Gill 1995; Castells 1996; Amin 1997). In the financial sector multinational banks are by far the major actors in global financial markets, playing a critical role in the management and organization of money and credit in the global economy (Walters 1993; Germain 1997). It is global corporate capital, rather than states, contend the globalists, that exercises decisive influence over the organization, location and distribution of economic power and resources in the contemporary global economy.

Contemporary patterns of economic globalization, the globalists also argue, have been accompanied by a new global division of labour brought about, in part, by the activities of multinationals themselves (Johnston et al. 1995; Hoogvelt 1997). The restructuring (deindustrialization) of OECD economies can be directly related to the outsourcing of manufacturing production by multinationals to the newly industrializing and transition economies of Asia, Latin America and Eastern Europe (Reich 1991; Wood 1994; Rodrik 1997). NICs now account for a significant proportion of global exports and, through integration into transnational production networks, have become extensions of, as well as competitors of, businesses in metropolitan economies. In this respect, globalization is reordering developing countries into clear winners and losers. Such restructuring is, moreover, replicated within countries, both North and South, as communities and particular locales closely integrated into global production networks reap significant rewards while the rest survive on the margins. Thus, contemporary economic globalization brings with it an increasingly unified world for elites – national, regional and global – but increasingly divided nations as the global workforce is segmented, within rich and poor countries alike, into winners and losers. The old North–South international division of labour is giving way, suggest the globalists, to a new global division of labour, which involves a reordering of interregional economic relations and a new pattern of wealth and inequality, transcending both post-industrial and industrializing economies (Reich 1991; Amin 1997; Hoogvelt 1997; Rodrik 1997; Castells 1998; Dicken 1998).

One of the central contradictions of this new order pertains to its governance. For the globalization of economic activity exceeds the regulatory reach of national governments while, at the same time, existing multilateral institutions of global economic governance have limited authority because states, jealously guarding their national sovereignty, refuse to cede them substantial power (Zürn 1995). Under these conditions, assert some of the more radical globalists, world markets effectively escape political regulation such that economic globalization is in danger of creating a 'runaway world' (Giddens 1999). Governments, therefore, have no real option other than to accommodate to the forces of economic globalization (Amin 1996; Cox 1997). Furthermore, the existing multilateral institutions of global economic governance, especially the IMF, World Bank and WTO, in so far as they advocate and pursue programmes which simply extend and deepen the hold of global market forces on national economic life, have become the agents of global capital and the G7 states (Gill 1995; Korten 1995; Cox 1996). For the most part, the governance structures of the global economy operate principally to nurture and reproduce the forces of economic globalization, while also acting to discipline this nascent 'global market civilization' (Gill 1995; Korten 1995; Burbach et al. 1997; Hoogvelt 1997; Scholte 1997).

While accepting many of the precepts of this radical globalist position, others conceive the governance structures of the global economy as having considerable autonomy from the dictates of global capital and/or the G7 states (Rosenau 1990; Shaw 1994; Shell 1995; Cortell and Davies 1996; Castells 1997; Hasenclever et al. 1997; Milner 1997; Herod et al. 1998). According to these authors, multilateral institutions have become increasingly important sites through which economic globalization is contested, by weaker states and the agencies of transnational civil society, while the G7 states and global capital find themselves on many occasions at odds with their decisions or rules. Moreover, the political dynamics of multilateral institutions tend to mediate great power control, for instance through consensual modes of decision-making, such that they are never merely tools of dominant states and social forces (Keohane 1984, 1998; Ruggie 1993a; Hasenclever et al. 1997; Roberts 1998). Alongside these global institutions also exist a parallel set of regional bodies, from MERCOSUR to the EU, which constitute another dimension to what is an emerging system of multilayered economic governance (Rosenau 1990, 1997; Ruggie 1993b). Within the interstices of this system operate the social forces of an emerging transnational civil society, from the International Chamber of Commerce to the Jubilee 2000 campaign, seeking to promote, contest and bring to account the agencies of economic globalization (Falk 1987; Ekins 1992; Scholte 1993; Burbach et al. 1997; Castells 1997; Rosenau 1997). In this respect, the politics of global economic governance is much more pluralistic than the sceptics admit in so far as global and regional institutions exercise considerable independent authority. Economic globalization has been accompanied by a significant internationalization of political authority associated with a corresponding globalization of political activity.

Since national governments are deeply embedded in this system of multilayered economic governance, their role and power continues to be qualified decisively by economic globalization (Reich 1991; Ohmae 1995; Sassen 1996; Rosenau 1997). Some fervent globalists regard nation-states as increasingly 'transitional modes of economic organization and regulation' since, in an age of global markets, it is believed they can no longer effectively manage or regulate their own national economies (Ohmae 1995). Sandwiched between the constraints of global financial markets and the exit options of mobile productive capital, national governments across the globe have been forced to adopt increasingly similar (neoliberal) economic strategies which promote financial discipline, limited government and sound economic management (Gill 1995;

Strange 1996; Amin 1997; Greider 1997; Hoogvelt 1997; Scholte 1997; Yergin and Stanislaw 1998; Luttwak 1999). As global competition intensifies, governments are increasingly unable to maintain existing levels of social protection or welfare state programmes without undermining the competitive position of domestic business and deterring much-needed foreign investment (Reich 1991; Cox 1997; Greider 1997; Scholte 1997; Gray 1998). Borrowing to increase public expenditure or raising taxes to do so are both equally constrained by the dictates of global financial markets (Gourevitch 1986; Frieden 1991; Garrett and Lange 1991; Cox 1997; Germain 1997). Some globalists interpret economic globalization as prefiguring the end of the welfare state and social democracy, while others point less dramatically to a growing convergence across the globe towards more limited welfare state regimes (Gourevitch 1986; Rodrik 1997; Gray 1998; Pieper and Taylor 1998). Nevertheless, there is agreement that the economic autonomy, sovereignty and social solidarity of contemporary states are being transformed by contemporary processes of economic globalization (Zacher 1992; Ohmae 1995; Cable 1996; Sassen 1996; Strange 1996; Altvater and Mahnkopf 1997; Amin 1997; Castells 1997; Cox 1997; Greider 1997; Jessop 1997; Rosenau 1997; Scholte 1997; Shaw 1997).

## V   Divided World, Divided Nations

Contemporary economic globalization, according to a recent UNDP report, is associated with an accelerating gap between rich and poor states, as well as between peoples, in the global economy (UNDP 1999). By determining the location and distribution of wealth and productive power in the world economy, globalization defines and reconfigures worldwide patterns of hierarchy and inequality. This has profound implications for human security and world order in so far as global inequalities condition the life chances of individuals and collectivities, not to mention creating the preconditions for a more unstable and unruly world (Herod et al. 1998; Hurrell 1999). Not surprisingly, the problem of global inequality has become one of the most pressing and contentious issues on the global agenda.

While there is considerable public and academic debate about global inequalities, the discussion does not readily crystallize into a neat dialogue between sceptics and globalists. There is much disagreement among both sceptics and globalists about the causes of, as well as the appropriate remedies for, global inequality.

In analysing contemporary patterns of global inequality, globalists tend to identify economic globalization as the primary culprit. In contrast, the sceptics tend to deny its significance, emphasizing instead the historical reality of imperialism and/or geopolitics. Yet, these contrasting interpretations are also associated within each camp with quite different ethical positions and distinctive assessments of the consequences of economic globalization for both national and international solidarity and, ultimately, the governance and stability of the present world order.

## One world or many?

Among those globalists of a neoliberal persuasion contemporary economic globalization is taken to embody the creation of a single global market which, through the operation of free trade, capital mobility and global competition, is the harbinger of modernization and development (Ohmae 1990, 1995; Perlmutter 1991). Pointing to the East Asian economic miracle and the Latin American experience of the early to mid 1990s (and, indeed, to the quick recovery of many of these economies from the economic turmoil of 1997–8), neoliberals emphasize that the solution to global inequalities is to be found in pursuing policies of openness to global capital and global competition, and in seeking closer integration within the global economy. While there is a recognition that economic globalization generates losers as well as winners, neoliberals stress the growing diffusion of wealth and affluence throughout the world economy. Global poverty, by historical standards, has fallen more in the last fifty years than in the past five hundred and the welfare of people in almost all regions has improved significantly over the last few decades (UNDP 1997). The world has become increasingly middle class. Rather than the old North–South fracture, a new worldwide division of labour is said to be replacing the traditional core–periphery model of global economic relations. As a result, the 'Third World' is becoming increasingly differentiated as more states, taking advantage of open global markets, become industrialized; South Korea, for instance, is now a member of the OECD, the Western club of 'rich' nations, while many other industrializing states aspire to membership. Recognizing both economic and moral limits to the pursuit of global equality, neoliberals remain willing to accept the 'natural' inequalities created by the global market when measured against the loss of liberty – and economic efficiency – entailed by multilateral intervention to redress the consequences of uneven economic globalization (Ohmae 1995).

Amongst neoliberals, economic globalization is associated with growing global affluence: extreme poverty and global inequality are regarded as transitional conditions that will evaporate with market-led global modernization. Economic globalization, it is argued, establishes the preconditions for a more stable and peaceful world order since enduring economic interdependence, as relations between Western states confirm, makes the resort to military force or war increasingly irrational and, therefore, increasingly unlikely (Mitrany 1975; Howard 1981; Mueller 1989; Russett 1993).

Those globalists of a social democratic or radical persuasion offer a rather different interpretation. Economic globalization, they argue, is directly responsible for widening disparities in life chances across the globe – a deepening polarization of income and wealth (Beetham 1995; Commission on Global Governance 1995; Falk 1995a; Gill 1995; Bradshaw and Wallace 1996; Castells 1997; Greider 1997; Hoogvelt 1997; Gray 1998; UNDP 1999). Three related patterns are evident: the segmentation of the global workforce into those who gain and those who lose from economic globalization; the growing marginalization of the losers from the global economy; and the erosion of social solidarity within nations as welfare regimes are unable, or governments unwilling, to bear the costs of protecting the most vulnerable (Lawrence 1996; Castells 1997; Cox 1997; Dicken 1998; Gray 1998; Scharpf 1999). Economic globalization creates a more affluent world for some at the expense of growing poverty for others. That poverty, however, is no longer confined to the South, the developing world, but is on the rise in sectors of the affluent North as well (Birdsall 1998; UNDP 1999).

Furthermore, globalization, it is argued, is responsible for the growing globalization of poverty, not simply inequality. Within OECD economies, unemployment and social exclusion have increased as many low-skilled and semi-skilled jobs have been relocated to more profitable ventures in developing countries (Rodrik 1997; Castells

1998). This global economic restructuring brings with it a horizontal segmentation of the workforce, within rich and poor countries alike, into winners and losers from global capitalism (Castells 1997). This divides nations, forcing some into poverty, and erodes the basis of social solidarity. In advanced economies global competition undermines the social and political coalitions necessary for strong welfare regimes and policies of social protection while, in the developing world, SAPs overseen by the IMF and World Bank severely limit government welfare spending. Today the globalization of poverty, it is suggested, is increasingly a matter of vital and shared global concern (Dickson 1997). By dividing states and peoples it engenders a deepening fragmentation of world order and societies, generating the conditions for a more unstable world. Unless economic globalization is tamed, so the argument goes, a new barbarism will prevail as poverty, social exclusion and social conflict envelop the world.

What is required is a new global ethic which recognizes 'a duty of care' beyond borders, as well as within them, and a global new deal between rich and poor states. This involves rethinking social democracy as a purely national project, recognizing that if it is to remain effective in a globalizing economy, it has to be embedded in a reformed and much stronger system of global governance which seeks to combine human security with economic efficiency (Held 1995; Giddens 1999; UNDP 1999). A reconstituted social democratic project requires the coordinated pursuit of national, regional and global programmes to regulate the forces of economic globalization – to ensure, in other words, that global markets begin to serve the world's peoples rather than vice versa. Extending social democracy beyond borders also depends on strengthening solidarities between those social forces, in different regions of the world, that seek to contest or resist the terms of contemporary economic globalization. Just as the Bretton Woods system established a world economic order conducive to the pursuit of national social democracy, a new global (social democratic) compact is required, argue many globalists, in order to tame the forces of economic globalization and to create a more just and humane world order.

## The challenge of enduring inequality

To the sceptics, especially of a traditional Marxist disposition, the prospect of a global New Deal is decidedly utopian. While acknowledging that contemporary capitalism is creating a more divided and unruly world, it is, many would argue, sheer political naivety to assume that those states, corporations and social forces that benefit most from the present liberal world order are ever likely to consent to its effective reform, let alone its transformation (Callinicos et al. 1994; Burbach et al. 1997). In this account, core and periphery – First World and Third World – remain very much a fundamental feature of the current world order. Rather than international capital creating 'one world' it has been accompanied by deepening global inequality through the marginalization of most Third World economies, as trade and investment flows among OECD economies intensify to the exclusion of much of the rest of the globe. Rather than a new global division of labour, this radical sceptical account points to a deepening North–South fracture (Burbach et al. 1997).

Central to this account is a conception of contemporary economic internationalization as a new mode of Western imperialism. Today 50 per cent of the world's population and two-thirds of its governments are bound by the disciplines of the IMF or the World

Bank (Pieper and Taylor 1998). As the East Asian crisis demonstrated, even the most affluent industrializing states are subject to the rule of G7 governments, particularly the US. Economic internationalization reinforces, rather than replaces, historical patterns of dominance and dependence such that the possibilities for real development remain effectively blocked. As poverty increases, the conflict between North and South deepens, while the affluent West, through various mechanisms from NATO to the World Bank, resorts to a form of 'global riot control' to consolidate its power and secure its economic fortunes. The internationalization of capital is creating an increasingly unruly and violent world in which poverty, deprivation and conflict are the daily reality for most of the world's peoples. In this context, reforming the architecture of the present economic order is a futile gesture when what is required to end imperialism is national revolutionary change in both the metropoles and the periphery. Only a socialist international order, in which socialist states are the essential building blocks, can eradicate global poverty through the determined redistribution of wealth and privilege (Callinicos et al. 1994).

By contrast, those sceptics of a more realist disposition regard such prescriptions as pure idealism, if not fantasy, in a world that has recently witnessed the complete collapse of state socialism. The problem of global inequality, they suggest, is actually one of the more intractable international issues on the global agenda and one which denies effective resolution (Krasner 1985). In this respect, while they may concede that economic internationalization is associated with a growing polarization between rich and poor states, they do not consider it to be the sole, or even primary, cause of growing inequality. National factors, from resource endowments to economic policies, are just as, if not more, important as determinants of the pattern of global inequality (Gilpin 1987). To presume that it can be moderated, let alone eradicated, through coordinated international intervention, or the creation of a socialist world order, is a categorical mistake. For inequality is inscribed in the very structure of world order since a global hierarchy of power is a consequence of a system which ranks states according to their national economic and military endowments (Gilpin 1981; Krasner 1985; Clark 1989; Krasner 1993; K. W. Thompson 1994). Moreover, the hierarchy of power, realists argue, is essential to the maintenance of a stable international order, since in an anarchic – that is, self-help – states system peace and security ultimately depend on the willingness of the most powerful states to police the system. Hierarchy, and thereby inequality, is a vital ingredient of the realist conception of world order, and the basis for effective international governance (Woods 1999). Moderating global inequalities may be a moral aspiration but it is not necessarily a rational one if it undermines the principal basis of international order. Nor, in a system in which states constantly struggle to maintain their power and influence over others, is it a feasible aspiration. Multilateral attempts to redress global inequalities, by taming the power of global markets, are doomed necessarily to failure, since the weak have no effective means to coerce the strong into taking actions which by definition threaten their power and wealth (Krasner 1985). For these reasons, among others, sceptics express a certain antipathy towards, and reservations about, grand projects to establish a more equal and just world order (Woods 1999). Paradoxically, they reason, such a world order is likely to be neither more secure nor more peaceful than the present unjust one. This does not mean that those of a realist persuasion necessarily regard rising inequality as either morally defensible or politically sustainable in the long run, but they consider that it remains a problem without any effective means of international resolution (Krasner 1985).

It is only within the borders of the nation-state – the nation as a moral community of fate – that legitimate and effective solutions to the problem of global inequality can be realized. Such solutions will always be partial and limited since governments cannot realistically aspire to redress all the external sources of domestic inequality. Although international cooperation between states may make it feasible to redress some of the worst excesses of the global market, in the end inequalities can only be moderated successfully and legitimately through the apparatus of national welfare regimes and the determined pursuit of national wealth and economic power. National governments, conclude the sceptics, remain the only proper and proven structures for mediating and redressing the worst consequences of uneven economic internationalization and, thereby, realizing the 'good community' (Hirst and Thompson 1999).

## VI  World Orders, Normative Choices

Throughout the modern period concepts of the political good have generally been elaborated at the level of state institutions and practices; the state has been at the intersection of intellectually and morally ambitious conceptions of political life (Dunn 1990: 142–60). Political theory, by and large, has taken the nation-state as a fixed point of reference and has sought to place the state at the centre of interpretations of the nature and proper form of the political good. Relations among states have of course been analysed; but they have rarely been examined, especially in recent times, as a central element of political theory and political philosophy. The central element has been the territorial political community and its many possible relations to what is desirable or politically good.

## The ethically bounded political community

The theory and practice of liberal democracy has added important nuances to this position. For within the framework of liberal democracy, while territorial boundaries and the nation-state demarcate the proper spatial limits of the political good, the articulation of the latter is directly linked to the citizenry. Theories of the modern state tend to draw a sharp contrast between the powers of the state and the power of the people (Skinner 1989). For theorists of the state such as Hobbes, the state is the supreme political reference point within a specific community and territory; it is independent of subjects and rulers, with distinctive political properties (1968: chs 16–19). By contrast, theorists of democracy tend to affirm the idea of the people as the active sovereign body with the capacity, in principle, to make or break governments. As Locke bluntly put it, 'the *Community* perpetually *retains a Supream Power*' over its lawmakers and legislature (1963: 413; see also 1963: 477). The political good inheres in, and is to be specified by, a process of political participation in which the collective will is determined through the medium of elected representatives (Bobbio 1989: 144). Rightful power or authority, that is, sovereignty, is vested in the people, subject to various entrenched rules, procedures and institutions which constitute national constitutional agreements and legal traditions. The democratic good unfolds in the context of these delimiting or self-binding mechanisms (Holmes 1988; Dahl 1989).

The theory of the political good in the modern territorial polity rests on a number of assumptions which repay an effort of clarification (see Miller 1999). These are that a political community is properly constituted and bounded when:

1   Its members have a common socio-cultural identity; that is, they share an understanding, explicit or implicit, of a distinctive culture, tradition, language and homeland, which binds them together as a group and forms a (if not the) basis (acknowledged or unacknowledged) of their activities.
2   There is a common framework of 'prejudices', purposes and objectives that generates a common political ethos; that is, an imagined 'community of fate' which connects them directly to a common political project – the notion that they form a people who should govern themselves.
3   An institutional structure exists – or is in the process of development – which protects and represents the community, acts on its behalf and promotes the collective interest.
4   'Congruence' and 'symmetry' prevail between a community's 'governors' and 'governed', between political decision-makers and decision-takers. That is to say, national communities exclusively 'programme' the actions, decisions and policies of their governments, and the latter determine what is right or appropriate for their citizens.
5   Members enjoy, because of the presence of conditions 1–4, a common structure of rights and duties, that is, they can lay claim to, and can reasonably expect, certain kinds of equal treatment, that is, certain types of egalitarian principles of justice and political participation.

According to this account, which in this context can be referred to as the sceptical analysis of the political good, appropriate conceptions of what is right for the political community and its citizens follow from its cultural, political and institutional roots, traditions and boundaries. These generate the resources – conceptual, ethical and organizational – for the determination of its fate and fortunes. Underpinning this understanding of the bounded community is a principle of justification which includes a significant communitarian line of thought: ethical discourse cannot be detached from the 'form of life' of a community; the categories of political discourse are integral to a particular tradition; and the values of such a community take precedence over individual or global requirements (Walzer 1983; Miller 1988; MacIntyre 1981, 1988).

## A global ethic

Globalists take issue with each of the above propositions, concluding that the political good today can only be disclosed by reflection on the diversity of the 'communities of fate' to which individuals and groups belong, and the way in which this diversity is reinforced by the political transformations globalization has brought in its wake. According to this globalist interpretation, the political good is entrenched in overlapping communities, and in an emergent transnational civil society and global polity. Disputes about the political good should be disputes about the nature and proper form of the developing global order. The basis of this globalist view can be grasped from a critique of the above five points.

First, shared identity in political communities historically has been the result of intensive efforts of political construction; it has never been a given (see pp. 14–16; cf. Gellner 1983; B. Anderson 1983; Smith 1986, 1995). Even within the boundaries of old-established communities, cultural and political identity is often disputed by and across social classes, gender divisions, local allegiances, ethnic groupings and the generations. The existence of a shared political identity cannot simply be read off vociferously proclaimed symbols of national identity. The meaning of such symbols is contested and the 'ethos' of a community frequently debated. The common values of a community may be subject to intense dispute. Justice, accountability, the rule of law and welfare are just a few terms around which there may appear to be a shared language, and yet fiercely different conceptions of these may be present (Held 1991: 11–21). In fact, if by a political consensus is meant normative integration within a community, then it is all too rare (Held 1996: part 2; and see below). Political identity is only by exception, for instance during wars, a singular, unitary phenomenon. Moreover, contemporary reflexive political agents, subject to an extraordinary diversity of information and communication, can be influenced by images, concepts, lifestyles and ideas from well beyond their immediate communities and can come to identify with groupings beyond their borders – ethnic, religious, social and political (J. B. Thompson 1995; Held et al. 1999: ch. 8; Keck and Sikkink 1998). And while there is no reason to suppose that they will uncritically identify with any one of these self-chosen ideas, commitments or relations may well be more important for some people's identity than 'membership in a community of birth' (J. Thompson 1998: 190; cf. Giddens 1991; Tamir 1993). Cultural and political identity today is constantly under review and reconstruction.

Second, the argument that locates the political good firmly within the terrain of the nation-state fails to consider or properly appreciate the diversity of political communities individuals can value; and the fact that individuals can involve themselves coherently in different associations or collectivities at different levels and for different purposes (J. Thompson 1998). It is perfectly possible, for example, to enjoy membership and voting rights in Scotland, the UK and Europe without necessarily threatening one's identification or allegiances to any one of these three political entities (see Archibugi et al. 1998). It is perfectly possible, in addition, to identify closely with the aims and ambitions of a transnational social movement – whether concerned with environmental, gender or human rights issues – without compromising other more local political commitments. Such a pluralization of political orientations and allegiances can be linked to the erosion of the state's capacity to sustain a singular political identity in the face of globalization. In the first instance, globalization is weakening the state's ability to deliver the goods to its citizens, thus eroding its legitimacy and the confidence of its citizens in its historic legacy. At the same time, the globalization of cultural processes and communications is stimulating new images of community, new avenues of political participation and new discourses of identity. Globalization is helping to create new communication and information patterns and a dense network of relations linking particular groups and cultures to one another, transforming the dynamics of political relations, above, below and alongside the state. Increasingly, successful political communities have to work with, not against, a multiplicity of identities, cultures and ethnic groupings. An overlapping consensus, which might underpin such communities, is often fragile and based purely on a commitment to common procedures – for instance, procedural mechanisms for the resolution of conflict – not a set of substantive, given values. A national political ethos may, at best, be skin-deep.

Third, globalization has 'hollowed out' states, undermining their sovereignty and autonomy. State institutions and political agents are increasingly like 'zombies', acting out the motions of politics but failing to determine any substantive, welfare-enhancing public good (Beck 1992, 1997). Contemporary political strategies involve easing adaptation to world markets and transnational economic flows. Adjustment to the international economy – above all, to global financial markets – becomes a fixed point of orientation in economic and social policy. The 'decision signals' of these markets, and of their leading agents and forces, become a, if not the, standard of rational decision-making. This position is linked, moreover, to the pursuit of distinctive supply-side measures – above all, to the use of education and training as tools of economic policy. Individual citizens must be empowered with cultural and educational capital to meet the challenges of increased (local, national, regional, global) competition and the greater mobility of industrial and financial capital. States no longer have the capacity and policy instruments they require to contest the imperatives of global economic change; instead, they must help individual citizens to go where they want to go via provision of social, cultural and educational resources. The terms of reference of public policy are set by global markets and corporate enterprise. The pursuit of the public good becomes synonymous with enhancing adaptation to this private end. Accordingly, the roles of the state as protector and representative of the territorial community, as a collector and (re)allocator of resources among its members, and as a promoter of an independent, deliberatively tested shared good are all in decline.

Fourth, the fate of a national community is no longer in its own hands. Regional and global economic, environmental and political processes profoundly redefine the content of national decision-making. In addition, decisions made by quasi-regional or quasi-supranational organizations such as the EU, WTO or the North Atlantic Treaty Organization (NATO) diminish the range of political options open to given national 'majorities'. In a similar vein, decisions by particular states – not just the most economically or militarily powerful nations – can ramify across borders, circumscribing and reshaping the political terrain. National governments by no means determine what is right or appropriate for their own citizens (Offe 1985). National policies with respect to interest rates, the harvesting of rainforests, the encouragement or restriction of the growing of genetically modified food, arms procurement and manufacture, incentive provisions to attract inward investment by multinational companies, along with decisions on a huge range of additional public matters from AIDS to the problems faced by a post-antibiotic culture, can have major consequences for those in neighbouring and distant lands. Political communities are thus embedded in a substantial range of processes which connect them in complex configurations.

Fifth, national communities are locked into webs of regional and global governance which alter and compromise their capacity to provide a common structure of rights, duties and welfare for their citizens. Regional and global processes, organizations and institutions undercut, circumscribe and delimit the kinds of entitlements and opportunities national states can offer and deliver. From human rights to trade regimes, political power is being rearticulated and reconfigured. Increasingly, contemporary patterns of globalization are associated with a multilayered system of governance, the diffusion of political power, and a widening gap between the influence of the richest and poorest communities. A complex constellation of 'winners' and 'losers' emerges. Locked into an array of geographically diverse forces, national governments are having to reconsider their roles and functions. Although the intensification of regional and global political relations has diminished the powers of national governments, it is recognized ever more that the nurturing and enhancement of the public good requires coordinated multilateral action, for instance, to prevent global recession and enhance sustainable growth, to protect human rights and intercede where they are grossly violated, to act to avoid environmental catastrophes such as ozone depletion or global warming. A shift is taking place from government to multilevel global governance. Accordingly, the institutional nexus of the political good is being reconfigured.

Each of the five propositions set forth by the sceptics – the theorists and advocates of the modern nation-state (see p. 33) – can be contrasted with positions held by the globalists. Thus, the political community and the political good need, on the global-ists' account, to be understood as follows:

1   Individuals increasingly have complex loyalties and multilayered identities, corresponding to the globalization of economic and cultural forces and the reconfiguration of political power. The movements of cultural goods across borders, hybridization and the intermingling of cultures create the basis of a transnational civil society and overlapping identities – a common framework of understanding for human beings, which progressively finds expression in, and binds people together into, interlocking collectivities capable of constructing and sustaining transnational movements, agencies and legal and institutional structures.
2   The continuing development of regional, international and global flows of resources and networks of interaction, along with the recognition by growing numbers of people of the increasing interconnectedness of political communities in diverse domains – including the social, cultural, economic and environmental – generate an awareness of overlapping 'collective fortunes' which require collective solutions. Political community begins to be reima-gined in both regional and global terms.
3   An institutional structure exists comprising elements of local, national, regional and global governance. At different levels, individual communities (albeit often imperfectly) are protected and represented; their collective interests require both multilateral advancement and domestic (local and national) adjustment if they are to be sustained and promoted.
4   Complex economic, social and environmental processes, shifting networks of regional and international agencies, and the decisions of many states and private organizations cut across spatially delimited, national locales with determinate consequences for their political agendas and strategic choices. Globalization decisively alters what it is that a national community can ask of its government, what politicians can promise and effectively deliver, and the range of people(s) affected by governmental actions. Political communities are 'reprogrammed'.
5   The rights, duties and welfare of individuals can only be adequately entrenched if, in addition to their proper articulation in national constitutions, they are underwritten by regional and global regimes, laws and institutions. The promotion of the political good and of egal-itarian principles of justice and political participation are rightly pursued at regional and global levels. Their conditions of possibility are inextricably linked to the establishment and development of robust transnational organizations and institutions of regional and global governance. In a global age, the latter are the necessary basis of cooperative relations and just conduct.

In contradistinction to the conception of the political good promulgated by advoc-ates of the modern nation-state, what is right for the individual political community and its citizens, in the globalists' account, must follow from reflection on the processes which generate an intermingling of national fortunes and fates. The growing fusion of worldwide economic, social, cultural and environmental forces requires a rethink-ing of the politically and philosophically 'isolationist' position of the communitarians and sceptics. For the contemporary world 'is not a world of closed communities with mutually impenetrable ways of thought, self-sufficient economies and ideally sovereign states' (O'Neill 1991: 282). Not only is ethical discourse separable from forms of life in a national community, but it is developing today at the intersection and interstices of overlapping communities, traditions and languages. Its categories are increasingly the result of the mediation of different cultures, communication processes and modes of understanding. There are not enough good reasons for allowing, in principle, the values of individual political communities to trump or take precedence over global principles of justice and political participation.

Of course, the globalists, like the sceptics, often have very different conceptions of what exactly is at stake here, that is, they hold very different views of what the global order should be like and the moral principles which might inform it. But they draw a clear-cut distinction between their conception of where the political good inheres and that of the sceptics. While for the latter ethical discourse is, and remains, firmly rooted in the bounded political community, for the former it belongs squarely to the world of 'breached boundaries' – the 'world community' or 'global village'.

## Conclusion

The great globalization debate, summarized in table 1, identifies some of the most fundamental issues of our time. Despite a propensity for hyperbole on both sides, the protagonists have generally elaborated highly important and carefully considered arguments. These pose key questions about the organization of human affairs and the trajectory of global social change. They also raise matters which go to the centre of political discussion, illuminating some of the strategic choices societies confront and the constraints which define the possibilities of effective political action.

Are the two main positions fundamentally at odds and contradictory in all respects, or is a productive synthesis possible? It is not the purpose of this Introduction, or of the volume for that matter, to answer this question. Indeed, we have sought to do this at length elsewhere and it would take us far beyond the scope of this volume to map out this terrain here (see Held et al. 1999; Held and McGrew 2002). A number of points, however, are worth emphasizing by way of a conclusion.

In the first instance, the debate raises profound questions of interpretation. But while it highlights that facts certainly do not speak for themselves, and depend for their meaning on complex interpretative frameworks, it would be wrong to conclude that the marshalled evidence is of secondary importance. There are clashes involving the conceptualization and interpretation of some of the most critical evidence. However, often the kind of evidence proffered by both sides differs markedly. For example, sceptics put primary emphasis on the organization of production and trade (stressing the geographical rootedness of MNCs and the marginal changes in trade–GDP ratios over the twentieth century), while globalists focus on financial deregulation and the explosive growth of global financial markets over the last twenty-five years. Sceptics stress the continuing primacy of the national interest and the cultural traditions of national communities which sustain their distinct identity, while globalists point to the growing significance of global political problems – such as worldwide pollution, global warming and financial crises – which create a growing sense of the common fate of humankind. A considered response to the debate would have to weigh all these considerations before coming to a settled view.

**Table 1** The great globalization debate: in sum

|   |   | Sceptics | Globalists |
|---|---|---|---|
| 1 | Concepts | Internationalization not globalization<br>Regionalization | One world, shaped by highly extensive, intensive and rapid flows, movements and networks across regions and continents |
| 2 | Power | The nation-state rules<br>Intergovernmentalism | Erosion of state sovereignty, autonomy and legitimacy<br>Decline of nation-state<br>Rise of multilateralism |
| 3 | Culture | Resurgence of nationalism and national identity | Emergence of global popular culture<br>Erosion of fixed political identities<br>Hybridization |
| 4 | Economy | Development of regional blocs<br>Triadization<br>New imperialism | Global informational capitalism<br>The transnational economy<br>A new global division of labour |
| 5 | Inequality | Growing North–South divide<br>Irreconcilable conflicts of interest | Growing inequality within and across societies<br>Erosion of old hierarchies |
| 6 | Order | International society of states<br>Political conflict between states inevitably persists<br>International governance and geopolitics<br>Primacy of the ethically bounded community | Multilayered global governance<br>Global civil society<br>Global polity<br>Cosmopolitan orientations |

Secondly, although there are, of course, very significant differences between (and within) each camp, there is some common ground. The debate does not simply comprise ships passing in the night. Indeed, both sides would accept that:

1 There has been some growth in recent decades in economic interconnectedness within and among regions, albeit with multifaceted and uneven consequences across different communities.
2 Interregional and global (political, economic and cultural) competition challenges old hierarchies and generates new inequalities of wealth, power, privilege and knowledge.
3 Transnational and transborder problems, such as the spread of genetically modified foodstuffs, mass terrorism and money laundering, have become increasingly salient, calling into question the traditional role, functions and institutions of accountability of national government.
4 There has been an expansion of international governance at regional and global levels – from the EU to the WTO – which poses significant normative questions about the kind of world order being constructed and whose interests it serves.

5   These developments require new modes of thinking about politics, economics and cultural change. They also require imaginative responses from politicians and policy-makers about the future possibilities and forms of effective political regulation and democratic accountability.

Thirdly, we believe that the debate highlights that there is much to be learned from both sides; it would be implausible to maintain that either side comprises mere rhetoric and ideology. The sceptical case has significant historical depth and needs to be carefully dissected if a globalist position is to be adequately defended. Many of the empirical claims raised by the sceptics' arguments, for example, concerning the historical significance of contemporary trade and direct investment flows, require detailed and rigorous examination. But having said that, globalism, in its various forms, does illuminate important transformations going on in the spatial organization of power – the changing nature of communication, the diffusion and speed-up of technical change, the spread of capitalist economic development, and so on – even if its understanding of these matters sometimes exaggerates their scale and impact.

Finally, the political issues raised by the debate are profound and merit the most serious consideration. We would like to reflect briefly on these now, and specify what we think of as the core challenges posed by globalization and its critics – challenges that will remain at the centre of the great globalization debate for some time to come.

## The challenges of globalization

(1) Contemporary processes of globalization and regionalization create overlapping networks of power which cut across territorial boundaries; as such, they put pressure on, and strain, a world order designed in accordance with the Westphalian principle of exclusive sovereign rule over a bounded territory.

(2) The locus of effective political power can no longer be assumed to be simply national governments – effective power is contested and bartered by diverse forces and agencies, public and private, at national, regional and international levels. Moreover, the idea of a self-determining people – or of a political community of fate – can no longer be located within the boundaries of a single nation-state. Some of the most fundamental forces and processes which determine the nature of life-chances are now beyond the reach and control of individual nation-states.

A distinctive aspect of this is the emergence of 'global politics' – the increasingly extensive form of political activity (see section II of this Introduction). Political decisions and actions in one part of the world can rapidly acquire worldwide ramifications. Sites of political action and/or decision-making can become linked through rapid communications into complex networks of political interaction. Associated with this 'stretching' of politics is a frequent intensification of global processes such that 'action at a distance' permeates the social conditions and cognitive worlds of specific places or policy communities (Giddens 1990: ch. 2). As a consequence, developments at the global level – whether economic, social or environmental – can acquire almost instantaneous local consequences, and vice versa.

The idea of global politics challenges the traditional distinctions between the domestic and the international, and between the territorial and the non-territorial, as embedded in modern conceptions of 'the political' (see Held et al. 1999: chs 1, 2 and 8). It highlights the richness and complexity of the interconnections which transcend states and societies in the global order. Global politics today, moreover, is anchored not just in traditional geopolitical concerns but also in a large diversity of economic, social and ecological questions. Pollution, drugs, human rights and terrorism are amongst an increasing number of transnational policy issues which cut across territorial jurisdictions and existing political alignments, and which require international cooperation for their effective resolution.

Nations, peoples and organizations are linked, in addition, by many new forms of communication which range across borders. The revolution in micro-electronics, in information technology and in computers has established virtually instantaneous worldwide links, which, when combined with the technologies of the telephone, television, cable and satellite, have dramatically altered the nature of political communication. The intimate connection between 'physical setting', 'social situation' and politics, which distinguished most political associations from premodern to modern times, has been ruptured; the new communication systems create new experiences, new modes of understanding and new frames of political reference independently of direct contact with particular peoples, issues or events.

In the past, nation-states principally resolved their differences over boundary matters by pursuing 'reasons of state' backed by diplomatic initiatives and, ultimately, by coercive means. But this power logic is singularly inadequate to resolve the many complex issues, from economic regulation to resource depletion and environmental degradation, which engender – at seemingly ever greater speeds – an intermeshing of 'national fortunes'. We are, as Kant most eloquently put it, 'unavoidably side by side'. In a world where powerful states make decisions not just for their peoples but for others as well, and where transnational actors and forces cut across the boundaries of national communities in diverse ways, the questions of who should be accountable to whom, and on what basis, do not easily resolve themselves.

(3) Existing political institutions, national and international, are weakened by three crucial regulatory and political gaps (Kaul et al. 1991: xixff.):

- a jurisdictional gap – the discrepancy between a regionalized and globalized world and national, discrete units of policy-making, giving rise to the problem of externalities such as the degradation of the global commons and who is responsible for them;
- a participation gap – the failure of the existing international system to give adequate voice to many leading global actors, state and non-state; and
- an incentive gap – the challenges posed by the fact that, in the absence of any supranational entity to regulate the supply and use of global public goods, many states will seek to free ride and/or fail to find durable collective solutions to pressing transnational problems.

(4) These political disjunctures are conjoined by an additional gap – what might be called a 'moral gap'; that is, a gap defined by:

- a world in which more than 1.2 billion people live on less than a dollar a day; 46 per cent of the world's population live on less than $2 a day; and 20 per cent of the world's population enjoy over 80 per cent of its income;
- commitments and values of, at best, 'passive indifference' to this, marked by UN expenditure per annum of $1.25 billion (minus peace-keeping), US per annum confectionery

expenditure of $27 billion, US per annum alcohol expenditure of $70 billion, and US per annum expenditure on cars that is through the roof (more than $550 billion).

This is not an anti-America statement, of course. Equivalent EU figures could have been highlighted.

Seemingly obvious questions arise. Would anyone freely choose such a state of affairs? Would anyone freely choose a distributional pattern of scarce goods and services, leading to hundreds of millions of people suffering serious harm and disadvantage independent of their will and consent (and 50,000 dying every day of malnutrition and poverty related causes), if these individuals did not already know that they had a privileged stake in the current social hierarchy? Would anyone freely endorse a situation in which the annual cost of supplying basic education to all children is $6 billion, of water and sanitation $9 billion, and of basic health to all $13 billion, while annually $4 billion is spent in the USA on cosmetics, nearly $20 billion on jewellery and $17 billion (in the US and Europe) on pet food?* Before an impartial court of moral reason (testing the reasonable rejectability of claims), it is hard to see how an affirmative answer to these questions could be defended. That global inequalities spark conflict and contestation can hardly be a surprise, especially given the visibility of the world's lifestyles in an age of mass media.

(5) There has been a shift from relatively discrete national communication and economic systems to their more complex and diverse enmeshment at regional and global levels, and from government to multilevel governance, as the globalists contend. This can be illustrated by a number of developments, including, most obviously, the rapid emergence of multilateral agencies and organizations. New forms of multilateral politics have been established involving governments, IGOs, a wide variety of transnational pressure groups and INGOs (see Union of International Associations 2001). In addition, there has been a very substantial development in the number of international treaties in force, as well as in the number of international regimes, altering the situational context of states (Held et al. 1999: chs 1–2). Political communities can no longer be conceived, if they ever could with any degree of accuracy, as simply discrete worlds or as self-enclosed political spaces; they are enmeshed in complex structures of overlapping forces, relations and networks.

Yet, as the sceptics argue, there are few grounds for thinking that a parallel 'globalization' of political identities has taken place. One exception to this is to be found among the elites of the global order – the networks of experts and specialists, senior administrative personnel and transnational business executives – and those who track and contest their activities – the loose constellation of social movements (including the anti-globalization movement), trade unionists and (a few) politicians and intellectuals. But these groups are not typical. Thus, we live with a challenging paradox – that governance is becoming increasingly a multilevel, intricately institutionalized and spatially dispersed activity, while representation, loyalty and identity remain stubbornly rooted in traditional ethnic, regional and national communities (Wallace 1999).

One important qualification needs to be added to the above arguments, one which focuses on generational change. While those who have some commitment to the global

---

* These figures are drawn from the US economic census (1997) and from http://www.wwlearning.co.uk/news/features 0000000 354-asp.

order as a whole and to the institutions of global governance constitute a distinct minority, a generational divide is evident. Compared to the generations brought up in the years prior to 1939, those born after World War II are more likely to see themselves as cosmopolitans, to support the UN system and to be in favour of the free movement of migrants and trade. Examining Eurobarometer data and findings from the World Values Survey (involving more than seventy countries), Norris concludes that 'cohort analysis suggests that in the long term public opinion is moving in a more international direction' (2000: p. 175). Generations brought up with Yahoo, MTV and CNN affirm this trend and are more likely to have some sense of global identification, although it remains to be seen whether this tendency crystallizes into a majority position and whether it generates a clearly focused political orientation, north, south, east and west.

Hence, the shift from government to multilayered governance, from national economies to economic globalization, is a potentially unstable shift, capable of reversal in some respects and certainly capable of engendering a fierce reaction – a reaction drawing on nostalgia, romanticized conceptions of political community, hostility to outsiders (refugees) and a search for a pure national state (e.g., in the politics of Haider in Austria, Le Pen in France and so on). But this reaction itself is likely to be highly unstable, and perhaps a relatively short- or medium-term phenomenon. To understand why this is so, nationalism has to be disaggregated.

(6) As 'cultural nationalism', it is, and in all likelihood will remain, central to people's identity; however, as political nationalism – the assertion of the exclusive political priority of national identity and the national interest – it cannot deliver, as noted previously, many sought-after public goods without seeking accommodation with others, in and through regional and global collaboration (see pp. 39–40). In this respect, only an international or, better still, cosmopolitan outlook can meet the challenges of a more global period, characterized by overlapping communities of fate and multilevel/multilayered politics. Unlike political nationalism, cosmopolitanism registers and reflects the multiplicity of issues, questions, processes and problems which affect and bind people together, irrespective of where they were born or reside. Whether cosmopolitanism can ever rival nationalism as a great cultural force is, however, at best an open question. Excessive optimism here would be a mistake and underestimate the severe political difficulties that lie ahead (see Part VI of this volume).

The Reader elaborates on these issues and positions, drawing on the most sophisticated arguments from both sides of the debate. The quality and originality of the contributions are of the highest order and they offer, together, a comprehensive introduction to the globalization literature.

## References

Albrow, M. (1996) *The Global Age*. Cambridge: Polity Press.
Altvater, E. and Mahnkopf, B. (1997) The world market unbound. *Review of International Political Economy* 4(3).
Amin, S. (1996) The challenge of globalization. *Review of International Political Economy* 2.
Amin, S. (1997) *Capitalism in the Age of Globalization*. London: Zed Press.
Anderson, B. (1983) *Imagined Communities: Reflections on the Origins and Spread of Nationalism*. London: Verso.

Anderson, K. and Blackhurst, R. (eds) (1993) *Regional Integration and the Global Trading System*. Brighton: Harvester.

Anderson, K. and Norheim, H. (1993) Is world trade becoming more regionalized? *Review of International Economics* 1.

Anderson, P. (1974) *Lineages of the Absolutist State*. London: New Left Books.

Archibugi, D., Held, D. and Köhler, M. (eds) (1998) *Re-imagining Political Community: Studies in Cosmopolitan Democracy*. Cambridge: Polity Press.

Ashford, D. (1986) *The Emergence of the Welfare State*. Oxford: Blackwell.

Axford, B. (1995) *The Global System*. Cambridge: Polity Press.

Barry, B. (1998) The limits of cultural politics. *Review of International Studies* 24(3).

Beck, U. (1992) *Risk Society: Towards a New Modernity*. London: Sage.

Beck, U. (1997) *The Reinvention of Politics*. Cambridge: Polity Press.

Beck, U. (1999) *What is Globalization?* Cambridge: Polity Press.

Beetham, D. (1995) What future for economic and social rights? *Political Studies* 48 (special issue).

Bentley, J. H. (1996) Cross-cultural interaction and periodization in world history. *American Historical Review* 101 (June).

Birdsall, N. (1998) Life is unfair: inequality in the world. *Foreign Policy* 111.

Bobbio, N. (1989) *Democracy and Dictatorship*. Cambridge: Polity Press.

Boyer, R. and Drache, D. (eds) (1996) *States against Markets*. London: Routledge.

Bozeman, A. B. (1984) The international order in a multicultural world. In H. Bull and A. Watson (eds), *The Expansion of International Society*, Oxford: Oxford University Press.

Bradshaw, Y. W. and Wallace, M. (1996) *Global Inequalities*. London: Pine Forge Press/Sage.

Braudel, F. (1984) *The Perspective of the World*. New York: Harper and Row.

Breuilly, J. (1992) *Nationalism and the State*. Manchester: Manchester University Press.

Brown, C. (1995) International political theory and the idea of world community. In K. Booth and S. Smith (eds), *International Relations Theory Today*, Cambridge: Polity Press.

Bull, H. (1977) *The Anarchical Society*. London: Macmillan.

Burbach, R., Núñez, O. and Kagarlitsky, B. (1997) *Globalization and its Discontents*. London: Pluto Press.

Buzan, B., Little, R. and Jones, C. (1993) *The Logic of Anarchy*. New York: Columbia University Press.

Cable, V. (1996) Globalization: can the state strike back? *The World Today* (May).

Callinicos, A. et al. (1994) *Marxism and the New Imperialism*. London: Bookmarks.

Castells, M. (1996) *The Rise of the Network Society*. Oxford: Blackwell.

Castells, M. (1997) *The Power of Identity*. Oxford: Blackwell.

Castells, M. (1998) *End of Millennium*. Oxford: Blackwell.

Clark, I. (1989) *The Hierarchy of States: Reform and Resistance in the International Order*. Cambridge: Cambridge University Press.

Clark, I. (2001) *The Post Cold War Order*. Oxford: Oxford University Press.

Clark, R. P. (1997) *The Global Imperative*. Boulder: Westview Press.

Commission on Global Governance (1995) *Our Global Neighbourhood*. Oxford: Oxford University Press.

Cooper, R. N. (1986) *Economic Policy in an Interdependent World*. Cambridge, Mass.: MIT Press.

Cortell, A. P. and Davies, J. W. (1996) How do international institutions matter? The domestic impact of international rules and norms. *International Studies Quarterly* 40.

Cox, R. (1996) Globalization, multilateralism and democracy. In R. Cox (ed.), *Approaches to World Order*, Cambridge: Cambridge University Press.

Cox, R. (1997) Economic globalization and the limits to liberal democracy. In A. McGrew (ed.), *The Transformation of Democracy? Globalization and Territorial Democracy*, Cambridge: Polity Press.

Crawford, J. and Marks, S. (1998) The global democracy deficit: an essay on international law and its limits. In Archibugi et al. 1998.

Dahl, R. A. (1989) *Democracy and its Critics*. New Haven: Yale University Press.

Dicken, P. (1998) *Global Shift*. London: Paul Chapman.

Dickson, A. (1997) *Development and International Relations*. Cambridge: Polity Press.

Dore, R. (ed.) (1995) *Convergence or Diversity? National Models of Production in a Global Economy*. New York: Cornell University Press.

Dunn, J. (1990) *Interpreting Political Responsibility*. Cambridge: Polity Press.

Dunning, J. (1993) *Multinational Enterprises and the Global Economy*. Wokingham: Addison-Wesley.

Ekins, P. (1992) *A New World Order: Grassroots Movements for Global Change*. London: Routledge.

Falk, R. (1969) The interplay of Westphalian and Charter conceptions of the international legal order. In R. Falk and C. Black (eds), *The Future of the International Legal Order*, vol. 1, Princeton: Princeton University Press.

Falk, R. (1987) The global promise of social movements: explorations at the edge of time. *Alternatives* 12.

Falk, R. (1995a) Liberalism at the global level: the last of the independent commissions? *Millennium* 24(3).

Falk, R. (1995b) *On Humane Governance: Toward a New Global Politics*. Cambridge: Polity Press.

Feldstein, M. and Horioka, C. (1980) Domestic savings and international capital flows. *Economic Journal* 90.

Fernández-Armesto, F. (1995) *Millennium*. London: Bantam.

Ferro, M. (1997) *Colonization: A Global History*. London: Routledge.

Frank, A. G. (1998) *Re-Orient: Global Economy in the Asian Age*. New York: University of California Press.

Frank, A. G. and Gills, B. K. (eds) (1996) *The World System*. London: Routledge.

Frieden, J. (1991) Invested interests: the politics of national economic policies in a world of global finance. *International Organization* 45(4).

Frost, M. (1986) *Towards a Normative Theory of International Relations*. Cambridge: Cambridge University Press.

Fukao, M. (1993) International integration of financial markets and the costs of capital. *Journal of International Securities Markets* 7.

Gagnon, J. and Unferth, M. (1995) Is there a world real interest rate? *Journal of International Money and Finance* 14.

Gamble, A. and Payne, A. (1991) Conclusion: the new regionalism. In A. Gamble and A. Payne (eds), *Regionalism and World Order*, London: Macmillan.

Garrett, G. (1996) Capital mobility, trade and the domestic politics of economic policy. In R. O. Keohane and H. V. Milner (eds), *Internationalization and Domestic Politics*, Cambridge: Cambridge University Press.

Garrett, G. (1998) Global markets and national politics. *International Organization* 52.

Garrett, G. and Lange, P. (1991) Political responses to interdependence: what's 'left' for the left? *International Organization* 45(4).

Garrett, G. and Lange, P. (1996) Internationalization, institutions and political change. In R. O. Keohane and H. V. Milner (eds), *Internationalization and Domestic Politics*, Cambridge: Cambridge University Press.

Gellner, E. (1983) *Nations and Nationalism*. Oxford: Blackwell.

Gereffi, G. and Korzeniewicz, M. (eds) (1994) *Commodity Chains and Global Capitalism*. Westport: Praeger.

Germain, R. (1997) *The International Organization of Credit*. Cambridge: Cambridge University Press.

Geyer, M. and Bright, C. (1995) World history in a global age. *American Historical Review* 100(4).

Giddens, A. (1985) *The Nation-State and Violence*, vol. 2 of *A Contemporary Critique of Historical Materialism*. Cambridge: Polity Press.

Giddens, A. (1990) *The Consequences of Modernity*. Cambridge: Polity Press.

Giddens, A. (1991) *Modernity and Self-Identity*. Cambridge: Polity Press.

Giddens, A. (1999) *The Third Way*. Cambridge: Polity Press.

Gill, S. (1992) Economic globalization and the internationalization of authority: limits and contradictions. *GeoForum* 23(3).

Gill, S. (1995) Globalization, market civilization and disciplinary neoliberalism. *Millennium* 24(3).

Gilpin, R. (1981) *War and Change in World Politics*. Cambridge: Cambridge University Press.

Gilpin, R. (1987) *The Political Economy of International Relations*. Princeton: Princeton University Press.

Gilroy, P. (1987) *There Ain't No Black in the Union Jack*. London: Hutchinson.

Godement, F. (1999) *The Downsizing of Asia*. London: Routledge.

Gordon, D. (1988) The global economy: new edifice or crumbling foundations? *New Left Review* 168.

Gourevitch, P. (1986) *Politics in Hard Times*. New York: Cornell University Press.

Graham, G. (1997) *Ethics and International Relations*. Oxford: Blackwell.

Gray, J. (1998) *False Dawn*. London: Granta.

Greider, W. (1997) *One World, Ready or Not: The Manic Logic of Global Capitalism*. New York: Simon and Schuster.

Haass, R. N. and Liton, R. E. (1998) Globalization and its discontents. *Foreign Affairs* (May–June).

Hall, S. (1992) The question of cultural identity. In S. Hall, D. Held and A. McGrew (eds), *Modernity and its Futures*, Cambridge: Polity Press.

Hanson, B. T. (1998) What happened to Fortress Europe? External trade policy liberalization in the European Union. *International Organization* 52(1) (Winter).

Hart, J. (1992) *Rival Capitalists: International Competitiveness in USA, Japan and Western Europe*. Princeton: Princeton University Press.

Harvey, D. (1989) *The Condition of Postmodernity*. Oxford: Blackwell.

Hasenclever, A., Mayer, P. and Rittberger, V. (1997) *Theories of International Regimes*. Cambridge: Cambridge University Press.

Held, D. (ed.) (1991) *Political Theory Today*. Cambridge: Polity Press.

Held, D. (1995) *Democracy and the Global Order: From the Modern State to Cosmopolitan Governance*. Cambridge: Polity Press.

Held, D. (1996) *Models of Democracy*, 2nd edn. Cambridge: Polity Press.

Held, D. and McGrew, A. (2002) *Globalization/Anti-Globalization*. Cambridge: Polity Press.

Held, D. and McGrew, A., Goldblatt, D. and Perraton, J. (1999) *Global Transformations: Politics, Economics and Culture*. Cambridge: Polity Press.

Helleiner, E. (1997) Braudelian reflections on economic globalization: the historian as pioneer. In S. Gill and J. Mittleman (eds), *Innovation and Transformation in International Studies*, Cambridge: Cambridge University Press.

Herod, A., Tuathail, G. O. and Roberts, S. M. (eds) (1998) *Unruly World? Globalization, Governance and Geography*. London: Routledge.

Hirst, P. (1997) The global economy: myths and realities. *International Affairs* 73(3) (July).

Hirst, P. and Thompson, G. (1996) *Globalization in Question*. Cambridge: Polity Press.

Hirst, P. and Thompson, G. (1999) *Globalization in Question*, 2nd edn. Cambridge: Polity Press.

Hobbes, T. (1968) *Leviathan*. Harmondsworth: Penguin.

Hodgson, M. G. S. (1993) The interrelations of societies in history. In E. Burke (ed.), *Rethinking World History: Essays on Europe, Islam and World History*, Cambridge: Cambridge University Press.

Hoffmann, Stanley (2002) Clash of globalizations. *Foreign Affairs* 81(4).

Holmes, S. (1988) Precommitment and the paradox of democracy. In J. Elster and R. Stagstad (eds), *Constitutionalism and Democracy*, Cambridge: Cambridge University Press.

Hoogvelt, A. (1997) *Globalization and the Postcolonial World: The New Political Economy of Development*. London: Macmillan.

Hoogvelt, Ankie (2001) *Globalization and the Postcolonial World*, 2nd edn. Basingstoke: Palgrave.

Howard, M. (1981) *War and the Liberal Conscience*. Oxford: Oxford University Press.

Hu, W. (1992) Global corporations are national firms with international operations. *California Management Review* 34.

Hurrell, A. (1999) Security and inequality. In A. Hurrell and N. Woods, *Inequality, Globalization and World Politics*, Oxford: Oxford University Press.

Hurrell, A. and Woods, N. (1995) Globalization and inequality. *Millennium* 2.

Jameson, F. (1991) *Postmodernism: The Cultural Logic of Late Capitalism*. London: Verso.

Jessop, B. (1997) Capitalism and its future: remarks on regulation, government and governance. *Review of International Political Economy* 4(3).

Johnston, R. J., Taylor, P. J. and Watts, M. J. (eds) (1995) *Geographies of Global Change*. Oxford: Blackwell.

Jones, R. J. B. (1995) *Globalization and Interdependence in the International Political Economy*. London: Frances Pinter.

Kaldor, M. (1998) *New and Old Wars*. Cambridge: Polity Press.

Kapstein, E. B. (1994) *Governing the Global Economy: International Finance and the State*. Cambridge, Mass.: Harvard University Press.

Kaul, I., Grunberg, I. and Stern, M. (1999) *Global Public Goods*. Oxford: Oxford University Press.

Keck, M. and Sikkink, K. (1998) *Activists beyond Borders*. New York: Cornell University Press.

Keohane, R. O. (1984) *After Hegemony*. Princeton: Princeton University Press.

Keohane, R. O. (1995) Hobbes's dilemma and institutional change in world politics: sovereignty in international society. In H.-H. Holm and G. Sørensen (eds), *Whose World Order?* Boulder: Westview Press.

Keohane, R. O. (1998) International institutions: can interdependence work? *Foreign Policy* (Spring).

Keohane, R. O. and Nye, J. S. (1972) *Transnational Relations and World Politics*. Cambridge, Mass.: Harvard University Press.

Keohane, R. and Nye, J. (1977) *Power and Interdependence*. Boston: Little, Brown.

Kofman, E. and Youngs, G. (eds) (1996) *Globalization: Theory and Practice*. London: Pinter.

Korten, D. C. (1995) *When Corporations Ruled the World*, Hartford: Kumerian Press.

Krasner, S. D. (1985) *Structural Conflict: The Third World against Global Liberalism*. Los Angeles: University of California Press.

Krasner, S. D. (1993) Economic interdependence and independent statehood. In R. H. Jackson and A. James (eds), *States in a Changing World*, Oxford: Oxford University Press.

Krasner, S. D. (1995) Compromising Westphalia. *International Security* 20(3).

Krugman, P. (1994) Does third world growth hurt first world prosperity? *Harvard Business Review* (July).

Krugman, P. (1995) Growing world trade: causes and consequences. *Brookings Papers on Economic Activity*.

Lacey, R. and Danziger, D. (1999) *The Year 1000*. London: Little, Brown.

Lawrence, R. (1996) *Single World, Divided Nations? International Trade and OECD Labor Markets*. Washington DC: Brookings Institution.

Liebes, T. and Katz, E. (1993) *The Export of Meaning: Cross-Cultural Readings of Dallas*. Cambridge: Polity Press.

Linklater, A. (1998) *The Transformation of Political Community*. Cambridge: Polity Press.

Lloyd, P. J. (1992) Regionalization and world trade. *OECD Economics Studies* 18 (Spring).

Locke, J. (1963) *Two Treatises of Government*. Cambridge: Cambridge University Press.

Luttwak, E. (1999) *Turbo-Capitalism*. New York: Basic Books.

McGrew, A. G. (1992) Conceptualizing global politics. In McGrew and Lewis et al. 1992.

McGrew, A. G. and Lewis, P. G. et al. (1992) *Global Politics*. Cambridge: Polity Press.

MacIntyre, A. (1981) *After Virtue*. London: Duckworth.

MacIntyre, A. (1988) *Whose Justice? Which Rationality?* London: Duckworth.

McLuhan, M. (1964) *Understanding Media: The Extension of Man*. London: Routledge and Kegan Paul.

Mann, M. (1986) *The Sources of Social Power*, vol. 1: *A History of Power from the Beginning to AD 1760*. Cambridge: Cambridge University Press.

Mann, M. (1987) Ruling strategies and citizenship. *Sociology* 21(3).

Mann, M. (1997) Has globalization ended the rise and rise of the nation-state? *Review of International Political Economy* 4.

Massey, D. and Jess, P. (eds) (1995) *A Place in the World? Culture, Places and Globalization*. Oxford: Oxford University Press.

Mazlish, B. and Buultjens, R. (eds) (1993) *Conceptualizing Global History*. Boulder: Westview Press.

Meyrowitz, J. (1985) *No Sense of Place*. Oxford: Oxford University Press.

Miller, D. (1988) The ethical significance of nationality. *Ethics* 98.

Miller, D. (1992) The young and the restless in Trinidad: a case of the local and the global in mass consumption. In R. Silverstone and E. Hirsch (eds), *Consuming Technology*, London: Routledge.

Miller, D. (1999) Justice and inequality. In A. Hurrell and N. Woods (eds), *Inequality, Globalization and World Politics*, Oxford: Oxford University Press.

Milner, H. V. (1997) *Interests, Institutions and Information: Domestic Politics and International Relations*. Princeton: Princeton University Press.

Mitrany, D. (1975) The progress of international government (1932). In P. Taylor (ed.), *The Functional Theory of Politics*, London: LSE/Martin Robertson.

Modelski, G. (1972) *Principles of World Politics*. New York: Free Press.

Morse, E. (1976) *Modernization and the Transformation of International Relations*. New York: Free Press.

Mueller, J. (1989) *Retreat from Doomsday: The Obsolescence of Major War*. New York: Basic Books.

Neal, L. (1985) Integration of international capital markets. *Journal of Economic History* 45 (June).

Nierop, T. (1994) *Systems and Regions in Global Politics*. London: John Wiley.

Norris, P. (2000) Global governance and cosmopolitan citizens. In J. S. Nye and J. D. Donahue (eds), *Governance in a Globalizing World*, Washington, DC: Brookings Institution Press.

O'Brien, R. (1992) *The End of Geography: Global Financial Integration*. London: Pinter.

OECD (1997) *Communications Outlook*. Paris: Organization for Economic Cooperation and Development.

Offe, C. (1985) *Disorganized Capitalism*. Cambridge: Polity Press.

Ohmae, K. (1990) *The Borderless World*. London: Collins.

Ohmae, K. (1995) *The End of the Nation State*. New York: Free Press.

O'Neill, O. (1991) Transnational justice. In D. Held (ed.), *Political Theory Today*, Cambridge: Polity Press.

Parekh, B. (1989) Between holy text and moral word. *New Statesman* 23 Mar.

Perlmutter, H. V. (1991) On the rocky road to the first global civilization. *Human Relations* 44(9).

Perraton, J., Goldblatt, D., Held, D. and McGrew, A. (1997) The globalization of economic activity. *New Political Economy* 2 (Spring).

Pieper, U. and Taylor, L. (1998) The revival of the liberal creed: the IMF, the World Bank and inequality in a globalized economy. In D. Baker, G. Epstein and R. Podin (eds), *Globalization and Progressive Economic Policy*, Cambridge: Cambridge University Press.

Piore, M. and Sabel, C. (1984) *The Second Industrial Divide*. New York: Basic Books.

Poggi, G. (1978) *The Development of the Modern State*. London: Hutchinson.

Porter, M. (1990) *The Competitive Advantage of Nations*. London: Macmillan.

Potter, D., Goldblatt, D., Kiloh, M. and Lewis, P. (eds) (1997) *Democratization*. Cambridge: Polity Press.

Reich, R. (1991) *The Work of Nations*. New York: Simon and Schuster.

Rheingold, H. (1995) *The Virtual Community*. London: Mandarin.

Rieger, E. and Liebfried, S. (1998) Welfare limits to globalization. *Politics and Society* 26(3).

Roberts, S. M. (1998) Geo-governance in trade and finance and political geographies of dissent. In Herod et al. 1998.

Robertson, R. (1992) *Globalization: Social Theory and Global Culture*. London: Sage.

Robins, K. (1991) Tradition and translation. In J. Corner and S. Harvey (eds), *Enterprise and Heritage: Crosscurrents of National Politics*, London: Routledge.

Rodrik, D. (1997) *Has Globalization Gone Too Far?* Washington DC: Institute for International Economics.

Rosenau, J. N. (1990) *Turbulence in World Politics*. Brighton: Harvester Wheatsheaf.

Rosenau, J. N. (1997) *Along the Domestic-Foreign Frontier*. Cambridge: Cambridge University Press.

Rowthorn, R. and Wells, J. (1987) *De-industrialization and Foreign Trade*. Cambridge: Cambridge University Press.

Ruggie, J. (1993a) Territoriality and beyond. *International Organization* 41(1).

Ruggie, J. (ed.) (1993b) *Multilateralism Matters*. New York: Columbia University Press.

Ruigrok, W. and Tulder, R. V. (1995) *The Logic of International Restructuring*. London: Routledge.

Russett, B. (1993) *Grasping the Democratic Peace: Principles for a Post-Cold War World*. Princeton: Princeton University Press.

Sandholtz, W. et al. (1992) *The Highest Stakes*. Oxford: Oxford University Press.

Sassen, S. (1996) *Losing Control? Sovereignty in an Age of Globalization*. New York: Columbia University Press.

Scharpf, F. (1991) *Crisis and Choice in European Social Democracy*. New York: Cornell University Press.

Scharpf, F. (1999) *Governing in Europe: Effective and Democratic?* Oxford: Oxford University Press.

Scholte, J. A. (1993) *International Relations of Social Change*. Buckingham: Open University Press.

Scholte, J. A. (1997) Global capitalism and the state. *International Affairs* 73(3) (July).

Shaw, M. (1994) *Global Society and International Relations*. Cambridge: Polity Press.

Shaw, M. (1997) The state of globalization: towards a theory of state transformation. *Review of International Political Economy* 4(3).

Shell, G. R. (1995) Trade legalism and international relations theory: an analysis of the WTO. *Duke Law Journal* 44(5).

Skinner, Q. (1978) *The Foundations of Modern Political Thought*, vol. 2. Cambridge: Cambridge University Press.

Skinner, Q. (1989) The state. In T. Ball, J. Farr and R. L. Hanson (eds), *Political Innovation and Conceptual Change*, Cambridge: Cambridge University Press.

Slater, D. (1995) Challenging western visions of the global: the geopolitics of theory and north–south relations. *European Journal of Development Research* 7(2).

Smith, A. D. (1986) *The Ethnic Origins of Nations*. Oxford: Blackwell.

Smith, A. D. (1990) Towards a global culture? In M. Featherstone (ed.), *Global Culture: Nationalism, Globalization and Modernity*, London: Sage.

Smith, A. D. (1995) *Nations and Nationalism in a Global Era*. Cambridge: Polity Press.

Sterling, R. W. (1974) *Macropolitics: International Relations in a Global Society*. New York: Knopf.

Strange, S. (1996) *The Retreat of the State*. Cambridge: Cambridge University Press.

Tamir, Y. (1993) *Liberal Nationalism*. Princeton: Princeton University Press.

Therborn, G. (1977) The rule of capital and the rise of democracy. *New Left Review* 13.

Thompson, G. (1998a) Globalization versus regionalism? *Journal of North African Studies*.

Thompson, G. (1998b) International competitiveness and globalization. In T. Baker and J. Köhler (eds), *International Competitiveness and Environmental Policies*, Brighton: Edward Elgar.

Thompson, G. and Allen, J. (1997) Think global and then think again: economic globalization in context. *Area* 29(3).

Thompson, J. (1998) Community identity and world citizenship. In Archibugi et al. 1998.

Thompson, J. B. (1990) *Ideology and Modern Culture*. Cambridge: Polity Press.

Thompson, J. B. (1995) *The Media and Modernity*. Cambridge: Polity Press.

Thompson, K. W. (1994) *Fathers of International Thought: The Legacy of Political Theory*. Baton Rouge: Louisiana State University Press.

Tilly, C. (ed.) (1975) *The Formation of National States in Western Europe*. Princeton: Princeton University Press.

Turner, B. S. (1986) *Citizenship and Capitalism*. London: Allen and Unwin.

Tyson, L. (1991) They are not us: why American ownership still matters. *American Prospect* (Winter).

UNCTAD (1998a) *The Least Developed Countries 1998*. Geneva: UN Conference on Trade and Development.

UNCTAD (1998b) *Trade and Development Report 1998*. Geneva: UN Conference on Trade and Development.

UNCTAD (1998c) *World Investment Report 1998*. Geneva: UN Conference on Trade and Development.

UNCTAD (2002) *World Investment Report 2002*. Geneva (www.unctad.org).

UNDP (1997) *Human Development Report 1997*. New York: Oxford University Press.

UNDP (1998) *Globalization and Liberalization*. New York: Oxford University Press.

UNDP (1999) *Globalization with a Human Face: Human Development Report 1999*. New York: Oxford University Press.

UNESCO (1950) *World Communications Report*. Paris: United Nations Educational, Scientific and Cultural Organization.

UNESCO (1986) *International Flows of Selected Cultural Goods*. Paris: United Nations Educational, Scientific and Cultural Organization.

UNESCO (1989) *World Communications Report*. Paris: United Nations Educational, Scientific and Cultural Organization.

Union of International Associations (2001) *Yearbook of International Organizations 2001/2002*, vol. IB. Munich: K. G. Saur.

Van der Pijl, K. (1999) *Transnational Classes and International Relations*. London: Routledge.

Wade, R. (1990) *Governing the Market: Economic Theory and the Role of Government in East Asian Industrialization*. Princeton: Princeton University Press.

Wallace, W. (1999) The sharing of sovereignty: the European paradox. *Political Studies* 47(3) (special issue).

Wallerstein, I. (1974) *The Modern World System*. New York: Academic Press.

Walters, A. (1993) *World Power and World Money*. Brighton: Harvester.

Waltz, K. (1979) *The Theory of International Politics*. New York: Addison-Wesley.

Walzer, M. (1983) *Spheres of Justice: A Defence of Pluralism and Equality*. Oxford: Martin Robertson.

Weiss, L. (1998) *State Capacity: Governing the Economy in a Global Era*. Cambridge: Polity Press.

Wood, A. (1994) *North–South Trade, Employment and Inequality*. Oxford: Oxford University Press.

Woods, N. (1999) Order, globalization and inequality in world politics. In A. Hurrell and N. Woods (eds), *Inequality, Globalization and World Politics*, Oxford: Oxford University Press.

WTO (2002) *Annual Report*. Geneva (www.wto.org).

Yergin, D. A. and Stanislaw, J. (1998) *The Commanding Heights*. New York: Simon and Schuster.

Young, O. (1972) The actors in world politics. In J. Rosenau, V. Davis and M. East (eds), *The Analysis of International Politics*, New York: Cornell University Press.

Zacher, M. (1992) The decaying pillars of the Westphalian temple. In J. N. Rosenau and O. E. Czempiel (eds), *Governance without Government*, Cambridge: Cambridge University Press.

Zevin, R. (1992) Are world financial markets more open? In T. Banuri and J. B. Schor (eds), *Financial Openness and National Autonomy*, Oxford: Oxford University Press.

Zürn, M. (1995) The challenge of globalization and individualization. In H. Holm and G. Sorensen (eds), *Whose World Order?* Boulder: Westview Press.

# Part I
# Understanding Globalization

Globalization, writes George Modelski, is the history of growing engagement between the world's major civilizations. It is best understood as a long-term historical process that can be traced back to the sporadic encounters amongst the earliest civilizations. However, it is modernity, and most especially the rise and global expansion of the West, which has shaped decisively the contemporary epoch of globalization. As the third millennium unfolds, the world's major civilizations find themselves enveloped in enduring webs of global economic, cultural, political and technological interconnectedness. Globalization, for Modelski, is a concept which captures this historical process of the widening and deepening of systemic interdependencies amongst nations, civilizations and political communities. It is a process which has come to define the contemporary condition and one which ultimately raises profound political questions as to whether it prefigures the emergence of a world society or global community.

For Tony Giddens too, globalization is largely synonymous with modernity, since in the modern era 'the intensification of worldwide social relations' is far greater than in any previous historical period. To understand globalization requires an examination of the driving forces of modernity; namely, how the intersecting processes of industrialization, capitalism, militarism and statism have an inherently globalizing impetus. This global momentum generates worldwide systems and infrastructures which now connect the lives and prospects of communities and households across distant parts of the globe. While the emergence of a global media infrastructure produces a developing awareness of how local and global events are interwoven, it is this dialectic between globalizing systems and local conditions which, in Giddens's analysis, constitutes the defining feature of the contemporary epoch.

David Held, Anthony McGrew and colleagues offer a distinctive conceptualization of globalization, along with a methodology for exploring its historically unique features. Defining globalization as 'a process which embodies a transformation in the spatial organization of social relations . . . generating transcontinental or interregional flows and networks', they advance an analytical framework which offers a methodology for comparing its various historical forms whilst avoiding a determinist account, i.e. a conceptualization of globalization understood as the progressive unification of humanity. In focusing attention on its spatial and organizational attributes, this approach provides insights into the unique character of contemporary patterns of globalization and its transformative consequences. Moreover, by explicating globalization in relation to power, the authors set out an approach to the subject which avoids a reductionist interpretation which portrays it as simply a spatial, rather than a social, process.

Robert Keohane and Joseph Nye further explore the unique aspects of contemporary globalization. Drawing upon an analytical distinction between globalization, as a process of heightening worldwide interdependence, and globalism, as the existence of multicontinental networks of interdependence, they elaborate the distinctive characteristics of the contemporary world order. They too argue that globalism today is very different from in the past – the networks of interdependence are much thicker or denser, whilst the speed and institutional velocity of global networks reflect a qualitative shift in communications technologies. One of the consequences of these developments, despite their unevenness, is the emergence of a new form of global politics which, in many parts of the world, corresponds more closely to reality 'than obsolete images of world politics as simply interstate relations'. Globalization is reshaping world politics, although, as Keohane and Nye warn, it is a trend which is contingent upon many factors such that it can be moderated or reversed by cataclysmic events, as 9/11 and its aftermath demonstrates.

Developing the concepts of globality and globalization, Jan Aart Scholte argues for a distinctive conceptualization of the latter. This conceptualization builds upon recent work in social geography which deals with the spatial form of contemporary social relations. Expanding upon the notion of 'deterritorialization', Scholte advances a conceptualization of globalization as supraterritoriality, defined by transworld flows and social relations which transcend borders and territorial space. Globalization as supraterritoriality refers to the emergence of 'transborder exchanges without distance' and, thus, to the 'relative deterritorialization of social life'. It involves both a reconfiguration of the social geography of modern life and requires a substantive rethinking of traditional social science approaches to understanding and explaining the contemporary human condition.

In a rather combative essay, Justin Rosenberg takes issue with the central propositions of the globalist account, as expressed in contributions like those above. 'Globalization theory', he argues, suffers from a fundamental contradiction in that it embodies a circular logic – globalization is conceived at one and the same time as both a cause and an outcome. Globalization is argued to be transforming societies and world order as well as being an expression of such transformations. Moreover, working from the premiss that the world has fundamentally changed, globalization theory overlooks the work of classical social theorists, such as Marx and Weber, who sought to explain patterns of global social change. The result is that globalization becomes little more than a descriptive category, whilst its novel attributes are exaggerated or reduced to a simple 'spatial fetishism'.

This sceptical voice is further amplified by the contribution of Paul Hirst and Grahame Thompson. Taking an historical approach, they conclude that the present era exhibits much weaker and less intense forms of global integration when compared with the high point of globalization during the *belle époque* (1890–1914). In so doing, they call into question the very validity of the concept of globalization as a valid term for understanding the contemporary world. Rather than the emergence of a singular world economy, they posit a world of highly uneven internationalization in which national borders retain their economic and political primacy. In so far as it fails to describe or explain the current economic realities, the widespread discourse of globalization has to be understood as a popular myth which gives some legitimacy to the project of neoliberal economic globalization by making the latter appear an inevitable product of historical forces. Globalization, in this regard, functions more as an ideology than an accurate account of the world of the twenty-first century.

For Stanley Hoffmann the exaggerated nature of globalization is evident in the changed world post-9/11. The terrorist attacks on the United States have demonstrated the reality of geopolitics, of the centrality of states and of military power to the maintenance of world order. The limits to globalization are now readily apparent. Moreover, the post-2001 waning of globalization demonstrates just how far the project itself was the specific creation of an internationalist American elite during the post-war era. But Western globalization and the globalization of terror have become intimately connected. Whereas the former provides the infrastructures and partial motivation for the latter, terror and the war on terror represent new barriers to, and constraints upon, global integration. Furthermore, these new limits to globalization are compounded by the unilateralist impulses of a preponderant USA. These developments demonstrate that 'globalization is neither inevitable nor irresistible' and, in so doing, could represent the inauguration of the post-globalization era.

By contrast, Joseph Nye offers a rather different account of the relationship between globalization and American power. Although he accepts that the present globalization project has been largely an American invention, the process itself has its own technological and economic dynamics. While the power of the USA is greatly enhanced by globalization, nevertheless 'it would be a mistake to envisage contemporary networks of globalism simply in terms of the hub and spokes of an American empire'. Indeed, though the USA promotes and benefits from globalization over the longer term, it will have to act to dilute its preponderant power, as other powers and regions acquire greater wealth and capabilities. To elide globalization with American power is an analytical as well as an empirical error.

This conclusion is reinforced by Michael Hardt's and Antonio Negri's article, the final selection in this section. In a radical reinterpretation of the concept of Empire, they argue that the present phase of globalized capitalism is creating a new global order. This order is best described as an Empire, not in the traditional sense of Imperial rule by a Great Power over subjugated territories and peoples, but rather as systems of global regulation which have no boundaries but which nonetheless embody relations of domination and subjugation. Moreover, the constitutionalization and institutionalization of this order, combined with a concurrent shift towards a new model of sovereignty, constitute an historically distinctive form of global governance. In this new Empire, the USA retains a privileged but not a preponderant position, since no single state can rule, whilst Imperialism, in its traditional form, is over. Globalization is central not only to the evolution of this new Empire but also to the mobilization of a counter-Empire – an alternative global society. For Hardt and Negri, the historical trajectory of contemporary globalization crucially will be determined by the contest between these two historical forces, namely Empire and counter-Empire.

# 1

# Globalization

## *George Modelski*

In clear contrast with all other historical societies, the contemporary world society is global. The process by which a number of historical world societies were brought together into one global system might be referred to as globalization. The nature and the shape assumed as a result of that process remain even today one of the basic factors of world politics.

Throughout recorded history, a trend can be observed toward the enlargement of the geographical scope of human communities; it has been one aspect of the increasing scale of social organization. Six thousand years ago, when a Great Society began to take form among the city states of Mesopotamia, the effective radius of its area may have been two or three hundred miles; two thousand years ago, when the Roman Empire dominated the Mediterranean basin, the radius of its control may have been one thousand miles or more (for a time it included Mesopotamia). The spread and enlargement of areas of civilization were at the same time occurring in the Chinese and Indian realms, so much so that what McNeill calls the "closure of the Eurasian ecumene" occurred between 500 BC and 200 AD,[1] some two millennia ago. Within that timespan, Hellenic culture reached India, while the Han Empire established a degree of contact with India and its missions established the existence of the Roman Empire. The epidemics that swept the ancient world around that time may have been the first practical consequence of the establishment of some pattern of interaction in the Old World. Generally, however, these interactions remained for a long time intermittent, indirect, nonpolitical, and not yet truly global.

## The Moslem World

At the opening of the period of globalization, at about 1000 AD, the nearest approximation to a worldwide political order was the Moslem world. Its origins lay in the Arab conquests of the seventh century, and its binding force was Islam. At that time it ranged from Spain and Morocco, through Damascus, Cairo and Baghdad, to Persia and the North of India; in the centuries that followed, it reached as far as the Indonesian islands, and Central and East Africa. Even by comparison with medieval Europe, it was a prosperous, productive and culturally rich world. Its cities, Baghdad and Cairo, were cosmopolitan and populous (Cairo had more than one million inhabitants during the medieval period), as well as being centers of artistic and literary creation. Its scholars and scientists were the true successors of Greek learning, while its universities predated Europe's by at least a century.

[ . . . ]

For several hundred years, the Moslem world was the true seat of civilization. In relation to it medieval Europe was for a long time not only politically on the defensive, but also economically and culturally inferior. Indeed, by occupying a central position in the Eurasian-African landmass and using it for their far-flung trade, the Moslems had already brought together the major centers of world civilization. Only the New World eluded them, and interoceanic shipping.

[ . . . ]

After 1500, the Moslem world was strategically outflanked by European naval operations, and its vitality continued to decline. While Islam continued to gain adherents in Asia and Africa, the brilliance of the medieval period did not return.

## The Expansion of Europe

The work of political unification of the world now fell to Europe. In one sense, the drive that produced it was a response to the prosperity of the Islamic world and the threat that was perceived to emanate from it. Leading that drive were the Portuguese and Spaniards, who had learned to respect and fear the Moslems during the centuries of the *Reconquista*. It was a genuine explosion of energy and vitality, of a breadth and scope hitherto unknown. Within a short space of time, soon after Copernicus reordered the heavens, men not only circumnavigated the globe, but followed up this feat with the establishment and maintenance of a permanent network of worldwide contacts.

The process of globalization was set in motion by people who lived in a small corner of the earth, not in the centers of world civilization. For the five hundred years that followed, it was they who determined the speed and the character of globalization; they also thereby shaped the structure of world politics.

By 1500, the characteristic features of modern world politics could already be discerned in embryo in Europe; in the course of globalization these features became characteristics of the entire global system.

[ . . . ]

## Some Other Features

One striking feature of the process of globalization has been the quality of arrogance and violence that fueled it. William McNeill notes the "deeprooted pugnacity and recklessness" which, in combination with advanced military technology and acquired immunity to a variety of diseases within a brief space of time, gave the Europeans of the Atlantic Seaboard the command of the oceans.[2] European warlikeness (even of the merchants who on the high seas easily assumed the role of pirates) was most pronounced when compared with the attitudes and aptitudes of all the other major world civilizations (except for the Moslems, another "community of will"). None of them could match the naked, if well-organized, force of their ruthless opponents. In the process of globalization, European warlikeness might well have become a dominant feature of the entire system of world politics.

[ . . . ]

A great expansion in state activity and efficiency may well have been the most profound influence of globalization. Royal governments in Portugal, Spain, England

and France organized and reaped the fruits of discovery and exploitation. In this, they learnt much from the Italian city states, Venice, Genoa and Florence: during the late medieval period, these were models of administrative organization and efficiency. But they soon had to expand their organization greatly in order to govern their newly acquired posts and territories – that is, efficiently to conduct higher-level administration at a distance. The Spanish Crown was the first to develop an elaborate machinery for the government of its American possessions; it thus gave employment to the rising number of graduates of law schools and universities. In turn, strong bureaucracies undermined tendencies toward popular rule, created a steady flow of revenue, and made the rulers independent of the control of assemblies, which had been so prominent in the earlier period. "Bureaucracy, like absolutism, strengthened its grip upon the kingdoms of Europe, in part at least as the consequence of the needs experienced and experiments conducted overseas."[3]

In military governmental operations, globalization was peculiarly favorable to, as well as dependent upon, the development of the navy. Effective naval operations over long distances require not only technology, but above all a sound political organization: a steady tax base, because they are expensive; a shipbuilding and supplies industry, geared to governmental demand; a manpower base that might be relatively small, but had to be loyal and well trained; and a governmental system that would be capable of coordinating these elements toward long-term goals. Governments that were capable of equipping fleets for sailing the world would also, as a rule, be efficient and strong governments, and it was they who set the tone of political organization.

Good navies were, for their part, closely dependent on the organization of commerce. The first Portuguese explorations were organized and financed by the Royal government; the monopoly of the spice trade that flowed from them was conducted entirely for the benefit of the King. This fusion of political and commercial activities probably contributed to the early decline of the trade. Spanish trade with the Americas was conducted by a monopoly of the merchants of Seville, with the financial backing of Italian and German houses, but it was less lucrative. It was the injection of Dutch and English enterprise, based on the long commercial experience of the cities of the Netherlands, that led to the development of specialized, corporate trade enterprises. The Dutch and English East Indies Companies became particularly famous, but there were many others. They all began as devices for pooling efforts to equip and supply fleets that sailed long distances. Voyages to the East, for instance, could last several years, and their profits were far from certain, although they could be spectacular. The organization, forethought, trust and care that were required for launching such expeditions were of a high order. Practices evolved in the organization and management of long-distance, hence higher-layered, trade and production activities became the bases of modern corporate organization.[4]

[ . . . ]

## An Appraisal

The way in which the world has been brought together was a spectacular enterprise, with a magnificence all its own. Its role in shaping human destiny has not often enough been appreciated, even though the tales of exploration and adventure have long held the fascination of European audiences. But the spectacle and the splendor also had their shadows, and some of these have been dark and long.

A most important characteristic of globalization was its marvelously uncontrolled character. Despite the force and impetus of the process, this was not an organized expansion of a centralized system, as were the contemporaneous Chinese expeditions to Africa. This was not an expansion of one entity, called Europe, seizing overseas territory; it was rather the spilling over of a multitude of enterprises from Europe onto the world. In turn, the impact of the process also changed Europe. No one empire emerged but rather a series of imperial domains, each in competition with the others. Despite attempts at monopolization, no one rule attained overwhelming superiority; conversely, no single empire gave its ruler sufficient power to establish dominion over the whole of Europe.

[ ... ]

Globalization helped to consolidate the system of independent states for Europe, and ultimately also for the world, by fostering the growth of a diversity of organizations, each one of which served as the seedbed of new autonomy and diversity. But above all, this process strengthened the state, and by doing so it markedly affected the course of future political development.

Who benefited from globalization? In a broad sense, the Western community did. During the past few centuries, the share of the European stock in the world's population has risen substantially.[5] In part, this is attributable to an earlier burst of population growth in Europe; but this early growth had also made possible large-scale migrations and the settlement of some of the world's most fertile and productive lands, in the attractive temperate zones, by people of European descent. The abundant lands and waters of North America, southern South America, South Africa and Australia became extensions of Europe, and their exploitation significantly altered the distribution of global wealth in favor of the European groups. As the result of globalization, the Europeans and their descendants today control the major part of cultivable land and the most productive sources of food, and they could also control the resources of the seas.[6]

Within Europe, those who benefited the most were those governments and states, and their subjects, that led and controlled the process. At first, the Iberian monarchies grew powerful on its proceeds, then the Dutch, the English and the French. Globalization altered the distribution of power away from Central Europe – including the cities of Northern Italy, the German lands and the Baltic area – to the coastlands of the North Atlantic. The process of growth redounded in the first place to the benefit of those who organized it.

Side by side with the benefits of globalization must be put its considerable costs and its range of adverse, indeed disintegrative effects. With regard to a number of human societies, its impact has been deadly, both in terms of social organization and for individual members of such societies, for whom the prospects of life declined tragically as the result of European impact. The societies of Mexico and Peru disintegrated, and in the century following the conquest the population of Central America declined catastrophically, through violence, disease and depression.[7] Similar disasters befell the Indian populations of North America, the inhabitants of many Pacific islands and the aboriginal populations of Australia.

[ ... ]

Most of the time globalization was a process of incorporating external parts into the ongoing fabric of Western-centered world politics. Those governments, societies, individuals that proved adept and adaptable enough were brought within the mainstream by means of cooptation. The great majority were either dominated, controlled, ignored or isolated. An alternative mode of adaptation – that of adjusting Western-type life patterns to the requirements of the rest of the world – has not been adequately considered. Cooptation certainly has been neither deep, rapid nor sufficiently extensive. Complementary adaptation is yet to be explored – for instance, through the selective slowing down of growth rates. The work of globalization could yet be carried to completion in unsuspected ways.

Globalization ultimately raises the problem of whether the large community, indeed the community of mankind, can be a good community. Renowned political thinkers have consistently opted for an ideal community that is small and intimate. By and large, contemporary political thought points to the lack of community in large-scale organizations.

The historical experience of globalization does not permit us to make any optimistic or easy conclusion. It offers no grounds for the opinion that the large community must, of necessity, create wide benefits; indeed, there are reasons for thinking that it may instead create opportunities for great dangers. But it also discloses no theoretical or practical considerations that show that the large community is inherently unable to be good. The large community is here and can no longer be avoided; perhaps it can be made better.

## Notes

1  W. H. McNeill, *The Rise of the West* (Chicago: Chicago University Press, 1963), ch. 7.
2  Ibid., pp. 623–4.
3  J. H. Parry, *The Age of Reconnaissance* (New York: New America Library, 1964), p. 320.
4  The prominence of corporate organization in the economic development of the United States may have had its origins in the early influence of such commercial corporations. Virginia was founded by an English chartered company; New York was a trading post of the Dutch West India Company; the Hudson Bay Company had been prominent in Canadian history for centuries.
5  C. M. Cipolla, *The Economic History of World Population* (Harmondsworth: Penguin, 1964), pp. 102–4, quoting Kuczynski, according to whom the white population of the earth was about 22 per cent of the human species in 1800 and about 35 per cent in 1930; more recently, this proportion may have been declining.
6  According to G. Borgstrom, *The Hungry Planet* (New York: Collier, 1965), "the privileged nations of the world" – which include the United States and account for some 450 million people – dispose of as many food calories per year as 1,300 million people at the bottom of the scale, who live in the least developed countries. "We like to think that we owe our abundance to our greater skill and ingenuity, completely forgetting that we owe it equally or maybe even to a greater extent to our good fortune in the great lottery of mankind, which has given us a disproportionate share of the world's agricultural resources" (p. 29).
7  Central Mexico had a population of 11 million in 1519 and one of 2.5 million in 1597 (quoted by Parry, *Age of Reconnaissance*, p. 246).

# 2

# The Globalizing of Modernity

## Anthony Giddens

Modernity is inherently globalizing – this is evident in some of the most basic characteristics of modern institutions, including particularly their disembeddedness and reflexivity. But what exactly is globalization, and how might we best conceptualize the phenomenon? I shall consider these questions at some length [ . . . ] since the central importance of globalizing processes today has scarcely been matched by extended discussions of the concept in the sociological literature. [ . . . ] The undue reliance which sociologists have placed upon the idea of 'society', where this means a bounded system, should be replaced by a starting point that concentrates upon analysing how social life is ordered across time and space – the problematic of time-space distanciation. The conceptual framework of time-space distanciation directs our attention to the complex relations between *local involvements* (circumstances of co-presence) and *interaction across distance* (the connections of presence and absence). In the modern era, the level of time-space distanciation is much higher than in any previous period, and the relations between local and distant social forms and events become correspondingly 'stretched'. Globalization refers essentially to that stretching process, in so far as the modes of connection between different social contexts or regions become networked across the earth's surface as a whole.

Globalization can thus be defined as the intensification of worldwide social relations which link distant localities in such a way that local happenings are shaped by events occurring many miles away and vice versa. This is a dialectical process because such local happenings may move in an obverse direction from the very distanciated relations that shape them. *Local transformation* is as much a part of globalization as the lateral extension of social connections across time and space. Thus whoever studies cities today, in any part of the world, is aware that what happens in a local neighbourhood is likely to be influenced by factors – such as world money and commodity markets – operating at an indefinite distance away from that neighbourhood itself. The outcome is not necessarily, or even usually, a generalized set of changes acting in a uniform direction, but consists in mutually opposed tendencies. The increasing prosperity of an urban area in Singapore might be causally related, via a complicated network of global economic ties, to the impoverishment of a neighbourhood in Pittsburgh whose local products are uncompetitive in world markets.

Another example from the very many that could be offered is the rise of local nationalisms in Europe and elsewhere. The development of globalized social relations probably serves to diminish some aspects of nationalist feeling linked to nation-states (or some states) but may be causally involved with the intensifying of more localized nationalist sentiments. In circumstances of accelerating globalization, the nation-state has become 'too small for the big problems of life, and too big for the small problems of life'.[1] At the same time as social relations become laterally stretched and as part of the same process, we see the strengthening of pressures for local autonomy and regional cultural identity.

## Two Theoretical Perspectives

Apart from the work of Marshall McLuhan and a few other individual authors, discussions of globalization tend to appear in two bodies of literature, which are largely distinct from one another. One is the literature of international relations, the other that of 'world-system theory', particularly as associated with Immanuel Wallerstein, which stands fairly close to a Marxist position.

Theorists of international relations characteristically focus upon the development of the nation-state system, analysing its origins in Europe and its subsequent worldwide spread. Nation-states are treated as actors, engaging with one another in the international arena – and with other organizations of a transnational kind (intergovernmental organizations or non-state actors). Although various theoretical positions are represented in this literature, most authors paint a rather similar picture in analysing the growth of globalization.[2] [...] Nation-states, it is held, are becoming progressively less sovereign than they used to be in terms of control over their own affairs – although few today anticipate in the near future the emergence of the 'world-state' which many in the early part of this century foresaw as a real prospect.

While this view is not altogether wrong, some major reservations have to be expressed. For one thing, it again covers only one overall dimension of globalization as I wish to utilize the concept here – the international coordination of states. Regarding states as actors has its uses and makes sense in some contexts. However, [...] treating states as actors having connections with each other and with other organizations in the international arena makes it difficult to deal with social relations that are not between or outside states, but simply cross-cut state divisions.

A further shortcoming of this type of approach concerns its portrayal of the increasing unification of the nation-state system. The sovereign power of modern states was not formed prior to their involvement in the nation-state system, even in the European state system, but developed in conjunction with it. Indeed, the sovereignty of the modern state was from the first *dependent upon the relations between states*, in terms of which each state (in principle if by no means always in practice) recognized the autonomy of others within their own borders. No state, however powerful, held as much sovereign control in practice as was enshrined in legal principle. The history of the past two centuries is thus not one of the progressive loss of sovereignty on the part of the nation-state. Here again we must recognize the dialectical character of globalization and also the influence of processes of uneven development. Loss of autonomy on the part of some states or groups of states has often gone along with an *increase* in that of others, as a result of alliances, wars, or political and economic changes of various sorts. [...]

Since the stance of world-system theory differs so much from international relations, it is not surprising to find that the two literatures are at arm's distance from one another. Wallerstein's account of the world system makes many contributions, in both theory and empirical analysis.[3] Not least important is the fact that he skirts the sociologists' usual preoccupation with 'societies' in favour of a much more embracing conception

of globalized relationships. He also makes a clear differentiation between the modern era and preceding ages in terms of the phenomena with which he is concerned. What he refers to as 'world economies' – networks of economic connections of a geographically extensive sort – have existed prior to modern times, but these were notably different from the world system that has developed over the past three or four centuries. Earlier world economies were usually centred upon large imperial states and never covered more than certain regions in which the power of these states was concentrated. The emergence of capitalism, as Wallerstein analyses it, ushers in a quite different type of order, for the first time genuinely global in its span and based more on economic than political power – the 'world capitalist economy'. The world capitalist economy, which has its origins in the sixteenth and seventeenth centuries, is integrated through commercial and manufacturing connections, not by a political centre. Indeed, there exists a multiplicity of political centres, the nation-states. The modern world system is divided into three components, the core, the semi-periphery, and the periphery, although where these are located regionally shifts over time.
[...]

Wallerstein successfully breaks away from some of the limitations of much orthodox sociological thought, most notably the strongly defined tendency to focus upon 'endogenous models' of social change. But his work has its own shortcomings. He continues to see only one dominant institutional nexus (capitalism) as responsible for modern transformations. World-system theory thus concentrates heavily upon economic influences and finds it difficult satisfactorily to account for just those phenomena made central by the theorists of international relations: the rise of the nation-state and the nation-state system. Moreover, the distinctions between core, semi-periphery, and periphery (themselves perhaps of questionable value), based upon economic criteria, do not allow us to illuminate political or military concentrations of power, which do not align in an exact way to economic differentiations.

## Dimensions of Globalization

I shall, in contrast, regard the world capitalist economy as one of four dimensions of globalization (see figure [1]).[4] The nation-state system is a second dimension; as the discussion above indicated, although these are connected in various ways, neither can be explained exhaustively in terms of the other.

If we consider the present day, in what sense can world economic organization be said to be dominated by capitalistic economic mechanisms? A number of considerations are relevant to answering this question. The main centres of power in the world economy are capitalist states – states in which capitalist economic enterprise (with the class relations that this implies) is the chief form of production. The domestic and international economic policies of these states involve many forms of regulation of economic activity, but, as noted, their institutional organization maintains an 'insulation' of the economic from the political. This allows wide scope for the global activities of business corporations, which always have a home base within a particular state but may develop many other regional involvements elsewhere.

Business firms, especially the transnational corporations, may wield immense economic power, and have the capacity to influence political policies in their home bases and elsewhere. The biggest transnational companies today have budgets larger than

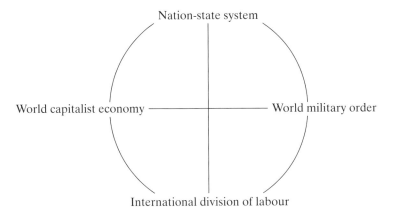

**Figure [1]**  The dimensions of globalization

those of all but a few nations. But there are some key respects in which their power cannot rival that of states – especially important here are the factors of territoriality and control of the means of violence. There is no area on the earth's surface, with the partial exception of the polar regions, which is not claimed as the legitimate sphere of control of one state or another. All modern states have a more or less successful monopoly of control of the means of violence within their own territories. No matter how great their economic power, industrial corporations are not military organizations (as some of them were during the colonial period), and they cannot establish themselves as political/legal entities which rule a given territorial area.

If nation-states are the principal 'actors' within the global political order, corporations are the dominant agents within the world economy. In their trading relations with one another, and with states and consumers, companies (manufacturing corporations, financial firms, and banks) depend upon production for profit. Hence the spread of their influence brings in its train a global extension of commodity markets, including money markets. However, even in its beginnings, the capitalist world economy was never just a market for the trading of goods and services. It involved, and involves today, the commodifying of labour power in class relations which separate workers from control of their means of production. This process, of course, is fraught with implications for global inequalities.

All nation-states, capitalist and state socialist, within the 'developed' sectors of the world, are primarily reliant upon industrial production for the generation of the wealth upon which their tax revenues are based. [ ... ] The pursuit of growth by both Western and East European societies inevitably pushes economic interests to the forefront of the policies which states pursue in the international arena. But it is surely plain to all, save those under the sway of historical materialism, that the material involvements of nation-states are not governed purely by economic considerations, real or perceived. The influence of any particular state within the global political order is strongly conditioned by the level of its wealth (and the connection between this and military strength). However, states derive their power from their sovereign capabilities, as Hans J. Morgenthau emphasizes.[5] They do not operate as economic machines, but as 'actors' jealous of their territorial rights, concerned with the fostering of national cultures, and having strategic geopolitical involvements with other states or alliances of states.

The nation-state system has long participated in that reflexivity characteristic of modernity as a whole. The very existence of sovereignty should be understood as something that is reflexively monitored, for reasons already indicated. Sovereignty is linked to the replacement of 'frontiers' by 'borders' in the early development of the nation-state system: autonomy inside the territory claimed by the state is sanctioned by the recognition of borders by other states. [ . . . ]

One aspect of the dialectical nature of globalization is the 'push and pull' between tendencies towards centralization inherent in the reflexivity of the system of states on the one hand and the sovereignty of particular states on the other. Thus, concerted action between countries in some respects diminishes the individual sovereignty of the nations involved, yet by combining their power in other ways, it increases their influence within the state system. The same is true of the early congresses which, in conjunction with war, defined and redefined states' borders – and of truly global agencies such as the United Nations. [ . . . ]

The third dimension of globalization is the world military order. In specifying its nature, we have to analyse the connections between the industrialization of war, the flow of weaponry and techniques of military organization from some parts of the world to others, and the alliances which states build with one another. Military alliances do not necessarily compromise the monopoly over the means of violence held by a state within its territories, although in some circumstances they certainly can do so.

In tracing the overlaps between military power and the sovereignty of states, we find the same push-and-pull between opposing tendencies noted previously. [ . . . ] [A]s a result of the massive destructive power of modern weaponry, almost all states possess military strength far in excess of that of even the largest of pre-modern civilizations. Many economically weak Third World countries are militarily powerful. In an important sense there is no 'Third World' in respect of weaponry, only a 'First World', since most countries maintain stocks of technologically advanced armaments and have modernized the military in a thoroughgoing way. Even the possession of nuclear weaponry is not confined to the economically advanced states.

The globalizing of military power obviously is not confined to weaponry and alliances between the armed forces of different states – it also concerns war itself. Two world wars attest to the way in which local conflicts became matters of global involvement. In both wars, the participants were drawn from virtually all regions (although the Second World War was a more truly worldwide phenomenon). In an era of nuclear weaponry, the industrialization of war has proceeded to a point at which [ . . . ] the obsolescence of Clausewitz's main doctrine has become apparent to everyone.[6] The only point of holding nuclear weapons – apart from their possible symbolic value in world politics – is to deter others from using them.

While this situation may lead to a suspension of war between the nuclear powers (or so we all must hope), it scarcely prevents them from engaging in military adventures outside their own territorial domains. [ . . . ]

The fourth dimension of globalization concerns industrial development. The most obvious aspect of this is the expansion of the global division of labour, which includes the differentiations between more and less industrialized areas in the world. Modern industry is intrinsically based on divisions of labour, not only on the level of job tasks but on that of regional specialization in terms of type of industry, skills, and the production of raw materials. There has undoubtedly taken place a major expansion of global interdependence in the division of labour since the Second World War. This has helped to bring about shifts in the worldwide distribution of production, including the deindustrialization of some regions in the developed countries and the emergence of the 'Newly Industrializing Countries' in the Third World. It has also undoubtedly served to reduce the internal economic hegemony of many states, particularly those with a high level of industrialization. It is more difficult for the capitalist countries to manage their economies than formerly was the case, given accelerating global economic interdependence. This is almost certainly one of the major reasons for the declining impact of Keynesian economic policies, as applied at the level of the national economy, in current times.

One of the main features of the globalizing implications of industrialism is the worldwide diffusion of machine technologies. The impact of industrialism is plainly not limited to the sphere of production, but affects many aspects of day-to-day life, as well as influencing the generic character of human interaction with the material environment.

Even in states which remain primarily agricultural, modern technology is often applied in such a way as to alter substantially pre-existing relations between human social organization and the environment. This is true, for example, of the use of fertilizers or other artificial farming methods, the introduction of modern farming machinery, and so forth. The diffusion of industrialism has created 'one world' in a more negative and threatening sense than that just mentioned – a world in which there are actual or potential ecological changes of a harmful sort that affect everyone on the planet. Yet industrialism has also decisively conditioned our very sense of living in 'one world'. For one of the most important effects of industrialism has been the transformation of technologies of communication.

This comment leads on to a further and quite fundamental aspect of globalization, which lies behind each of the various institutional dimensions that have been mentioned and which might be referred to as cultural globalization. Mechanized technologies of communication have dramatically influenced all aspects of globalization since the first introduction of mechanical printing into Europe. They form an essential element of the reflexivity of modernity and of the discontinuities which have torn the modern away from the traditional.

The globalizing impact of media was noted by numerous authors during the period of the early growth of mass circulation newspapers. Thus one commentator in 1892 wrote that, as a result of modern newspapers, the inhabitant of a local village has a broader understanding of contemporary events than the prime minister of a hundred years before. The villager who reads a paper 'interests himself simultaneously in the issue of a revolution in Chile, a bush-war in East Africa, a massacre in North China, a famine in Russia'.[7]

The point here is not that people are contingently aware of many events, from all over the world, of which previously they would have remained ignorant. It is that the global extension of the institutions of modernity would be impossible were it not for the pooling of knowledge which is represented by the 'news'. This is perhaps less obvious on the level of general cultural awareness than in more specific contexts. For example, the global money markets of today involve direct and simultaneous access to pooled information on the part of individuals spatially widely separated from one another.

## Notes

1   Daniel Bell, 'The world and the United States in 2013', *Daedalus* 116 (1987).
2   See for example James N. Rosenau, *The Study of Global Interdependence* (London: Pinter, 1980).
3   Immanuel Wallerstein, *The Modern World System* (New York: Academic, 1974).
4   This figure (and the discussion which accompanies it) supersedes that which appears on p. 277 of Giddens, *Nation-State and Violence* (Cambridge: Polity Press, 1985).
5   H. J. Morgenthau, *Politics among Nations* (New York: Knopf, 1960).
6   Clausewitz was a subtle thinker, however, and there are interpretations of his ideas which continue to insist upon their relevance to the present day.
7   Max Nordau, *Degeneration* (1892; New York: Fertig, 1968), p. 39.

# 3

# Rethinking Globalization

## *David Held and Anthony McGrew,*
## *David Goldblatt and Jonathan Perraton*

[ . . . ]

### Rethinking Globalization: An Analytical Framework

What is globalization? Although in its simplest sense globalization refers to the widening, deepening and speeding up of global interconnectedness, such a definition begs further elaboration. Despite a proliferation of definitions in contemporary discussion – among them 'accelerating interdependence', 'action at a distance' and 'time–space compression'[1] (see, respectively, Ohmae 1990; Giddens 1990; Harvey 1989) – there is scant evidence in the existing literature of any attempt to specify precisely what is 'global' about globalization. For instance, all the above definitions are quite compatible with far more spatially confined processes such as the spread of national or regional interconnections. In seeking to remedy this conceptual difficulty, this study commences from an understanding of globalization which acknowledges its distinctive spatial attributes and the way these unfold over time.

Globalization can be located on a continuum with the local, national and regional.[2] At the one end of the continuum lie social and economic relations and networks which are organized on a local and/or national basis: at the other end lie social and economic relations and networks which crystallize on the wider scale of regional and global interactions. Globalization can be taken to refer to those spatio-temporal processes of change which underpin a transformation in the organization of human affairs by linking together and expanding human activity across regions and continents. Without reference to such expansive spatial connections, there can be no clear or coherent formulation of this term.

Accordingly, the concept of globalization implies, first and foremost, a *stretching* of social, political and economic activities across frontiers such that events, decisions and activities in one region of the world can come to have significance for individuals and communities in distant regions of the globe. In this sense, it embodies transregional interconnectedness, the widening reach of networks of social activity and power, and the possibility of action at a distance. Beyond this, globalization implies that connections across frontiers are not just occasional or random, but rather are regularized such that there is a detectable *intensification*, or growing magnitude, of interconnectedness, patterns of interaction and flows which transcend the constituent societies and states of the world order. Furthermore, growing extensity and intensity of global interconnectedness may also imply a *speeding up* of global interactions and processes as the development of worldwide systems of transport and communication increases the potential velocity of the global diffusion of ideas, goods, information, capital and people.

And the growing *extensity*, *intensity* and *velocity* of global interactions may also be associated with a deepening enmeshment of the local and global such that the *impact* of distant events is magnified while even the most local developments may come to have enormous global consequences. In this sense, the boundaries between domestic matters and global affairs may be blurred. A satisfactory definition of globalization must capture each of these elements: extensity (stretching), intensity, velocity and impact. And a satisfactory account of globalization must examine them thoroughly. We shall refer to these four elements henceforth as the 'spatio-temporal' dimensions of globalization.

By acknowledging these dimensions a more precise definition of globalization can be offered. Accordingly, globalization can be thought of as

> *a process (or set of processes) which embodies a transformation in the spatial organ-ization of social relations and transactions – assessed in terms of their extensity, intensity, velocity and impact – generating transcontinental or interregional flows and networks of activity, interaction, and the exercise of power.*

In this context, flows refer to the movements of physical artefacts, people, symbols, tokens and information across space and time, while networks refer to regularized or patterned interactions between independent agents, nodes of activity, or sites of power (Modelski 1972; Mann 1993; Castells 1996).

This formulation helps address the failure of existing approaches to differentiate globalization from more spatially delimited processes – what we can call 'localization', 'nationalization', 'regionalization' and 'internationalization'. For as it is defined above, globalization can be distinguished from more restricted social developments. Localization simply refers to the consolidation of flows and networks within a specific locale. Nationalization is the process whereby social relations and transactions are developed within the framework of fixed territorial borders. Regionalization can be denoted by a clustering of transactions, flows, networks and interactions between functional or geographical groupings of states or societies, while internationalization can be taken to refer to patterns of interaction and interconnectedness between two or more nation-states irrespective of their specific geographical location (see Nierop 1994; Buzan 1998). Thus contemporary globalization describes, for example, the flows of trade and finance between the major regions in the world economy, while equival-ent flows within them can be differentiated in terms of local, national and regional clusters.

In offering a more precise definition of these concepts it is crucial to signal that globalization is not conceived here in opposition to more spatially delimited processes but, on the contrary, as standing in a complex and dynamic relationship with them. On the one hand, processes such as regionalization can create the necessary kinds of economic, social and physical infrastructures which facilitate and complement the deepen-ing of globalization. In this regard, for example, economic regionalization (for instance, the European Union) has not been a barrier to the globalization of trade and pro-duction but a spur. On the other hand, such processes can impose limits to global-ization, if not encouraging a process of deglobalization. However, there is no a priori reason to assume that localization or regionalization exist in an oppositional or con-tradictory relationship to globalization. Precisely how these processes interrelate in economic and other domains is more an empirical matter [ . . . ].

## Historical forms of globalization

Sceptics of the globalization thesis alert us to the fact that international or global inter-connectedness is by no means a novel phenomenon; yet they overlook the possibility that the particular form taken by globalization may differ between historical eras. To distinguish the novel features of globalization in any epoch requires some kind of ana-lytical framework for organizing such comparative historical enquiry. For without such a framework it would be difficult to identify the most significant features, continuities or differences between epochs. Thus the approach developed here centres on the idea of *historical forms of globalization* as the basis for constructing a systematic com-parative analysis of globalization over time. Utilizing this notion helps provide a mechanism for capturing and systematizing relevant differences and similarities. In this context, historical forms of globalization refer to

> *the spatio-temporal and organizational attributes of global interconnectedness in discrete historical epochs.*

To say anything meaningful about either the unique attributes or the dominant fea-tures of contemporary globalization requires clear analytical categories from which such descriptions can be constructed. Building directly on our earlier distinctions, historical forms of globalization can be described and compared initially in respect of the four spatio-temporal dimensions:

- the extensity of global networks;
- the intensity of global interconnectedness;
- the velocity of global flows;
- the impact propensity of global interconnectedness.

Such a framework provides the basis for both a *quantitative* and a *qualitative* assessment of historical patterns of globalization. For it is possible to analyse (1) the extensive-ness of networks of relations and connections; (2) the intensity of flows and levels of activity within these networks; (3) the velocity or speed of interchanges; and (4) the impact of these phenomena on particular communities. A systematic assessment of how these phenomena have evolved provides insights into the changing historical forms of globalization; and it offers the possibility of a sharper identification and com-parison of the key attributes of, and the major disjunctures between, distinctive forms of globalization in different epochs. Such a historical approach to globalization avoids the current tendency to presume either that globalization is fundamentally new, or that there is nothing novel about contemporary levels of global economic and social interconnectedness since they appear to resemble those of prior periods.

Of course, the very notion of historical forms of globalization assumes that it is feasible to map, in an empirical sense, the extensity, intensity, velocity and impact propensity of global flows, networks and transactions across time. [ ... ] But one par-ticular dimension of globalization is especially difficult to operationalize: the impact propensity of global flows, networks and transactions. Yet without some clear under-standing of the nature of impact, the notion of globalization would remain imprecise. How should impact propensity be conceived?

For the purpose of this study, we distinguish between four analytically distinct types of impacts: *decisional, institutional, distributive* and *structural*. Decisional impacts refer to the degree to which the relative costs and benefits of the policy choices confronting governments, corporations, collectivities and households are influenced by global forces and conditions. Thus globalization may make some policy options or courses of action more or less costly and, in so doing, condition the outcome of individual or organizational decision-making. Depending on decision-makers' and collectivities' sensitivity or vulnerability to global conditions, their policy choices will be constrained or facilitated to a greater or lesser degree.[3] Decisional impacts can be assessed in terms of high impact (where globalization fundamentally alters policy preferences by transforming the costs and benefits of different courses of action) and low impact (where policy preferences are only marginally affected).

But the impact of globalization may not always be best understood in terms of decisions taken or forgone, since it may operate less transparently by reconfiguring the agenda of decision-making itself and, consequently, the available choices which agents may or may not realistically make. In other words, globalization may be associated with what Schattschneider referred to as the 'mobilization of bias' in so far as the agenda and choices which governments, households and corporations confront are set by global conditions (1960: 71). Thus, while the notion of decisional impacts focuses attention on how globalization directly influences the preferences and choices of decision-makers, the notion of institutional impact highlights the ways in which organizational and collective agendas reflect the effective choices or range of choices available as a result of globalization. In this respect, it offers insights into why certain choices may never even be considered as options at all.

Beyond such considerations, globalization may have considerable consequences for the distribution of power and wealth within and between countries. Distributional impacts refer to the ways in which globalization shapes the configuration of social forces (groups, classes, collectivities) within societies and across them. Thus, for instance, trade may undermine the prosperity of some workers while enhancing that of others. In this context, some groups and societies may be more vulnerable to globalization than others.

Finally, globalization may have discernible structural impacts in so far as it conditions patterns of domestic social, economic and political organization and behaviour. Accordingly, globalization may be inscribed within the institutions and everyday functioning of societies (Axford 1995). For instance, the spread of Western conceptions of the modern state and capitalist markets has conditioned the development of the majority of societies and civilizations across the globe. They have forced or stimulated the adaptation of traditional patterns of power and authority, generating new forms of rule and resource allocation. The structural consequences of globalization may be visible over both the short and the long term in the ways in which states and societies accommodate themselves to global forces. But such accommodation is, of course, far from automatic. For globalization is mediated, managed, contested and resisted by governments, agencies and peoples. States and societies may display varying degrees of sensitivity or vulnerability to global processes such that patterns of domestic structural adjustment will vary in terms of their degree and duration.

In assessing the impact of globalization on states and communities, it is useful to emphasize that the four types of impact can have a direct bearing on them, altering their form and modus operandi, or an indirect bearing, changing the context and balance of forces with which states have to contend. Decisional and institutional impacts tend to be direct in this regard, although they can have consequences for the economic and social circumstances in which states operate. Distributional and structural impacts tend to be indirect but, of course, none the less significant for that.

There are other important features of historical forms of globalization which should be distinguished. In addition to the spatio-temporal dimensions which sketch the broad shape of globalization, there are four dimensions which map its specific organizational profile: *infrastructures*, *institutionalization*, *stratification* and *modes of interaction*. Mapping the extensity, intensity, velocity and impact propensity of networks of global interconnectedness necessarily involves mapping the *infrastructures* which facilitate or carry global flows, networks and relations. Networks cannot exist without some kind of infrastructural support. Infrastructures may be physical, regulative/legal, or symbolic, for instance, a transportation infrastructure, the law governing war, or mathematics as the common language of science. But in most domains infrastructures are constituted by some combination of all these types of facility. For example, in the financial realm there is a worldwide information system for banking settlements, regulated by a regime of common rules, norms and procedures, and working through its own technical language via which its members communicate.

Infrastructures may facilitate or constrain the extensity and intensity of global connectedness in any single domain. This is because they mediate flows and connectivity: infrastructures influence the overall level of interaction capacity in every sector and thus the potential magnitude of global interconnectedness. Interaction capacity, understood as the potential scale of interaction defined by existing technical capabilities, is determined primarily, but not exclusively, by technological capacity and communications technology (see Buzan et al. 1993: 86). For instance, the interaction capacity of the medieval world system, constrained as it was by limited means of communication, among other things, was considerably less than that of the contemporary era, in which satellites and the Internet facilitate instant and almost real-time global communication (Deibert 1997). Thus changes in infrastructure have important consequences for the development and evolution of global interaction capacity.

Infrastructural conditions also facilitate the *institutionalization* of global networks, flows and relations. Institutionalization comprises the regularization of patterns of interaction and, consequently, their reproduction across space and time. To think in terms of the institutionalization of patterns of global connections (trade, alliances, etc.) is to acknowledge the ways in which global networks and relations become regularized and embedded in the practices and operations of the agencies (states, collectivities, households, individuals) in each social domain, from the cultural to the criminal (see Giddens 1979: 80). [ . . . ]

Discussion of infrastructures and institutionalization links directly to the issue of power. By power is meant the capacity of social agents, agencies and institutions to maintain or transform their circumstances, social or physical; and it concerns the resources which underpin this capacity and the forces that shape and influence its exercise. Accordingly, power is a phenomenon found in and between all groups, institutions and societies, cutting across public and private life. While 'power', thus understood, raises a number of complicated issues, it usefully highlights the nature of power as a universal dimension of human life, independent of any specific site or set of institutions (see Held 1989, 1995).

But the power of an agent or agency or institution, wherever it is located, never exists in isolation. Power is always exercised, and political outcomes are always determined, in the context of the relative capabilities of parties. Power has to be understood as a relational phenomenon (Giddens 1979: ch. 2; Rosenau 1980: ch. 3). Hence, power expresses at one and the same time the intentions and purposes of agencies and institutions and the relative balance of resources they can deploy with respect to each other. However, power cannot simply be conceived in terms of what agents or agencies do or do not do. For power is also a structural phenomenon, shaped by and in turn shaping the socially structured and culturally patterned behaviour of groups and the practices of organizations (Lukes 1974: 22). Any organization or institution can condition and limit the behaviour of its members. The rules and resources which such organizations and institutions embody rarely constitute a neutral framework for action, for they establish patterns of power and authority and confer the right to take decisions on some and not on others; in effect, they institutionalize a power relationship between 'rulers' and 'ruled', 'subjects' and 'governors' (McGrew 1988: 18–19).

Globalization transforms the organization, distribution and exercise of power. In this respect, globalization in different epochs may be associated with distinctive patterns of global *stratification*. In mapping historical forms of globalization, specific attention needs to be paid to patterns of stratification. In this context, stratification has both a social and a spatial dimension: hierarchy and unevenness, respectively (see Falk 1990: 2–12). Hierarchy refers to asymmetries in the control of, access to and enmeshment in global networks and infrastructures, while unevenness denotes the asymmetrical effects of processes of globalization on the life chances and well-being of peoples, classes, ethnic groupings and the sexes. These categories provide a mechanism for identifying the distinctive relations of global domination and control in different historical periods.

There are important differences too in the dominant *modes of interaction* within each epoch of globalization. It is possible to distinguish crudely between the dominant types of interaction – imperial or coercive, cooperative, competitive, conflictual – and the primary instruments of power, for example, military vs economic instruments. Thus, arguably, in the late nineteenth-century era of Western expansion, imperialism and military power were the dominant modes and instruments of globalization, whereas in the late twentieth century economic instruments, competition and cooperation appear to take precedence over military force (Morse 1976).

---

**Box 1**   Historical forms of globalization: key dimensions

*Spatio-temporal dimensions*
1   the extensity of global networks
2   the intensity of global interconnectedness
3   the velocity of global flows
4   the impact propensity of global interconnectedness

*Organizational dimensions*
5   the infrastructure of globalization
6   the institutionalization of global networks and the exercise of power
7   the pattern of global stratification
8   the dominant modes of global interaction

All in all, historical forms of globalization can be analysed in terms of eight dimensions: see box 1. Collectively, they determine the shape of globalization in each epoch.

## Notes

1 By 'accelerating interdependence' is understood the growing intensity of international enmeshment among national economies and societies such that developments in one country impact directly on other countries. 'Action at a distance' refers to the way in which, under conditions of contemporary globalization, the actions of social agents (individuals, collectivities, corporations, etc.) in one locale can come to have significant intended or unintended consequences for the behaviour of 'distant others'. Finally, 'time–space compression' refers to the manner in which globalization appears to shrink geographical distance and time; in a world of instantaneous communication, distance and time no longer seem to be a major constraint on patterns of human social organization or interaction.

2 Regions refer here to the geographical or functional clustering of states or societies. Such regional clusters can be identified in terms of their shared characteristics (cultural, religious, ideological, economic, etc.) and high level of patterned interaction relative to the outside world (Buzan 1998).

3 'Sensitivity involves degrees of responsiveness within a policy-framework – how quickly do changes in one country bring costly changes in another and how great are the costly effects ... Vulnerability can be defined as an actor's liability to suffer costs imposed by external events even after policies have been altered' (Keohane and Nye 1977: 12).

## References

Axford, B. (1995) *The Global System*. Cambridge: Polity Press.

Buzan, B. (1998) The Asia-Pacific: what sort of region, in what sort of order? In McGrew and Brook 1998.

Buzan, B., Little, R. and Jones, C. (1993) *The Logic of Anarchy*. New York: Columbia University Press.

Castells, M. (1996) *The Rise of the Network Society*. Oxford: Blackwell.

Deibert, R. (1997) *Parchment, Printing and Hypermedia*. New York: Columbia University Press.

Falk, R. (1990) Economic dimensions of global civilization. Working paper prepared for the Cairo meeting of the Global Civilization Project, Center for International Studies, Princeton University.

Giddens, A. (1979) *Central Problems in Social Theory: Action, Structure and Contradiction in Social Analysis*. London: Macmillan.

Giddens, A. (1990) *The Consequences of Modernity*. Cambridge: Polity Press.

Harvey, D. (1989) *The Condition of Postmodernity*. Oxford: Blackwell.

Held, D. (1989) *Political Theory and the Modern State*. Cambridge: Polity Press.

Held, D. (1995) *Democracy and the Global Order: From the Modern State to Cosmopolitan Governance*. Cambridge: Polity Press.

Keohane, R. O. and Nye, J. (1977) *Power and Interdependence*. Boston: Little, Brown.

Lukes, S. (1974) *Power: A Radical View*. London: Macmillan.

McGrew, A. G. (1988) Conceptualising Global Politics. Unit 1 in A. G. McGrew (ed.), *Global Politics*, Milton Keynes: Open University.

McGrew, A. G. and Brook, C. (eds) (1998) *Asia-Pacific in the New World Order*. London: Routledge.

Mann, M. (1993) *The Sources of Social Power*, vol. 2: *The Rise of Classes and Nation-States, 1760–1914*. Cambridge: Cambridge University Press.

Modelski, G. (1972) *Principles of World Politics*. New York: Free Press.

Morse, E. (1976) *Modernization and the Transformation of International Relations*. New York: Free Press.

Nierop, T. (1994) *Systems and Regions in Global Politics: An Empirical Study of Diplomacy, International Organization and Trade 1950–1991*. Chichester: John Wiley.

Ohmae, K. (1990) *The Borderless World*. London: Collins.

Rosenau, J. (1980) *The Study of Global Interdependence*. London: Frances Pinter.

Schattschneider, E. F. (1960) *The Semi-Sovereign People: A Realist View of Democracy in America*. New York: Rinehart and Winston.

# 4

# Globalization: What's New? What's Not? (And So What?)

*Robert O. Keohane and Joseph S. Nye Jr.*

"Globalization" emerged as a buzzword in the 1990s, just as "interdependence" did in the 1970s, but the phenomena it refers to are not entirely new. Our characterization of interdependence more than 20 years ago now applies to globalization at the turn of the millennium: "This vague phrase expresses a poorly understood but widespread feeling that the very nature of world politics is changing." Some skeptics believe such terms are beyond redemption for analytic use. Yet the public understands the image of the globe, and the new word conveys an increased sense of vulnerability to distant causes. For example, as helicopters fumigated New York City in 1999 to eradicate a lethal new virus, the press announced that the pathogen might have arrived in the bloodstream of a traveler, in a bird smuggled through customs, or in a mosquito that had flown into a jet. Fears of "bioinvasion" led some environmental groups to call for a reduction in global trade and travel.

Like all popular concepts meant to cover a variety of phenomena, both "interdependence" and "globalization" have many meanings. To understand what people are talking about when they use the terms and to make them useful for analysis, we must begin by asking whether interdependence and globalization are simply two words for the same thing, or whether there is something new going on.

## The Dimensions of Globalism

The two words are not exactly parallel. Interdependence refers to a condition, a state of affairs. It can increase, as it has been doing on most dimensions since the end of World War II; or it can decline, as it did, at least in economic terms, during the Great Depression of the 1930s. Globalization implies that something is increasing: There is more of it. Hence, our definitions start not with globalization but with "globalism," a condition that can increase or decrease.

Globalism is a state of the world involving networks of interdependence at multicontinental distances. The linkages occur through flows and influences of capital and goods, information and ideas, and people and forces, as well as environmentally and biologically relevant substances (such as acid rain or pathogens). Globalization and deglobalization refer to the increase or decline of globalism.

Interdependence refers to situations characterized by reciprocal effects among countries or among actors in different countries. Hence, globalism is a type of interdependence, but with two special characteristics. First, globalism refers to networks of connections (multiple relationships), not to single linkages. We would refer to economic or military interdependence between the United States and Japan, but not to globalism between the United States and Japan. U.S.–Japanese interdependence is part of contemporary globalism, but is not by itself globalism.

Second, for a network of relationships to be considered "global," it must include multicontinental distances, not simply regional networks. Distance is a continuous variable, ranging from adjacency (between, say, the United States and Canada) to opposite sides of the globe (for instance, Great Britain and Australia). Any sharp distinction between long-distance and regional interdependence is therefore arbitrary, and there is no point in deciding whether intermediate relationships – say, between Japan and India or between Egypt and South Africa – would qualify. Yet globalism would be an odd word for proximate regional relationships. Globalization refers to the shrinkage of distance on a large scale [ . . . ]. It can be contrasted with localization, nationalization, or regionalization.

Some examples may help. Islam's rapid diffusion from Arabia across Asia to what is now Indonesia was a clear instance of globalization, but the initial movement of Hinduism across the Indian subcontinent was not. Ties among the countries of the Asia Pacific Economic Cooperation forum qualify as multicontinental interdependence, because these countries include the Americas as well as Asia and Australia; but ties among members of the Association of Southeast Asian Nations are regional.

Globalism does not imply universality. At the turn of the millennium, more than a quarter of the American population used the World Wide Web compared with one hundredth of 1 percent of the population of South Asia. Most people in the world today do not have telephones; hundreds of millions live as peasants in remote villages with only slight connections to world markets or the global flow of ideas. Indeed, globalization is accompanied by increasing gaps, in many respects, between the rich and the poor. It implies neither homogenization nor equity.

Interdependence and globalism are both multidimensional phenomena. All too often, they are defined in strictly economic terms, as if the world economy defined globalism. But there are several, equally important forms of globalism:

- *Economic globalism* involves long-distance flows of goods, services, and capital, as well as the information and perceptions that accompany market exchange. It also involves the organization of the processes that are linked to these flows, such as the organization of low-wage production in Asia for the U.S. and European markets.
- *Military globalism* refers to long-distance networks of interdependence in which force, and the threat or promise of force, are employed. A good example of military globalism is the "balance of terror" between the United States and the Soviet Union during the cold war. The two countries' strategic interdependence was acute and well recognized. Not only did it produce world-straddling alliances, but either side could have used intercontinental missiles to destroy the other within 30 minutes. Their interdependence was distinctive not because it was totally new, but because the scale and speed of the potential conflict arising from it were so enormous.
- *Environmental globalism* refers to the long-distance transport of materials in the atmosphere or oceans, or of biological substances such as pathogens or genetic materials, that affect human health and well-being. The depletion of the stratospheric ozone layer as a result of ozone-depleting chemicals is an example of environmental globalism, as is the spread of the AIDS virus from west equatorial Africa around the world since the end of the 1970s. Some environmental globalism may be entirely natural, but much of the recent change has been induced by human activity.

- *Social and cultural globalism* involves the movement of ideas, information, images, and people (who, of course, carry ideas and information with them). Examples include the movement of religions or the diffusion of scientific knowledge. An important facet of social globalism involves the imitation of one society's practices and institutions by others: what some sociologists refer to as "isomorphism." Often, however, social globalism has followed military and economic globalism. Ideas, information, and people follow armies and economic flows, and in doing so, transform societies and markets. At its most profound level, social globalism affects the consciousness of individuals and their attitudes toward culture, politics, and personal identity. Indeed, social and cultural globalism interacts with other types of globalism, because military, environmental, and economic activity convey information and generate ideas, which may then flow across geographical and political boundaries. In the current era, as the growth of the Internet reduces costs and globalizes communications, the flow of ideas is increasingly independent of other forms of globalization.

This division of globalism into separate dimensions is inevitably somewhat arbitrary. Nonetheless, it is useful for analysis, because changes in the various dimensions of globalization do not necessarily occur simultaneously. One can sensibly say, for instance, that economic globalization took place between approximately 1850 and 1914, manifested in imperialism and increased trade and capital flows between politically independent countries; and that such globalization was largely reversed between 1914 and 1945. That is, economic globalism rose between 1850 and 1914 and fell between 1914 and 1945. However, military globalism rose to new heights during the two world wars, as did many aspects of social globalism. The worldwide influenza epidemic of 1918–19, which took 30 million lives, was propagated in part by the flows of soldiers around the world. So did globalism decline or rise between 1914 and 1945? It depends on what dimension of globalism one is examining.

## Contemporary Globalism

When people speak colloquially about globalization, they typically refer to recent increases in globalism. In this context, comments such as "globalization is fundamentally new" make sense but are nevertheless misleading. We prefer to speak of globalism as a phenomenon with ancient roots and of globalization as the process of increasing globalism, now or in the past.

The issue is not how old globalism is, but rather how "thin" or "thick" it is at any given time. As an example of "thin globalization," the Silk Road provided an economic and cultural link between ancient Europe and Asia, but the route was plied by a small group of hardy traders, and the goods that were traded back and forth had a direct impact primarily on a small (and relatively elite) stratum of consumers along the road. In contrast, "thick" relations of globalization, as described by political scientist David Held and others, involve many relationships that are intensive as well as extensive: long-distance flows that are large and continuous, affecting the lives of many people. The operations of global financial markets today, for instance, affect people from Peoria to Penang. Globalization is the process by which globalism becomes increasingly thick.

Globalism today is different from globalism of the 19th century, when European imperialism provided much of its political structure, and higher transport and communications costs meant fewer people were directly involved. But is there anything about globalism today that is fundamentally different from just 20 years ago? To say that something is "fundamentally" different is always problematic, since absolute discontinuities do not exist in human history. Every era builds on others, and historians can always find precursors for phenomena of the present. Journalist Thomas Friedman argues that contemporary globalization goes "farther, faster, deeper, and cheaper..." The degree of thickening of globalism may be giving rise to three changes not just in degree but in kind: increased density of networks, increased "institutional velocity," and increased transnational participation.

## Density of networks

Economists use the term "network effects" to refer to situations where a product becomes more valuable once many people use it – take, for example, the Internet. Joseph Stiglitz, former chief economist of the World Bank, has argued that a knowledge-based economy generates "powerful spillover effects, often spreading like fire and triggering further innovation and setting off chain reactions of new inventions." Moreover, as interdependence and globalism have become thicker, systemic relationships among different networks have become more important. There are more interconnections. Intensive economic interdependence affects social and environmental interdependence; awareness of these connections in turn affects economic relationships. For instance, the expansion of trade can generate industrial activity in countries with low environmental standards, mobilizing environmental activists to carry their message to these newly industrializing but environmentally lax countries. The resulting activities may affect environmental interdependence (for instance, by reducing cross-boundary pollution) but may generate resentment in the newly industrializing countries, affecting social and economic relations.

The worldwide impact of the financial crisis that began in Thailand in July 1997 illustrates the extent of these network interconnections. Unexpectedly, what first appeared as an isolated banking and currency crisis in a small "emerging market" country had severe global effects. It generated financial panic elsewhere in Asia, particularly in South Korea and Indonesia; prompted emergency meetings at the highest level of world finance and huge "bail-out" packages orchestrated by the International Monetary Fund (IMF); and led eventually to a widespread loss of confidence in emerging markets and the efficacy of international financial institutions. Before that contagious loss of confidence was stemmed, Russia had defaulted on its debt, and a U.S.-based hedge fund had to be rescued suddenly through a plan brokered by the Federal Reserve Bank of New York. Even after recovery had begun, Brazil required an IMF loan, coupled with a devaluation, to avoid financial collapse in 1999.

Economic globalism is nothing new. Indeed, the relative magnitude of cross-border investment in 1997 was not unprecedented. Capital markets were by some measures more integrated at the beginning than at the end of the 20th century. The net outflow of capital from Great Britain in the four decades before 1914 averaged 5 percent of gross domestic product, compared with 2 to 3 percent for Japan over the last decade. The financial crisis of 1997–99 was not the first to be global in scale: "Black Tuesday" on Wall Street in 1929 and the collapse of Austria's Creditanstalt bank in 1931 triggered a worldwide financial crisis and depression. In the 1970s, skyrocketing oil prices prompted the Organization of Petroleum Exporting Countries to lend surplus funds to developed nations, and banks in those countries made a profit by relending that money to developing countries in Latin America and Africa (which needed the money to fund expansionary fiscal policies). But the money dried up with the global recession of 1981–83: by late 1986, more than 40 countries worldwide were mired in severe external debt.

But some features of the 1997–99 crisis distinguish it from previous ones. Most economists, governments, and international financial institutions failed to anticipate the crisis, and complex new financial instruments made it difficult to understand. Even countries that had previously been praised for their sound economic policies and performance were no less susceptible to the financial contagion triggered by speculative attacks and unpredictable changes in market sentiment. The World Bank had recently published a report entitled "The East Asian Miracle" (1993), and investment flows to Asia had risen rapidly to a new peak in 1997, remaining high until the crisis hit. In December 1998, Federal Reserve Board Chairman Alan Greenspan said: "I have learned more about how this new international financial system works in the last 12 months than in the previous 20 years." Sheer magnitude, complexity, and speed distinguish contemporary globalization from earlier periods: Whereas the debt crisis of the 1980s was a slow-motion train wreck that took place over a period of years, the Asian meltdown struck immediately and spread over a period of months.

The point is that the increasing thickness of globalism – the density of networks of interdependence – is not just a difference in degree. Thickness means that different relationships of interdependence intersect more deeply at more points. Hence, the effects of events in one geographical area, on one dimension, can have profound effects in other geographical areas, on other dimensions. As in scientific theories of "chaos," and in weather systems, small events in one place can have catalytic effects, so that their consequences later, and elsewhere, are vast. Such systems are difficult to understand, and their effects are therefore often unpredictable. Furthermore, when these are human systems, people are often hard at work trying to outwit others, to gain an economic, social, or military advantage precisely by acting in unpredictable ways. As a result, globalism will likely be accompanied by pervasive uncertainty. There will be continual competition between increased complexity and uncertainty, and efforts by governments, market participants, and others to comprehend and manage these increasingly complex interconnected systems.

Globalization, therefore, does not merely affect governance; it is affected by governance. Frequent financial crises of the magnitude of the crisis of 1997–99 could lead to popular movements to limit interdependence and to a reversal of economic globalization. Chaotic uncertainty is too high a price for most people to pay for somewhat higher average levels of prosperity. Unless some of its aspects can be effectively governed, globalization may be unsustainable in its current form.

## Institutional velocity

The information revolution is at the heart of economic and social globalization. It has made possible the transnational organization of work and the expansion of markets, thereby facilitating a new international division of labor. As Adam Smith famously declared in *The Wealth of Nations*, "the division of labor is limited by the extent of the market." Military globalism predated the information revolution, reaching its height during World War II and the cold war; but the nature of military interdependence has been transformed by information technology. The pollution that has contributed to environmental globalism has its sources in the coal-oil-steel-auto-chemical economy that was largely created between the middle of the 19th and 20th centuries and has become globalized only recently; but the information revolution may have a major impact on attempts to counter and reverse the negative effects of this form of globalism.

Sometimes these changes are incorrectly viewed in terms of the velocity of information flows. The biggest change in velocity came with the steamship and especially the telegraph: the transatlantic cable of 1866 reduced the time of transmission of information between London and New York by over a week – hence, by a factor of about a thousand. The telephone, by contrast, increased the velocity of such messages by a few minutes (since telephone messages do not require decoding), and the Internet, as compared with the telephone, by not much at all. The real difference lies in the reduced cost of communicating, not in the velocity of any individual communication. And the effects are therefore felt in the increased intensity rather than the extensity of globalism. In 1877 it was expensive to send telegrams across the Atlantic, and in 1927 or even 1977 it was expensive to telephone transcontinentally. Corporations and the rich used transcontinental telephones, but ordinary people wrote letters unless there was an emergency. But in 2000, if you have access to a computer, the Internet is virtually free and transpacific telephone calls may cost only a few cents per minute. The volume of communications has increased by many orders of magnitude, and the intensity of globalism has been able to expand exponentially.

Markets react more quickly than before, because information diffuses so much more rapidly and huge sums of capital can be moved at a moment's notice. Multinational enterprises have changed their organizational structures, integrating production more closely on a transnational basis and entering into more networks and alliances, as global capitalism has become more competitive and more subject to rapid change. Nongovernmental organizations (NGOs) have vastly expanded their levels of activity.

With respect to globalism and velocity, therefore, one can distinguish between the velocity of a given communication – "message velocity" – and "institutional velocity." Message velocity has changed little for the population centers of relatively rich countries since the telegraph became more or less universal toward the end of the 19th century. But institutional velocity – how rapidly a system and the units within it change – is a function not so much of message velocity than of the intensity of contact – the "thickness" of globalism. In the late 1970s, the news cycle was the same as it had been for decades: people found out the day's headlines by watching the evening news and got the more complete story and analysis from the morning paper. But the introduction of 24-hour cable news in 1980 and the subsequent emergence of the Internet have made news cycles shorter and have put a larger premium on small advantages in speed. Until recently, one newspaper did not normally "scoop" another by receiving and processing information an hour earlier than another: as long as the information could be processed before the daily paper "went to bed," it was timely. But in 2000, an hour – or even a few minutes – makes a critical difference for a cable television network in terms of being "on top of a story" or "behind the curve." Institutional velocity has accelerated more than message velocity. Institutional velocity reflects not only individual linkages but networks and interconnections among networks. This phenomenon is where the real change lies.

## Transnational participation and complex interdependence

Reduced costs of communications have increased the number of participating actors and increased the relevance of "complex interdependence." This concept describes a hypothetical world with three characteristics: multiple channels between societies, with multiple actors, not just states; multiple issues, not arranged in any clear hierarchy; and the irrelevance of the threat or use of force among states linked by complex interdependence.

We used the concept of complex interdependence in the 1970s principally to describe emerging relationships among pluralist democracies. Manifestly it did not characterize relations between the United States and the Soviet Union, nor did it typify the politics of the Middle East, East Asia, Africa, or even parts of Latin America. However, we did argue that international monetary relations approximated some aspects of complex interdependence in the 1970s and that some bilateral relationships – French–German and U.S.–Canadian, for example – approximated all three conditions of complex interdependence. In a world of complex interdependence, we argued, politics would be different. The goals and instruments of state policy – and the processes of agenda setting and issue linkage – would all be different, as would the significance of international organizations.

Translated into the language of globalism, the politics of complex interdependence would be one in which levels of economic, environmental, and social globalism are high and military globalism is low. Regional instances of security communities – where states have reliable expectations that force will not be used – include Scandinavia since the early 20th century. Arguably, intercontinental complex interdependence was limited during the cold war to areas protected by the United States, such as the Atlantic security community. Indeed, U.S. power and policy were crucial to the construction of postwar international institutions, ranging from NATO to the IMF, which protected and supported complex interdependence. Since 1989, the decline of military globalism and the extension of social and economic globalism to the former Soviet empire have implied the expansion of areas of complex interdependence, at least to the new and aspiring members of NATO in Eastern Europe. Moreover, economic and social globalism seem to have created incentives for leaders in South America to settle territorial quarrels, out of fear both of being distracted from tasks of economic and social development and of scaring away needed investment capital.

Even today complex interdependence is far from universal. Military force was used by or threatened against states throughout the 1990s, from the Taiwan Strait to Iraq, from Kuwait to the former Yugoslavia; from Kashmir to Congo. Civil wars are endemic in much of sub-Saharan Africa and sometimes have escalated into international warfare, as when the Democratic Republic of Congo's civil war engulfed five neighboring countries. The information revolution and the voracious appetite of television viewers for dramatic visual images have heightened global awareness of some of these civil conflicts and made them more immediate, contributing to pressure for humanitarian intervention, as in Bosnia and Kosovo. The various dimensions of globalization – in this case, the social and military dimensions – intersect, but the results are not necessarily conducive to greater harmony. Nevertheless, interstate use and threat of military force have virtually disappeared in certain areas of the world – notably among the advanced, information-era democracies bordering the Atlantic and the Pacific, as well as among a number of their less wealthy neighbors in Latin America and increasingly in Eastern-Central Europe.

The dimension of complex interdependence that has changed the most since the 1970s is participation in channels of contact among societies. There has been a vast expansion of such channels as a result of the dramatic fall in the costs of communication over large distances. It is no longer necessary to be a rich organization to be able to communicate on a real-time basis with people around the globe. Friedman calls this change the "democratization" of technology, finance, and information, because diminished costs have made what were once luxuries available to a much broader range of society.

"Democratization" is probably the wrong word, however, since in markets money votes, and people start out with unequal stakes. There is no equality, for example, in capital markets, despite the new financial instruments that permit more people to participate. "Pluralization" might be a better word, suggesting the vast increase in the number and variety of participants in global networks. The number of international NGOs more than quadrupled from about 6,000 to over 26,000 in the 1990s alone. Whether they are large organizations such as Greenpeace or Amnesty International, or the proverbial "three kooks with modems and a fax machine," NGOs can now raise their voices as never before. In 1999, NGOs worldwide used the Internet to coordinate a massive protest against the World Trade Organization meeting in Seattle. Whether these organizations can forge a coherent and credible coalition has become the key political question.

This vast expansion of transnational channels of contact, at multicontinental distances, generated by the media and a profusion of NGOs, has helped expand the third dimension of complex interdependence: the multiple issues connecting societies. More and more issues are up for grabs internationally, including regulations and practices – ranging from pharmaceutical testing to accounting and product standards to banking regulation – that were formerly regarded as the prerogatives of national governments. The Uruguay Round of multilateral trade negotiations of the late 1980s and early 1990s focused on services, once virtually untouched by international regimes; and the financial crisis of 1997–99 led to both public and private efforts to globalize the transparent financial reporting that has become prevalent in advanced industrialized countries.

Increased participation at a distance and greater approximation of complex interdependence do not imply the end of politics. On the contrary, power remains important. Even in domains characterized by complex interdependence, politics reflects asymmetrical economic, social, and environmental interdependence, not just among states but also among nonstate actors, and through transgovernmental relations. Complex interdependence is not a description of the world, but rather an ideal concept abstracting from reality. It is, however, an ideal concept that increasingly corresponds to reality in many parts of the world, even at transcontinental distances – and that corresponds more closely than obsolete images of world politics as simply interstate relations that focus solely on force and security.

So what really is new in contemporary globalism? Intensive, or thick, network interconnections that have systemic effects, often unanticipated. But such thick globalism is not uniform: it varies by region, locality, and issue area. It is less a matter of communications message velocity than of declining cost, which does speed up what we call systemic and institutional velocity. Globalization shrinks distance, but it does not make distance irrelevant. And the filters provided by domestic politics and political institutions play a major role in determining what effects globalization really has and how well various countries adapt to it. Finally, reduced costs have enabled more actors to participate in world politics at greater distances, leading larger areas of world politics to approximate the ideal type of complex interdependence.

Although the system of sovereign states is likely to continue as the dominant structure in the world, the content of world politics is changing. More dimensions than ever – but not all – are beginning to approach our idealized concept of complex inter-dependence. Such trends can be set back, perhaps even reversed, by cataclysmic events, as happened in earlier phases of globalization. History always has surprises. But history's surprises always occur against the background of what has gone before. The surprises of the early 21st century will, no doubt, be profoundly affected by the processes of contemporary globalization that we have tried to analyze here.

# 5

# What is 'Global' about Globalization?

## Jan Aart Scholte

[ . . . ]

Probably the most common usage in everyday language has conceived of globalization as internationalization. As such, globalization refers to increases of interaction and interdependence between people in different countries. Considerable rises in cross-border exchanges have indeed occurred in recent decades, so it is understandable that the term globalization has come for many to mean internationalization.

However, interconnections between countries have also intensified at various earlier times during the 500-year history of the modern states-system. In particular, [ . . . ] the late nineteenth century witnessed levels of cross-border migration, direct investment, finance and trade that, proportionately, are broadly comparable with those of the present. No vocabulary of 'globalization' was needed on previous occasions of internationalization, and the terminology of 'international relations' arguably remains quite sufficient to examine contemporary cross-border transactions and interlinkages. We should reserve the new word to designate something different.

A second definition – used especially by neoliberals as well as some of their more vociferous critics – has identified globalization as liberalization. In these cases a global world is one without regulatory barriers to transfers of resources between countries. In recent history we have indeed witnessed many reductions of statutory constraints on cross-border movements of goods, services, money and financial instruments. Hence, as with the first definition, it is understandable that people might associate globalization with liberalization.

Yet this second notion is also redundant. The long-established liberal discourse of 'free' trade is quite adequate to convey these ideas. 'Global-speak' was not needed in earlier times of widespread liberalization like the third quarter of the nineteenth century. There seems little need now to invent a new vocabulary for this old phenomenon. Again, let us look for a distinctive meaning of globalization.

A third common conception – globalization as universalization – also fails the test of providing new insight. True, more people and cultural phenomena than ever have in recent history spread to all habitable corners of the planet. However, moves toward universalization are hardly new to the contemporary world. For example, Clive Gamble writes of 'our global prehistory', arguing that the transcontinental spread of the human species – begun a million years ago – constitutes the initial instance of globalization (1994: ix, 8–9). Closer to our present, several world religions have for a thousand years and more extended across large expanses of the earth. Transoceanic trade has for centuries distributed various goods in 'global' (read world-scale) markets. Yet the pre-existent vocabulary of 'universality' and 'universalization' is quite adequate to describe these age-old conditions. In this regard, too, a new terminology of 'globalization' is unnecessary.

What of a fourth definition, that of globalization as westernization? This usage has arisen particularly in various arguments about post-colonial imperialism. Often in these cases globalization is associated with a process of homogenization, as all the world becomes western, modern and, more particularly, American. Such a conception is not surprising at a time when Madison Avenue and Hollywood have acquired such a planetary reach.

However, intercontinental westernization, too, has unfolded since long before the recent emergence of globe-talk. Concepts of 'modernization' or (for those who prefer an explicitly radical term) 'imperialism' are more than sufficient to convey ideas of westernization, Europeanization and Americanization. We do not need a new vocabulary of globalization to remake an old analysis. [ ... ]

## A Distinctive Concept of Globalization

Yet can *all* talk of globality be dismissed as fad and hype? Are ideas of globalization *always* reducible to internationalization, liberalization, universalization or westernization? If new terminology spreads so far and attracts so much attention, might it not be more than a synonym for pre-existent vocabulary? Can we distinguish and specify such a distinctive concept of globalization?

Important new insight into relatively new conditions is in fact available from a fifth type of definition. This conceptualization identifies globalization as deterritorialization – or, as I would prefer, the growth of 'supraterritorial' relations between people. In this usage, 'globalization' refers to a far-reaching change in the nature of social space. The proliferation and spread of supraterritorial – or what we can alternatively term 'transworld' or 'transborder' – connections brings an end to what could be called 'territorialism', that is, a situation where social geography is entirely territorial. Although, as already stressed, territory still matters very much in our globalizing world, it no longer constitutes the whole of our geography.

A reconfiguration of social space has far-reaching significance. After all, space is one of the primary dimensions of social relations. Geography ranks on a par with culture, ecology, economy, politics and psychology as a core determinant of social life. The spatial contours of a society strongly influence the nature of production, governance, identity and community in that society – and vice versa. For example, differences between the lives of desert nomads, mountain villagers and island seafarers are largely attributable to contrasts in the places that they inhabit. The spatial and other primary aspects of social relations are deeply interconnected and mutually constitutive. If the character of society's map changes, then its culture, ecology, economics, politics and social psychology are likely to shift as well.

To be sure, we are referring here to questions of *macro* social space, that is, relating to the geographical setting of larger collective life: districts, countries, etc. Social space also has *micro* aspects that lie within a person's realm of direct sensory experience, such as the built environment. However, micro spaces are not of immediate concern to a discussion of globalization. [ ... ]

Each of the four other conceptions of globality discussed above is reconcilable with territorialist constructions of social space. In other words, these definitions presume that the map of society is solely and completely territorial. In territorial geography, relations between people are mapped on the earth's surface and measured on a three-dimensional grid of longitude, latitude and altitude. In a territorial framework, 'place' refers to a fixed location on such a map; 'distance' refers to the length of a track that connects points on this map; and 'border' refers to a line on this map which divides tracts on the earth's surface from each other. Territorialism implies that macro social space is wholly organized in terms of units such as districts, towns, provinces, countries and regions. In times of *statist* territorialism more particularly, countries have held pride of place above the other kinds of territorial realms.

Until recently, social geography across the world had a territorialist character. Indeed, even today many people use the terms 'geography' and 'territory' interchangeably, as if to exclude the possibility that space could be nonterritorial. Under conditions of territorialism, people identify their 'place' in the world primarily in relation to territorial locations. (In most cases this territorial reference point is fixed, though for nomadic groups the spot may shift.) In times of nationalism, the foremost territorial 'home' has usually been a country. Moreover, in a territorialist world the length of territorial distances between places and the presence or absence of territorial (especially state) borders between places tends heavily to influence the general frequency and significance of contacts that people at different sites might have with each other. Thus people normally have most of their interactions and affiliations with others who share the same territorial space: for example, the same village, the same county, the same country, or the same continent.

Yet current history has witnessed a proliferation of social connections that are at least partly – and often quite substantially – detached from a territorial logic of the kind just described. Take, for instance, telephone calls, electronic finance and the depletion of stratospheric ozone. Such phenomena cannot be situated at a fixed territorial location. They operate largely without regard of territorial distance. They substantially bypass territorial borders. Thus, technologically speaking, a telephone conversation can occur across an ocean as readily as across a street. Today money deposited with a major bank is mostly stored in 'placeless' cyberspace rather than in a vault. Ozone depletion exists everywhere on earth at the same time, and its relative distribution across different parts of the world shifts without regard to territorial distances or borders. The geography of these *global* conditions cannot be understood in terms of territoriality alone; they also reside in the world as a single place – that is, in a *transworld* space.

Understood in this sense, globality marks a distinct kind of space–time compression, and one that is mostly new to contemporary history. To be sure, the world has long been 'shrinking', as territorial distances have been covered in progressively shorter time intervals. Thus, whereas Marco Polo took years to complete his journey across Eurasia in the thirteenth century, by 1850 a sea voyage from South East Asia to North West Europe could be completed in 59 days. In the twentieth century, motorized ships and land vehicles took progressively less time again to link territorial locations. Nevertheless, such transport still requires measurable time spans to cross territorial distances, and these movements still face substantial controls at territorial frontiers. Although speed has markedly increased, proximity in these cases is still closely related to territorial distance and borders.

In the case of global transactions, in contrast, 'place' is not territorially fixed, territorial distance is covered in effectively no time, and territorial boundaries present no particular impediment. Satellite television, the US dollar, the women's movement, the anthropogenic greenhouse effect and many other contemporary conditions have a pronounced *supraterritorial* quality. Globality (as supraterritoriality) describes circumstances where territorial space is substantially transcended. Phenomena like Coca-Cola and faxes 'touch down' at territorial locations, but they are also global in the sense that they can extend anywhere in the world at the same time and can unite locations anywhere in effectively no time. The geography of, for instance, Visa credit cards and world service broadcasts has little to do with territorial distances, and these *transborder* flows – that is, relations that transcend territorial frontiers – largely escape controls at state boundaries. Likewise, where, using specific and fixed territorial coordinates, could we situate Special Drawing Rights (SDRs), the Rushdie affair, the magazine *Elle*, the debt of the Brazilian government, karaoke, the production of a Ford automobile, and the law firm Clifford Chance?

All such circumstances reside at least partly across the planet as one more or less seamless sphere. Global conditions like Internet connections can and do surface simultaneously at any point on earth that is equipped to host them. Global phenomena like a news flash can and do move almost instantaneously across any distance on the planet.

Place, distance and borders only retrieve vital significance in respect of global activities when the earth is contrasted to extraterrestrial domains. Thus, for example, the 'border' of the New York Stock Exchange lies at the communications satellites that orbit the earth and instantaneously transmit messages from investors the world over to Wall Street. Time again becomes a significant factor in respect of radio signals when they have to cover interplanetary and longer distances. However, within the domain of our planet, location, distance and borders place no insurmountable constraints on supraterritorial relations. In this sense they are suitably called 'global' phenomena.

Various researchers across a range of academic disciplines have discerned a rise of supraterritoriality in contemporary history without using that precise word. Already at mid-century, for example, the philosopher Martin Heidegger proclaimed the advent of 'distancelessness' and an 'abolition of every possibility of remoteness' (1950: 165–6). Forty years later the geographer David Harvey described 'processes that so revolutionize the objective qualities of space and time that we are forced to alter, sometimes in quite radical ways, how we represent the world to ourselves' (1989: 240). The sociologist Manuel Castells has distinguished a 'network society', in which a new 'space of flows' exists alongside the old 'space of places' (1989: 348; 1996–7). In the field of International Relations, John Ruggie has written of a 'nonterritorial region' in contemporary world affairs (1993: 172).

Hence globality in the sense of transworld simultaneity and instantaneity – in the sense of a single world space – refers to something distinctive that other vocabulary does not cover. Some readers may cringe at the apparent jargon of 'globality', 'supraterritoriality', 'transworld' connections and 'transborder' relations. Yet preexistent words like 'international', 'supranational' and 'transnational' do not adequately capture the key *geographical* point at issue. New terminology is unavoidable.

As already intimated, the present analysis employs the four adjectives 'global', 'supraterritorial', 'transworld' and 'transborder' as synonyms. Partly this practice is a stylistic device that permits some variation of vocabulary. More importantly, however, different readers may find that one or the other of these words – or their use in combination – is more effective in denoting the distinctive type of social geography that is under discussion here.

The difference between globality and internationality needs in particular to be stressed. Whereas international relations are *inter*territorial relations, global relations are *supra*territorial relations. International relations are *cross*-border exchanges *over* distance, while global relations are *trans*border exchanges *without* distance. Thus global economics is different from international economics, global politics is different from international politics, and so on. Internationality is embedded in territorial space; globality transcends that geography.

In addition, global (as *trans*border) relations are not the same as *open*-border transactions. True, contemporary liberalization has sometimes occurred in tandem with globalization. The recent large-scale removal of statutory restrictions on transactions between countries has both responded to and facilitated the rise of supraterritoriality. However, the two trends remain distinct. Liberalization is a question of regulation, whereas globalization (as relative deterritorialization) is a question of geography.

Global events are also distinct from universal circumstances. Universality means being spread worldwide, while globality implies qualities of transworld concurrence and coordination. True, universalization has sometimes transpired in tandem with globalization, both encouraging and being encouraged by the growth of supraterritoriality. However, the two trends remain distinct. Universality says something about territorial extent, whereas globality says something about space–time relations.

Likewise, global conditions are not by definition the same as western, European, American or modern conditions. To be sure [ . . . ], modern social forces like rationalist knowledge, capitalist production and machine technology have done much to propel the rise of supraterritoriality. In addition, governments, firms and other actors based in Western Europe and the USA have ranked among the most enthusiastic promoters of globalization. However, globality and modernity are not equivalent. At most it might be argued that globalization marks an advanced phase of modernization, although, as noted earlier, some analyses associate globalization with a move to postmodernity.

To stress this key point once more: globalization as it is understood here is *not* the same thing as internationalization, liberalization, universalization or modernization. It is crucial to note that commentators who reject the novelty and transformative potential of 'globalization' have almost invariably conflated the term with one of the four redundant usages. To appreciate the arguments put forward [here], the logic and the evidence must be assessed in the light of a fifth, different definition of globalization as the rise of supraterritoriality and, therefore, a relative deterritorialization of social life.

[ . . . ]

## Farewell to Methodological Territorialism?

If contemporary social geography is not territorialist, then we need to adjust traditional approaches of social research. In other words, we must change the prevailing methodology, the established ways of conducting social inquiry. Methodological territorialism has had a pervasive and deep hold on the conventions of social research; thus globalization (when understood as the spread of supraterritoriality) implies a major reorientation of approach.

Methodological territorialism refers here to the practice of understanding the social world and conducting studies about it through the lens of territorial geography. Territorialist method means formulating concepts and questions, constructing hypotheses, gathering and interpreting empirical evidence, and drawing conclusions all in a territorial spatial framework. These habits are so engrained in prevailing methodology that most social researchers reproduce them unconsciously.

Methodological territorialism lies at the heart of mainstream conceptions of geography, economy, governance, community and society. Thus geographers have traditionally conceived of the world in terms of bordered territorial (especially country) units. Likewise, macroeconomists have normally studied production and distribution in relation to national (read territorial) and international (read interterritorial) activity. Students of politics have automatically treated governance as a territorial question (i.e. of local and national governments, with the latter sometimes meeting in so-called 'international' organizations). Similarly, anthropologists have usually conceived of culture and community with reference to territorial units (i.e. local and national peoples). Finally, territorialist habits have had most sociologists presume that 'society' by definition takes a territorial form: 'Chilean society', 'Iranian society', 'Hungarian society', etc.

Like any analytical device, methodological territorialism involves simplification. It offered a broadly viable intellectual shortcut in an earlier day of social inquiry. After all, the Westphalian states-system that arose in the seventeenth century and spread worldwide by the middle of the twentieth century was quintessentially territorial. Likewise, the mercantile and industrial activity that dominated capitalism during this period operated almost exclusively in territorial space. Similarly, the main forms of collective identities during these times (namely, ethnic groups and state-nations) had pronounced territorial referents. Nor did anthropogenic global ecological changes occur on any significant scale prior to the mid-twentieth century. Hence methodological territorialism reflected the social conditions of a particular epoch when bordered territorial units, separated by distance, formed far and away the overriding geographical framework for macro-level social organization.

However, territorialist analysis is not a timeless method. On the contrary, no scholarly research undertaken a thousand years ago made reference to bounded territorial spaces. After all, countries, states, nations and societies did not in that earlier epoch exist as clearly delineated territorial forms. Indeed, the world was not mapped as a sphere until the fourth century BC (by Dicaerchus in Sicily), and a grid to locate points on a map was not introduced until the second century AD (by Zhang Heng in China) (Douglas, 1996: 22). Maps showing the continents in anything like the territorial shape that we would recognize today were not drawn before the late fifteenth century. It took a further two hundred years before the first maps depicting bordered country units appeared (Campbell, 1987; Whitfield, 1994). Not until the high tide of colonialism in the late nineteenth and early twentieth centuries did a territorialist logic extend across all regions of human habitation on earth.

If methodological territorialism is a historical phenomenon, then it has an end as well as a beginning. There is no reason why, once installed, territorialist assumptions should last in perpetuity. The emergence of the states-system, the growth of mercantile and industrial capitalism, and the rise of national identities all understandably prompted the development of methodological territorialism several centuries ago. However, today widespread and accelerated globalization may stimulate another reconceptualization. If contemporary human circumstances have gained a substantial global dimension, then we need to develop an alternative, nonterritorialist cartography of social life.

[ ... ]

## Globality and Territoriality

That said, we should not replace territorialism with a globalist methodology that neglects territorial spaces. The end of territorial*ism* owing to globalization has not meant the end of territoriali*ty*. To say that social geography can no longer be understood in terms of territoriality *alone* is not to say that territoriality has become irrelevant. We inhabit a global*izing* rather than a fully global*ized* world. Indeed, the rise of supraterritoriality shows no sign of producing an end to territoriality. [ ... ]

The wording [here] has been deliberately formulated to indicate the continuing importance of territoriality next to spreading globality. For example, it has been explicitly said that globalization brings a *relative* rather than a complete deterritorialization of social life. Global relations have *substantially* rather than totally transcended territorial space. They are *partly* rather than wholly detached from territorial logics. Although territoriality places no *insurmountable* constraints on global circumstances, supraterritorial phenomena still have to engage at some level with territorial places, territorial governments and territorial identities. Much more globalization – more than is in prospect for a long time to come – would need to take place before territorial space became irrelevant. [ ... ]

Finally, globalization is not antithetical to territoriality insofar as the trend can be linked to many processes of *reterritorialization*. Such developments occur when certain territorial units decline in significance and other territorial configurations obtain increased importance. For example, [ ... ] globalization has in various ways encouraged the concurrent contemporary trend of regionalization. In addition, the spread of supraterritorial circumstances has in many countries helped local authorities to gain greater autonomy vis-à-vis the national state. Furthermore, [ ... ] globalization has contributed to ethnic revivals which have encouraged the disintegration of pre-existent territorial states (like the former Czechoslovakia, Soviet Union and Yugoslavia) and their replacement with new ones.

The preceding paragraphs have highlighted the continuing relevance of territoriality in the contemporary globalizing world. At the same time, it is clear that territory acquires different kinds of significance when it intersects with global spaces. The move from three-dimensional geography (longitude, latitude and altitude) to four-dimensional space (these three plus globality) fundamentally changes the map of social relations. [ ... ] [T]his reconfiguration of geography has important implications for structures of production, governance, community and knowledge. We no longer inhabit a territorial*ist* world, and this change requires substantial shifts in the ways that we theorize and practise politics.

## References

Campbell, T. (1987) *The Earliest Printed Maps 1472–1500*. London: British Library.

Castells, M. (1989) *The Informational City: Information Technology, Economic Restructuring, and the Urban-Regional Process*. Oxford: Blackwell.

Douglas, I. R. (1996) 'The Myth of Globali[z]ation: A Poststructural Reading of Speed and Reflexivity in the Governance of Late Modernity'. Paper presented to the 38th Annual Convention of the International Studies Association, San Diego, 16–20 April.

Gamble, C. (1994) *Timewalkers: The Prehistory of Global Colonization*. Cambridge, MA: Harvard University Press.

Harvey, D. (1989) *The Condition of Postmodernity: An Enquiry into the Conditions of Cultural Change*. Oxford: Blackwell.

Heidegger, M. (1950) 'The Thing'. In *Poetry, Language, Thought*. New York: Harper and Row, 1971, pp. 165–82.

Ruggie, J. G. (1993) 'Territoriality and Beyond: Problematizing Modernity in International Relations. *International Organization*, vol. 47, no. 1 (Winter): 139–74.

Whitfield, P. (1994) *The Image of the World: 20 Centuries of World Maps*. London: British Library.

# 6

# The Problem
# of Globalisation Theory

## *Justin Rosenberg*

[...] Globalisation is said to signal not only a truly basic social change – 'the supplanting of modernity with globality'[1] – but also, as a result of this change, the redundancy of some of the founding ideas of classical social theory, extending even to the very concept of 'society' itself. Even more dramatically, globalisation has necessitated a wholesale 'spatialization of social theory'[2] on the basis of a 'retrospective discovery'[3] of the centrality of speed of communication in the constitution of social orders:

> It suddenly seems clear that the divisions of the continents and of the globe as a whole were the function of distances made once imposingly real thanks to the primitiveness of transport and the hardships of travel. ... 'distance' is a social product; its length varies depending on the speed with which it may be overcome. ... All other socially produced factors of constitution, separation and the maintenance of collective identities – like state borders or cultural barriers – seem in retrospect merely secondary effects of that speed ...[4]

In short, for some writers – referred to below as 'globalisation theorists' – globalisation has now become 'the central thematic for social theory',[5] and 'a key idea by which we understand the transition of human society into the third millennium'.[6]

## The General Problem

On any sober intellectual reckoning, this is a curious outcome indeed. For the very idea of globalisation as an explanatory schema in its own right is fraught with difficulties. The term 'globalisation', after all, is at first sight merely a descriptive category, denoting either the geographical extension of social processes or possibly, as in Giddens' definition, 'the intensification of worldwide social relations'.[7] Now, since no-one denies that 'worldwide social relations' do indeed exist today in ways and to a degree that they never did before, there can be no objection to calls for a theory of globalisation, if that means an explanation of how and why these have come about. But such an explanation, if it is to avoid empty circularity, must fall back on some more basic social theory which could explain why the phenomena denoted by the term have become such a distinctive and salient feature of the contemporary world. (Globalisation as an outcome cannot be explained simply by invoking globalisation as a process tending towards that outcome.) Yet if that were so, and if, for example, time–space compression were to be explained as an emergent property of a particular historical type of social relations, then the term 'globalisation' would not denote a theory in its own right at all – instead it would function merely as a measure of how far and in what ways this historical process had developed. And the globalisation theorists clearly intend something more than this. By asserting that the emergence of a single global space as the arena of social action increasingly outweighs in its consequences other kinds of causality which have traditionally been invoked to explain social phenomena; by extrapolating the geographical dimension of this process into an alternative, spatio-temporal problematic for social science; and finally, by pitting this new problematic not simply against competing perspectives in the contemporary social sciences, but also against the classical foundations of modern social thought as a whole – in all these ways, they have raised their sights beyond any purely descriptive role for the concept. In the logical structure of their argumentation, what presents itself initially as the *explanandum* – globalisation as the developing outcome of some historical process – is progressively transformed into the *explanans*: it is globalisation which now explains the changing character of the modern world – and even generates 'retrospective discoveries' about past epochs in which it must be presumed not to have existed.

This inversion of *explanans* and *explanandum* cannot easily be rejected on purely logical grounds. After all, the consequences of a particular historical development may indeed go on to become significant causes in their own right, generating in turn further consequences which can no longer be derived from the original historical development. This is intrinsic to the nature of historical change. In this way, for example, Marx believed that the analysis of capitalist social relations had become fundamental to understanding modern societies, however much these relations were originally the product of other, necessarily pre-capitalist, causes. In fact, Marx also believed that the experience of capitalist society was an enabling condition of the intellectual formulation of the 'materialist conception of history', a new problematic, on the basis of which he too asserted the possibility of making 'retrospective discoveries' about the (pre-capitalist) past.[8] This comparison suggests that the claims of globalisation theory cannot simply be dismissed *a priori*. But it also alerts us to the real character of these claims. As Ankie Hoogvelt puts it, in one of the milder formulations which nonetheless captures nicely the kind of intellectual shift involved:

> [W]hat is being argued here is that, owing to the present reconstitution of the world into a single *social* space, that self-same historical process [which produced globalisation] has now lifted off and moved into a new ballpark. If, previously, global integration in the sense of a growing unification and interpenetration of the human condition was driven by the economic logic of capital accumulation, today it is the unification of the human condition that drives the logic of further capital accumulation.[9]

Within this shift we may identify the basic distinction which will be used in what follows, between a theory of globalisation and globalisation theory: the former might be constructed out of anything presumed to generate the spatio-temporal phenomena involved; the latter, by contrast, must derive its explanatory mechanism within those phenomena themselves: in short, it needs – even presupposes – a spatio-temporal reformulation of social theory itself. And it is this latter discourse of globalisation theory – an increasingly confident discourse within the literature – which will be interrogated in the pages which follow.

[ . . . ]

But the purpose is by no means entirely negative. Globalisation theory, for all its intellectual tribulations, has this virtue: it throws into new relief two things which are worth debating and defending. The first of these is the status of classical social theory – represented in these pages above all by Karl Marx and, secondarily, Max Weber – in the continuing enterprise of social science. Since this enterprise itself has meaning only in relation to an evolving historical reality, the question of whether and how far ideas developed in the nineteenth and early twentieth century can still retain their relevance to the contemporary world is entirely legitimate. More, it is this questioning which compels adherents of what C. Wright Mills called the tradition of Classic Social Analysis[10] to refresh and extend that tradition by trying to demonstrate how its methods and insights can illuminate an historical reality which might indeed seem to have moved decisively beyond their analytical reach. [ ... ]

The second issue which is thrown into new relief by the debate over globalisation is the idea of 'the international' as a significant and distinctive dimension of the social world of modernity. The sometimes rather extreme dismissal of this by globalisation theory forces us to take stock of the notion, and to clarify what, if anything, should be preserved within it. What is at stake here?

## 'International Relations' and Globalisation Theory

If 'the divisions of the continents and of the globe as a whole' are indeed breaking down, and if the claims of globalisation theory are the legitimate theoretical implication of this, then it is not only the notion of 'society' as a territorially bounded entity which must give way to the emergent reality. International theory too – traditionally defined as the study of interactions across, between and among such entities – must also be subjected to fundamental modification. Thus Jan Aart Scholte holds that a 'methodological territorialism' is written into the very definition of 'inter-national' relations. This, he argues, blinds academics and policy-makers alike to the 'supraterritorial' character of contemporary global challenges. For these are increasingly constituted not in the territorial space of the 'Westphalian states-system' but rather in that 'distanceless space' promoted by modern financial markets, satellite communications and computer networks. Urgent intellectual rectification is now required: 'it is arguably dangerous to give methodological territorialism further lease on life in a globalising world.'[11]

The rectification of international theory has not proceeded as far or as fast as globalisation theorists in other disciplines would advocate. According to Malcolm Waters, international theory has proved unable so far to move beyond 'a proto-theory of globalization'[12] in which attention to processes of transnational integration co-exist problematically with claims for the continuing significance of the sovereign state: this 'dualism remains the bottom line for political science and international relations versions of globalization'.[13] Yet if the battle for globalisation theory has not yet been won in this field, still the tocsin has sounded. And a proliferation of books and articles has indeed appeared in recent years taking up the new nomenclature and proclaiming the end of the 'Westphalian System'.[14] In varying degrees and with differing nuances, these writings have claimed that the organisation of the world by and around a system of sovereign, territorial nation-states is gradually submerging beneath new kinds of (non-territorial) linkages. The intensification of these linkages is in turn producing a new spatial and institutional configuration of social power – a 'postinternational' system[15] – whose shape corresponds less and less to the interstate model provided by orthodox International Relations.

In the discussion which follows below, two lines will be drawn in the sand concerning this matter. First, it will be argued that the prior existence of a 'Westphalian System', which serves as the crucial historical foil for the theoretical significance of contemporary claims about globalisation, is actually quite mythical. Defining the modern international system purely in terms of geopolitical norms of interaction between states, it derives in fact from the (sociologically) narrowest of international theories – political realism. And it has always stood in the way of a much richer understanding of the international derived from analysis of the wider historical process of capitalist world development – a process rendered invisible, or at any rate irrelevant, by the notion of a Westphalian System. [ . . . ]

Yet if the first line to be drawn points to a critique of the discipline of International Relations, the second, perhaps surprisingly, will cross over the first to mount an equally emphatic defence. For the merging in globalisation theory of the idea of 'the international' with the belief in a (now fading) Westphalian System passes all too easily into an outright denial of any remaining analytical determinacy to those general questions which are raised – in different ways in different historical epochs – by interrelations across, between and among human societies. It passes, that is, into the rejection of what might be called 'the problematic of the international', which is conventionally taken to compose the distinctive subject matter of international theory. This is a rejection endorsed, in his own complicated way, by Rob Walker in his book *Inside/Outside: International Relations as Political Theory*.[16] [ . . . ]

That said, however, the fundamental problem with globalisation theory lies not in the difficulties of its encounter with International Relations, but rather in the deeper contradiction already alluded to at the level of social theory itself: the attempt to construct 'globalisation' as an *explanans* leads to a conceptual inflation of 'the spatial' which is both difficult to justify ontologically and liable to produce not explanations but reifications. And yet we have also said that this charge is impossible to substantiate *a priori*. How, then, should we proceed? The answer can only be that we must examine the outcome of these assumptions in the texts of the globalisation theorists themselves. Is it really true that globalisation theory makes its adherents dependent on such large theoretical claims about the significance of space? If so, how do they seek to ground those claims? And in any case, do these claims, in turn, really lie at the heart of the explanatory difficulties which they experience? We have to look and see.

If any one of the three key assertions we are making – the necessity to globalisation theory of the conceptual inflation of space, the impossibility of its grounding in an alternative problematic for social theory, the inevitability of its reificatory consequences for concrete explanations – is contradicted by the evidence we find, then our overall intellectual case against globalisation theory will fail.

If, on the other hand, they are all confirmed, then we may perhaps make the following prediction. The more vigorously and systematically the case for globalisation as an *explanans* is pursued, the more explicitly and disruptively those inherent problems will manifest themselves. In the end, the intellectual cost of this will prove so high that one of two outcomes must result. Either the claims of globalisation theory will be *tacitly* withdrawn (after successive attempts at substantiation have failed), within the very process of the argumentation itself. This, we shall attempt to show in some detail, is what happens in Giddens' *Consequences of Modernity*. Alternatively, those claims will be from the start the object of such powerful intellectual equivocations that the authors will prevent themselves, perhaps wisely, from allowing them free rein. The consequence of this latter policy, however, strongly illustrated in the case of Jan Aart Scholte, is that no clear, definitive argument can be permitted to emerge at all. Prevented from reaching their full height, yet asserted nonetheless in some necessarily tumbledown form, these claims will come to resemble instead the intellectual equivalent of an architectural folly.

Yet if globalisation theory necessarily has this self-confounding quality, why take the trouble to subject it to a scholarly critique? Why not simply wait for it to collapse of its own accord? The answer is twofold. First, our suspicions and predictions remain at this stage only suspicions and predictions. They have yet to be substantiated. And second, the current fashionability of globalisation theory has not come without a price. For arguably the claims which it makes, if taken seriously, combine to exercise a kind of theoretical veto over other, more valuable resources for understanding both the contemporary world in general and its international politics in particular. Before we move on [ . . . ], we should therefore pause to spell out what this veto comprises.

It seems to have three main elements. First, insofar as it represents the contemporary world as having moved decisively beyond the imaginative reach of classical writers such as Karl Marx and Max Weber, globalisation theory in fact jettisons a vital resource for understanding exactly the spatio-temporal phenomena which it deems so significant. Once cut off from the rich explanatory schemas of classical social theory, these phenomena are instead converted into irreducible causes in their own right – unavoidably renaturalising the very things which it was the achievement of those earlier writers to problematise and demystify. A central feature of this process is the systematic fetishising of spatial categories, a possibility latent in the term 'globalisation' itself, but fully activated only by the role which it is now called upon to play in the construction of social explanation. This in turn produces a paradoxical *reduction* in the explanatory claims of social science. For the deepest level of the classical interrogation of modernity – the one at which its most dramatic and counter-intuitive discoveries were made – is now increasingly sealed off anew by the progressive rehabilitation of old reifications in a new technical language.

Second, by conflating the general intellectual issue of relations between societies with a specific historical form of those relations, caricatured as 'the Westphalian System', globalisation theory mistakes a subsequent evolution in that form for the obsolescence of the problematic of the international itself. In this respect, far from achieving an advance on existing international theory, it simply abandons the field, and haplessly reproduces many of the fallacies of liberal idealism – thereby joining the latter in the particular ideological division of labour through which the realist orthodoxy has for so long secured its place. The 'realist' response, when it comes, will presumably be as devastating for globalisation theory as it has always been for alternative approaches which have left untheorised the terrain of geopolitics where the intellectual counter-attack traditionally mobilises.

Finally, by embodying nonetheless the dominant site of convergence today between sociological thought and International Relations, globalisation theory constitutes the latest, and in some ways the most disruptive, obstacle to the great desideratum of this field: a genuinely social theory of the international system. And that, as already suggested, is no longer (if it ever was) a matter of concern to international theorists alone. Despite its origins in sociology and its attention to international processes, globalisation theory thus does neither credit to the one nor justice to the other.

Any one of these problems on its own would tell against the wisdom of embracing such an approach as 'the central thematic for social theory'. In combination, however, and when added to the obfuscatory role which the term plays in public debate, they surely warrant a more active and critical diagnosis. [ ... ]

## Notes

1   M. Albrow, *The Global Age*, Cambridge 1996, p. 4.
2   M. Featherstone and S. Lash, 'Globalization, Modernity and the Spatialization of Social Theory: An Introduction', in M. Featherstone, S. Lash and R. Robertson (eds), *Global Modernities*, London 1995, p. 1.
3   Z. Bauman, *Globalization: The Human Consequences*, Cambridge 1998, p. 15.
4   Ibid., pp. 12 and 15.
5   Featherstone and Lash, 'Globalization, Modernity', in Featherstone et al. (eds), *Global Modernities*, p. 1.
6   M. Waters, *Globalization*, London 1995, p. 1.
7   A. Giddens, *The Consequences of Modernity*, Stanford 1990, p. 64.
8   See, for example, his discussion of the category of 'labour' in the 1857 'General Introduction', *Grundrisse*, trans. M. Nicolaus, Harmondsworth 1973, pp. 103ff.
9   A. Hoogvelt, *Globalisation and the Postcolonial World: The New Political Economy of Development*, Basingstoke 1997, p. 121. This announcement comes at the end of a brief discussion of Giddens' work, specifically *The Consequences of Modernity*.
10  C. Wright Mills, *The Sociological Imagination*, Oxford 1959. For an attempt to relate Mills' arguments directly to the concerns of IR theory, see J. Rosenberg, 'The International Imagination: IR Theory and Classic Social Analysis', *Millennium*, 23 (1), Spring 1994.
11  J. A. Scholte, 'Globalisation: Prospects for a Paradigm Shift', in M. Shaw (ed.), *Politics and Globalisation*, London 1999, p. 18.
12  Waters, *Globalization*, p. 27.
13  Ibid., p. 28.
14  For an overview of these works, see I. Clark, *Globalization and International Relations Theory*, Oxford 1999.
15  James Rosenau, cited in Waters, *Globalization*, p. 30.
16  Cambridge 1993.

# 7

# Globalization – A Necessary Myth?

## *Paul Hirst and Grahame Thompson*

Globalization has become a fashionable concept in the social sciences, a core dictum in the prescriptions of management gurus, and a catch-phrase for journalists and politicians of every stripe. It is widely asserted that we live in an era in which the greater part of social life is determined by global processes, in which national cultures, national economies and national borders are dissolving. Central to this perception is the notion of a rapid and recent process of economic globalization. A truly global economy is claimed to have emerged or to be in the process of emerging, in which distinct national economies and, therefore, domestic strategies of national economic management are increasingly irrelevant. The world economy has internationalized in its basic dynamics, it is dominated by uncontrollable market forces, and it has as its principal economic actors and major agents of change truly transnational corporations that owe allegiance to no nation-state and locate wherever on the globe market advantage dictates.

This image is so powerful that it has mesmerized analysts and captured political imaginations. But is it the case? [ . . . ]

We began this investigation with an attitude of moderate scepticism. It was clear that much had changed since the 1960s, but we were cautious about the more extreme claims of the most enthusiastic globalization theorists. In particular it was obvious that radical expansionary and redistributive strategies of national economic management were no longer possible in the face of a variety of domestic and international constraints. However, the closer we looked the shallower and more unfounded became the claims of the more radical advocates of economic globalization. In particular we began to be disturbed by three facts. First, the absence of a commonly accepted model of the new global economy and how it differs from previous states of the international economy. Second, in the absence of a clear model against which to measure trends, the tendency to casually cite examples of the internationalization of sectors and processes as if they were evidence of the growth of an economy dominated by autonomous global market forces. Third, the lack of historical depth, the tendency to portray current changes as unique and without precedent and firmly set to persist long into the future.

To anticipate, as we proceeded our scepticism deepened until we became convinced that globalization, as conceived by the more extreme globalizers, is largely a myth. Thus we argue that:

1 The present highly internationalized economy is not unprecedented: it is one of a number of distinct conjunctures or states of the international economy that have existed since an economy based on modern industrial technology began to be generalized from the 1860s. In some respects, the current international economy is *less* open and integrated than the regime that prevailed from 1870 to 1914.

2   Genuinely transnational companies appear to be relatively rare. Most companies are based nationally and trade multinationally on the strength of a major national location of assets, production and sales, and there seems to be no major tendency towards the growth of truly international companies.

3   Capital mobility is not producing a massive shift of investment and employment from the advanced to the developing countries. Rather foreign direct investment (FDI) is highly concentrated among the advanced industrial economies and the Third World remains marginal in both investment and trade, a small minority of newly industrializing countries apart.

4   As some of the extreme advocates of globalization recognize, the world economy is far from being genuinely 'global'. Rather trade, investment and financial flows are concentrated in the Triad of Europe, Japan and North America and this dominance seems set to continue.

5   These major economic powers, the G3, thus have the capacity, especially if they coordinate policy, to exert powerful governance pressures over financial markets and other economic tendencies. Global markets are thus by no means beyond regulation and control, even though the current scope and objectives of economic governance are limited by the divergent interests of the great powers and the economic doctrines prevalent among their elites.

We should emphasize that this [article] challenges the strong version of the thesis of *economic* globalization, because we believe that without the notion of a truly globalized economy many of the other consequences adduced in the domains of culture and politics would either cease to be sustainable or become less threatening. Hence most of the discussion here is centred on the international economy and the evidence for and against the process of globalization.

[ ... ]

## Models of the International Economy

We can only begin to assess the issue of globalization if we have some relatively clear and rigorous model of what a global economy would be like and how it represents both a new phase in the international economy and an entirely changed environment for national economic actors. Globalization in its radical sense should be taken to mean the development of a new economic structure, and not just conjunctural change towards greater international trade and investment within an existing set of economic relations. An extreme and one-sided ideal type of this kind enables us to differentiate *degrees* of internationalization, to eliminate some possibilities and to avoid confusion between claims. Given such a model it becomes possible to assess it against evidence of international trends and thus enables us more or less plausibly to determine whether or not this phenomenon of the development of a new supranational economic system is occurring. In order to do this we have developed two basic contrasting ideal types of international economy, one that is fully globalized, and an open international economy that is still fundamentally characterized by exchange between relatively distinct national economies and in which many outcomes, such as the competitive performance of firms and sectors, are substantially determined by processes occurring at the national level. These ideal types are valuable in so far as they are useful in enabling us to clarify the issues conceptually, that is, in specifying the difference between a new global economy and merely extensive and intensifying international economic relations. Too often evidence compatible with the latter is used as though it substantiated the former. With a few honourable exceptions, the more enthusiastic advocates of globalization have failed to specify that difference, or to specify what evidence would be decisive in pointing to a structural change towards a global economy. Increasing salience of foreign trade and considerable and growing international flows of capital are not *per se* evidence of a new and distinct phenomenon called 'globalization'. [ . . . ]

## Type 1: An inter-national economy

We shall first develop a simple and extreme version of this type. An *inter-national economy* is one in which the principal entities are national economies. Trade and investment produce growing interconnection between these still national economies. Such a process involves the increasing integration of more and more nations and economic actors into world market relationships. Trade relations, as a result, tend to take on the form of national specializations and the international division of labour. The importance of trade is, however, progressively replaced by the centrality of investment relations between nations, which increasingly act as the organizing principle of the system. The form of interdependence between nations remains, however, of the 'strategic' kind. That is, it implies the continued relative separation of the domestic and the international frameworks for policy-making and the management of economic affairs, and also a relative separation in terms of economic effects. Interactions are of the 'billiard ball' type; inter-national events do not directly or necessarily penetrate or permeate the domestic economy but are refracted through national policies and processes. The international and the domestic policy fields either remain relatively separate as distinct levels of governance, or they work 'automatically'. In the latter case adjustments are not thought to be the subject of policy by public bodies or authorities, but are a consequence of 'unorganized' or 'spontaneous' market forces.

Perhaps the classic case of such an 'automatic' adjustment mechanism remains the Gold Standard, which operated at the height of the Pax Britannica system from mid-nineteenth century to 1914. Automatic is put in inverted commas here to signal the fact that this is a popular caricature. The actual system of adjustment took place very much in terms of overt domestic policy interventions. [ . . . ]

Great Britain acted as the political and economic hegemon and the guarantor of this system. But it is important to recognize that the Gold Standard and the Pax Britannica system was merely one of several structures of the international economy in this century. Such structures were highly conditional on major sociopolitical conjunctures. Thus the First World War wrecked British hegemony, accelerating a process that would have occurred far more slowly merely as a consequence of British industrial decline. It resulted in a period of protectionism and national autarchic competition in the 1930s, followed by the establishment of American hegemony after the Second World War and by the reopened international economy of the Bretton Woods system. This indicates the danger of assuming that current major changes in the international economy are unprecedented and that they are inevitable or irreversible. The lifetime of a prevailing system of international economic relations in this century has been no more than thirty to forty years. Indeed, given that most European currencies did not become fully convertible until the late 1950s, the full Bretton Woods system after the Second World War only lasted upwards of thirteen to fourteen years. Such systems have been transformed by major changes in the politico-economic balance of power and the conjunctures that have effected these shifts have been large-scale conflicts between the major powers. In that sense, the international economy has been determined as to its structure and the distribution of power within it by the major nation-states.

[ ... ]

The point of this ideal type drawing on the institutions of the *belle époque* is not, however, a historical analogy: for a simple and automatically governed international economic system *like* that before 1914 is unlikely to reproduce itself now. The current international economy is relatively open, but it has real differences from that prevailing before the First World War: it has more generalized and institutionalized free trade through the WTO, foreign investment is different in its modalities and destinations – although a high degree of capital mobility is once again a possibility – the scale of short-term financial flows is greater, the international monetary system is quite different and freedom of labour migration is drastically curtailed. The pre-1914 system was, nevertheless, genuinely international, tied by efficient long-distance communications and industrialized means of transport.

The communications and information technology revolution of the late twentieth century has further developed a trading system that could make day-to-day world prices: it did not create it. In the second half of the nineteenth century the submarine intercontinental telegraph cables enabled the integration of world markets (Standage 1998). Modern systems dramatically increase the possible volume and complexity of transactions, but we have had information media capable of sustaining a genuine international trading system for over a century. The difference between a trading system in which goods and information moved by sailing ship and one in which they moved by steam ships and electricity is qualitative. If the theorists of globalization mean that we have an economy in which each part of the world is linked by markets sharing close to real-time information, then that began not in the 1970s but in the 1870s.

## Type 2: A globalized economy

A *globalized economy* is a distinct ideal type from that of the inter-national economy and can be developed by contrast with it. In such a global system distinct national economies are subsumed and rearticulated into the system by international processes and transactions. The inter-national economy, on the contrary, is one in which processes that are determined at the level of national economies still dominate and international phenomena are outcomes that emerge from the distinct and differential performance of the national economies. The inter-national economy is an aggregate of nationally located functions. Thus while there is in such an economy a wide and increasing range of international economic interactions (financial markets and trade in manufactured goods, for example), these tend to function as opportunities or constraints for nationally located economic actors and their public regulators.

The global economy raises these nationally based interactions to a new power. The international economic system becomes autonomized and socially disembedded, as markets and production become truly global. Domestic policies, whether of private corporations or public regulators, now have routinely to take account of the predominantly international determinants of their sphere of operations. As systemic interdependence grows, the national level is permeated by and transformed by the international. In such a globalized economy the problem this poses for public authorities of different countries is how to construct policies that coordinate and integrate their regulatory efforts in order to cope with the systematic interdependence between their economic actors.

The first major consequence of a globalized economy would thus be that its governance is fundamentally problematic. Socially decontextualized global markets would be difficult to regulate, even supposing effective cooperation by the regulators and a coincidence of their interests. The principal difficulty is to construct both effective and integrated patterns of national and international public policy to cope with global market forces. The systematic economic interdependence of countries and markets would by no means necessarily result in a harmonious integration enabling world consumers to benefit from truly independent, allocatively efficient market mechanisms. On the contrary, it is more than plausible that the populations of even successful and advanced states and regions would be at the mercy of autonomized and uncontrollable (because global) market forces. Interdependence would then readily promote *dis-integration* – that is, competition and conflict – between regulatory agencies at different levels. Such conflict would further weaken effective public governance at the global level. Enthusiasts for the efficiency of free markets and the superiority of corporate control compared with that of public agencies would see this as a rational world order freed from the shackles of obsolete and ineffective national public interventions. Others, less sanguine but convinced globalization *is* occurring, like Cerny (1998), see it as a world system in which there can be no generalized or sustained public reinsurance against the costs imposed on localities by unfavourable competitive outcomes or market failures.

Even if one does not accept that the full process of globalization is taking place, this ideal type can help to highlight some aspects of the importance of greater economic integration within the major regional trade blocs. Both the European Union (EU) and the North American Free Trade Area (NAFTA) will soon be highly integrated markets of continental scale. Already in the case of the EU it is clear that there are fundamental problems of the integration and coordination of regulatory policies between the different public authorities at Union, national and regional level.

It is also clear that this ideal type highlights the problem of weak public governance for the major corporations. Even if such companies were truly global, they would not be able to operate in all markets equally effectively and, like governments, would lack the capacity to reinsure against unexpected shocks relying on their own resources alone. Governments would no longer be available to assist as they have been for 'national champions'. Firms would therefore seek to share risks and opportunities through intercorporate investments, partnerships, joint ventures, etc. Even in the current internationalized economy we can recognize such processes emerging.

A second major consequence of the notion of a globalizing international economy would be the transformation of multinational companies (MNCs) into transnational companies (TNCs) as the major players in the world economy.[1] The TNC would be genuine footloose capital, without specific national identification and with an internationalized management, and at least potentially willing to locate and relocate anywhere in the globe to obtain either the most secure or the highest returns. In the financial sector this could be achieved at the touch of a button and in a truly globalized economy would be wholly dictated by market forces, without deference to national monetary policies. In the case of primarily manufacturing companies, they would source, produce and market at the global level as strategy and opportunities dictated. The company would no longer be based on one predominant national location (as with the MNC) but would service global markets through global operations. Thus the TNC, unlike the MNC, could no longer be controlled or even constrained by the policies of particular national states. Rather it could escape all but the commonly agreed and enforced international regulatory standards. National governments could not adopt particular and effective regulatory policies that diverged from these standards to the detriment of TNCs operating within their borders. The TNC would be the main manifestation of a truly globalized economy.

Julius (1990) and Ohmae (1990, 1993), for example, both consider this trend towards true TNCs to be well established. Ohmae argues that such 'stateless' corporations are now the prime movers in an interlinked economy (ILE) centred on North America, Europe and Japan. He contends that macroeconomic and industrial policy intervention by national governments can only distort and impede the rational process of resource allocation by corporate decisions and consumer choices on a global scale. Like Akio Morita of Sony, Ohmae argues that such corporations will pursue strategies of 'global localization' in responding on a worldwide scale to specific regionalized markets and locating effectively to meet the varying demands of distinct localized groups of consumers. The assumption here is that TNCs will rely primarily on foreign direct investment and the full domestication of production to meet such specific market demands. This is in contrast to the strategy of flexibly specialized core production in the company's main location and the building of branch assembly plants where needed or where dictated by national public policies. The latter strategy is compatible with nationally based companies. The evidence from Japanese corporations which are the most effective operators in world markets favours the view that the latter strategy is predominant (Williams et al. 1992). Japanese companies appear to have been reluctant to locate core functions like R&D or high value-added parts of the production process abroad. Thus national companies with an international scope of operations currently and for the foreseeable future seem more likely to be the pattern than the true TNCs. Of course, such multinational companies, although they are nationally based, are internationally orientated. Foreign markets influence their domestic strategies and foreign competitors their production processes. Although MNCs continue to trade substantially *within* their national economies, significant percentages of foreign sales influence their actions. The point, however, is that this is not new; companies in the long boom period after 1945 were influenced in this way too, and were successful only if they met the standards of international competition.

A third consequence of globalization would be the further decline in the political influence and economic bargaining power of organized labour. Globalized markets and TNCs would tend to be mirrored by an open world market in labour. Thus while companies requiring highly skilled and productive labour might well continue to locate in the advanced countries, with all their advantages, rather than merely seek areas where wages are low, the trend towards the global mobility of capital and the relative national fixity of labour would favour those advanced countries with the most tractable labour forces and the lowest social overheads relative to the benefits of labour competence and motivation. 'Social democratic' strategies of enhancement of working conditions would thus be viable only if they assured the competitive advantage of the labour force, without constraining management prerogatives, and at no more overall cost in taxation than the average for the advanced world. Such strategies would

clearly be a tall order and the tendency of globalization would be to favour management at the expense of even strongly organized labour, and, therefore, public policies
sympathetic to the former rather than the latter. This would be the 'disorganized
capitalism' of Lash and Urry (1987) with a vengeance, or it could be seen as placing
a premium on moderate and defensive strategies where organized labour remains locally
strong (Scharpf 1991, 1997).

A final and inevitable consequence of globalization is the growth in fundamental
multipolarity in the international political system. In the end, the hitherto hegemonic
national power would no longer be able to impose its own distinct regulatory objectives in either its own territories or elsewhere, and lesser agencies (whether public or
private) would thus enjoy enhanced powers of denial and evasion *vis-à-vis* any aspir-
ant 'hegemon'. A variety of bodies from international voluntary agencies to TNCs
would thus gain in relative power at the expense of national governments and, using
global markets and media, could appeal to and obtain legitimacy from consumers/
citizens across national boundaries. Thus the distinct disciplinary powers of national
states would decline, even though the bulk of their citizens, especially in the advanced
countries, remained nationally bound. In such a world, national military power would
become less effective. It would no longer be used to pursue economic objectives because
'national' state control in respect of the economy would have largely disappeared. The
use of military force would be increasingly tied to non-economic issues, such as
nationality and religion. A variety of more specific powers of sanction and veto in the
economic sphere by different kinds of bodies (both public and private) would thus
begin to compete with national states and begin to change the nature of international
politics. As economics and nationhood pulled apart, the international economy would
become even more 'industrial' and less 'militant' than it is today. War would be increasingly localized; wherever it threatened powerful global economic interests the war-
ring parties would be subject to devastating economic sanction.

## The Argument in Outline

[ . . . ]

The strong concept of a globalized economy outlined above acts as an ideal type
which we can compare to the actual trends within the international economy. This
globalized economy has been contrasted to the notion of an inter-national economy
in the above analysis in order to distinguish its particular and novel features. The opposition of these two types for conceptual clarity conceals the possibly messy combination
of the two in reality. This makes it difficult to determine major trends on the basis
of the available evidence. These two types of economy are not inherently mutually
exclusive; rather in certain conditions the globalized economy would *encompass and
subsume* the inter-national economy. The globalized economy would rearticulate
many of the features of the inter-national economy, transforming them as it reinforced
them. If this phenomenon occurred there would thus be a complex combination of
features of both types of economy present within the present conjuncture. The problem in determining what is happening is to identify the dominant trends: either the
growth of globalization or the continuation of the existing inter-national patterns.

It is our view that such a process of hybridization is not taking place, but it would
be cavalier not to consider and raise the possibility. Central in this respect is the

evidence [ . . . ] for the weak development of TNCs and the continued salience of MNCs, and also the ongoing dominance of the advanced countries in both trade and FDI. Such evidence is consistent with a continuing inter-national economy, but much less so with a rapidly globalizing hybrid system. Moreover, we should remember that an inter-national economy is one in which the major nationally based manufacturers and the major financial trading and service centres are strongly externally oriented, emphasizing international trading performance. The opposite of a globalized economy is not thus a nationally inward-looking one, but an open world market based on trading nations and regulated to a greater or lesser degree by both the public policies of nation-states and supranational agencies [ . . . ]. Such an economy has existed in some form or another since the 1870s, and has continued to re-emerge despite major setbacks, the most serious being the crisis of the 1930s. The point is that it should not be confused with a global economy. [ . . . ]

## Note

1   This distinction between MNCs and TNCs is not usual. There is a tendency to use them interchangeably, increasingly with the use of TNC as a generally accepted term for both types. Where we use the term TNC it should be clear that we are referring to a *true* TNC in the context of discussing the strong globalizers' view.

## References

Cerny, P. (1998) Neomedievalism, civil war and the new security dilemma: globalization as a durable disorder. *Civil Wars* 1(1): 36–64.

Julius, D. (1990) *Global Companies and Public Policy*. London: RIIA, Pinter.

Lash, S. and Urry, J. (1987) *The End of Organized Capitalism*. Cambridge: Polity Press.

Ohmae, K. (1990) *The Borderless World*. London and New York: Collins.

Ohmae, K. (1993) The rise of the region state. *Foreign Affairs* (Spring): 78–88.

Scharpf, F. (1991) *Crisis and Choice in European Social Democracy*. Ithaca: Cornell University Press.

Scharpf, F. (1997) Negative and positive integration in the political economy of European welfare states. In G. Marks (ed.), *Governance in the European Union*, London: Sage.

Standage, T. (1998) *The Victorian Internet: The Remarkable Story of the Telegraph and the Nineteenth Century Online Pioneers*. London: Weidenfeld and Nicolson.

Williams, K., Haslem, C., Williams, J. and Adcroft, A. (1992) Factories as warehouses: Japanese manufacturing, foreign direct investment in Britain and the United States. University of East London Occasional Paper on Business, Economy and Society, no. 6.

# 8

# Clash of Globalizations

## Stanley Hoffmann

## A New Paradigm?

[ . . . ]
Everybody has understood the events of September 11 as the beginning of a new era. But what does this break mean? In the conventional approach to international relations, war took place among states. But in September, poorly armed individuals suddenly challenged, surprised, and wounded the world's dominant superpower. The attacks also showed that, for all its accomplishments, globalization makes an awful form of violence easily accessible to hopeless fanatics. Terrorism is the bloody link between interstate relations and global society. As countless individuals and groups are becoming global actors along with states, insecurity and vulnerability are rising. To assess today's bleak state of affairs, therefore, several questions are necessary. What concepts help explain the new global order? What is the condition of the interstate part of international relations? And what does the emerging global civil society contribute to world order?

## Sound and Fury

Two models [ . . . ] still have adherents. The "realist" orthodoxy insists that nothing has changed in international relations since Thucydides and Machiavelli: a state's military and economic power determines its fate; interdependence and international institutions are secondary and fragile phenomena; and states' objectives are imposed by the threats to their survival or security. Such is the world described by Henry Kissinger. Unfortunately, this venerable model has trouble integrating change, especially globalization and the rise of nonstate actors. Moreover, it overlooks the need for international cooperation that results from such new threats as the proliferation of weapons of mass destruction (WMD). And it ignores what the scholar Raymond Aron called the "germ of a universal consciousness": the liberal, promarket norms that developed states have come to hold in common.

Taking Aron's point, many scholars today interpret the world in terms of a triumphant globalization that submerges borders through new means of information and communication. In this universe, a state choosing to stay closed invariably faces decline and growing discontent among its subjects, who are eager for material progress. But if it opens up, it must accept a reduced role that is mainly limited to social protection, physical protection against aggression or civil war, and maintaining national identity. The champion of this epic without heroes is the *New York Times* columnist Thomas Friedman. He contrasts barriers with open vistas, obsolescence with modernity, state control with free markets. He sees in globalization the light of dawn, the "golden strait-jacket" that will force contentious publics to understand that the logic of globalization is that of peace (since war would interrupt globalization and therefore progress) and democracy (because new technologies increase individual autonomy and encourage initiative).

## Back to Reality

These models come up hard against three realities. First, rivalries among great powers (and the capacity of smaller states to exploit such tensions) have most certainly not disappeared. For a while now, however, the existence of nuclear weapons has produced a certain degree of prudence among the powers that have them. The risk of destruction that these weapons hold has moderated the game and turned nuclear arms into instruments of last resort. But the game could heat up as more states seek other WMD as a way of narrowing the gap between the nuclear club and the other powers. The sale of such weapons thus becomes a hugely contentious issue, and efforts to slow down the spread of all WMD, especially to dangerous "rogue" states, can paradoxically become new causes of violence.

Second, if wars between states are becoming less common, wars within them are on the rise – as seen in the former Yugoslavia, Iraq, much of Africa, and Sri Lanka. Uninvolved states first tend to hesitate to get engaged in these complex conflicts, but they then (sometimes) intervene to prevent these conflicts from turning into regional catastrophes. The interveners, in turn, seek the help of the United Nations or regional organizations to rebuild these states, promote stability, and prevent future fragmentation and misery.

Third, states' foreign policies are shaped not only by realist geopolitical factors such as economics and military power but by domestic politics. Even in undemocratic regimes, forces such as xenophobic passions, economic grievances, and transnational ethnic solidarity can make policymaking far more complex and less predictable. Many states – especially the United States – have to grapple with the frequent interplay of competing government branches. And the importance of individual leaders and their personalities is often underestimated in the study of international affairs.

For realists, then, transnational terrorism creates a formidable dilemma. If a state is the victim of private actors such as terrorists, it will try to eliminate these groups by depriving them of sanctuaries and punishing the states that harbor them. The national interest of the attacked state will therefore require either armed interventions against governments supporting terrorists or a course of prudence and discreet pressure on other governments to bring these terrorists to justice. Either option requires a questioning of sovereignty – the holy concept of realist theories. The classical realist universe of Hans Morgenthau and Aron may therefore still be very much alive in a world of states, but it has increasingly hazy contours and offers only difficult choices when it faces the threat of terrorism.

At the same time, the real universe of globalization does not resemble the one that Friedman celebrates. In fact, globalization has three forms, each with its own problems. First is economic globalization, which results from recent revolutions in technology, information, trade, foreign investment, and international business. The main actors are companies, investors, banks, and private services industries, as well as states and international organizations. This present form of capitalism, ironically foreseen by Karl Marx and Friedrich Engels, poses a central dilemma between efficiency and fairness. The specialization and integration of firms make it possible to increase aggregate wealth, but the logic of pure capitalism does not favor social justice. Economic globalization has thus become a formidable cause of inequality among and within states, and the concern for global competitiveness limits the aptitude of states and other actors to address this problem.

Next comes cultural globalization. It stems from the technological revolution and economic globalization, which together foster the flow of cultural goods. Here the key choice is between uniformization (often termed "Americanization") and diversity. The result is both a "disenchantment of the world" (in Max Weber's words) and a reaction against uniformity. The latter takes form in a renaissance of local cultures and languages as well as assaults against Western culture, which is denounced as an arrogant bearer of a secular, revolutionary ideology and a mask for U.S. hegemony.

Finally there is political globalization, a product of the other two. It is characterized by the preponderance of the United States and its political institutions and by a vast array of international and regional organizations and transgovernmental networks (specializing in areas such as policing or migration or justice). It is also marked by private institutions that are neither governmental nor purely national – say, Doctors Without Borders or Amnesty International. But many of these agencies lack democratic accountability and are weak in scope, power, and authority. Furthermore, much uncertainty hangs over the fate of American hegemony, which faces significant resistance abroad and is affected by America's own oscillation between the temptations of domination and isolation.

The benefits of globalization are undeniable. But Friedmanlike optimism rests on very fragile foundations. For one thing, globalization is neither inevitable nor irresistible. Rather, it is largely an American creation, rooted in the period after World War II and based on U.S. economic might. By extension, then, a deep and protracted economic crisis in the United States could have as devastating an effect on globalization as did the Great Depression.

Second, globalization's reach remains limited because it excludes many poor countries, and the states that it does transform react in different ways. This fact stems from the diversity of economic and social conditions at home as well as from partisan politics. The world is far away from a perfect integration of markets, services, and factors of production. Sometimes the simple existence of borders slows down and can even paralyze this integration; at other times it gives integration the flavors and colors of the dominant state (as in the case of the Internet).

Third, international civil society remains embryonic. Many nongovernmental organizations reflect only a tiny segment of the populations of their members' states. They largely represent only modernized countries, or those in which the weight of the state is not too heavy. Often, NGOs have little independence from governments.

Fourth, the individual emancipation so dear to Friedman does not quickly succeed in democratizing regimes, as one can see today in China. Nor does emancipation prevent public institutions such as the International Monetary Fund, the World Bank, or the World Trade Organization from remaining opaque in their activities and often arbitrary and unfair in their rulings.

Fifth, the attractive idea of improving the human condition through the abolition of barriers is dubious. Globalization is in fact only a sum of techniques (audio and videocassettes, the Internet, instantaneous communications) that are at the disposal of states or private actors. Self-interest and ideology, not humanitarian reasons, are what drive these actors. Their behavior is quite different from the vision of globalization as an Enlightenment-based utopia that is simultaneously scientific, rational, and universal. For many reasons – misery, injustice, humiliation, attachment to traditions, aspiration to more than just a better standard of living – this "Enlightenment" stereotype of globalization thus provokes revolt and dissatisfaction.

Another contradiction is also at work. On the one hand, international and transnational cooperation is necessary to ensure that globalization will not be undermined by the inequalities resulting from market fluctuations, weak state-sponsored protections, and the incapacity of many states to improve their fates by themselves. On the other hand, cooperation presupposes that many states and rich private players operate altruistically – which is certainly not the essence of international relations – or practice a remarkably generous conception of their long-term interests. But the fact remains that most rich states still refuse to provide sufficient development aid or to intervene in crisis situations such as the genocide in Rwanda. That reluctance compares poorly with the American enthusiasm to pursue the fight against al Qaeda and the Taliban. What is wrong here is not patriotic enthusiasm as such, but the weakness of the humanitarian impulse when the national interest in saving non-American victims is not self-evident.

## Imagined Communities

Among the many effects of globalization on international politics, three hold particular importance. The first concerns institutions. Contrary to realist predictions, most states are not perpetually at war with each other. Many regions and countries live in peace; in other cases, violence is internal rather than state-to-state. And since no government can do everything by itself, interstate organisms have emerged. The result, which can be termed "global society," seeks to reduce the potentially destructive effects of national regulations on the forces of integration. But it also seeks to ensure fairness in the world market and create international regulatory regimes in such areas as trade, communications, human rights, migration, and refugees. The main obstacle to this effort is the reluctance of states to accept global directives that might constrain the market or further reduce their sovereignty. Thus the UN's powers remain limited and sometimes only purely theoretical. International criminal justice is still only a spotty and contested last resort. In the world economy – where the market, not global governance, has been the main beneficiary of the state's retreat – the network of global institutions is fragmented and incomplete. Foreign investment remains ruled by bilateral agreements. Environmental protection is badly ensured, and issues such as migration and population growth are largely ignored. Institutional networks are not powerful enough to address unfettered short-term capital movements, the lack of international regulation on bankruptcy and competition, and primitive coordination among rich countries. In turn, the global "governance" that does exist is partial and weak at a time when economic globalization deprives many states of independent monetary and fiscal policies, or it obliges them to make cruel choices between economic competitiveness and the preservation of social safety nets. All the while, the United States displays an increasing impatience toward institutions that weigh on American freedom of action. Movement toward a world state looks increasingly unlikely. The more state sovereignty crumbles under the blows of globalization or such recent developments as humanitarian intervention and the fight against terrorism, the more states cling to what is left to them.

Second, globalization has not profoundly challenged the enduring national nature of citizenship. Economic life takes place on a global scale, but human identity remains national – hence the strong resistance to cultural homogenization. Over the centuries, increasingly centralized states have expanded their functions and tried to forge a sense of common identity for their subjects. But no central power in the world can do the same thing today, even in the European Union. There, a single currency and advanced economic coordination have not yet produced a unified economy or strong central institutions endowed with legal autonomy, nor have they resulted in a sense of postnational citizenship. The march from national identity to one that would be both national and European has only just begun. A world very partially unified by technology still has no collective consciousness or collective solidarity. What states are unwilling to do, the world market cannot do all by itself, especially in engendering a sense of world citizenship.

Third, there is the relationship between globalization and violence. The traditional state of war, even if it is limited in scope, still persists. There are high risks of regional explosions in the Middle East and in East Asia, and these could seriously affect relations between the major powers. Because of this threat, and because modern arms are increasingly costly, the "anarchical society" of states lacks the resources to correct some of globalization's most flagrant flaws. These very costs, combined with the classic distrust among international actors who prefer to try to preserve their security alone or through traditional alliances, prevent a more satisfactory institutionalization of world politics – for example, an increase of the UN's powers. This step could happen if global society were provided with sufficient forces to prevent a conflict or restore peace – but it is not.

Globalization, far from spreading peace, thus seems to foster conflicts and resentments. The lowering of various barriers celebrated by Friedman, especially the spread of global media, makes it possible for the most deprived or oppressed to compare their fate with that of the free and well-off. These dispossessed then ask for help from others with common resentments, ethnic origin, or religious faith. Insofar as globalization enriches some and uproots many, those who are both poor and uprooted may seek revenge and self-esteem in terrorism.

## Globalization and Terror

Terrorism is the poisoned fruit of several forces. It can be the weapon of the weak in a classic conflict among states or within a state, as in Kashmir or the Palestinian territories. But it can also be seen as a product of globalization. Transnational terrorism is made possible by the vast array of communication tools. Islamic terrorism, for example, is not only based on support for the Palestinian struggle and opposition to an invasive American presence. It is also fueled by a resistance to "unjust" economic globalization and to a Western culture deemed threatening to local religions and cultures.

If globalization often facilitates terrorist violence, the fight against this war without borders is potentially disastrous for both economic development and globalization.

Antiterrorist measures restrict mobility and financial flows, while new terrorist attacks could lead the way for an antiglobalist reaction comparable to the chauvinistic paroxysms of the 1930s. Global terrorism is not the simple extension of war among states to nonstates. It is the subversion of traditional ways of war because it does not care about the sovereignty of either its enemies or the allies who shelter them. It provokes its victims to take measures that, in the name of legitimate defense, violate knowingly the sovereignty of those states accused of encouraging terror. (After all, it was not the Taliban's infamous domestic violations of human rights that led the United States into Afghanistan; it was the Taliban's support of Osama bin Laden.)

But all those trespasses against the sacred principles of sovereignty do not constitute progress toward global society, which has yet to agree on a common definition of terrorism or on a common policy against it. Indeed, the beneficiaries of the antiterrorist "war" have been the illiberal, poorer states that have lost so much of their sovereignty of late. Now the crackdown on terror allows them to tighten their controls on their own people, products, and money. They can give themselves new reasons to violate individual rights in the name of common defense against insecurity – and thus stop the slow, hesitant march toward international criminal justice.

Another main beneficiary will be the United States, the only actor capable of carrying the war against terrorism into all corners of the world. Despite its power, however, America cannot fully protect itself against future terrorist acts, nor can it fully overcome its ambivalence toward forms of interstate cooperation that might restrict U.S. freedom of action. Thus terrorism is a global phenomenon that ultimately reinforces the enemy – the state – at the same time as it tries to destroy it. The states that are its targets have no interest in applying the laws of war to their fight against terrorists; they have every interest in treating terrorists as outlaws and pariahs. The champions of globalization have sometimes glimpsed the "jungle" aspects of economic globalization, but few observers foresaw similar aspects in global terrorist and antiterrorist violence.

Finally, the unique position of the United States raises a serious question over the future of world affairs. In the realm of interstate problems, American behavior will determine whether the nonsuperpowers and weak states will continue to look at the United States as a friendly power (or at least a tolerable hegemon), or whether they are provoked by Washington's hubris into coalescing against American preponderance. America may be a hegemon, but combining rhetorical overkill and ill-defined designs is full of risks. Washington has yet to understand that nothing is more dangerous for a "hyperpower" than the temptation of unilateralism. It may well believe that the constraints of international agreements and organizations are not necessary, since U.S. values and power are all that is needed for world order. But in reality, those same international constraints provide far better opportunities for leadership than arrogant demonstrations of contempt for others' views, and they offer useful ways of restraining unilateralist behavior in other states. A hegemon concerned with prolonging its rule should be especially interested in using internationalist methods and institutions, for the gain in influence far exceeds the loss in freedom of action.

[ . . . ]

# 9
# Globalization and American Power
## Joseph S. Nye Jr.

With the end of the Cold War, the United States became more powerful than any state in recent history. Globalization contributed to that position, but it may not continue to do so throughout the century. Today globalization reinforces American power; over time it may dilute that power. Globalization is the child of both technology and policy. American policy deliberately promoted norms and institutions such as GATT, the World Bank, and the IMF that created an open international economic system after 1945. For forty-five years, the extent of economic globalization was limited by the autarkic policies of the communist governments. The end of the Cold War reduced such barriers, and American economic and soft power benefited both from the related ascendance of market ideology and the reduction of protectionism.

The United States plays a central role in all dimensions of contemporary globalization. Globalization at its core refers to worldwide networks of interdependence. A network is simply a series of connections of points in a system, but networks can take a surprising number of shapes and architectures. An airline hub and spokes, a spiderweb, an electricity grid, a metropolitan bus system, and the Internet are all networks, though they vary in terms of centralization and complexity of connections. Theorists of networks argue that under most conditions, centrality in networks conveys power – that is, the hub controls the spokes.[1] Some see globalism as a network with an American hub and spokes reaching out to the rest of the world. There is some truth in this picture, as the United States is central to all four forms of globalization: economic (the United States has the largest capital market), military (it is the only country with global reach), social (it is the heart of pop culture), and environmental (the United States is the biggest polluter, and its political support is necessary for effective action on environmental issues). As argued above, the United States has played a central role in the current phase of globalization for a variety of reasons, including its syncretic culture, market size, the effectiveness of some of its institutions, and its military force. And this centrality has in turn benefited American hard and soft power. In this view, being the hub conveys hegemony.

Those who advocate a hegemonic or unilateralist foreign policy are attracted to this image of global networks. Yet there are at least four reasons it would be a mistake to envisage contemporary networks of globalism simply in terms of the hub and spokes of an American empire that creates dependency for smaller countries. This metaphor is useful as one perspective on globalization, but it does not provide the whole picture.

First, the architecture of networks of interdependence varies according to the different dimensions of globalization. The hub-and-spokes metaphor fits military globalism more closely than economic, environmental, or social globalism because American dominance is so much greater in that domain. Even in the military area, most states are more concerned about threats from neighbors than from the United States, a fact that leads many to call in American global power to redress local balances. The American presence is welcome in most of East Asia as a balance to rising Chinese power. That is, the hub-and-spokes metaphor fits power relations better than it portrays threat relations, and [ . . . ] balancing behavior is heavily influenced by perceptions of threat. If instead of the role of welcome balancer, the United States came to be seen as a threat, it would lose the influence that comes from providing military protection to balance others. At the same time, in economic networks a hub-and-spokes image is inaccurate. In trade, for example, Europe and Japan are significant alternative nodes in the global network. Environmental globalization – the future of endangered species in Africa or the Amazonian rain forest in Brazil – is also less centered around the United States. And where the United States is viewed as a major ecological threat, as in production of carbon dioxide, it is less welcome, and there is often resistance to American policies.

Second, the hub-and-spokes image may mislead us about an apparent absence of reciprocity or two-way vulnerability. Even militarily, the ability of the United States to strike any place in the world does not make it invulnerable, as we learned at high cost on September 11, 2001. Other states and groups and even individuals can employ unconventional uses of force or, in the long term, develop weapons of mass destruction with delivery systems that would enable them to threaten the United States. Terrorism is a real threat, and nuclear or mass biological attacks would be more lethal than hijacked aircraft. [ . . . ] [G]lobal economic and social transactions are making it increasingly difficult to control our borders. When we open ourselves to economic flows, we simultaneously open ourselves to a new type of military danger. And while the United States has the largest economy, it is both sensitive and potentially vulnerable to the spread of contagions in global capital markets, as we discovered in the 1997 "Asian" financial crisis. In the social dimension, the United States may export more popular culture than any other country, but it also imports more ideas and immigrants than most countries. Managing immigration turns out to be an extremely sensitive and important aspect of the response to globalism. Finally, the United States is environmentally sensitive and vulnerable to actions abroad that it cannot control. Even if the United States took costly measures to reduce emissions of carbon dioxide at home, it would still be vulnerable to climate change induced by coal-fired power plants in China.

A third problem with the simple hub-and-spokes dependency image that is popular with the hegemonists is that it fails to identify other important connections and nodes in global networks. New York is important in the flows of capital to emerging markets, but so are London, Frankfurt, and Tokyo. In terms of social and political globalization, Paris is more important to Gabon than Washington is; Moscow is more important in Central Asia. Our influence is often limited in such situations. The Maldive Islands, only a few feet above sea level in the Indian Ocean, are particularly sensitive to the potential effects of producing carbon dioxide in the rest of the world. They are also completely vulnerable, since their sensitivity has to do with geography, not policy. At some time in the future, China will become more relevant to the Maldives than the United States is, because they will eventually outstrip us in the production of greenhouse gases. For many countries, we will not be the center of the world.

Finally, as the prior example suggests, the hub-and-spokes model may blind us to changes that are taking place in the architecture of the global networks. Network theorists argue that central players gain power most when there are structural holes – gaps in communications – between other participants. When the spokes cannot communicate with each other without going through the hub, the central position of the hub provides power. When the spokes can communicate and coordinate directly with each other, the hub becomes less powerful. The growth of the Internet provides these inexpensive alternative connections that fill the gaps.[2]

As the architecture of global networks evolves from a hub-and-spokes model to a widely distributed form like that of the Internet, the structural holes shrink and the structural power of the central state is reduced. It is true, for now, that Americans are central to the Internet; at the beginning of the twenty-first century, they comprise more than half of all Internet users. But by 2003, projections suggest, the United States will have 180 million Internet users, and there will be 240 million abroad.[3] This will be even more pronounced two decades hence, as Internet usage continues to spread. English is the most prevalent language on the Internet today, but by 2010, Chinese Internet users are likely to outnumber American users.[4] The fact that Chinese web sites will be read primarily by ethnic Chinese nationals and expatriates will not dethrone English as the web's lingua franca, but it will increase Chinese power in Asia by allowing Beijing "to shape a Chinese political culture that stretches well beyond its physical boundaries."[5] And China will not be alone. With the inevitable spread of technological capabilities, more-distributed network architectures will evolve. At some time in the future, when there are a billion Internet users in Asia and 250 million in the United States, more web sites, capital, entrepreneurs, and advertisers will be attracted to the Asian market.

The United States now seems to bestride the world like a colossus, to use *The Economist*'s phrase.[6] Looking more closely, we see that American dominance varies across realms and that many relationships of interdependence go both ways. Large states such as the United States – or, to a lesser extent, China – have more freedom than do small states, but they are rarely exempt from the effects of globalization. And states are not alone [ ... ] [ – ] organizations, groups, and even individuals are becoming players. For both better and worse, technology is putting capabilities within the reach of individuals that were solely the preserve of government in the past.[7] Falling costs are increasing the thickness and complexity of global networks of interdependence. The United States promotes and benefits from economic globalization. But over the longer term, we can expect globalization itself to spread technological and economic capabilities and thus reduce the extent of American dominance.

[ ... ]

## Notes

1   Daniel Brass and Marlene Burckhardt, "Centrality and Power in Organizations," in Nitin Nohria and Robert Eccles (eds.), *Networks and Organizations* (Boston: Harvard Business School Press, 1992); John Padgett and Christopher Ansell, "Robust Actors and the Rise of the Medici, 1400–1434," *American Journal of Sociology*, May 1993. I am indebted to David Lazer and Jane Fountain for help on this point.

2   Ronald Burt, *Structural Holes: The Social Structure of Competition* (Cambridge, MA: Harvard University Press, 1992), Chapter 1.

3   Alec Klein, "Seeking to Conquer the Globe, AOL Is Local Advertising Appeal," *International Herald Tribune*, May 31, 2001: 1.

4   "Graphiti," *Red Herring*, January 30, 2001: 39.
5   Tony Saich, "Globalization, Governance, and the Authoritarian State: China," in Joseph S. Nye Jr. and John D. Donahue (eds.), *Governance in a Globalizing World* (Washington DC: Brookings Institution Press, 2000), p. 224.
6   "America's World," *The Economist*, October 23, 1999: 15.
7   Bill Joy et al., "Why the Future Doesn't Need Us," *Wired*, April 2000.

# 10
# Globalization as Empire

*Michael Hardt and Antonio Negri*

Empire is materializing before our very eyes. Over the past several decades, as colonial regimes were overthrown and then precipitously after the Soviet barriers to the capitalist world market finally collapsed, we have witnessed an irresistible and irreversible globalization of economic and cultural exchanges. Along with the global market and global circuits of production has emerged a global order, a new logic and structure of rule – in short, a new form of sovereignty. Empire is the political subject that effectively regulates these global exchanges, the sovereign power that governs the world.

Many argue that the globalization of capitalist production and exchange means that economic relations have become more autonomous from political controls, and consequently that political sovereignty has declined. Some celebrate this new era as the liberation of the capitalist economy from the restrictions and distortions that political forces have imposed on it; others lament it as the closing of the institutional channels through which workers and citizens can influence or contest the cold logic of capitalist profit. It is certainly true that, in step with the processes of globalization, the sovereignty of nation-states, while still effective, has progressively declined. The primary factors of production and exchange – money, technology, people, and goods – move with increasing ease across national boundaries; hence the nation-state has less and less power to regulate these flows and impose its authority over the economy. Even the most dominant nation-states should no longer be thought of as supreme and sovereign authorities, either outside or even within their own borders. The decline in sovereignty of nation-states, however, does not mean that sovereignty as such has declined.

Throughout the contemporary transformations, political controls, state functions, and regulatory mechanisms have continued to rule the realm of economic and social production and exchange. Our basic hypothesis is that sovereignty has taken a new form, composed of a series of national and supranational organisms united under a single logic of rule. This new global form of sovereignty is what we call Empire.

The declining sovereignty of nation-states and their increasing inability to regulate economic and cultural exchanges is in fact one of the primary symptoms of the coming of Empire. The sovereignty of the nation-state was the cornerstone of the imperialisms that European powers constructed throughout the modern era. By "Empire," however, we understand something altogether different from "imperialism." The boundaries defined by the modern system of nation-states were fundamental to European colonialism and economic expansion: the territorial boundaries of the nation delimited the center of power from which rule was exerted over external foreign territories through a system of channels and barriers that alternately facilitated and obstructed the flows of production and circulation. Imperialism was really an extension of the sovereignty of the European nation-states beyond their own boundaries. Eventually, nearly all the world's territories could be parceled out and the entire world map could be coded in European colors: red for British territory, blue for French, green for Portuguese, and so forth. Wherever modern sovereignty took root, it constructed a Leviathan that overarched its social domain and imposed hierarchical territorial boundaries, both to police the purity of its own identity and to exclude all that was other.

The passage to Empire emerges from the twilight of modern sovereignty. In contrast to imperialism, Empire establishes no territorial center of power and does not rely on fixed boundaries or barriers. It is a decentered and deterritorializing apparatus of rule that progressively incorporates the entire global realm within its open, expanding frontiers. Empire manages hybrid identities, flexible hierarchies, and plural exchanges through modulating networks of command. The distinct national colors of the imperialist map of the world have merged and blended in the imperial global rainbow. The transformation of the modern imperialist geography of the globe and the realization of the world market signal a passage within the capitalist mode of production. Most significant, the spatial divisions of the three Worlds (First, Second, and Third) have been scrambled so that we continually find the First World in the Third, the Third in the First, and the Second almost nowhere at all. Capital seems to be faced with a smooth world – or really, a world defined by new and complex regimes of differentiation and homogenization, deterritorialization and reterritorialization. The construction of the paths and limits of these new global flows has been accompanied by a transformation of the dominant productive processes themselves, with the result that the role of industrial factory labor has been reduced and priority given instead to communicative, cooperative, and affective labor. In the postmodernization of the global economy, the creation of wealth tends ever more toward what we will call biopolitical production, the production of social life itself, in which the economic, the political, and the cultural increasingly overlap and invest one another.

Many locate the ultimate authority that rules over the processes of globalization and the new world order in the United States. Proponents praise the United States as the world leader and sole superpower, and detractors denounce it as an imperialist oppressor. Both these views rest on the assumption that the United States has simply donned the mantle of global power that the European nations have now let fall. If the nineteenth century was a British century, then the twentieth century has been an American century; or really, if modernity was European, then postmodernity is American. The most damning charge critics can level, then, is that the United States is repeating the practices of old European imperialists, while proponents celebrate the United States as a more efficient and more benevolent world leader, getting right what the Europeans got wrong. Our basic hypothesis, however, that a new imperial form of sovereignty has emerged, contradicts both these views. The United States does not, and indeed no nation-state can today, form the center of an imperialist project. Imperialism is over. No nation will be world leader in the way modern European nations were.

The United States does indeed occupy a privileged position in Empire, but this privilege derives not from its similarities to the old European imperialist powers, but from its differences. These differences can be recognized most clearly by focusing on the properly imperial (not imperialist) foundations of the United States constitution, where by "constitution" we mean both the formal constitution, the written document along with its various amendments and legal apparatuses, and the material constitution, that is, the continuous formation and re-formation of the composition of social forces. Thomas Jefferson, the authors of the Federalist, and the other ideological founders of the United States were all inspired by the ancient imperial model; they believed they were creating on the other side of the Atlantic a new Empire with open, expanding frontiers, where power would be effectively distributed in networks. This imperial idea has survived and matured throughout the history of the United States constitution and has emerged now on a global scale in its fully realized form.

We should emphasize that we use "Empire" here not as a metaphor, which would require demonstration of the resemblances between today's world order and the Empires of Rome, China, the Americas, and so forth, but rather as a concept, which calls primarily for a theoretical approach. The concept of Empire is characterized fundamentally by a lack of boundaries: Empire's rule has no limits. First and foremost, then, the concept of Empire posits a regime that effectively encompasses the spatial totality, or really that rules over the entire "civilized" world. No territorial boundaries limit its reign. Second, the concept of Empire presents itself not as a historical regime originating in conquest, but rather as an order that effectively suspends history and thereby fixes the existing state of affairs for eternity. From the perspective of Empire, this is the way things will always be and the way they were always meant to be. In other words, Empire presents its rule not as a transitory moment in the movement of history, but as a regime with no temporal boundaries and in this sense outside of history or at the end of history. Third, the rule of Empire operates on all registers of the social order extending down to the depths of the social world. Empire not only manages a territory and a population but also creates the very world it inhabits. It not only regulates human interactions but also seeks directly to rule over human nature. The object of its rule is social life in its entirety, and thus Empire presents the paradigmatic form of biopower. Finally, although the practice of Empire is continually bathed in blood, the concept of Empire is always dedicated to peace – a perpetual and universal peace outside of history.

The Empire we are faced with wields enormous powers of oppression and destruction, but that fact should not make us nostalgic in any way for the old forms of domination. The passage to Empire and its processes of globalization offer new possibilities to the forces of liberation. Globalization, of course, is not one thing, and the multiple processes that we recognize as globalization are not unified or univocal. Our political task, we will argue, is not simply to resist these processes but to reorganize them and redirect them toward new ends.

The creative forces of the multitude that sustain Empire are also capable of autonomously constructing a counter-Empire, an alternative political organization of global flows and exchanges. The struggles to contest and subvert Empire, as well as those to construct a real alternative, will thus take place on the imperial terrain itself – indeed, such new struggles have already begun to emerge. Through these struggles and many more like them, the multitude will have to invent new democratic forms and a new constituent power that will one day take us through and beyond Empire.

The genealogy we follow in our analysis of the passage from imperialism to Empire will be first European and then Euro-American, not because we believe that these regions are the exclusive or privileged source of new ideas and historical innovation, but simply because this was the dominant geographical path along which the concepts and practices that animate today's Empire developed – in step, as we will argue, with the development of the capitalist mode of production. Whereas the genealogy of Empire is in this sense Eurocentric, however, its present powers are not limited to any region. Logics of rule that in some sense originated in Europe and the United States now invest practices of domination throughout the globe. More important, the forces that contest Empire and effectively prefigure an alternative global society are themselves not limited to any geographical region. The geography of these alternative powers, the new cartography, is still waiting to be written – or really, it is being written today through the resistances, struggles, and desires of the multitude.

[ . . . ]

# Part II
# Political Power and Civil Society: A Reconfiguration?

One thousand years ago, a modern political map of the world would have been incomprehensible. This is not just because much of the world was still to be 'discovered'. People simply did not think of political power as something divided by clear-cut boundaries and unambiguous territorial domains. Modern politics emerged with and was shaped by the development of political communities tied to specific pieces of land, and formed into a nation-state. This saw political power centralized within Europe, state structures created and eventually the emergence of a new order among states. Forms of democracy were developed within certain political communities, while at the same time the creation of empires helped forestall the development of democratic accountability in many places. Today, questions arise as to whether we are living through another political transformation which might be as important as the creation of the nation-state. Is the exclusive link between territory and political power being broken by globalization?

The modern nation-state is the principal form of political rule across the globe, and is likely to remain so, the sceptics argue. The seventeenth century marked the beginning of the contemporary international system – the key parts of which are sovereign states claiming exclusive authority within their own geographic boundaries. This system is characterized by territorial states which settle their differences privately and sometimes by force; which seek to place their own national interest above all others; and which recognize no superior authority to themselves. Changes in international law, regional associations and global institutions in the last century did not alter the fundamental form and shape of this state system. For the division of the globe into nation-states, with distinctive sets of geopolitical interests, was built into institutions of regional and global governance; for instance, the veto powers granted to leading states (the US, Russia, Britain, France and China) in the Security Council of the United Nations. Furthermore, the new challenges of growing internationalism do not diminish the state-centric world. Sceptics discount the presumption that internationalization prefigures the emergence of a new, less state-centric world order. Far from considering national governments as becoming immobilized by international imperatives, they point to their growing centrality in the active promotion and regulation of cross-border activity.

Globalists take issue with these contentions. At the heart of the globalist thesis is the conviction that globalization is transforming the nature and form of political power today. Globalists argue that the right of most states to rule within circumscribed territories – their sovereignty – is on the edge of transformation, as is the practical nature of this entitlement – the actual capacity of states to rule. According to these authors, contemporary processes of globalization are historically unprecedented; and governments and societies across the globe are having to adjust to a world in which there is no longer a clear distinction between international and domestic, external and internal affairs.

Globalization involves a 'massive shake-out' of societies, economies and the institutions of governance. For some globalists, contemporary globalization is reconstituting the power, functions and authority of national government. In this world, national governments are relegated to little more than transmission belts for global economic change, or, at best, intermediate institutions and mechanisms sandwiched between increasingly powerful local, regional and global mechanisms of power and authority. Other globalists take a less radical view. They talk less in terms of 'the end of the state', and more in terms of a new spectrum of political developments and adjustment strategies in which the state finds itself relocated in multiple regional and global political networks.

The extracts which follow reflect this complex debate and offer important refinements of the arguments on both sides. Susan Strange takes a strong globalist standpoint. Her view is that politicians and governments have lost the authority they used to have and that their command over outcomes has diminished. Her argument is that 'the impersonal forces of world markets, integrated over the post-war period more by private enterprise in finance, industry and trade than by cooperative decisions of governments, are now more powerful than states'. Both the authority and legitimacy of states are in decline and, as a consequence, a serious vacuum is opening up in the international order; 'a yawning hole of non-authority, ungovernance it might be called'.

Assessing directly globalist arguments about the end of the nation-state, Michael Mann analyses four supposed 'threats' – global capitalism, environmental danger, identity politics and post-nuclear geopolitics. He sets out how all four impact differently on nation-states in different regions, and contain both 'state weakening and strengthening tendencies, and increase the significance of inter-national as well as transnational networks'. In this highly differentiated analysis Mann points to the diverse impacts of these threats, and their variable outcomes. He suggests that the patterns are too varied to allow one simply to argue that the nation-state and the nation-state system are strengthening or weakening. And he concludes that while 'human interaction networks are now penetrating the globe', they are doing so in 'multiple, variable and uneven ways'.

Robert Keohane takes a somewhat parallel view, but he argues the case quite differently. He begins his chapter by examining what he calls 'Hobbes's dilemma'. Hobbes thought that since people are egotistical and self-interested, and always seek more intensive pleasure and gain, no security is possible in the political and social worlds. Moreover, since there is no good reason to suppose that rulers will behave any differently from the ruled, there is a high risk that states will be predatory and oppressive. While accepting fundamental elements of this 'realist' characterization of the nature of humankind and state activity, Keohane argues that institutions can shape and alter the nature of this dilemma and its outcomes; and that, historically, the sovereign constitutional state has in fact done this. But what interests him above all is the place of sovereignty under contemporary conditions of 'complex interdependence'; that is, areas where there are 'multiple channels of contact existing among pluralistic societies' and where war is excluded as a primary means of resolving policy and political outcomes.

In these circumstances, Keohane argues, neither states nor transnational relations will replace one another; for sovereignty neither remains intact under existing forms of complex interdependence nor is it wholly eroded. Rather, sovereignty today is increasingly transformed, as it has become 'less a territorially defined barrier' and more 'a bargaining resource for a politics characterized by complex transnational networks'. Keohane traces out this development taking into account different developmental levels of complex interdependence around the world. He concludes that, while the institution of sovereign statehood is being modified, it is not likely to be superseded, and that Hobbes's dilemma will never be resolved entirely. Nevertheless, in the context of an intensification of economic globalization, the end of the Cold War, and the emergence of marked domains of peace as well as conflict, one thing is certain; we are entering a period of increasing diversity which will require the further development of international institutions to facilitate cooperation across economic, political and cultural domains.

There are globalists who believe that the rules governing the states system are changing fundamentally and that a new universal constitutional order is in the making, with profound implications for the constituent units, competencies, structure and standing of the international legal order. On the other side, there are those who are profoundly sceptical of any such transformation; they hold that states remain the leading source of all international rules – the limiting factor that ensures that international relations are shaped by, and remain anchored to, the politics of the sovereign state. Reflecting on this debate, David Held argues in the next chapter that significant transformations are under way in the international legal and political realms. He contends that there has been a transition from the classic regime of sovereignty, which gave the state free rein in the constitution of political and economic relations, to an order of liberal international sovereignty, which seeks to limit the nature and scope of state power. As a result, sovereignty can no longer be understood in terms of the categories of untrammelled effective power. Rather, a legitimate state must increasingly be understood through the language of democracy and human rights: legitimate authority has become linked, in moral and legal terms, with the maintenance of human rights values and democratic standards. Held concludes by assessing the strengths and weaknesses of this transformation, and points to a number of key deficiencies in the regime of liberal international sovereignty.

Ian Clark argues in the next chapter that globalization is creating a 'new security agenda' and transforming the nature and form of the organization of violence. If it can be shown that national security today is increasingly a collective or multilateral affair, then the one thing that did most to give modern states a clear rationale and purpose is in question. This has significant implications for the proper nature and scope of political community. Clark examines these concerns by exploring four interrelated arguments: the detachment of security from territory; the interconnectedness of security issues and global markets; the emergence of a new security agenda; and the alleged diminished capacity of states under conditions of globalization to provide security for their citizens. He concludes that a fundamental transformation is taking place between the state and the realm of security. Globalization is not just impinging on security matters from 'outside' but from within the heart of the state itself. In Clark's assessment, 'we should speak less about globalization and the security state and think more about the globalization of the security state'. The political organization of coercive power is changing its shape and dynamics.

The litany of threats to state sovereignty is often stated: global financial flows, multinational corporations, global media empires, the Internet and so on. Globalists assert that state power is increasingly enfeebled by these developments, which lead to the permeability of state borders. States were the primary actors, and multilateral international conventions, negotiated over many years, were the main expression of interstate cooperation. But, Anne-Marie Slaughter argues, this all suggests too static a conception of the state itself. As she puts it, 'the state is not disappearing; it is dis-aggregating into its component institutions'. The primary actors in the international order are 'no longer foreign ministries and heads of state, but the same government institutions that dominate domestic politics: administrative agencies, courts, and legis-latures'. The unitary state has given way to the disaggregated state and the rise of government networks. While these networks take many forms and perform a variety of different functions, they herald 'a new era of transgovernmental regulatory coopera-tion' and define transgovernmentalism 'as a distinctive mode of global governance: horizontal rather than vertical, composed of national government officials rather than international bureaucrats, decentralized and informal rather than organized and rigid'. Slaughter examines this new political phenomenon, and explores its many implications – positive as well as negative. Her assessment is that regulatory networks are the medium for the Information Age and through them political power will be recast – not simply eroded or undermined.

The application of the concept of networks is extended in the next chapter by Jessica Mathews. The end of the Cold War marks, she maintains, a new distribution of power among states, markets and civil society. Nothing less than a 'power shift' is taking place. New information technologies have helped drive the expansion of business, citizen, IGO and INGO networks, which now share power with governments. The hierarch-ical organization of the latter is increasingly ill-equipped to manage and regulate the new divisions of economic, social and cultural resources. Although it is not easy to 'imagine political entities that could compete with the emotional attachment of a shared landscape, national history, language, flag, and currency', new geographic and func-tional entities are emerging which might challenge the state's hegemony in these areas. The development of global cities, sub-national regions and new political formations like the EU, alongside the explosive growth of INGOs and social movements, suggests new forms of hybrid allegiances and identities. It is possible that continuing global-ization 'may well spark a vigorous reassertion of economic and cultural nationalism', but the new networks of business, INGOs and IGOs solve problems, from economic management to environmental tasks, which governments cannot solve alone. Hence, the 'power shift' is likely to continue, and reinforce the relative decline of state power.

Are regionalization and globalization contradictory forces and processes, or could they be complementary in fundamental respects? The emergence of regional systems of states and political linkages, preoccupied with increasing cooperation and regula-tion within transborder territorial domains, is a notable development of the post-Second World War era. The leading examples of this trend are the EU, NAFTA and APEC. While these are very diverse phenomena with very distinctive forms of regionalist governance (respectively, multilevel governance, hub-and-spoke institutions and market-led organizations), they can all be interpreted, Anthony Payne contends, as state pro-jects which 'intersect' with globalization. For the regional bodies that have emerged all 'typically seek to accelerate, to modify, or occasionally to reverse the direction of social change' engendered by globalization. Payne shows how globalization generates new forms of regional and global governance and might even be said to require them, but that it is far from creating a uniform pattern of governance at these levels. Significant, deeply rooted differences exist in the economic and political formation of regions, and these are likely to continue to have an important influence on forms of governance at all levels, including the global.

The heterogeneous and at times contradictory character of global governance is the principal theme of the final chapter in this section, by James Rosenau. He argues that 'world affairs can be conceptualized as governed through a bifurcated system – what can be called the two worlds of world politics – one an interstate system of states and their national governments that has long dominated the course of events and the other a multi-centric system of diverse types of other collectivities . . . who collectively form a highly complex system of global governance'. Developing the concept of multiple 'spheres of authority', Rosenau explores how governance comes about in a world that is both rapidly integrating and fragmenting under the pressures of globalization. While this 'fragmegration' will be with us for a long time and many of its tensions will intensify, Rosenau believes that the collective will to preserve and use the new horizontal forms of authority is not lacking and that global governance is and will remain central to the effective management of human affairs. However, in this time of continuing and profound transformations too much 'remains murky to project beyond the immediate present and anticipate long-term trajectories'. One cannot conclude with any confidence precisely what the political paths will be in the century ahead.

# 11
# The Declining Authority of States

## Susan Strange

Today it seems that the heads of governments may be the last to recognise that they and their ministers have lost the authority over national societies and economies that they used to have. Their command over outcomes is not what it used to be. Politicians everywhere talk as though they have the answers to economic and social problems, as if they really are in charge of their country's destiny. People no longer believe them. Disillusion with national leaders brought down the leaders of the Soviet Union and the states of central Europe. But the disillusion is by no means confined to socialist systems. Popular contempt for ministers and for the head of state has grown in most of the capitalist countries – Italy, Britain, France and the United States are leading examples. Nor is the lack of confidence confined to those in office; opposition parties and their leaders are often no better thought of than those they wish to replace. In the last few years, the cartoonists and the tabloid press have been more bitter, less restrained critics of those in authority in government than at any other time this century. Although there are exceptions – mostly small countries – this seems to be a worldwide phenomenon of the closing years of the twentieth century, more evident in some places than others, but palpable enough to suggest that some common causes lie behind it.

This [ ... ] is written in the firm belief that the perceptions of ordinary citizens are more to be trusted than the pretensions of national leaders and of the bureaucracies who serve them; that the commonsense of common people is a better guide to understanding than most of the academic theories being taught in universities. The social scientists, in politics and economics especially, cling to obsolete concepts and inappropriate theories. These theories belong to a more stable and orderly world than the one we live in. It was one in which the territorial borders of states really meant something. But it has been swept away by a pace of change more rapid than human society had ever before experienced.

For this reason I believe the time has come to reconsider a few of the entrenched ideas of some academic colleagues in economics, politics, sociology and international relations. The study of international political economy has convinced me that we have to rethink some of the assumptions of conventional social science, and especially of the study of international relations. These concern: firstly, the limits of politics as a social activity; secondly, the nature and sources of power in society; thirdly, the necessity and also the indivisibility of authority in a market economy; and fourthly, the anarchic nature of international society and the rational conduct of states as the unitary actors within that society. The first and second are assumptions commonly taken for granted in political science. The third is an assumption of much liberal, or neo-classical economic science. And the last is an assumption of much so-called realist or neo-realist thinking in international relations. Each of these assumptions will be examined more closely later [ . . . ].

But first it may help to outline briefly the argument [ . . . ] as a whole. That will show the context in which these more fundamental questions about politics and power arise and have to be reconsidered. The argument put forward is that the impersonal forces of world markets, integrated over the postwar period more by private enterprise in finance, industry and trade than by the cooperative decisions of governments, are now more powerful than the states to whom ultimate political authority over society and economy is supposed to belong.

Where states were once the masters of markets, now it is the markets which, on many crucial issues, are the masters over the governments of states. And the declining authority of states is reflected in a growing diffusion of authority to other institutions and associations, and to local and regional bodies, and in a growing asymmetry between the larger states with structural power and weaker ones without it.

There are, to be sure, some striking paradoxes about this reversal of the state–market balance of power. One, which disguises from many people the overall decline of state power, is that the *intervention* of state authority and of the agencies of the state in the daily lives of the citizen appears to be growing. Where once it was left to the individual to look for work, to buy goods or services with caution in case they were unsafe or not what they seemed to be, to build or to pull down houses, to manage family relationships and so on, now governments pass laws, set up inspectorates and planning authorities, provide employment services, enforce customer protection against unclean water, unsafe food, faulty buildings or transport systems. The impression is conveyed that less and less of daily life is immune from the activities and decisions of government bureaucracies.

That is not necessarily inconsistent with my contention that state *power* is declining. It is less effective on those basic matters that the market, left to itself, has never been able to provide – security against violence, stable money for trade and investment, a clear system of law and the means to enforce it, and a sufficiency of public goods like drains, water supplies, infrastructures for transport and communications. Little wonder that it is less respected and lacks its erstwhile legitimacy. The need for a political authority of some kind, legitimated either by coercive force or by popular consent, or more often by a combination of the two, is the fundamental reason for the state's existence. But many states are coming to be deficient in these fundamentals. Their deficiency is not made good by greater activity in marginal matters, matters that are optional for society, and which are not absolutely necessary for the functioning of the market and the maintenance of social order. Trivialising government does not make its authority more respected; often, the contrary is true.

The second paradox is that while the governments of established states, most notably in North America and western Europe, are suffering this progressive loss of real authority, the queue of societies that want to have their own state is lengthening. This is true not only of ethnic groups that were forcibly suppressed by the single-party government of the former Soviet Union. It is true of literally hundreds of minorities and aboriginal peoples in every part of the world – in Canada and Australia, in India and Africa, even in the old so-called nation-states of Europe. Many – perhaps the majority – are suppressed by force, like the Kurds or the Basques. Others – like the Scots or the Corsicans – are just not strong enough or angry enough to offer a serious challenge to the existing state. Still others such as the native Americans, the Aboriginals, the Samis or the Flemish are pacified by resource transfers or by half-measures that go some way to meet their perceived need for an independent identity. Only a few, such as the Greenlanders, the Slovaks or Slovenes or the unwanted, unviable Pacific island-states, have succeeded in getting what they wanted – statehood. But once achieved, it does not seem to give them any real control over the kind of society or the nature of their economy that they might have preferred. In short, the desire for ethnic or cultural autonomy is universal; the political means to satisfy that desire within an integrated world market economy is not. Many, perhaps most, societies have to be content with the mere appearance of autonomy, with a facade of statehood. The struggle for independence has often proved a pyrrhic victory.

The final paradox which can be brought as evidence against my basic contention about the hollowness of state authority at the end of this century is that this is a western, or even an Anglo-Saxon phenomenon, and is refuted by the Asian experience of the state. The Asian state, it is argued, has in fact been the means to achieve economic growth, industrialisation, a modernised infrastructure and rising living standards for the people. Singapore might be the prime example of a strong state achieving economic success. But Japan, Korea, Taiwan are all states which have had strong governments, governments which have successfully used the means to restrict and control foreign trade and foreign investment, and to allocate credit and to guide corporate development in the private sector. Is it not premature – just another instance of Eurocentrism therefore – to assume the declining authority of the state?

There are two answers to this third paradox. One is that all these Asian states were exceptionally fortunate. They profited in three ways from their geographical position on the western frontier of the United States during the Cold War. Their strategic importance in the 1950s and after was such that they could count on generous military and economic aid from the Americans, aid which was combined with their exceptionally high domestic savings and low patterns of consumption. The combination gave a head start to rapid economic development. Secondly, and also for strategic reasons, they could be – almost had to be – exempted from the pressure to conform to the norms of the open liberal economy. They were allowed, first formally and then informally, to limit foreign imports and also to restrict the entry of the foreign firms that might have proved too strong competitors for their local enterprises. At the same time, they were given relatively open access first to the large, rich US market for manufactures, and later, under some protest, to the European one. And thirdly, the technology necessary to their industrialisation was available to be bought on the market, either in the form of patents, or in the person of technical advisors from Europe and America or through corporate alliances which brought them the technology without the loss of managerial control.

Now, I would argue, these special dispensations are on the way out, and not only because the Cold War is over. The Asian governments will be under increasing pressure from Washington to adopt more liberal non-discriminatory policies on trade and investment. And they will also be under pressure from within to liberalise and to allow more competition, including foreign competition, for the benefit of consumers and of other producers. In short, the exceptionalism of the Asian state during the Cold War has already been substantially eroded, and will continue to be so. As it has been at other times, and in other places, there will be contests for control over the institutions and agencies of government in most of the Asian countries. There will be contests between factions of political parties, between vested interests both in the private sectors and in the public sector. There will be power struggles between branches of the state bureaucracy. Both the unity and the authority of government are bound to suffer.

# The Neglected Factor – Technology

The argument [I want to make] depends a good deal on the accelerating pace of technological change as a prime cause of the shift in the state–market balance of power. Since social scientists are not, by definition, natural scientists, they have a strong tendency to overlook the importance of technology which rests, ultimately, on advances in physics, in chemistry and related sciences like nuclear physics or industrial chemistry. In the last 100 years, there has been more rapid technological change than ever before in human history. On this the scientists themselves are generally agreed. It took hundreds – in some places, thousands – of years to domesticate animals so that horses could be used for transport and oxen (later heavy horses) could be used to replace manpower to plough and sow ground for the production of crops in agriculture. It has taken less than 100 years for the car and truck to replace the horse and for aircraft to partly take over from road and rail transport. The electric telegraph as a means of communication was invented in the 1840s and remained the dominant system in Europe until the 1920s. But in the next eighty years, the telegraph gave way to the telephone, the telephone gave way to radio, radio to television and cables to satellites and optic fibres linking computers to other computers. No one under the age of thirty or thirty-five today needs convincing that, just in their own lifetime, the pace of technological change has been getting faster and faster. The technically unsophisticated worlds of business, government and education of even the 1960s would be unrecognisable to them. No fax, no personal computers, no accessible copiers, no mobile phones, no video shops, no DNA tests, no cable TV, no satellite networks connecting distant markets, twenty-four hours a day. The world in which their grandparents grew up in the 1930s or 1940s is as alien to them as that of the Middle Ages. There is no reason to suppose that technological change in products and processes, driven by profit, will not continue to accelerate in future.

This simple, everyday, commonsense fact of modern life is important because it goes a long way to explaining both political and economic change. It illuminates the changes both in the power of states and in the power of markets. Its dynamism, in fact, is basic to my argument, because it is a continuing factor, not a once-for-all change.

For the sake of clarity, consider first the military aspects of technical change, and then the civilian aspects – although in reality each spills over into the other. In what are known as strategic studies circles, no one doubts that the development of the atom bomb in the middle of the twentieth century, and later of nuclear weapons carried by intercontinental missiles, has brought about a major change in the nature of warfare between states. Mutual assured destruction was a powerful reason for having nuclear weapons – but equally it was a good reason for not using them. After the paradoxical long peace of the Cold War, two things began to change. The expectation that, sooner or later, nuclear war would destroy life on the planet began to moderate. And confidence began to wane that the state could, by a defensive strategy, prevent this happening. Either it would or it wouldn't, and governments could do little to alter the probabilities. Thus, technology had undermined one of the primary reasons for the existence of the state – its capacity to repel attack by others, its responsibility for what Adam Smith called 'the defence of the realm'.

At the same time technology has had its effect on civilian life. Medical technology has made human life both longer and more comfortable. Electrical technology has liberated millions of women from the drudgery that imprisoned previous generations in the day-long labour of preparing food, keeping the family's clothes clean and mended, and houses clean and warm. As washing machines, vacuum cleaners, dishwashers, central heating and refrigerators and freezers spread down the income levels, more people had more to lose from inter-state conflict. Comfort bred conservatism in politics. Moreover, the new wealth was being acquired by the Germans and the Japanese, who had actually been defeated in World War II. Acquiring territory was no longer seen as a means to increase wealth. Losing territory did not mean the state became poorer or weaker. Gaining market shares in the world outside the territorial borders of the state, however, did enable formerly poor countries like Japan, Taiwan or Hong Kong to earn the foreign exchange with which to buy capital goods, foreign technology and the necessary resources of energy and raw materials. As John Stopford and I have argued, competition for world market shares has replaced competition for territory, or for control over the natural resources of territory, as the 'name of the game' between states (Stopford and Strange 1991; Strange in Rizopoulos 1990). In this new game, the search for allies among other states goes on, but not for their added military capabilities. It is for the added bargaining power conferred by a larger economic area.

Moreover, the search for allies is not confined to other states or inter-governmental organizations. It is supplemented by a search for allies among foreign-owned firms. These firms may be persuaded, in exchange for access to the national market, to raise the finance, apply their technology, provide the management and the access to export markets – in short, to take all the steps necessary to locate production of goods or services within the territory of the host state. In most developing or ex-socialist countries, the prospect of new jobs and extra export earnings brought by such investments have become powerful reasons for a change of attitude toward the so-called 'multinationals'.

## The Second Neglect – Finance

Not the least of the TNC's attractions to host states is its ability to raise finance both for the investment itself and – even more important – for the development of new technology. Another key part of the argument [ . . . ] is that, besides the accelerating pace of technological change, there has been an escalation in the capital cost of most technological innovations – in agriculture, in manufacturing and the provision of services, and in new products and in new processes. In all of these, the input of capital has risen while the relative input of labour has fallen. It is this increased cost which has raised the stakes, as it were, in the game of staying up with the competition. This is so whether we look at competition from other firms who are also striving for larger market shares, or whether we look at governments trying to make sure that the economies for whose performance they are held responsible stay up with the competition in wealth-creation coming from other economies. Thus, to the extent that a government can benefit from a TNC's past and future investments without itself bearing the main cost of it, there are strong reasons for forging such alliances.

But the escalating costs of technological change are also important for a more fundamental reason, and not just because it explains the changing policies of host states to TNCs. It has to do with change in the world system. The cost of new technology in the production structure has added to the salience of money in the international political economy. It is no exaggeration to say that, with a few notable exceptions, scholars in international relations for the past half-century have grossly neglected the political aspects of credit-creation, and of changes in the global financial structure.[1] In much theorising about international relations or even international political economy there is no mention at all of the financial structure (as distinct from the international monetary order governing the exchange relations of national currencies). Briefly, the escalating capital costs of new technologies could not have been covered at all without, firstly, some very fundamental changes in the volume and nature of credit created by the capitalist market economy; and secondly, without the added mobility that in recent years has characterised that created credit. The *supply* of capital to finance technological innovation (and for other purposes) has been as important in the international political economy as the *demand* from the innovators for more money to produce ever more sophisticated products by ever more capital-intensive processes of production.

These supply and demand changes take place, and take effect, in the market. And it is markets, rather than state–state relations, that many leading texts in international political economy tend to overlook. Much more emphasis is put on international monetary relations between governments and their national currencies. To the extent that attention is paid at all to the institutions creating and marketing credit in the world economy, they are held to be important chiefly for the increased volatility they may cause to exchange rates, or to the impact they may have on the ability of governments to borrow abroad to finance development or the shortfall between revenue and spending, or between export earnings and import bills.

More significant in the long run, however, when it comes to evolving better theories to explain change in the international political economy is the accompanying neglect of the three-way connections between the supply side of international finance (credit), the demand side from firms, and the political intervention of governments as regulators of banking and financial markets and as borrowers or lenders, at home and abroad. There are theories to explain each of the three, but no unifying theory to explain their mutual connections.

[ ... ]

Awareness of this failure of inter-connection between bodies of theory relating to political and economic change customarily treated by social scientists in isolation from each other has powerfully motivated [this work]. My exploration of the phenomenon of diffuse authority over the global political economy is necessarily sketchy and incomplete. Yet by drawing attention to both the theoretical lacunae in social science and to the empirical evidence of the increasing exercise of non-state authority, my hope is that further work will be inspired to develop at both the theoretical and the empirical level.

## Politics, Power and Legitimacy

There are three premises underlying the argument [here]. Each relates directly to – indeed, challenges – some of the conventional assumptions of economics, social and political science and international relations. The first premise is that politics is a common activity; it is not confined to politicians and their officials. The second is that power over outcomes is exercised impersonally by markets and often unintentionally by those who buy and sell and deal in markets. The third is that authority in society and over economic transactions is legitimately exercised by agents other than states, and has come to be freely acknowledged by those who are subject to it.

[ . . . ]

[T]hree general propositions about the patterns of legitimate authority now developing in the international political economy towards the end of the twentieth century [can be established]. One is that there is growing asymmetry among allegedly sovereign states in the authority they exercise in society and economy. In international relations, back to Thucydides, there has always been some recognition of a difference between small states and great powers, in the way each behaves to others and in the options available to them in their relations with other states. But there has been a tendency all along to assume a certain uniformity in the nature and effectiveness of the control which each state has over social and economic relations within their respective territorial boundaries. The attributes of domestic sovereignty, in other words, were assumed automatically to go with the regulation accorded each state by its peers. Now, I shall argue, that assumption can no longer be sustained. What was regarded as an exceptional anomaly when in 1945 the United States conceded two extra votes in the UN General Assembly for the Soviet Union – one for the 'sovereign' republic of the Ukraine and one for Byelorussia – now hardly attracts comment. The microstates of Vanuatu and the Republic of San Marino are admitted to the select circle of member-states of the United Nations. But no one really believes that recognition of their 'sovereignty' is more than a courteous pretence. It is understood that there is only a difference of degree between these and many of the smaller and poorer members of the international society of states who are established occupants of seats in the UN.

The second proposition is that the authority of the governments of all states, large and small, strong and weak, has been weakened as a result of technological and financial change and of the accelerated integration of national economies into one single global market economy. Their failure to manage the national economy, to maintain employment and sustain economic growth, to avoid imbalances of payments with other states, to control the rate of interest and the exchange rate is not a matter of technical incompetence, nor moral turpitude nor political maladroitness. It is neither in any direct sense their fault, nor the fault of others. None of these failures can be blamed on other countries or on other governments. They are, simply, the victims of the market economy.

The third proposition complements the second. It is that some of the fundamental responsibilities of the state in a market economy – responsibilities first recognised, described and discussed at considerable length by Adam Smith over 200 years ago – are not now being adequately discharged by anyone. At the heart of the international political economy, there is a vacuum, a vacuum not adequately filled by intergovernmental institutions or by a hegemonic power exercising leadership in the common interest. The polarisation of states between those who retain some control over their destinies and those who are effectively incapable of exercising any such control does not add up to a zero-sum game. What some have lost, others have not gained. The diffusion of authority away from national governments has left a yawning hole of non-authority, ungovernance it might be called.

[ . . . ]

## Note

1  The notable exceptions include Veseth 1990; Wachtel 1986; Frieden 1987; Moffitt 1984; Calleo 1982. I should add that we all owe big debts to the economic historians such as Kindleberger, Cipolla, Feis and de Cecco, and more recently Cain and Hopkin; to the practitioners such as Volcker and Gyoten; and not least to journalists such as the late Fred Hirsch and Yoichi Funabashi.

## References

Calleo, D. (1982) *The Imperious Economy*. Cambridge, Mass.: Harvard University Press.

Frieden, Jeffry (1987) *Banking on the World: The Politics of American International Finance*. New York: Harper and Row.

Moffitt, M. (1984) *The World's Money: International Banking from Bretton Woods to the Brink of Insolvency*. London: Joseph.

Rizopoulos, N. (ed.) (1990) *Sea-Changes: American Foreign Policy in a World Transformed*. New York: Council on Foreign Relations.

Stopford, John and Strange, Susan (1991) *Sterling and British Policy: A Political Study of an International Currency in Decline*. Oxford: Oxford University Press.

Veseth, Michael (1990) *Mountains of Debt: Crisis and Change in Renaissance Florence, Victorian Britain and Post-war America*. Oxford: Oxford University Press.

Wachtel, Howard (1986) *The Money Mandarins: The Making of a New Supranational Economic Order*. New York: Pantheon Books.

# 12

# Has Globalization Ended the Rise and Rise of the Nation-State?

## *Michael Mann*

## Introduction

The human sciences seem full of enthusiasts claiming that a new form of human society is emerging.

[ . . . ]

But is it [ . . . ]? To suggest that it is, various groups of enthusiasts advance four main theses.

1   Capitalism, now become global, transnational, post-industrial, 'informational', consumerist, neoliberal and 'restructured', is undermining the nation-state – its macroeconomic planning, its collectivist welfare state, its citizens' sense of collective identity, its general caging of social life.
2   New 'global limits', especially environmental and population threats, producing perhaps a new 'risk society', have become too broad and too menacing to be handled by the nation-state alone.
3   'Identity politics' and 'new social movements', using new technology, increase the salience of diverse local and transnational identities at the expense of both national identities and those broad class identities which were traditionally handled by the nation-state. For this and for the previous reason we are witnessing the stirrings of a new transnational 'civil society', social movements for peace, human rights and environmental and social reform which are becoming truly global.
4   Post-nuclearism undermines state sovereignty and 'hard geopolitics', since mass mobilization warfare underpinned much of modern state expansion yet is now irrational. [ . . . ]

So the empirical part of this article will investigate whether these four nation-state-weakening theses are correct. Since they downplay political power relations, it also considers two political counter-theses.

A   State institutions, both domestic and geopolitical, still have causal efficacy because they too (like economic, ideological and military institutions) provide necessary conditions for social existence: the regulation of aspects of social life which are distinctively 'territorially centred' (see Mann 1986: ch. 1). Thus they cannot be the mere consequence of other sources of social power.
B   Since states vary greatly, if (A) is true, these variations will cause variations in other spheres of social life. Even within Europe states differ in size, power, geography and degree of centralization. Across the globe, variations dramatically increase: in degree of democracy, level of development, infrastructural power, geopolitical power, national indebtedness, etc. They also inhabit very different regional settings. Can contemporary capitalism, even

if reinforced by environmental limits, 'cultural postmodernity' and demilitarization, render all this variation irrelevant, and have the *same* effects on all countries? Or will these variations cause variation among these forces, and so limit globalization?

Only the most breathless of enthusiasts would deny all validity to these counter-theses – or to the survival of the nation-state as wielder of some economic, ideological, military and political resources. The task is to establish *degrees* of relative causality: to what extent is the nation-state being transformed, to what extent is it declining – or even perhaps still growing?

But to establish this we must also make some conceptual distinctions. We can roughly distinguish five socio-spatial networks of social interaction in the world today:

1  *local* networks – which for present purposes just means subnational networks of interaction;
2  *national* networks, structured or (more neutrally) bounded by the nation-state;
3  *inter-national* networks, that is relations between nationally constituted networks. Most obviously, these include the 'hard geopolitics' of inter-state relations which centre on war, peace and alliances. But they also include 'soft geopolitics' between states – negotiations about more peaceable and particular matters like air transport communications, tax treaties, air pollution, etc. And they include relations between networks that are more nationally than state-constituted: for example, the emergence of 'national champions' playing on a broader playing-field – whether these are football teams or giant corporations;
4  *transnational* networks, passing right through national boundaries, being unaffected by them. These might not be very extensive – perhaps a religious sect organized across two neighbouring countries – or they might be continent-wide or even worldwide. Many transnational arguments about contemporary society rest on a 'macroregional' base. Examples are the frequent distinctions between 'Liberal/Anglo-Saxon', 'Nordic/Social Democratic' or 'Christian Democratic/corporatist' forms of contemporary social organization;
5  *global* networks cover the world as a whole – or, perhaps more realistically, they cover most of it. But we should distinguish between networks which radiate universalistically or particularistically across the globe. The feminist movement may spread through almost all countries, but usually only among rather particular, smallish groups. The Catholic Church has some presence in all continents but only has quite a narrow base across Asia, while being near-universal across Latin America. The capitalism evoked by many of the enthusiasts is a universal global network, evenly diffusing through economic and social life just about everywhere. Thus global networks might be formed by either a single universal network or by a more segmented series of networks between which existed rather particularistic relations.

Over the last centuries local interaction networks have clearly diminished in relative weight; while longer-distance networks – national, inter-national and transnational – have become denser, structuring more of people's lives. Genuinely global networks have emerged relatively recently. Note that global networks need not be the same as transnational networks, though many enthusiasts equate them. Nor are they necessarily economic in nature. Global networks may be constituted by geopolitics [ . . . ] or by ideological movements like a religion or socialism or feminism or neoliberalism – the combination amounting perhaps to a new transnational civil society.

Since national and inter-national networks are constituted or fundamentally constrained by the nation-state, the future of the nation-state thus turns critically upon the answer to two questions: *Is the social significance of national and inter-national networks declining relative to some combination of local and transnational networks? And to the extent that global networks are emerging, what is the relative contribution to them of national/inter-national versus local/transnational networks?*

## The 'Modest Nation-State' of the North

I start with the most familiar and dominant form of state in the world today. In the 'west', or more precisely the 'northwest' of western Europe and its white colonies, arose a state claiming formal political sovereignty over 'its' territories and a legitimacy based on the 'people' or 'nation' inhabiting them. This is what we mean by the nation-state.

The regulatory powers of such states expanded through several centuries. First, from the end of the Middle Ages they increasingly plausibly claimed a monopoly of judicial regulation and military force. Then, in the eighteenth and especially the nineteenth centuries they sponsored integrating communications infrastructures and basic control of the poor. The twentieth century saw welfare states, macroeconomic planning and the mobilization of mass citizen nationalism. All the while more states legitimated themselves in terms of 'the people', either 'representing' the people (liberal democracies) or 'organically embodying' it (authoritarian regimes), with varying degrees of civil, political and social citizenship. To a degree, therefore, northwesterners became 'caged' into national interaction networks, and these became supplemented by the inter-national relations between nation-states which we know by the term 'geopolitics'.

This is the now familiar story of 'the rise and rise' of the nation-state and the nation-state system – to which I have contributed myself (Mann 1986, 1993).

[ . . . ]

Since 1945 the [nation-state] further diffused across almost all the rest of 'the north', i.e. the whole European continent and increasing regions of East and South Asia. Its formal trappings have also dominated 'the south', while all states meet in a forum called 'The United Nations'. The [ . . . ] nation-state might seem to dominate the entire globe. In some limited senses it actually does. Only a few states do not base their legitimacy on the nation, or lack a monopoly of domestic coercion or real territorial boundedness. Almost all manage to implement policies oriented towards basic population control, health and education. Plunging mortality and rising literacy have multiple causes but some lie in the realm of effective public policy. For these reasons I will go ahead and describe contemporary states as nation-states. Yet most of them actually possess rather limited control over their territories and boundaries, while their claims to represent the nation are often specious. For much of the world a *true* nation-state remains more aspiration for the future than present reality. The nation-state's rise has been global, but modest and very uneven. The modest nation-state came to dominate the 'north', has been part of its expansion and represents a desired future for the bulk of the world's people. Is all this now threatened?

## The Capitalist Threat

The enthusiasts have correctly identified many important transformations of capitalism. It is not necessary here to document capitalism's use of new 'informational' and 'post-industrial' technology to expand through much of the world and penetrate more of social life. But how great is its threat to the nation-state? And just how 'global' and/or 'transnational' is it?

In a formal geographic sense capitalism *is* now more or less global. Two great geo-political events permitted massive extension. First, decolonization largely ended the segmentation of the world economy into separate imperial zones. Second, the collapse of Soviet autarchy opened up most of Eurasia to capitalist penetration. Only Iran, China and a handful of smaller communist countries now maintain partial blockages, and these are declining or may be expected to start declining soon. China retains distinct property forms (mixing private with varieties of public ownership and control), and there still also remain (declining) areas of subsistence economy scattered through the world. Yet capitalist commodity exchange clearly dominates. With no confident adversary in sight, capitalism is becoming – at least minimally – global. That was not so in 1940, or even in 1980. It is obviously a major transformation.

But are its global networks 'pure' in the sense of being singularly universal, or do other more particularistic principles of social organization also help constitute them? An economy may be global, but this may be conferred by help from national and inter-national networks of interaction.

[ . . . ]

[M]ost 'transnational' economic relations cannot be necessarily equated with a global universalism. The bulk of capitalist activity is more 'trilateral' than global, being concentrated in the three regions of the advanced 'north': Europe, North America and East Asia. These contain over 85 per cent of world trade, over 90 per cent of production in advanced sectors like electronics, plus the headquarters of all but a handful of the top 100 multinationals (including banks). This does not necessarily mean capitalism is not global. It may only indicate that the north is rich, the south is poor – and that both are locked together in a global network of interaction. But it does suggest that capitalism retains a geo-economic order, dominated by the economies of the advanced nation-states. Clusters of nation-states provide the stratification order of globalism. Among other consequences, this protects the citizens of the north: the poorly educated child of an unskilled worker in Britain or the United States will enjoy far better material conditions of existence (including twenty more years of life) than will his/her counterpart in Brazil or India. True, inequalities within all these nation-states are widening, yet it is almost inconceivable that the bulk of the privileges of national citizens in northern countries could be removed. That would cause such social disorder as to be incommensurate with a stable and profitable capitalism. The nation-state provides some of the structure, and some of the stratification structure, of the global networks of capitalism. If the commodity rules, it only does so entwined with the rule of – especially northern – citizenship.

The global economy is also subject to loose and predominantly 'soft' inter-national regulation in the shape of organizations like G7, GATT, the World Bank or the IMF. These are also northern-dominated. Some of these are involved in seemingly endless negotiations of trade liberalization – and these are likely to drag on a lot longer since national governments have been recently raising non-tariff barriers. We are nowhere near global free trade, but we may be moving a little closer and this is at present ideologically dominant. But is this just another liberalization phase in the normal historical oscillation around the middle zone between the free trade and protectionist poles? That depends on the resolution of other tendencies discussed in this article.

So, at the moment and probably also for the near future, a rapidly globalizing economy does not only acquire its character from transnational networks of inter-action. What adds up to the global is a very complex mix of the local, the national, the inter-national (represented in my discussion mostly by northern trilateralism) – and the truly transnational. The *transnational* commodity does not rule the globe.

Over time some of these national and inter-national structurings may decline. Northern domination of the world economy may diminish because of the pressures of comparative advantage. Apart from very high-tech activities, much productive enterprise may migrate to the lower costs of the south, producing more globalization (though not necessarily much reducing inequality). But so far migration has operated not by some 'transnational' logic (of random walk?) but by some combination of four other principles: the possession of useful natural resources, geographical propinquity (neighbouring countries), geopolitical alliances (friendly countries), and state and civil society stability (predictable countries). Whereas the first factor is found fairly randomly through the world – and so oil alone can develop rather backward, distant countries – the last three factors are generally interconnected. The historical development of the major northern economies emerged amid broader regional settings, from which neighbouring states and societies also benefited. Thus expansion has mostly been to the Koreas and the Mexicos, friendly neighbours with relatively developed nations and states, rather than, say, to most African countries. Nor does most growth take a regional, 'enclave' pattern within states (except where raw materials matter, or where extension is over a border and the neighbouring government sponsors 'enterprise zones'). Development then tends to diffuse across the core territories of these states, aiding the development of their overall civil societies and their drift towards becoming nation-states. Thus extension of the north – and so globalization – has depended upon, and in turn reinforced, the nation-states benefiting from it. This form of globalization reinforces national networks of interaction.

Since finance capital seems more transnational than industrial capital, its constraints upon the nation-state are usually those most emphasized by the enthusiasts. Its mobility and velocity produce financial movements which dwarf the fiscal resources of states and which constrain two of the three props of post-war state fiscal policy – interest rates and currency valuation (taxation being less affected). Yet it is difficult to assess the overall significance of this, for two reasons. First, the numbers do not offer real precision about power relations. Since currencies, shares, futures, etc. can be traded many times over in a single day, the paper value of 'financial flows' vastly exceeds that of world trade, and continues to grow. But power cannot be simply read off such sums. What are being traded are property rights to raw materials, manufactured goods and (increasingly) services, almost all of which have much greater fixity of location and therefore presumably a degree of national identity.

Second, it is not clear how effective macroeconomic planning ever was in the northwest. It *seemed* effective while massive growth was occurring and governments had access to surpluses. Many were able to be mildly interventionist (though selective incentives were generally more effective than physical controls). But since then we have seen the collapse not only of Keynesian economics but also of economic theory in general. Economists now more or less admit they have no explanation of any of the great booms or slumps of the twentieth century (or at least one that does not depend on singular events like great world wars). Macroeconomic planning was a general ideology surrounding some highly abstract concepts, from which were precariously derived some technical tools (including, most fundamentally, national accounting) and policies (which in fact also depended on contingencies). Macroeconomic planning still contains such a mixture, though its emphasis has changed. The ideological pretensions and the ability to expand spending have certainly declined. Thus we may expect looser and fiscally more cautious national/inter-national (i.e. trilateral) macroeconomic policies: a proliferation of G7 and GATT guidelines and piecemeal liberalizing agreements; MITI-style [the highly interventionist Japanese Ministry of Trade and Industry] collaboration and incentive programmes more than nationalization or direct state investment; central banks more than politicians; less the pretence of controlling markets than of signalling intentions to them; and, above all, no increases in taxation masquerading as grandiose economic theory.

Nor are the reasons for these less than dramatic power reductions easy to interpret. [ . . . ]

[N]ational economies [ . . . ] vary considerably – in their prosperity, their cohesion and their power. Consider [ . . . ] the three main regions of the north. North America is dominated by its superpower, the USA. This has an unusual state, dominated by its unique war machine and (rather meagre) social security system. Most other governmental activities which in most other northern countries are mainly the province of the central state (criminal justice, education and most welfare programmes) are the concern of fifty separate 'states' or local governments in the USA. Three major industries are closely entwined with the federal government, agriculture, the military-industrial complex and health care, and may be said to be somewhat (if particularistically) planned. They are likely to remain so – though the current plan is to downsize the military by just under a quarter over two decades. Many other industries have closer relations with 'state' and local governments, for example property development and construction. Federal legislation has been traditionally tight in the area of labour relations and monopolies, especially restraining the growth of US unions and banks. But there has been little macroeconomic planning by any level of government. The principal 'planning' agency (over interest rates) is the Federal Reserve Bank, which is largely autonomous of government. There is no serious American industrial policy; this is left to the post-war powerhouses of the US economy, the large corporations. Much of this is due to the radical separation of powers enshrined by the US constitution. A coordinated political economy cannot easily be run by a President and his cabinet, two Houses of Congress, a Supreme Court and fifty 'states' (which are also fragmented by the same separation of powers) – especially when they belong to different political parties. Thus it is difficult to see much of a weakening of US government powers, since these were never exercised very actively. [ . . . ]

East Asia is at present also dominated by a single nation-state, though Japan is not a military superpower. Japanese political economy differs from both North American and European, with far more coordination between the state and capitalist corporations (and, in a more dependent role, the labour unions): 'Governing the market', Wade (1990) calls it; 'Governed interdependence', say Weiss and Hobson (1995). Such national coordination has been adapted in varying forms across the smaller economies of East Asia. These include active industrial policies centring on selective tax rates or conditional subsidies for key or export sectors, public absorbing of risk for innovation and government coordination of inter-firm collaboration for technology upgrading (Weiss 1995). These countries also have political stability and an advanced civil, i.e. 'national', society which is stable, literate and broadly honest. They have also experienced phenomenal growth[, t]hough growth is stuttering [ . . . ].
[ . . . ]

East Asia offers different combinations of capitalist transformation and nation-states.

Europe is the only one of the three regions to have experienced significant political transformation. [ ... ]

The original impetus for [ ... ] this was mainly geopolitical and military: to prevent a third devastating war in the continent, more specifically to bind Germany into a peaceful concert of nation-states. The United States had its own, primarily geopolitical, reasons for encouraging it. Thus the 'Six' and the 'Nine' were being bound together before much of the capitalist transformation had occurred. But since the chosen mechanisms of binding were [to begin with] primarily economic, they were then intensified by this transformation. The economy of Europe has thus been substantially transnationalized.

Yet the European Union also remains an association between nation-states, an international network of interaction. Specific geopolitical agreements between Germany and France, with the support of their client Benelux states, have always been its motor of growth. Germany and France, like the other states, have lost many particularistic autonomies. But, when allied, they remain the masters on most big issues. [ ... ] The minor and economically weaker states may seem to have lost more, but their sovereignty on the big issues was more limited in the past. Britain has stood to lose most, because of its historic geopolitical independence from the rest of Europe. And they vote and acquire ministries based on a combination of their population size and economic muscle. 'They' are states and national economies, represented by statesmen (and women) and national technocrats and business leaders. This is not traditional 'hard' geopolitics, since the agenda is primarily economic and the participants believe war between them is unthinkable. It is 'soft' geopolitics structured by much denser inter-national (plus the remaining national) networks of interaction.
[ ... ]

But suppose that the drift of the economy is towards more and more transnational globalism, that free trade is largely achieved as the EU, NAFTA, the Asian and Pacific Conference countries and other trade groups merge under the loose umbrella of GATT, that multinationals become more cosmopolitan, that development of the south becomes more diffuse, less nation-state-centric. Would this amount to a single transnational/global economy in which the commodity and the single market ruled universally?

The answer is both yes and no. All goods and services would then have a price on a single market and capitalist enterprises would organize their financing, production and exchange. 'Consumerism' already dominates, some of the enthusiasts say; business accountancy practices spread through previously insulated institutions like civil services or universities; and athletes sell their skills to the highest bidder on free and relatively new markets. Such commodity penetration would broaden.

But even so, the rules of those markets might still have their particularities, some being the effects of national and inter-national networks of interaction. Though a far broader range of goods are now bought and sold, many of the most important ones are not actually sold as commodities on free markets. None of the three biggest industries in the US economy, defence, health care and (probably) illicit drugs, are simply dominated by commodity production, though all involve considerable transnational networks. In defence [for example] the government is a monopolistic customer for hi-tech weapons systems and it decides what other states (friendly ones) will be allowed as customers; supply is not very competitive (sometimes only one manufacturer will 'tender' and sometimes profit is calculated on a cost-plus basis). The weapons embody more 'use' than 'exchange' value – the USA *must* have them, almost regardless of cost, and the corporation can produce them without much thought of market risk. [...]

Though the capitalist economy is now significantly global, its globalism is 'impure', a combination of both the transnational and the inter-national. The potential universalism of the former is undercut by the particularisms of nation-states – and indeed also by the particularisms of human social practices at large.

## Environmental Limits, New Social Movements and a New Transnational Civil Society

Through population growth, soil and plant erosion, water shortages, atmospheric pollution and climate change, we encounter a second form of globalism – reinforced by the dangers of biological, chemical and nuclear warfare alluded to later. We are indeed living in Beck's 'risk society' (though this is not the only society we are living in) and have only done so in the second half of the twentieth century. On some of these issues the traditional 'solution' of letting the south or the poor starve can endure. But on others, humanity together faces severe risks. These are not identical to the risks of capitalism, though the two are deeply entwined (since capitalism is now the dominant form of economic production). The 'mastery' and 'exploitation' of nature, and the enormous increase in human potentiality to do so throughout the globe, are also attributable to industrialism and to the other modes of production developed in the modern period. State socialism (and fascism too) was even more destructive of the environment, while the petty commodity production of small peasants has also been forced into many destructive practices. Nation-states, scientific establishments and (until the last few years) virtually all modern institutions contributed their piece of destruction. And rampant population growth also has sources other than capitalism, for example military, religious and patriarchal practices. To deal with these risks responses must go beyond the nation-state and capitalism alike.

Present responses on environmental issues seem mainly two-fold. First, organizations are already in action embodying variant forms of the famous environmental maxim 'Think globally, act locally'. These are mainly mixed local-transnational pressure groups and NGOs, some of them formal pressure groups (like Greenpeace), others carried by professional and scientific networks (of soil scientists, ornithologists, demographers, etc.). They are more 'modern' than 'postmodern', since they reject scientific-material exploitation of nature on primarily scientific and social-scientific grounds. Though their elites originated in the north, they have increasingly spread globally, among both highly educated southern elites and among diverse, and rather particular, groups threatened by real material problems. Such networks use the most modern and global means of communication. In exploiting these, they sometimes outflank national government and international capital alike – as consumers mobilized through western Europe to boycott Shell, humiliate the British government, and force the towing back of the Brent Spar oil platform in 1995. We may expect more of this.

Is this a 'global civil society'? Its structure is not entirely new: in the early twentieth century socialists (and, to a lesser extent, anarchists, pacifists and fascists) also generated extensive transnational networks covering much of the globe, using similarly advanced technology (printing presses, immediate translation, dictaphones, etc. – see Trotsky's remarkable study in Mexico City). The socialists launched a wave of revolutions, some successful, most unsuccessful. Many of the more idealistic proponents of the notion of a new civil society expect its scale eventually to dwarf such historical analogies.

Second, however, there is also increasing deployment of intergovernmental agencies: macroregional and continental agencies, UN conferences, etc. Their key participants, those who could implement coordinated policy decisions, are representatives of nation-states. 'Soft geopolitics' is becoming denser in this arena too. The other main delegates are the 'experts' mentioned two paragraphs above, who lead a double life. Though nurtured in transnational professional associations, they must adopt the perspective of the nation-state, persuading governments that global concerns are actually in the national interest. Some hit on excellent wheezes. Some American ornithologist managed to persuade the State Department to insert into its aid programme to Belize a requirement to protect a rare bird of which the Belize planners had not previously heard. More significantly, feminists involved in development agencies are pressuring reactionary dictators in the south to put more resources into the education of women since this will reduce the birth rate (one of the primary goals of almost all southern governments).

Thus environmental issues mainly encourage dual networks of interaction, one a potentially local/transnational civil society, the other inter-national, in the form of 'soft' geopolitics. The former may transcend the nation-state, the latter co-ordinate states more tightly together, though perhaps in partly consensual terms which are not incompatible with a gradual spread of a civil society. Again it is a mixed story.

And this is also the case with others among the 'new social movements'. It is usually argued that those concerned with the 'new politics' of identity – of gender, sexuality, lifestyle, age cohort, religion and ethnicity – weaken national (and nationally regulated class) identities, replacing or supplementing them with local-cum-transnational sources of identity. Ethnic politics are too variable to be dealt with in a few paragraphs (and I am writing about them at length elsewhere). So one sentence will do here: ethnic politics may fragment existing states, but – given the defeat of alternative multinational and socialist states – they fragment them into more, supposedly more authentic, nation-states. But for other social movements based on identity politics, I wish to argue that on balance they strengthen existing nation-states.
[ . . . ]

Feminists, gays, religious fundamentalists, etc. use emerging global networks of communication and NGOs, and they focus energies on the UN as well as their own state. However, most contending actors demand *more* regulation by their own nation-state through its legal or welfare agencies: to restrict or liberalize abortion, pre-marital conception and single parenting; to clarify harassment, child abuse and rape and the evidence needed to prosecute them; to guarantee or restrict the rights of those with unorthodox sexual preferences or lifestyles. Since authoritative social regulation remains overwhelmingly the province of the nation-state, the emergence of new identities may ultimately reinvigorate its politics and broaden its scope. New social movements claim to be turned off by class politics. Perhaps class politics will decline – but not national politics in general.

## Post-militarism and a New World Order

As Martin Shaw argues, it is in the realm of hard geopolitics that the northern nation-states have experienced the most radical transformation – because this is where they learned the bitterest lessons [Shaw 1997]. In the two great northern wars (more commonly called the world wars) they suffered perhaps 70–80 million dead – as a direct consequence of the nation-state system. Through those wars they also pioneered weapons so devastating that they could no longer be actually used for any rational 'hard geopolitical' purpose. Northern states are now less willing to engage themselves in wholesale war than almost any states in history. The original backbone of the nation-state is turning to jelly.

But again our three regions vary. None are more reluctant militarists than the Europeans, the guilty perpetrators of both wars, reliant for their defence for the last fifty years on the USA and presently faced by no serious threat to their security. Though the EU contains two nuclear powers, has its Franco-German brigade and its curious Western European [Defence] Union, all this is less significant than the unprecedented virtual absence of serious 'hard geopolitics' within Europe. Germans remain the most constrained of all by anti-militarism. The determination to break with the terrible character of European history is probably the most causally determining modern transformation of all, and the one which is most encroaching upon traditional national sovereignties. But to make European history the general pattern of the world would be ethnocentric in the extreme. And if it was, then the analogy would require more than just a restructuring of capitalism reinforced by a 'cultural turn'. The analogy would require future wars killing many millions of people in other regions of the world, before they too cried 'enough'.

Yet most Japanese may also have cried 'enough'. They are at present reluctant militarists. Some Japanese politicians are bolder than their German counterparts in expressing nationalism, but they still get slapped down. Yet East Asia is potentially an insecure region. The United States differs again. It suffered little during the two great northern wars – indeed its economy greatly benefited. It is a military superpower, still projects a standing armed force of 1,200,000 into the next century, and still modernizes its hardware. It remains the global policeman, a role which European and Japanese governments are keen to see continue and may even help finance. But even in the USA defence cuts have been sizeable and it is doubtful that the American electorate has the stomach for warfare in which many American lives would be lost. In any case these northern regions dominate the world without war.

The world nonetheless remains conflict-ridden, with a substantial place for 'hard' geopolitics. Consider this list: rising ethnic separatism, conflict between potentially nuclear states like India and Pakistan or the two Chinas, China's geopolitical role incommensurate with its real strength, the instability of Russia and some smaller well-armed powers, the prevalence of military regimes in the world, the likely proliferation of nuclear weapons and the largely uncontrolled current spread of chemical and biological weapons through the world. Who knows what eco-tensions, resulting from water shortages, foreign-dominated exploitation of a country's habitat, etc. might lurk around the corner? It is unlikely militarism or war will just go away. All these threats constitute serious obstacles to the diffusion of transnational and universal global networks.
[ . . . ]

# Conclusion

This article has analysed four supposed 'threats' to contemporary nation-states: capitalist transformation, environmental limits, identity politics and post-militarism. We must beware the more enthusiastic of the globalists and transnationalists. With little sense of history, they exaggerate the former strength of nation-states; with little sense of global variety, they exaggerate their current decline; with little sense of their plurality, they downplay inter-national relations. In all four spheres of 'threat' we must distinguish: (a) differential impacts on different types of state in different regions; (b) trends weakening *and* some trends strengthening nation-states; (c) trends displacing national regulation to inter-national as well as to transnational networks; (d) trends simultaneously strengthening nation-states *and* transnationalism.

I have hazarded some generalizations. Capitalist transformation seems to be somewhat weakening the most advanced nation-states of the north yet successful economic development would strengthen nation-states elsewhere. The decline of militarism and 'hard geopolitics' in the north weakens its traditional nation-state core there. Yet the first three supposed 'threats' should actually intensify and make more dense the inter-national networks of 'soft geopolitics'. And identity politics may (contrary to most views) actually strengthen nation-states. These patterns are too varied and contradictory, and the future too murky, to permit us to argue simply that the nation-state and the nation-state system are *either* strengthening *or* weakening. It seems rather that (despite some postmodernists), as the world becomes more integrated, it is *local* interaction networks that continue to decline – though the fragmentation of some presently existing states into smaller ethnically defined states would be something of a counter-trend, i.e. the reduction of the nation-state to a more local level.

Global interaction networks are indeed strengthening. But they entwine three main elements. First, part of their force derives from the more global scale of transnational relations originating principally from the technology and social relations of capitalism. But these do not have the power to impose a singular universalism on global networks. Thus, second, global networks are also modestly segmented by the particularities of nation-states, especially the more powerful ones of the north. Third, that segmentation is mediated by inter-national relations. These include some 'hard' politics, and if these turned again to major wars or international tensions, then segmentation would actually increase. Yet at present the expansion of 'soft' geopolitics is more striking, and this is rather more congenial to transnationalism. Is this a single 'global society'? Not in the strongest sense often implied by the more enthusiastic theorists. These global networks contain no singular, relatively systemic principle of interaction or integration. My own view of 'society' is less demanding, since I conceive of human societies as always formed of multiple, overlapping and intersecting networks of interaction. Globalism is unlikely to change this. Human interaction networks are now penetrating the globe, but in multiple, variable and uneven fashion.

## References

Mann, M. (1986) *From the Beginning to* AD *1760*, vol. 1 of *The Sources of Social Power*. Cambridge: Cambridge University Press.

Mann, M. (1993) *The Rise of Classes and Nation-States*, vol. 2 of *The Sources of Social Power*. Cambridge: Cambridge University Press.

Shaw, M. (1997) The state of globalization: towards a theory of state transformation. *Review of International Political Economy* 4(3) (Autumn).

Wade, R. (1990) *Governing the Market: Economic Theory and the Rise of the Market in East Asian Industrialization*. Princeton: Princeton University Press.

Weiss, L. (1995) Governed interdependence: rethinking the government–business relationship in East Asia. *Pacific Review* 8.

Weiss, L. and Hobson, J. (1995) *States and Economic Development: A Comparative Historical Analysis*. Cambridge: Polity Press.

# 13

# Sovereignty in International Society

## *Robert O. Keohane*

[ . . . ] [A]ny coherent attempt to understand contemporary international relations must include an analysis of the impact of two factors: long-term tendencies toward globalization – the intensification of transnational as well as interstate relations – and the more immediate effects of the end of the Cold War and the collapse of the Soviet Union. For the United States, accustomed to being both relatively autonomous and a leader of a "free world" coalition, both of these changes have immediate impact. Indeed, the very concept of world leadership is up for grabs as it has not been since World War II. [ . . . ] I do not expect the end of the Cold War to lead to a new world order, which President George Bush sought to celebrate in 1991. Voltaire is reputed to have said that the Holy Roman Empire was neither holy, nor Roman, nor an empire, and one could say about the new world order that it is neither new, nor global in scope, nor an order. A focus on the effects of the end of the Cold War, and of globalization [ . . . ] is more fruitful.

As a result of the end of the Cold War, the United States is likely to reduce its global ambitions and be disinclined to enter into new alliances, although US policymakers will continue to seek to enhance the role of NATO and US leadership in it. US economic rivalry with former Cold War allies will no longer be muted by the need to remain united in the face of a Soviet threat, as Joanne Gowa anticipated on theoretical grounds before the end of the Cold War.[1] Severe competitive pressures on major US corporations, resulting both from the rapidity of technological change and from globalization, are combining with anxiety about rapid increases in Japanese (and more generally, East Asian) economic capabilities relative to those of the United States to increase policymakers' concern about the competitive position of the United States in the world economy. Economic strength is ultimately the basis for economic and military power, and the United States can no longer take its economic preponderance for granted. US domestic policies will increasingly be oriented toward maintaining competitiveness in the world economy, which in turn requires technological leadership and may also involve further attempts to organize a trade and investment bloc, as in the North American Free Trade Agreement (NAFTA). Increasing concern in the United States about its commercial competitiveness was evident before the end of the Cold War but has been accentuated by the collapse of the Soviet Union. The Soviet collapse reduces both the US need for allies against another superpower and the incentive for US commercial rivals to defer to US leadership.

During the early years of the Cold War, world politics was unusually hierarchical in structure. The United States was to a remarkable degree economically and militarily self-sufficient: at least for some time, it could have managed to be quite autarchic. However, US policymakers viewed autarchy as unattractive, since it would have forced the United States to forgo the economic benefits of foreign trade and investment, and it could have led to the creation of a coalition against the United States that included the potential power centers of China, Japan, and Western Europe. The impact of autarchy on US political institutions, Assistant Secretary of State Dean Acheson told Congress in 1945, would be severe: "If you wish to control the entire trade and income of the United States, which means the life of the people, you could probably fix it so that everything produced here would be consumed here, but that would completely change our Constitution, our relations to property, human liberty, our very conception of law."[2]

The decision by the United States in 1945 to maintain a capitalist economy with increasing openness (measured by such indicators as trade and investment as shares of gross domestic product) has been a crucial source of the globalization – the increasingly global character of social, economic, and political transactions – that we now experience. And the outward orientation of US policy clearly owes a great deal to the Soviet challenge and the Cold War. Now that the Cold War is over, globalization continues apace and has implications for sovereignty that affect the United States as well as other capitalist democracies.

Yet globalization coexists with an older feature of world politics: states are independent entities with diverse interests and have no guarantees that other states will act benignly toward them or even keep their commitments. World politics is a "self-help system," as Kenneth N. Waltz has expressed it, in which states seek to maintain and insofar as feasible expand their power and in which they are concerned about their power relative to others as well as about their own welfare.[3] One of the earliest and most powerful expressions of these assumptions about human nature and human interactions was enunciated by Thomas Hobbes in the seventeenth century. Hobbes, who was thinking principally about domestic politics and civil strife but who referred also to international relations, developed an argument for unified sovereignty and authoritarian rule that led to what I will refer to as Hobbes's dilemma. Hobbes's dilemma encapsulates the existential tragedy that results when human institutions collapse and people expect the worst from each other, whether this occurs in Somalia, Bosnia, or the Corcyrean Revolution described by Thucydides: "Death thus ranged in every shape. . . . There was no length to which violence did not go. . . . Reckless audacity came to be considered as the courage of a loyal ally; prudent hesitation, specious cowardice; moderation was seen to be a cloak for unmanliness; ability to see all sides of a question, inaptness to act on any. . . . The cause of all these evils was the lust for power arising from greed and ambition."[4]

However, Hobbes's dilemma is not a statement of immutable fact, since it can be avoided; indeed, it can be seen as an expression of the dead end to which Hobbesian assumptions can lead. Properly appreciated, it is less an insightful key to world politics than a metaphor of the "realist trap."[5] Adopting an institutionalist perspective, I suggest that one way out of the realist trap is to explore further the concept of *sovereignty*. Sovereignty is often associated with realist thinking; and globalist writers sometimes argue that its usefulness and clarity have been diminished in the modern world.[6] In contrast, I will argue that sovereign statehood is an *institution* – a set of persistent and connected rules prescribing behavioral roles, constraining activity, and shaping expectations[7] – whose rules significantly modify the Hobbesian notion of anarchy. We can understand this institution by using a rationalistic argument: its evolution can be understood in terms of the rational interests of the elites that run powerful states, in view of the institutional constraints that they face. Our prospects for understanding the present conjuncture – globalization, the end of the Cold War, the dubious prospects for a new world order – will be enhanced if we understand the nature of sovereignty.

The first section covers Hobbes's dilemma and the failure of Hobbes's solution to it and includes a brief summary of institutionalist responses at the domestic and international levels of analysis. In the section on sovereignty under conditions of high interdependence I develop an argument about how sovereignty is changing in those areas of the world characterized by "complex interdependence," areas within which multiple channels of contact exist among pluralistic societies and between which war is excluded as a means of policy.[8] In the section on zones of peace and conflict I introduce a cautionary note by arguing that we are entering a period of great diversity in world politics, with zones of conflict as well as a zone of peace, and therefore emphasizing the limits to institutionalist solutions to Hobbes's dilemma. [ . . . ]

In this chapter I do not sketch a vision of what the world should be like – if I were to do so, I would outline a Rawlsian utopia or offer a political strategy for change. Rather, as a social scientist I seek to analyze some of the actual changes in the international system from the standpoint of the United States and the institutionalist international relations theory that I have sought to develop. Rather than speculate on current events, I have sought to identify a major institution, that of sovereign statehood, and ask in light of past experience how it is changing. Hence I do not try to survey recent changes but to focus on sovereignty both as a lens through which to view the contemporary world and as a concept with implications for international relations theory. My hope is that what may appear idiosyncratic in my account will lead to some insights even if it does not command universal acceptance.

## Hobbes's Dilemma and the Institutionalist Response

We can summarize Hobbes's dilemma in two propositions:

1 *Since people are rational calculators, self-interested, seeking gain and glory, and fearful of one another, there is no security in anarchy.* Concentrated power is necessary to create order; otherwise, "the life of man [is] solitary, poor, nasty, brutish and short."[9]

2 *But precisely because people are self-interested and power-loving, unlimited power for the ruler implies a predatory, oppressive state.* Its leaders will have ex post incentives to renege on commitments; ex ante, therefore, they will find it difficult to persuade their subjects to invest for the long term, lend the state money, and otherwise create the basis for wealth and power. This is what Martin Wight calls "the Hobbesian paradox": "The classic Realist solution to the problem of anarchy is to concentrate power in the hands of a single authority and to hope that this despot will prove a partial exception to the rule that men are bad and should be regarded with distrust."[10]

Hobbes firmly grasped the authoritarian-predatory state horn of his dilemma. Partly because he regarded reason as the servant of the passions, he was pessimistic about prospects for cooperation among people not controlled by a centralized power. His solution is to establish "Leviathan," a centralized, unified state enabled "by terror . . . to form the wills of them all to peace at home and mutual aid against their enemies abroad."[11] Yet Hobbes's solution to the problem of domestic anarchy reproduces his dilemma at the international level: *The Hobbesian solution creates a "war of all against all."* Sovereigns, "because of their independency, are in continual jealousies and in the state and posture of gladiators."[12] Under neither general anarchy nor the Hobbesian solution to it can international trade or other forms of economic exchange flourish: property rights are in both circumstances too precarious.

For Hobbes, the fact that war is reproduced at the international level is not debilitating, since by fighting each other the sovereigns "uphold the industry of their subjects." That is, the gains from international economic exchange that are blocked by warfare are dwarfed by the gains from internal economic exchange; and the "hard shell" of the nation-state, described over 30 years ago by John Herz, protects subjects from most direct depredations of international war.[13] Since it is not necessary to overcome anarchy at the international level, the contradiction inherent in the Hobbesian paradox does not pose the problems for Hobbes's approach to international relations that it poses for his solution to problems of domestic anarchy.

In much realist thought Hobbes's international solution has been reified as if it were an essential quality of the world. Yet by his own argument about the consequences of anarchy, its implications seem morally unacceptable. Only the ad hoc assumption that rulers can protect their subjects appears superficially to save his solution from condemnation by his own argument. Even in the seventeenth century, the Hobbesian external solution – anarchy tempered by the ability to defend territory – only worked for island countries such as England. The Thirty Years' War devastated much of Germany, killing a large portion of the population; the population of the state of Württemberg fell from 450,000 in 1620 to under 100,000 in 1639, and the great powers are estimated to have suffered 2,000,000 battle deaths.[14] If the result of accepting realist pessimism is inevitable military conflict among the great powers, locked into a mutually destructive competition from which they cannot escape, then rather than celebrating our awareness of tragedy, we had better look for a way out of the realist trap.

Both of Hobbes's solutions to his dilemma are deficient. Indeed, their deficiencies stem from the same cause: the lack of attention to how institutions can profoundly affect self-interested action by changing constraints and incentives. Institutions are not a substitute for self-interest, but they shape self-interest, both domestically and internationally.[15]

[ . . . ]

## Institutions: Constitutional Government and Sovereignty

The historically successful answer to Hobbes's dilemma at the internal level – constitutional government – is very different from that proposed by Hobbes. Liberal thinkers have sought to resolve Hobbes's dilemma by building reliable representative institutions, with checks on the power of rulers, hence avoiding the dilemma of accepting either anarchy or a "predatory state."[16] These institutions presuppose the establishment of a monopoly of force within a given territory; hence the emphasis of realist international relations theory on the role of state power helps to explain their existence. However, regardless of institutions' dependence on state power, liberal insights are in my view important for understanding contemporary world politics. Changes in the nature of states profoundly affect international relations, and although world politics falls short of the normative standards of liberalism, it is more highly institutionalized than realists think.

For liberals, constitutional government must be combined with a framework of stable property rights that permit markets to operate in which individual incentives and social welfare are aligned with one another.

> Individuals must be lured by incentives to undertake the socially desirable activities [that constitute economic growth]. Some mechanism must be devised to bring social and private rates of return into closer parity.... A discrepancy between private and social benefits or costs means that some third party or parties, without their consent, will receive some of the benefits or incur some of the costs. Such a difference occurs when property rights are poorly defined, or are not enforced. If the private costs exceed the private benefits, individuals ordinarily will not be willing to undertake the activity even though it is socially profitable.[17]

The political argument of constitutionalism is familiar: constitutionalism is to constrain the ruler, thus creating order without arbitrariness or predation. Economically, constitutional government created institutions that could make sovereigns' promises credible, thereby reducing uncertainty, facilitating the operation of markets, and lowering interest rates for loans to sovereigns, thus directly creating power resources for states with constitutional governments.[18] Constitutionalism involved a modification of the traditional conception of sovereignty, dating to the thought of Jean Bodin and reflected in that of Hobbes. This conception linked sovereignty to will, "the idea that there is a final and absolute authority in the political community."[19] This notion, however, was challenged by theorists such as Locke and Montesquieu, whose ideas were developed and applied by the American revolutionaries. The debates between 1763 and 1775 in the American colonies over relations with Britain "brought into question the entire concept of a unitary, concentrated, and absolute governmental sovereignty."[20] As James Madison put it in a letter of 1787 to Thomas Jefferson: "The great desideratum of Government is, so to modify the sovereignty as that it may be sufficiently neutral between different parts of the Society to control one part from invading the rights of another, and at the same time sufficiently controuled itself, from setting up an interest adverse to that of the entire Society."[21] Thus internal sovereignty became pluralized and constitutionalized in liberal polities.

Externally, Hobbes's dilemma of internal anarchy versus international anarchy was traditionally dealt with, if not resolved, by the institution of sovereignty. Internationally, formal sovereignty can be defined, as Hans J. Morgenthau did, as "the supreme legal authority of the nation to give and enforce the law within a certain territory and, in consequence, independence from the authority of any other nation and equality with it under international law."[22] This doctrine is traditionally seen as an outcome of the Peace of Westphalia, although Stephen Krasner has recently argued convincingly that this "Westphalian system" was not inherent in the treaties signed in 1648.[23] As Martin Wight and the English school of international relations have shown, the function of the concept of sovereignty changed over time: "It began as a theory to justify the king being master in his new modern kingdom, absolute internally. Only subsequently was it turned outward to become the justification of equality of such sovereigns in the international community."[24] By the eighteenth and nineteenth centuries, as Hedley Bull explains, the conception of sovereignty as reflecting equality and reciprocity had become the core principle of international society. The exchange of recognition of sovereignty had become "a basic rule of coexistence within the states system," from which could be derived corollaries such as the rule of nonintervention and the rights of states to domestic jurisdiction.[25]

This is not to imply that rulers were either altruistic or that they followed norms of international society that were in conflict with their conceptions of self-interest. On the contrary, I assume that self-interest, defined in the traditional terms of maintenance of rule, extension of power, and appropriation of wealth, constitutes the best explanatory principle for rulers' behavior. However, the institution of sovereignty served their interests by restraining intervention. Intervention naturally led to attempts to foster disunion and civil war and therefore reduced the power of monarchs vis-à-vis civil society. Hence, agreement on principles of nonintervention represented a cartel-type solution to a problem of collective action: in specific situations, the dominant strategy was to intervene, but it made sense to refrain *conditional on others' restraint.* With respect to intervention, as well as logically, sovereignty and reciprocity were closely linked. Traditional sovereign statehood was an international institution prescribing fairly clear rules of behavior. Indeed, between the late seventeenth and the mid-twentieth centuries it was the central institution of international society, and it continues to be so in much of the world. It is true that world politics was "anarchic" in the specific sense that it lacked common government and states had to rely on their own strategies and resources, rather than outside authority, to maintain their status and even, in extreme situations, their existence. But this "anarchy" was institutionalized by general acceptance of the norm of sovereignty. To infer from the lack of common government that the classical Western state system lacked accepted norms and practices is to caricature reality and to ignore what Bull and Wight referred to as international society.[26]

International institutions include organizations, formal rules (regimes), and informal conventions. The broad institutional issue to which traditional sovereignty was an appropriate response is how to preserve and extend order without having such severe demands placed on the institutions that they either collapse or produce more disorder. The key question is how well a set of institutions is adapted to underlying conditions, especially the nature and interests of the interacting units. The Westphalian system was well adapted, since the essential principle of sovereignty was consistent with the demand for freedom of action by states, relatively low levels of interdependence, and the desire of rulers to limit intervention that could jeopardize their control over their populations. As reductions in the cost of transportation increased the potential benefits from international trade, adaptations in the institution of sovereign statehood were made to permit powerful states to capture these gains. Colonialism enabled European states to capture such gains in the nineteenth century, but it was premised on the assumptions that intraimperial gains from trade would outweigh losses from interimperial barriers; that resistance by colonized peoples would be minimal; and that colonialism would retain legitimacy in the metropoles. By 1945 all of these premises were being challenged, not least in the United States. Oceanic hegemony, established first by Britain, then by the United States, constituted another response to the need for a set of enforceable rules to control opportunism, but it proved to be vulnerable to the consequences of its own success: the rapid growth of other countries and their resistance to hegemonic dominance. Yet as noted earlier, the restoration of traditional sovereignty would not create the basis for large-scale economic exchange under conditions of high interdependence. Fundamental contracting problems among sovereign states therefore generate a demand for international regimes: sets of formal and informal rules that facilitate cooperation among states.[27] Such regimes can facilitate mutually beneficial agreements – even though they fall far short of instituting rules that can guarantee the ex ante credibility of commitments.

## Sovereignty under Conditions of High Interdependence

To judge from renewed debates about the concept, traditional notions of sovereignty seem to be undergoing quite dramatic change. On issues as diverse as ratification of the Maastricht Treaty for European integration and the role of the United Nations in Iraq, sovereignty has once again become a contested concept.

One way of thinking about this process has been articulated eloquently by Alexander Wendt, who puts forward the hypothesis that interactions among states are changing their concepts of identity and their fundamental interests. States will "internalize sovereignty norms," and this process of socialization will teach them that "they can afford to rely more on the institutional fabric of international society and less on individual national means" to achieve their objectives.[28] Georg Sørensen sees this process of socialization as breaking the neorealists' automatic link between anarchy and self-help.[29]

Wendt himself has modestly and perceptively acknowledged that the force of his argument depends on "how important interaction among states is for the constitution of their identities and interests."[30] Furthermore, for rational leaders to rely more on international institutions to maintain their interests, these institutions need to be relatively autonomous – that is, not easily manipulated by other states. Yet evidence seems plentiful that in contemporary pluralistic democracies, state interests reflect the views of dominant *domestic* coalitions, which are constituted increasingly on the basis of common interests with respect to the world political economy.[31] And the history of the European Community – the most fully elaborated and authoritative multilateral institution in modern history – demonstrates that states continue to use international institutions to achieve their own interests, even at the expense of their partners.

At a more basic theoretical level, no one has yet convincingly traced the micro-foundations of a socialization argument: how and why those individuals with influence over state policy would eschew the use of the state as agent for their specific interests in order to enable it to conform to norms that some self-constituted authorities proclaimed to be valid. The only major attempt in recent centuries to found an international institution on untested belief – the League of Nations – was a tragic failure. The League could only have succeeded if governments had genuinely believed that peace was indivisible and that this belief was shared sufficiently by others that it would be safe to rely "on the institutional fabric of international society." But in fact, that belief was not shared by key elites, and in light of long experience with the weakness of international institutions, it is hard to blame them.[32] Idealists hope to transmute positive beliefs into reality; but the conditions for the success of this strategy are daunting indeed.

Despite the wishful thinking that seems to creep into idealistic institutionalism, its proponents usefully remind us that sovereign statehood is an institution whose meaning is not fixed but has indeed changed over time. And they have shown convincingly that sovereignty has never been simply a reflection, at the level of the state, of international anarchy, despite Kenneth Waltz's definition, which equates sovereignty with autonomy.[33] If idealistic institutionalism does not provide an answer to questions about the evolution of sovereignty, it certainly helps open the door to a discussion of these issues.

I propose a rational-institutionalist interpretation of changes in sovereignty. Just as cooperation sometimes emerges from discord, so may intensified conflict under conditions of interdependence fundamentally affect the concept of sovereignty and its functions. The concept of sovereignty that emerges, however, may be very different in different parts of the world: no linear notion of progress seems applicable here. In this section I will just sketch the argument for changes in sovereignty under conditions of complex interdependence.

Sovereignty has been most thoroughly transformed in the European Community (EC). The legal supremacy of community over national law makes the EC fundamentally different, in juridical terms, from other international organizations. Although national governments dominate the decisionmaking process in Europe, they do so within an institutional context involving the pooling and sharing of sovereignty, and in conjunction with a commission that has a certain degree of independence. As in the United States, it is difficult to identify "the sovereign institution" in the European Community: there is no single institutional expression of the EC's will. Yet unlike in the United States, the constituent parts retain the right to veto amendments to the constitutional document (in the EC case the Treaty of Rome), and there is little doubt that secession from the community would not be resisted by force. So the European Community is not by any means a sovereign state, although it is an unprecedented hybrid, for which the traditional conception of sovereignty is no longer applicable.[34]

Interdependence is characterized by continual discord within and between countries, since the interests of individuals, groups, and firms are often at odds with one another. As global economic competition among sectors continues to increase, so will policy contention. Indeed, such discord reflects the responsiveness of democracies to constituency interests. A stateless competitive world market economy, in which people as well as factors of production could move freely, would be extremely painful for many residents of rich countries: the quasi-rents they now receive as a result of their geographical location would disappear. Matters would be even worse for people not protected by powerful governments who had to face economic agents wielding concentrated power or supported by state policy. It is not surprising, therefore, that people around the world expect protective action from their governments – and in Europe from the European Community and its institutions – and that free trade is more a liberal aspiration than a reality. In a bargaining situation, concentrating resources is valuable, and only the state can solve the collective-action problem for millions of individuals. Hence as global competition intensifies with technological change and the decline of natural barriers to exchange, public institutions are likely to be used in an increasing variety of ways to provide advantages for their constituents. In most of the world, the state is the key institution: the state is by no means dead. In Europe, supranational and intergovernmental institutions play a significant role, along with states. Economic conflict between the EC and other major states, and among states (within and outside the EC), is likely to be accentuated by the end of the Cold War, which has reduced incentives to cooperate on economic issues for the sake of political solidarity.[35]

The mixture to be expected of multilateral cooperation and tough interstate bargaining is exemplified by recent patterns in international trade. During the 1980s the GATT dispute-settlement procedure was more actively employed than ever in the past; and it frequently led to the settlement of trade issues.[36] Furthermore, the Uruguay Round of GATT will subject many service sectors and agriculture to multilateral regulation to which they have not been subject previously and should thus lead to substantial liberalization of world trade. However, bilateralism appears to have grown during the 1980s with the negotiation of formal bilateral agreements by the United States as well as the maintenance of so-called voluntary export restraints and the use of bilateral agreements to resolve issues on which major countries such as the United States have taken aggressive unilateral action. Between 10 and 20 percent of OECD imports are subject to nontariff measures; in some sectors such as textiles the figures approach 50 percent. In December 1993 the Uruguay Round GATT negotiations were brought to a successful conclusion after having continued for almost three years beyond their original deadline of December 1990. But we simultaneously observe increases in globalization and in mercantilist policy.[37] Yet I expect that the OECD democracies will continue to have sufficient interest in securing the benefits of the international division of labor such that full-scale economic warfare, much less military conflict, will remain unlikely.

Under these conditions of complex interdependence, and even outside of the institutions of the EC, the meaning of sovereignty changes. Sovereignty no longer enables states to exert effective supremacy over what occurs within their territories: decisions are made by firms on a global basis, and other states' policies have major impacts within one's own boundaries. Reversing this process would be catastrophic for investment, economic growth, and electoral success. What sovereignty does confer on states under conditions of complex interdependence is legal authority that can either be exercised to the detriment of other states' interests or be bargained away in return for influence over others' policies and therefore greater gains from exchange. Rather than connoting the exercise of supremacy within a given territory, sovereignty provides the state with a legal grip on an aspect of a transnational process, whether involving multinational investment, the world's ecology, or the movement of migrants, drug dealers, and terrorists. *Sovereignty is less a territorially defined barrier than a bargaining resource for a politics characterized by complex transnational networks.* Although this shift in the function of sovereignty is a result of interdependence, it does not necessarily reduce discord, since there are more bargaining issues between states that are linked by multiple channels of contact than between those with barriers between them. Such discord takes place within a context from which military threats are excluded as a policy option, but distributional bargaining is tough and continuous.

I suggest, therefore, that within the OECD area the principle and practice of sovereignty are being modified quite dramatically in response to changes in international interdependence and the character of international institutions. In the European Community the relevant changes in international institutions have a juridical dimension; indeed, one implication of European Community law is that bargaining away sovereignty to the EC may be effectively irreversible, since the EC takes over the authority formerly reserved to states. In other parts of the OECD area, states accept limits on their formerly sovereign authority as a result of agreeing to multilateral regimes with less organizational or legal authority than the EC; and sovereignty may therefore be easier to recapture, albeit at a cost, in the future. In the aspiring democracies of Eastern Europe, some of my colleagues have recently observed a pattern of "anticipatory adaptation," by which one of these countries unilaterally adopts "norms associated with membership in an [international] organization prior to its actually being accorded full status in that organization."[38] We can understand the pattern of often conflictual cooperation among the economically advanced democracies as one of "cooperation under anarchy" if we are very careful about what anarchy means, but it may be more useful to see it as a question of institutional change.[39] The institution of sovereign statehood, which was well adapted for the Westphalian system, is being modified, although not superseded, in response to the interests of participants in a rapidly internationalizing political economy.

## Zones of Peace and Conflict: A Partially Hobbesian World

Unfortunately, the institutionalist solution to Hobbes's dilemma is difficult to implement both domestically and internationally.
[ . . . ]
   What seems [ . . . ] likely is that domestic and international political institutions will remain highly varied in form, strength, and function in different parts of the world. The OECD area, or much of it, will remain characterized by complex interdependence. Nationalism may be strengthened in some countries but will not threaten the status of the OECD area as a zone of peace in which pluralistic conflict management is successfully institutionalized. International regimes will continue to provide networks of rules for the management of both interstate and transnational relationships, although increased economic competition is likely to both limit the growth of these regimes and provide grounds for sharp disagreements about how their rules should be applied. The domestic institutional basis for these regimes will be provided by the maintenance of pluralist, constitutional democracies that will not fight each other, whose governments are not monolithic, and between which there is sufficient confidence that agreements can be made.[40] As argued in the previous section, sovereignty is likely, in these areas, to serve less as a justification of centralized territorial control and a barrier to intervention and more as a bargaining tool for influence over transnational networks. It will be bargained away in somewhat different ways within different contexts involving security, economic issues, arrangements for political authority, and cultural linkages among countries.[41]

   In other parts of the world complex interdependence will not necessarily prevail. Some of these areas may be moving toward a situation in which force is not employed and in which the domestic conditions for democracy are emerging: this seems to be true in much of East Asia and Latin America. In others relatively stable patterns of authoritarian rule may emerge or persist. For much of the developing world, therefore, some shift toward sovereignty as a bargaining resource in transnational networks will be observable. For instance, the developing countries were able to use their ability to withhold consent to the Montreal Protocol on depletion of the ozone layer to secure a small fund to facilitate the transition to production of less harmful substitutes for chlorofluorocarbons (CFCs).[42]

   In much of the former Soviet Union and in parts of Africa, the Middle East, and Asia, however, neither domestic institutions nor prospects of economic gain are likely to provide sufficient incentives for international cooperation. In these zones of conflict, military conflict will be common. The loyalties of populations of states may be divided, as in Bosnia, along ethnic or national lines, and no state may command legitimacy. Secessionist movements may prompt intervention from abroad, as in Georgia. Governments of neighboring countries may regard shifts of power in nearby states as threatening to them and be prompted therefore to intervene to prevent these changes. New balances of power and alliances, offensive as well as defensive, may emerge in a classic and often bloody search for power and order. Since traditional security risks – involving fears of cross-border attacks, civil wars, and intervention – will remain paramount, sovereignty will remain highly territorial and the evolution toward sovereignty as a bargaining resource in transnational relations that is taking place in the OECD area will be retarded. Intervention and chaos may even ensue.[43]

We do not know precisely which regions, much less countries, will be characterized by endemic strife. On the basis of past conflict or ethnic division, the Middle East, much of Africa, the southern tier of the former Soviet Union, and parts of South Asia would seem to be in the greatest danger.
[ . . . ]

# Conclusion

Globalization and the end of the Cold War have created a new situation in world politics. In some ways, the new world is more like traditional world politics than was the world from 1945 to the mid-1980s: political alignments will become more fragmented and fluid, and economic competition will not be muted by alliance cooperation. In other respects, however, the new world will be very different from the world before World War II. Globalization seems irreversible with all its implications for the permeability of borders and the transformation of sovereignty among the economically advanced democracies; and international institutions have become central to the political and military as well as the economic policies of the major states.[44]

Yet Hobbes's dilemma cannot be ignored. Without well-developed constitutional institutions, the alternatives in many countries lie between anarchy and predation, neither of which is attractive. The extensive patterns of agreement characteristic of complex interdependence depend on pluralist democratic institutions. Less ambitious forms of world order, relatively peaceful but not necessarily so cooperative, depend on stable domestic institutions, although whether they depend on democracy is not yet entirely clear. At any rate, predatory authoritarian states are likely to become involved in international conflict, and intensely divided states are particularly prone to do so. The latter are likely targets for intervention by the former. It seems unlikely not only that democracy will sweep the world but also that all states will be governed by stable institutions, even authoritarian ones. Hence "world order" does not seem to be impending: a global security community is unlikely soon to come into existence.
[ . . . ]

The key problem of world order now is to seek to devise institutional arrangements that are consistent both with key features of international relations and the new shape of domestic politics in key countries. It will be very difficult to construct such institutions. They must be built not only by governments but by international civil society under conditions of globalization. They must be constructed not by a single hegemonic power but by several countries whose interests conflict in multiple ways. Nevertheless, among advanced democracies appropriate institutions could facilitate political and economic exchange by reducing transaction costs, providing information, and making commitments credible. The resulting benefits will accrue not only to governments but to transnational corporations and professional societies, and to some workers as well, in both developing and developed countries. But adjustment costs will be high, hence there will be losers in the short run; there may also be long-run losers, since globalization will continue to put downward pressure on wages for those workers in developed countries who can be replaced by workers in poorer parts of the world or who compete in national labor markets with such workers. Hence domestic institutions that provide retraining, that spread the costs of adjustment, and perhaps that redistribute income on a continuing basis to globally disadvantaged groups will be essential corollaries to maintaining and strengthening international institutions in an age of globalization.

[ … ]

Social scientists viewing the new world order should be humble on two dimensions. Our failure to foresee the end of the Cold War should make us diffident about our ability to predict the future. And the weakness of our knowledge of the conditions for constitutional democracy and for peace should make us reluctant to propose radical new plans for global democratization or peacekeeping. Nevertheless, we can go beyond the Hobbesian solution to Hobbes's dilemma of anarchy and order: we can focus on how institutions embodying the proper incentives can create order without predation within societies, and how even much weaker international institutions can moderate violence and facilitate cooperation in international relations. Strong institutions cannot be suddenly created: both constitutional democracy and a reciprocity-laden conception of sovereignty emerged over a period of centuries. Nevertheless, it is imperative to avoid the magnitude of violence and dysfunction that occurred in the West. We should encourage the creation and maintenance of institutions, domestic and international, that provide incentives for the moderation of conflict, coherent decisionmaking to provide collective goods, and the promotion of economic growth. It is in such lasting institutions that our hopes for the future lie.

## Notes

1   Joanne Gowa, "Bipolarity, Multipolarity and Free Trade," *American Political Science Review* 83(4) (Dec. 1989): 1245–56.
2   US House Special Committee on Post-War Economic Policy and Planning, *Hearings* (Washington DC: GPO, 1945), p. 1082. Cited in Gabriel Kolko, *The Politics of War: The World and United States Foreign Policy, 1943–1945* (New York: Vintage Books of Random House, 1968), p. 254.
3   Kenneth N. Waltz, *Theory of International Politics* (Reading, Mass.: Addison Wesley, 1979).
4   Thucydides, *The Peloponnesian War*, Book 3, paras 81–2.
5   On the "realist trap," see Robert O. Keohane, "Theory of World Politics: Structural Realism and Beyond," in Keohane, *International Institutions and State Power: Essays in International Relations Theory* (Boulder: Westview Press, 1989), pp. 35–73, esp. pp. 65–6.
6   Hans-Henrik Holm and Georg Sørensen, "A New World Order: The Withering Away of Anarchy and the Triumph of Individualism? Consequences for IR-Theory," *Cooperation and Conflict* 28(3) (1993): 265–301.
7   For this definition, see Keohane, *International Institutions and State Power*, pp. 3–7 and ch. 7.

8   Robert O. Keohane and Joseph S. Nye, Jr, *Power and Interdependence: World Politics in Transition* (Boston: Little, Brown, 1977 and 1989).

9   Thomas Hobbes, *Leviathan* (Paris, 1651), Book 1, ch. 13.

10  Martin Wight, *International Theory: The Three Traditions* (New York: Holmes & Meier, 1992), p. 35.

11  *Leviathan*, part 2, ch. 17.

12  *Leviathan*, part 1, ch. 13.

13  John M. Herz, *International Politics in the Atomic Age* (New York: Columbia University Press, 1959).

14  Evan Luard, *War in International Society* (New Haven: Yale University Press, 1987), p. 247, says that perhaps 40 percent of the rural and town population of Germany may have died, although this estimate may be too high. On battle deaths, see Charles Tilly, *Coercion, Capital and European States, AD 990–1990* (Oxford: Blackwell, 1990), p. 165.

15  Sovereign statehood in my view has helped shape states' conceptions of self-interest. For instance, great-power intervention in Africa during the Cold War was focused on helping the great power's clients gain power within unified states, rather than on promoting fragmentation. The one major attempt to change boundaries by war – Somalia's invasion of Ethiopia in the late 1970s – led to withdrawal of US support for Somalian military actions and a resounding defeat. For an astute analysis, see Robert H. Jackson and Carl G. Rosberg, "Why Africa's Weak States Persist: The Empirical and the Juridical in Statehood," *World Politics* 35(1) (Oct. 1982): 1–24.

16  See Margaret Levi, *Of Rule and Revenue* (Berkeley: University of California Press, 1988), esp. ch. 1.

17  Douglass C. North and Robert Paul Thomas, *The Rise of the Western World* (Cambridge: Cambridge University Press, 1973), pp. 2–3.

18  Charles P. Kindleberger, *A Financial History of Western Europe* (London: Allen and Unwin, 1984); Douglass C. North and Barry R. Weingast, "Constitutions and Commitment: The Evolution of Institutions Governing Public Choice in Seventeenth-Century England," *Journal of Economic History* 49(4) (Dec. 1989): 803–32.

19  F. H. Hinsley, *Sovereignty*, 2nd edn (Cambridge: Cambridge University Press, 1986), p. 1.

20  Bernard Bailyn, *The Ideological Origins of the American Revolution* (Cambridge: Belknap Press of Harvard University Press, 1967), pp. 201–29.

21  Madison to Jefferson, October 24, 1787, J. P. Boyd (ed.), *The Papers of Thomas Jefferson* (Princeton: Princeton University Press, 1955), pp. 278–9.

22  Hans J. Morgenthau, *Politics among Nations*, 4th edn (New York: Knopf, 1967), p. 305.

23  Stephen D. Krasner, "Westphalia and All That," draft chapter (Oct. 1992) for Judith Goldstein and Robert O. Keohane (eds), *Ideas and Foreign Policy: Beliefs, Institutions and Political Change* (Ithaca: Cornell University Press, 1993).

24  Wight, *International Theory*, pp. 2–3.

25  Hedley Bull, *The Anarchical Society* (New York: Columbia University Press, 1977), pp. 34–7. Martin Wight makes this connection between sovereignty and reciprocity explicit by saying that "reciprocity was inherent in the Western conception of sovereignty." *Systems of States* (Leicester: Leicester University Press, 1977), p. 135.

26  One difficulty with realist characterizations of anarchy is that they conflate three different meanings of the terms: (1) lack of common government; (2) insignificance of institutions; and (3) chaos, or Hobbes's "war of all against all." Only the first meaning can be shown to be true in general of international relations. For a good discussion of anarchy in international relations, see Helen V. Milner, "The Assumption of Anarchy in International Relations Theory: A Critique," *Review of International Studies* 17(1) (Jan. 1991): 67–86.

27  Robert O. Keohane, *After Hegemony: Cooperation and Discord in the World Political Economy* (Princeton: Princeton University Press, 1984); Stephen D. Krasner (ed.), *International*

*Regimes* (Ithaca: Cornell University Press, 1982). Note that a demand for international regimes does not create its own supply; hence a functional theory does not imply, incorrectly, that efficient institutions always emerge or that we live in the (institutionally) best of all possible worlds.

28  Alexander Wendt, "Anarchy Is What States Make of It," *International Organization* 46(2) (Spring 1992): 414–15.

29  Georg Sørensen, "The Limits of Neorealism: Western Europe after the Cold War," paper presented at the Nordic International Studies Association (NISA) Inaugural Conference, Oslo, Aug. 18–19, 1993, p. 9.

30  Wendt, "Anarchy Is What States Make of It," p. 423.

31  Peter J. Katzenstein, *Small States in World Markets* (Ithaca: Cornell University Press, 1984); Peter Gourevitch, *Politics in Hard Times* (Ithaca: Cornell University Press, 1986); Helen V. Milner, *Resisting Protectionism* (Princeton: Princeton University Press, 1988); Ronald Rogowski, *Commerce and Coalitions* (Princeton: Princeton University Press, 1989); Jeffry A. Frieden, "National Economic Policies in a World of Global Finance," *International Organization* 45(4) (Autumn 1991): 425–52; Andrew Moravcsik, "Liberalism and International Relations Theory," Working Paper, no. 92–6, Center for International Affairs, Harvard University, Oct. 1992.

32  See Inis L. Claude, *Power and International Relations* (New York: Random House, 1962).

33  For Waltz a sovereign state "decides for itself how it will cope with its internal and external problems." That is, sovereignty is the equivalent of self-help, which derives from anarchy. Waltz, *Theory of International Politics*, p. 96. A brilliant critique of Waltz's failure to incorporate a historical dimension in his theory is by John Gerard Ruggie, "Continuity and Transformation in the World Polity: Toward a Neorealist Synthesis," *World Politics* 35 (Jan. 1983): 261–85. For Ruggie's chapter, other commentaries, and a reply by Waltz, see Robert O. Keohane (ed.), *Neorealism and its Critics* (New York: Columbia University Press, 1986).

34  For general discussions see Robert O. Keohane and Stanley Hoffmann, *The New European Community: Decisionmaking and Institutional Change* (Boulder: Westview Press, 1991); and Alberta M. Sbragia (ed.), *Europolitics: Institutions and Policymaking in the "New" European Community* (Washington DC: Brookings, 1992). On the European Court of Justice and neofunctional theory, see Anne-Marie Burley and Walter Mattli, "Europe Before the Court: A Political Theory of Legal Integration," *International Organization* 47(1) (Winter 1993): 41–76. It is not clear that the Maastricht Treaty, even if ratified, will fundamentally alter practices relating to sovereignty in the EC. On Maastricht, see Wayne Sandholtz, "Choosing Union: Monetary Politics and Maastricht," *International Organization* 47(1) (Winter 1993): 1–40.

35  For a general argument about the "security externalities" of agreements to open borders to free trade, see Gowa, "Bipolarity, Multipolarity and Free Trade."

36  Robert E. Hudec, Daniel L. M. Kennedy, and Mark Sgarabossa, "A Statistical Profile of GATT Dispute Settlement Cases: 1948–1990," MS, University of Minnesota Law School, 1992.

37  See Helge Hveem, "Hegemonic Rivalry and Antagonistic Interdependence: Bilateralism and the Management of International Trade," paper presented at the First Pan-European Conference in International Studies, Heidelberg, Sept. 16–20, 1992. His figures come from the UNCTAD database on trade control measures. On p. 16 Hveem quotes Robert Gilpin about the "complementary development" of globalization and mercantilism, citing "The Transformation of the International Political Economy," *Jean Monnet Chair Papers* (European Policy Unit at the European University Institute, Firenze).

38  Stephan Haggard, Marc A. Levy, Andrew Moravcsik, and Kalypso Nicolaides, "Integrating the Two Halves of Europe: Theories of Interests, Bargaining and Institutions," in Robert O. Keohane, Joseph S. Nye, and Stanley Hoffmann (eds), *After the Cold War:*

*International Institutions and State Strategies in Europe, 1989–1991* (Cambridge, Mass.: Harvard University Press, 1993), p. 182.

39  Kenneth A. Oye (ed.), *Cooperation under Anarchy* (Princeton: Princeton University Press, 1986).

40  Democratic pluralism is necessary for the multiple channels of contact between societies characteristic of complex interdependence. With respect to restraints on the use of force, it seems clear from the large literature on democracy and war that democracies have rarely, if ever (depending on one's definition), fought one another, although they vigorously fight nondemocracies. However, nondemocracies have often been at peace with one another, so democracy is certainly not necessary to peace. Furthermore, until recently democracies have been relatively few and either scattered or allied against a common enemy (or both); so the empirical evidence for the causal impact of mutual democracy is weak. Among the OECD countries peace seems ensured by a combination of mutual economic and political interests, lack of territorial conflict, and mutual democracy. On theoretical grounds, however, no one has yet succeeded in showing that mutual democracy is sufficient: to do so, one would have to develop and test a convincing theory of why democracies should not fight one another. For some of this literature, see Michael Doyle, "Kant, Liberal Legacies and Foreign Affairs," *Philosophy and Public Affairs* 12 (1983): 205–35 and 323–53 (two-part article); Zeev Maos and Nasrin Abdolali, "Regime Types and International Conflict," *Journal of Conflict Resolution* 33 (1989): 3–35; and Georg Sørensen, "Kant and Processes of Democratization: Consequences for Neorealist Thought," *Journal of Peace Research* 29 (1992): 397–414. My thinking on this issue has been affected by a stimulating talk given at the Harvard Center for International Affairs by Professor Joanne Gowa of Princeton University on May 6, 1993, and by a just-completed Ph.D. dissertation at Harvard University by John Owen on sources of "democratic peace."

41  My characterization of emerging patterns of world politics has much in common with the stimulating discussion of "plurilateralism" offered by Philip G. Cerny in "Plurilateralism: Structural Differentiation and Functional Conflict in the Post-Cold War World Order," *Millennium: Journal of International Studies* 22 (Spring 1993): 27–52.

42  Edward A. Parson, "Protecting the Ozone Layer," in Peter M. Haas, Robert O. Keohane, and Marc A. Levy (eds), *Institutions for the Earth: Sources of Effective International Environmental Protection* (Cambridge, Mass.: MIT Press, 1993), pp. 49–50.

43  For a similar argument, contrasting a liberal core and a realist periphery, see James M. Goldgeier and Michael McFaul, "A Tale of Two Worlds: Core and Periphery in the Post-Cold War Era," *International Organization* 46(1) (Spring 1992): 467–92.

44  On international institutions, see Keohane, Nye, and Hoffmann, *After the Cold War*.

# 14

# The Changing Structure of International Law: Sovereignty Transformed?

*David Held*

## Classic Sovereignty

[ . . . ]

The doctrine of sovereignty developed in two distinct dimensions: the first concerned with the "internal," the second with the "external" aspects of sovereignty. The former involves the claim that a person, or political body, established as sovereign rightly exercises the "supreme command" over a particular society. Government – whether monarchical, aristocratic, or democratic – must enjoy the "final and absolute authority" within a given territory. The latter involves the assertion that there is no final and absolute authority above and beyond the sovereign state. States must be regarded as independent in all matters of internal politics and should in principle be free to determine their own fate within this framework. External sovereignty is a quality that political societies possess in relationship to one another; it is associated with the aspiration of a community to determine its own direction and politics without undue interference from other powers (Hinsley 1986).

The sovereign states system became entrenched in a complex of rules that evolved, from the seventeenth century, to secure the concept of an order of states as an international society of sovereign states (Bull 1977). The emergence of a "society" of states, first in Europe and later across the globe, went hand in hand with a new conception of international law that can be referred to as the "Westphalian regime" (after the peace treaties of Westphalia of 1648), but that I simply refer to as the classic regime of sovereignty. The regime covers the period of international law and regulation from 1648 to the early twentieth century (although elements of it, it can be argued plausibly, still have application today). Not all of its features were intrinsic to the settlement of Westphalia; rather, they were formed through a normative trajectory in international law that did not receive its fullest articulation until the late eighteenth and early nineteenth centuries, when territorial sovereignty, the formal equality of states, non-intervention in the domestic affairs of other recognized states, and state consent as the basis of international legal obligation became the core principles of international society (see Crawford and Marks 1998).

The classic regime of sovereignty highlights the development of a world order in which states are nominally free and equal; enjoy supreme authority over all subjects and objects within a given territory; form separate and discrete political orders with their own interests (backed by their organization of coercive power); recognize no temporal authority superior to themselves; engage in diplomatic initiatives but otherwise in limited measures of cooperation; regard cross-border processes as a "private matter" concerning only those immediately affected; and accept the principle of effectiveness, that is, the principle that might eventually makes right in the international world – appropriation becomes legitimation (see Falk 1969; Cassese 1986, 396–9; Held 1995, p. 78).

To emphasize the development of the classic regime of sovereignty is not to deny, of course, that its reality was often messy, fraught, and compromised (see Krasner 1995, 1999). But acknowledging the complexity of the historical reality should not lead one to ignore the structural and systematic shift that took place from the late sixteenth century in the principles underlying political order, and their often bloody reality. States struggled to contain and manage people, territories, and resources – a process exemplified both by European state formation in the seventeenth and eighteenth centuries and by the rapid carving out of colonies by European powers in the nineteenth century.

Four important corollaries to the development of the classic regime of sovereignty should be emphasized. In the first instance, the crystallization of international law as interstate law conferred on heads of state or government the capacity to enter into agreements with the representatives of other states without regard to the constitutional standing of such figures; that is, without regard to whether or not heads of state were entitled by specific national legal arrangements to commit the state to particular treaty rights and duties. Second, interstate law was indifferent to the form of national political organization. It accepted "a *de facto* approach to statehood and government, an approach that followed the facts of political power and made few inquiries into how that power was established" (Crawford and Marks 1998, 72). Absolutist regimes, constitutional monarchies, authoritarian states, and liberal democratic states were all regarded as equally legitimate types of polity.

The third corollary involved the creation of a disjuncture between the organizing principles of national and international affairs. In principle and practice, the political and ethical rules governing these two spheres diverged. As liberal democratic nation-states became slowly entrenched in the West, so did a political world that tolerated democracy in nation-states and nondemocratic relations among states; the entrenchment of accountability and democratic legitimacy inside state boundaries and the pursuit of reasons of state (and maximum political advantage) outside such boundaries; democracy and citizenship rights for those regarded as "insiders" and the frequent negation of these for those beyond their borders (Held 1999, 91). The gulf between *Sichtlichkeit* and *Realpolitik* was taken for granted.

The fourth corollary to the classic regime of sovereign international law concerns the delegitimation of all those groups and nonstate actors who sought to contest territorial boundaries, with paradoxical consequences. Stripped of traditional habitats and territories by colonial powers and hegemonic interests, such groups often had no alternative but to resort to coercion or armed force in order to press their claims to secure homelands. For they too had to establish "effective control" over the area they sought as their territory if they were going to make their case for international recognition (see Baldwin 1992, 224–5).

The retreat and defeat of European empires from the late nineteenth century, the spread of democratic ideas throughout the world's regions in the twentieth century, and the establishment of new transnational and multilateral forms of organization and activity throughout the last one hundred years have altered the political and legal landscape (see Held and McGrew, Goldblatt, and Perraton 1999, chs. 1, 2). The questions are: Has a new framework of international law been established? Has the balance changed between the claims made on behalf of the states system and those made on behalf of alternative political and normative positions?

## Liberal International Sovereignty

The hold of the classic regime of sovereignty was dislodged within the boundaries of nation-states by successive waves of democratization (Potter et al. 1997). While these were primarily aimed at reshaping the national polity, they had spillover effects for the interstate system (Bull 1977). Although it was not until after the Second World War that a new model of international regulation fully crystallized, the regime of liberal international sovereignty has origins which can be traced back further. Its beginning is marked by attempts to extend the processes of delimiting public power to the international sphere and by attempts thereafter to transform the meaning of legitimate political authority from effective control to the maintenance of basic standards or values that no political agent, whether a representative of a government or state, should, in principle, be able to abrogate. Effective power is challenged by the principles of self-determination, democracy, and human rights as the proper basis of sovereignty. It is useful to highlight some of the legal transformations that have taken place – in the domains of war, war crimes, human rights, democratic participation, as well as the environment – which underlie this shift. In the main, these transformations have been ushered in with the approval and consent of states, but the delegation and changes in sovereignty have, it will be seen, acquired a status and momentum of their own.

## Rules of warfare and weaponry

The formation of the rules of warfare has been based on the presupposition that, while war cannot be completely abolished, some of its most appalling consequences, for soldiers and citizens alike, should be made illegal. The aim of these rules is to limit conduct during war to minimum standards of civilized behavior that will be upheld by all parties to an armed conflict. While the rules of warfare are, of course, often violated, they have served in the past to provide a brake on some of the more indiscriminate acts of violence. The major multilateral conventions governing war date back to the Declaration of Paris of 1856, which sought to limit sea warfare by prohibiting privateering, and to specify the conditions under which a blockade could be said to be effective with determinate legal consequences. Important milestones include the Geneva Convention of 1864 (revised in 1906), the Hague Conventions of 1899 and 1907, and the Geneva Conventions of 1929 and 1949 which, together, helped codify humane treatment for the wounded in the field, acceptable practices of land warfare, the rights and duties of the parties to a conflict and of neutral states and persons, and a plethora of rules governing the treatment of prisoners and the protection of civilians. In addition to these and other regional treaties, the behavior of belligerents is, in principle, circumscribed by elements of customary international law and by a general acknowledgment of a "law of humanity" forbidding "unwarranted cruelty or other actions affronting public morality" (Plano and Olton 1988, 193; see Byers 1999).

The rules of warfare form an evolving framework of regulations seeking to restrain the conduct of parties to an international armed conflict. The rules are premised on the "dual notion that the adverse effects of war should be alleviated as much as possible (given military necessities), and that the freedom of the parties to resort to methods and means of warfare is not unlimited" (Dinstein 1993, 966). These guiding orientations and the agreements to which they have given rise mark, in principle, a significant change over time in the legal direction of the modern state; for they challenge the principle of military autonomy and question national sovereignty at one of its most delicate points – the relation between the military and the state (what it is that each can legitimately ask of the other) and the capacity of both to pursue their objectives irrespective of the consequences.

Conventions on the conduct of war have been complemented by a series of agreements on the use of different types of weapons, from the rules governing the use of dumdum bullets (the Hague Convention, 1907) and the use of submarines against merchant ships (the Paris Protocol of 1936) to a whole range of recently negotiated agreements on conventional and nuclear, chemical, and biological weapons (see SIPRI 1999). As a result, arms control and regulation have become a permanent feature of international politics. Agencies for arms control and disarmament (or sections within foreign ministries) now exist within all the world's major states, managing what has become a continuous diplomatic and regulatory process (see Held and McGrew, Goldblatt, and Perraton 1999, 123–33). Many recent agreements, moreover, have created mechanisms of verification or commitments that intrude significantly on national sovereignty and military autonomy. For example, the 1993 Chemical Weapons Convention, a near-universal disarmament treaty, creates an international inspectorate to oversee its implementation (anxiety about which filled the U.S. Senate with complaints about "surrendered sovereignty" (Wright 2000)). Accordingly, it is not unreasonable to claim that the international laws of war and weapons control have shaped and helped nurture a global infrastructure of conflict and armaments regulation.

## War crimes and the role of the individual

The process of the gradual delimitation of state power can be illustrated further by another strand in international legal thinking that has overturned the primacy of the state in international law and buttressed the role of the individual in relation to and with responsibility for systematic violence against others. In the first instance, by recognizing the legal status of conscientious objection, many states have acknowledged there are clear occasions when an individual has a moral obligation beyond that of his or her obligation as a citizen of a state (see Vincent 1992, 269–92). The refusal to serve in national armies triggers a claim to a "higher moral court" of rights and duties. Such claims are exemplified as well in the changing legal position of those who are willing to go to war. The recognition in international law of the offenses of war crimes, genocide, and crimes against humanity makes clear that acquiescence to the commands of national leaders will not be considered sufficient grounds for absolving individual guilt in these cases. A turning point in this regard was the decisions taken by the International Tribunal at Nuremberg (and the parallel tribunal in Tokyo). The tribunal laid down, for the first time in history, that when *international rules* that protect basic humanitarian values are in conflict with *state laws*, every individual must transgress the state laws (except where there is no room for "moral choice," i.e., when a gun is being held to someone's head) (Cassese 1988, 132). Modern international law has generally endorsed the position taken by the tribunal and has affirmed its rejection of the defense of obedience to superior orders in matters of responsibility for crimes against peace and humanity. As one commentator has noted: "since the Nuremberg Trials, it has been acknowledged that war criminals cannot relieve themselves of criminal responsibility by citing official position or superior orders. Even obedience to explicit national legislation provides no protection against international law" (Dinstein 1993, 968).

The most notable recent extension of the application of the Nuremberg principles has been the establishment of the war crimes tribunals for the former Yugoslavia (established by the UN Security Council in 1993) and for Rwanda (set up in 1994) (cf. Chinkin 1998; *The Economist* 1998). The Yugoslav tribunal has issued indictments against people from all three ethnic groups in Bosnia and is investigating crimes in Kosovo, although it has encountered serious difficulty in obtaining custody of the key accused. (Significantly, of course, ex-President Slobodan Milosevic has recently been arrested and brought before The Hague war crimes tribunal.) Although neither the Rwandan tribunal nor the Yugoslav tribunal have had the ability to detain and try more than a small fraction of those engaged in atrocities, both have taken important steps toward implementing the law governing war crimes and, thereby, reducing the credibility gap between the promises of such law, on the one hand, and the weakness of its application, on the other.

Most recently, the proposals put forward for the establishment of a permanent international criminal court are designed to help close this gap in the longer term (see Crawford 1995; Dugard 1997; Weller 1997). Several major hurdles remain to its successful entrenchment, including the continuing opposition from the United States (which fears its soldiers will be the target of politically motivated prosecutions) and dependency upon individual state consent for its effectiveness (Chinkin 1998, 118–19). However, [...] the court will be formally established and will mark another significant step away from the classic regime of sovereignty and toward the firm entrenchment of the framework of liberal international sovereignty.

The ground which is being staked out now in international legal agreements suggests that the containment of armed aggression and abuses of power can be achieved only through both the control of warfare and the prevention of the abuse of human rights. For it is only too apparent that many forms of violence perpetrated against individuals and many forms of abuse of power do not take place during declared acts of war. In fact, it can be argued that the distinctions between war and peace and between aggression and repression are eroded by changing patterns of violence (Kaldor 1998a and b). The kinds of violence witnessed in Bosnia and Kosovo highlight the role of paramilitaries and of organized crime and the use of parts of national armies that may no longer be under the direct control of a state. What these kinds of violence signal is that there is a very fine line between explicit formal crimes committed during acts of war and major attacks on the welfare and physical integrity of citizens in situations that may not involve a declaration of war by states. While many of the new forms of warfare do not fall directly under the classic rules of war, they are massive violations of international human rights. Accordingly, the rules of war and human rights law can be seen as two complementary forms of international rules that aim to circumscribe the proper form, scope, and use of coercive power (see Kaldor 1998b, chs. 6, 7). For all the limitations of its enforcement, these are significant changes that, when taken together, amount to the rejection of the doctrine of legitimate power as effective control, and its replacement by international rules that entrench basic humanitarian values as the criteria for legitimate government.

## Human rights, democracy and minority groups

At the heart of this shift is the human rights regime (see Held 1995, ch. 5; Held and McGrew, Goldblatt, and Perraton 1999, ch. 1). The basic elements of this regime [ . . . ] are set out in table 1. [ . . . ] Three interrelated features of the regime are worth dwelling on: (1) the constitutive human rights agreements; (2) the role of self-determination and the democratic principle that were central to the framework of decolonization; and (3) the recent recognition of the rights of minority groups.

On (1): The human rights regime consists of overlapping global, regional, and national conventions and institutions (see Donnelly 1998; Evans 1997). At the global level, human rights are firmly entrenched in the International Bill of Human Rights, the building blocks of which are the UN Declaration of Human Rights of 1948 and the Covenants on Civil and Political Rights, and on Economic, Social and Cultural Rights, which were

**Table 1**  A selected list of human rights initiatives and agreements

| Date | |
| --- | --- |
| Jun 1945 | Charter of the United Nations |
| Jun 1946 | UN Commission on Human Rights |
| Dec 1948 | Genocide Convention/Universal Declaration of Human Rights |
| Nov 1950 | European Convention on Human Rights |
| Jul 1951 | Convention Relating to the Status of Refugees |
| Dec 1952 | Convention on the Political Rights of Women |
| Sep 1954 | Convention on the Status of Stateless Persons |
| Sep 1956 | Convention Abolishing Slavery |
| Jun 1957 | ILO's Convention on the Abolition of Forced Labor |
| Nov 1962 | Convention on Consent to Marriage |
| Dec 1965 | Convention on the Elimination of Racial Discrimination |
| Dec 1966 | International Covenants on Economic, Social, and Cultural Rights/Civil and Political Rights; Optional Protocol |
| Nov 1973 | Convention on the Suppression of Apartheid |
| Jun 1977 | Two additional protocols to the Geneva Conventions |
| Dec 1979 | Convention on the Elimination of all Forms of Discrimination against Women |
| Dec 1984 | Convention against Torture |
| Nov 1989 | Convention on the Rights of the Child |
| May 1993 | International Criminal Tribunal for the Former Yugoslavia |
| Nov 1994 | International Criminal Tribunal for Rwanda |
| Jul 1998 | UN conference agrees treaty for a permanent International Criminal Court |

*Source*: UN and *The Economist* 1998

adopted in 1966 and came into force in 1976. These were complemented in the late 1970s and 1980s by the Convention on the Elimination of Discrimination against Women and the Convention on the Rights of the Child. The UN Commission on Human Rights is responsible for overseeing this system and bringing persistent abuses to the attention of the UN Security Council. In addition, the International Labor Organization is charged, in principle, with policing the area of labor and trade union rights.

Within most of the world's regions there is an equivalent legal structure and machinery. The European Convention for the Protection of Human Rights and Fundamental Freedoms (1950) is particularly significant. For it was designed to take the first steps toward the "collective enforcement," as its preamble states, of certain of the rights enumerated in the Universal Declaration. The European agreement, in allowing individual citizens to initiate proceedings against their own governments, is a most remarkable legal innovation. Although its implementation has been far from straightforward and is fraught with bureaucratic complexities, it seeks to prevent its signatories from treating their citizens as they think fit, and to empower citizens with the legal means to challenge state policies and actions that violate their basic liberties. Human rights have also been promoted in other regions of the world, notably in Africa and the Americas. The American Convention on Human Rights, which came into force in 1978, and the African (Banjul) Charter of Human and People's Rights (1981), were useful steps in this regard. But perhaps as important in promoting human rights, if not more so, have been the multiplicity of political and international nongovernmental organizations (INGOs) that have actively sought to implement these agreements and, thereby, to reshape the ordering principles of public life (see Held and McGrew, Goldblatt, and Perraton 1999, ch. 1).

On (2): There is a notable tendency in human rights agreements to entrench the notion that a legitimate state must be a state that upholds certain core democratic values (see Crawford and Marks 1998). For instance, in Article 21 the Universal Declaration of Human Rights asserts the democratic principle along with enumerated rights as a common standard of achievement for all peoples and nations (see UN 1988, 2, 5). Although this principle represented an important position to which anticolonial movements could appeal, the word "democracy" does not itself appear in the Declaration and the adjective "democratic" appears only once, in Article 29. By contrast, the 1966 UN International Covenant on Civil and Political Rights (enacted 1976) elaborates this principle in Article 25, making a number of different declarations and other instruments into a binding treaty (see UN 1988, 28). According to Article 25 of the Covenant:

> Every citizen shall have the right and the opportunity, without . . . unreasonable restrictions:
>
> (a)  to take part in the conduct of public affairs, directly or through freely chosen representatives;
> (b)  to vote and to be elected at genuine periodic elections which shall be by universal and equal suffrage and shall be held by secret ballot, guaranteeing the free expression of the will of the electors;
> (c)  to have access, on general terms of equality, to public service in his country.

The American Convention on Human Rights, along with other regional conventions, contains clear echoes of Article 21 of the Universal Declaration as well as of Article

25 of the Covenant on Civil and Political Rights, while the European Convention on Human Rights is most explicit in connecting democracy with state legitimacy, as is the statute of the Council of Europe, which makes a commitment to democracy a condition of membership. Although such commitments often remain fragile, they signal a new approach to the concept of legitimate political power in international law.

On (3): Since 1989 the intensification of interethnic conflict has created an urgent sense that specific minorities need protection (renewing concerns voiced clearly during the interwar period). In 1992 the United Nations General Assembly adopted a Declaration on the Rights of Persons Belonging to National, Ethnic, Religious and Linguistic Minorities. Proclaiming that states "shall protect the existence and national, cultural, religious and linguistic identity of minorities," the Declaration sets out rights for members of minorities to be able "to participate effectively in cultural, religious, social and public life." While the Declaration is not legally binding, it is widely regarded in the UN system and in some leading INGOs (Amnesty International, Oxfam) as establishing a future trajectory of international legal change. In other contexts, the impetus to secure protection for minority rights is also apparent. Within the Council of Europe, a Charter for Regional and Minority Languages and a Framework Convention for the Protection of National Minorities have been elaborated. Moreover, the Organization for Security and Cooperation in Europe has adopted a series of instruments affirming minority rights and has founded the office of High Commissioner for National Minorities to provide "early warning" and "early action" with respect to "tensions involving national minority issues" (Crawford and Marks 1998, 76–7).

Changes in human rights law have placed individuals, governments, and nongovernmental organizations under new systems of legal regulation – regulation that, in principle, is indifferent to state boundaries. This development is a significant indicator of the distance that has been traveled from the classic, state-centric conception of sovereignty to what amounts to a new formulation for the delimitation of political power on a global basis. The regime of liberal international sovereignty entrenches powers and constraints, and rights and duties, in international law that – albeit ultimately formulated by states – go beyond the traditional conception of the proper scope and boundaries of states, and can come into conflict, and sometimes contradiction, with national laws. Within this framework, states may forfeit claims to sovereignty if they violate the standards and values embedded in the liberal international order; and such violations no longer become a matter of morality alone. Rather, they become a breach of a legal code, a breach that may call forth the means to challenge, prosecute, and rectify it (see Habermas 1999). To this end, a bridge is created between morality and law where, at best, only stepping stones existed before. These are transformative changes that alter the form and content of politics, nationally, regionally, and globally. They signify the enlarging normative reach, extending scope, and growing institutionalization of international legal rules and practices – the beginnings of a "universal constitutional order" in which the state is no longer the only layer of legal competence to which people have transferred public powers (Crawford and Marks 1998, 2; Weller 1997, 45).

But a qualification needs to be registered at this stage in order to avoid misunderstanding. The regime of liberal international sovereignty should not be understood as having simply weakened the state in regional and global legal affairs. The intensification of international law and the extension of the reach of human rights instruments do not signal alone the demise of the state or even the erosion of its powers. For in many respects, the changes under way represent the extension of the classic liberal concern to define the proper form, scope, and limits of the state in the face of the processes, opportunities, and flux of civil life. In the extension of the delimitation of public powers, states' competencies and capacities have been, and are being, reconstituted or reconfigured – not merely eroded (see Held and McGrew, Goldblatt, and Perraton 1999, "Conclusion"). [ . . . ]

## Environmental law

The final legal domain to be examined in this section is the law governing the environment, wildlife, and the use of natural resources. Within this sphere the subject and scope of international law embrace not just humankind as individuals but the global commons and our shared ecosystems. While attempts to regulate the trade and use of rare species date back over a hundred years, the pace of initiatives in environmental regulation has quickened since the end of the Second World War (Hurrell and Kingsbury 1992). The first convention on the regulation of international whaling was signed in 1946, and early treaties on the international carriage of toxic substances, minor habitat protection schemes, and some regulation of the international nuclear cycle were agreed in the 1950s and 1960s. However, it was only in the late 1960s and early 1970s that the extent and intensity of international environmental regulation began to increase significantly (see Held and McGrew, Goldblatt, and Perraton 1999, ch. 8). The key moment in this regard was the 1972 Stockholm conference on the international environment sponsored by the UN Environment Program. This was the first occasion at which multilateral agencies and national governments gathered to consider the whole panoply of shared environmental problems and the proper scope of the response.

Throughout the 1970s and 1980s, the regulation of international waters and the control of marine pollution became extensively institutionalized with the adoption and ratification of the London Dumping Convention (1972), the MARPOL convention on ship pollution (1978), the UN Convention on the Law of the Sea (1982), and a multiplicity of regional seas agreements on cooperation and control of pollution (the Helsinki, Barcelona, Oslo, and Paris conventions as well as the UN regional seas program). At the heart of the classic conception of sovereignty, natural resources were regarded as legitimately falling under the sovereign authority of states on the condition that whoever possessed a resource, and exercised actual control over it, secured a legal title (see Cassese 1986, 376–90). Although this principle has been extended in recent times to cover the control of resources in a variety of areas (including the continental shelf and "economic zones" that stretch up to 200 nautical miles from coastal states), a new concept was expounded in 1967 as a means for rethinking the legal basis of the appropriation and use of resources – the "common heritage of mankind."

Among the key elements of this concept are the exclusion of a right of appropriation; the duty to use resources in the interest of the whole of humanity; and the duty to explore and exploit resources for peaceful purposes only. The notion of the "common heritage" was subject to intense debate in the United Nations and elsewhere; it was, nevertheless, enshrined in two seminal treaties, the 1979 Convention on the Moon and Other Celestial Bodies and the 1982 Convention on the Law of the Sea.

Introduced as a way of thinking about the impact new technologies would have on the further exploitation of natural resources – resources that were beyond national jurisdiction on the seabed or on the moon and other planets – its early advocates saw it as a basis for arguing that the vast domain of hitherto untapped resources should be developed for the benefit of all, particularly developing nations. As such, the introduction of the concept was a turning point in legal considerations, even though there was considerable argument over where and how it might be applied. It was significantly revised and qualified by the 1996 Agreement relating to the Implementation of Part XI (of the Law of the Sea).

Further significant conventions were signed in the 1980s and 1990s to combat the risks flowing from degraded resources and other environmental dangers, including the international movement of hazardous wastes (the Basel Convention in 1989), air pollution involving the emission of CFCs (the Vienna and Montreal Protocols in 1985 and 1987) as well as a range of treaties regulating transboundary acid rain in Europe and North America. Alongside these agreements, environmental issues became points of contention and the focus of regional cooperation and regulation in the EU, the Nordic Council, NAFTA, APEC, MERCOSUR, and other areas.

Against the background of such developments, the impetus was established for the 1992 Rio conference (and for the Kyoto meeting in 1997). Conducted under the auspices of the UNEP and involving negotiations between almost every member state of the UN, Rio sought to establish the most far-reaching set of global environmental agreements ever arrived at. The Rio Declaration took as its primary goal the creation of "a new and equitable global partnership through the creation of new levels of cooperation among states, key sectors of societies and people" (UNEP 1993, vol. 1, 3). Principle 7 of the Declaration demanded that states cooperate "in a spirit of global partnership to conserve, protect and restore the health and integrity of the Earth's ecosystem"; and Principle 12 called for "environmental measures addressing transboundary or global environmental problems" which should, "as far as possible, be based on an international consensus" (1993, 4, 5). The results included conventions on biodiversity, climate change and greenhouse emissions, the rain forests, and the establishment of international arrangements for transferring technology and capital from the North to the South for environmental programs (see UNEP 1993).

Rio committed all states to engage "in a continuous and constructive dialogue," to foster "a climate of genuine cooperation," and to achieve "a more efficient and equitable world economy" (UNEP 1993, 14; and cf. 111, 238). Traces of the concept of the "common heritage" can be found in its many documents, as it sought to create a new sense of transborder responsibility for the global commons and signaled the urgency of establishing a legal order based on cooperation and equity. Implementation of its many agreements has, of course, been another story. Agreement on the scope and scale of environmental threats was difficult to achieve, as was anything resembling a consensus on who is responsible for creating these and how the costs should be allocated to ameliorate them. Even where agreement was possible, international organizations have lacked the authority to ensure it is upheld. Other than through moral pressure, no mechanism exists for forcing recalcitrant states into line, and the latter retain an effective veto over environmental policy via inaction and indecision. The Rio Declaration had a great deal to say about "the new global partnership" tackling transborder problems that escape national jurisdiction, but it offered little precision on the principles of accountability and enforcement. Accordingly, while international environmental law constitutes a large and rapidly changing corpus of rules, quasi-rules, and precedents that set down new directions in legal thinking, the implications of these for the balance between state power and global and regional authority remain fuzzy in many respects. International environmental treaties, regimes, and organizations have placed in question elements of the sovereignty of modern states – that is, their entitlement to rule exclusively within delimited borders – but have not yet locked the drive for national self-determination and its related "reasons of state" into a transparent, effective, and accountable global framework. The limits of the liberal international order may have been reached. For while this order seeks the means and mechanisms to delimit and divide public power, it does not have a legitimate and adequate basis to tackle the transborder overspill of national decisions and policies, and the collective problems that emerge from the overlapping fortunes of national communities. Whether this is a contingent inadequacy or a necessary feature of the conceptual resources of liberalism is a matter to which this paper will return.

## The Achievements of Liberal Sovereignty

The classic regime of sovereignty has been recast by changing processes and structures of regional and global order. States are locked into diverse, overlapping, political and legal domains – that can be thought of as an emerging multilayered political system. National sovereignty and autonomy are now embedded within broader frameworks of governance and law in which states are increasingly but one site for the exercise of political power and authority. While this is, in principle, a reversible shift, the classic regime of state sovereignty has undergone significant alteration. [ . . . ] It is useful to rehearse and emphasize the most substantial changes before reflecting on the difficulties, dilemmas, and limitations of these processes.

The most substantial points can be put briefly. Sovereignty can no longer be understood in terms of the categories of untrammeled effective power. Rather, a legitimate state must increasingly be understood through the language of democracy and human rights. Legitimate authority has become linked, in moral and legal terms, with the maintenance of human rights values and democratic standards. The latter set a limit on the range of acceptable diversity among the political constitutions of states (Beitz 1979, 1994, 1998). [ . . . ]

At the beginning of the twenty-first century, each of the four main corollaries of the system of interstate law is open to revaluation – that is, recognition of heads of state irrespective of their constitutional standing; international law's de facto approach to sovereignty; the disjuncture between considerations of appropriate rules and organizations for domestic politics and those thought applicable in the realm of *Realpolitik*; and the refusal to bestow legitimacy or confer recognition on those who forcefully challenge established national regimes or existing boundaries. Today, the legitimacy of state leadership cannot be taken for granted and, like the constitutional standing of a national polity, is subject to scrutiny and tests with respect to human rights and liberal democratic standards (Crawford and Marks 1998, 84–5). In addition, the growth of regional and global governance, with responsibility for areas of increasing transborder concern from pollution and health to trade and financial matters, has helped close the gap between the types of organization thought relevant to national and transnational life. Finally, there have been important cases where governments within settled borders (such as the Southern Rhodesian government after its unilateral declaration of independence in 1965) have remained unrecognized by the international community while, at the same time, national liberation movements have been granted new levels of recognition or respect (for example, the ANC in the late 1980s during the closing stages of apartheid in South Africa). In addition, some struggles for autonomy have been accepted by significant powers, for instance the Croatian struggle for nationhood, prior to borders being redrawn and recast.

Boundaries between states are of decreasing legal and moral significance. States are no longer regarded as discrete political worlds. International standards breach boundaries in numerous ways. Within Europe the European Convention for the Protection of Human Rights and Fundamental Freedoms and the EU create new institutions and layers of law and governance that have divided political authority; any assumption that sovereignty is an indivisible, illimitable, exclusive, and perpetual form of public power – entrenched within an individual state – is now defunct (Held 1995, 107–13). Within the wider international community, rules governing war, weapon systems, war crimes, human rights, and the environment, among other areas, have transformed and delimited the order of states, embedding national polities in new forms and layers of accountability and governance (from particular regimes such as the Nuclear Nonproliferation Agreement to wider frameworks of regulation laid down by the UN Charter and a host of specialized agencies) (see Held and McGrew, Goldblatt, and Perraton 1999, chs. 1, 2). [ . . . ]

## An Assessment of Liberal Sovereignty

The political and legal transformations of the last fifty years have gone some way toward circumscribing and delimiting political power on a regional and global basis. Several major difficulties remain, nonetheless, at the core of the liberal international regime of sovereignty that create tensions, if not faultiness, at its center. In the first instance, any assessment of the cumulative impact of the legal and political changes must acknowledge their highly differentiated character because particular types of impact – whether on the decisional, procedural, institutional, or structural dimensions of a polity – are not experienced uniformly by all states and regions.

Second, while the liberal political order has gone some way toward taming the arrogance of princes and princesses and curbing some of their worst excesses within and outside their territories, the spreading hold of the regime of liberal international sovereignty has compounded the risks of arrogance in certain respects. This is so because in the transition from prince to prime minister or president, from unelected governors to elected governors, from the aristocratic few to the democratic many, political arrogance has been reinforced by the claim of the political elites to derive their support from that most virtuous source of power – the *demos*. Democratic princes can energetically pursue public policies – whether in security, trade, technology, or welfare – because they feel, and to a degree are, mandated so to do. The border spillover effects of their policies and agendas are not prominent in their minds or a core part of their political calculations. Thus, for example, some of the most significant risks of Western industrialization and energy use have been externalized across the planet. Liberal democratic America, geared to domestic elections and vociferous interest groups, does not weigh heavily the ramifications across borders of its choice of fuels, consumption levels, or type of industrialization – George W. Bush's refusal after his election in 2001 to ratify the Kyoto agreement on greenhouse gas omissions being a case in point. From the location of nuclear plants, the management of toxic waste, and the regulation of genetically modified foodstuffs, to the harvesting of scarce resources (e.g., the rain forests) and the regulation of trade and financial markets, governments by no means simply determine what is right or appropriate for their own citizens, and national communities by no means exclusively "program" the actions and policies of their own governments.

Third, the problem of spillover consequences is compounded by a world increasingly marked by "overlapping communities of fate" – where the trajectories of each and every country are more tightly entwined than ever before. While democracy remains rooted in a fixed and bounded territorial conception of political community, contemporary regional and global forces disrupt any simple correspondence between national territory, sovereignty, political space, and the democratic political community. These forces enable power and resources to flow across, over, and around territorial boundaries and escape mechanisms of national democratic control. Questions about who should be accountable to whom, which socioeconomic processes should be regulated at what levels (local, national, regional, global) and on what basis do not easily resolve themselves and are left outside the sphere of liberal international thinking.

Fourth, while many pressing policy issues, from the regulation of financial markets to the management of genetic engineering, create challenges that transcend borders and generate new transnational constituencies, existing intergovernmental organizations are insufficient to resolve these – and resolve them legitimately. Decision-making in leading IGOs, for instance the World Trade Organization (WTO) and the International Monetary Fund (IMF), is often skewed to dominant geopolitical and geo-economic interests whose primary objective is to ensure flexible adjustment in and to the international economy (downplaying, for example, the external origins of a country's difficulties and the structural pressures and rigidities of the world economy itself). Moreover, even when such interests do not prevail, a crisis of legitimacy threatens these institutions. For the "chains of delegation" from national states to multilateral bodies are too long, the basis of representation often unclear, and the mechanisms of accountability of the technical elites themselves who run the IGOs are weak or obscure (Keohane 1998). Agenda-setting and decision procedures frequently lack transparency, key negotiations are held in secret, and there is little or no wider accountability to the UN system or to any democratic forum more broadly. Problems of transparency, accountability, and democracy prevail at the global level. Whether "princes" and "princesses" rule in cities, states, or multilateral bodies, their power will remain arbitrary unless tested and redeemed through democratic processes that embrace all those significantly affected by them.

Fifth, serious deficiencies can, of course, be documented in the implementation and enforcement of democratic and human rights, and of international law more generally. Despite the development and consolidation of the regime of liberal international sovereignty, massive inequalities of power and economic resources continue to grow. There is an accelerating gap between rich and poor states as well as between peoples in the global economy (UNDP 1999). The human rights agenda often has a hollow ring. The development of regional trade and investment blocs, particularly the Triad (NAFTA, the EU, and Japan), has concentrated economic transactions within and between these areas (Thompson 2000). The Triad accounts for two thirds to three quarters of world economic activity, with shifting patterns of resources across each region. However, one further element of inequality is particularly apparent: a significant proportion of the world's population remains marginal or excluded from these networks (Pogge 1999, 27; see UNDP 1997, 1999; Held and McGrew 2000).

Does this growing gulf in the life circumstances and life chances of the world's population highlight intrinsic limits to the liberal international order? Or should this disparity be traced to other phenomena – the particularization of nation-states or the inequalities of regions with their own distinctive cultural, religious, and political problems? The latter are contributors to the disparity between the universal claims of the human rights regime and its often tragically limited impact (see Pogge 1999; Leftwich 2000). But one of the key causes of the gulf lies, in my judgment, elsewhere – in the tangential impact of the liberal international order on the regulation of economic power and market mechanisms. The focus of the liberal international order is on the curtailment of the abuse of political power, not economic power. It has few, if any, systematic means to address sources of power other than the political (see Held 1995, pt. 3). Its conceptual resources and leading ideas do not suggest or push toward the pursuit of self-determination and autonomy in the economic domain; they do not seek the entrenchment of democratic rights and obligations outside the sphere of the political. Hence, it is hardly a surprise that liberal democracy and flourishing economic inequalities exist side by side. [See chapter 44 for an exploration of the implications of these arguments.]

## References

Baldwin, T. (1992) The Territorial State. In H. Gross and T. R. Harrison (eds), *Jurisprudence, Cambridge Essays*, Oxford: Clarendon Press.

Beitz, C. (1979) *Political Theory and International Relations*. Princeton: Princeton University Press.

Beitz, C. (1994) Cosmopolitan Liberalism and the States System. In C. Brown (ed.), *Political Restructuring in Europe: Ethical Perspectives*, London: Routledge.

Beitz, C. (1998) Philosophy of International Relations. In *The Routledge Encyclopedia of Philosophy*, London: Routledge.

Bull, H. (1977) *The Anarchical Society*. London: Macmillan.

Byers, M. (1999) *Custom, Power and the Power of Rules*. Cambridge: Cambridge University Press.

Cassese, A. (1986) *International Law in a Divided World*. Oxford: Clarendon Press.

Cassese, A. (1988) *Violence and Law in the Modern Age*. Cambridge: Polity Press.

Chinkin, C. (1998) International Law and Human Rights. In T. Evans (ed.), *Human Rights Fifty Years On: A Reappraisal*, Manchester: Manchester University Press.

Crawford, J. (1995) Prospects for an International Criminal Court. In M. D. A. Freeman and R. Halson (eds), *Current Legal Problems 1995*, 48, pt 2, collected papers, Oxford: Oxford University Press.

Crawford, J. and Marks, S. (1998) The Global Democracy Deficit: An Essay on International Law and Its Limits. In D. Archibugi et al. (eds), *Re-Imagining Political Community: Studies in Cosmopolitan Democracy*, Cambridge: Polity Press.

Dinstein, Y. (1993) Rules of War. In J. Krieger (ed.), *The Oxford Companion to Politics of the World*, Oxford: Oxford University Press.

Donnelly, J. (1998) *International Human Rights*, 2nd edn. Boulder, CO: Westview Press.

Dugard, J. (1997) Obstacles in the Way of an International Criminal Court. *Cambridge Law Journal* 56.

*The Economist* (1998) A Survey of Human Rights. December 5.

Evans, T. (1997) Democratization and Human Rights. In A. McGrew (ed.), *The Transformation of Democracy?* Cambridge: Polity Press.

Falk, R. (1969) The Interplay of Westphalian and Charter Conceptions of the International Legal Order. In R. Falk and C. Black (eds), *The Future of the International Legal Order*, vol. 1, Princeton, NJ: Princeton University Press.

Habermas, J. (1999) Bestiality and Humanity. *Constellations* 6: 3.

Held, D. (ed.) (1995) *Democracy and the Global Order: From the Modern State to Cosmopolitan Governance*. Cambridge: Polity Press.

Held, D. (1999) The Transformation of Political Community: Rethinking Democracy in the Context of Globalization. In I. Shapiro and C. Hacker-Cordón (eds), *Democracy's Edges*, Cambridge: Cambridge University Press.

Held, D. and McGrew, A. (eds) (2000) *The Global Transformation Reader*. Cambridge: Polity Press.

Held, D. and McGrew, A., Goldblatt, D., and Perraton, J. (1999) *Global Transformations: Politics, Economics and Culture*. Cambridge: Polity Press.

Hinsley, F. H. (1986) *Sovereignty*, 2nd edn. Cambridge: Cambridge University Press.

Hurrell, A. and Kingsbury, B. (eds) (1992) *The International Politics of the Environment*. Oxford: Oxford University Press.

Kaldor, M. (1998a) Reconceptualizing Organized Violence. In D. Archibugi et al. (eds), *Re-Imagining Political Community: Studies in Cosmopolitan Democracy*, Cambridge: Polity Press.

Kaldor, M. (1998b) *New and Old Wars*. Cambridge: Polity Press.

Keohane, R. O. (1998) International Institutions: Can Interdependence Work? *Foreign Policy* Spring, 82–96.

Krasner, S. (1995) Compromising Westphalia. *International Security* 20: 115–51.

Krasner, S. (1999) *Sovereignty: Organized Hypocrisy*. Princeton, NJ: Princeton University Press.

Leftwich, A. (2000) *States of Development*. Cambridge: Polity Press.

Plano, J. C. and Olton, R. (1988) *The International Relations Dictionary*. Santa Barbara, CA: ABC Clio.

Pogge, T. (1999) Economic Justice and National Borders. *Revision* 22: 27–34.

Potter, D., Goldblatt, D., Kiloh, M., and Lewis, P. (eds) (1997) *Democratization*. Cambridge: Polity Press.

SIPRI (1999) *SIPRI Yearbook 1999: Armaments, Disarmament and International Security*. Oxford: Oxford University Press.

Thompson, G. (2000) Economic Globalization? In D. Held (ed.), *A Globalizing World? Culture, Economics and Politics*, London: Routledge.

UN (1988) *Human Rights: A Compilation of International Instruments*. New York: United Nations.

UNDP (1997) *Human Development Report 1997*. New York: Oxford University Press.

UNDP (1999) *Globalization with a Human Face: Human Development Report 1999*. New York: Oxford University Press.

UNEP (1993) *Report of the United Nations Conference on Environment and Development*, 3 vols. New York: United Nations.

Vincent, J. (1992) Modernity and Universal Human Rights. In A. McGrew and P. Lewis (eds), *Global Politics*, Cambridge: Polity Press.

Weller, M. (1997) The Reality of the Emerging Universal Constitutional Order: Putting the Pieces Together. *Cambridge Review of International Studies* Winter/Spring, 40–63.

Wright, R. (2000) Continental Drift: World Government Is Caring. *New Republic* January 25.

# 15

# The Security State

*Ian Clark*

[ . . . ] There is a [ . . . ] link between globalization and both the substance and mode of attainment of security. In parallel with [ . . . ] other spheres, the most common depiction of this relationship is that of globalization impinging upon the state from the outside and transforming the security environment within which it operates. As a result, the state is portrayed as having a diminished capacity to produce security: globalization of security presents yet another policy challenge to the already embattled state. Such accounts are [ . . . ] deeply flawed and misleading. They conjure an image of globalization as a disembodied process occurring over and beyond states, and simply impacting upon them as a new constraining influence from the outside.

As will be argued [ . . . ], changes in the substance of security reflect deep-seated 'internal' transformations as well. The claim about globalization in general, that it is 'not just an "out there" phenomenon' but also an 'in here' development (Giddens 1998: 311), is thus specifically applicable to globalized security. This is symptomatic of revamped societal bargains under way within individual states, and not simply of a logic of state activity dictated by new systemic structures 'outside'. Let there be no mistaking, however, how critical these new societal bargains are. As has been pointed out, 'in the implicit contract between individuals and the state . . . the most fundamental service purchased . . . is security' (Holsti 1996: 108). How tenable are such contracts if it is true, as claimed of Northern states' pronounced reluctance to go to war, that the 'original backbone of the nation-state is turning to jelly' (Mann 1997: 492)? Hence, one astute commentator raises the essential issue that 'there would seem to be a close relationship between the relative decline of inter-state violence and the weakening of the role of states in the global process' (Laidi 1998: 94). The loss of the state's identity as the principal unit of war-making is symptomatic of what appears to be its more general decline elsewhere.

However, the new security order is as much a measure of state performance as of non-performance in this area. [ . . . ] The new security agenda is not entailed simply by the declining capacity of states to produce security of the traditional variety. It is instead revealing of the changing social contracts within states and these are, at the same time, part of the changing logic of state functionality in a globalized setting. Neither can be explained in separation from the other. Globalization, to echo one similar judgement, does not change merely 'the external context within which states operate', but reflects also change in 'the very nature of states' (Guehenno 1998/9: 7).
[ . . . ]

Of all the potential manifestations of globalization, those in the security domain have been the least systematically explored. This in itself is perhaps surprising, since globalization 'does not seem so new to the world of strategy' (Guehenno 1998/9: 5). The bases of the claim to the impact of globalization on security will be set out in detail below. At the outset, we can make some attempt to distinguish its effects from those engendered by more modest moves towards internationalization. In general, even within traditionalist conceptions of 'military security', there has been widespread recognition of this tendency towards 'internationalization' of security (Held and McGrew 1993: 267). Obviously in this context, the meaning of 'internationalization' is not the same as that of globalization, and perhaps connotes little more than a suggestion of multi-lateralism. States are now less than ever inclined to pursue their security within a unilateralist framework. For this reason, analysts have developed a concept of 'world' as opposed to 'national' security, drawing attention to high levels of interdependence as the reason why security is no longer 'sustainable through unilateral means' (Klare and Thomas 1994: 3). In so far as this is the case, we are witnessing a diminution of the 'go-it-alone' mentality that has been the distinctive hallmark of national security in the recent historical epoch, and a corresponding shift towards what has been called 'the transnationalization of legitimate violence' (Kaldor 1998: 103). Of course, there may be many explanations for this tendency – such as the sophistication of military technology and its consequent cost, the restructuring of the defence-industrial base, the inability of most states to deploy the whole range of military capabilities, and the drift towards collective legitimation of military action. Cumulatively, these trends suggest a decline in the role of the state as an independent producer of security, in favour of a shift towards its 'cartelization'. In the production of security, globaliza-tion denotes a move away from the age of laissez-faire to an era of oligopoly.

This does not mean that the selective recourse to collective security, by itself, is evidence for a globalization of security. The relevance of collective security to the dis-cussion of globalization has been questioned on the basis that it is an overly state-centric concept and thus ill suited for embracing other social forces: 'the notion of an international collective as a single fabric of like units', it is asserted, 'becomes ques-tionable' (Latham 1996: 91–2). On this account, collective security has been overtaken by the rise of non-state security actors. This point may well have force. But even were it possible to incorporate other actors within collective security structures, the sub-stantive change in security mapped out by this tendency would still be of a lesser order than that assumed within the context of globalization. The fundamental reason for this is that globalization requires a change in the nature of the security state itself, not simply of the setting in which it finds itself. By contrast, [ . . . ] this is not a neces-sary condition of multilateralism or internationalism. States can opt into, or out of, collective defence and collective security arrangements without experiencing funda-mental change to themselves. In sharp contrast, it is this focus on the simultaneous transformation of the state and its environment that sets globalization apart from those other trends.

[ . . . ]

We can now review the standard bodies of evidence appealed to in support of the claim that security is being reshaped by the impact of globalization. For purposes of presentation, this evidence will be divided into four interrelated sets of arguments. These are commonly presented as follows: the detachment of security from territori-ality; the enmeshment of security in global networks; the creation by globalization of a new security agenda; and the diminished capacity of the state to provide secur-ity for its citizens. These are the principal ways in which security and globalization have been related to each other. It remains to assess the force of these respective arguments [ . . . ].

## The Globalization of Security

Within the traditional literature of IR, there can be few topics that have been regarded as more territorialized than security itself. Security has normally been defined as the protection of vital interests within a sovereign space. It is thus territory that 'ties down' security, and supplies the traditional referent for its enjoyment. Without it, we have a conceptual difficulty in specifying the subject of security. And yet it is precisely this territorial dimension that globalization calls into question. By doing so, it poses a frontal challenge to existing frameworks for understanding security as well.

If this is the case, there is a compelling argument that the globalization of security be traced back to the introduction of nuclear weapons, as John Herz (1973) pointed out long ago and others have since reinforced. It was the capacity for territorial defence that was most directly challenged by the nuclear weapon, and indeed by other forms of aerial bombardment. As Harknett concedes in his reworking of Herz's argument, 'the pre-nuclear conceptualization of territoriality as a hard-shell of defence in which protection was achieved by planning to repulse an offensive attack has indeed been undermined by nuclear weapons' (Harknett 1996: 145–6). More generally, Ruggie has acutely drawn attention to what he terms the 'unbundling of territoriality'. For all that there has been a remorseless trend towards sovereign partition of territory, international society has itself required exceptions to it. Extraterritoriality is the prime example, but Ruggie characterizes the process more broadly: 'International regimes, common markets, political communities, and the like constitute additional institutional forms through which territoriality has become unbundled' (1998: 190–1). Without question, globalization helps explain this unbundling or, more accurately, globalization *is* this process of unbundling, even when authored by actors in addition to states. If Ruggie's unbundling is driven by states in quest of a working interstate system, the wider unbundling has been encouraged by other social actors seeking viable non-territorial networks of activity and giving rise, even if inadvertently, to the rudiments of a global society.

The instances of this de-emphasis of territoriality are manifold and need not be described in detail. They include new military agendas in which military forces are now less exercised by the requirement for defence of national territory, narrowly construed. Sorensen locates this favoured motif of globalization – 'the irrelevance of borders' – within the security debate: 'armed forces are increasingly assigned tasks which have nothing to do with national defence in the traditional sense', he comments, and illustrates the claim with reference to 'humanitarian intervention in domestic conflicts and the defence of basic human rights' (1997: 267). Others envisage the emergence of new security communities that are no longer territorially defined. These are described as *cognitive regions* within which the threat of war has been all but eliminated (Adler 1997: 254).

This is not to deny the qualifications that need to be entered against all such claims. The evidence for globalization of security is much more ambiguous than in other spheres, and we must guard against any temptation to present security in radically de-territorialized terms, no matter how significant some of the trends in that direction might be. Three caveats will be entered at this point, each of which touches on profound theoretical issues that pervade this discussion. The first follows Freedman.

Although couched as part of a slightly different argument, his observations have relevance in the present context. He dissents from any belief that the revolution in military technology holds out a prospect of war reduced to the 'virtual', in which pain and inconvenience can be minimized. Freedman correctly reminds us that 'territory, prosperity, identity, order, values – they all still matter' (1998: 78). To this extent, traditionalist notions of security, and of the role of force within it, are far from irrelevant, even if they are now joined by additional concerns. Secondly, as a corrective to the impression of the end of territoriality, it must also be remembered that territoriality remains a powerful form of defence within the international system, and nowhere more so than amongst its weakest members. It is on this basis that Third World writers question the tendency within Western security literature to emphasize the new agenda, with its explicit shift in focus away from the state and towards the individual. Ayoob, for example, restates the common view that within the South, strong territorially organized states are the only available bulwark against penetrating forces from the North (1997: 139–40). Finally, there is ambivalence at the core of the security developments of the past decade. Cox provides a compelling account of this. He neatly suggests that 'The United States stands at the heart of the contradiction between these two principles: it is the champion of globalization, yet its role as military enforcer is territorially based' (Cox 1996: 292). The relationship between globalization, territoriality, and security is thus more complex than some writers on the subject would have us believe.

The second category is really a set of arguments, rather than a single position, but is unified around the central claim that security is increasingly structured into global networks. The content of these networks varies from one account to another, but collectively they contribute to a new conception of security, given the state's reduced capacity to act autonomously in its pursuit. This is the security argument which most directly parallels those already encountered above, such as the general 'loss of sovereignty' thesis, or the inability of the state to sustain its own macro-economic policy given conditions of intense capital mobility. In the present context, globalizing networks are deemed to have hollowed out the security state.

What form do these networks take? They are, in fact, specific instances of the more general forms of globalization hitherto described. In that sense, they derive from those tendencies [ . . . ] towards globalization of production and exchange, systems of global communications, and the restructuring of state responsibilities for its own citizenry.

The application of these developments to security can be undertaken most conveniently, albeit somewhat narrowly, in the setting of defence hardware and technology. In this case, issues pertaining to security are subsumed under the more general discussion of globalization of production. Supply of military equipment is very much a part of this global system of production, as well as of exchange. Moreover, the individual state, as supplier and consumer, has less control over either of these systems. From this perspective, various ideas that were central to cold war concepts of national security have come to be challenged, such as the protection of the national-defence industrial base, of national industrial champions, and of technological skills required for military equipment. These imperatives no longer make the same kind of sense given the degree of privatization that has taken place, the escalating costs of military technology, and the relative internationalization of the defence industry.

Crawford usefully develops this line of analysis and draws attention to the 'encroachment of the market on the allocation of goods and services necessary to military strength, and the subsequent chipping away at the state's ability to control the allocation of those resources' (1995: 159). So significant is this transition that she sees it as marking a historical watershed. 'The trend in increasing state control over those resources, evident since the late nineteenth century,' she attests, 'would seem to have reversed itself in the late twentieth century' (1995: 159). The importance of this trend is further magnified by the interlocking of civilian and military technologies, with the balance shifting in favour of civilian technology, upon which the military is now increasingly dependent, rather than the military providing the spin-offs for the civilian sector (Crawford 1995: 155).

The impact of globalization upon security can also be conceived in a much wider framework, operative within a notion of systemic security whereby security itself is part of an interlinked network, the whole impacting upon the individual parts. Such a notion is appealed to in the viewpoint that 'the relative security of the inhabitants of the North is purchased at the price of chronic insecurity for the vast majority of the world population' (Wyn Jones 1996: 203). States consume security as best they can, but the system rations their varying degrees of access to it.

There are, as always, qualifications that need to be entered against all such claims. At the very least, there is the respectable interpretation that the world's security system has become less, not more, integrated since the end of the cold war. It was during the cold war that the two superpowers took the leading role in integrating the security perceptions and policies of their respective blocs. Also, because of its bipolar nature, the cold war ensured that the workings of a single balance of power would impinge upon all regional security structures around the globe. Set against this experience, the end of the cold war has amounted to an act of liberation, although not necessarily beneficent in its consequences. It represented the removal of the constraints of a global contest (Walker 1993: 7), as a result of which there has been some 'unbundling' of strategy itself (Guehenno 1998/9: 8). This has allowed the possible 'emergence of regional powers dominating regional sub-systems' (Hoffmann 1995/6: 32). Such notions of growth in regional autonomy call into question facile assumptions about the intensity of globalization of contemporary security. At the very least, they remind us that globalization may reveal itself in a variety of localized forms.

The third possible manifestation of globalization is in the setting of new security agendas and the creation of new security problems. These pertain, particularly if not exclusively, to issues of identity. In short, it may be thought that globalization is part of the complex of forces leading to the emergence of non-state-centric paradigms, and the reintroduction of societal dimensions of security. Generically, these are manifestations of the so-called twin assaults on the state from above and below – from globalization without and from fragmentation within. Such a stark opposition is again misleading but serves to introduce the general theme. In the words of one writer, 'secular changes in technology, economic relations, social epistemes, and institutions are causing globalising and localising pressures that are squeezing the nation-state from both above and below' (Adler 1997: 250). The consequence of these antagonistic tendencies is the destabilization of existing identities. In terms of globalization, they generate feelings of threat and encourage ' "local" resistance to homogenization which produces the exacerbation of a feeling of insecurity together with a fear of losing one's own national identity' (Guibernau 1996: 135). Bretherton likewise refers to the antagonism between globalization and cultural particularism, and depicts the latter as a defensive reaction to the former (1996: 105).

Under the heading of this new security agenda, three examples can be briefly described and linked to the globalization thesis, as illustrations of the process in general. These are the challenges represented by: ethnic identity; population movements; and the emergence of new forms of economic insecurity. The first of these has already been alluded to and is too familiar to require detailed elaboration. It depicts the most highly visible, if still somewhat contentious, aspect of international security in the 1990s. Through Eastern Europe and the Balkans, the former Soviet Union and parts of Africa, there has developed what has been described as the 'imperialism of parochialism' which has 'come to take centre stage in many theatres of military security' (Chipman 1993: 143). To the extent that this agenda of ethnic struggle has its roots in global pressures, the link to security can be made in a very direct, and disturbing, way.

Secondly, a prominent feature of the globalization landscape is the reality of, and even greater potential for, considerable movements of populations. There is, of course, much that needs to be said against this. There are more politico-legal restrictions on human movement today than at any time in the past hundred years, and so if there is a globalization of human mobility, its manifestations are deeply paradoxical indeed. And yet, for all that, there are significant movements, driven by both short-term emergencies leading to influxes of refugees (Rwanda's overspill into Zaire, Albania's drift across the Adriatic to Italy), and long-term structural factors concerning economic opportunity and encouraging quality-of-life migrations. Bretherton makes the general point when she refers to migration as a 'global phenomenon which has, itself, been identified as an important aspect of the globalization thesis with the potential, ultimately, for blurring national and ethnic differences' (1996: 123). This long-term potential notwithstanding, the pressure for population movement creates shorter-term tensions and insecurities, and itself exacerbates the politics of identity. In some cases, it does so by contributing to the (narrower) redefinition of citizenship.

Thirdly, globalization is linked to the emergence of new security issues by way of its economic agenda. While from the perspective of the global economy, the organization of production might seem 'placeless', from the point of view of individual states this is scarcely so. The very ease with which phases of production can be transferred globally, and the tenacity with which mobile capital searches out new theatres of investment, can induce economic insecurities. As has been said, there is now a 'heightened fear of *economic* competition among industrialized states as they search for ways to ensure that innovative activity takes place on *their* territory and not elsewhere' (Crawford 1995: 158). Systemically, globalized production may be relatively placeless, but in terms of its material consequences it remains firmly rooted. Indeed, the penalties at the national level for failure to compete are more severe than ever. This too is part of the insecurity syndrome of the present age.

Finally, the subject can be examined in the framework of the retreat of the state from the provision of security. Perhaps surprisingly, the globalization literature has paid much less attention to this aspect of state endeavour than to the other functional areas. While the perceived retreat of the state is widely noted in the literature on sovereignty, economy, and democracy, it is a relatively underdeveloped notion in the context of international security (Harknett 1996: 139). This is in itself a striking omission, given the widely recognized connection between the historical development of the state and its military functionality.

When the reduction of state capacity for security is alluded to, it is within a range of differing contexts. Thus the diminished security state can be construed narrowly to refer mainly to its loss of control over defence production and technology. This is the argument of Crawford, already encountered, that 'military resources – especially high-technology ones – are increasingly found in global commercial markets over which states have little control' (1995: 150). The most dramatic illustration of this kind is the demise of the Soviet Union. This event can be graphically portrayed as an instance of catastrophic defence failure engendered by globalization. 'The story of the Soviet demise', writes Crawford, 'is, thus, partly one of how the Soviet state first lost out on the capabilities acquired through the international diffusion of technology and, subsequently, how it became dependent on markets controlled by the West as its own defense industrial base became subject to the forces of globalization' (1995: 167). In this case, the inability to cope with profound changes in the production of defence technology was a contributing factor, not only in reduced security capacity, but also to the failure of the state itself.

Another dimension of state decline can be substantiated by the ongoing privatization of security provision: 'a dramatic growth in private security', one commentator remarks, 'could challenge this control and eventually may threaten global order with military force that is less accountable and controllable than state militarism' (Howe 1998: 1). In parallel with the retreat of the state from a range of social and welfare services, and the withdrawal of the state from what were once deemed to be its core industries, such as energy and transport, analysts also discern the privatization of security (Shearer 1998). 'The privatization of warfare' has been referred to as another example of the 'contracting-out of responsibilities and services traditionally identified with or provided by the state' (Kritsiotis 1998: 11). Of course, there are mundane and literal examples of this in the privatization of some state (domestic) security functions – such as custody and transport of prisoners – as well as privatization of key elements of defence or defence-related industries. However, the notion of privatization of security must extend beyond such cases if it is to be understood within a context of globalization. The role of mercenaries would be one case in point (Kritsiotis 1998). More generally, the argument perhaps finds expression in the suggestion that, in present circumstances, states 'have a monopoly on the ability to *legitimize* violence, but they do not have the ability to *monopolize* violence' (Deudney 1995: 97). The activities of private security companies – such as Military Professional Resources Incorporated, Executive Outcomes, and Sandline – loom large in any such discussion (Howe 1998: 2–6). What this suggests is both a security leakage to other bodies, and a degree of devolution of the security function to private companies. In this sense, it may be possible to conceptualize recent trends in international security as the counterpart to the deregulation that has taken place in the economic sphere.

However, there are more deep-seated arguments about state capabilities that go well beyond such market-centred analyses. These pertain to new bargains between state and civil society, and to the types of security that states are now required to produce. They also relate to the apparently reduced reliance of states upon the military mobilization of their own societies. It is within this context of fundamental state restructuring that appeals to the imagery of the incapacity of states appear at their most superficial. The relationship between globalization and security is much more complex than any such simplistic account would have us believe.

According to the school of sociological realists (Giddens 1985; Tilly 1985; Hall 1986; Mann 1986, 1993), the military is one of the institutional clusters that have left their distinctive imprint on the formation of the modern state. Indeed, some would go so far as to define the modern state in terms of its great success in extracting resources for war-making activities (Tilly 1985). It is but a small step from such historical accounts to the classical conceptions of the state as the institution which has monopolized the legitimate resort to violence, both internally and externally. Thus conceived, the relationship between the state and its security function is an essentialist one, and any change in the latter can be assumed to have dramatic consequences for the former. As has been suggested, a 'security materialist' approach to the subject holds that 'states and state systems emerge, persist, and are replaced according to whether they are, in the long term, viable or functional as providers of security' (Deudney 1995: 89). If this were the case, the globalization of security would reach to the very centres of state power and legitimacy. Thus it is that legitimacy has become a key site for detecting the presence of globalization.

It is precisely on the basis of the state's inability to perform its traditional security functions that a number of analysts have claimed to discern a growing legitimacy deficit. 'Legitimacy deficits and crises can also be expected', writes Deudney, 'in situations where a significant gap exists between the state apparatus' obligated promise and its potential performance in meeting the security needs . . . of the members of civil society' (1995: 101–2). Such a deficit was first diagnosed as a consequence of nuclear weapons: these were deemed to have undercut the state's capacity to protect its own territory and citizens since 'defence', in the classical understanding of it, was no longer possible against them. In the nuclear age, the 'state apparatus can no longer relate to civil society as the effective protector of civil society from destruction' (Deudney 1995: 99). Others, writing in similar vein, insist that the consequent 'level of vulnerability produced by the threat of nuclear attack is such that territoriality must be rethought' (Harknett 1996: 148). Such diagnoses are, in terms of strategic theory, largely uncontroversial and accord with the standard distinction about the nuclear-age move from defence to postures of deterrence. States, on this reckoning, could no longer prevent damage to themselves by physical means but could at best dissuade, by threats of retaliation, those who might seek to inflict it.

There is, however, a more subtle implication for security in the nuclear age that has been less noticed. This is the claim, particularly developed by Martin Shaw, that nuclear technology makes states less dependent on society as the instrument of security. 'From the mid-1950s onwards', he contends, 'nuclear weaponry has had an accelerating influence on war-preparation. Its primary effect has been to demobilize societies' (1994: 146). This is in the sense that the human and industrial potential of society may now have much less relevance for the outcome of wars than was the case in the world wars earlier in this century. As with other forms of technological innovation, nuclear weapons have created structural unemployment in the security industry, and society has been increasingly 'laid off'.

Such a claim is contentious on a number of counts, not least in so far as nuclear weapons are now less salient elements of post-cold war security. It might then be thought to follow that the state once more has to fall back upon increased reliance on societal resources. However, there is also much historical evidence against this proposition, even as an interpretation of the cold war period itself. Simply because of the demands of the cold war, which overlapped with the formative years of the nuclear age, the major nuclear protagonists arguably did much more, not less, by way of mobilizing their societies than had hitherto been the case. Such a development can hardly be denied as regards the Soviet Union, but is also widely recognized as a portrayal of the 'national security state' in the United States.

But even if Shaw's point is questionable as a specific account of the consequences of nuclear weapons, at least in the short term, it might yet have force as a more general interpretation of the changing framework of security in an age of globalization. Even if societies were not immediately stood down from the mid-1950s as a result of the nuclear revolution, is there not persuasive evidence that they have increasingly come to be so from the 1990s onwards? The logic to which this responds is not that of nuclear redundancy alone, but the more general futility of attempting to fight total wars by mobilizing all the resources of a *national* society, when resources can no longer be harnessed on any such recognizable basis. If the great wars of this century were fought and won as clashes of resources and production, how are total wars to be fought in conditions of globalized production? And what are the implications for state capacity of any such reduced dependence on national society for the production of security?

The point can be pursued by highlighting two trends that have become conspicuous in recent years, at least in the context of the military policies of the developed democratic states. The first is a package of tendencies associated with the promise of military high technology, and often run together under the general rubric of the revolution in military affairs (RMA). Freedman has tellingly investigated this topic, and provides a succinct summary of its rationale. 'The series of developments that are brought together in the RMA', he concludes, 'have the connecting theme of the separation of the military from the civilian, of combatants from non-combatants, of fire from society, of organised violence from everyday life' (1998: 17). One is necessarily led to ponder whether it is just a military logic, and the potential of smart technology, which lies behind such tendencies, or whether there might also be a more deep-seated socio-political and economic transformation under way. If total wars are no longer possible – as societies can make less contribution to them – it makes sense to redefine warfare as the sphere of military activity, segregated as much as possible from the life of society.

At the same time, there is a second, and equally conspicuous, tendency. This is the widely remarked sensitivity to incurring any appreciable level of military casualties, as clearly demonstrated at the time of the Gulf War. This reluctance is most visible in the United States, but is a common feature in the majority of contemporary developed states. States, then, are increasingly reluctant to put not only the lives of their civilians on the line, but also those of their soldiers. Is this a contradictory development, or does a consistent logic make sense of both trends? One writer neatly poses the issue in his comment that it is 'perhaps ironic that in the nuclear age concern about the safety of the individual soldier has reached new heights' (Spybey 1996: 127). Is it ironic that such a principle of 'combatant immunity' should be under development? And is it paradoxical that there should be a trend towards the separation of the military from society, at the same time as there is also a trend to minimize for the soldier what might hitherto have been deemed the inescapable hazards of the profession? If security is being re-professionalized, and society demobilized, is it not inconsistent at the same time to seek to evade the professional responsibilities that the military are supposed to accept?

Alternatively, we are forced to consider whether there is not a single logic that can account for both movements simultaneously. What seems to be questioned by these developments is where the security buck stops. Accordingly, it can be suggested that the reason for the trend towards the segregation of the military from society is, in fact, the very same reason pushing for a lessening of the risks incurred by the military as well. Any such analysis must focus upon the notion of a changing societal bargain or compact. If it is broadly true, as Shaw suggests, that in the historical development of the state, the 'incorporation of the workers into parliamentary democracy was itself largely a trade-off for universal military service' (1994: 145), then it would follow that the abandonment of universal military service betokens a new trade-off. This, in turn, might entail a growing divergence within Shaw's implicit association of 'political rights with military duty'. Political rights, and by extension social and economic rights, thereby become further separated from the citizen's obligation to bear arms. At the same time, it might also be thought that the soldier's obligation to make the ultimate sacrifice is also reduced. Precisely because the state now provides less – security, welfare, economic benefits, sovereignty – it is led to make fewer demands on both its civilians *and* its soldiers.

The same conclusion might be reached from an 'externalist' perspective. What traditionally legitimized the demands the state could make of its own society was the bargain whereby, in return, the state would provide a range of social goods, above all the security of their enjoyment. Symptomatically, the altered terms of these domestic compacts call into question the basis on which the resort to violence can be legitimized. Revealingly, analysts do claim to detect a shift of this nature, especially since the end of the cold war. The drift from security unilateralism to multilateralism itself draws attention to the extent to which 'the use of force is subject to greater collective legitimation' (Ruggie 1998: 197). This is not to suggest that, *in extremis*, a state can no longer act individually, but the emerging norm is evidently to act as part of a coalition, both as a matter of practicality and also as the policy of preference. If states still have the monopoly on legitimation of violence, they now express this multilaterally if at all. Ruggie locates these developments in the context of his argument about 'territorial unbundling' which, as suggested above, seems to be a fair description of the very nature of globalization. What this then implies is that legitimation of violence is indeed ceasing to be monopolized by individual states, at the very same time as the provision of social goods is thought to derive increasingly from globalized processes.

This seems like a compelling case of form following function. Since the state can no longer take all the credit for this provision, the social compacts are being reconfigured on a multilateral or transnational basis, and the state is less entitled to legitimize violence on its own account. It follows also that it cannot require its citizens to make undue sacrifice for its cause. To this extent, security is becoming disembedded from the specific national compacts that have been so characteristic of the history of the previous century. If this is now true of strong states, it has in a sense always been the case for weak states and this, in turn, might imply a greater uniformity in future of state underproduction of security.
[ . . . ]
On security as elsewhere, globalization impinges not simply from the outside in, but also from the inside out. If globalization is a factor in changing security, it operates within both realms simultaneously – both re-creating the state and setting new agendas as part of a single political process. We should speak less about globalization *and* the security state and think more about the globalization *of* the security state.

# References

Adler, E. (1997) Imagined (security) communities: cognitive regions in international relations. *Millennium*, 26 (2).

Ayoob, M. (1997) Defining security: a subaltern realist perspective. In K. Krause and M. C. Williams (eds), *Critical Security Studies: Concepts and Cases*, London.

Bretherton, C. and Ponton, G. (eds) (1996) *Global Politics: An Introduction*. Oxford.

Chipman, J. (1993) Managing the politics of parochialism. *Survival*, 35 (1).

Cox, R. W. (1996) Production and security. In R. W. Cox, *Approaches to World Order*, Cambridge.

Crawford, B. (1995) Hawks, doves, but no owls: international economic interdependence and construction of the new security dilemma. In R. D. Lipschutz (ed.), *On Security*, New York.

Deudney, D. (1995) Political fission: state structure, civil society, and nuclear security politics in the United States. In R. D. Lipschutz (ed.), *On Security*, New York.

Freedman, L. (1998) *The Revolution in Strategic Affairs*, Adelphi Paper 318. Oxford.

Giddens, A. (1985) *The Nation-state and Violence*. Cambridge.

Giddens, A. (1998) Affluence, poverty and the idea of a post-scarcity society. In K. Booth (ed.), *Statecraft and Security: The Cold War and Beyond*, Cambridge.

Guehenno, J.-M. (1998/9) The impact of globalisation on strategy. *Survival*, 40 (4).

Guibernau, M. (1996) *Nationalisms: The Nation-state and Nationalism in the Twentieth Century*. Cambridge.

Hall, J. A. (ed.) (1986) *States in History*. Oxford.

Harknett, R. J. (1996) Territoriality in the nuclear era. In E. Kofman and G. Youngs (eds), *Globalization: Theory and Practice*, London.

Held, D. and McGrew, A. (1993) Globalization and the liberal democratic state. *Government and Opposition*, 28 (2).

Herz, J. (1973) *The Nation-state and the Crisis of World Politics*. New York.

Hoffmann, S. (1995/6) The politics and ethics of military intervention. *Survival*, 37 (4).

Holsti, K. J. (1996) *The State, War and the State of War*. Cambridge.

Howe, H. M. (1998) Global order and the privatization of security. *Fletcher Forum of World Affairs*, 22 (2).

Kaldor, M. (1998) Reconceptualizing organized violence. In D. Archibugi, D. Held and M. Kohler (eds), *Re-imagining Political Community: Studies in Cosmopolitan Democracy*, Cambridge.

Klare, M. T. and Thomas, D. C. (1994) *World Security: Challenges for a New Century*, 2nd edn. New York.

Kritsiotis, D. (1998) Mercenaries and the privatization of warfare. *Fletcher Forum of World Affairs*, 22 (2).

Laidi, Z. (1998) *A World without Meaning: The Crisis of Meaning in International Politics*. London.

Latham, R. (1996) Getting out from under: rethinking security beyond liberalism and the levels-of-analysis problem. *Millennium*, 25 (1).

Mann, M. (1986) *The Sources of Social Power. Vol. I: A History of Power from the Beginning to AD 1760*. Cambridge.

Mann, M. (1993) *The Sources of Social Power. Vol. II: The Rise of Classes and Nation-states, 1760–1914*. Cambridge.

Mann, M. (1997) Has globalization ended the rise and rise of the nation-state? *Review of International Political Economy*, 4 (3).

Ruggie, J. G. (1998) *Constructing the World Polity: Essays on International Institutionalization*. London.

Shaw, M. (1994) *Global Society and International Relations*. Oxford.

Shearer, D. (1998) *Private Armies and Military Intervention*, Adelphi Paper 316. Oxford.

Sørensen, G. (1997) An analysis of contemporary statehood: consequences for conflict and cooperation. *Review of International Studies*, 23 (3).

Spybey, T. (1996) *Globalization and World Society*. Cambridge.

Tilly, C. (1985) War making and state making as organized crime. In P. B. Evans, H. K. Jacobson and R. D. Putnam (eds), *Bringing the State Back In*, Cambridge.

Walker, R. B. J. (1993) *Inside/Outside: International Relations as Political Theory*. Cambridge.

Wyn Jones, R. (1996) 'Travel without maps': thinking about security after the cold war. In M. J. Davis (ed.), *Security Issues in the Post-Cold War World*, Cheltenham.

# 16

# Governing the Global Economy Through Government Networks

*Anne-Marie Slaughter*

How can States regulate an increasingly global economy? The litany of threats to State sovereignty is familiar: global financial flows, global corporations, global television, global computing, and global transportation networks. The generally accepted account of how such threats render State borders increasingly permeable and thus State power increasingly feeble conceives of sovereignty itself as a curiously static attribute, as if State power depended on maintaining territory as a hermetically sealed sphere. However, as Abram and Antonia Chayes point out, sovereignty in the post-Cold War and even the post-Second World War world is increasingly defined not by the power to insulate but by the power to participate – in international institutions of all kinds.[1] As globalization literally turns the world inside-out, nationalizing international law and internationalizing national law, the opportunities for such participation expand exponentially. What is new is that the resulting institutions are as likely to be transgovernmental as they are international or supranational. The result is indeed a 'power shift', but more within the State than away from it.[2]

Traditional conceptions of international law and international relations assume that States are the primary actors on the international stage and that States themselves are unitary, opaque, and capable of rational calculation. This is the image that gives rise to familiar metaphors such as billiard balls and black boxes; it is the assumption that feeds critical attacks on the liberal projection of the unitary individual onto the international system. As a unitary actor, the State speaks with one voice through the mouth of the head of state or chief executive. The assumption is not that the chief executive speaks only on his or her own account; on the contrary, he or she may be but a spokesperson for an outcome reached as the result of a complex interplay of domestic institutions and interests. Nevertheless, it is the head of state who is the embodiment and representative of the State in the international system, the gatekeeper for all interactions, both domestic and international.

Furthermore, it follows from this conception of the international system and of States as the primary actors within it that the rules governing international life must be a product of either State practice or negotiation. The resulting rules and institutions are described as being by States, for States, and of States. The paradigm is the multilateral international convention, negotiated over many years in various international watering holes, signed and ratified with attendant flourish and formality, and given continuing life through the efforts of an international secretariat whose members prod and assist ongoing rounds of negotiation aimed at securing compliance with obligations already undertaken and at expanding the scope and precision of existing rules.

The rules and institutions described by the traditional conceptions of international law are indeed important for the regulation of international conflict and the facilitation of international co-operation. In short, they are important for the creation and maintenance of international order. However, they apply to part only, and arguably a diminishing part, of the rules and institutions that are generated outside any one national legal system but that directly regulate individuals and groups in both their domestic and foreign interactions.

The conventional debate over globalization and the attendant decline of State power is handicapped by this traditional conception of States and State institutions. In fact, the State is not disappearing; it is disaggregating into its component institutions. The primary State actors in the international realm are no longer foreign ministries and heads of state, but the same government institutions that dominate domestic politics: administrative agencies, courts, and legislatures. The traditional actors continue to play a role, but they are joined by fellow government officials pursuing quasi-autonomous policy agendas. The disaggregated State, as opposed to the mythical unitary State, is thus hydra-headed, represented and governed by multiple institutions in complex interaction with one another abroad as well as at home.

The corollary of the disaggregation of the State in foreign relations is the rise of government networks. Courts, administrative agencies, legislators, and heads of State are all networking with their foreign counterparts. Each of these institutions has the capacity not only to represent 'the national interest' in interactions with its foreign counterparts, but also to act on a subset of interests arising from its particular domestic function that are likely to be shared by its foreign counterparts. The resulting networks take a variety of forms and perform a variety of functions, some of which will be elaborated in the rest of this chapter. But they are all the tangible manifestation of a new era of transgovernmental regulatory co-operation. More broadly still, they define transgovernmentalism as a distinctive mode of global governance: horizontal rather than vertical, composed of national government officials rather than international bureaucrats, decentralized and informal rather than organized and rigid.

Against this backdrop, it is worth returning to the question posed at the beginning of this chapter: how can States regulate an increasingly global economy? The answer is through government networks. When President Clinton called for a co-ordinated institutional response to the burgeoning global economic crisis, he immediately deployed not his Secretary of State, but the Secretary of the Treasury and the Chairman of the Federal Reserve to contact their foreign counterparts and co-ordinate a global interest rate cut. International networks of these officials are already well established. Indeed, in many cases they have formed their own organizations, which bear little resemblance to traditional international organizations. Steadily growing economic interdependence, at both the macro and micro levels, has forced economic regulators to work with one another transnationally in order to perform their domestic jobs more effectively. They are thus at the forefront of transgovernmental initiatives.

This chapter will focus on two particular types of government networks among financial regulators: central bankers, securities regulators, insurance commissioners, and antitrust officials. The first type are the relatively more formal transgovernmental regulatory organizations (TROs). The members of these organizations are domestic agencies, or even subnational agencies such as provincial or State regulators, in contrast to conventional international organizations, which are [made up] primarily, or solely, of nation-states. These transgovernmental organizations tend to operate with a minimum of physical and legal infrastructure. Most lack a foundational treaty, and operate under only a few agreed objectives or by-laws. Nothing they do purports to be legally binding on their members and mechanisms for formal enforcement or implementation are rare. Instead, these functions are left to the members themselves. But despite this informal structure and loose organization, these organizations have had an important influence on international financial regulatory co-operation.

The second type of government network consists of agreements between the domestic regulatory agencies of two or more States. The last few decades have witnessed the emergence of a vast network of such agreements, which effectively institutionalize channels of regulatory co-operation between specific countries. These agreements embrace principles that can be implemented by the regulators themselves. Widespread use of Memoranda of Understanding (MOUs) and even less formal initiatives has sped the growth of governmental networks. Further, while these agreements are most commonly bilateral arrangements, they may also evolve into plurilateral arrangements, offering greater flexibility with less formality than traditional international organizations.

Government networks have many advantages. They are fast, flexible, cheap, and potentially more effective, accountable, and inclusive than existing international institutions. They can spring up virtually overnight, address a host of issues, and form 'mega-networks' that link existing networks. As international actors from non-governmental organizations (NGOs) to corporations have already recognized, globalization and the information technology revolution make networking the organizational form of choice for a rapidly changing and varied environment. In comparison, formal international organizations increasingly resemble slow-moving dinosaurs. Government networks also offer more scope for experimentation. For example, they facilitate the development of potential solutions by small groups of countries, which can then be tested before being adopted more generally in a more traditional multilateral form.

In addition, government networks comprise national government officials rather than international officials, which avoids any need for two-level adoption or implementation of international rules. The actors who make the rules or formulate the principles guiding government networks are the same actors who have the power to enforce them. This attribute of government networks can work to enhance both effectiveness and accountability. Regarding effectiveness, the nature of international regulation increasingly requires States to assume obligations that involve commitments concerning the way in which, and the degree to which, they enforce their own national laws. Implementation of international agreements will thus become increasingly difficult unless the relevant national officials are involved from the beginning. Government networks bypass a great deal of cumbersome and formal international negotiating procedure.

Regarding accountability, government networks certainly pose problems, but are likely to emerge as the lesser of two evils. As domestic political resistance to globalization in many countries triggers a backlash against both existing international institutions and the prospect of new ones, transgovernmental activity by elected or even appointed national officials will seem less threatening than a burgeoning supranational bureaucracy. In Robert Kuttner's dark formulation: '[i]f the Federal Reserve operates domestically at one remove from democratic accountability, the IMF and the World Bank operate at two removes'.[3] More optimistically, government networks tend to be functionally oriented and easy to expand, meaning that they can include any actors who perform similar functions, whether private or public, national or supranational, regional or local. The result is a vast array of opportunities for participation in rule-making by an eclectic mix of actors.

These are rosy scenarios. Government networks also have disadvantages and worrisome features. Most of these fall under the heading of accountability, both domestic and international. First is the concern that government networks reflect technocracy more than democracy, that their purported effectiveness rests on shared functional values rather than on responsiveness to underlying social and political issues. Such concerns spawn a need to build mechanisms for accountability to domestic constituencies in countries participating in government networks. Second, however, is a set of concerns about global accountability: concerns about the politics of insulation and the politics of imposition. On the one hand, many developing countries are likely to see government networks as simply the latest effort to insulate the decisions of the powerful from the input of the weak. On the other hand, other countries, both developed and developing, may see government networks as a device whereby the most powerful countries penetrate the defences of national sovereignty to impose their policy templates on everyone else.

In addition to concerns about accountability, critics of government networks have also charged them with reflecting if not encouraging a minimalist global agenda and displacing traditional international organizations. Both of these claims are overblown and overlook the extent to which government networks can and do coexist with international organizations. The agenda pursued by government networks is generally a transnational regulatory agenda rather than a more traditional agenda devoted to providing global public goods, but they are hardly a *cause* of the asserted decline in resources allocated to combating global poverty, to human rights, and health care. Moreover, to the extent that they are displacing traditional international organizations, it is either because those organizations have proved relatively ineffective or, more frequently, because government networks are better adapted to a host of contemporary tasks and the technology available to accomplish them. Finally, government networks may be particularly well suited to the exercise of 'soft power', a form of influence and persuasion that requires States genuinely to interact with and learn from each other in a non-hierarchical setting.

[ . . . ]

## Regulating the Global Economy through Government Networks: Implications and Problems

What are the implications of government networks? At the most general level, they offer a new vision of global governance: horizontal rather than vertical, decentralized rather than centralized, and composed of national government officials rather than a supranational bureaucracy. They are *potentially* both more effective and more accountable than traditional international institutions, at least for some purposes. They simultaneously strengthen the power of the State and equip State actors to interact meaningfully and innovatively with a host of other actors. These include public actors at the supranational, subnational, and regional levels, private actors such as corporations and NGOs, and 'mixed' actors that are privately organized but increasingly perform public functions. Further, government networks are optimally adapted to the technology of the Information Age, existing more in virtual than real space. Finally, as the form of governance changes, function is likely to follow suit, enabling government networks to deploy resources away from command and control regulation and towards a variety of catalysing and supporting roles.[4]

Yet government networks trigger both suspicion and anxiety. The suspicion is of a burgeoning global technocracy, insensitive to political choices driven by more than functional considerations and unresponsive to existing mechanisms of democratic governance at the national or international levels. The anxiety is a function of many of the same network attributes that are positively evaluated above. As any feminist who has battled 'the old boy network' will quickly recognize, the informality, flexibility, and decentralization of networks means that it is very difficult to establish precisely who is acting and when. Influence is subtle and hard to track; important decisions may be made in very informal settings. As Martti Koskenniemi argues [ . . . ], giving up form and validity is ceding fundamental constraints on power.[5]

At this stage, systematic empirical observations of government networks are so limited that both camps can see what they want to see, or at least what they are primed to look for. Existing networks differ in many ways, both within and across issue areas; even where the literature is fairly extensive, as in the documentation of new forms of financial regulation, it is often quite technical and silent on questions such as accountability. Further, different government networks have different relationships with existing international or supranational organizations. Similarly, their members have a range of different relationships with various national supervisory bodies such as legislative committees. Both international lawyers and political scientists could usefully engage in case studies and systematic research across issue areas.

At this stage of the analysis, a review of some of the principal criticisms of government networks that have been advanced in print and in public audiences, together with some tentative responses, may help guide future research agendas. This section distils three such criticisms: lack of accountability; promotion of a minimalist and exclusionary policy agenda; and marginalization and displacement of traditional international organizations. After reviewing each critique, I set forth some initial responses, many of which will also pose questions for further study.

## A new technocratic élite

The sharpest criticisms of government networks emphasize their lack of accountability. According to Philip Alston, if [Slaughter's] analysis 'is correct . . . , [i]t implies the marginalisation of governments as such and their replacement by special interest groups . . . It suggests a move away from arenas of relative transparency into the back rooms . . . and the bypassing of the national political arenas to which the United States and other proponents of the importance of healthy democratic institutions attach so much importance'.[6] Antonio Perez, identifying a related argument about networks among national and international bureaucrats in Abram and Antonia Chayes's *The New Sovereignty*, accuses them of adopting 'Platonic Guardianship as a mode of transnational governance', an open 'move toward technocratic elitism'.[7] And Sol Picciotto, who also chronicles the rise of government networks but from a more explicitly critical perspective, argues: 'A chronic lack of legitimacy plagues direct international contacts at the sub-State level among national officials and administrators.'[8] He attributes this lack of legitimacy to their informality and confidentiality, precisely the attributes that make them so attractive to the participants.[9]

Such charges are much easier to make than to prove. To begin with, concerns about accountability assume that government networks are developing and implementing substantive policies in ways that differ significantly from outcomes that would be reached as the result of purely national processes or of negotiations within traditional international institutions. Although reasons exist to accept this premiss with regard to policy initiatives such as the 1988 Capital Accord adopted by the Basle Committee,[10] it is less clear regarding other networks, even within the financial arena. Network initiatives are theoretically subject to the normal political constraints on domestic policy-making processes once they have been introduced at the domestic level. Arguments that they circumvent these constraints rest on the presumed ability of national officials in the same issue area to collude with one another in ways that strengthen their respective positions *vis-à-vis* bureaucratic rivals or legislative overseers back home. This presumption is often contested by experts in the different fields of financial regulation and requires further research on a case by case basis.

More generally, many government networks remain primarily talking shops, dedicated to the sharing of information, the cross-fertilization of new ideas, and the development of common principles based on the respective experiences of participating members. The power of information is soft power, persuasive rather than coercive.[11] It is 'the ability to get desired outcomes because others want what you want'.[12] Specific government institutions may still enjoy a substantial advantage over others due to the quality, quantity, and credibility of the information they have to exchange.[13] But in giving and receiving this information, even in ways that may significantly affect their thinking, government officials are not exercising power in the traditional ways which polities find it necessary to hold them accountable for. We may need to develop new metrics or even new conceptions of accountability geared towards the distinctive features of power in the Information Age.

A second and related response raises the question whether and when direct accountability is necessary for legitimate government. Some domestic institutions, such as courts and central banks, are deemed to act legitimately without direct accountability. Legitimacy may be conferred or attained independent of mechanisms of direct accountability – performance may be measured by outcomes as much as by process. Insulated institutions are designed to counter the voters' changing will and whim, in order to garner the benefits of expertise and stability and to protect minorities. Many of the policy arenas in which government networks are likely to be most active are those in which domestic polities have agreed that a degree of insulation and expertise is desirable. Thus, it is not automatically clear that the transgovernmental extension of these domestic activities poses legitimacy problems.

A third response is: 'accountable compared to what?' The presumed accountability or lack thereof of government networks must be contrasted with the accountability of international organizations on the one hand and NGOs on the other. International organizations are widely perceived as being accountable only to diplomats and international lawyers, which helps explain their relative disrepute in many countries. And accountable to whom? The United Nations suffers from the perennial perception that it is answerable primarily to its own bureaucracy; the International Monetary Fund and, to a lesser extent, the World Bank are widely seen as fronts for the United States; European Union institutions have been in crisis over a purported 'democracy deficit'

for much of this decade; the World Trade Organization draws populist fire for privil-
eging free trade, and hence the large corporate interests best positioned to benefit
from free trade, over the employment, welfare, environmental, and cultural interests
of large numbers of voters.[14]

NGOs hardly fare better. Although they must routinely sing for their supper and
thus depend on their ability to persuade individual and institutional contributors of
the worth of their activities, many, if not most, are single issue groups who target a
particular demographic and political segment of society and may well wield power quite
disproportionate to the number of their supporters. Further, their contributors rarely
have any direct control over policy decisions once the contribution has been made,
or, equally important, any means of ensuring how their contribution was spent.

In this context, government networks have a number of potential advantages.
First, they are composed of the same officials who make and implement regulations
domestically. To the extent that these networks do actually make policy, and to the
extent that the policies made and subsequently adopted at the national level differ
significantly from the outcome of a purely domestic regulatory process, it is reasonable to expect that other domestic political institutions – legislators, courts, or other
branches of the bureaucracy – will extend their normal oversight functions to transgovernmental as well as domestic activities. Alston rejects this claim as excessively
optimistic, arguing that all the organs of the State have been significantly weakened
by globalization and the neo-liberal economic agenda that has accompanied it.[15] That,
however, is a separate argument, which is considered separately below. It is also an
argument with far broader implications: if the State is really so weakened, then the
prospects of enhancing the accountability of any of the important actors in international life are slim indeed.

A promising development that suggests that State institutions with a more directly
representative mandate are not yet dead is the growth of legislative networks: links
among those national officials who are most directly responsible for ensuring bureaucratic accountability. In some areas, national legislation has been used to facilitate the
growth of government networks.[16] In others, such as human rights and the environ-
ments, national legislators are increasingly recognizing that they have common interests.
In the European Union, governments are increasingly having to submit their European
policies to special parliamentary committees, who are themselves networking.[17] The
result, according to German international relations scholar Karl Kaiser, is the 'repar-
liamentarization' of national policy.[18] In addition, legislative networks can be used to
strengthen national legislative institutions. For example, the Association of African
Election Authorities was founded in 1997. It is composed both of government officials
and leaders of NGOs directly involved in monitoring and assisting elections.

Other examples include legislative networks contained within international organizations, as discussed further below. These networks allow the regulators or parliaments of weak States to participate in global governance, and thereby serve the functions
both of setting a good example for fragile institutions and of lending their strength
and status to the organization in question. The OSCE Parliamentary Assembly, for
example, has played an important role in legitimizing Eastern European parliaments
by monitoring elections and including parliamentarians in all OSCE deliberations. The
controversy surrounding the OSCE's rejection of a Belarussian delegation in July 1997
demonstrates that membership in the Assembly has become a symbol of governmental legitimacy.[19]

A final response to the accountability critique is that the critics are missing a more significant point about the changing nature of power itself. Government networks are far better suited to exercising 'soft power' than 'hard power' – that is, the power flowing from an ability to convince others that they want what you want rather than an ability to compel them to forgo their preferences by using either threats or rewards.[20] Soft power rests much more on persuasive than coercive authority, a base that may in turn require a capacity for genuine engagement and dialogue with others. To the extent that government officials seek to persuade but then find that they must in turn allow themselves to be persuaded in their interactions with their foreign counterparts, what should mechanisms of accountability be designed to accomplish?

If a judge, or a regulator, or even a legislator, learns about alternative approaches to a problem facing him or her in the process of disseminating his or her own country's solution, and views that solution more critically thereafter, is there an accountability problem? The answer is likely to be that an accountable government does not seek to constrain the sources of knowledge brought to bear on a particular governance problem, but rather the ways in which that knowledge is acted upon. Fair enough, but many government officials will think and act differently as a result of their participation in transgovernmental networks in ways that we cannot, and arguably should not, control.

## A minimalist global agenda

A second major critique of government networks is that they instantiate a radically scaled-back global policy agenda. Alston observes that the formulation of the transgovernmental policy agenda focuses on issues that are essentially spillovers from the domestic policy agendas of the industrialized world, leaving out global poverty, malnutrition, human rights, refugees, the persecution of minority groups, and disease.[21] On a superficial level, he is right. The formulation of the policy agenda in my own previous writing on transgovernmentalism and in an article by Michael Reisman[22] who makes a number of similar points does focus more on the extension of a national regulatory agenda than on more traditional international issues. In this sense the 'real new world order', to quote from my own work, is more about the globalization of national regulatory problems and solutions than the extension of traditional international institutions that was apparently initially envisaged by George Bush.

But that is a rhetorical flourish, a point advanced as provocatively as possible. Alston is making a more important point, arguing that the transgovernmental regulatory agenda is *displacing* the traditional internationalist agenda of providing public goods to solve international collective action problems. That is a much more serious charge, but it confuses the symptoms with the disease. How can the emergence of transgovernmental regulatory networks addressing domestic policy issues that have become globalized be adduced as a *cause* of declining interest in an older but perennial set of international problems? Frustration with international bureaucracy, doubt about the value received for money already spent, neo-liberal economics as a (dubious) domestic solution that in many countries is projected on to the national sphere, the converse crisis of the social democratic (liberal, in the United States) welfare State – surely these are the real culprits. The resulting issues demand introspection and innovation, on all our parts.

More generally, the problems Alston identifies are best addressed at the level of changing domestic State preferences. It is national officials who must be motivated to renew their commitment to the global public issues he identifies. They must also be convinced that at least partial solutions to problems such as poverty, disease, famine, human rights abuses (including women's and children's rights) are achievable and worth pursuing on a global rather than a purely national scale. Focusing on networks of national government officials, many of whom are grappling with these problems within their own countries, is a sensible strategy for pursuing this agenda, and possibly the optimal strategy. Even if traditional international institutions are the best mechanisms for implementing a revived maximalist global agenda, a question addressed in the next section, it is States and thus government officials who must set and fund that agenda.

## Displacing international institutions

The third critique of government networks is that they are displacing international institutions. Alston makes this charge by again equating government networks with the values of globalization and then lamenting the impact of those values on international organizations.[23] However, a broader critique along the same lines emerges not only from the contrast that I and others have drawn between traditional liberal internationalism and transgovernmentalism, but also from the perception that government networks offer some States a way of escaping or circumventing undesirable aspects of international organizations. In particular, government networks can be seen as a way of avoiding the universality of international organizations and the cumbersome formality of their procedures that is typically designed to ensure some measure of equality of participation. Members of a government network can pick and choose new members, establish tiers of membership, or simply design procedures that ensure that power is concentrated among some members. Networks that fit this description fuel fears that their members are engaging in a politics of insulation from the global community.

These are genuine and potentially serious concerns that may well be warranted in respect of some government networks at least some of the time. But at this level, the debate is too general to have much bite. The charges of insulating powerful States at the expense of weaker States will have to be demonstrated and rebutted in the context of specific networks. The much larger point, however, is that the apparent opposition between government networks and international organizations is likely to prove a false dichotomy. Transgovernmentalism represents an alternative paradigm of global governance, but, like all paradigms, its purity is quickly stained in practice. Further, continuing to frame the debate in these terms will obscure an extraordinary set of opportunities to design new hybrid forms of governance that build on network concepts as well as on more traditional modes of organization.

In some issue areas, a real choice is emerging between regulation through government networks and through either existing or new international organizations. In international antitrust regulation, for example, the United States is actively pushing for transgovernmental co-operation, albeit under the auspices of the Organization for Economic Co-operation and Development, rather than intergovernmental harmonization through an organization like the World Trade Organization or the United Nations or a new international antitrust authority.[24] In such cases the claim that government networks will displace international organizations carries weight, although the international organization risking displacement will not be a promoter of the global agenda that champions of traditional international organizations appear to have in mind. Nevertheless, the outcome of such debates will depend on the relative merit not only of the institutional values fostered by competing institutional forms (speed, flexibility, and policy autonomy versus universality, formality, and deliberation), but also of the substantive regulatory outcomes each form is supposed to promote in the issue area in question (mutual recognition versus harmonization).

In many other issue areas, however, government networks will exist alongside or even within international institutions and are very likely to complement their functions. The NAFTA environmental enforcement network, for instance, is an example of a 'nested network', in which a government network implements the agenda of an international organization that is at least semi-traditional. Networks of national officials operating within the World Intellectual Property Organization, at least for the purposes of negotiating new approaches to international intellectual property regulation, offer another example. The real research questions will ultimately involve efforts to determine which organizational forms are best suited to which governance functions. It may even be possible to develop a principle of global subsidiarity, designed to facilitate the allocation of functions between international organizations and national officials operating within government networks, or some combination of the two.[25] In the meantime, the threat of competition from government networks will add the spur of competition to salutary efforts to reform existing international organizations.

A final critique of government networks implicates an idea, and perhaps an ideal, of internationalism: a distinction between international and domestic politics that is embodied in and protected by a conception of national sovereignty. However much their agendas now address issues once of purely domestic concern, international organizations still operate in a self-consciously international space. They employ independent international bureaucrats, whose loyalty is supposed to shift away from their national governments. And when they convene meetings of relevant national officials, as they frequently do, those officials are at the very least wearing dual hats, formally representing their governments in external affairs. As a result, the resolutions or even rules adopted can be resisted at the national level as being external and imposed.

One of the major advantages of government networks, at least from the perspective of those who are often frustrated by the difficulty of ensuring compliance with international rules and norms, is that they directly engage the national officials who have the power to implement domestic policy changes. As a result, the policies they adopt, implement, or at least promote are much harder to combat on grounds of national sovereignty. From a theoretical perspective, government networks straddle and ultimately erase the domestic/international divide. But from the perspective of some governments, such as the Mexican environmental officials participating in the North American Free Trade Agreement (NAFTA) 'environmental enforcement network', the result is a politics of imposition that is but the latest face of imperialism, or at least hegemony.

This critique must also be contextualized. In many international issue areas, such as human rights or environmental regulation, or even many types of financial regulation, the point is precisely to penetrate national sovereignty. The policy decisions that are the subject of international concern are being made at the domestic level. Conversely, rules and principles being adopted in the international or transgovernmental sphere are supposed to shape governments' relations with their own systems. Further, these goals are often shared by many domestic actors. Thus, to say that government networks are particularly effective at penetrating the face of national sovereignty and defusing opposition based on the 'imposition' of foreign or international rules and institutions is as likely to be praise as censure.

## Advantages of government networks: bringing the (disaggregated) state back in

The danger in responding to specific criticisms is always that of losing sight of the forest. In this case, much of the critique of transgovernmentalism betrays reflexive hostility and poverty of imagination – a defensive attachment to a liberal internationalist agenda that champions international organizations either as ends in themselves or as the only means to achieve transcendent policy goals. For many, even those who share the underlying policy goals, this agenda is nothing more than yesterday's *status quo*: the welfare State at home, international bureaucracy abroad. Transgovernmentalism may in some cases be associated with other policy agendas, such as neo-liberal economics. But it also reflects the rise of an organizational form as a mode of adaptation to a host of factors, from technology to the decline of inter-State conflict, that cannot be wished or argued away. It is a choice, of course, whether to celebrate or lament this development. But here again, the choice even to frame transgovernmentalism as an issue offers numerous advantages that its critics apparently have not stopped to ponder.

First, and most important, transgovernmentalism is all about bringing the State back in as an important international actor. As emerges repeatedly in Alston's analysis, his underlying concern is the decline of State power. He argues: 'Several parallel developments are working to reduce the powers of the state, of national legislatures, and of international organisations, while private power (that of corporations rather than NGOs) is taking up even more of the slack left by the emergence of the minimalist state.'[26] This has certainly been the conventional wisdom for much of the past decade. But a new consensus is emerging on the importance of a strong State. Gerard Helman and Steven Ratner began by pointing out the terrible consequences of 'failed States', an argument that was reviled for its neo-colonial overtones in suggesting international substitutes for domestic State power, but that can be read equally as highlighting the importance of a well-functioning State.[27] Stephen Holmes has followed suit with his diagnosis of the disasters flowing from 'weak-State liberalism' in the former Soviet Union.[28] And as Alston himself acknowledges, even the World Bank is recognizing 'that the backlash against the state . . . has gone too far'.[29]

The point of presenting transgovernmentalism as a 'new world order', in contrast to the claims of liberal internationalists who seek to devolve power ever upward to international organizations and 'new medievalists' who predict or even call for the demise of the Westphalian system, was to argue that State power was disaggregating rather than disappearing. State actors are exercising their power by different means and through different channels. Alston is quite right to claim that this is a partial image – 'one . . . layer out of a much more complex set of strata'.[30] But singling out this layer is a reminder that the State is not standing still. Further, thinking about global policy issues – in all areas – in terms of networks of State actors that compete with, complement, and even bridge the gap to networks of supranational, subnational, and private actors opens the door to a host of new ways in which State actors can address global problems.

A final example is in order. The arrest and requested extradition of General Augusto Pinochet from Britain to Spain to stand trial for crimes against humanity committed in Chile illustrates the impact of transnational judicial networks. A Spanish judge not only requests the British government to proceed with arrest and extradition under applicable British and European law, but specifically addresses arguments to his British counterparts by tailoring his extradition request to take account of objections raised in an initial judgment blocking extradition by a lower British court. Furthermore, other European magistrates – from France, Switzerland, Belgium, Luxembourg, and Sweden – all quickly voiced their support of the Spanish position by announcing potential extradition requests of their own. Judges in each country have been reinforced in their interpretation of international and domestic law by an awareness of their counterparts abroad, lending substance to the idea of a global community of law. The substance of their achievement in helping to bring a notorious human rights violator to justice might be even greater with the added assistance of an international institution such as the projected international criminal court. But disaggregated State actors, interacting with the political branches but maintaining their own autonomy, have not done so badly.

A second major advantage of government networks concerns the ways in which they can be used to strengthen individual State institutions without labelling the State as a whole as 'weak', 'failed', 'illiberal', or anything else. Networks target specific institutions, imposing particular conditions or at least goals regarding the level and quality of their functioning and often providing direct information and even material aid. The SEC, for example, distributes considerable technical assistance through its network of MOUs with other securities regulation agencies.[31] The criteria for participation have little to do with the political system as a whole and a great deal to do with technical or professional competence. While it may seem odd to praise the act of turning a blind eye to abuses and worse elsewhere in a national political system, the concept of a disaggregated State recognizes that wholesale labels are likely to be misleading and/or counter-productive. States are not unitary actors inside or out; absent revolution, they are likely to evolve and change in complex institutional patterns. Government networks may be exclusionary in various ways, but they are also inclusive in ways that some international organizations cannot afford to be.

On a more theoretical level, Abram and Antonia Chayes argue that 'the new sovereignty' is actually 'status – the vindication of the state's existence in the international system'.[32] They demonstrate that in contemporary international relations, sovereignty has been redefined to mean 'membership . . . in the regimes that make up the substance of international life'.[33] Disaggregating the State makes it possible to disaggregate sovereignty as well, helping specific State institutions derive strength and status from participation in a transgovernmental order. The net cost or benefit of this development will depend on the values transmitted through any particular government network, but no values are inherent in the organizational form itself. However, the potential to be gained from piercing the sovereign veil and targeting specific institutions is enormous.

## Conclusion

Many international lawyers will not like the message of this chapter. It seems an assault on all that internationalists have laboured so painstakingly to build in the twentieth century. It offers a horizontal rather than a vertical model of global governance, an informal and frequently selective set of institutions in place of formal and highly scripted fora in which each State is accorded an equal voice. Alternatively, government networks may appear trendy but inconsequential – talking shops at best and opportunities for foreign junkets at worst. After all, international institutions have proliferated over the past decades and seem sufficiently robust that at least one noted political scientist has posed the question 'Why do they never die?'[34]

In fact, government networks are here to stay and will assume increasing importance in all areas of international life. They are the optimal form of organization for the Information Age. Note the responses to the East Asian financial crisis; amid calls for a new Bretton Woods agreement to craft and implement a new international architecture, the real forum for policy innovation and implementation is the G22. Governmental networks are less likely to displace international organizations than to infiltrate and complement them; they will also be the ideal fora for pioneering initiatives and pilot projects among smaller groups of States. In economic regulation in particular, they develop easily as they are based on shared technical expertise among regulators and the escalating demands of a globalized economy among both the richest States and the most promising emerging markets.

The provenance of current government networks should not limit their applicability, however. They offer an important governance alternative to both traditional international institutions and 'new medievalist' networks of non-State, regional, local, and supranational actors. It is an alternative that can be promoted and used in imaginative ways, from bolstering legislative and judicial networks to 'nesting networks' within existing international institutions and creating standing links between government networks and NGO networks. Such initiatives will simultaneously have to address rising questions of the accountability of transgovernmental actors: how to define it and how to implement it.

Perhaps the sharpest challenge that proponents of and participants in government networks will have to surmount comes from those who see them as the newest blind for the projection of United States power. In its crudest form, the claim is that as international institutions have become too constraining, the United States has moved away from its traditional liberal internationalist agenda and begun promoting more informal co-operation through government networks which allow individual United States government institutions to play a dominant role. From this perspective, networks are an optimal organizational form only in so far as a United States institution remains the central node.

In contrast to this critique, however, United States policy-makers are beginning to find that in some areas networks create their own demands. In the areas of data privacy and cultural policy, for example, the United States is being excluded from transgovernmental co-operation because it does not have domestic government institutions concerned with these issues. Participation in a transgovernmental network requires a national node, but creation of such a node carries its own implications, and dangers, from the perspective of those who oppose such policy altogether. Thus, just as United

States securities regulators encourage the creation of at least quasi-autonomous securities commissions in emerging markets as the price of entry into both bilateral and plurilateral network relations, the United States executive and legislature is facing a similar choice in policy areas more foreign to United States traditions.

Finally, different organizational forms have their own impact on the ways in which power is most effectively exercised. The informality and flexibility of government networks privileges the expertise and superior resources of United States government institutions in many ways. At the same time, however, the absence of formal voting rules or even of established institutional protocols prevents the United States or any other powerful State from actually imposing its will. The dominant currency is engagement and persuasion, built on long-term relationships and trust. United States government officials from regulators to judges to legislators are likely to find themselves enmeshed in networks even as they try to engineer them.

Every age needs its own idealistic vision: the Information Age will celebrate the exchange of ideas over the imposition of ideology. Networks are the medium for that exchange, a medium that, like others before it, will itself become the message. The result will be the effective adaptation of national governments to the growth of networks among the private and semi-public actors they supposedly govern. The State will thus be able to retain its position as a primary locus of political, economic, and even social power in the international system, but shifts in both the organization and the nature of that power will ultimately transform the State itself.

## Notes

1   Abram and Antonia Chayes, *The New Sovereignty* (Cambridge, Mass.: Harvard University Press, 1996).
2   See Jessica T. Mathews, 'Power Shift' (1997) 1 *Foreign Affairs*, 76.
3   Robert Kuttner, 'Globalism Bites Back' (Mar.–Apr. 1998) 6 *The American Prospect*, 7.
4   The public management section of the OECD (called PUMA) has launched a major regulatory reform initiative that operates through a 'regulatory management and reform network'. A major focus of reform efforts is the shift away from 'command and control regulations' to a wide range of alternative instruments, many of them market-based or relying on self-regulation incentives. For an overview of this programme, see the PUMA website at http://www.oecd.org/puma/regref/work.htm. In the United States similar work has been done under Vice President Al Gore's 'Reinventing Government' initiative.
5   Koskenniemi, in M. Byers (ed.), *The Role of International Law in International Politics* (Oxford: Oxford University Press), chapter 3.
6   Philip Alston, 'The Myopia of the Handmaidens: International Lawyers and Globalisation' (1997) 8 *European Journal of International Law*, 435, 441.
7   Antonio Perez, 'Who Killed Sovereignty? Or: Changing Norms Concerning Sovereignty In International Law' (1996) 14 *Wisconsin International Law Journal*, 463, 476.
8   Sol Picciotto, 'Networks in International Economic Integration: Fragmented States and the Dilemmas of Neo-Liberalism' (1996–7) 17 *Northwestern Journal of International Law and Business*, 1014, 1047.
9   Ibid., at 1049.
10  Ethan B. Kapstein, *Supervising International Banks: Origins and Implications of the Basle Accord* (Princeton: Department of Economics, Princeton University, 1991).
11  Robert O. Keohane and Joseph S. Nye Jr., 'Power and Interdependence in the Information Age' (1998) 77 *Foreign Affairs*, 81, 86.
12  Ibid.
13  See ibid., at 89–92 (discussing 'the politics of credibility').

14   Consider the following passage from political scientist Henry Nau, which sounds virtually the same themes as Alston's critique of government networks: 'Whose political interests [are] being served by international institutions? Realists said State interests, but the major States today are democracies and consist of many societal and special interests that do not reflect a single government, let alone national interest. Critics of international institutions suspect that these special interests, especially corporate and bureaucratic élites with stakes in globalization, now dominate international organizations and use them to circumvent democratic accountability.' Nau, 'Institutional Skepticism', Letter to the Editor (Summer 1998) 111 *Foreign Policy*, 168.

15   Alston, 'Myopia of the Handmaidens', at 442.

16   MOUs between the SEC and its foreign counterparts, for example, have been directly encouraged and facilitated by several United States statutes passed expressly for the purpose. Faith T. Teo, 'Memoranda of Understanding among Securities Regulators: Frameworks for Cooperation, Implications for Governance' (1998), 29–43 (ms on file with author, Harvard Law School).

17   Shirley Williams, 'Sovereignty and Accountability in the European Union', in Robert Keohane and Stanley Hoffmann (eds), *The New European Community* (Boulder, Colo.: Westview Press, 1991).

18   Karl Kaiser, 'Globalisierung als Problem der Demokratie' (Apr. 1998) *Internationale Politik*, 3.

19   Aleksandr Potemkin, *Session of OSCE Parliamentary Assembly ends in Moscow*, ITAR-TASS News Agency, 9 July 1997.

20   Keohane and Nye, 'Power and Interdependence', at 86.

21   Alston, 'Myopia of the Handmaidens', at 439.

22   Michael Reisman, 'Designing and Managing the Future of the State' (1997) 8 *European Journal of International Law*, 409.

23   Alston, 'Myopia of the Handmaidens', at 444.

24   According to Spencer Weber Waller, '[Transgovernmental] [c]ooperation is currently in vogue because it *increases* national power. Substantive harmonization and true international antitrust law, in contrast, promise the diminution of both national lawmaking and enforcement power. Not surprisingly, the United States, although the current leader in pushing for cooperation, is the most reluctant harmonizer on the international scene.' 'The Internationalization of Antitrust Enforcement' (1997) 77 *Boston University Law Review*, 343, 378.

25   As a starting-point, one might argue that co-operative networks of national regulatory officials can and should focus on the issues which they are best equipped to address – the extension of their domestic policy briefs. International institutions should address those issues which either no one State is adequately equipped to address or which fail to be addressed at all at the national level, either as a result of collective action problems, or because of other reasons for resistance.

26   Alston, 'Myopia of the Handmaidens', at 442.

27   See e.g. Gerald Helman and Steven Ratner, 'Saving Failed States' (1992–3) 89 *Foreign Policy*, 3.

28   Stephen Holmes, 'What Russia Teaches Us Now' (July–Aug. 1997) *American Prospect*, 30; see also Grigory Yavlinsky, 'Russia's Phoney Capitalism' (May/June 1998) *Foreign Affairs*, 67.

29   Alston, 'Myopia of the Handmaidens', at 444.

30   Ibid., at 441.

31   Teo, 'Memoranda', at 23–4.

32   Chayes and Chayes, *The New Sovereignty*, at 27.

33   Ibid.

34   Susan Strange, 'Why Do International Organizations Never Die?', in B. Reinalda and V. Verbeek (eds), *Autonomous Policy Making by International Organizations* (London: Routledge, 1998), 213.

# 17
# Power Shift

*Jessica T. Mathews*

## The Rise of Global Civil Society

The end of the Cold War has brought no mere adjustment among states but a novel redistribution of power among states, markets, and civil society. National governments are not simply losing autonomy in a globalizing economy. They are sharing powers – including political, social, and security roles at the core of sovereignty – with businesses, with international organizations, and with a multitude of citizens' groups, known as nongovernmental organizations (NGOs). The steady concentration of power in the hands of states that began in 1648 with the Peace of Westphalia is over, at least for a while.

The absolutes of the Westphalian system – territorially fixed states where everything of value lies within some state's borders; a single, secular authority governing each territory and representing it outside its borders; and no authority above states – are all dissolving. Increasingly, resources and threats that matter, including money, information, pollution, and popular culture, circulate and shape lives and economies with little regard for political boundaries. International standards of conduct are gradually beginning to override claims of national or regional singularity. Even the most powerful states find the marketplace and international public opinion compelling them more often to follow a particular course.

[...]

The most powerful engine of change in the relative decline of states and the rise of nonstate actors is the computer and telecommunications revolution, whose deep political and social consequences have been almost completely ignored. Widely accessible and affordable technology has broken governments' monopoly on the collection and management of large amounts of information and deprived governments of the deference they enjoyed because of it. In every sphere of activity, instantaneous access to information and the ability to put it to use multiplies the number of players who matter and reduces the number who command great authority. The effect on the loudest voice – which has been government's – has been the greatest.

By drastically reducing the importance of proximity, the new technologies change people's perceptions of community. Fax machines, satellite hookups, and the Internet connect people across borders with exponentially growing ease while separating them from natural and historical associations within nations. In this sense a powerful globalizing force, they can also have the opposite effect, amplifying political and social fragmentation by enabling more and more identities and interests scattered around the globe to coalesce and thrive.

These technologies have the potential to divide society along new lines, separating ordinary people from elites with the wealth and education to command technology's power. Those elites are not only the rich but also citizens' groups with transnational interests and identities that frequently have more in common with counterparts in other countries, whether industrialized or developing, than with countrymen.

Above all, the information technologies disrupt hierarchies, spreading power among more people and groups. In drastically lowering the costs of communication, consultation, and coordination, they favor decentralized networks over other modes of organization. In a network, individuals or groups link for joint action without building a physical or formal institutional presence. Networks have no person at the top and no center. Instead, they have multiple nodes where collections of individuals or groups interact for different purposes. Businesses, citizens' organizations, ethnic groups, and crime cartels have all readily adopted the network model. Governments, on the other hand, are quintessential hierarchies, wedded to an organizational form incompatible with all that the new technologies make possible.

Today's powerful nonstate actors are not without precedent. The British East India Company ran a subcontinent, and a few influential NGOs go back more than a century. But these are exceptions. Both in numbers and in impact, nonstate actors have never before approached their current strength. And a still larger role likely lies ahead.

## Dial Locally, Act Globally

No one knows how many NGOs there are or how fast the tally is growing. Published figures are badly misleading. One widely cited estimate claims there are 35,000 NGOs in the developing countries; another points to 12,000 irrigation cooperatives in South Asia alone. In fact, it is impossible to measure a swiftly growing universe that includes neighborhood, professional, service, and advocacy groups, both secular and church-based, promoting every conceivable cause and funded by donations, fees, foundations, governments, international organizations, or the sale of products and services. The true number is certainly in the millions, from the tiniest village association to influential but modestly funded international groups like Amnesty International to larger global activist organizations like Greenpeace and giant service providers like CARE, which has an annual budget of nearly $400 million.

Except in China, Japan, the Middle East, and a few other places where culture or authoritarian governments severely limit civil society, NGOs' role and influence have exploded in the last half-decade. Their financial resources and – often more important – their expertise approximate and sometimes exceed those of smaller governments and of international organizations. "We have less money and fewer resources than Amnesty International, and we are the arm of the UN for human rights," noted Ibrahima Fall, head of the UN Centre for Human Rights, in 1993. "This is clearly ridiculous." Today NGOs deliver more official development assistance than the entire UN system (excluding the World Bank and the International Monetary Fund). In many countries they are delivering the services – in urban and rural community development, education, and health care – that faltering governments can no longer manage.

The range of these groups' work is almost as broad as their interests. They breed new ideas; advocate, protest, and mobilize public support; do legal, scientific, technical, and policy analysis; provide services; shape, implement, monitor, and enforce national and international commitments; and change institutions and norms.

Increasingly, NGOs are able to push around even the largest governments. When the United States and Mexico set out to reach a trade agreement, the two governments planned on the usual narrowly defined negotiations behind closed doors. But NGOs had a very different vision. Groups from Canada, the United States, and Mexico wanted to see provisions in the North American Free Trade Agreement on health and safety, transboundary pollution, consumer protection, immigration, labor mobility, child labor, sustainable agriculture, social charters, and debt relief. Coalitions of NGOs formed in each country and across both borders. The opposition they generated in early 1991 endangered congressional approval of the crucial "fast track" negotiating authority for the US government. After months of resistance, the Bush administration capitulated, opening the agreement to environmental and labor concerns. Although progress in other trade venues will be slow, the tightly closed world of trade negotiations has been changed forever.

Technology is fundamental to NGOs' new clout. The nonprofit Association for Progressive Communications provides 50,000 NGOs in 133 countries access to the tens of millions of Internet users for the price of a local call. The dramatically lower costs of international communication have altered NGOs' goals and changed international outcomes. Within hours of the first gunshots of the Chiapas rebellion in southern Mexico in January 1994, for example, the Internet swarmed with messages from human rights activists. The worldwide media attention they and their groups focused on Chiapas, along with the influx of rights activists to the area, sharply limited the Mexican government's response. What in other times would have been a bloody insurgency turned out to be a largely nonviolent conflict. "The shots lasted ten days," José Angel Gurría, Mexico's foreign minister, later remarked, "and ever since, the war has been . . . a war on the Internet."

NGOs' easy reach behind other states' borders forces governments to consider domestic public opinion in countries with which they are dealing, even on matters that governments have traditionally handled strictly between themselves. At the same time, cross-border NGO networks offer citizens' groups unprecedented channels of influence. Women's and human rights groups in many developing countries have linked up with more experienced, better funded, and more powerful groups in Europe and the United States. The latter work the global media and lobby their own governments to pressure leaders in developing countries, creating a circle of influence that is accelerating change in many parts of the world.

## Out of the Hallway, Around the Table

In international organizations, as with governments at home, NGOs were once largely relegated to the hallways. Even when they were able to shape governments' agendas, as the Helsinki Watch human rights groups did in the Conference on Security and Cooperation in Europe in the 1980s, their influence was largely determined by how receptive their own government's delegation happened to be. Their only option was to work through governments.

All that changed with the negotiation of the global climate treaty, culminating at the Earth Summit in Rio de Janeiro in 1992. With the broader independent base of public support that environmental groups command, NGOs set the original goal of negotiating an agreement to control greenhouse gases long before governments were ready to do so, proposed most of its structure and content, and lobbied and mobilized public pressure to force through a pact that virtually no one else thought possible when the talks began.

More members of NGOs served on government delegations than ever before, and they penetrated deeply into official decision-making. They were allowed to attend the small working group meetings where the real decisions in international negotiations are made. The tiny nation of Vanuatu turned its delegation over to an NGO with expertise in international law (a group based in London and funded by an American foundation), thereby making itself and the other sea-level island states major players in the fight to control global warming. *ECO*, an NGO-published daily newspaper, was negotiators' best source of information on the progress of the official talks and became the forum where governments tested ideas for breaking deadlocks.

Whether from developing or developed countries, NGOs were tightly organized in a global and half a dozen regional Climate Action Networks, which were able to bridge North–South differences among governments that many had expected would prevent an agreement. United in their passionate pursuit of a treaty, NGOs would fight out contentious issues among themselves, then take an agreed position to their respective delegations. When they could not agree, NGOs served as invaluable back channels, letting both sides know where the other's problems lay or where a compromise might be found.

As a result, delegates completed the framework of a global climate accord in the blink of a diplomat's eye – 16 months – over the opposition of the three energy superpowers, the United States, Russia, and Saudi Arabia. The treaty entered into force in record time just two years later. Although only a framework accord whose binding requirements are still to be negotiated, the treaty could force sweeping changes in energy use, with potentially enormous implications for every economy.

The influence of NGOs at the climate talks has not yet been matched in any other arena, and indeed has provoked a backlash among some governments. A handful of authoritarian regimes, most notably China, led the charge, but many others share their unease about the role NGOs are assuming. Nevertheless, NGOs have worked their way into the heart of international negotiations and into the day-to-day operations of international organizations, bringing new priorities, demands for procedures that give a voice to groups outside government, and new standards of accountability.

## One World Business

The multinational corporations of the 1960s were virtually all American, and prided themselves on their insularity. Foreigners might run subsidiaries, but they were never partners. A foreign posting was a setback for a rising executive.

Today, a global marketplace is developing for retail sales as well as manufacturing. Law, advertising, business consulting, and financial and other services are also marketed internationally. Firms of all nationalities attempt to look and act like locals wherever they operate. Foreign language skills and lengthy experience abroad are an asset, and increasingly a requirement, for top management. Sometimes corporate headquarters are not even in a company's home country.

Amid shifting alliances and joint ventures, made possible by computers and advanced communications, nationalities blur. Offshore banking encourages widespread evasion of national taxes. Whereas the fear in the 1970s was that multinationals would become an arm of government, the concern now is that they are disconnecting from their home countries' national interests, moving jobs, evading taxes, and eroding economic sovereignty in the process.

The even more rapid globalization of financial markets has left governments far behind. Where governments once set foreign exchange rates, private currency traders, accountable only to their bottom line, now trade $1.3 trillion a day, 100 times the volume of world trade. The amount exceeds the total foreign exchange reserves of all governments, and is more than even an alliance of strong states can buck.

Despite the enormous attention given to governments' conflicts over trade rules, private capital flows have been growing twice as fast as trade for years. International portfolio transactions by US investors, 9 percent of US GDP in 1980, had grown to 135 percent of GDP by 1993. Growth in Germany, Britain, and elsewhere has been even more rapid. Direct investment has surged as well. All in all, the global financial market will grow to a staggering $83 trillion by 2000, a 1994 McKinsey & Co. study estimated, triple the aggregate GDP of the affluent nations of the Organization for Economic Cooperation and Development.

Again, technology has been a driving force, shifting financial clout from states to the market with its offer of unprecedented speed in transactions – states cannot match market reaction times measured in seconds – and its dissemination of financial information to a broad range of players. States could choose whether they would belong to rule-based economic systems like the gold standard, but, as former Citicorp chairman Walter Wriston has pointed out, they cannot withdraw from the technology-based marketplace, unless they seek autarky and poverty.

More and more frequently today, governments have only the appearance of free choice when they set economic rules. Markets are setting de facto rules enforced by their own power. States can flout them, but the penalties are severe – loss of vital foreign capital, foreign technology, and domestic jobs. Even the most powerful economy must pay heed. The US government could choose to rescue the Mexican peso in 1994, for example, but it had to do so on terms designed to satisfy the bond markets, not the countries doing the rescuing.

The forces shaping the legitimate global economy are also nourishing globally integrated crime – which UN officials peg at a staggering $750 billion a year, $400 billion to $500 billion of that in narcotics, according to US Drug Enforcement Agency estimates. Huge increases in the volume of goods and people crossing borders and competitive pressures to speed the flow of trade by easing inspections and reducing paperwork make it easier to hide contraband. Deregulation and privatization of government-owned businesses, modern communications, rapidly shifting commercial alliances, and the emergence of global financial systems have all helped transform local drug operations into global enterprises. The largely unregulated multi-trillion-dollar pool of money in supranational cyberspace, accessible by computer 24 hours a day, eases the drug trade's toughest problem: transforming huge sums of hot cash into investments in legitimate business.

Globalized crime is a security threat that neither police nor the military – the state's traditional responses – can meet. Controlling it will require states to pool their efforts and to establish unprecedented cooperation with the private sector, thereby compromising two cherished sovereign roles. If states fail, if criminal groups can continue to take advantage of porous borders and transnational financial spaces while governments are limited to acting within their own territory, crime will have the winning edge.

## Born-Again Institutions

Until recently, international organizations were institutions of, by, and for nation-states. Now they are building constituencies of their own and, through NGOs, establishing direct connections to the peoples of the world. The shift is infusing them with new life and influence, but it is also creating tensions.

States feel they need more capable international organizations to deal with a lengthening list of transnational challenges, but at the same time fear competitors. Thus they vote for new forms of international intervention while reasserting sovereignty's first principle: no interference in the domestic affairs of states. They hand international organizations sweeping new responsibilities and then rein them in with circumscribed mandates or inadequate funding. With states ambivalent about intervention, a host of new problems demanding attention, and NGOs bursting with energy, ideas, and calls for a larger role, international organizations are lurching toward an unpredictable, but certainly different, future.

International organizations are still coming to terms with unprecedented growth in the volume of international problem-solving. Between 1972 and 1992 the number of environmental treaties rocketed from a few dozen to more than 900. While collaboration in other fields is not growing at quite that rate, treaties, regimes, and intergovernmental institutions dealing with human rights, trade, narcotics, corruption, crime, refugees, antiterrorism measures, arms control, and democracy are multiplying. "Soft law" in the form of guidelines, recommended practices, nonbinding resolutions, and the like is also rapidly expanding. Behind each new agreement are scientists and lawyers who worked on it, diplomats who negotiated it, and NGOs that back it, most of them committed for the long haul. The new constituency also includes a burgeoning, influential class of international civil servants responsible for implementing, monitoring, and enforcing this enormous new body of law.

At the same time, governments, while ambivalent about the international community mixing in states' domestic affairs, have driven some gaping holes in the wall that has separated the two. In the triumphant months after the Berlin Wall came down, international accords, particularly ones agreed on by what is now the Organization for Security and Cooperation in Europe and by the Organization of American States (OAS), drew explicit links between democracy, human rights, and international security, establishing new legal bases for international interventions. In 1991 the UN General Assembly declared itself in favor of humanitarian intervention without the request or consent of the state involved. A year later the Security Council took the unprecedented step of authorizing the use of force "on behalf of civilian populations" in Somalia. Suddenly an interest in citizens began to compete with, and occasionally override, the formerly unquestioned primacy of state interests.

Since 1990 the Security Council has declared a formal threat to international peace and security 61 times, after having done so only six times in the preceding 45 years. It is not that security has been abruptly and terribly threatened; rather, the change reflects the broadened scope of what the international community now feels it should poke its nose into. As with Haiti in 1992, many of the so-called Chapter VII resolutions authorizing forceful intervention concerned domestic situations that involved awful human suffering or offended international norms but posed little if any danger to international peace.

Almost as intrusive as a Chapter VII intervention, though always invited, election monitoring has also become a growth industry. The United Nations monitored no election in a member state during the Cold War, only in colonies. But beginning in 1990 it responded to a deluge of requests from governments that felt compelled to prove their legitimacy by the new standards. In Latin America, where countries most jealously guard their sovereignty, the OAS monitored 11 national elections in four years.

And monitoring is no longer the passive observation it was in earlier decades. Carried out by a close-knit mix of international organizations and NGOs, it involves a large foreign presence dispensing advice and recommending standards for voter registration, campaign law, campaign practices, and the training of clerks and judiciaries. Observers even carry out parallel vote counts that can block fraud but at the same time second-guess the integrity of national counts.

International financial institutions, too, have inserted themselves more into states' domestic affairs. During the 1980s the World Bank attached conditions to loans concerning recipient governments' policies on poverty, the environment, and even, occasionally, military spending, a once sacrosanct domain of national prerogative. In 1991 a statement of bank policy holding that "efficient and accountable public sector management" is crucial to economic growth provided the rationale for subjecting to international oversight everything from official corruption to government competence.

Beyond involving them in an array of domestic economic and social decisions, the new policies force the World Bank, the International Monetary Fund, and other international financial institutions to forge alliances with business, NGOs, and civil society if they are to achieve broad changes in target countries. In the process, they have opened themselves to the same demands they are making of their clients: broader public participation and greater openness in decision-making. As a result, yet another set of doors behind which only officials sat has been thrown open to the private sector and to civil society.

## Leaps of Imagination

After three and a half centuries, it requires a mental leap to think of world politics in any terms other than occasionally cooperating but generally competing states, each defined by its territory and representing all the people therein. Nor is it easy to imagine political entities that could compete with the emotional attachment of a shared landscape, national history, language, flag, and currency.

Yet history proves that there are alternatives other than tribal anarchy. Empires, both tightly and loosely ruled, achieved success and won allegiance. In the Middle Ages, emperors, kings, dukes, knights, popes, archbishops, guilds, and cities exercised overlapping secular power over the same territory in a system that looks much more like a modern, three-dimensional network than the clean-lined, hierarchical state order that replaced it. The question now is whether there are new geographic or functional entities that might grow up alongside the state, taking over some of its powers and emotional resonance.

The kernels of several such entities already exist. The European Union is the most obvious example. Neither a union of states nor an international organization, the EU leaves experts groping for inadequate descriptions like "post-sovereign system" or "unprecedented hybrid." It respects members' borders for some purposes, particularly in foreign and defense policy, but ignores them for others. The union's judiciary can override national law, and its Council of Ministers can overrule certain domestic executive decisions. In its thousands of councils, committees, and working groups, national ministers increasingly find themselves working with their counterparts from other countries to oppose colleagues in their own government; agriculture ministers, for example, ally against finance ministers. In this sense the union penetrates and to some extent weakens the internal bonds of its member states. Whether Frenchmen, Danes, and Greeks will ever think of themselves first as Europeans remains to be seen, but the EU has already come much further than most Americans realize.

Meanwhile, units below the national level are taking on formal international roles. Nearly all 50 American states have trade offices abroad, up from four in 1970, and all have official standing in the World Trade Organization (WTO). German *Länder* and British local governments have offices at EU headquarters in Brussels. France's Rhône-Alpes region, centered in Lyon, maintains what it calls "embassies" abroad on behalf of a regional economy that includes Geneva, Switzerland, and Turin, Italy.

Emerging political identities not linked to territory pose a more direct challenge to the geographically fixed state system. The WTO is struggling to find a method of handling environmental disputes in the global commons, outside all states' boundaries, that the General Agreement on Tariffs and Trade, drafted 50 years ago, simply never envisioned. Proposals have been floated for a Parliamentary Assembly in the United Nations, parallel to the General Assembly, to represent the people rather than the states of the world. Ideas are under discussion that would give ethnic nations political and legal status, so that the Kurds, for example, could be legally represented as a people in addition to being Turkish, Iranian, or Iraqi citizens.

Further in the future is a proposed Global Environmental Authority with independent regulatory powers. This is not as far-fetched as it sounds. The burden of participating in several hundred international environmental bodies is heavy for the richest governments and is becoming prohibitive for others. As the number of international agreements mounts, the pressure to streamline the system – in environmental protection as in other areas – will grow.

The realm of most rapid change is hybrid authorities that include state and non-state bodies such as the International Telecommunications Union, the International Union for the Conservation of Nature, and hundreds more. In many of these, businesses or NGOs take on formerly public roles. The Geneva-based International Standards Organization, essentially a business NGO, sets widely observed standards on everything from products to internal corporate procedures. The International Securities Markets Association, another private regulator, oversees international trade in private securities markets – the world's second-largest capital market after domestic government bond markets. In another crossover, markets become government enforcers when they adopt treaty standards as the basis for market judgments. States and NGOs are collaborating ad hoc in large-scale humanitarian relief operations that involve both military and civilian forces. Other NGOs have taken on standing operational roles for international organizations in refugee work and development assistance. Almost unnoticed, hybrids like these, in which states are often the junior partners, are becoming a new international norm.

[ . . . ]

## Dissolving and Evolving

Might the decline in state power prove transitory? Present disenchantment with national governments could dissipate as quickly as it arose. Continuing globalization may well spark a vigorous reassertion of economic or cultural nationalism. By helping solve problems governments cannot handle, business, NGOs, and international organizations may actually be strengthening the nation-state system.

These are all possibilities, but the clash between the fixed geography of states and the nonterritorial nature of today's problems and solutions, which is only likely to escalate, strongly suggests that the relative power of states will continue to decline. Nation-states may simply no longer be the natural problem-solving unit. Local government addresses citizens' growing desire for a role in decision-making, while transnational, regional, and even global entities better fit the dimensions of trends in economics, resources, and security.

[ ... ]

# 18

# Globalization and Modes of Regionalist Governance

## *Anthony Payne*

## Introduction

This chapter constitutes an attempt to link the concept of globalization to that of governance via the notion of regionalism. [ . . . ] [I]t defines regionalism [ . . . ] as 'a state-led or states-led project designed to reorganise a particular regional space along defined economic and political lines' (Payne and Gamble, 1996: 2). The leading current examples of such projects are the European Union (EU), the North American Free Trade Agreement (NAFTA) and Asia-Pacific Economic Cooperation (APEC). The adjective 'regionalist' used in the title thus derives from the noun 'regionalism', as defined above and as used in relation to the three cases identified, and is to be distinguished from the adjective 'regional' which derives from the noun 'region' (incidentally, a much more difficult category to define). This is no doubt an obvious distinction, but it is nevertheless one that is often not made in these sorts of discussions. [ . . . ]

At first sight, the trend towards globalization seems to be contradicted by the emergence of regionalist projects such as the EU, NAFTA, and APEC. In conventional readings these diverse initiatives have been typically constructed into a prevailing 'regional bloc scenario' which is then used to stoke fears of 'trade wars' between the blocs leading in time to 'real wars'. The problem with this line of interpretation, which is admittedly quite arresting as a 'headline' reading of some current international trends, is that it is grounded intellectually in a particular body of mainstream [international political economy] (IPE) theory which is itself seriously flawed. The so-called 'hegemonic stability thesis', which is at the core of neo-realist and neo-liberal IPE, does indeed argue that, in the absence of an effective hegemon to keep order, the world will degenerate into conflict which in the present era is most likely to be manifested between regional blocs of states. But such arguments are derived from narrow presumptions about the systemic tendency for interstate relations to be governed by the problematic of anarchy and they certainly make no allowance for the various changes in the nature of the world economy highlighted by the process of globalization. As Andrew Gamble and I [once] suggested, [ . . . ] a more sensible organizing claim was that 'the relationship between these two apparently competing tendencies in the contemporary world political economy – regionalism as a statist project and globalisation as a social process – appears still to be in the balance and indeed there is no reason to assume that one must necessarily triumph over the other' (Payne and Gamble, 1996: 2). [ . . . ] [After careful research,] we were prepared to go further and claim that 'state projects like regionalism typically seek to accelerate, to modify, or occasionally to reverse the direction of social change' associated with globalization (Gamble and Payne, 1996: 250). In other words, the argument was that regionalism, far from being in contradiction with globalization, was in fact an essential part of the phenomenon. 'In practice', as we put it, 'regionalism as a set of state projects intersects with globalisation' (Gamble and Payne, 1996: 250). There is not the space here to set out the various ways in which this has occurred in relation to the EU, NAFTA, and APEC. However, the two points to insist on are: first, that the analysis of regionalist projects has to be undertaken in the context of an awareness of globalization (for, if this is not done, they will be misunderstood); and, second, that the various projects are all, albeit in different ways, centrally concerned with the reorganization of the dominant form of state operative in their region. [ . . . ]

## 'New Medievalism' and the Turn Towards Governance

The main concept that IPE has come up with to characterize the new global scene is the 'new medievalism'. This was a phrase first used by the late Hedley Bull as long ago as 1977 in suggesting that one alternative to the modern state system (the others were world government or an ideologically homogeneous cosmopolitan society) might be 'a modern and secular equivalent of the kind of universal political organization that existed in Western Christendom in the Middle Ages' (Bull, 1977: 254). Bull grounded his speculation on an insightful appreciation of five major trends which, in his view, gave rise to the possible emergence of a 'new medievalism'. The first was the trend towards regional integration, as best exemplified by the European Community, in respect of which Bull anticipated the likelihood, now more prominent in the literature, that the Community was pioneering a new, hybrid form of political organization. The second was the disintegration of existing states as a result of secessionism, although he noted that this would only be of significance for 'new medievalism' if the disintegration stopped short of the creation of new states. The third trend was the revival of private international violence, specifically terrorism, which potentially challenged the claim to the legitimate monopoly of the means of coercion conventionally associated with state sovereignty. The fourth was the growth of transnational organizations with which states were increasingly being forced to share power and authority, and the fifth was the technological unification of the world, particularly in respect of communications, transport, and cultural networks, a theme which, as we have seen, has been amply highlighted in the much more recent globalization discourse.

Nevertheless, as intriguing as his analysis undoubtedly was, Bull himself ultimately remained sceptical as to how far any of these trends would actually lead to permanent changes, as opposed to marginal adjustments, in the international state system. Accordingly, his exploration of the notion of a 'new medievalism' was largely forgotten for several years until it was picked up in the early 1990s by a number of writers to highlight both the variegated nature of the political actors currently operational in international politics and the apparently common ideological discourse of a liberal democratic political economy (à la Fukuyama) within which they have now to act. For example, Robert Cox, the founding figure of 'new' IPE, drew attention to a number of features of what he called 'global *perestroika*'. The old state system, he suggested, was resolving itself into a complex of political–economic entities, including micro-regions, traditional states and macro-regions with institutions of greater or lesser functional scope; world cities were emerging as the 'keyboards' of the global economy; and multi-lateral processes were providing regulation and service in an increasing number of areas of policy. All in all, he went on, specifically citing Bull in the associated end-note, 'the whole picture resembles the multi-level order of medieval Europe more than the Westphalian model of a system of sovereign independent states that has hereto-fore been the paradigm of international relations' (Cox, 1996: 308).

This argument was then taken even further by John Ruggie, who argued that the term 'new medievalism' was useful precisely because it highlighted the fact that the world is moving through a transition as significant as that between the medieval and modern eras. He accepted the arguments of such as Jameson (1984) and Harvey (1989) that it was not just that the Westphalian state system was in crisis, but rather that modernity itself was being reconfigured by the spatial and temporal implosion of the globe (the key theme in the new sociology of globalization). Ruggie's complaint was that most of this analysis was silent on the future of the state and the state-system. In his view, the old mode of differentiation of the international political system, namely territorial sovereignty, is being 'unbundled' by globalization. It is not adequate any longer to view political relations from the single-point perspective characteristic of the age of modernity; instead political and other forms of analysis must open up the 'multiperspectival' nature of reality and appreciate, for example, that the EU 'may constitute nothing less than the emergence of the first truly postmodern international political form' (Ruggie, 1993: 140). In this sense the intellectual approach required is actually closer to that of medieval times in Europe than of the modern period. At any rate, the implied association with the sort of distinctions drawn by Hirst and Thompson in relation to economic issues is clear [see chapter 7]. The 'inter-national' economy coexisted with Westphalian states; a 'globalized' or 'globalizing' economy is consistent with 'new medievalist' political structures.

As will be apparent, the 'new medievalist' analogy is above all a metaphor and, as such, it works well enough. However, viewed as prospective political analysis, it remains no more than an hypothesis and, even as that, it needs considerable fleshing out. Simon Bromley, for one, has rightly referred to much of the talk of 'new medievalism' as 'jejune' (Bromley, 1996: 132). Its great merit, though, is that it does recognize that there is a pressing need to analyse how the globalizing economy affects political structures and the political behaviour that goes on within them. As Andrew Gamble has said, 'the advantage of new medievalism is that it does focus attention on systems of rule, which globalisation does not' (Gamble, 1997: 14). In short, the con-cept raises the very matter of the *governance* of a globalizing economy and thus begins to demand of us precisely the shift from the IPE to the comparative politics and pub-lic policy literature which I believe to be necessary. As many have pointed out, there has already been an extensive debate in these fields of study about the meaning of the concept of governance – ranging from 'old' notions of governance understood as the 'steering' done by governments to the 'new governance' defined by Rhodes as 'governing without government' via 'self-organizing, interorganizational networks' (Rhodes, 1996: 660). Although these formulations are not without their interest, the exercise in hand here needs to adopt a significantly broader (and possibly therefore also admittedly looser) notion of governance than this specialist literature allows. The best formal conceptualization is provided by James Rosenau who uses the term to refer to 'spheres of authority . . . at all levels of human activity . . . that amount to systems of rule in which goals are pursued through the exercise of control' (Rosenau, 1997: 145).

Conceived in this fashion, the question before us can be reformulated very straight-forwardly as follows: what are the systems of rule by which globalization is enabled to go about its business? Entry into this debate can obviously be made in a variety of ways and at a number of levels. Indeed, it is a central part of the 'new medievalist' hypothesis that this must be so. There is, for example, an important literature just now emerging on forms of global governance and there is also a huge amount being said also on local and other sub-national forms of governance in the context of glob-alization. I choose to continue to focus for the moment on the regionalist level and in the rest of the chapter I concern myself therefore with the question of 'regionalist governance'.

## Theories of Regionalist Governance

The immediate problem to be faced is that the theoretical discussion of governance at the regionalist level has – until very recently – been remarkably sterile and unhelp-ful. The main source is the long-running debate conducted between the neo-functionalists and the intergovernmentalists in the context of attempts to explain the dynamics of post-war European integration (Caporaso and Keeler, 1995). Neo-functionalists emphasize an incremental and gradual process of change driven fundamentally by the logic of self-sustaining processes which cause integration in one sector to 'spill over' into others. They privilege social and political elites acting across state boundaries but are generally less interested in specifying the key agents than in identifying the political process involved. Intergovernmentalists focus on the outcomes of interstate bargains. They see national governments as the principal agents advancing or block-ing regional integration but incorporate the influence of domestic politics by conceiving of regionalist politics as a series of 'two-level games' where national governments serve as the crucial link between the domestic and international levels. The trouble is that neither camp can escape from the conventional concept of a Westphalian state which is able to enjoy both internal and external sovereignty. The intergovernmentalists self-evidently assert their attachment to such a view, whilst the neo-functionalists fall into the same trap by failing to conceive of the 'supra-nationalism', which is the sup-posed end-result of the spillover process, in any fundamentally different fashion.

Rescue is, however, at hand. Whilst this debate has been pursued, blow by blow, in the narrow world of European Community studies (which has always separated itself off rather too much from the intellectual worlds of both comparative politics/policy analysis *and* international relations/IPE), these other literatures have each moved on in a fashion which now offers up the prospect of forging a powerful blend of theories which, in harness, can at last provide a more or less satisfactory set of tools with which to analyse the behaviour of agents in and around state-led regionalist projects. I am thinking here, first, of the perceived convergence of contemporary theories of the state in the comparative politics literature and, second, of the revival of the old interest in transnational and transgovernmental relations in the international relations literature. Each has a lot of potential value to say about contemporary modes of governance and so let me now briefly explore the latest developments in these two fields.

The comparative politics strand draws attention to the extent to which there has lately developed a convergence between pluralist, elitist, and Marxist schools of thought in their thinking about the relationship between the state and civil society (Marsh, 1995). This is not to go so far as to suggest the emergence of a consensus. But, according to this argument, pluralists have increasingly come to accept that political competition does not take place on a level playing field and that there is such a thing as structured privilege which can be enjoyed by a particular individual or group on a number of bases. Equally, modern elite theorists do not see such clear and unchanging patterns in the circulation of elites as did their classical predecessors and modern Marxists have moved substantially away from the view that agents can only be understood as 'bearers' of structures to the point where they have largely embraced the notion that power relationships are contingent and thus require empirical explanation. In short, the effect has been to create a good deal of common theoretical ground whereby it is agreed that the state needs to be taken seriously, then located socially, disaggregated institutionally, and decomposed into its various component policy networks. All this, it hardly needs to be said, is a long way from Westphalia.

The international relations strand connects nicely with these conclusions because it resuscitates an interest in transnational relations without collapsing these into a society-centred view of the world which underplays the role of states. Keohane and Nye launched this line of enquiry in the 1970s, distinguishing between transnational relations, defined as transboundary relations involving a non-state actor, and trans-governmental relations, defined as transboundary relations involving sub-units of national governments (Keohane and Nye, 1971, 1974, and 1977). Yet the novelty of this approach was never fully exploited, even by its two instigators, both of whom were quickly drawn back into mainstream work. The subject has, however, recently been revived by Risse-Kappen in a way which focuses on the interaction between states and their internal institutional structures, on the one hand, and transnational relations, on the other (Risse-Kappen, 1995). This serves very effectively to 'transnationalize' many of the insights of contemporary state theory and renders them much more usable as research tools in international contexts.

To sum up, then, recent theorizing in these two separate parts of the terrain of political studies *together* provides a useful starting point for attempts to get to grips with the politics of regionalist governance. They take us beyond the tired exchanges of neo-functionalism versus intergovernmentalism and open up the possibility of discerning a number of different modes of regionalist governance. The next and last substantive section of the chapter constitutes an early effort in this direction. It draws on an emerging literature in respect of the EU and tries at least to ask the right questions in respect of NAFTA and APEC.

## Comparative Modes of Regionalist Governance

### 'Multilevel governance' in the EU

Over the last few years a number of scholars in different countries have started to conceptualize the EU as a multilevel structure of governance within which state and sub-state, public and private, transnational and supra-national actors all deal with each other in complex networks of varying horizontal and vertical density. This argument does not necessarily contest the claim that state executives and state arenas are still important or even that they remain the *most* important parts of the EU decision-making system. But it does firmly suggest that the state no longer monopolizes either in European-level policy-making or in domestic interest aggregation in member states. As a consequence, a new kind of polity is seen as being in process of formation, characterized according to Gary Marks and colleagues by the following key features:

> First . . . decision making competencies are shared by actors at different levels rather than monopolized by state executives. That is to say, supranational institutions . . . have independent influence in policy making that cannot be derived from their role as agents of state executives. Second, collective decision making among states involves a significant loss of control for individual state executives [with] lowest common denominator outcomes . . . available only on a sub-set of EU decisions. Third, political arenas are interconnected rather than nested . . . Subnational actors . . . act directly both in national and supranational arenas, creating transnational associations in the process. States do not monopolize links between domestic and European actors, but are one among a variety of actors contesting decisions that are made at a variety of levels (Marks, Hooghe, and Blank, 1995: 4–5).

In this vision, the EU is thus presented as a dynamic, evolving arena of political interaction, not a stable order which can be reduced either to an intergovernmental or neo-functionalist logic.

Analytically, the implication of this approach is that reified state-centric accounts which set out the preferences and bargaining strategies of whole countries have necessarily to be complicated by attention to the particular preferences of particular actors at a variety of points in the multilevel structure. As Marks, Hooghe, and Blank put it, 'there is no fixed recipe for disaggregating the state; it depends on the policy issue at hand' (Marks, Hooghe, and Blank, 1995: 8). Equally, there is no fixed recipe for assessing the role of the non-state actors who press themselves upon the various policy networks. However, what this also of course means is that there may still be policy areas where something closer to the old intergovernmentalist model remains appropriate. The baby does not have to be, and should not be, completely thrown out with the bath-water. Rather, the next step forward must be the elaboration and testing of hypotheses about the different conditions under which multilevel governance begins to take precedence over more traditional methods of government-to-government bargaining. A first stab at this has recently been essayed by Risse-Kappen (Risse-Kappen, 1996).

## 'Hub and spoke' governance in North America

As yet, no literature of any substance has emerged which seeks to analyse the institutional structure of NAFTA. This is partly just a matter of time (NAFTA was only inaugurated on 1 January 1994), but also reflects the very limited nature of the organizational apparatus which has been established to manage the treaty. Apart from regular meetings of trade ministers, environment ministers, and the like, this does not extend much beyond some rather frail dispute-mediation mechanisms and two commissions on different aspects of environmental co-operation, the significance or activism of which it is still somewhat early to judge.

However, if the focus of enquiry is widened somewhat, it is possible to argue that a nascent mode of governance is emerging in North America – and I deliberately say 'in North America' rather than in NAFTA. The key insight here is that the power of the US state is decisive in shaping the contours of governance in North America. Yet, as is well known, the US state is composed of a myriad of different actors open to the influence of a complex range of social actors. One might even want to describe it as a multilevel structure of governance in its own right. In any deep analysis of US 'state strategy' it is thus clearly necessary to consider the relationship of US state policy-makers to the power of US national and transnational capital, to assess the role of various domestic and foreign pressure groups, to bear in mind all the time the balance of power between the legislature, the executive and the judiciary and between the different parts of the federal system, to weigh up the competing bureaucratic claims to represent the US of the White House, the State Department, the Pentagon, the CIA, the Treasury, the Federal Reserve, the Drugs Enforcement Agency and so on – in sum, to move on and away from the easy notion of there ever being a single US policy towards anywhere or anything and grapple instead with the many contradictions and variables – the many messy policies – that actually exist.

At the same time, as is equally well known, the US state structure is relatively easy to penetrate. US-based pressure groups have long understood this. But what has lately happened with increasing force and significance is that sub-state, state, and non-state actors outside the US but within North America (and thus deeply affected by all that the US state does or does not do) have caught on to the opportunity which this represents and have started to lobby their cases with the US *within* the US political system. Most particularly, other states in North America have realized that they have other options than to seek to relate to the US, foreign minister to foreign minister or diplomat to diplomat. Canadian state and other actors lobbied their positions extensively in Washington in the run-up to the negotiation of the US-Canada free trade agreement (as well as negotiating hard in the formal talks); the Mexican state did this brilliantly in the difficult months before the passage of NAFTA through the US Congress (Presland, 1997); and some of the small Caribbean states, which are much concerned about their trading position in the region after NAFTA, are slowly realizing that they may have a better chance of influencing US trade policy via a close collaboration with the two US senators from Florida than ritual twenty-minute meetings with President Clinton which is all that their size and relative importance to the White House can usually generate (Sutton and Payne, 1992).

I conceptualize this emerging process as a form of 'hub and spoke' governance to highlight the fact that ultimately the channels flow in and out of Washington DC and the reality that it is the policy of the hub state that matters. But it is significant that a number of US states (of the union) are beginning to position themselves, as it were, as entry-points to the spokes, linking the US outwards, say, to Canada, Mexico, and the Caribbean Basin but also acting back upon the US policy process in good part on behalf of those other parts of North America with which, for geographical reasons, they have particular and often very sensitive social, economic and political connections (Munton and Kirton, 1996). From this point of view, an interesting comparative piece of research would be to examine, explicitly within the context of a notion of North American governance, the respective roles of political actors in Washington state vis-à-vis Canada, Texas vis-à-vis Mexico and Florida vis-à-vis the Caribbean Basin.

## Pre-governance in Asia–Pacific

The academic literature on the political linkage between the domestic and international arenas within Asia–Pacific economic co-operation, whether defined broadly or by specific reference to APEC itself, is largely confined to the work of Richard Higgott (Higgott, 1993, 1994, and 1995). In a series of articles he has demonstrated that APEC is a form of 'market-led regionalism'; that, 'despite some institutional characteristics', it is as yet 'neither an institution nor a regime' (Higgott, 1995: 369); and that the act of con-ceding policy autonomy to a supra-national body is not even contemplated in the region. On a more positive note, what has driven the process forward has been the evolution of a region-wide dialogue about the merits of liberal economic co-operation dating back to the 1960s and encompassing in turn the Pacific Trade and Development Conferences (PAFTAD), the Pacific Basin Economic Committee (PBEC) and the Pacific Economic Co-operation Council (PECC). According to Higgott, this network of civil servants, university economists, and policy entrepreneurs has some of the character-istics of what Peter Haas has called an epistemic community. This was defined by Haas as 'a network of professionals with recognized expertise and competence in a par-ticular domain and an authoritative claim to policy-relevant knowledge within that domain or issue-area' (Haas, 1992: 3). However, the problem with the literature on epistemic communities is that it lacks a theory of domestic politics and the state capable of indicating when and why such communities of professionals have an impact on policy formation. Higgott is thus surely right to assert that the 'network' which has emerged in Asia–Pacific around the concept of market-led regionalism is far from being a full-fledged regional policy network of the type recognized and analysed so extensively by pluralist writers on Europe and North America. Nor, it can be swiftly said, is there any prospect of the Japanese state playing the hub role in a regional governance system along the lines previously identified in respect of the US state within North America. In present and foreseeable circumstances, then, it seems appropriate to describe Asia–Pacific regionalism as being, at best, in 'pre-governance' mode.

## Conclusions

[ … ]
I will confine myself to making just three summary points.

The first is that globalization clearly does allow for new forms of governance. Indeed, it might even require such forms of governance. For whether the various new insti-tutions of governance serve to facilitate the process of globalization, or to check and control it, or both, remains to be investigated in any depth. But even to pose the ques-tion is to strike a marked contrast to the picture of a world order that has slipped beyond the management of state actors favoured by proponents of the strongest ver-sion of the globalization thesis. I repeat, therefore, that it is an error to view global-ization in too essentialistic or fatalistic a fashion. It should be viewed at root as a political process, as having an ideological character, and as giving rise to diverse, as yet largely uncharted, forms of governance. In short, research on globalization in the field of polit-ical studies must proceed in partnership with the notion of governance, using many of the conceptual tools set out in the earlier discussion.

The second point is that, manifestly, much of this governance now goes on at what I have called the regionalist level. Nobody can deny the political significance in the new global order of the EU, NAFTA, and even APEC. They collectively represent something new. However, as we have seen, no single mode of regionalist governance has emerged. Nor are any yet stable, with clear lines of political development laid down. Nor is there likely to be some linear process of development by which supposedly less advanced forms follow in the wake of the more advanced. It is a mistake, often implicitly made in the analysis of regionalism, to operate as if the EU was somehow showing the face of the future to other regionalist bodies. More comparative research unquestionably needs to be done, but it must be grounded in the realization that each of the three regionalist projects highlighted here (not to mention the many other existing *sub*-regionalist projects (Hook and Kearns, forthcoming)) has grown out of particular regional histories and cultures. In short, their differences (as between Europe, North America, and Asia–Pacific) are, and seem bound to remain, as striking as their similarities (deriving from the common regionalist thrust).

The third and final point relates to the overall picture, the overarching form of governance at the global level, likely to emerge from the globalization process. By virtue of its focus on the regionalist level, this chapter is limited in what it can hope to say in answer to this question. But what is apparent is that there will not be achieved any easy 'meshing' of the modes of governance in existence in the three major triadic regions of the world order, with the result that the option held out by some of building global governance in part via a 'minilateralization' of three structures of governance (as opposed to a larger number of states in conventional 'multilateralism') will be very difficult to realize. As we have described them, the polities being brought into being via the various modes of governance of the EU, North America, and Asia–Pacific are not the 'like units' that states are deemed to be in conventional neo-realist international relations theory. As such, the vision of some kind of 'super G3' directorate being created out of the building blocks of the current three major regionalist projects is too simplistic and probably misconceived. Given the range of other players (state and non-state) and other levels of action (global, sub-regional, national, sub-national, local) that need to be encompassed in the analysis, a much more likely scenario is that the political economy of globalization will be accompanied by the emergence of a highly complex, 'plurilateral' system of governance (Cerny, 1993). What is certain is that, within such a system, regionalist governance is positioned to play a major role.

## References

Bromley, S. (1996) Feature Review of Paul Hirst and Grahame Thompson's *Globalization in Question. New Political Economy* 1: 129–33.

Bull, H. (1977) *The Anarchical Society. A Study of Order in World Politics.* New York: Columbia University Press.

Caporaso, J. A., and Keeler, J. T. S. (1995) The European Union and Regional Integration Theory. In C. Rhodes and S. Mazey (eds), *The State of the European Union.* Vol. 3: *Building a European Polity?* Boulder, Colo.: Lynne Rienner.

Cerny, P. G. (1993) Plurilateralism: Structural Differentiation and Functional Conflict in the Post-Cold War World Order. *Millennium: Journal of International Studies* 22: 27–51.

Cox, R. W. (1996) Global Perestroika. In R. W. Cox, with T. J. Sinclair, *Approaches to World Order,* Cambridge: Cambridge University Press.

Gamble, A. M. (1997) The New Medievalism, paper delivered to an Anglo-Japanese seminar. The Kobe Institute, Kobe.

Gamble, A. M., and Payne, A. J. (1996) Conclusion: The New Regionalism. In A. M. Gamble and A. J. Payne (eds), *Regionalism and World Order*, London: Macmillan.

Haas, P. (1992) Introduction: Epistemic Communities and International Policy Coordination. *International Organization* 46: 1–35.

Harvey, D. (1989) *The Condition of Postmodernity*. Oxford: Blackwell.

Higgott, R. (1993) Asia Pacific Economic Cooperation: Theoretical Opportunities and Practical Constraints. *The Pacific Review* 6: 103–17.

Higgott, R. (1994) Ideas, Identity and Policy Coordination in the Asia Pacific. *The Pacific Review* 7: 367–80.

Higgott, R. (1995) Economic Cooperation in the Asia Pacific: A Theoretical Comparison with the European Union. *Journal of European Public Policy* 2: 361–83.

Hirst, P., and Thompson, G. (1996) *Globalization in Question: The International Economy and the Possibilities of Governance*. Cambridge: Polity Press.

Hook, G. D., and Kearns, I. P. (eds) (forthcoming) *Sub-regionalism and World Order*. London: Macmillan.

Jameson, F. (1984) Postmodernism, or the Cultural Logic of Late Capitalism. *New Left Review* 146: 53–92.

Keohane, R. O., and Nye, J. S. (eds) (1971) *Transnational Relations and World Politics*. Cambridge, Mass.: Harvard University Press.

Keohane, R. O., and Nye, J. S. (eds) (1974) Transgovernmental Relations and International Organizations. *World Politics* 27: 39–62.

Keohane, R. O., and Nye, J. S. (eds) (1977) *Power and Interdependence*. Boston: Little, Brown.

Marks, G., Hooghe, L., and Blank, K. (1995) European Integration since the 1980s: State-centric versus Multi-level Governance. Paper delivered to the American Political Science Association annual conference, Chicago.

Marsh, D. (1995) The Convergence between Theories of the State. In D. Marsh and G. Stoker (eds), *Theory and Methods in Political Science*, London: Macmillan.

Munton, D., and Kirton, J. (1996) Beyond and Beneath the Nation-state: Province–State Interactions and NAFTA. Paper delivered to the International Studies Association annual conference, San Diego, California.

Payne, A. J., and Gamble, A. M. (1996) Introduction: The Political Economy of Regionalism and World Order. In A. M. Gamble and A. J. Payne (eds), *Regionalism and World Order*, London: Macmillan.

Presland, S. (1997) The Neoliberal Alliance in the Passage of NAFTA. Unpublished Ph.D. thesis, University of Sheffield, Sheffield.

Rhodes, R. A. W. (1996) The New Governance: Governing without Government. *Political Studies* 44: 652–67.

Risse-Kappen, T. (ed.) (1995) *Bringing Transnational Relations Back In: Non-State Actors, Domestic Structures and International Institutions*. Cambridge: Cambridge University Press.

Risse-Kappen, T. (1996) Exploring the Nature of the Beast: International Relations Theory and Comparative Policy Analysis Meet the European Union. *Journal of Common Market Studies* 34: 53–80.

Rosenau, J. (1997) *Along the Domestic-Foreign Frontier: Exploring Governance in a Turbulent World*. Cambridge: Cambridge University Press.

Ruggie, J. G. (1993) Territoriality and Beyond: Problematizing Modernity in International Relations. *International Organization* 47: 139–74.

Sutton, P. K., and Payne, A. J. (1992) Commonwealth Caribbean Diplomacy: A New Strategy for a New World Order. *Caribbean Affairs* 5: 47–63.

# 19

# Governance in a New Global Order

*James N. Rosenau*

We live in a messy world. There are far too many people who survive on or below the poverty line. There are far too many societies paralysed by division. There is too much violence within and between countries. Terrorists are too successful. In many places there is too little water and too many overly populated, pollution-ridden cities. And, most conspicuously, there is all too little effective governance capable of ameliorating, if not resolving, these and numerous other problems that crowd high on the global agenda. Perhaps even more troubling, our generation lacks [ ... ] the orientations necessary to sound assessments of how the authority of governance can be brought to bear on the challenges posed by the prevailing disarray.

Consequently, with the end of the Cold War and the stability inherent in the super-power rivalry, the messiness of world and domestic affairs has led to pervasive uncertainties. People are unsettled by the realization that deep changes are unfolding in every sphere of life, that events in any part of the world can have consequences for developments in every other part of the world, that the internet and other technologies have collapsed time and distance, that consequently national states and their governments are not as competent as they once were, that their sovereignty and boundaries have become increasingly porous, and that therefore the world has moved into a period of extraordinary complexity. In effect, diverse and contradictory forces have been unleashed that can be summarized in the clash between globalization, centralization and integration on the one hand, and localization, decentralization and fragmentation on the other. The clashes between these forces – what I call 'fragmegration' in order to capture the intricate links between the polarities (Rosenau, 1997, ch. 6) – underlie the many huge challenges to humankind's capacity to lessen the messiness unfolding throughout the world and intensify movement towards acceptable levels of peace and prosperity.

In short, reinforced by the collapse of time and distance, the weaknesses of states, the vast movements of people and the ever greater complexities of modern life, the question of how to infuse a modicum of order, a measure of effective authority and a potential for improving the human condition into the course of events looms as increasingly urgent. It is being asked at every level of community as fragmegrative tensions intensify and as citizens and officials alike ponder how to conduct their affairs in the face of transformative dynamics that are often bewildering and seemingly out of control.

Much of the bewilderment derives from the fast-paced dynamics of fragmegration. As suggested by linking in a single phrase the interactions between worldwide forces pressing for fragmentation and those exerting pressure for integration, fragmegrative dynamics are pervaded with contradictions and tensions. They tug people and institutions at every level of community in opposite directions, often forcing choices favouring localizing or globalizing goals. Indeed, it can be reasonably postulated that every increment of fragmentation gives rise to an increment of integration, and vice versa. This pervasiveness of fragmegrative dynamics is readily traceable in a wide variety of situations, from cultural sensitivities to inroads from abroad to fears of jobs lost through the demise of trade barriers, from linguistic distortions fostered by the Internet to environmental degradation generated by expanded productive facilities, and so on across all the situations that mark our transformative epoch. To grasp the underpinnings of modern life, in other words, there is considerable clarity to be had in viewing all its issues through fragmegrative lenses.

To proceed in this fashion, however, is not to answer the question of how to develop the order and authority needed for an improvement of the human condition. Perhaps the most frequent answer to the question is a two-word phrase that may appear to make sense, but that upon reflection can seem vague and vacuous. The phrase is 'global governance'. What does the phrase mean, one can reasonably ask? Does it refer to a central authority that can exercise control over far-flung situations on a global scale? Or is it limited to the exercise of authority in particular situations, such as environmental threats or outbreaks of widespread violence, which may be global in scope and especially dire? Or does it connote the sum of all the diverse efforts of communities at every level to move towards goals while preserving their coherence from one moment in time to the next? The ensuing pages are founded on a clear-cut response to these alternatives: global governance is a summarizing phrase for all the sites in the world where efforts to exercise authority are undertaken. It neither posits a highest authority nor anticipates that one is likely to evolve in the long run. On the contrary, it argues that an irreversible process is under way wherein authority is increasingly disaggregated, resulting in a system of global governance that comprises more and more centres of authority in every corner of the world and at every level of community.

## The Concept of Global Governance

If one appreciates that widespread use of the word 'governance' is essentially a recent phenomenon – indeed, it does not exist in some languages (such as German) – it is not surprising that its wider usage has paralleled the advent of globalization. With but few exceptions, in fact, governance tends to be employed when it is modified by the adjective 'global'. Otherwise, for any scale short of the global – whether local, provincial, national or regional – 'government' is usually treated as the entity through which order is sought and goals framed and implemented. And why have 'global' and 'governance' become inextricably linked in public discourse? The answer strikes me as rather obvious: for a long time the world was described as increasingly interdependent, but only since the end of the Cold War have the dynamics of interdependence tended to have consequences that are global in scope. The problem of global warming, for example, knows no boundaries and reaches into every corner of the globe. Likewise, genocidal policies and practices in Rwanda and Kosovo have been experienced as challenges to all of humankind, as have financial crises and a growing gap between the rich and poor in developing countries. As the advent of such situations has accelerated at a seemingly ever more rapid rate, the notion has quickly spread that interdependence is characteristic of the world as a whole. Accordingly, persuaded that many problems cannot be allowed to fester and endanger the well-being of people everywhere, and eager to bring a modicum of order and direction to the uncertainties and dislocations inherent in the vast degrees of interdependence, analysts have quite naturally begun to talk of the need for global governance and the processes and structures that might foster and sustain it.

Both governance and government consist of rule systems, of steering mechanisms through which authority is exercised in order to enable systems to preserve their coherence and move towards desired goals. While the rule systems of governments can be thought of as structures, those of governance are social functions or processes that can be performed or implemented in a variety of ways at different times and places (or even at the same time) by a wide variety of organizations. To govern, whether as structure or function, is thus to exercise authority. To have authority is to be recognized as having the right to govern, to issue directives that are heeded by those encompassed by the directives. Rule systems acquire authority in a variety of ways. These range from steering mechanisms that are structures endowed with authority through constitutions, bylaws and other formally adopted instruments of rule, to those that are processes informally created through repeated practices that are regarded as authoritative even though they may not be constitutionally sanctioned. Both the formal and informal rule systems consist of what I call 'spheres of authority' (SOAs) that define the range of their capacity to generate compliance on the part of those persons towards whom their directives are issued. Compliance, in other words, is the key to ascertaining the presence of an SOA.

Viewed in terms of their compliance-generating capacities, the steering mechanisms that undertake governance may be just as effective (or ineffective) as those of governments. While governments generate compliance through formal prerogatives such as sovereignty and constitutional legitimacy, the effectiveness of governance rule systems derives from traditional norms and habits, informal agreements, shared premises, and a host of other practices that lead people to comply with their directives. Thus, as the demand for governance increases with the proliferation of complex interdependencies, rule systems can be found in non-governmental organizations, corporations, professional societies, business associations, advocacy groups, and many other types of collectivities that are not considered to be governments.

It follows that world affairs can be conceptualized as governed through a bifurcated system – what can be called the two worlds of world politics – one an interstate system of states and their national governments that has long dominated the course of events, and the other a multicentric system of diverse types of other collectivities that has lately emerged as a rival source of authority with actors that sometimes cooperate with, often compete with, and endlessly interact with the state-centric system (Rosenau, 1990, ch. 10). Viewed in the context of proliferating centres of authority, the global stage is thus dense with actors, large and small, formal and informal, economic and social, political and cultural, national and transnational, international and subnational, aggressive and peaceful, liberal and authoritarian, who collectively form a highly complex system of global governance.

To repeat, despite the vast differences among them, what the disparate collectivities in the two worlds of world politics have in common is that they all sustain rule systems that range across the concerns of their members and that constitute the boundaries of their SOAs (Rosenau, forthcoming, ch. 13). When collectivities in the two worlds cooperate across the divide between them, as often they must, to advance shared interests in particular issue areas, the hybrid institutions they form to coordinate their SOAs are considered to constitute a 'regime' (Krasner, 1983, p. 2).

Does the advent of a bifurcated system imply that states are in a process of disintegration? Not at all. Doubtless the interstate system will continue to be central to world affairs for decades and centuries to come. To stress that collectivities other than states have emerged as important SOAs is not in any way to suggest that states are headed for demise. Analysts differ over the degree to which the national state has been weakened by the dynamics of fragmegration, but few contend that the weakening amounts to a trend line that will culminate in total collapse. States are still among the main players on the global stage, but they are no longer the only main players.[1] Many of them are deep in crisis, by which I do not mean pervasive street riots, but rather cross-cutting conflicts that paralyse policy-making processes and result in stalemate and stasis, in the avoidance of decisions that would at least address the challenges posed by a fragmegrative world undergoing vast and continuous changes. Yes, most states still control their banking systems and maintain legitimate monopoly over the use of force. Yes, states have undergone transformation into managerial entities and are thus still able to exercise a measure of control over the course of events. And yes, the aspiration to statehood is still shared widely in many parts of the world. But for all its continuing authority and legitimacy, key dimensions of the power of the modern state have undergone considerable diminution. In the words of one analyst, 'As wealth and power are increasingly generated by private transactions that take place across the borders of states rather than within them, it has become harder to sustain the image of states as the preeminent actors at the global level' (Evans, 1997, p. 65).

Analysts also differ over the notion of global governance as disaggregated centres of authority. Some argue that positing the global stage as ever more crowded with SOAs is such a broad conception as to make it 'virtually meaningless both for theory construction and social action' (Väyrynen, 1999, p. 25). Here this argument is found wanting. Opting for a narrow conception may facilitate analysis, but doing so is also misleading in that it ignores the vast proliferation of SOAs that has emerged as a prime characteristic of the system of global governance since the end of the Cold War. [ . . . ]

## Domestic-Foreign Boundaries

It is not a simple matter to grasp global governance as congeries of diverse collectivities in the two worlds of world politics. Such a perspective requires one to wrench free of the long-standing and unquestioned premise that the boundaries separating countries are firm and impassable without the permission of the states that preside over them. This wrenching task is not easily accomplished. Our analytic capacities are rooted in methodological territorialism (Scholte, 2000, pp. 56–8), in a long-standing, virtually unconscious habit of probing problems in a broad, geographic or spatial context. This habit poses an acute problem because of the ever growing porosity of domestic-foreign boundaries (Rosenau, 1997) that has rendered territoriality much less pervasive than it used to be even as all the social sciences construct their inquiries, develop their concepts, formulate their hypotheses and frame their evidence-gathering procedures through spatial lenses. Nor are officials free to think in alternative contexts: as one analyst put it, 'Trapped by the territoriality of their power, policy makers in traditional settings often have little choice but to address the symptoms rather than the causes of public problems' (Reinicke, 1999–2000, p. 45).

Yet breaking out of the conceptual jail imposed by methodological territorialism is imperative because a prime characteristic of fragmegration is that its processes readily span foreign-domestic boundaries. Fragmegrative dynamics are such that states can exercise little control over the flows of ideas, money, goods, pollution, crime, drugs and terrorism; and they have only slightly greater control over the flow of people. Why? Because their capacities have been weakened by a pervasive trend towards ever greater complexity – by microelectronic technologies that have rendered what used to be remote ever more proximate; by a continuing proliferation of networked organizations; by a variety of incentives that lead huge numbers of people, everyone from the tourist to the terrorist, to move widely around the world; by the globalization of national economies and the neoliberal economic policies that have enhanced the relevance of markets and the power of multinational corporations; by a skill revolution that has everywhere linked people ever more closely to the course of events; and by divisive politics that have fostered authority crises which inhibit many states from framing and implementing goals appropriate to the dilemmas they face. In short, a host of dynamics have greatly increased transborder flows and rendered domestic-foreign boundaries ever more porous. With the collapse of time and distance, subnational organizations and governments that once operated within the confines of national boundaries are now so inextricably connected to far-off parts of the world that the legal and geographic jurisdictions in which they are located matter less and less. What matters, instead, are the spheres of authority to which their members are responsive.

## Compliance

As previously noted, if the world is conceived to be a vast multiplicity of SOAs that collectively constitute a new global order, the key to understanding their various roles in global governance lies not in focusing on their legal prerogatives, but rather in assessing the degree to which they are able to evoke the compliance of the people whom they seek to mobilize through the directives they issue. Achieving compliance is the key to leadership and politics, and it is not readily accomplished. The more complex societies and the world become, the more difficult it is to get people to respond to efforts to generate their compliance. States have an advantage in this regard because they have the legitimate right to employ force if their citizens fail to comply. But to stress this distinctive quality of states is to ignore the underpinnings of compliance. Most notably perhaps, it ignores the large degree to which compliance is rooted in habit, in an unthinking readiness to respond to directives issued by the authorities to which one has been socialized to be committed and loyal, and the large degree to which such habits are no longer encompassed by the clear-cut province of states. With the proliferation of SOAs and the declining relevance of domestic-foreign boundaries, with the emergence of alternative authorities to which people can transfer their compliance habits, states are less and less able to rely on the effectiveness of their directives.

Put differently, many states today are ensconced in paralysing authority crises that inhibit their governing capacities. This is not to refer to those states plagued with internal wars (such as Colombia) or to rioting protesters in the streets of national capitals. Some do experience such moments on occasion (as in Yugoslavia or the Philippines), but more often than not authority crises involve stalemate, an inability to frame goals, to implement them, to realize them. Governments in many countries, from Russia to Israel, from Peru to China, from the Congo to Indonesia, from the United States to Belgium, are riven by deep divisions and thus often have difficulty raising taxes, preserving societal harmony, ameliorating deep-seated conflicts, expanding their economies, recruiting or retaining members of their armed forces, or otherwise maintaining a level of compliance that sustains their effectiveness.

It follows that global governance today is characterized by an extensive disaggregation of authority, by growing numbers of SOAs in the two worlds of world politics that immensely complicate the tasks of coordination necessary to establish a humane and stable world. Put differently, SOAs proliferate because increasingly people are capable of shouldering and managing multiple identities that lessen their allegiance to their states. As they get involved in more and more networks in the multi-centric world, so their loyalties fractionate and become issue and object specific. Yet history in this era of fragmegration does record pockets of successful coordination among states in the state-centric world and among collectivities in the multi-centric world that are able to generate meaningful compliance. Even though SOAs vary widely in their ability to evoke compliance and thus in their contribution to the processes of global governance, some do manage to gain a measure of control over fragmegrative tensions. Rule systems developed through negotiation among national governments – such as the United Nations, the Kyoto Protocol on the Environment, the World Trade Organization, or the European Union – have the widest scope and, consequently, make perhaps the most substantial contribution to governance processes. Steering mechanisms maintained by SOAs in the multi-centric world – such as the calculations of credit-rating agencies that estimate the reliability of national economies, the rulings of truth commissions designed to enable countries racked by civil strife to heal their wounds, or the practices of the insurance industry to offset climate changes (Carlsson and Stripple, 2000) – exemplify effective instruments of governance with respect to specific issues.[2] No less important, many successful efforts at global governance result from cooperation among collectivities in the state-centric and multi-centric worlds. In the words of one knowledgeable observer, 'global regimes are increasingly the product of negotiations among state and non-state actors' (Zacher, 1999, p. 48).

For every example of rule systems in the two worlds of world politics that achieve meaningful coordination and compliance, however, innumerable cases can be cited in which efforts to maintain effective steering mechanisms fail to generate the compliance necessary for governance. Indeed, such failures may well be more the rule than the exception in world affairs today. Our messy world is littered with paralysed or stalemated governments and non-governmental SOAs that fall far short of evoking the compliance appropriate to their goals and policies. Given the continuing processes wherein authority is undergoing disaggregation and rendering compliance more elusive, it is easy to be pessimistic about the prospects for global governance and the probabilities of continuing disarray in world affairs.

## Leadership

Some analysts contend that the disarray is not as great as it may seem, that tendencies in this direction are held in check – and in some cases reversed – by the leadership of the United States as the dominant actor in the post-Cold War arrangement of world politics. Frequently referred to as 'hegemonic stability' or a 'unipolar structure', the dominance of the United States and the democratic values it espouses is conceived to be a form of global governance. It is a conception that presumes that the capabilities of the US are so unrivalled that it can generate the compliance necessary to preserve stability on a global scale even as it promotes human rights, democracy and open markets. As I see it, such an approach is misguided. Not only does it ignore the reluctance of the American people to play an active role in the processes of global governance – a reluctance which takes the form of not paying in full its dues to the United Nations or otherwise not participating in numerous international rule systems to which most countries have agreed – but even more important it is a perspective that takes no account of the large degree to which authority is undergoing disaggregation. If the preceding analysis is correct that the global stage is ever more crowded with SOAs capable of independently pursuing their goals, then obviously hegemonic leadership can neither flourish nor endure. Much as many people in the US, ordinary citizens as well as leaders, might prefer to pursue unilateral policies, for example, in most situations the country is forced to work within and through multilateral institutions and, in so doing, it often has to accept modification of its goals. And when it does not accept any modifications, when it proceeds unilaterally – as in the case of its war on drugs – its policies tend to flail aimlessly at best, or fail at worst. The world is simply too interdependent, and authority is too dispersed, for any one country to command the global scene as fully as was the case in the past.

## The Advent of Networks

While a number of dynamics have contributed to the diminution of state capacities, certainly one of the most important of these has been the shifting balance between hierarchical and network forms of organization, between vertical and horizontal flows of authority. Greatly facilitated by the Internet, people now converge electronically as equals, or at least not as superiors and subordinates. They make plans, recruit members, mobilize support, raise money, debate issues, frame agendas, and undertake collective action, amounting to steering mechanisms founded on horizontal rather than hierarchical channels of authority. Indeed, it has been argued, with reason, that:

> The rise of network forms of organization – particularly 'all channel networks', in which every node can communicate with every other node – is one of the single most important effects of the information revolution for all realms: political, economic, social, and military. It means that power is migrating to small, non-state actors who can organize into sprawling networks more readily than can traditionally hierarchical nation-state actors. It means that conflicts will increasingly be waged by 'networks', rather than by 'hierarchies'. It means that whoever masters the network form stands to gain major advantages in the new epoch. (Arquilla and Ronfeldt, 1997, p. 5)

In other words, not only has the advent of network forms of organization undermined the authority of states, but in the context of our concern with global governance, it has also had even more important consequences. Most notably, networks have contributed to the disaggregation of authority as well as the formation of new collectivities not founded on hierarchical principles.

If the notion that new rule systems can be founded on horizontal as well as vertical structures of authority seems awkward, it warrants reiterating that the core of effective authority lies in the compliance of those towards whom it is directed. If people ignore, avoid, or otherwise do not heed the compliance sought by 'the' authorities, then it can be said that for all practical purposes the latter are authorities in name only, that their authority has evaporated. Authority is thus profoundly relational. It links – or fails to do so, or does so somewhat – those who issue directives and those for whom the directives are intended. Stated more elaborately, authority needs to be treated as a continuum wherein at one extreme full compliance is evoked and at the other extreme it is not. The viability of all collectivities can be assessed by ascertaining where they are located on the continuum. The closer they are to the compliance extreme, the greater will be their viability and effectiveness, just as the nearer they are to the non-compliance extreme, the greater is the likelihood that they will be ineffective and falter. Accordingly, it becomes possible to conceive of collectivities held together through horizontal flows of authority – through compliance with electronic messages cast as requests rather than as directives – and it is precisely this possibility that underlies the bifurcation of global structures into state-centric and multi-centric worlds, the proliferation of SOAs, the growing relevance of NGOs, and the increased attention paid to the possibility that a global civil society may be emerging.

## The Governance of Fragmegration

As previously indicated, there is no lack of either variety or number in the extant systems of governance. On the contrary, it is difficult to overestimate how crowded the global stage has become as the world undergoes a multiplication of all kinds of governance, from formal to multilevel governments, from formally sanctioned entities such as arbitration boards to informal SOAs, from emergent supranational entities such as the European Union to emergent issue regimes, from regional bodies to international governmental organizations (IGOs), from transnational corporations to neighbourhood associations, from humanitarian groups to ad hoc coalitions, from certifying agencies to social movements, and so on across an ever widening array of activities and concerns.

Notwithstanding the increasing difficulty of generating compliance posed by the world's greater complexity, not every fragmegrative situation on the global agenda lacks governance. There are innumerable situations involving localizing responses to globalizing stimuli that are marked by a high, or at least an acceptable, quality of governance and that thus need not be of concern here. The vast proliferation of rule systems in recent decades includes a trend to devolve governance so that its steering mechanisms are closer to those who experience its policies. This trend is most conspicuously marked by the evolution of what has been called 'multilevel' governance, a form of rule system in which authority is voluntarily and legally dispersed among the various levels of community where problems are located and local needs require attention. The European Union exemplifies multilevel governance, as does Scotland, Wales, the French provinces, US welfare programmes, and many other federal systems in which previously centralized authority has been redistributed to provincial and municipal rule systems. Such systems are not lacking in tensions and conflicts, but relatively speaking the quality of governance is such that the tensions do not lead to violence, the loss of life, the deterioration of social cohesion, or the degradation of people. In short, in and of itself no fragmegrative process is inherently negative or destructive.

For all kinds of reasons, however, some fragmegrative situations are fragile, dele-terious, violence-prone, and marked by publics who resent, reject or otherwise resist the intrusion of global values, policies, actors or institutions into their local affairs. It is these situations that pose problems for global governance. To be sure, some of the global intrusions can be, depending on one's values, welcomed and applauded. The world's intrusion into the apartheid rule system, for example, was clearly worthwhile. But in many cases – in those where fragmegrative situations involve local reactions to globalizing dynamics that result in internal fighting, external aggression, intensified crime, repressed minorities, exacerbated cleavages, sealed boundaries, glorified but exclusionary ideals, pervasive corruption, and a host of other patterns that run coun-ter to human dignity and well-being – corrective steering mechanisms that upgrade the quality of governance seem urgently needed. Put more moderately, given the worldwide scope of such situations, effective mechanisms for global governance seem eminently desirable.

Part of the problem of achieving governance over deleterious fragmegrative situations, of course, is that often they require the use of external force against local authorities, a practice that has long been contrary to international law and only lately undergone revision, most notably with respect to Kosovo. But international military interventions into domestic arenas are only one part – and a small one at that – of the challenge of establishing rule systems for unwanted fragmegrative conditions. There are many situations in which organized violence is not the response to global-izing dynamics, but which are nonetheless woefully lacking in appropriate steering mech-anisms and thus in need of enlightened rule systems. The list of such circumstances is seemingly endless: they can involve situations in which boundaries are sealed, minor-ities silenced, crime tolerated, majorities deceived, societies ruptured, law flouted, tyrants enhanced, corruption ignored, oppositions jailed, people trafficked, pollution accepted, elections rigged, and thought controlled – to cite only the more conspicu-ous practices that are often protected by the conventions of sovereignty and that one would like to see subjected to at least some effective and humane mechanisms of global governance. The thwarted aspirations of the Falun Gong, the people of Burma, the women of Afghanistan, and the Kurds are only among the more conspicuous of many examples of continuing fragmegrative situations that elude efforts towards steerage in enlightened directions.

Nor are the protections of sovereignty the only hindrance to decent global govern-ance. Governance on a global scale is also difficult because the globalizing and local-izing interactions often occur across both cultures and issue areas. For instance, while national governments can address – though not necessarily alleviate – the fears of their workers over the loss of jobs resulting from foreign trade with relative ease because they have some jurisdiction over both the well-being of their workers and the con-tents of trade legislation, the global scale of fragmegrative dynamics can also involve situations in which the parties to them are not located in the same jurisdiction, with the result that any attempt to steer them must be undertaken by diverse authorities that often have different interests and goals. Indeed, not infrequently a globalizing political or economic stimulus can provoke localizing cultural reactions far removed from the country, region or issue area in which the stimuli were generated; contrariwise, local events such as protest marches, coups d'état or severe economic downturns can have widespread consequences in distant places. The rapid spread of currency crises, for example, often seems ungovernable because authority for coping with the crises is so widely dispersed in this issue area and because much of the action takes place beyond the reach of any extant governments, in cyberspace. Put more strongly, the processes of imitative, emulative and isomorphic spread, as well as those that are direct and not circuitous, are so pervasive and powerful that developing steering mechanisms that prevent, or at least minimize, their unwanted consequences seems a staggering task under the best of circumstances.

[ . . . ]

# Conclusions

[ . . . ] Will the proliferation of rule systems, the disaggregation of authority and the greater density of the global stage enhance or diminish the effectiveness of the over-all system of global governance? While there doubtless will be pockets of ineffectiveness and breakdown, will the emergent system, on balance, make for more humane and sensitive governance? [ . . . ]

As an optimist, I am inclined to note three aspects of an upbeat answer if one is willing to look beyond the immediate present. In the first place, more than a little truth attaches to the aphorism that there is safety in numbers. That is, the more pluralistic and crowded the global stage gets with SOAs and their diverse steering mechanisms, the less can any one of them, or any coalition of them, dominate the course of events and the more will all of them have to be sensitive to how sheer numbers limit their influence. Every rule system, in other words, will be hemmed in by all the others, thus conducing to a growing awareness of the virtues of cooperation and the need to contain the worst effects of deleterious fragmegration.

Secondly, there is a consciousness of and intelligence about the processes of globalization that is spreading widely to every corner of the earth. What has been designated as 'reflexivity' (Giddens and Pierson, 1998, pp. 115–17) and what I call 'the globalization of globalization' (Rosenau, 2000) is accelerating at an extraordinary rate – from the ivory towers of academe to the halls of government, from the conference rooms of corporations to the peasant homes of China (where the impact of the WTO is an intense preoccupation), people in all walks of life have begun to appreciate their interdependence with others as time and distance shrink. For some, maybe even many, the rush into a globalized world may be regrettable, but few are unaware that they live in a time of change and thus there is likely to be a growing understanding of the necessity to confront the challenges of fragmegration and to be open to new ways of meeting them. [ . . . ]

Third, the advent of networks and the flow of horizontal communications has brought many more people into one or another aspect of the ongoing dialogue. The conditions for the emergence of a series of global consensuses never existed to quite the extent they do today. The skills of individuals and the orientations of the organizations they support are increasingly conducive to convergence around shared values. To be sure, the battle of Seattle and subsequent skirmishes between advocates and critics of globalization – quintessential instances of fragmegration – point to a polarization around two competing consensuses, but aside from those moments when their conflicts turn violent, the very competition between the opposing camps highlights a potential for dialogue that may lead to compromises and syntheses. Already there are signs that the attention of international institutions such as the World Bank, the World Economic Forum, the WTO and the IMF has been arrested by the complaints of their critics and that they are pondering the challenges posed by the growing gap between rich and poor people and nations.

None of this is to suggest, however, that nirvana lies ahead. Surely it does not. Surely fragmegration will be with us for a long time and surely many of its tensions will intensify. But the collective will to preserve and use the new, horizontal forms of authority is not lacking and that is not a trivial conclusion.

## Notes

1   Some analysts suggest that conceptions of the state trace a pendulum-like pattern that swings back and forth between notions of strong and weak states. See, for example, Evans (1997, p. 83), who cites Dani Rodrik as observing that 'excessive optimism about what the state would be able to accomplish was replaced by excessive pessimism'.
2   For a host of other examples of effective governance in the multi-centric world, see Cutler, Haufler and Porter, 1999.

## References

Arquilla, John and Ronfeldt, David (1997) A new epoch – and spectrum – of conflict. In John Arquilla and David Ronfeldt (eds), *In Athena's Camp: Preparing for Conflict in the Information Age*, Santa Monica: RAND.

Carlsson, Sverker and Stripple, J. (2000) Climate governance beyond the state – contributions from the insurance industry. Paper presented at the International Political Science Association, Quebec City, 1–5 Aug.

Cutler, A. Claire, Haufler, Virginia and Porter, Tony (eds) (1999) *Private Authority in International Affairs*. Albany: State University of New York Press.

Evans, Peter (1997) The eclipse of the state? Reflections on stateness in an era of globalization. *World Politics*, 50 (Oct.): 62–87.

Giddens, Anthony and Pierson, Christopher (1998) *Conversations with Anthony Giddens: Making Sense of Modernity*. Cambridge: Polity.

Krasner, Stephen A. (ed.) (1983) *International Regimes*. Ithaca: Cornell University Press.

Reinicke, Wolfgang H. (1999–2000) The other world wide web: global public policy networks. *Foreign Policy* (Winter): 44–57.

Rosenau, James N. (1990) *Turbulence in World Politics: A Theory of Change and Continuity*. Princeton: Princeton University Press.

Rosenau, James N. (1997) *Along the Domestic-Foreign Frontier: Exploring Governance in a Turbulent World*. Cambridge: Cambridge University Press.

Rosenau, James N. (2000) The globalization of globalization. Paper presented at the International Studies Association, Los Angeles, 16 Mar.

Rosenau, James N. (forthcoming) *Distant Proximities: Dynamics beyond Globalization*.

Scholte, Jan Aart (2000) *Globalization: A Critical Introduction*. London: Macmillan.

Väyrynen, Raimo (1999) Norms, compliance, and enforcement in global governance. In Raimo Väyrynen (ed.), *Globalization and Global Governance*, Lanham: Rowman and Littlefield.

Zacher, Mark (1999) Uniting nations: global regimes and the United Nations systems. In Raimo Väyrynen (ed.), *Globalization and Global Governance*, Lanham: Rowman and Littlefield.

# Part III
# The Fate of National Culture in an Age of Global Communication

The movement of cultures is linked with the movement of people. The earliest movements of people took their cultures with them across regions and continents. The globalization of culture has, accordingly, a long history. The great world religions showed how ideas and beliefs can cross the continents and transform societies. No less important were the great premodern empires which, in the absence of direct military and political control, held their domains together through a common culture of ruling elites.

However, there is something quite distinctive, globalists argue, about the sheer scale, intensity and speed of global cultural communications today. This can be linked to many factors. First, the twentieth century witnessed a wave of technological innovations in communication and transportation, along with the transformation of older technologies, which together generated functioning global infrastructures. These have opened up a massive series of communication channels that cross national borders, increasing the range and type of communications to and from all the world's regions. Second, contemporary patterns of cultural globalization have created a far greater intensity of images and practices, moving with far greater extensity and at a far greater velocity than in earlier periods. At both the domestic and the international level, cultures, societies and economies are becoming more information dense. This process is compounded by the fact that new global communication systems are used for business and commercial purposes. While there remain significant differences in information density and velocity in different parts of the globe, it is becoming increasingly difficult for people to live in any place culturally isolated from the wider world.

Against such propositions the sceptics argue that there is little sign as yet that national cultures are in terminal decline. They point out that the key supposed agents of cultural globalization – Coca-Cola, McDonald's, Microsoft and so on – are in the business of making profits and pursuing commerce, not in the business of creating alternative centres of political identity and legitimacy. The world remains a place of competing cultures, all investing in their own symbolic resources, and seeking to enlarge their spheres of influence. There is little basis for global cultural projects to flourish. Just as the territorial state is far more resilient than globalists suggest, so too are national cultures. In fact, the resilience of national cultures is an important part of the explanation of why territorial states persist and continue to play such a key part in the determination of the shape of international order.

The contours of the debate about cultural globalization are set out and explained in this section. In the first paper, by Kevin Robins, the growing mobility of goods and commodities, information and communication products and services across borders is introduced. The complexity of this phenomenon and of its diverse impacts is emphasized. Robins seeks to set out how and why it is that cultural globalization involves an unequal and uneven set of processes, which call into question old certainties and hierarchies of identity. In such a world, the cultural meaning of boundaries is transformed and cultural continuities are disrupted. Examining these processes further, John Thompson retraces the emergence of globalization in the sphere of communication. When did it begin? How did it develop? In seeking to answer these questions, Thompson provides a systematic survey of the emergence of global communication networks. After dwelling on some of the structural characteristics of globalized processes of communication, he investigates 'the creative interface between the globalized diffusion of media products and their localized appropriation'. Thompson concludes by arguing that while the globalization of communication has altered the nature of symbolic exchange and transformed certain aspects of the life conditions of people throughout the world, it has not done so straightforwardly at the expense of local and national cultural life. The importance which media messages have for individuals depends crucially 'on the contexts of reception and on the resources that recipients bring to bear on the reception process'. But he emphasizes as well that the localized appropriation of global media products can also be a source of tension and conflict. Global media products may expand people's horizons of understanding and interpretation; but they can also lead to antagonism between local, national and global forces.

The chapter which follows, by Robert McChesney, provides a succinct overview of media globalization, focusing on the trend to global corporate media consolidation, and economic deregulation and its uneven consequences and risks. McChesney outlines how the deregulation of media ownership, the privatization of television in lucrative European and Asian markets and new communication technologies have all combined to stimulate the emergence of media giants who can establish powerful distribution and production networks within and among nations. He examines how the global media market has become dominated by a few transnational corporations, and how these are interlinked with a second tier of regional and national corporate powerhouses. McChesney believes that the global media system is 'fundamentally non-competitive in any meaningful economic sense of the term' and that there are grave risks to autonomous cultural formation from the growing consolidation of 'a commercial model of communication'. This type of communication tends to create a culture of entertainment and to erode the development of public life which is so important for democratic politics. Against this, McChesney finds some evidence that there could be increasing 'widespread opposition to these trends', although there is nothing inevitable about this.

Globalization is frequently claimed to be destructive of cultural identity and, in particular, of patterns of national identity. But, John Tomlinson contends, this argument is fundamentally mistaken; globalization is 'the most significant force in *creating and proliferating* cultural identity'. Tomlinson argues that the intensification of globalization has coincided with a dramatic rise of social movements based around identity – gender, sexuality, religion, ethnicity and nationality – and that this is partly to be understood as a result of processes internal to globalization. For the 'institutional social life of [western] modernity' is spread by globalization itself. The latter distributes over space and time the core institutions of modern life, including the nation-state, urbanism and explicit locally based identity patterns. Globalization has problematized 'identity' in many parts of the world, where previously the routines of everyday life were such that 'identity was not a central concern'. Loose, contingent and tacit forms of attachment and belonging are more complex than the concept of a self-conscious 'identity' often allows. By spreading the institutions of modernity, globalization promotes particular forms of imagination linked to place and community, including nationality, which became institutionalized and regularized. Thus, 'in so far as globalization distributes the institutional features of modernity across all cultures', it 'produces "identity" where none existed – where before there were perhaps more particular, more inchoate, less socially-policed belongings'. However, globalization also produces other effects, challenging forms of national identity as well, as many have noted. Thus, we are inevitably faced with, and will continue to face, the necessity to negotiate great cultural and political complexity.

For all those who hold the view that a global culture is emerging, Anthony Smith's article provides a most telling challenge. Not only is the idea of a global culture vague and imprecise, but there is very little evidence, he suggests, that national cultures are being swept aside. The latter remain the obstinate bases of collective cultural identity. National sentiments and values in respect of a sense of continuity, shared memories and a common destiny still pervade many given collectivities which have had a common experience and distinctive history. As Smith puts it, 'vernacular mobilization; the politicization of cultures; the role of intelligentsia and other strata; and the intensification of cultural wars . . . are some of the reasons . . . why national cultures . . . continue to divide our world into discrete cultural blocks, which show little sign of homogenization, let alone amalgamation'. Despite global shifts in the technical and linguistic infrastructures of communication, it is highly unlikely that any kind of global culture will supersede the world of nations.

Is there any evidence that the populations of the world are becoming more 'cosmopolitan'; that is, more broadly sympathetic to international issues and concerns, and less preoccupied with the claim that national identity must always trump other more global considerations? There are some good reasons for thinking that the elites of the global order – the networks of experts and specialists, international bureaucrats and multinational business executives – and those who track and contest their activities – social movements, trade unionists and some politicians and intellectuals – are more global in their orientations and more absorbed by transborder questions. But is there any reason for thinking that people's identity in general is anything other than rooted in traditional ethnic, regional and national communities, as Smith maintains? Pippa Norris's chapter explores these issues systematically and looks at some important and interesting evidence. While she finds that those who have a commitment to the global order as a whole and to international institutions are a distinctive minority, she argues that the evidence reveals an important generational divide which ought not to be neglected. Those born after the Second World War are more likely to interpret their politics as internationalist, to support the UN system and to lend their support to the free trade system and the free movement of migrants. Norris shows that age cohort analysis indicates that over the long term public opinion is moving in a more international direction. Younger generations, brought up with MTV, CNN and the Internet, and living in a world defined from the outset by significant global issues such as environmental degradation, express some sense of global identification. However, whether this emerges into a strong trend and a majority position is an open question – and clearly a contested political matter, nationally, regionally and globally.

# 20
# Encountering Globalization

## *Kevin Robins*

[ . . . ]

Globalization is about growing mobility across frontiers – mobility of goods and commodities, mobility of information and communications products and services, and mobility of people. Walk down your local high street and you will be aware of global chains such as McDonald's or Benetton. You may buy the global products of Sony, Procter and Gamble or the Coca-Cola Corporation. In your local supermarkets you will buy more or less exotic fruits and vegetables from almost anywhere in the world, along with ingredients for curries, stir-fries, pizzas, and other 'world foods'. If you go out to eat you can choose from restaurants providing a whole range of 'ethnic' cuisines (Italian, Chinese, Indian, Korean, Thai, etc.). Go to the off-licence and you cannot but be aware of the increasing globalization of the market for wines (not just French or Spanish, but now South African, Chilean, Australian, and even Crimean varieties) and beers (Italian, American, Indian, Brazilian, Japanese, and more). Your coat might be produced in Turkey, your hi-fi in Japan, and your car in Korea. And, of course, we could push this analysis back one stage further, for the various inputs into the production of these commodities (raw materials, labour, components, finance) are also likely to come from a range of geographical sources.

Through the development of satellite and cable services, and on the basis of more liberal media regulation, the television market is moving from national to trans-national scale. CNN can bring you 'real-time' access to news stories across the world, as we clearly saw at the time of the Gulf War in 1991. The Disney Channel is targeted at a global audience. 'It's an MTV World' is the cover story of a recent issue of *Newsweek* magazine (24 April 1995) [ . . . ] – itself now a global media enterprise. The main headline: 'Rock around the clock and around the world with the ultimate New Age multinational'. Through the new telecommunications networks – from voice through to fax and e-mail – we can now enter into global communications 'at the touch of a button' (though paying for them is, of course, another matter). And if you have access to the Internet and the World Wide Web, you may gain access to global databases, and you can choose to become a member of a global user group. Instantaneous and ubiquitous communication is giving substance to the Canadian philosopher Marshall McLuhan's idea, first put forward in the 1960s, that the world is now becoming a 'global village'.

There are gathering flows of people, too, not just of physical and information products and goods. Members of the international business elite now undertake international travel on a routine and regular basis, constituting themselves as a global community of frequent-flier cosmopolitans. Far more numerous are those whose mobility and movement are precipitated by need or by despair, the migrants who take advantage of a cheap plane or train to seek work in the world's more affluent centres, establishing themselves there as minority communities in exile. Leisure pursuits, too, like the pursuit of employment, are associated with accelerating flows. If where you live is a tourist resort, you will be familiar with visitors from Europe or from the United States, increasingly from Japan and the Far East, and now, too, from Eastern Europe and Russia. And you will doubtless be aware of the relative ease with which you can undertake holiday travel, not just to the South of France, or the Costa Brava, but now to Florida Disneyland, or to Goa or the Caribbean. [ . . . ] Mobility has become ordinary in the emerging global order. But it is also possible to see the world without having to move. For now 'the world' is able to come to where we are. As the writer Simon Winchester puts it in his introduction to Martin Parr's collection of photographs, *Small World*:

> A whole new industry has been born from the manufacturing of . . . foreign-theme entertainment parks, the world brought to your doorstep by, first, the Americans (with both the outer world, and outer space, tucked into the more exotic corners of Disneyland) and then by the Japanese – who went on to develop the idea to a fine art, settling outside Tokyo an English village that is more brimming with thatch and swimming in bitter beer than anywhere in the Cotswolds. Soon the Europeans are to have such a *parc international*, with little great walls of China and petit Taj Mahals constructed in fields convenient for the fun-filled charabancs that converge on Cherbourg. (Parr 1995)

[ . . . ]

With mobility, comes encounter. In many respects, this may be stimulating and productive. Global encounters and interactions are producing inventive new cultural forms and repertoires. Musical culture provides an excellent example: Salma and Sabine are Pakistani sisters who sing Abba songs in Hindi; Rasta-Cymru is a Welsh-speaking reggae band; El Vez is a Latino Elvis impersonator with attitude; Cartel is a Turkish–German group appropriating US West-coast rap music and style. The anthropologist Jan Nederveen Pieterse reflects on the significance of such musical and other cultural intermixtures:

> How do we come to terms with phenomena such as Thai boxing by Moroccan girls in Amsterdam, Asian rap in London, Irish bagels, Chinese tacos and Mardi Gras Indians in the United States, or Mexican schoolgirls dressed in Greek togas dancing in the style of Isadora Duncan? How do we interpret Peter Brook directing the Mahabharata, or Ariane Mnouchkine staging a Shakespeare play in Japanese Kabuki style for a Paris audience in the Théâtre du Soleil? (Nederveen Pieterse 1995: 53)

Nederveen Pieterse describes these phenomena in terms of the origination of 'third cultures', the 'creolization of global culture', the development of an 'intercontinental crossover culture'. Globalization, from this perspective, is conceived in terms of a process of creative and conjoining *hybridization*.

Of course, this is only one aspect of the logic of globalization. The encounter between cultures can produce tension and friction. The globalization process can equally be associated with confrontation and the collision of cultures. At the present time, we can see some of the stresses of global change in the difficult relations between Western and Islamic worlds. It is there in the conflict between French people and Algerian migrants, or in the divisions between Germans and their Turkish 'guest workers'. The building of Europe's largest mosque in Rome, the historical centre of Christendom, has had some problematical repercussions. In Britain, the 'Rushdie affair' has testified to the difficulty of intercultural understanding. The Iranian government has sought to block American satellite broadcasting to prevent the 'Westoxification' of Iranian society (while many Iranians have been actively seeking to acquire satellite dishes in order to see Western programmes such as *Baywatch* and *Beavis and Butthead*). In August 1995, the socialist mayor of Courcouronnes, south of Paris, put a ban on satellite dishes to prevent the reception of programmes from North Africa. 'Integration', he maintained, 'does not mean transforming France into a nation of the Maghreb' (*Observer*, 17 Sept. 1995).

But there are also cultural confrontations within the Western world itself. It is apparent in the ambivalence and anxiety felt in Europe towards American cultural exports: in 1995, the Uruguay Round of GATT (General Agreement on Tariffs and Trade) negotiations almost broke down on account of French intransigence about maintaining restrictive quotas on US film and television products. 'Are we all Americans now?' Andrew Billen wondered (*Observer*, 17 Sept. 1995), as the Disney Channel arrived in Britain. There is the clear sense in some quarters that 'Americanization' – from Hollywood to Coke and McDonald's – is a threat to the integrity of European cultural life (see Tomlinson 1997). In these defensive and protective responses to cultural encounter, we are a long way from the celebration of cultural hybridization.

## Complexities of Globalization

Having argued that globalization and global encounter constitute a new logic of economic and cultural development, I want now to make two important qualifications to what would otherwise risk being too facile an argument. [ . . . ]

The first point of qualification [ . . . ] is that globalization does not supersede and displace everything that preceded it. As well as recognizing social innovation, we must have regard to the evident continuities in social and cultural life. Globalization may be seen in terms of an accumulation of cultural phenomena, where new global elements coexist alongside existing and established local or national cultural forms. [ . . . ]

[Second] I want to emphasize [globalization's] complexity and diversity (which make it particularly unamenable to ideal-type categorizations). The processes of global change are multifarious, and they are also experienced differentially by all those who confront them.

[ . . . ]

There are more and less benign encounters with the forces of globalization. The geographer Doreen Massey captures this inequality well in relation to the experience of human mobility and movement. [ . . . ] At one end of the spectrum, she argues, there are those 'at the forefront' of what is going on: 'the jet-setters, the ones sending and receiving the faxes and the e-mail, holding the international conference calls, the ones distributing the films, controlling the news, organizing the investments and the international currency transactions'. At the other end are those who are out of control:

The refugees from El Salvador or Guatemala and the undocumented migrant workers from Michoacán in Mexico crowding into Tijuana to make perhaps a fatal dash for it across the border into the USA to grab a chance of a new life. Here the experience of movement, and indeed of a confusing plurality of cultures, is very different. And, there are those from India, Pakistan, Bangladesh and the Caribbean, who come halfway round the world only to get held up in an interrogation room at Heathrow. (Massey 1993: 61–2)

'Some initiate flows and movement,' Massey observes, 'others don't; some are more on the receiving end of it than others; some are effectively imprisoned by it' (1993: 61). Globalization is an uneven and an unequal process.
[ . . . ]

# A World of Difference

[ . . . ] I want [ . . . ] to look at some broader aspects of globalization in relation to culture and identity. For it is surely clear that the global shift – associated with the creation of world markets, with international communication and media flows, and with international travel – has profound implications for the way we make sense of our lives and of the changing world we live in. For some, the proliferation of shared or common cultural references across the world evokes cosmopolitan ideals. There is the sense that cultural encounters across frontiers can create new and productive kinds of cultural fusion and hybridity. But, where some envisage and enjoy cosmopolitan complexities, others perceive, and often oppose, what they see as cultural homogenization and the erosion of cultural specificity. Globalization is also linked to the revalidation of particular cultures and identities. Globalization is, then, transforming our apprehension of the world in sharply contrasting ways. It is provoking new senses of disorientation and of orientation, giving rise to new experiences of both placeless and placed identity.

Old certainties and hierarchies of identity are called into question in a world of dissolving boundaries and disrupted continuities. Thus, in a country that is now a container of African and Asian cultures, can the meaning of what it is to be British ever again have the old confidence and surety it might once have had? And what does it mean now to be European in a continent coloured not only by the cultures of its former colonies, but also by American and Japanese cultures? Is not the very category of identity itself problematical? Is it at all possible, in global times, to sustain a coherent and unified sense of identity? Continuity and historicity of identity are challenged by the immediacy and intensity of global cultural confrontations. Of course, we should not believe that these developments are entirely unprecedented [ . . . ] a great many cultures have historical experience of global intrusion [ . . . ]. Nonetheless we should have regard to what is without precedent at the end of the twentieth century: the scale, the extent, the comprehensive nature, of global integration. We should consider [ . . . ] the particular complexities of global encounter at this century's end.

One very powerful dimension of global cultural change has been that which has sought to dissolve the frontiers and divisions between different cultures. It has been actively promoted by global corporate interests [ . . . ] – it is an ideal that is particularly sympathetic to those members of the class of symbolic analysts working in the creative areas of media, advertising, and so on. We could consider it in terms of the global culture and philosophy associated with 'McDonaldization' or 'Coca-colonization'. But a particularly good example – because it is so explicit and self-aware about its objectives – is that of Benetton advertising. Through its 'United Colors of Benetton' slogan, the company has actively promoted the idea of the 'global village', associated with global consumer citizenship. What is advocated is the ideal of a new, 'universal' identity that transcends old, particularistic attachments. But transcendence is through incorporation, rather than through dissolution. Michael Shapiro describes it as 'a globalizing, ecumenical impulse':

> Ever since [Oliviero] Toscanini [the artistic creator of the campaigns] produced the slogan, *The United Colors of Benetton*, the Benetton company has made explicit its desire to dominate the mediascape with a symbolism that comprehends nationalities, ethnicities, religions, and even tribal affiliations. The world of geopolitical boundaries – boundaries transversed by Benetton's enterprises – is no impediment to the production of media-carried global symbolism. (Shapiro 1994: 442)

This global corporate philosophy is further refined in Benetton's most recent campaign, concerned with global threats and disasters:

> In this case, the interpretative work locates the observer in a global community, trying to make sense of the violent clashes of ethno-nationalists. This global self-identification is precisely the difference-effacing stance that Benetton is trying to achieve. The interpretative contemplation of global threats and catastrophes cuts across ethnicities, nationalities, and tribalisms, allowing Benetton to position its products in a universalizing thematic that transcends cultural inhibitions. (1994: 448)

What the example of Benetton makes clear is the resourcefulness of global advertising, both incorporating and effacing cultural difference in its endeavours to put in place the new global acumen.

A second dimension of cultural globalization that we should consider is that which promotes cultural encounter and interaction. Here, in stark contrast with the first dimension that we have just looked at, we are concerned with the active interpenetration, combination and mixture of cultural elements. These processes are, as Akbar Ahmed makes clear, a consequence of both communication flows and human flows:

> The mixing of images, interlocking of cultures, juxtaposition of different peoples, availability of information are partly explained because populations are mobile as never before. The mobility continues in spite of increasingly rigid immigration controls. Filipino maids in Dubai, Pakistani workers in Bradford, the Japanese buying Hollywood studios, Hong Kong Chinese entrepreneurs acquiring prime property in Vancouver testify to this. The swirling and eddying of humanity mingles ideas, cultures and values as never before in history. (Ahmed 1992: 26)

Cultures are transformed by the incorporations they make from other cultures in the world. Salman Rushdie (1991: 394) has famously written of 'the transformation that comes of new and unexpected combinations of human beings, cultures, ideas, politics, movies, songs'; '*Mélange*, hotchpotch,' he declares, 'a bit of this and a bit of that is *how newness enters the world*.' This process of hybridization is particularly apparent now in developments within popular culture. The sociologist Les Back (1994: 14) describes the bhangramuffin music of the singer/songwriter Apache Indian as 'a meeting place where the languages and rhythms of the Caribbean, North America and India mingle, producing a new and vibrant culture'. 'Artists like Apache Indian are expressing and defining cultural modes that are simultaneously local and global,' Back observes. 'The music manifests itself in a connective supplementarity – raga plus bhangra plus England plus India plus Kingston plus Birmingham' (p. 15). Places too can be characterized in terms of hybridity: places of encounter, meeting places, crucibles in which cultural elements are turned into new cultural compounds. Doreen Massey (1993: 66) argues for the recognition of 'a sense of place which is extraverted, which includes a consciousness of its links with the wider world, which integrates in a positive way the global and the local'. A 'global sense of place' involves openness to global dynamics and also an acceptance of cultural diversity and the possibilities of cultural encounter within.

The third dimension of cultural globalization that I want to [emphasize] concerns developments that apparently involve a rejection or turning away from the turbulent changes associated with global integration. These developments express themselves in a turn, or return, to what are seen as traditional and more fundamental loyalties. In the recent period, we have become increasingly aware of the resurgence of national, regional, ethnic and territorial attachments. In Eastern Europe, particularly in the former Yugoslavia, we have witnessed the growth of neo-nationalism in its most militant form, but it has also been a feature of Western Europe, with the assertion of Basque, Breton or Scottish identities. It has now become a journalistic commonplace to describe such regionalist or nationalist reassertion in terms of a reversion or regression to tribal loyalties. These loyalties and attachments seem to go against the grain of globalization; they appear to articulate the desire and need for stability and order, as a refuge from the turbulence and upheaval of global transformation. And, of course, there is a great deal of truth in this theory of resistance through roots. But we might, at the same time, also see this as itself an expression of the globalization process – Anthony Smith (1991: 143) writes of the 'globalization of nationalism'. Resurgent nations are also seeking to position themselves in the new global space.

We may see the same contradictory relation to the globalization process in the case of resurgent religious cultures and identities. While there has been a return to fundamentals within Hinduism, Judaism and Christianity, it is the case of Islamic fundamentalism that has been made to stand out for its opposition to global times. The attempts by some Islamic countries to ban satellite television have seemed to symbolize resistance to global information and communication flows [ . . . ]. A *Guardian* headline (5 Aug. 1994) expressed it perfectly: 'As satellite television shrinks the world, traditionalists from Tehran to Bollywood [India] take on the dishes in a war of the heavens.' At one level, of course, this does indeed represent a defensive and protective response to the disruptions of global modernity. As Akbar Ahmed (himself a Muslim) makes clear in his book *Postmodernism and Islam*, we must see such actions in the context of the struggle by traditional cultures, and particularly Islam, to come to terms with Western globalization:

> The West, though the dominant global civilization, will continue to expand its boundaries to encompass the world; traditional civilizations will resist in some areas, accommodate to change in others. In the main, only one, Islam, will stand firm in its path. Islam, therefore, appears to be set on a collision course with the West. (Ahmed 1992: 264)

But we must see this as far more than just closure and retreat from global culture. What we must also recognize is the aspiration to create a space within global culture.

For many Muslims, Ahmed argues, the objective is 'to participate in the global civilization without their identity being obliterated' (ibid.). As Peter Beyer (1994) argues, the 'revitalization of religion is a way of asserting a particular (group) identity, which in turn is a prime method of competing for power and influence in the global system' (p. 4); the 'central thrust is to make Islam and Muslims more determinative in the world system, not to reverse globalization. The intent is to shape global reality, not to negate it' (p. 3). The point is to create a global civilization on a different basis from that which is being elaborated by the symbolic analysts of the West.

What I am trying to bring out in all of this is the factor of diversity and difference in the cultural experience of global modernity: new forms of universal culture, new kinds of particularism, new hybrid developments, all of them gaining their significance from their new global context. We should not think of globalization in terms of homogenization, then, in line with what is commonly believed and feared.

But nor should we see it just in terms of diversity and differentiation, which is the opposite temptation that many more critical spirits have succumbed to. What globalization in fact brings into existence is a new basis for thinking about the relation between cultural convergence and cultural difference.

[ . . . ]

The globalization process must be seen in terms of the complex interplay of economic and cultural dynamics, involving confrontation, contestation and negotiation. The global future is therefore sure to have surprises in store for us.

## References

Ahmed, A. (1992) *Postmodernism and Islam*. London: Routledge.

Back, L. (1994) The sounds of the city. *Anthropology in Action* 1(1): 11–16.

Beyer, P. (1994) *Religion and Globalization*. London: Sage.

Massey, D. (1993) Power-geometry and a progressive sense of place. In J. Bird et al. (eds), *Mapping the Future: Local Cultures, Global Change*, London: Routledge.

Nederveen Pieterse, J. (1995) Globalization as hybridization. In M. Featherstone, S. Lash and R. Robertson (eds), *Global Modernities*, London: Sage.

Parr, M. (1995) *Small World*. Stockport: Dewi Lewis.

Rushdie, S. (1991) *Imaginary Homelands*. London: Granta/Penguin.

Shapiro, M. (1994) Images of planetary danger: Luciano Benetton's ecumenical fantasy. *Alternatives* 19(4): 433–54.

Smith, A. D. (1991) *National Identity*. Harmondsworth: Penguin.

Tomlinson, J. (1997) Internationalization, globalization and media imperialism. In K. Thompson (ed.), *Media and Cultural Regulation*, London: Sage/The Open University.

# 21

# The Globalization of Communication

## John B. Thompson

One of the salient features of communication in the modern world is that it takes place on a scale that is increasingly global. Messages are transmitted across large distances with relative ease, so that individuals have access to information and communication which originates from distant sources. Moreover, with the uncoupling of space and time brought about by electronic media, the access to messages stemming from spatially remote sources can be instantaneous (or virtually so). Distance has been eclipsed by proliferating networks of electronic communication. Individuals can interact with one another, or can act within frameworks of mediated quasi-interaction, even though they are situated, in terms of the practical contexts of their day-to-day lives, in different parts of the world.

The reordering of space and time brought about by the development of the media is part of a broader set of processes which have transformed (and are still transforming) the modern world. These processes are commonly described today as 'globalization'. The term is not a precise one, and it is used in differing ways in the literature.[1] In the most general sense, it refers to the growing interconnectedness of different parts of the world, a process which gives rise to complex forms of interaction and interdependency. Defined in this way, 'globalization' may seem indistinguishable from related terms such as 'internationalization' and 'transnationalization', and these terms are often used interchangeably in the literature. But while these various notions refer to phenomena that are closely connected, the process of globalization, as I shall understand it here, involves more than the expansion of activities beyond the boundaries of particular nation-states. Globalization arises only when (a) activities take place in an arena which is global or nearly so (rather than merely regional, for example); (b) activities are organized, planned or coordinated on a global scale; and (c) activities involve some degree of reciprocity and interdependency, such that localized activities situated in different parts of the world are shaped by one another. One can speak of globalization in this sense only when the growing interconnectedness of different regions and locales becomes systematic and reciprocal to some degree, and only when the scope of interconnectedness is effectively global.

[ . . . ]

There can be no doubt that the organization of economic activity and concentrations of economic power have played a crucial role in the process of globalization. But all forms of power – economic, political, coercive and symbolic – have both contributed to and been affected by this process. If one retraces the process of globalization, one finds that these various forms of power overlap with one another in complex ways, sometimes reinforcing and sometimes conflicting with one another, creating a shifting interplay of forms of power. In this chapter I shall focus primarily on the social organization of symbolic power and the ways in which it has contributed to and been transformed by the process of globalization. But this will necessarily involve some discussion of economic, political and coercive power as well.

[ . . . ]

## The Emergence of Global Communication Networks

The practice of transmitting messages across extended stretches of space is not new. [ . . . ] Elaborate networks of postal communication were established by political authorities in the Roman Empire and by political, ecclesiastical and commercial elites in medieval Europe. With the development of printing in the late fifteenth century, books, pamphlets and other printed materials were circulated well beyond the locales of their production, frequently crossing the frontiers of the emerging nation-states. Moreover, as European powers developed trading relations with other parts of the world, communication channels were established between Europe and those regions of the world that were drawn increasingly into the spheres of European colonial expansion.

It was only in the nineteenth century, however, that communication networks were systematically organized on a global scale. It was in the nineteenth century, therefore, that the globalization of communication took hold. This was partly due to the development of new technologies which enabled communication to be dissociated from physical transportation. But it was also linked directly to economic, political and military considerations. I shall examine the beginnings of the globalization of communication by focusing on three key developments of the late nineteenth and early twentieth centuries: (1) the development of underwater cable systems by the European imperial powers; (2) the establishment of international news agencies and their division of the world into exclusive spheres of operation; and (3) the formation of international organizations concerned with the allocation of the electromagnetic spectrum.

(1) The telegraph was the first medium of communication which successfully exploited the communication potential of electricity. Experiments with early forms of telegraphy took place in the late eighteenth and early nineteenth centuries, but the first electromagnetic telegraphs were developed in the 1830s. In 1831 Joseph Henry of Albany, New York, succeeded in transmitting signals over a mile-long circuit, and by 1837 usable systems had been developed by Cooke and Wheatstone in England and Morse in the United States. The system devised by Cooke and Wheatstone, which used needles that could be read visually, was initially installed along the railway between Paddington and West Drayton in July 1839. But Morse's system, which used a dot–dash code for the transmission of messages, eventually proved to be the most successful. In 1843 Morse built his first practical telegraph line between Washington and Baltimore with funds provided by the US Congress. Subsequently the telegraph industry developed rapidly in the United States and in Europe, stimulated by demand from the railways, the press, and the business and financial sectors.

The early telegraph systems were land-based and therefore restricted in terms of their geographical scope. It was not until the 1850s that reliable methods of underwater telegraphy were developed. The early submarine cables were generally made of copper wire coated with gutta percha, a natural insulating material made from the sap of a Malayan tree.[2] In 1851–2 submarine cables were successfully laid across the English Channel and between England and Ireland. In 1857–8 the first attempt was made to lay a cable across the Atlantic Ocean, though it ended in failure. The first attempts to link Britain with India were similarly unsuccessful. In 1864, however, a submarine cable was successfully laid between Karachi and the Persian Gulf; the line was then connected by land-based cables to Constantinople and Europe. By 1865 a telegraph link between Britain and India was complete. A year later, a transatlantic cable was successfully laid.

Following these early successes, the submarine cable industry developed rapidly. In the early 1870s, cables were laid throughout South-East Asia, so that Europe was linked to China and Australia. Cables were also laid between Europe and South America, and along the coasts of Africa. Most of the cables were produced, laid and operated by private companies, although these companies often received substantial financial assistance from governments. London was the centre of this expanding communication network and was the principal source of finance for the international submarine cable business. By 1900, approximately 190,000 miles of submarine cable had been laid throughout the world. British firms owned 72 per cent of these cables, and a substantial proportion were owned by one firm – the Eastern and Associated Companies founded by the Manchester merchant John Pender, who had been involved in the submarine cable industry since the 1860s.

The early submarine cable networks were used primarily for commercial and business purposes, although political and military concerns also played an important role in their development. As leaders of the most extensive empire of the late nineteenth century, British officials were well aware of the strategic value of rapid communications. The British Admiralty and the Colonial, War and Foreign Offices placed pressure on the government to construct additional submarine cables which did not cross non-British territories, and which would therefore be less vulnerable in times of crisis. One such cable was laid between Britain and the Cape of Good Hope in 1899–1901, and was used during the Boer War. This line was subsequently extended to Mauritius, Ceylon, Singapore and Australia, thereby connecting Britain to South-East Asia and Australia via a route which avoided the Middle East.

The submarine cable networks developed in the second half of the nineteenth century thus constituted the first global system of communication in which the capacity to transmit messages was clearly separated from the time-consuming processes of transportation. Individuals located in the major urban centres of Europe and North America acquired the means to communicate almost instantaneously with other parts of the world. The contrast with earlier forms of transport-based communication was dramatic. Up to the 1830s, a letter posted in England took five to eight months to reach India; and due to monsoons in the Indian Ocean, it could take two years for a reply to be received.[3] In the 1870s, a telegram could reach Bombay in five hours, and the answer could be back on the same day. And in 1924, at the British Empire Exhibition, King George V sent himself a telegram which circled the globe on all-British lines in 80 seconds. Rapid communication on a global scale – albeit along routes that reflected the organization of economic and political power – was a reality.

(2) A second development of the nineteenth century which was of considerable significance for the formation of global communication networks was the establishment

of international news agencies. The significance of news agencies in this context was threefold. First, the agencies were concerned with the systematic gathering and dissemination of news and other information over large territories – primarily in Europe to begin with, but soon extending to other parts of the world. Second, after an initial period of competitive rivalry, the major news agencies eventually agreed to divide up the world into mutually exclusive spheres of operation, thus creating a multilateral ordering of communication networks which was effectively global in scope. Third, the news agencies worked closely with the press, providing newspapers with stories, extracts and information which could be printed and diffused to a wide audience. Hence the news agencies were tied into networks of communication which, via print (and later radio and television), would reach a significant and growing proportion of the population.

The first news agency was established in Paris by Charles Havas in 1835.[4] A wealthy entrepreneur, Havas acquired what was primarily a translating office, the *Correspondance Garnier*, and turned it into an agency which collected extracts from various European papers and delivered them daily to the French press. By 1840 the agency catered for clients in London and Brussels as well, supplying news by coach and by means of a regular pigeon service. In the late 1840s, rival news-gathering services were set up in London by Paul Julius Reuter and in Berlin by Bernard Wolff. The agencies took advantage of the development of telegraph cable systems, which made it possible to transmit information over ever-greater distances at great speed. Competition among the three agencies intensified in the 1850s, as each agency sought to secure new clients and to expand its sphere of operation. However, in order to avoid damaging conflicts, the agencies eventually decided to cooperate by dividing the world up into mutually exclusive territories. By virtue of the Agency Alliance Treaty of 1869, Reuter obtained the territories of the British Empire and the Far East; Havas acquired the French Empire, Italy, Spain and Portugal; and Wolff was granted the exclusive right to operate in German, Austrian, Scandinavian and Russian territories. While the agencies were independent commercial organizations, their domains of operation corresponded to the spheres of economic and political influence of the major European imperial powers. Each agency worked closely with the political and commercial elites of the country which served as its home base, enjoying some degree of political patronage and providing information which was valuable for the conduct of trade and diplomacy.

The triple agency cartel dominated the international collection and dissemination of news until the outbreak of the First World War. Other news agencies were established in the late nineteenth and early twentieth centuries, but most had aligned themselves with one of the three principals. In the wake of the First World War, however, the triple agency cartel was broken by the expansion of two American agencies, Associated Press (AP) and the United Press Association (UPA, subsequently transformed into United Press International or UPI). Associated Press was a cooperative established in 1848 by six New York daily newspapers. AP joined the European cartel in 1893, agreeing to supply the European agencies with news from America in return for the exclusive right to distribute news in the United States. The United Press Association was founded by E. W. Scripps in 1907, partly in order to break the hold of AP in the domestic US news market. In addition to serving the US market, UPA set up offices in South America and sold news to South American and Japanese newspapers. During the First World War and its aftermath, both AP and UPA expanded their activities worldwide, placing increasing pressure on the cartel arrangements. By the early 1930s the triple agency cartel was effectively at an end; in 1934 Reuters signed a new agreement with AP which gave the American agencies a free hand to collect and distribute news throughout the world. While the American agencies expanded rapidly and Reuters maintained a strong position in the global market, the other European agencies underwent major changes. The capitulation of France in 1940 brought about the dissolution of Havas, although it was eventually replaced by a new agency, the Agence France-Presse (AFP), which took over many of the assets and connections of its predecessor. With the rise of Nazism and the subsequent defeat and partition of Germany following the Second World War, the Wolff agency lost its position of influence in the international domain and eventually disappeared.

Since the Second World War, the four major agencies – Reuters, AP, UPI and AFP – have maintained their positions of dominance in the international system for the collection and dissemination of news and other information. Many other agencies have been established and expanded their spheres of operation; and some agencies, such as TASS and the Deutsche Presse Agentur, acquired (at least temporarily) a prominent international role. But the four majors remain the key actors in the global information order. Many newspapers and broadcasting organizations throughout the world depend heavily on them for international news, as well as for news of their own geopolitical region, and many of the smaller agencies are affiliated to them. The major news agencies have also expanded and diversified their activities, taking advantage of new developments in information and communication technology and emerging as central players in the new global market for information and data of various kinds, including information relating to financial and commercial transactions.[5]

The dominance of the major news agencies, combined with other inequalities in the international flow of information and communication, has led to calls from various quarters for a reorganization of the global information order. A series of conferences and commissions sponsored by UNESCO in the 1970s and early 1980s generated a wide-ranging debate on the theme of a 'New World Information and Communication Order' (NWICO). The proponents of NWICO were seeking a more equitable balance in the international flow and content of information, as well as a strengthening of the technological infrastructures and productive capacities of less developed countries in the sphere of communication. But the UNESCO initiatives met with considerable resistance from certain governments and interest groups in the West. In 1984 the United States withdrew from UNESCO, followed by the United Kingdom in 1985; together this deprived UNESCO of around 30 per cent of its budget and greatly limited the effectiveness of any policy recommendations.[6] Nevertheless, the NWICO debate helped to increase awareness of the issues raised by the dominance of the major news agencies and, more generally, by the inequalities associated with the globalization of communication. It also helped to stimulate the development of various forms of cooperation among so-called Third World countries, including the expansion of regional and non-aligned news agencies in Africa and elsewhere.[7]

(3) A third development which played an important role in the globalization of communication also stems from the late nineteenth century: it concerns the development of new means of transmitting information via electromagnetic waves and the succession of attempts to regulate the allocation of the electromagnetic spectrum. [ . . . ] The use of electromagnetic waves for the purposes of communication greatly expanded the capacity to transmit information across large distances in a flexible and cost-efficient

way, dispensing with the need to lay fixed cables over land or under sea. But the increasing use of electromagnetic waves also created a growing need to regulate the allocation of spectrum space both within and between countries. Each country developed its own legislative framework for spectrum allocation and selective licensing. Initially one of the key concerns of the authorities entrusted with the task of allocating spectrum space was to set aside a segment of the spectrum for military and security purposes, thereby minimizing interference from amateur radio users. But as the commercial potential of the new medium became increasingly clear, political authorities became directly involved in the selective licensing of broadcasting organizations, which were granted exclusive rights to broadcast at designated frequencies in particular regions. The practices of selective licensing were shaped not only by the technical constraints of spectrum scarcity but also by a broader set of political considerations concerning the proper nature and role of broadcasting organizations, considerations which varied greatly from one country to another.[8]

The international frameworks for the management of spectrum space were less effective. The key organization in this regard was the International Telegraph Union, subsequently transformed into the International Telecommunication Union (ITU). Originally formed in 1865 under a convention signed by 20 European states, the union was concerned primarily with the establishment of international standards and the resolution of technical problems.[9] At its 1906 Berlin conference, it dealt with radio for the first time and agreed to allocate certain sections of the spectrum to specific services, such as the frequencies used by ships at sea. Subsequently the ITU convened a regular conference – the World Administrative Radio Conference or WARC – to address problems of spectrum allocation and related issues. In the early phase of these international activities, frequencies were generally allocated on a first come, first served basis.[10] Users simply notified the ITU of the frequencies they were using or wished to use, and they thereby acquired a 'squatter's right'. But as demands on the radio spectrum increased, the ITU gradually adopted a more active stance. Sections of the spectrum were allocated to particular services, and the world was divided into three broad regions – Europe and Africa, the Americas, and Asia and the South Pacific – which could each be planned in more detail. The systems developed by the ITU have none the less come under increasing pressure in recent years, partly as a result of rising demands by existing users and partly due to new demands by countries hitherto largely excluded from the domain of international telecommunications.

The development of technologies capable of transmitting messages via electromagnetic waves, together with the emergence of national and international organizations concerned with the management of spectrum space, marked a decisive advance in the globalization of communication. It was now possible to transmit increasing quantities of information over large distances in an efficient and virtually instantaneous way. Moreover, the messages transmitted by electromagnetic waves were potentially accessible to anyone who was within range of the signals and who had the equipment to receive them – a fact which was of enormous significance for the commercial exploitation of the medium. However, during the first half of the twentieth century most communication by electromagnetic transmission remained confined to specific geographical locales, such as particular urban areas, nation-states or the regions between land and ships at sea. It was not until the 1960s, with the launching of the first successful geo-stationary communication satellites, that communication by electromagnetic transmission became fully global in scope. I shall return to this development shortly.

## Patterns of Global Communication Today: An Overview

While the origins of the globalization of communication can be traced back to the mid-nineteenth century, this process is primarily a phenomenon of the twentieth. For it is during the twentieth century that the flow of information and communication on a global scale has become a regularized and pervasive feature of social life. There are, of course, many dimensions to this process; the twentieth century has witnessed an unparalleled proliferation of the channels of communication and information diffusion. The rapid development of systems of radio and television broadcasting throughout the world has been an important but by no means the only aspect of this process. The globalization of communication has also been a structured and uneven process which has benefited some more than others, and which has drawn some parts of the world into networks of global communication more quickly than other parts. Since the late 1960s, the characteristics of global communication flows have been studied in some detail by researchers in international communication – well before the term 'globalization' gained currency in the social sciences.[11] In this section I shall draw on this literature for the purpose of analysing some of the main patterns of global communication today. I shall not attempt to analyse these patterns in a detailed and comprehensive fashion, but merely to identify some of the main dimensions of globalized communication processes; and I shall be concerned above all to highlight their structured and uneven character. While the range of relevant issues is potentially very wide, I shall restrict my attention to four themes: (1) the emergence of transnational communication conglomerates as key players in the global system of communication and information diffusion; (2) the social impact of new technologies, especially those associated with satellite communication; (3) the asymmetrical flow of information and communication products within the global system; and (4) the variations and inequalities in terms of access to the global networks of communication.

(1) The globalization of communication in the twentieth century is a process that has been driven primarily by the activities of large-scale communication conglomerates. The origins of these conglomerates can be traced back to the transformation of the press in the nineteenth century [ . . . ]. The change in the economic basis of newspapers, precipitated and promoted by the introduction of new methods of production, set in motion a long-term process of accumulation and concentration in the media industries. In the course of the twentieth century, this process has increasingly assumed a transnational character. Communication conglomerates have expanded their operations in regions other than their countries of origin; and some of the large industrial and financial concerns have, as part of explicit policies of global expansion and diversification, acquired substantial interests in the information and communication sector. Through mergers, acquisitions and other forms of corporate growth, the large conglomerates have assumed an ever-greater presence in the global arena of the information and communication trade.

The names of some of the largest communication conglomerates are well known: Time Warner, formed by the merger of Time, Inc., and Warner Communications in 1989 and now the largest media enterprise in the world, has subsidiaries in Australia, Asia, Europe and Latin America. The German-based Bertelsmann group, with strong interests in publishing, television, music and high-tech information systems, has operations in Europe, the United States and Latin America. Rupert Murdoch's News Corporation, which has substantial interests in publishing, television and film, probably has the most extensive reach, with subsidiaries in Europe, the United States, Australia and Asia. These and other large communication conglomerates operate increasingly in a worldwide market and organize their activities on the basis of strategies which are effectively global in design. But nearly all of the large conglomerates are based in North America, Western Europe, Australia or Japan; very few are based in Third World countries, although the latter provide important markets for their goods and services.[12] Hence the development of communication conglomerates has led to the formation of large concentrations of economic and symbolic power which are privately controlled and unevenly distributed, and which can deploy massive resources to pursue corporate objectives in a global arena. It has also led to the formation of extensive, privately controlled networks of communication through which information and symbolic content can flow.

The nature and activities of some of the large communication conglomerates have been documented in the literature and I shall not examine them further here.[13] There is a need, however, for more up-to-date comparative research on the activities of these conglomerates, on the ways in which they are adapting to the changing economic and political circumstances of the 1990s, and on their exploitation of new technological developments.

(2) The development of new technologies has played an important role in the globalization of communication in the late twentieth century, both in conjunction with the activities of communication conglomerates and independently of them. Three interrelated developments have been particularly important. One is the deployment of more extensive and sophisticated cable systems which provide much greater capacity for the transmission of electronically encoded information. A second development is the increasing use of satellites for the purposes of long-distance communication, often in conjunction with land-based cable systems. The third development – in many ways the most fundamental – is the increasing use of digital methods of information processing, storage and retrieval. The digitalization of information, combined with the development of related electronic technologies (microprocessors, etc.), has greatly increased the capacity to store and transmit information and has created the basis for a convergence of information and communication technologies, so that information can be converted relatively easily between different communication media.

All three of these technological developments have contributed in fundamental ways to the globalization of communication. Most obviously, the use of telecommunications satellites, positioned in geosynchronous orbits and interlinked, has created a system of global communication which is virtually instantaneous and which dispenses with the need for terrestrial relays and transmission wires. Since their development in the early 1960s, telecommunications satellites have been used for a variety of purposes.[14] The needs of the military and of large commercial organizations have always played an important role, and many multinational corporations make extensive use of satellite communication. Satellites have also been increasingly integrated into the normal telecommunications networks, carrying a growing proportion of the international traffic in telephone, telex, fax, electronic mail and related communication services.

From the outset, telecommunications satellites were also used as relay stations and distribution points for television broadcasting. They formed an integral part of national network systems in the USA, the former USSR and elsewhere, and they were used as distribution points to supply cable systems on a national and international basis. In recent years, however, the development of more sophisticated satellites, capable of transmitting stronger, well-targeted signals, has made possible the introduction of direct broadcasting by satellite (or DBS). The first DBS systems began transmitting programmes in the USA in 1975, and the first European systems began operating in 1986; by the early 1990s, a variety of DBS systems were operating or planned in other parts of the world. Part of the significance of DBS is that it creates new distribution systems outside of the established terrestrially based networks of broadcasting – systems which are often privately owned and controlled and in which the large communication conglomerates may have a substantial stake. Moreover, these new distribution systems are inherently transnational since, from a technical point of view, there is no reason why the reception area (or 'footprint') of a DBS satellite should correspond even roughly to the territorial boundaries of a particular nation-state.

In addition to creating new transnational distribution networks, the development of DBS and other technologies (including cable and videocassette recorders) has expanded the global market for media products. The international flow of films, TV programmes and other materials has increased as producers and distributors seek to exploit the lucrative markets created by satellite and cable channels and by videocassette rentals and sales. This expansion of the global market should be viewed against the backcloth of earlier trends in the international flow of media products.

(3) A central feature of the globalization of communication is the fact that media products circulate in an international arena. Material produced in one country is distributed not only in the domestic market but also – and increasingly – in a global market. It has long been recognized, however, that the international flow of media products is a structured process in which certain organizations have a dominant role, and in which some regions of the world are heavily dependent on others for the supply of symbolic goods. Studies carried out in the early 1970s by Nordenstreng and Varis showed a clear asymmetry in the international flow of television programmes: there was, to a large extent, a one-way traffic in news and entertainment programmes from the major exporting countries to the rest of the world.[15] The United States was (and remains) the leading exporter in television programming, selling far more material to other countries (especially to Latin America, Europe, Canada, Australia and Japan) than it imports from abroad. Some European countries, such as Britain and France, were also major exporters (and remain so); but, unlike the United States, they also imported a significant quantity of programming from abroad (mainly from the US). Subsequent studies by Varis and others have tended to confirm the unevenness of flow, although they have also produced a more complex picture and have highlighted the growing importance of intraregional trade (for instance, countries like Mexico and Brazil have emerged as major producers and exporters of programming material to other parts of Latin America).[16]

The structured character of the international flow of symbolic goods is the outcome of various historical and economic factors. In the domain of news, the patterns of dependence reflect the legacy of the international news agencies established in London, Paris and New York (although the precise significance of Western-based news agencies remains a matter of some dispute[17]). In the sphere of entertainment, the economic power of Hollywood continues to exert a major influence on the international flow of films and

TV programmes. Many television stations in less developed countries do not have the resources to produce extensive programming of their own. The import of American serials, at prices negotiated on a country-by-country basis, is a relatively inexpensive (and financially very attractive) way to fill broadcasting schedules.

While some of the broad patterns of international flow have been documented over the years, the research remains fragmentary. There are many sectors of the information and communication industries which have yet to be studied in detail from this point of view. And the ways in which existing patterns of international flow will be affected by new technological developments – such as those associated with satellite and cable systems, or those linked more generally to the digitalization of information – is a question which demands a good deal more research. Given the complexity of global networks of transmission and trade and the huge volume of material which passes through them, it is unlikely that our understanding of patterns of international flow will ever be more than partial. But further research could help to shed light on some of the more significant trends.

(4) In addition to analysing the patterns of international flow, it is essential to consider the patterns of access to and uptake of material transmitted through global networks. Much of the research on patterns of international flow has been based on the content analysis of television broadcasting schedules in different countries. But in some parts of the world, access to television broadcasting services was restricted for many years to the relatively small proportion of the population which lived in the major urban areas. For the rural population, which comprises 70–90 per cent of the population in many Third World countries, radio has probably been a more important medium of communication than television.[18] Of course, this situation is changing continuously as more resources are devoted to the development of television services and as more individuals and families are able to gain access to them. But significant inequalities remain in terms of the capacity of individuals in different parts of the world, and in different parts and social strata of the same country, to gain access to the materials which are diffused through global networks.

Quite apart from these inequalities of access, globalized symbolic materials are subjected to different patterns of uptake. Taken on its own, the content analysis of programming schedules tells us relatively little about who watches which programmes, how long they watch them for, etc., and hence tells us relatively little about the extent of uptake of globally distributed material.[19] Moreover, if we wish to explore the impact of the globalization of communication, we must consider not only the patterns of uptake but also the *uses* of globalized symbolic materials – that is, what recipients do with them, how they understand them, and how they incorporate them into the routines and practices of their everyday lives.
[ ... ]

## Globalized Diffusion, Localized Appropriation: Towards a Theory of Media Globalization

[ ... ]

We have already shed some light on the global–local axis by examining some of the patterns of global diffusion. I now want to develop this analysis further by focusing on the process of appropriation and pursuing three interrelated themes. The first theme is this: given the hermeneutical character of appropriation, it follows that the significance which media messages have for individuals and the uses to which mediated symbolic materials are put by recipients depend crucially on the contexts of reception and on the resources that recipients bring to bear on the reception process. This is well illustrated by the Liebes and Katz study of the reception of *Dallas*. It is also vividly demonstrated by the perceptive account by Sreberny-Mohammadi and Mohammadi of the role of communication media in the Iranian Revolution.[20] During the 1970s, traditional religious language and imagery were used in Iran as symbolic weapons in the struggle against the Shah, who was associated with the corrupting importation of Western culture. Although Khomeini was in exile, his speeches and sermons were recorded and smuggled into Iran on audiocassettes, which were easily reproduced and widely diffused. But with the development of an Islamic regime in the post-revolutionary period, Western cultural products began to assume a very different significance for many Iranians. Videos of Western films and tapes of Western pop music circulated as part of a popular cultural underground, taking on a subversive character; they helped to create an alternative cultural space in which individuals could take some distance from a regime experienced by many as oppressive.[21] Examples such as these illustrate well the contextually bounded character of the process of appropriation. As symbolic materials circulate on an ever-greater scale, locales become sites where, to an ever-increasing extent, globalized media products are received, interpreted and incorporated into the daily lives of individuals. Through the localized process of appropriation, media products are embedded in sets of practices which shape and alter their significance.

Let us now consider a second theme: how should we understand the social impact of the localized appropriation of globalized media products? Here I want to emphasize one key feature of this process. I want to suggest that the appropriation of globalized symbolic materials involves what I shall describe as *the accentuation of symbolic distancing from the spatial-temporal contexts of everyday life*. The appropriation of symbolic materials enables individuals to take some distance from the conditions of their day-to-day lives – not literally but symbolically, imaginatively, vicariously. Individuals are able to gain some conception, however partial, of ways of life and life conditions which differ significantly from their own. They are able to gain some conception of regions of the world which are far removed from their own locales.

The phenomenon of symbolic distancing is brought out well by James Lull in his study of the impact of television in China.[22] Television became a widespread medium in China only in the course of the 1980s. In the 1960s and 1970s relatively few television sets were sold in China; they were very expensive relative to normal wages and were generally restricted to the more privileged urban elites. In the 1980s, however, domestic television production increased dramatically; by 1990 most urban families owned at least one TV set, and there was about one set for every eight people nation-wide.[23] Broadcasting is dominated by the national network, Central China Television (CCTV), which supplies a large proportion of the programming material to the various regional and local stations operating throughout the country.

What sense do Chinese viewers make of the programmes they watch? Lull pursues this question through a series of extended interviews with families in Shanghai, Beijing, Guangzhou and Xian. Among other things, he shows that, while many

Chinese viewers are critical of the programmes available to them, they value television for the way that it offers new vistas, new lifestyles and new ways of thinking. 'In
our daily lives we just go to work and come home, so we want to see something that
is different from our own life. TV gives us a model of the rest of the world':[24] this
comment by a 58-year-old accountant from Shanghai captures well the effect of symbolic distancing in the age of global communication. Chinese viewers are drawn to
programmes imported from Japan, Taiwan, Europe and the United States not only
for their information and entertainment value, but also because they give a glimpse
– albeit a fleeting and partial one – of what life is like elsewhere. When people watch
international news, for instance, they may pay as much attention to street scenes, housing and clothing as to the commentary which accompanies the pictures from foreign
lands.

[ . . . ]

   In emphasizing the phenomenon of symbolic distancing, I do not want to suggest,
of course, that this is the *only* aspect of the process of appropriation which is worthy
of consideration. On the contrary, in the actual circumstances of day-to-day life, it is
likely that the appropriation of globalized media products will interact with localized
practices in complex ways and may, in some respects, serve to consolidate established
relations of power or, indeed, to create new forms of dependency. [ . . . ]

   This brings us to a third theme that I want briefly to consider: the localized appropriation of globalized media products is also a source of tension and potential conflict.
It is a source of tension partly because media products can convey images and
messages which clash with, or do not entirely support, the values associated with a
traditional way of life. In some contexts this discordance may be part of the very appeal
of media products: they help individuals to take a distance, to imagine alternatives,
and thereby to question traditional practices. So, for instance, it seems that Egyptian
soap operas are of interest to young Bedouin women in the Western Desert precisely
because they present a set of lifestyles – such as the possibility of marrying for love
and living separately from the extended family – which diverge from the set of
options traditionally available to them.[25]

[ . . . ]

   It would be imprudent to claim that the localized appropriation of globalized
media products has been a major factor in stimulating broader forms of social conflict
and social change in the modern world; most forms of social conflict are extremely
complex and involve many diverse factors. But it could be plausibly argued that the
increasingly globalized diffusion of media products has played a role in triggering
off some of the more dramatic conflicts of recent years. Lull contends that the stream
of domestic and international television programmes transmitted throughout China
in the 1980s created a cultural reservoir of alternative visions, encouraging people to
question traditional values and official interpretations and helping them to imagine
alternative ways of living. By itself, this certainly did not bring about the audacious
demonstration in Tiananmen Square, nor did it determine the course of the subsequent confrontation. But in the absence of television it seems unlikely that the
events of Tiananmen Square would have unfolded in the way they did, nor would
they have been witnessed by millions of individuals in China and throughout the
world.

[ . . . ]

## Notes

1  For a review of different usages, see Roland Robertson, *Globalization: Social Theory and Global Culture* (London: Sage, 1992), esp. ch. 1.

2  See Daniel R. Headrick, *The Tools of Empire: Technology and European Imperialism in the Nineteenth Century* (Oxford: Oxford University Press, 1981), ch. 11; Bernard S. Finn, *Submarine Telegraphy: The Grand Victorian Technology* (Margate: Thanet Press, 1973).

3  Headrick, *The Tools of Empire*, p. 130.

4  For more detailed accounts of the development of the major news agencies, see Graham Storey, *Reuters' Century 1851–1951* (London: Max Parrish, 1951); Oliver Boyd-Barrett, *The International News Agencies* (London: Constable, 1980); Anthony Smith, *The Geopolitics of Information: How Western Culture Dominates the World* (London: Faber, 1980).

5  The growth and diversification of Reuters in the 1970s and 1980s was particularly pronounced. In 1963, two-thirds of Reuters' revenue of £3 million came from media subscribers. In 1989, the media accounted for only 7 per cent of Reuters' revenue; 55 per cent was derived from the money market, 19 per cent from securities, 8 per cent from commodities and 11 per cent from client services. By 1990 Reuters' overall revenue had risen to £1,369 million, of which 82.5 per cent was earned overseas. (See Jeremy Tunstall and Michael Palmer, *Media Moguls* (London and New York: Routledge, 1991), p. 56.)

6  For a detailed account of the NWICO debate and the role of UNESCO, see Thomas L. McPhail, *Electronic Colonialism: The Future of International Broadcasting and Communication*, 2nd edn (Newbury Park, Calif.: Sage, 1987).

7  On the development of news agencies and other mechanisms of information exchange in Third World countries, see Oliver Boyd-Barrett and Daya Kishan Thussu, *Contra-Flow in Global News: International and Regional News Exchange Mechanisms* (London: John Libbey, 1992).

8  For further discussion of the institutional frameworks of broadcasting, see John B. Thompson, *Ideology and Modern Culture: Critical Social Theory in the Era of Mass Communication* (Cambridge: Polity Press, 1991), pp. 183–92.

9  See McPhail, *Electronic Colonialism*, ch. 5; John Howkins, 'The management of the spectrum', *InterMedia* 7(5) (Sept. 1979): 10–22.

10  Howkins, 'The management of the spectrum', p. 14.

11  Among the most important and influential of the early studies were the UNESCO-sponsored surveys carried out by Nordenstreng and Varis in 1971–3 and by Varis in 1983. See Kaarle Nordenstreng and Tapio Varis, *Television Traffic – A One-Way Street? A Survey and Analysis of the International Flow of Television Programme Material*, Reports and Papers on Mass Communication, no. 70 (Paris: UNESCO, 1974); Tapio Varis, *International Flow of Television Programmes*, Reports and Papers on Mass Communication, no. 100 (Paris: UNESCO, 1986). Numerous other studies have been carried out. For useful discussions of the relevant literature, see Jeremy Tunstall, *The Media Are American: Anglo-American Media in the World* (London: Constable, 1977); Elihu Katz and George Wedell, *Broadcasting in the Third World: Promise and Performance* (Cambridge, Mass.: Harvard University Press, 1977); Smith, *The Geopolitics of Information*; Ralph Negrine and S. Papathanassopoulos, *The Internationalization of Television* (London: Pinter, 1990); Preben Sepstrup, *Transnationalization of Television in Europe* (London: John Libbey, 1990); Annabelle Sreberny-Mohammadi, 'The global and the local in international communications', in James Curran and Michael Gurevitch (eds), *Mass Media and Society* (London: Edward Arnold, 1991); Geoffrey Reeves, *Communications and the 'Third World'* (London: Routledge, 1993).

12  A recent UNESCO report on world communications showed that, of the 78 largest communication conglomerates ranked according to total media turnover, 39 were based in the United States, 25 in Western Europe, 8 in Japan, 5 in Canada and 1 in Australia; none

were based in the Third World. (See *World Communication Report* (Paris: UNESCO, 1989), pp. 104–5.)

13  See, for example, Ben H. Bagdikian, *The Media Monopoly*, 4th edn (Boston: Beacon Press, 1992); Anthony Smith, *The Age of Behemoths: The Globalization of Mass Media Firms* (New York: Priority Press, 1991); Tunstall and Palmer, *Media Moguls*.

14  For further discussion of historical and technical aspects of satellite communications, see Abram Chayes, James Fawcett, Masami Ito, Alexandre-Charles Kiss et al., *Satellite Broadcasting* (London: Oxford University Press, 1973); Jonathan F. Galloway, *The Politics and Technology of Satellite Communications* (Lexington: D. C. Heath, 1972).

15  Nordenstreng and Varis, *Television Traffic*; see also Tapio Varis, 'Global traffic in television', *Journal of Communication* 24 (1974): 102–9.

16  See Varis, *International Flow of Television Programmes*; Annabelle Sreberny-Mohammadi, 'The "World of the News" study: results of international cooperation', *Journal of Communications* 34 (1984): 121–34; Sepstrup, *Transnationalization of Television in Europe*.

17  Some commentators have argued that the influence of Western-based news agencies has been exaggerated. See, for example, Robert L. Stevenson, 'The "World of the News" study: pseudo debate', *Journal of Communications* 34 (1984): 134–8; Michael Tracey, 'The poisoned chalice? International television and the idea of dominance', *Daedalus* 114 (1985): 17–55.

18  See Katz and Wedell, *Broadcasting in the Third World*, ch. 1.

19  For a discussion of some of the issues involved in studying patterns of consumption in relation to the globalization of communication, see Sepstrup, *Transnationalization of Television in Western Europe*, ch. 4.

20  See Annabelle Sreberny-Mohammadi and Ali Mohammadi, *Small Media, Big Revolution: Communication, Culture, and the Iranian Revolution* (Minneapolis: University of Minnesota Press, 1994).

21  Ibid., pp. 186–8.

22  See James Lull, *China Turned On: Television, Reform, and Resistance* (London: Routledge, 1991).

23  Ibid., p. 23.

24  Quoted in ibid., p. 171.

25  See Lila Abu-Lughod, 'Bedouins, cassettes and technologies of public culture', *Middle East Report* 159(4) (1989): 7–11, 47.

# 22
# The New Global Media

*Robert W. McChesney*

The nineties have been a typical *fin de siècle* decade in at least one important respect: the realm of media is on the brink of a profound transformation. Whereas previously media systems were primarily national, in the past few years a global commercial-media market has emerged. "What you are seeing," says Christopher Dixon, media analyst for the investment firm PaineWebber, "is the creation of a global oligopoly. It happened to the oil and automotive industries earlier this century; now it is happening to the entertainment industry."

Together, the deregulation of media ownership, the privatization of television in lucrative European and Asian markets, and new communications technologies have made it possible for media giants to establish powerful distribution and production networks within and among nations. In short order, the global media market has come to be dominated by the same eight transnational corporations, or TNCs, that rule US media: General Electric, AT&T/Liberty Media, Disney, Time Warner, Sony, News Corporation, Viacom and Seagram, plus Bertelsmann, the Germany-based conglomerate [see table 1]. At the same time, a number of new firms and different political and social factors enter the picture as one turns to the global system, and the struggle for domination continues among the nine giants and their closest competitors. But as in the United States, at a global level this is a highly concentrated industry; the largest media corporation in the world in terms of annual revenues, Time Warner (1998 revenues: $27 billion), is some fifty times larger in terms of annual sales than the world's fiftieth-largest media firm.

A few global corporations are horizontally integrated; that is, they control a significant slice of specific media sectors, like book publishing, which has undergone extensive consolidation in the late nineties. "We have never seen this kind of concentration before," says an attorney who specializes in publishing deals. But even more striking has been the rapid *vertical* integration of the global media market, with the same firms gaining ownership of content and the means to distribute it. What distinguishes the dominant firms is their ability to exploit the "synergy" among the companies they own. Nearly all the major Hollywood studios are owned by one of these conglomerates, which in turn control the cable channels and TV networks that air the movies. Only two of the nine are not major content producers: AT&T and GE. But GE owns NBC, AT&T has major media content holdings through Liberty Media, and both firms are in a position to acquire assets as they become necessary [see table 2].

The major media companies have moved aggressively to become global players. Even Time Warner and Disney, which still get most of their revenues in the United States, project non-US sales to yield a majority of their revenues within a decade. The point is to capitalize on the potential for growth abroad – and not get outflanked by competitors – since the US market is well developed and only permits incremental

**Table 1**  And then there were nine

| Disney | AT&T | Sony |
|---|---|---|
| Annual revenues: $23 billion (FY 1998)<br><br>Non-US sales: 21%<br><br>Non-US sales in 1984: 8.4%<br><br>Disney has established a strong presence in China, Japan, Europe and Latin America. Its ESPN International is broadcast in twenty-one languages to 155 million households in 182 nations. | Annual revenues: $53 billion (FY 1998)/$1.5 billion (Liberty)<br><br>Non-US sales: n/a<br><br>As part of its merger with Tele-Communications Inc., AT&T acquired Liberty Media, which has holdings in South America and Asia in cable, satellite and broadcast television. It also owns stakes in Time Warner, News Corporation, CNBC and Sprint PCS Group. | Annual revenues: $56.6 billion (FY 1999)/$10.4 billion (media)<br><br>Non-Japan sales: 78.2%<br><br>Non-Japan sales in 1989: 68.6%<br><br>Among Sony's global media activities are local-language film production in Europe and Asia, television programming on five continents and Sony Music Entertainment sales in Latin America, Asia and Europe. |

| General Electric | News Corporation | Seagram |
|---|---|---|
| Annual revenues: $100 billion (FY 1998)/ $5.3 billion (NBC)<br><br>Non-US sales: 43%<br><br>Non-US sales in 1988: 22%<br><br>GE's media assets include NBC and CNBC. Its channels in Europe and Asia reach 70 million households. | Annual revenues: $13.6 billion (FY 1999)<br><br>Non-US sales: 26%<br><br>Still the biggest English-language newspaper producer in the world, News Corporation's US TV stations reach some 40 percent of the viewing population. Murdoch is expanding his media properties in Asia and Latin America but News Corporation will receive the majority of its income from the United States for at least another decade. | Annual revenues: $12.3 billion (FY 1999)/$7.4 billion (media)<br><br>Non-US sales: 50% (co. est.)<br><br>Seagram's Universal Music Group is the largest recorded-music firm in the world. In 1998 the company purchased Polygram for $10.4 billion. Seagram also owns Universal Studios, with theme parks in Asia and TV channels throughout Europe and Latin America. |

| Time Warner | Viacom | Bertelsmann |
|---|---|---|
| Annual revenues: $26.8 billion (FY 1998)<br><br>Non-US sales: 21%<br><br>With 200 subsidiaries, Time Warner is a major global player in virtually every media sector except newspapers and radio. Two examples: CNN International reaches 200 nations, and HBO has expanded throughout Europe, Latin America and most of Asia. | Annual revenues: $12.1 billion (FY 1998)/$6.8 billion (CBS)<br><br>Non-US sales: 23%<br><br>Non-US sales in 1988: .006%<br><br>Viacom's Paramount Pictures and MTV distribute heavily outside the United States. It owns Nickelodeon, which operates customized channels from Uzbekistan to the Philippines, and Blockbuster, which has 6,000 stores in twenty-seven countries. Its purchase of CBS is pending approval. | Annual revenues: $16.4 billion (FY 1998)<br><br>Non-Germany sales: 72%<br><br>The Germany-based Bertelsmann is the largest TV and radio firm in Europe. Bertelsmann's BMG Music does considerable business in Asia, South Africa and Brazil. It owns Random House in the United States and publishing companies in Germany, Britain and Argentina. |

*Source*: *Rich Media, Poor Democracy*, by Robert W. McChesney. Additional research: Alison Mann.

**Table 2** Who owns the movies? The major Hollywood studios, all but one owned by the nine mega-conglomerates, make more than half of their money outside the United States. Here are the top four movies in selected countries, with ownership information

| Country | Films | Country | Film company | Affiliated media conglomerate (if any) |
|---------|-------|---------|--------------|----------------------------------------|
| Brazil | *Titanic* | US | Fox/Paramount | NewsCorp/Viacom |
| | *Armageddon* | US | BVI/Touchstone | Disney |
| | *Devil's Advocate* | US | Warner Brothers | Time Warner |
| | *The Mask of Zorro* | US | Sony Pictures Entertainment | Sony |
| France | *Titanic* | US | Fox/Paramount | NewsCorp/Viacom |
| | *Le Dîner de Cons* | France | Gaumont | Gaumont Multimedia |
| | *Les Couloirs de Temps (The Visitors II)* | France | Gaumont | Gaumont Multimedia |
| | *Taxi* | France | ARP/TF1 | |
| Italy | *Titanic* | US | Fox/Paramount | NewsCorp/Viacom |
| | *Tre Uomini e una Gambia* | Italy | Medusa | Mediaset |
| | *La Vita è Bella* | Italy | Cecchi Gori | Cecchi Gori Group |
| | *Cosi è La Vita* | Italy | Medusa | Mediaset |
| Japan | *Titanic* | US | Fox/Paramount | NewsCorp/Viacom |
| | *Deep Impact* | US | Paramount/Dream Works | Viacom |
| | *Pokémon* | Japan | Shogakukan Productions Co., Ltd. | |
| | *Godzilla* | US | Sony/TriStar | Sony |
| Mexico | *Titanic* | US | Fox/Paramount | NewsCorp/Viacom |
| | *Godzilla* | US | Sony/TriStar | Sony |
| | *Armageddon* | US | BVI/Touchstone | Disney |
| | *A Bug's Life* | US | BVI/Disney | Disney |
| Poland | *Titanic* | US | Fox/Paramount | NewsCorp/Viacom |
| | *Armageddon* | US | Buena Vista/Touchstone | Disney |
| | *Godzilla* | US | Sony/TriStar | Sony |
| | *As Good As It Gets* | US | Columbia/TriStar | Sony |

**Table 2**   (*Cont'd*)

| Country | Films | Country | Film company | Affiliated media conglomerate (if any) |
|---|---|---|---|---|
| Russia | *Titanic* | US | Fox/Paramount | NewsCorp/Viacom |
|  | *Armageddon* | US | Buena Vista/ Touchstone | Disney |
|  | *Godzilla* | US | Sony/TriStar | Sony |
|  | *Deep Impact* | US | Paramount/ DreamWorks | Viacom |
| South Africa | *Tomorrow Never Dies* | US–UK | MGM/United Artists | Disney |
|  | *Armageddon* | US | BVI/Touchstone | Disney |
|  | *There's Something About Mary* | US | 20th Century Fox | NewsCorp |
|  | *Deep Impact* | US | Paramount/ DreamWorks | Viacom |
| South Korea | *Titanic* | US | Fox/Paramount | NewsCorp/Viacom |
|  | *Armageddon* | US | BVI/Touchstone | Disney |
|  | *Mulan* | US | BVI/Disney | Disney |
|  | *A Promise* | Korea | Shincine | Samsung |

*All sources: Screen International* 1998 except Japan (*Variety*). Research: Jillian K. Dunham.

expansion. As Viacom CEO Sumner Redstone has put it, "Companies are focusing on those markets promising the best return, which means overseas." Frank Biondi, former chairman of Seagram's Universal Studios, asserts that "99 percent of the success of these companies long-term is going to be successful execution offshore."

Prior to the eighties and nineties, national media systems were typified by domestically owned radio, television and newspaper industries. Newspaper publishing remains a largely national phenomenon, but the face of television has changed almost beyond recognition. Neoliberal free-market policies have opened up ownership of stations as well as cable and digital satellite TV systems to private and transnational interests, producing scores of new channels operated by the media TNCs that dominate cable ownership in the United States. The channels in turn generate new revenue streams for the TNCs: the major Hollywood studios, for example, expect to generate $11 billion from global TV rights to their film libraries in 2002, up from $7 billion in 1998.

While media conglomerates press for policies to facilitate their domination of markets throughout the world, strong traditions of protection for domestic media and cultural industries persist. Nations ranging from Norway, Denmark and Spain to Mexico, South Africa and South Korea keep their small domestic film production industries alive with government subsidies. In the summer of 1998 culture ministers from twenty nations, including Brazil, Mexico, Sweden, Italy and Ivory Coast, met in Ottawa to discuss how they could "build some ground rules" to protect their cultural fare from "the Hollywood juggernaut." Their main recommendation was to keep culture out of the control of the World Trade Organization. A similar 1998 gathering, sponsored by the United Nations in Stockholm, recommended that culture be granted special exemptions in global trade deals.

Nevertheless, the trend is clearly in the direction of opening markets. Proponents of neoliberalism in every country argue that cultural trade barriers and regulations harm consumers, and that subsidies inhibit the ability of nations to develop their own competitive media firms. There are often strong commercial-media lobbies within nations that perceive they have more to gain by opening up their borders than by maintaining trade barriers. In 1998, for example, when the British government proposed a voluntary levy on film theater revenues (mostly Hollywood films) to benefit the British commercial film industry, British broadcasters, not wishing to antagonize the firms who supply their programming, lobbied against the measure until it died.

The global media market is rounded out by a second tier of four or five dozen firms that are national or regional powerhouses, or that control niche markets, like business or trade publishing. About half of these second-tier firms come from North America; most of the rest are from Western Europe and Japan. Each of these second-tier firms is a giant in its own right, often ranking among the thousand largest companies in the world and doing more than $1 billion per year in business. The roster of second-tier media firms from North America includes Dow Jones, Gannett, Knight-Ridder, Hearst and Advance Publications, and among those from Europe are the Kirch Group, Havas, Mediaset, Hachette, Prisa, Canal Plus, Pearson, Reuters and Reed Elsevier. The Japanese companies, aside from Sony, remain almost exclusively domestic producers.

This second tier has also crystallized rather quickly; across the globe there has been a shakeout in national and regional media markets, with small firms getting eaten by medium firms and medium firms being swallowed by big firms. Many national and regional conglomerates have been established on the backs of publishing or television empires, as in the case of Denmark's Egmont. The situation in most nations is similar to the one in the United States: compared with ten or twenty years ago, a much smaller number of much larger firms now dominate the media. Indeed, as most nations are smaller than the United States, the tightness of the media oligopoly can be even more severe. The situation may be most stark in New Zealand, where the newspaper industry is largely the province of the Australian-American Rupert Murdoch and the Irishman Tony O'Reilly, who also dominates New Zealand's commercial-radio broadcasting and has major stakes in magazine publishing. Murdoch controls pay television and is negotiating to purchase one or both of the two public TV networks, which the government is aiming to sell. In short, the rulers of New Zealand's media system could squeeze into a closet.

Second-tier corporations are continually seeking to reach beyond national borders. Australian media moguls, following the path blazed by Murdoch, have the mantra "Expand or die." As one puts it, "You really can't continue to grow as an Australian supplier in Australia." Mediaset, the Berlusconi-owned Italian TV power, is angling to expand into the rest of Europe and Latin America. Perhaps the most striking example of second-tier globalization is Hicks, Muse, Tate and Furst, the US radio/publishing/TV/billboard/movie theater power that has been constructed almost overnight. In 1998 it spent well over $1 billion purchasing media assets in Mexico, Argentina, Brazil and Venezuela.

Thus second-tier media firms are hardly "oppositional" to the global system. This is true as well in developing countries. Mexico's Televisa, Brazil's Globo, Argentina's Clarin and Venezuela's Cisneros Group, for example, are among the world's sixty or seventy largest media corporations. These firms tend to dominate their own national and regional media markets, which have been experiencing rapid consolidation as well. They have extensive ties and joint ventures with the largest media TNCs, as well as with Wall Street investment banks. And like second-tier media firms elsewhere, they are also establishing global operations, especially in nations that speak the same language. As a result, they tend to have distinctly pro-business political agendas and to support expansion of the global media market, which puts them at odds with large segments of the population in their home countries.

Together, the sixty or seventy first- and second-tier giants control much of the world's media: book, magazine and newspaper publishing; music recording; TV production; TV stations and cable channels; satellite TV systems; film production; and motion picture theaters. But the system is still very much in formation. New second-tier firms are emerging, especially in lucrative Asian markets, and there will probably be further upheaval among the ranks of the first-tier media giants. And corporations get no guarantee of success merely by going global. The point is that they have no choice in the matter. Some, perhaps many, will falter as they accrue too much debt or as they enter unprofitable ventures. But the chances are that we are closer to the end of the process of establishing a stable global media market than to the beginning. And as it takes shape, there is a distinct likelihood that the leading media firms in the world will find themselves in a very profitable position. That is what they are racing to secure.

The global media system is fundamentally noncompetitive in any meaningful economic sense of the term. Many of the largest media firms have some of the same major shareholders, own pieces of one another or have interlocking boards of directors. When *Variety* compiled its list of the fifty largest global media firms for 1997, it observed that "merger mania" and cross-ownership had "resulted in a complex web of inter-relationships" that will "make you dizzy." The global market strongly encourages corporations to establish equity joint ventures in which the media giants all own a part of an enterprise. This way, firms reduce competition and risk and increase the chance of profitability. As the CEO of Sogecable, Spain's largest media firm and one of the twelve largest private media companies in Europe, expressed it to *Variety*, the strategy is "not to compete with international companies but to join them." In some respects, the global media market more closely resembles a cartel than it does the competitive marketplace found in economics textbooks.

Global conglomerates can at times have a progressive impact on culture, especially when they enter nations that had been tightly controlled by corrupt crony media systems (as in much of Latin America) or nations that had significant state censorship over media (as in parts of Asia). The global commercial-media system is radical in that it will respect no tradition or custom, on balance, if it stands in the way of profits. But ultimately it is politically conservative, because the media giants are significant beneficiaries of the current social structure around the world, and any upheaval in property or social relations – particularly to the extent that it reduces the power of business – is not in their interest.

While the "Hollywood juggernaut" and the specter of US cultural imperialism remains a central concern in many countries, the notion that corporate media firms are merely purveyors of US culture is ever less plausible as the media system becomes increasingly concentrated, commercialized and globalized. The global media system is better understood as one that advances corporate and commercial interests and values and denigrates or ignores that which cannot be incorporated into its mission. There is no discernible difference in the firms' content, whether they are owned by shareholders in Japan or Belgium or have corporate headquarters in New York or Sydney. Bertelsmann CEO Thomas Middelhoff bristled when, in 1998, some said it was improper for a German firm to control 15 percent of the US book-publishing market. "We're not foreign. We're international," Middelhoff said. "I'm an American with a German passport."

As the media conglomerates spread their tentacles, there is reason to believe they will encourage popular tastes to become more uniform in at least some forms of media. Based on conversations with Hollywood executives, *Variety* editor Peter Bart concluded that "the world filmgoing audience is fast becoming more homogeneous." Whereas action movies had once been the only sure-fire global fare – and comedies had been considerably more difficult to export – by the late nineties comedies like *My Best Friend's Wedding* and *The Full Monty* were doing between $160 million and $200 million in non-US box-office sales.

When audiences appear to prefer locally made fare, the global media corporations, rather than flee in despair, globalize their production. This is perhaps most visible in the music industry. Music has always been the least capital-intensive of the electronic media and therefore the most open to experimentation and new ideas. US recording artists generated 60 percent of their sales outside the United States in 1993; by 1998 that figure was down to 40 percent. Rather than fold their tents, however, the five media TNCs that dominate the world's recorded-music market are busy establishing local subsidiaries in places like Brazil, where "people are totally committed to local music," in the words of a writer for a trade publication. Sony has led the way in establishing distribution deals with independent music companies from around the world [see table 3].

With hypercommercialism and growing corporate control comes an implicit political bias in media content. Consumerism, class inequality and individualism tend to be taken as natural and even benevolent, whereas political activity, civic values and antimarket activities are marginalized. The best journalism is pitched to the business class and suited to its needs and prejudices; with a few notable exceptions, the journalism reserved for the masses tends to be the sort of drivel provided by the media giants on their US television stations. This slant is often quite subtle. Indeed, the genius of the commercial-media system is the general lack of overt censorship. As George Orwell noted in his unpublished introduction to *Animal Farm*, censorship in free societies is infinitely more sophisticated and thorough than in dictatorships, because "unpopular ideas can be silenced, and inconvenient facts kept dark, without any need for an official ban."

Lacking any necessarily conspiratorial intent and acting in their own economic self-interest, media conglomerates exist simply to make money by selling light escapist entertainment. In the words of the late Emilio Azcarraga, the billionaire head of Mexico's Televisa: "Mexico is a country of a modest, very fucked class [ . . . ]. Television has the obligation to bring diversion to these people and remove them from their sad reality and difficult future."

It may seem difficult to see much hope for change. As one Swedish journalist noted in 1997, "Unfortunately, the trends are very clear, moving in the wrong direction on virtually every score, and there is a desperate lack of public discussion of the

**Table 3** Who owns the music? Overseas sales of US recording artists are declining, but the media giants are establishing subsidiaries around the world to produce and distribute local music. Here are the top four recording artists in selected countries, with ownership information

| Country | Artist | Title | Label | Company and home base |
|---------|--------|-------|-------|-----------------------|
| Brazil | E O Tchan | E O Tchan do Brasil | Universal | Seagram (Canada) |
| | Pe. Marcelo Rossi | Musicas para Louvar A. Senhor | Universal | Seagram (Canada) |
| | Grupo Molejo | Brincadeira de Crianca | Warner | Time Warner (US) |
| | Leandro & Leonardo | Un Sonhador | BMG | Bertelsmann (Germany) |
| France | Original Soundtrack | Notre Dame de Paris | Sony | Sony (Japan) |
| | Original Soundtrack | Titanic | Sony | Sony (Japan) |
| | Louise Attaque | Louise Attaque | Sony | Sony (Japan) |
| | Celine Dion | S'il Suffisait d'Aimer | Sony | Sony (Japan) |
| Japan | B'z | B'z The Best Pleasure | Rooms Records | Being, Inc. (Japan) |
| | B'z | B'z The Best Treasure | Rooms Records | Being, Inc. (Japan) |
| | Every Little Thing | Time to Destination | Avex | Avex Group (Japan) |
| | Yumi Matsutoya | Neue Music | Toshiba/EMI | EMI (Japan) |
| Mexico | Los Temerarios | Como te Recuerdo | Fonovisa | Televisa (Mexico) |
| | Mecano | Ana, Jose, Nacho | BMG | Bertelsmann (Germany) |
| | Juan Gabriel | Celebración de los 25 años | BMG | Bertelsmann (Germany) |
| | Mana | Sueños Liquidos | Warner | Time Warner (US) |
| Poland | Original Soundtrack | Titanic | Sony | Sony (Japan) |
| | Celine Dion | Let's Talk About Love | Sony | Sony (Japan) |
| | Modern Talking | Back for Good | BMG | Bertelsmann (Germany) |
| | Era | Ameno | Universal | Seagram (Canada) |
| Russia | Depeche Mode | Ultra | Mute | Mute (UK) |
| | Enigma | Le Roi Est Mort, Vive le Roi! | EMI | EMI |
| | George Michael | Older | EMI | EMI |
| | Paul McCartney | Flaming Pie | EMI | EMI |
| South Africa | Whitney Houston | My Love Is Your Love | Arista | Bertelsmann (North America) |
| | Boyzone | By Request | Polygram | Seagram (Canada) |
| | Vengaboys | Greatest Hits Bonus | EMI | EMI (South Africa) |
| | Ricky Martin | Ricky Martin | Sony/Columbia | Sony (Japan) |
| South Korea | Seo Tae-Ji | Take 5 | Samsung | Samsung |
| | H.O.T. | Set a Line (vol. 4) | Shinnara | (South Korea) |
| | Ryu Seung-Joon Ryu | Seung-Joon 2 | Seoul | (South Korea) |
| | Cool | Sorrow | Samsung | Samsung |

*All sources*: IFPI (International Federation of Phonographic Industry) except South Africa (Bryan Pearson). Research: Jillian K. Dunham.

long-term implications of current developments for democracy and accountability."
But there are indications that progressive political movements around the world are
increasingly making media issues part of their political platforms. From Sweden, France
and India to Australia, New Zealand and Canada, democratic left political parties are
making structural media reform – breaking up the big companies, recharging nonprofit
and noncommercial broadcasting and media – central to their agenda. They are
finding out that this is a successful issue with voters.

At the same time, the fate of the global media system is intricately intertwined with
that of global capitalism, and despite the self-congratulatory celebration of the free
market in the US media, the international system is showing signs of weakness. Asia,
the so-called tiger of twenty-first-century capitalism, fell into a depression in 1997, and
its recovery is still uncertain. Even if there is no global depression, discontent is brew-
ing in those parts of the world and among those segments of the population that have
been left behind in this era of economic growth. Latin America, the other vaunted
champion of market reforms since the eighties, has seen what a World Bank official
terms a "big increase in inequality." While the dominance of commercial media
makes resistance more difficult, it is not hard to imagine widespread opposition to
these trends calling into question the triumph of the neoliberal economic model and
the global media system it has helped create.

# 23
# Globalization and Cultural Identity

## John Tomlinson

It is fair to say that the impact of globalization in the cultural sphere has, most generally, been viewed in a pessimistic light. Typically, it has been associated with the destruction of cultural identities, victims of the accelerating encroachment of a homogenized, westernized, consumer culture. This view, the constituency for which extends from (some) academics to anti-globalization activists (Shepard and Hayduk 2002), tends to interpret globalization as a seamless extension of – indeed, as a euphemism for – western cultural imperialism. In the discussion which follows I want to approach this claim with a good deal of scepticism.

I will not seek to deny the obvious power of globalized capitalism to distribute and promote its cultural goods in every corner. Nor will I take up the argument – now very commonly made by critics of the cultural imperialism thesis (Lull 2000; Thompson 1995; Tomlinson 1991) that a deeper cultural impact cannot be easily inferred from the presence of such goods. What I will try to argue is something more specific: that cultural identity, properly understood, is much more the *product* of globalization than its victim.

## Identity as Treasure

To begin, let me sketch the implicit (for it is usually implicit) reasoning behind the assumption that globalization destroys identities. Once upon a time, before the era of globalization, there existed local, autonomous, distinct and well-defined, robust and culturally sustaining connections between geographical place and cultural experience. These connections constituted one's – and one's community's – 'cultural identity'. This identity was something people simply 'had' as an undisturbed existential possession, an inheritance, a benefit of traditional long dwelling, of continuity with the past. Identity, then, like language, was not just a description of cultural belonging; it was a sort of collective treasure of local communities. But it was also discovered to be something fragile that needed protecting and preserving, that could be lost. Into this world of manifold, discrete, but to various degrees vulnerable, cultural identities there suddenly burst (apparently around the middle of the 1980s) the corrosive power of globalization. Globalization, so the story goes, has swept like a flood tide through the world's diverse cultures, destroying stable localities, displacing peoples, bringing a market-driven, 'branded' homogenization of cultural experience, thus obliterating the differences between locality-defined cultures which had constituted our identities. Though globalization has been judged as involving a *general* process of loss of cultural diversity, some of course did better, some worse out of this process. Whilst those cultures in the mainstream of the flow of capitalism – those in the West and, specifically, the United States – saw a sort of standardized version of their cultures exported worldwide, it was the 'weaker' cultures of the developing world that have been most threatened. Thus the economic vulnerability of these non-western cultures is assumed to be matched by a cultural vulnerability. Cultural identity is at risk everywhere with the depredations of globalization, but the developing world is particularly at risk.

This, then, is the story that implicates globalization in the destruction of cultural identity, and in the threat to that particular subset of cultural identity that we call 'national identity'. But another, quite contradictory, story can be told: that globalization, far from destroying it, has been perhaps the most significant force in *creating and proliferating* cultural identity. This story involves a rather different understanding of the idea of 'identity' than the somewhat reified understanding of an individual or collective possession. And it also involves a rather more complex understanding of the globalization process: one, at least, which allows for a degree of unpredictability in its consequences.

## Identity as Cultural Power

Let us begin with identity, a concept which surely lies at the heart of our contemporary cultural imagination. It is not, in fact, difficult in the prolific literature of analysis of the concept to find positions which contest the story of identity as the victim of globalization that I sketched above. To take just one example, Manuel Castells devoted an entire volume of his celebrated analysis of 'The Information Age' to the proposition that: 'Our world and our lives are being shaped by the conflicting trends of globalization and identity.' For Castells, the primary *opposition* to the power of globalization lies in 'the widespread surge of powerful expressions of collective identity that challenge globalization . . . on behalf of cultural singularity and people's control over their lives and environment' (1997: 2). Far from being the fragile flower that globalization tramples, identity is seen here as the upsurging *power* of local culture that offers (albeit multi-form, disorganized and sometimes politically reactionary) *resistance* to the centrifugal force of capitalist globalization.

This more robust view of the 'power of identity' is one to which anyone surveying the dramatic rise of social movements based around identity positions (gender, sexuality, religion, ethnicity, nationality) might easily subscribe. So, recognizing the significant cultural sources of resistance to the power of globalization goes a long way towards getting this power in perspective. The impact of globalization thus becomes, more plausibly, a matter of the *interplay* of an institutional-technological impetus towards globality with counterpoised 'localizing' forces. The drive towards 'globality' combines a logic of capitalist expansion with the rapid development of deterritorializing media and communications technologies. But this drive is opposed by various processes and practices expressing different orders of 'locality'. Amongst these we can count the cultural identity movements that Castells focuses on, but also less formally organized expressions of identity, for example, those involved in local consumption preferences (Howes 1996). And, on quite another level, we have to add the considerable cultural effort exercised by nation-states in binding their populations into another cultural-political order of local identification.

This more complex formulation clearly implies that cultural identity is not likely to be the easy prey of globalization. This is because identity is not in fact merely some fragile communal-psychic attachment, but a considerable dimension of *institutional-ized* social life in modernity. Particularly in the dominant form of *national identity*, it is the product of deliberate cultural construction and maintenance via both the regulatory and the socializing institutions of the state: in particular, the law, the education system and the media. The deterritorializing force of globalization thus meets a structured opposition in the form of what Michael Billig (1995) has called 'banal nationalism' – the everyday minute reinforcement; the continuous routinized 'flagging' of national belonging, particularly through media discourse – sponsored by developed nation-states.

Of course this is not to deny that nation-states are, to varying degrees, *compromised* by globalization in their capacity to maintain exclusivity of identity attachments, just as they are in their capacity independently to regulate national economies within a global market. For example, the complexities and tensions introduced by the multi-ethnic constitution of societies arising from global population movements – a chronic feature of all modern nation-states (Smith 1995; Geertz 2000) – pose obvious prob-lems for the continued cultural 'binding' of twenty-first-century nations into coherent identity positions. This problem is, moreover, more dramatic in its consequences for some nations of the developing world, where multi-ethnic composition arising from the crude territorial divisions of colonial occupation combines with comparatively weak state structures to produce a legacy of often bloody political instability and inter-ethnic violence.

But notice that none of these problems conforms to the scenario of the general *destruction* of identities by globalization. Rather, they attest to an *amplification* of the significance of identity positions in general produced by globalization. It is this proliferation of identity that causes problems for the nation-state's hegemony over its population's sense of cultural attachment.

## Identity and Institutional Modernity

This brings me to my central claim that globalization actually proliferates rather than destroys identities. In this respect I depart somewhat from Castells's position: in set-ting identity as a sort of autonomous cultural dynamic, surging up from the grassroots as an oppositional force to globalization, Castells really fails to see the rather com-pelling *inner logic* between the globalization process and the institutionalized construction of identities. This, I think, lies in the nature of the institutions of modernity that glob-alization distributes. To put the matter simply: globalization is really the globalization of modernity, and modernity is the harbinger of identity.

It is a common assumption that identity-formation is a universal feature of human experience. Castells seems implicitly to take this view when he writes: 'Identity is people's source of meaning and experience' (1997: 6). But whilst it is true that the construction of meaning via cultural practices is a human universal, it does not follow that this invariably takes the form of identity construction as we currently understand it in the global-modern West. This form of ethnocentric assumption has been recently criticized both by anthropologists and media and cultural critics. For example, David Morley, commenting on Roger Rouse's study of Mexican labour migrants to the United States, points out that these people 'moved from a world in which . . . *identity was not a central concern*, to one in which they were pressed . . . to adopt a particular form of personhood (as bearers of individual identities) and of identity as a member of a collective or "community" . . . which *was quite at odds with their own understanding of their situation and their needs*' (Morley 2000: 43 – emphasis added).

Understanding that what we call 'identity' may not be a universal, but just one particular, modern, way of socially organizing – and indeed regulating – cultural experience takes some of the wind from the sails of the argument that globalization inevitably destroys identity. The social-psychology of attachment to locality is a powerful phenomenon, but it is also a complex one, with different possible modes of articulation and different consequent implications for people's sense of self and of existential well-being. And these differences are all relative to cultural context. The assumption that these various attachments can and must be focused through the western-modern prism of 'identity' is no less short-sighted than the corollary assumption that these attachments have remained unchanged across time in 'traditional' societies. And this is, of course, related to the common mistake, criticized by anthropologists such as James Clifford (1997), of regarding 'traditional' societies as, *by nature* and not merely in comparison to modern ones, static and immobile.

The implication of understanding identity as a specifically modern cultural imagination is sufficient to undermine the simple idea that globalization destroys identity. But the stronger claim that globalization actually generates identity – and, indeed, the danger that, in some circumstances, it produces *too much* identity – requires more elaboration.

## Globalization and Modernity

To appreciate this, it is necessary to take a more complex view of the globalization process than is often adopted – certainly in the polemical discourses of the anti-globalization movement, where globalization is essentially understood as the globalization of capitalism, achieved in its cultural aspect via a complicitous western-dominated media system. This more complex, multidimensional conceptualization, which views globalization as operating simultaneously and interrelatedly in the economic, technological-communicational, political and cultural spheres of human life, is in fact relatively uncontentious – at least in principle – within academic discourses. But the cultural implication, rather less easily swallowed by some, is that globalization involves not the simple enforced distribution of a particular western (say, liberal, secular, possessive-individualist, capitalist-consumerist) lifestyle, but a more complicated dissemination of the entire range of institutional features of cultural modernity.

Modernity is a complex and much contested idea, but in this context it means, above all, the *abstraction* of social and cultural practices from contexts of local particularity, and their *institutionalization and regulation* across time and space (Giddens 1990). The examples of such institutionalization that most readily spring to mind are the organization and policing of social territory (the nation-state, urbanism), or of production and consumption practices (industrialization, the capitalist economy).

But modernity also institutionalizes and regulates cultural practices, including those by which we imagine attachment and belonging to a place or a community. The *mode* of such imagination it promotes is what we have come to know as 'cultural identity' – self and communal definitions based around specific, usually politically inflected, differentiations: gender, sexuality, class, religion, race and ethnicity, nationality. Some of these differentiations of course existed before the coming of modernity, some – like nationality – are specifically modern imaginings. But the force of modernity is as much in the *substance* of these categories of imagined belonging as in the very fact of their institutionalization and regulation. In modern societies we live our lives within structures that orchestrate existential experience according to well-policed boundaries. We 'live' our gender, our sexuality, our nationality and so forth as publicly institutionalized, discursively organized belongings. What could be a much looser, contingent, particular and tacit sense of belonging becomes structured into an array of identities, each with implications for our material and psychological well-being, each, thus, with a 'politics'. This is what I mean by saying that modernity is the harbinger of identity.

And in so far as globalization distributes the institutional features of modernity across all cultures, globalization produces 'identity' where none existed – where before there were perhaps more particular, more inchoate, less socially policed belongings. This, rather than the sheer obliteration of identities, is the most significant cultural impact of globalization, an impact felt at the *formal* level of cultural experience. This impact might, on a narrow reading, be seen as 'cultural imperialism' – in that this modern institutionalization of cultural attachments clearly arose first in the West. But, more interestingly, it can be understood as part of the cultural package, mixed in its blessings, that is global modernity.

## Identity and Deterritorialization

One broad approach to this 'package' is in terms of the 'deterritorializing' character of the globalization process – its property of diminishing the significance of social-geographical location to the mundane flow of cultural experience (Garcia-Canclini 1995; Tomlinson 1999). What this idea implies is not that globalization destroys localities – as, for example, in the crude homogenization thesis, everywhere becoming blandly culturally uniform – but that cultural experience is in various ways 'lifted out' of its traditional 'anchoring' in particular localities. One way of understanding this is to think about the places we live in as being increasingly 'penetrated' by the connectivity of globalization. We may live in places that retain a high degree of distinctiveness, but this particularity is no longer – as it may have been in the past – the most important determinant of our cultural experience. The idea of deterritorialization, then, grasps the way in which events outside of our immediate localities – in Anthony Giddens's terse definition of globalization, 'action(s) at a distance' – are increasingly consequential for our experience. Modern culture is less determined by location because location is increasingly penetrated by 'distance'.

The more obvious examples of this sort of penetration of localities are in such areas of mundane cultural experience as our interaction with globalizing media and communications technologies – television, mobile phones, email, the Internet – or in the transformation of local into increasingly 'international' food cultures (Tomlinson 1999). What is at stake in such examples is a transformation in our routine pattern of cultural existence which brings globalized influences, forces, experiences and outlooks into the core of our locally situated lifeworld. Television news brings distant conflicts into the intimate spaces of our living-rooms, 'exotic' tastes become routinely mixed with domestic ones, assumptions we make about the health and security of our families now routinely factor in an awareness, however vague, of global contingencies such as environmental risk or stock-market stability. But we can add to these a more subtle example of deterritorialization: precisely, the reach of the institutional-modern form of identity into cultural life.

For the remaining part of this discussion, I shall try to sketch some of the implications of what we can call this proliferating but 'uneven' generation of identity, focusing on the key issue of the challenge this poses to the coherence of national identities.

Since the eighteenth century, national identity has been the most spectacularly successful modern mode of orchestrating belonging. And the fact that virtually all of the world's six billion population today either enjoy or claim a national identity is itself testament to the power of the globalization of modernity. It is clear from this that the nation and national identity are not in danger of imminent collapse. But the very dynamism and complexity of globalization is such that the stability of this form of identification is not guaranteed indefinitely. The very dynamic which established national identity as the most powerful cultural-political binding force of modernity may now be unravelling some of the skeins that tie us in securely to our national 'home'. The kernel of truth in the claim that national identity is threatened by globalization lies in the fact that the proliferation of identity positions may be producing challenges to the dominance of national identity.

The most remarked examples of this sort of challenge are, naturally enough, the most immediately destructive ones: the violence and chaos of ethnic and religious confrontations with the nation-state. The repercussions of the fall of Eastern European communism – most dramatically in the former Yugoslavia – in the final decade of the twentieth century are an obvious case in point. The collapse of communism is often interpreted in political-economic terms as a reaction to a step change in the global advance of capitalism. The increasing power and integration of the global capitalist market made it impossible for the control economies of the eastern bloc to survive outside of this indisputably dominant economic world system. Although the capitulation of these regimes was most immediately due to internal pressures for liberalization across both the political and the economic spheres, the impetus towards this lay – so the economistic story goes – in a combination of the external economic forces which were rapidly undermining the economic bases of these countries, and the demonstration, via a globalizing media, of the attractions of western consumer culture ineluctably associated with both economic and democratic liberalism.

But the ensuing conflicts in Croatia, Bosnia-Herzegovina and Kosovo could not, on any reasonable interpretation, be judged as the fall-out from an exclusively political-economic process. What the 'opening up' of globalization meant in this context was not the engagement with a global market system, but the unleashing of violent cultural forces – ethnic/nationalist factionalism – which had been, apparently, artificially contained under the communist federal regime. The rapid disintegration of the Yugoslav Federation revealed deep divisions in cultural and religious identities – Serbs, Croats, Bosnians, ethnic Albanians; Christians and Muslims – which became rapidly inflamed into what Mary Kaldor (1999) has aptly called the 'new wars' of the era of globalization. The key point in Kaldor's analysis of these 'globalization wars' is that they are fought around a vicious, particularistic form of 'identity politics' in which 'movements . . . mobilize around ethnic, racial or religious identity for the purpose of claiming state power' (1999: 76).

Such examples of the violent assertion of, and the struggle over, cultural identity seem, on the one hand, to fit the argument about the generation of modern institutionalized forms of identity rather well. For, far from being simply atavistic reversions, the deliberate aim of such ethnic conflicts is, as Kaldor says, to claim state power – that is, to institutionalize a particular cultural identity in a modern political form. But, on the other hand, we might view such instances as less of a fundamental challenge to the dominant *form* of identity as national identity, than as struggles for dominance within this form (Tomlinson 2000).

There are, of course, examples of projects of cultural 'reterritorialization' – the claiming and reclaiming of localities – which don't inevitably involve claims to state power. For example, the land rights movements of aboriginal groups in Australia, the USA, Canada and elsewhere that have come to prominence in recent years. Though in such examples the claims of identity are inextricably mixed with issues of political and economic justice, there is the indication that what is being argued for is a right to an ethnic 'homeland' that is conceived as coexistent and compatible with a national identity. What is interesting about such projects is that, again, they exemplify a particularly modern cultural sensibility: the very notion of a juridical contestation of rights linked to identity seems understandable only within the sort of global-modern institutional form of identity which we have identified.

But for evidence of a more fundamental shift in the grip of the nation-state over our cultural imagination, we may have to look for more gentle, subtle, long-term shifts in identification. The most discussed aspect of this sort of shift – particularly within cultural studies and in post-colonial studies – is the emergence of 'hybrid' cultural identities as a consequence both of the multicultural constitution of modern nation-states and of the emergence of transnational forms of popular culture (Nederveen Pieterse 1995; Werbner and Modood 1997). Significant as this trend is, there is a danger that the concept of hybridity may be expected to do too much explanatory work and, indeed, that the idea of continual hybridization as the destination of global cultures may be overstated (Tomlinson 1999: 141f.). So, to conclude, I want to present an example, in the form of a little vignette, of a modest popular-cultural consequence of globalization that does not fit into either of the usual schemas of homogenization or hybridization.

## The Revival of the *Qipau*

In the fashionable *Dong An* shopping centre in the Wang Fu Jing district of Beijing you will find a small boutique called *Mu Zhen Liao*. Here, young, discriminating and upwardly mobile Beijingers come to choose clothes, not from the designer labels of the West, but 'classical' Chinese clothing: elegant *qipaus*, *cheongsams* and finely tailored jackets in beautiful silks and other traditional fabrics. These clothes display all the detail and finesse of the fashions favoured by the wealthy Manchurian elite in the Qing dynasty of the seventeenth to nineteenth centuries. But they are not in any simple sense 'traditional' clothes. The young women wearing them in the streets will turn as many heads amongst the locals as amongst the western tourists. For the fact is that ten or fifteen years ago a shop like *Mu Zhen Liao* would not have existed in China. Its appearance amongst the new up-market stores, and the Starbucks cafés, of the *Dong An* centre is a small but interesting consequence of China's open-door economic policy introduced by Deng Xiaoping in the early 1980s. Effectively, Deng's policy opened up both Chinese economic and cultural life to the process of globalization

– culminating in China's entry into the WTO in 2001. *Mu Zhen Liao* – a chain store with branches in many of the provincial capitals – exists, in cultural as in economic terms, as a consequence of globalization.

Fashion is a significant expression of cultural identity. But what sort of identity does this 'classic' dress style represent for the affluent younger generation of Chinese who choose it in preference to the European fashions or American sportswear brands with which it competes? It is not easy to pin down. Certainly, this is not a national identity (or a reaction to 'westernization') in the simple sense of expressing the version of 'Chineseness' sponsored by the Chinese state. For a rather bland, dull, conservative western style seems, if anything, to be the mainstream dress code smiled upon by China's political leaders. Indeed, after the disastrous experiment in cultural engineering symbolized in the so-called 'Mao Jacket' uniform of the Cultural Revolution, it might seem that China has simply lost confidence in a symbolically 'traditional' dress code. There are some interesting subtleties here, however. What in the West was called the 'Mao Jacket' in fact developed out of the *Zhong Shan* style of clothing invented by the revolutionary leader Sun Yat-sen at the start of the first Chinese Republic in 1912. Sun based this design upon a blend of western 'modern' dress with Chinese styles from as early as the Tang dynasty. This was intended to express both modern republican and at the same time 'authentic' Chineseness, in contrast to the dress of the hated Manchu rulers of the collapsing Qing dynasty. The *qipau*, then, is a Manchurian, as distinct from a 'Chinese' (Han) style. It is doubtful, of course, that any of the young women purchasing *qipaus* consciously wish to express a Manchu identity. But at some level below the mere appeal of fashion, they are surely expressing a form of Chineseness that contrasts with the drab, dominant 'People's Republic' version, and the cultural hegemony under which their parents lived. Globalization here does not so much directly challenge, as promote, new and complex versions of national identity.

And this is not, of course, just a problem for bureaucratic regimes such as China, trying to maintain political control over a vast population experiencing rapid economic and cultural transformation. All nation-states now contain and seek to govern populations whose identities are both multiple and *complex*. This complexity does not by any means necessarily entail the diminishing significance of identification with the nation: identity is not a zero-sum game. But it does suggest that the way in which national identity is experienced within globalization is, like everything else, in flux. Political subjects can now experience and express, without contradiction, both attachments to the nation, multi-ethnic allegiances *and* cosmopolitan sensibilities. The really interesting cultural-political question that emerges is of how nimble and reflexively attuned state apparatuses are capable of becoming in response to these changes.

## References

Billig, M. (1995) *Banal Nationalism*. London: Sage.

Castells, M. (1997) *The Power of Identity*, vol. II of *The Information Age: Economy, Society and Culture*. Oxford: Blackwell.

Clifford, J. (1997) *Routes: Travel and Translation in the Late Twentieth Century*. Cambridge, Mass.: Harvard University Press.

Garcia Canclini, N. (1995) *Hybrid Cultures: Strategies for Entering and Leaving Modernity*. Minneapolis: University of Minnesota Press.

Geertz, C. (2000) *Available Light: Anthropological Reflections on Philosophical Topics*. Princeton, NJ: Princeton University Press.

Giddens, A. (1990) *The Consequences of Modernity*. Cambridge: Polity Press.

Howes, D. (ed.) (1996) *Cross-Cultural Consumption: Global Markets, Local Realities*. London: Routledge.

Kaldor, M. (1999) *New and Old Wars*. Cambridge: Polity Press.

Lull, J. (2000) *Media, Communication, Culture: A Global Approach*. Cambridge: Polity.

Morley, D. (2000) *Home Territories: Media, Mobility and Identity*. London: Routledge.

Nederveen Pieterse, J. (1995) Globalization as Hybridization. In M. Featherstone et al. (eds), *Global Modernities*, London: Sage, pp. 45–68.

Shepard, B. and Hayduk, R. (eds) (2002) *From ACT UP to the WTO: Urban Protest and Community Building in the Era of Globalization*. London: Verso.

Smith, A. (1995) *Nations and Nationalism in a Global Era*. Cambridge: Polity Press.

Thompson, J. B. (1995) *The Media and Modernity*. Cambridge: Polity.

Tomlinson, J. (1991) *Cultural Imperialism: A Critical Introduction*. London: Pinter.

Tomlinson, J. (1999) *Globalization and Culture*. Cambridge: Polity Press.

Tomlinson, J. (2000) Proximity Politics. *Information, Communication and Society*, 3(3): 402–14.

Werbner, P. and Modood, T. (eds) (1997) *Debating Cultural Hybridity*. London: Zed Books.

# 24

# Towards a Global Culture?

## *Anthony D. Smith*

The initial problem with the concept of a 'global culture' is one of the meaning of terms. Can we speak of 'culture' in the singular? If by 'culture' is meant a collective mode of life, or a repertoire of beliefs, styles, values and symbols, then we can only speak of cultur*es*, never just culture; for a collective mode of life, or a repertoire of beliefs, etc., presupposes different modes and repertoires in a universe of modes and repertoires. Hence, the idea of a 'global culture' is a practical impossibility, except in interplanetary terms. Even if the concept is predicated of *homo sapiens*, as opposed to other species, the differences between segments of humanity in terms of lifestyle and belief-repertoire are too great, and the common elements too generalized, to permit us to even conceive of a globalized culture.

Or are they? Can we not at last discern the lineaments of exactly that world culture which liberals and socialists alike had dreamed of and hoped for since the last century? [ . . . ]

What is the content of such a [ . . . ] 'global culture'? How shall we picture its operations? Answers to such questions usually take the form of extrapolation from recent western cultural experiences of 'postmodernism'. Beneath a modernist veneer, we find in practice a pastiche of cultural motifs and styles, underpinned by a universal scientific and technical discourse. A global culture, so the argument runs, will be eclectic like its western or European progenitor, but will wear a uniformly streamlined packaging. Standardized, commercialized mass commodities will nevertheless draw for their contents upon revivals of traditional, folk or national motifs and styles in fashions, furnishings, music and the arts, lifted out of their original contexts and anaesthetized. So that a global culture would operate at several levels simultaneously: as a cornucopia of standardized commodities, as a patchwork of denationalized ethnic or folk motifs, as a series of generalized 'human values and interests', as a uniform 'scientific' discourse of meaning, and finally as the interdependent system of communications which forms the material base for all the other components and levels.[1]

It might be argued that there is nothing especially new about a 'global culture', that earlier cultural imperialisms were every whit as eclectic and simultaneously standardized. After all, the hellenization that Alexander's armies carried throughout the ancient Near East drew on a variety of local motifs as well as giving them expression in the Greco-Macedonian forms of theatre, assembly, marketplace and gymnasium. And the same was true of the pax Romana throughout the Mediterranean world (see Tcherikover 1970; Balsdon 1979).

Yet, those pre-modern cultural imperialisms were neither global nor universal. They were ultimately tied to their places of origin, and carried with them their special myths and symbols for all to recognize and emulate. Today's emerging global culture is tied to no place or period. It is context-less, a true melange of disparate components drawn from everywhere and nowhere, borne upon the modern chariots of global telecommunications systems.

There is something equally timeless about the concept of a global culture. Widely diffused in space, a global culture is cut off from any past. As the perennial pursuit of an elusive present or imagined future, it has no history. A global culture is here and now and everywhere, and for its purposes the past only serves to offer some decontextualized example or element for its cosmopolitan patchwork.

This sense of timelessness is powerfully underlined by the pre-eminently technical nature of its discourse. A global culture is essentially calculated and artificial, posing technical problems with technical solutions and using its folk motifs in a spirit of detached playfulness. Affectively neutral, a cosmopolitan culture reflects a technological base made up of many overlapping systems of communications bound by a common quantitative and technical discourse, manned by an increasingly technical intelligentsia, whose 'culture of critical discourse' replaces the social critique of its earlier humanistic counterparts (see Gouldner 1979).

## Memory, Identity and Cultures

Eclectic, universal, timeless and technical, a global culture is seen as pre-eminently a 'constructed' culture, the final and most imposing of a whole series of human constructs in the era of human liberation and mastery over nature. In a sense, the nation too was just such a construct, a sovereign but finite 'imagined community'.

Nations were 'built' and 'forged' by state elites or intelligentsias or capitalists; like the Scots kilt or the British Coronation ceremony, they are composed of so many 'invented traditions', whose symbols we need to read through a process of 'deconstruction', if we are to grasp the hidden meanings beneath the 'text' of their discourse. The fact, therefore, that a global culture would need to be constructed, along with global economic and political institutions, should occasion no surprise; nor should we cavil at the eclecticism with which such a cosmopolitan culture is likely to make use of bits and pieces of pre-existing national and folk cultures.[2]

Let us concede for the moment that nations are, in some sense, social 'constructs' and 'imagined' communities. Is it because of this 'constructed' quality that they have managed to survive and flourish so well? Are we therefore justified in predicting the same bright future for an equally well crafted 'global culture'?

To answer affirmatively would require us to place the whole weight of demonstration on the common characteristic of human construction and imagination, at the expense of those characteristics in which nations and national cultures differ markedly from our description of the qualities of a global culture. The obstinate fact is that national cultures, like all cultures before the modern epoch, are *particular*, *timebound* and *expressive*, and their eclecticism operates within strict cultural constraints. As we said at the outset, there can in practice be no such thing as 'culture', only specific, historical cultures possessing strong emotional connotations for those who share in the particular culture. It is, of course, possible to 'invent', even manufacture, traditions as commodities to serve particular class or ethnic interests. But they will only survive and flourish as part of the repertoire of national culture if they can be made continuous with a much longer past that members of that community presume to constitute their 'heritage'.

In other words, 'grafting' extraneous elements must always be a delicate operation; the new traditions must evoke a popular response if they are to survive, and that means hewing close to vernacular motifs and styles. That was the instinct which guided most nationalists and helped to ensure their lasting successes. The success of the nineteenth-century British Coronation ceremony or the Welsh Eisteddfodau owed much to the ability of those who revived them to draw on much older cultural motifs and traditions, memories of which were still alive; though in one sense 'new', these revivals were only able to flourish because they could be presented, and were accepted, as continuous with a valued past (see Hobsbawm and Ranger 1983).

If cultures are historically specific and spatially limited, so are those images and symbols that have obtained a hold on human imagination. Even the most imperialist of those images – emperor, Pope or Tsar – have drawn their power from the heritage of Roman and Byzantine symbolism. It is one thing to be able to package imagery and diffuse it through world-wide telecommunications networks. It is quite another to ensure that such images retain their power to move and inspire populations, who have for so long been divided by particular histories and cultures, which have mirrored and crystallized the experiences of historically separated social groups, whether classes or regions, religious congregations or ethnic communities. The meanings of even the most universal of imagery for a particular population derive as much from the historical experiences and social status of that group as from the intentions of purveyors, as recent research on the national reception of popular television serials suggests (see Schlesinger 1987). [ ... ]

In other words, images and cultural traditions do not derive from, or descend upon, mute and passive populations on whose *tabula rasa* they inscribe themselves. Instead, they invariably express the identities which historical circumstances have formed, often over long periods. The concept of 'identity' is here used, not of a common denominator of patterns of life and activity, much less some average, but rather of the subjective feelings and valuations of any population which possesses common experiences and one or more shared cultural characteristics (usually customs, language or religion). These feelings and values refer to three components of their shared experiences:

1  a sense of continuity between the experiences of succeeding generations of the unit of population;
2  shared memories of specific events and personages which have been turning-points of a collective history; and
3  a sense of common destiny on the part of the collectivity sharing those experiences.

By a collective cultural identity, therefore, is meant those feelings and values in respect of a sense of continuity, shared memories and a sense of common destiny of a given unit of population which has had common experiences and cultural attributes. [ ... ]

It is in just these senses that 'nations' can be understood as historic identities, or at least deriving closely from them, while a global and cosmopolitan culture fails to relate to any such historic identity. Unlike national cultures, a global culture is essentially memoryless. Where the 'nation' can be constructed so as to draw upon and revive latent popular experiences and needs, a 'global culture' answers to no living needs, no identity-in-the-making. It has to be painfully put together, artificially, out of the many existing folk and national identities into which humanity has been so long divided. There are no 'world memories' that can be used to *unite* humanity; the most global experiences to date – colonialism and the World Wars – can only serve to remind us of our historic cleavages. (If it is argued that nationalists suffered selective amnesia in order to construct their nations, the creators of a global culture would have to suffer total amnesia, to have any chance of success!)

The central difficulty in any project to construct a global identity, and hence a global culture, is that collective identity, like imagery and culture, is always historically specific because it is based on shared memories and a sense of continuity between generations.

To believe that 'culture follows structure', that the techno-economic sphere will provide the conditions and therefore the impetus and content of a global culture, is to be misled once again by the same economic determinism that dogged the debate about 'industrial convergence', and to overlook the vital role of common historical experiences and memories in shaping identity and culture. Given the plurality of such experiences and identities, and given the historical depth of such memories, the project of a global culture, as opposed to global communications, must appear premature for some time to come.

## 'Ethno-history' and Posterity

If it proves difficult to envisage a point of departure for this project in common human experiences and memories, the universal stumbling-block to its construction is not far to seek. That ubiquitous obstacle is embodied in the continued presence of pre-modern ties and sentiments in the modern epoch. Indeed, just as a 'postmodern' era awaits its liberation from the modern industrial world, so the latter is still weighed down by the burden of pre-modern traditions, myths and boundaries. I have argued elsewhere that many of today's nations are built up on the basis of pre-modern 'ethnic cores' whose myths and memories, values and symbols shaped the culture and boundaries of the nation that modern elites managed to forge. Such a view, if conceded, must qualify our earlier acceptance of the largely 'constructed' quality of modern nations. That nationalist elites were active in inculcating a sense of nationality in large sections of 'their' populations who were ignorant of any national affiliations is well documented (see Kedourie 1960; Breuilly 1982). It does not follow that they 'invented nations where none existed', as Gellner had once claimed, even where they used pre-existing materials and even when nations are defined as large, anonymous, unmediated, co-cultural units (see Gellner 1964: ch. 7; also Gellner 1983: ch. 5).

Nationalists, like others, found themselves constrained by accepted cultural traditions, from which they might select, and by popular responses, which they hoped to channel, if not manipulate. But their room for cultural manoeuvre was always limited by those cultural traditions and popular, vernacular repertoires of myth, memory, symbol and value. For nationalists, the 'nation-to-be' was not any large, anonymous, co-cultural unit. It was a community of history and culture, possessing a compact territory, unified economy and common legal rights and duties for all members. If 'nationalism creates nations' in its own image, then its definition of the nation was of a piece with its aspirations for collective autonomy, fraternal unity and distinctive identity. The identity and unity that was sought was of and for an existing historic culture-community, which the nationalists thought they were reviving and returning to a 'world of nations'. It depended, therefore, in large measure on the rediscovery of the community's 'ethno-history', its peculiar and distinctive cultural contribution to the worldwide fund of what Weber called 'irreplaceable culture values'. This was the nationalist project, and it is one that has by no means run its course, even as signs of its supersession by wider projects are on the horizon. In fact, it can be argued that nationalist and post-nationalist projects feed off each other, and are likely to do so for some time to come.

In fact, the success of the nationalist project depended not only on the creative skills and organizational ability of the intelligentsia, but on the persistence, antiquity and resonance of the community's ethno-history. The more salient, pervasive and enduring that history, the firmer the cultural base it afforded for the formation of a modern nation. Once again, these are largely subjective aspects. It is the salience of that history in the eyes of the community's members, and the *felt* antiquity of their ethnic ties and sentiments, which give an ethno-history its power and resonance among wide strata. It matters little whether the communal events recounted happened in the manner purveyed, or if heroes acted nobly as tradition would have us believe; the Exodus, William Tell, Great Zimbabwe, derive their power not from a sober historical assessment, but from the way events, heroes and landscapes have been woven by myth, memory and symbol into the popular consciousness. For the participants in this drama, ethno-history has a 'primordial' quality, or it is powerless (Smith 1988).[3]

Why do such myths and memories retain their hold, even today, to fuel the nationalist project? There is no single answer; but two considerations must take priority. The first is the role of ethno-history, its myths, values, memories and symbols, in assuring collective dignity (and through that some measure of dignity for the individual) for populations which have come to feel excluded, neglected or suppressed in the distribution of values and opportunities. By establishing the unity of a submerged or excluded population around an ancient and preferably illustrious pedigree, not only is the sense of bonding intensified, but a reversal of collective status is achieved, at least on the cognitive and moral levels. [ . . . ]

The second consideration is even more important. With the attenuation of the hold of traditional cosmic images of another, unseen existence beyond the everyday world, the problem of individual oblivion and collective disintegration becomes more pressing and less easily answered. Loss of social cohesion feeding off an increasing sense of individual meaninglessness, in a century when the old 'problem of evil' has been posed in unparalleled ways, drives more and more people to discover new ways of understanding and preserving 'identity' in the face of annihilation. For many, the only guarantee of preservation of some form of identity is in the appeal to 'posterity', to the future generations that are 'ours', because they think and feel as 'we' do, just as our children are supposed to feel and think like each of us individually. With the dissolution of all traditional theodicies, only the appeal to a collective posterity offers hope of deliverance from oblivion (see Smith 1970; Anderson 1983: ch. 1).

[ . . . ]

## Vernacular Mobilization and Cultural Competition

There are also more specific reasons for the continuing hold of national cultures with their ethnic myths and memories in an increasingly interdependent world.

Perhaps the most common way in which nations have been, and are being, formed is through processes of 'vernacular mobilization' and 'cultural politicization'. Where ethnic communities (or *ethnie*) lack states of their own, having usually been incorporated in wider polities in an earlier epoch, they risk dissolution in the transition to modernity, unless an indigenous intelligentsia emerges, strong enough to mobilize wider sections of 'their' community on the basis of a rediscovered ethno-history and vernacular culture. The success of the intelligentsia largely hinges on their ability to discover a convincing cultural base, one that can find a popular response, at least among educated strata. The intelligentsia are populist to the extent that they make use of (some) popular culture and a living communal history, even where they stop short of mobilizing actual peasants. The important task is to convince immediate followers, and enemies outside, of the cultural viability of the nation-to-be. The richer, more fully documented the ethno-history, the more widely spoken the vernacular tongue and the more widely practised the native customs and religion, the less difficult will it be to convince others, friends and enemies, of the actuality of the 'nation'; for it can be made to 'flow' coterminously with the demotic *ethnie* and seem its reincarnation after a long period of presumed death. Conversely, the scantier the records of ethno-history and less widely spoken the vernacular and practised the customs, the harder will it be to convince others of the viability of the national project, and the more it will be necessary to find new ways of overcoming doubt and hostility. Hence the appeal to lost epics and forgotten heroes – an Oisin or Lemminkainen – to furnish a noble pedigree and sacred landscape for submerged or neglected communities (see Hutchinson 1987; Branch 1985: Introduction).

To create the nation, therefore, it is not enough simply to mobilize compatriots. They must be taught who they are, where they came from and whither they are going. They must be turned into co-nationals through a process of mobilization into the vernacular culture, albeit one adapted to modern social and political conditions. Only then can the old-new culture become a political base and furnish political weapons in the much more intense cultural competition of a world of nations. Old religious sages and saints can now be turned into national heroes, ancient chronicles and epics become examples of the creative national genius, while great ages of achievement in the community's past are presented as the nation's 'golden age' of pristine purity and nobility. The former culture of a community, which had no other end beyond itself, now becomes the talisman and legitimation for all manner of 'national' policies and purposes, from agricultural villagization to militarism and aggrandisement. Ethnicity is nationalized (see Seton-Watson 1977: chs 2–4; Smith 1986: ch. 8).

Though the intelligentsia tend to be the prime beneficiaries of the politicization of culture, other strata share in the realization of the national project. Peasants and workers are not immune, even if they are rarely prime movers, particularly where a marxisant 'national communism' holds sway. On the whole, it is the nationalist motifs which tap peasant energies most effectively, particularly where a foreign threat can be convincingly portrayed, as when China was invaded by Japan (see Johnson 1969; Smith 1979: ch. 5). Because of this 'multi-class' character, the national project retains a popularity that is the envy of other ideological movements; for it appears to offer each class not just a tangible benefit, but the promise of dignity and unity in the 'superfamily' of the nation (see Nairn 1977: ch. 9; Horowitz 1985: ch. 2).

One other reason for the continuing power of the national idea today needs to be remembered. This is the accentuation of that idea and of the several national cultures across the globe by their competition for adherents and prestige. I am not simply referring here to the way in which such cultures have become interwoven with the rivalry of states in the international arena. The cultures themselves have been thrown into conflict, as communities in their struggle for political rights and recognition have drawn upon their cultural resources – music, literature, the arts and crafts, dress, food and so on – to make their mark in the wider political arena, regionally and internationally, and continue to do so by the use of comparative statistics, prestige projects, tourism and the like. These are veritable 'cultural wars', which underline the polycentric nature of our interdependent world, as each community discovers afresh its 'national essence' in its 'irreplaceable culture values' (Weber 1968: ch. 5).

Vernacular mobilization; the politicization of cultures; the role of the intelligentsia and other strata; and the intensification of cultural wars: here are some of the reasons, briefly sketched, why national cultures inspired by rediscovered ethno-histories continue to divide our world into discrete cultural blocks, which show little sign of harmonization, let alone amalgamation. When we add the sharply uneven nature of the distributions of both a 'rich' ethno-history and economic and political resources between nations and *ethnie* today, the likelihood of an early 'supersession' of nationalism appears remote. Feeding on each other, ethnic nationalisms seem set to multiply and accentuate national and ethnic boundaries and the uneven distribution of cultural and economic resources, at least in those areas where there remain a multitude of unsatisfied ethno-national claims. If the various regional inter-state systems appear strong enough (for how long?) to contain conflicting ethno-nationalist movements, even in Africa and Asia, the number and intensity of current and potential ethnic conflicts hardly suggests a global diminution of the power of nationalism or the hold of national cultures in the next few decades.

[ ... ]

## Conclusion

From the standpoint of both global security and cosmopolitan culture, this is a bleak conclusion. There is, however, another side to the overall picture, which may over the longer term help to mitigate some of the worst effects of intensified and proliferating ethno-national conflicts. I refer to the growing importance of the lingua franca and of various 'culture areas'.

[ ... ]

Such culture areas are, of course, a far cry from the ideal of a global culture which will supersede the many national cultures that still divide the world so resoundingly. Their loose patchwork quality and mixture of cultures do not as yet offer a serious challenge to the still fairly compact, and frequently revived, national cultures. [ ... ]

[ ... ] We are still far from even mapping out the kind of global culture and cosmopolitan ideal that can truly supersede a world of nations, each cultivating its distinctive historical character and rediscovering its national myths, memories and symbols in past golden ages and sacred landscapes. A world of competing cultures, seeking to improve their comparative status rankings and enlarge their cultural resources, affords little basis for global projects, despite the technical and linguistic infrastructural possibilities.

At the same time, the partial mixing of cultures, the rise of a lingua franca and of wider 'Pan' nationalisms, though sometimes working in opposed directions, have created the possibility of 'families of culture' which portend wider regional patchwork culture-areas.

Such culture-areas may perhaps serve as models in the more long-term future for even broader inter-continental versions. Even in such distant scenarios, it is hard to envisage the absorption of ethno-national cultures, only a diminution in their political relevance. So attenuated a cosmopolitanism is unlikely to entail the supersession of national cultures.

## Notes

1   I have brought together different phases of twentieth-century Western culture in this sketch, in particular, the modernist trends of the 1960s, the 'postmodern' reactions of the 1960s and 1970s, and the technical 'neutrality' of the mass computer revolution of the 1980s. Of course, these trends and phases overlap: Stravinsky's pastiche dates from the early 1920s, while 'modernism' still exerts profound influences till today. The main point is that this Western image of 'things to come' is composed of several contradictory layers.

2   For the idea that nations should be conceived as sovereign but limited 'imagined communities', see Anderson (1983). His analysis, which gives pride of place to the 'technology of print capitalism' and the 'administrative pilgrimages' of provincial (read 'national' today) elites (to Washington, Moscow, Brussels?), could indeed shed light on the chances, and obstacles, to the rise of wider 'regional' cultures today.

3   This should not be construed as an argument for 'primordialism', the view that ethnicity and nationality are somehow 'givens' of human existence and/or history. For a discussion of the issues involved, see the essays by Brass and Robinson in Taylor and Yapp (1979); cf. also A. D. Smith (1984).

## References

Anderson, Benedict (1983) *Imagined Communities: Reflections on the Origins and Spread of Nationalism*. London: Verso and New Left Books.

Balsdon, J. V. (1979) *Romans and Aliens*. London: Duckworth.

Branch, Michael (ed.) (1985) *Kalevala: The Land of Heroes*, trans. W. F. Kirby. London: Athlone.

Breuilly, John (1982) *Nationalism and the State*. Manchester: Manchester University Press.

Gellner, Ernest (1964) *Thought and Change*. London: Weidenfeld and Nicolson.

Gellner, Ernest (1983) *Nations and Nationalism*. Oxford: Blackwell.

Gouldner, Alvin (1979) *The Rise of the Intellectuals and the Future of the New Class*. London: Macmillan.

Hobsbawm, Eric and Ranger, Terence (eds) (1983) *The Invention of Tradition*. Cambridge: Cambridge University Press.

Horowitz, Donald (1985) *Ethnic Groups in Conflict*. Berkeley: University of California Press.

Hutchinson, John (1987) *The Dynamics of Cultural Nationalism; The Gaelic Revival and the Creation of the Irish Nation State*. London: Allen and Unwin.

Johnson, Chalmers (1969) Building a communist nation in China. In R. A. Scalapino (ed.), *The Communist Revolution in Asia*, Englewood Cliffs: Prentice Hall.

Kedourie, Elie (1960) *Nationalism*. London: Hutchinson.

Nairn, Tom (1977) *The Break-up of Britain*. London: New Left Books.

Schlesinger, Philip (1987) On national identity: some conceptions and misconceptions criticised. *Social Science Information* 26(2): 219–64.

Seton-Watson, Hugh (1977) *Nations and States: An Inquiry into the Origins of Nations and the Politics of Nationalism*. London: Methuen.

Smith, Anthony D. (1970) Modernity and evil: some sociological reflections on the problem of meaning. *Diogenes* 71: 65–80.

Smith, Anthony D. (1979) *Nationalism in the Twentieth Century*. Oxford: Martin Robertson.

Smith, Anthony D. (1984) Ethnic myths and ethnic revivals. *European Journal of Sociology* 25: 283–305.

Smith, Anthony D. (1986) *The Ethnic Origins of Nations*. Oxford: Blackwell.

Smith, Anthony D. (1988) The myth of the 'modern nation' and the myths of nations. *Ethnic and Racial Studies* 11(1): 1–26.

Taylor, David and Yapp, Malcolm (eds) (1979) *Political Identity in South Asia*. London and Dublin: Centre of South Asian Studies, SOAS, Curzon Press.

Tcherikover, Victor (1970) *Hellenistic Civilisation and the Jews*. New York: Athenaeum.

Weber, Max (1968) *Economy and Society*, vol. 1, ed. G. Roth and C. Wittich. New York: Bedminster Press.

# 25

# Global Governance and Cosmopolitan Citizens

## *Pippa Norris*

[ … ]

The impact of [globalization and of] global governance upon national identities has raised many hopes and fears. On the one hand, theorists ranging from Auguste Comte and John Stuart Mill to Karl Marx and Anthony Giddens have expressed optimism that humanity will eventually transcend national boundaries by moving toward a global culture and society. In this perspective, we can expect the globalization of markets, governance, and communications to strengthen a *cosmopolitan* orientation, broadening identities beyond national boundaries to a world community, and increasing awareness of the benefits of transnational collaboration within regional associations and international institutions.

Hence theorists such as Ohmae believe that we are witnessing the "end of the nation state," with the modern period representing a new historical era dominated by the growth of world market forces and the forces of Western consumerism, a tide against which national governments and economies have become increasingly powerless.[1] Anthony Giddens claims that contemporary globalization is historically unprecedented, reshaping modern societies, economies, governments, and the world order.[2] David Held argues that nation-states are drawing together by complex processes of interdependence on problems such as AIDS, migration, human rights, crime, trade, environmental pollution, and new challenges to peace, security, and economic prosperity that spill over national boundaries.[3] This process has gone furthest within the European Union, where the future of sovereignty and autonomy within nation-states has been most strongly challenged by European integration, but he argues that all of the world's major regions are affected, producing overlapping *"communities of fate."* The association of nationalism with some of the most disruptive forces in twentieth-century history – from Hitler and Mussolini to recent conflict in the Balkans – has led many to applaud this development, although others deplore the loss of distinct national communities to the homogenizing cultural embrace of McDonald's, Disney, and Cable News Network (CNN).

Yet alternatively those who adopt a more skeptical perspective doubt whether the nation-state has been seriously weakened, and whether there is any evidence of an emerging "cosmopolitan identity" to replace the visceral appeals of nationalism. Structural developments in world economies and governance may have occurred without fundamentally eroding, indeed perhaps even strengthening, deep-rooted attitudes toward nationalism and the nation-state. In Anthony Smith's view, "We are still far from even mapping out the kind of global culture and cosmopolitan ideals that can truly supersede the world of nations."[4] Mann argues that, far from weakening nationalism, a reaction to globalization may have served to strengthen national identities.[5] Along similar lines, Hirst and Thompson argue that the nation-state retains its power in the modern era, and the main trend has been toward the growth of regional blocs, where nation-states remain the primary actors, not the emergence of a new world order that transcends states.[6]

What is the evidence to substantiate these arguments? The most systematic empirical work has examined whether nationalism has declined within the European Union. The process of economic and political integration, with people working, living, studying, and traveling in different member states, can be expected to have broken down some of the traditional cultural barriers between member states, particularly among the early joiners. Public opinion has been closely monitored in Eurobarometer surveys since early 1970. Successive studies have found that the public's identification with Europe has fluctuated over time, often in response to specific political events like the Maastricht agreement, the "mad cow" dispute, and the launch of the euro under the European Economic and Monetary Union (EMU). The process of European integration has been gradually strengthening, deepening, and widening the Union, yet there is little evidence that this process has generated a growing sense of European identity and community among its citizens, even among the public in long-standing member states like Germany.[7] Related attitudes also display a pattern of trendless fluctuations since the early 1970s, rather than growing public affection for the European project, including approval of EU policies, satisfaction with the performance of the Union, and confidence in EU institutions like the commission and Parliament. Persistent cross-national differences continue between states like Ireland and Belgium that are relatively positive across most indicators, and deep-seated Euro-skeptics like the British.[8] Moreover in the 1990s, British public opinion drifted in an ever more Euro-skeptic direction; almost half the public now opts for complete withdrawal.[9]

If there is little evidence of growing cosmopolitan identities within the EU, what is the situation elsewhere? We generally know far less about trends in public opinion concerning other institutions of global governance, such as attitudes toward NATO, the UN, or the World Trade Organization (WTO), in large part because systematic cross-national survey evidence is sparse beyond Western Europe, and largely non-existent in most of the developing world, although polls are available within particular countries.[10] One of the most thorough studies of attitudes toward international organizations, by Philip Evert, suggests a similar pattern to that already observed toward the EU. Evert found that support for the EU, NATO, and the UN is essentially multi-dimensional, with attitudes influenced by responses to specific issues and events, rather than being arrayed on a general continuum stretching from nationalism to internationalism. Fluctuations over time in the public's approval of NATO displayed no secular trends, although there were also persistent differences in support between member states.[11]

Therefore despite plausible theories that the rise of global governance may lead toward growing cosmopolitanism, most of the available empirical studies lean toward a skeptical perspective. At least within Europe, national publics vary significantly in their support for the institutions and policies of the new world order, and the past thirty years have not seen the rise of a more internationalist orientation. Nevertheless evidence remains limited. We lack systematic comparative studies to understand trends in many countries outside of the EU, particularly in the developing world, and it remains possible that some underlying fundamental transformation of national identities will take far longer to become apparent.

## Evidence for Cosmopolitanism

The concepts of "cosmopolitan" and "national" identities are particularly complex. In this study, "national identity" is understood to mean the existence of communities with bonds of "blood and belonging" arising from sharing a common homeland, cultural myths, symbols and historical memories, economic resources, and legal-political rights and duties.[12] Nationalism can take "*civic*" forms, meaning ties of soil based on citizenship within a shared territory and boundaries delineated by the nation-state, or it may take "*ethnic*" forms, drawing on more diffuse ties of blood based on religious, linguistic, or ethnic communities.[13] National identities are usually implicit and may only rise to the surface in response to an "other," in which (rather like Simone de Beauvoir's *Second Sex*) we know what we are by virtue of what we are not. Hence as a minority, Scottish nationalism is currently explicit and self-assertive, while English identity remains dormant and inert, perhaps even slightly embarrassed.[14] In the modern world, national identities underpin the state and its institutions exercising political authority within a given territory, although there are many multinational states like the United Kingdom as well as stateless nations like the Kurds. *Nationalists* can be understood as those who identify strongly with their nation-state, who have little confidence in multilateral and international institutions, and who favor policies of national economic protectionism over the free trade of goods and services.

In contrast, *cosmopolitans* can be understood as those who identify more broadly with their continent or with the world as a whole, and who have greater faith in the institutions of global governance. The nationalism–cosmopolitan dimension can be expected to crosscut traditional ideological cleavages, although there may be some overlap. If leaning rightward, cosmopolitans can be expected to support policies designed to dismantle protectionist economic barriers, while those on the left may favor other measures like stricter global environmental regulations and greater spending on overseas aid. Cosmopolitans can be expected to be comfortable living and working in different countries, familiar with travel well beyond their national boundaries, and fluent in languages, as well as connected to international networks through global communications.[15] In previous eras this process mainly influenced the elite, like the European aristocracy finishing their education in Paris and Rome on the eighteenth century Grand Tour, but the most recent wave of globalization in communications may have encouraged a resurgence of cosmopolitanism to spread well beyond elite circles to the mass public.[16] If this hypothesis were correct, we would expect to find that cosmopolitan identities would supplement traditional national and ethnic allegiances, producing a broader identification with neighboring countries, citizens, and regions of the world.

What evidence would allow us to examine claims of a growing cosmopolitan consciousness? Previous analysis of public opinion toward these issues has relied largely on the Eurobarometer, monitoring the fifteen member states, as well as the annual International Social Survey Program (ISSP), covering eighteen to twenty democracies.[17] These are invaluable sources for monitoring trends over time, but the most comprehensive comparative data, which include a range of developing postcommunist and postindustrial societies, are available from the World Values Survey.[18] The 1990–91 and 1995–97 waves are combined for this analysis, allowing the comparison of seventy nations. The survey contains long-established democracies, consolidating regimes, and various types of authoritarian states, and includes societies ranging in per capita income from $300 to $30,000 a year. This study is still the only comparative survey that aims at global coverage, including 70 out of 174 independent nation-states in the world and the majority of the world's population. All the surveys used face-to-face interviews using a multistage random sample, and the data are weighted for analysis to compensate for obvious deviations from national populations.

One limitation of the survey is that the first wave in 1980–83 only included Western industrialized nations, so it cannot be used to study trends over time in postcommunist and developing societies. Cohort analysis can be employed, however, dividing the sample by decade of birth, to examine whether successive generations have become progressively more cosmopolitan in their orientations. Of course attitudes could be interpreted as a life-cycle effect, if younger people become more deeply rooted in their local or national communities as they age and settle down. We cannot resolve this issue with the available data, but it seems more plausible to understand age-related differences primarily as cohort effects, reflecting each generation's distinctive experiences of the major developments in international affairs in the twentieth century, as different generations acquire their attitudes and identities during their formative years prior to the Great War, the interwar era, or the postwar decades.

Public opinion can be monitored at three levels to distinguish among identification with the global community, confidence in the institutions of global governance, and approval of the policy mechanisms.[19] First, at the most diffuse level, theories suggest that the growth of global governance may have gradually eroded *national identities* and produced more cosmopolitans, understood as essentially "citizens of the world" with a broad internationalist outlook. Equally plausibly, theories suggest that globalization may have changed public attitudes toward the *institutions* of international and multilateral governance, notably the United Nations, which has rapidly expanded its role as an active player in peacekeeping operations, as well as the new regional associations like the EU, ASEAN, and NAFTA, which have strengthened economic links among member states. Lastly, at the most specific level, globalization may have altered public support for the *policy mechanisms* designed to dismantle national barriers, including policies promoting free trade and open labor markets for migrant workers.

## The erosion of national identities

The strength of national and cosmopolitan identities is gauged by people's attachment to different territorial areas, an approach commonly used in previous studies.[20] In the World Values Surveys, people were asked the following:

> *"To which of these geographical groups would you say you belong first of all? And the next?*
> *The locality or town where you live*
> *The state or region of the country in which you live*
> *Your country [The US, France, etc.] as a whole**

*The continent in which you live [North America/Europe/Asia/Latin America, and so on]\**
*The world as a whole."*
*\*[Each specific nation and continent substituted for these labels.]*

People could give two responses, allowing overlapping and multiple identities if, for example, they feel they belong most strongly to their local community and then to their country, or if they identify with their country and then with their continent, and so on. The replies can be combined to provide a cosmopolitan identity scale ranging on a continuum from the most localized identities to the most cosmopolitan.[21]

Table [1] shows the response when people were asked their primary identification ("which geographic groups do you belong to *first of all?*"). The most striking finding to emerge is how far local and national identities remain far stronger than any cosmopolitan orientation. Almost half the public (47 percent) see themselves as belonging primarily to their locality or region of the country, while more than one-third (38 percent) say they identify primarily with their nation. Nevertheless, one-sixth of the public (15 percent) feels close to their continent or "the world as a whole" in their primary identity. The proportion of cosmopolitans is therefore small but not insignificant.

If we combine the first and second choices, altogether one-fifth of the public can be classified as pure localists, who identified only with their local-regional community (table [2]). In contrast, only 2 percent are pure cosmopolitans, who expressed only a continental-world identity. The remainder had mixed multiple identities, for example, seeing themselves as belonging to their region and country or to their country and continent. The overall results therefore serve to support the skeptical thesis that sees citizens as deeply rooted in their traditional communities, with strong ties of blood and soil, despite (or even because of?) all the structural changes produced by globalizing forces.

How do attitudes vary by type of society? Perhaps the most common explanation for differences in the rise of cosmopolitanism regards the process of socioeconomic development as the primary driving force. Postmodernization theory certainly advances these claims. Traditional societies are facing increasing financial volatility and economic insecurities produced by opening up markets to global forces, illustrated by the East Asian financial crisis in 1997–99, throwing millions into unemployment and slowing down investments in Latin America. Since 1980, the majority of countries in Sub-Saharan Africa, many in Latin America, and most in transition have experienced disastrous failures in growth, with setbacks in human security and growing poverty.[22] Ronald Inglehart predicts that in a situation of growing insecurities traditional societies may experience a resurgence in feelings of nationalism and identification with the nation-state. In contrast, in postindustrial societies, with high levels of affluence and economic growth during recent decades, Inglehart argues that the tendency is to transfer authority from the nation-state simultaneously downward toward more local and regional communities, as in Quebec, Scotland, and Catalonia, and also upward toward broader transnational ties.[23] If this account were correct, then we would expect cosmopolitanism to be most widespread in postindustrial societies. Countries like the United States, Germany, and the United Kingdom have been transformed most radically by the process of technological change, new communications, and open markets in goods and services, as well as by high levels of education and affluence produced by

**Table [1]**  Primary type of territorial identity (percent)

| Profile | Variable | World-continent | National | Local-regional |
|---|---|---|---|---|
| All | | 15 | 38 | 47 |
| Type of society | Postindustrial | 15 | 41 | 44 |
| | Postcommunist | 16 | 32 | 53 |
| | Developing | 14 | 37 | 49 |
| Cohort | 1905–14 | 6 | 33 | 62 |
| | 1915–24 | 10 | 35 | 55 |
| | 1925–34 | 10 | 38 | 53 |
| | 1935–44 | 11 | 38 | 51 |
| | 1945–54 | 19 | 37 | 44 |
| | 1955–64 | 17 | 35 | 48 |
| | 1965–78 | 21 | 34 | 44 |
| Continent | North America | 16 | 43 | 41 |
| | South America | 17 | 37 | 45 |
| | North Europe | 11 | 36 | 53 |
| | Northwestern Europe | 13 | 25 | 62 |
| | Southwestern Europe | 13 | 23 | 64 |
| | Eastern Europe | 8 | 34 | 58 |
| | Former Soviet Union | 15 | 32 | 53 |
| | Middle East | 12 | 49 | 39 |
| | Asia | 13 | 32 | 55 |
| | Africa | 9 | 41 | 49 |
| Education | Highest | 18 | 42 | 40 |
| | Lowest | 7 | 29 | 64 |
| Gender | Men | 16 | 40 | 45 |
| | Women | 14 | 36 | 49 |
| Size of town | Low (less than 2,000) | 11 | 34 | 55 |
| | High (more than 500,000) | 21 | 36 | 43 |
| Type of culture | Northern European | 12 | 36 | 53 |
| | English | 19 | 41 | 41 |
| | Catholic European | 13 | 24 | 64 |
| | Confucian | 5 | 44 | 52 |
| | Central European | 7 | 33 | 60 |
| | Soviet | 16 | 31 | 53 |
| | Latin American | 8 | 50 | 43 |
| | Southeast Asian | 8 | 29 | 63 |
| | African | 9 | 41 | 49 |
| Postmaterialism | Materialist | 12 | 38 | 50 |
| | Mixed | 16 | 39 | 45 |
| | Postmaterialist | 20 | 37 | 43 |
| Type of democracy | Free | 16 | 39 | 45 |
| | Partly free | 15 | 32 | 53 |
| | Nonfree | 10 | 32 | 58 |

*Source*: World Values Surveys combined waves 1990–91 and 1995–97, weighted data (N = 147319)
*Note*: "To which of these geographical groups would you say you belong *first of all*?
  The locality or town where you live
  The state or region of the country in which you live
  Your country [*The US, France*, and so on] as a whole
  The continent in which you live [*North America/Europe/Asia/Latin America*, and so on]
  The world as a whole."

**Table [2]**   Multiple territorial identities (percent of total)

| Belong first (row) | Belong second (column) | | | | | |
|---|---|---|---|---|---|---|
|  | Local | Region | Nation | Continent | World | All first |
| Local |  | 15.5 | 17.5 | 1.0 | 2.6 | 36.7 |
| Region | 4.1 |  | 5.9 | 0.5 | 0.8 | 11.2 |
| Nation | 18.0 | 9.4 |  | 3.6 | 6.1 | 37.1 |
| Continent | 0.5 | 0.5 | 1.3 |  | 0.4 | 2.7 |
| World | 3.5 | 1.2 | 5.9 | 1.6 |  | 12.2 |
| All second | 26.1 | 26.6 | 30.6 | 6.8 | 9.9 | 100.0 |

*Source*: World Values Surveys combined waves 1990–91 and 1995–97, weighted data (N = 147319)
*Note*: "To which of these geographical groups would you say you belong *first of all?* And the next?
   The locality or town where you live
   The state or region of the country in which you live
   Your country [*The US, France*, and so on] as a whole
   The continent in which you live [*North America/Europe/Asia/Latin America*, and so on]
   The world as a whole."

socioeconomic development. Nationalism can be expected to remain stronger in less developed societies, such as those in southeast Asia and Africa, as well as in post-communist states struggling with the disruptive process of economic and political transitions in Central and Eastern Europe.

Table [1] shows how national identities vary in different types of societies.[24] The results show few major differences in cosmopolitan orientations among postindustrial, postcommunist, and developing societies, in contrast to Inglehart's hypotheses. Contrary to popular perceptions, nationalism proved weakest in postcommunist states, where local-regional identities prevail. Therefore globalization may well have had a differential impact on developed and developing countries, especially the "winners" and "losers" from the globalizations of markets, but it is not evident that so far this has affected the public's national identities.

Alternatively if the latest wave of globalization is a historical process, then plausibly the process of *generational* change may influence attitudes. As globalization is a gradual development, though one that has accelerated in the late twentieth century, it can be expected to affect the younger generation most strongly, brought up in a world of MTV, Yahoo, and McDonald's. In contrast, the prewar and interwar generation can be expected to retain stronger national allegiances and be most distrustful of the new forms of regional and global governance. The theory of postmoderniza-tion developed by Ronald Inglehart presents the strongest argument that pervasive structural trends are transforming the basic values of the younger generation; with the net result that intergenerational population replacement is producing cultural change.[25]

The results strongly confirm this thesis (table [1]).[26] The oldest cohort, born at the turn of the last century, display by far the strongest nationalism while the younger cohorts, the baby boomers born after World War II, are most likely to have a sense of global identification. The generation gap means that cosmopolitans are more than three times as likely among the baby boomers than the pre-Great War generations.

Moreover, this pattern was not just confined to postindustrial societies, as it was also equally evident among the younger cohorts in postcommunist and developing countries. If understood as a generational and not a life-cycle effect, and if we can extrapolate from these patterns, they provide important evidence that in the long term, secular trends will eventually reduce the balance of support for nationalism and move the public in a more cosmopolitan direction. The results suggest that the more optimistic scenarios of a global society and culture are indeed greatly exaggerated at present, but there is good evidence to believe that these hopes (and fears) may well be realized in the future as younger populations gradually replace older groups. The younger generations, backpacking with Eurail passes, volunteering for the Peace Corps, or working with environmental NGOs around the world, are most cosmopolitan in their orientation.

What are the other characteristics of the cosmopolitans? Table [1] shows that this group is broadly distributed by continent, although stronger in North and South America than in Europe, and weakest in Eastern Europe and Africa. Previous studies have emphasized that educational attainment is strongly associated with a sense of belonging to the European Union.[27] The comparison confirms that education strongly predicts a cosmopolitan identity, with twice as many people identifying with the world or continent in the highest than in the lowest educational group. There is a modest gender gap, with women marginally more localized than men. Not surprisingly, urbanization also has a significant impact, with far more localists in rural areas and more cosmopolitans living in large towns and cities. Among the cultural zones, cosmopolitanism was most clearly evident among those sharing an English-speaking background, while lower levels were found among those who shared a Confucian tradition. Postmaterial attitudes operated in the expected direction, with far more globalists among the postmaterialist category, while the type of democracy also had a modest association. We can conclude that perhaps the most significant indicator of an emerging cosmopolitan orientation comes from the generational patterns that we have observed, rather than from any major differences between postindustrial and developing societies. The postwar generation who grew up in conditions of relative peace and security seem most at home in the world, more comfortable with cosmopolitan identities than their fathers or grandfathers. Still it needs to be stressed that claims that we are all becoming citizens of the world remain exaggerated, since most people in most societies, continents, and cultures remain rooted in the older forms of belonging through their local community or nation-state.
[ . . . ]

## The Future of Cosmopolitan Citizenship

[ . . . ] Has globalization increased the number of cosmopolitans, citizens of the world who feel comfortable traveling, living, and working within different societies, or in reaction has there been a resurgence of nationalism or even localism? Growing cultural globalism is often assumed, but beyond aggregate indicators, such as trends in news flows, movie receipts, or the number of McDonald's around the world [ . . . ], we know little about what it means for how people feel about the world and whether structural changes have altered fundamental identities. As David McCrone and Paula Surridge remark, "National identity is one of the most discussed but least understood

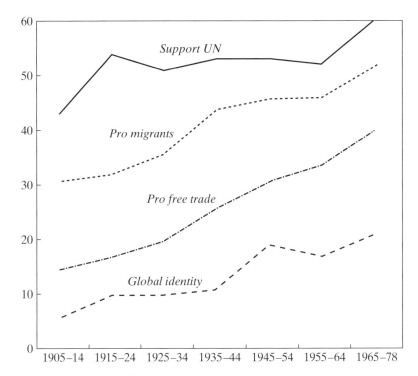

**Figure [1]**   Cosmopolitan attitudes by cohort

*Source*: World Values Surveys, early–mid-1990s

concepts of the late twentieth century."[28] The idea of cosmopolitanism is even more elusive and complex.

The results of this study are of the "cup half empty" or the "cup half full" variety. Interpretations of the evidence can be used to support both sides of the debate about nationalism. On the one hand, it is true that cosmopolitans remain a distinct minority, and most people remain strongly rooted to the ties of local, regional, and national communities that give people a sense of blood and belonging. When asked, more people are likely to see themselves as living in Berlin, Prague, or Athens, rather than sharing a more diffuse feeling of being Europeans, still less citizens of the world. The globalization linking us through networks of mass communications, the flow of goods and capital, and the forces of mass tourism and travel has not yet destroyed local ties.

Yet, on the other hand, the most important indicators of cultural change found in this chapter are the persistent differences in international attitudes held by different generations. The more optimistic claims of some theorists concerning the decline of the nation-state and erosion of nationalism are not yet evident – but at the same time cohort analysis suggests that in the long term public opinion is moving in a more internationalist direction (figure [1]). Most strikingly, almost one-fifth of the baby boomers born after World War II see themselves as cosmopolitan citizens of the globe, identifying with their continent or the world as a whole, but this is true of only one in ten of the group brought up in the interwar years, and of even fewer of the prewar generation. A similar generational divide is evident across the attitudes like support for the institutions of global governance and the policies of free trade and open labor markets. If this trend is maintained, we can expect to see a rising tide of popular support for globalization in future decades, through the gradual process of generational turnover. Growing urbanization and rising educational levels can also be expected to contribute toward this general development. This cultural shift has important implications for the democratic legitimacy of international organizations like the United Nations and the European Union, as well as for the gradual breakdown of some of the deep-rooted barriers dividing nation against nation. In short, the younger generation brought up in the postwar era is less nationalistic than its mothers and fathers, and it remains to be seen whether its children maintain this trend.

## Notes

1  K. Ohmae, *The End of the Nation State* (New York: Free Press, 1995).
2  Anthony Giddens, *The Consequences of Modernity* (Cambridge: Polity Press, 1990).
3  David Held and others, *Global Transformations: Politics, Economics and Culture* (Stanford: Stanford University Press, 1999), pp. 444–6.
4  Anthony Smith, "Towards a Global Culture?" in Michael Featherstone (ed.), *Global Culture* (London: Sage, 1995).
5  M. Mann, "Has Globalization Ended the Rise and Rise of the Nation-State?" *Review of International Political Economy*, vol. 4 (1997).
6  P. Hirst and G. Thompson, *Globalization in Question: The International Economy and the Possibilities of Governance* (Cambridge: Polity Press, 1996).
7  Sophie Duchesne and André-Paul Frognier, "Is There a European Identity?" in Oskar Niedermayer and Richard Sinnott (eds), *Public Opinion and Internationalized Governance* (Oxford: Oxford University Press, 1995); Angelika Scheuer, "A Political Community?" in Hermann Schmitt and Jacques Thomassen (eds), *Political Representation and Legitimacy in the European Union* (Oxford: Oxford University Press, 1999); and B. Nelson, D. Roberts and W. Veit (eds), *The Idea of Europe: Problems of National and Transnational Identity* (Oxford: Berg, 1982).
8  Pippa Norris, "The Political Regime," in Schmitt and Thomassen (eds), *Political Representation and Legitimacy in the European Union* (Oxford: Oxford University Press, 1995). See also Mattei Dogan, "The Decline of Nationalism within Western Europe," *Comparative Politics*, vol. 20 (1994), pp. 281–5.
9  Geoffrey Evans, "Europe: A New Electoral Cleavage?" in Geoffrey Evans and Pippa Norris (eds), *Critical Elections: British Parties and Voters in Long-Term Perspective* (London: Sage, 1999); and Geoffrey Evans, "How Britain Views the EU," in Roger Jowell and others, *British Social Attitudes: The 15th Report* (Aldershot: Dartmouth/SCPR, 1998).
10  Although a detailed case study of the impact of NAFTA can be found in Ronald Inglehart, Neil Nevitte, and Migual Basanez, *Cultural Change in North America? Closer Economic, Political and Cultural Ties between the United States, Canada and Mexico* (New York: De Gruyter, 1996).
11  Philip Evert, "NATO, the European Community, and the United Nations," in Oskar Niedermayer and Richard Sinnott (eds), *Public Opinion and Internationalized Governance* (Oxford: Oxford University Press, 1995).
12  There is a large literature on the concepts of nationalism and national identity. See, for example, Michael Ignatieff, *Blood and Belonging* (London: Chatto and Windus, 1993); Benedict Anderson, *Imagined Communities: Reflections on the Origin and Spread of Nationalism* (London: Verso, 1983); Anderson, *Banal Nationalism* (London: Sage, 1995); and Ernest Gellner, *Nations and Nationalism* (Oxford: Blackwell, 1983).

13  Anthony D. Smith, *National Identity* (London: Penguin, 1991), chap. 7. For a discussion of some of these issues, see Pippa Norris, "Ballots not Bullets: Testing Consociational Theories of Ethnic Conflict, Electoral Systems and Democratization," in Andrew Reynolds (ed.), *Institutional Design, Conflict Management and Democracy*, forthcoming.

14  Bridget Taylor and Katarina Thomson (eds), *Scotland and Wales: Nations Again?* (University of Wales Press, 1999).

15  For a more detailed discussion of this distinction, see Pippa Norris, "Towards a More Cosmopolitan Political Science?" *European Journal of Political Research*, vol. 30, no. 1 (1997).

16  See Michael Featherstone (ed.), *Global Culture* (London: Sage, 1995).

17  For an earlier study based on the ISSP module on nationalism, see, for example, Pippa Norris, "Global Communications and Cultural Identities," *Harvard International Journal of Press/Politics*, vol. 4, no. 4 (1999), pp. 1–7. The most thorough empirical work on orientations within Europe from 1973 to 1990 using the Eurobarometer surveys can be found in Oskar Niedermayer and Richard Sinnott, *Public Opinion and Internationalized Governance* (Oxford: Oxford University Press, 1995).

18  The author is most grateful to the principal investigator, Ronald Inglehart, and all the collaborators on the World Values Surveys for release of this dataset.

19  David Easton, *A Framework for Political Analysis* (Prentice Hall, 1965); and Easton, "A Reassessment of the Concept of Political Support," *British Journal of Political Science*, vol. 5 (1975), pp. 435–57.

20  Ronald Inglehart, *The Silent Revolution: Changing Values and Political Styles among Western Nations* (Princeton: Princeton University Press, 1977); and Sophie Duchesne and André-Paul Frognier, "Is There a European Identity?" in Oskar Niedermayer and Richard Sinnott (eds), *Public Opinion and Internationalized Governance* (Oxford: Oxford University Press, 1995).

21  Because of the size of the combined dataset (with more than 147,000 cases) all the differences between groups are statistically significant by conventional tests like ANOVA. As a result, tests of statistical significance are not reported in the presentation of the analysis.

22  UNDP, *Human Development Report 1999*, p. 99.

23  Ronald Inglehart, *Modernization and Post-Modernization* (Princeton: Princeton University Press, 1997), pp. 303–5.

24  Developing societies were classified as those with a "medium" or "low" human development index in 1997. See UNDP, *Human Development Report 1999*, table 1, pp. 134–7.

25  Inglehart, *Modernization and Post-Modernization*.

26  The analysis is based on factor analysis not reported here.

27  Inglehart, *The Silent Revolution*.

28  David McCrone and Paula Surridge, "National Identity and National Pride," in Roger Jowell and others (eds), *British and European Social Attitudes, the 15th Report* (Aldershot: Ashgate, 1998).

# Part IV
# A Global Economy?

Three sets of interrelated issues have come to frame the scholarly debate concerning economic globalization. The first of these issues concerns the extent of global economic integration or, more crudely, whether it is accurate to talk of a single borderless global economy. This is associated with a further issue, namely whether a new form or epoch of global capitalism has evolved, sustaining a new global division of labour and transforming the location and distribution of economic power. The third set of issues revolves around the political implications of economic globalization, specifically the extent to which states have become subjugated to global market forces, placing new constraints on progressive economic policy and the welfare state.

Globalists consider that the pattern and intensity of contemporary economic globalization is historically unprecedented; a single global economy can be said to be in the making. Driven by the third industrial revolution – the new electronic, information order – and a neoliberal economic agenda, the transnational organization of economic power and activity now outstrips the regulatory capacity of states, even the most powerful. While global markets do not entail the end of the state as an economic unit (few think that they do), they nevertheless severely erode national economic sovereignty and impose on all governments conservative fiscal policies and market-friendly economic strategies.

By contrast, the sceptics consider such accounts to exaggerate the level of global economic integration as well as the power of global capital. Globalists, they argue, overlook the centrality of states – especially the great powers – in engineering global markets. Far from international markets bringing about the end of the welfare state and national economic policy, both have become increasingly more salient. This is because most economic activity is still rooted in nation-states; multinationals remain essentially national companies with international operations; and national economic policies are still critical to the creation of wealth and prosperity. Rather than a single global economy, the world is breaking up into three major regional blocs in which states retain control, competing for economic advantage. There is no new global capitalist order. As many sceptics argue, the world economy was far more integrated at the beginning of the twentieth century than it is at the beginning of the twenty-first century.

Central to this debate about contemporary globalization is the question of economic power: namely, whether the transnational organization of finance, production and commerce is creating a borderless world economy. For globalists, such as Peter Dicken and Manuel Castells, the new geography of the world economy, produced by the growing integration of economic activity across national borders, constitutes the emergence of a 'single, planetary scale worldwide economy'. For Dicken this new geo-economy is principally the product of the globalization of production, engineered by transnational corporations in the form of global production chains. Although geography is not yet dead, Dicken argues that it is the deepening integration of the global and local scales of production, in real geographical space, which makes the present era historically distinct.

Castells affirms this conclusion, arguing that the existence of global (real-time) markets, manifest most clearly in twenty-four-hour-a-day trading across world financial centres, embeds national production, financial and commercial activity within worldwide networks of economic organization. Multinational corporations and global production networks, in fields as diverse as computer chips and apparels, are reorganizing economic activity on a global scale, creating a new global economy which operates according to a quite different logic from that found in the international economy of the *belle époque* or in the Imperial economies of earlier centuries. What is novel about this new global informational capitalism is that, mediated by global infrastructures of instantaneous communications and information technologies, it increasingly enables the functioning and operation of a real-time planetary economy. This is not to argue that this planetary economy is entirely universal in its scope since, as Castells goes on to describe, it is highly regionally differentiated and segmented, involving a new global division of labour – one that excludes or marginalizes many. Moreover, Castells notes that the new architecture of the global economy is unstable, since the dynamics of global competition and technological diffusion induce a 'creative chaos' challenging established economic and political structures. Within this creative chaos the role of states and local competitive advantages becomes increasingly significant, despite constraints imposed by the operation of global markets.

A heated and intense exchange of views has developed concerning the empirical accuracy and validity of this globalist characterization of the world economy. Paul Hirst's and Grahame Thompson's contribution presents a powerful sceptical case, conceptually and empirically, against the new global economy thesis. Making a careful analytical distinction between the idea of an international economy (links between separate national economies) and a universal global economy (economic organization without borders), they dismiss the central claims of the economic globalists. By comparison with the *belle époque*, the world today is significantly less economically integrated. Moreover, the empirical evidence indicates that the new 'global economy' is far less geographically inclusive than the economic system of the *belle époque*. There is little evidence of a new international division of labour. Rather, there is evidence of a growing exclusion or marginalization of many states and populations in the South from international economic activity. In effect, world economic activity has become increasingly concentrated amongst OECD or Western economies to the exclusion of much of the South. It is also the case that the world economy is becoming increasingly regionalized, rather than globalized, as trade and investment flows have become concentrated within – rather than between – the three major blocs of the world economy, namely Europe, Asia-Pacific and North America.

This sceptical analysis is amplified by Robert Gilpin's contribution, which, although a more cautious account in many respects, nevertheless concludes that 'economic globalization is much more limited than many realize'. Gilpin reaffirms the verdict that the world was much more economically interdependent at the beginning of the twentieth century than it is today. Furthermore, he dismisses many of the alleged consequences of globalization as the mistaken product of confused analyses. Governments, whether in respect of macroeconomic or welfare policy, are not nearly so constrained by an open world economy as the globalists think. Managing the national economy undoubtedly has become more complicated. But it is certainly not the case that economic sovereignty has been eroded. On the contrary, access to global finance enables governments to borrow more freely to finance expansionary economic policies or the welfare state. Governments have never been so powerful or so crucial to the management of their national economies or the world economy. In these respects, globalists greatly exaggerate the impact of globalization on the state.

Björn Hettne takes up this issue of state power. He is also somewhat sceptical of the claim that globalization necessarily undermines the state and the effective management of domestic affairs. Although his contribution acknowledges that there has been a major expansion of global market forces, it argues that regionalism provides a new mechanism for mediating these forces through new regional institutions of political accountability and control. For Hettne, regionalism can and does moderate the expanding scope and reach of global economic forces. Moreover, he maintains that while political and economic trends point towards growing regionalization, the processes of globalization and of regionalization are, in contrast to Hirst's and Thompson's understanding, complementary. Seeking to unpack the changing relationship between the 'forces of globalization' and the 'forces of regionalization', Hettne explores a growing shift from the territorial logic of state control to the emergence of regional systems of states preoccupied with regulation and accountability in a wider context. It is in this development that he sees strong grounds for asserting that regionalization and globalization are mutually reinforcing processes – strengthening, rather than eroding, state power.

This optimistic view of the new regionalism is contested by Fritz Scharpf's extract. Scharpf accepts the assertion that globalization and regionalization are in fundamental respects mutually reinforcing, but he draws a quite different conclusion from that reached by Hettne. Rather than regionalism providing a new political mechanism for regulating globalization, it has, especially in the European context, effectively reinforced the global economic constraints and competitive pressures bearing on national economies. In the process, national governments and, especially, the social democratic project have been decisively compromised. Although he does not go so far as to conclude that, under conditions of globalization and regionalization, we are witnessing the end of the welfare state, he does suggest that, at least for EU states, 'their capacity to defend existing patterns of national policy is reduced to a much greater degree than is generally implied by the pressures of global economic competition'.

At issue here is the question of whether there has been an erosion in national economic sovereignty and the power of the modern state to regulate economic activity for the national good. Since capital is increasingly mobile, significant constraints, it is often said, are created on the power of national governments to pursue progressive economic policies or redistributive social policies. It is not that all capital is necessarily 'footloose', but the fact that capital and production could be moved to alternative investment opportunities which creates strong pressures to market appeasing and market supporting policies. For Dani Rodrik, economic globalization imposes significant new constraints upon welfare regimes, whilst simultaneously generating new demands for enhanced social protection amongst those most vulnerable faced with the vagaries of global competition. In his view, the central problem today is how the tension between globalization and welfare protection can be moderated. In this respect, economic globalization does not necessarily spell the demise of the welfare state but, rather, the end of traditional approaches to welfare. New approaches involve investment in human capital, education and technical skills as articulated in the social programmes of the Neue Mitte, the Third Way and the New Democrats. Unless the tensions between globalization and social protection are resolved effectively, the globalization project itself, argues Rodrik, will be endangered by tendencies towards national fragmentation and the protectionist impulses of disadvantaged groups.

Taking issue with this conclusion, Geoffrey Garrett's contribution argues that growing international economic independence has not eroded or compromised the welfare state or national economic sovereignty in any significant way. States and national politics still matter, and, somewhat curiously perhaps, more so than ever. As economies become more open to global market forces, their workers seek greater social protection from the consequences of foreign competition. In the light of this, there has not been a notable end to 'progressive politics' but, on the contrary, a strengthening or revival of social democracy, as governments seek to respond to their citizens' demands. Global markets have not triumphed over states and remain subject to strong national intervention and regulation. The welfare state is not the victim of globalization but, instead, remains central to the success of the globalization project.

This sceptical argument is further reinforced by Duane Swank's detailed and comprehensive empirical analysis of the relationship between economic openness, taxation and welfare funding. Swank's analysis contests many of the globalist claims that globalization reduces the state's tax base, restricts expansionary and interventionary economic policies and leads to welfare retrenchment. He concludes that international capital mobility and economic openness have not created any significant pressures for welfare retrenchment amongst OECD states. Nor has globalization reduced the policy autonomy of states in respect of generous welfare regimes. But he qualifies these conclusions by suggesting that the internationalization of markets has had limited, indirect effects on welfare regimes and the efficacy of social democracy. Even so, he concludes that 'globalization has not been irrelevant' for the social democratic project and the welfare state.

# 26

# A New Geo-economy

*Peter Dicken*

## *Something* is Happening Out There

[ ... ]
The most significant development in the world economy during the past few decades has been the *increasing internationalization – and, arguably, the increasing globalization – of economic activities*. The internationalization of economic activities is nothing new. Some commodities have had an international character for centuries; an obvious example being the long-established trading patterns in spices and other exotic goods. Such internationalization was much enhanced by the spread of industrialization from the eighteenth century onwards in Europe. Nevertheless until very recently the production process itself 'was primarily organized *within* national economies or parts of them. International trade ... developed primarily as an exchange of raw materials and foodstuffs ... [with] ... products manufactured and finished in single national economies ... *In terms of production, plant, firm and industry were essentially national phenomena*' (Hobsbawm 1979: 313, emphasis added).

The nature of the world economy has changed dramatically, however, especially since the 1950s. National boundaries no longer act as 'watertight' containers of the production process. Rather, they are more like sieves through which extensive leakage occurs. The implications are far-reaching. Each one of us is now more fully involved in a global economic system than were our parents and grandparents. Few, if any, industries now have much 'natural protection' from international competition whereas in the past, of course, geographical distance created a strong insulating effect. Today, in contrast, fewer and fewer industries are oriented towards local, regional or even national markets. A growing number of economic activities have meaning only in a global context. Thus, whereas a hundred or more years ago only rare and exotic products and some basic raw materials were involved in truly international trade, today virtually everything one can think of is involved in long-distance movement. And because of the increasingly complex ways in which production is organized across national boundaries, rather than contained within them, the actual origin of individual products may be very difficult to ascertain.
[ ... ]

What these developments imply is the emergence of a *new global division of labour* which reflects a change in the geographical pattern of specialization at the global scale. Originally, as defined by the eighteenth-century political economist Adam Smith, the 'division of labour' referred simply to the specialization of workers in different parts of the production process. It had no explicitly geographical connotations at all. But quite early in the evolution of industrial economies the division of labour took on a geographical dimension. Some areas came to specialize in particular types of economic activity. Within the rapidly evolving industrial nations of Europe and the United States regional specialization – in iron and steel, shipbuilding, textiles, engineering and so on – became a characteristic feature. At the global scale the broad division of labour was between the industrial countries on the one hand, producing manufactured goods, and the non-industrialized countries on the other, whose major international function was to supply raw materials and agricultural products to the industrial nations and to act as a market for some manufactured goods. Such geographical specialization – structured around a *core*, a *semi-periphery* and a *periphery* – formed the underlying basis of much of the world's trade for many years.

This relatively simple pattern (although it was never quite as simple as the description above suggests) no longer applies. During the past few decades trade flows have become far more complex. The straightforward exchange between core and peripheral areas, based upon a broad division of labour, is being transformed into a highly complex, kaleidoscopic structure involving the *fragmentation* of many production processes and their *geographical relocation* on a global scale in ways which slice through national boundaries. In addition, we have seen the emergence of new centres of industrial production in the newly industrializing economies (NIEs). Both old and new industries are involved in this re-sorting of the global jigsaw puzzle in ways which also reflect the development of technologies of transport and communications, of corporate organization and of the production process. The technology of production itself is undergoing substantial and far-reaching change as the emphasis on large-scale, mass-production, assembly-line techniques is shifting to a more flexible production technology. And just as we can identify a new international division of labour in production so, too, we can identify a 'new international financial system', based on rapidly emerging twenty-four-hour global transactions concentrated primarily in the three major financial centres of New York, London and Tokyo.

## A 'New' Geo-economy? The Globalization Debate

So, something is undoubtedly happening 'out there'. But precisely what that 'something' might be – and whether it really represents something new – is a subject of enormous controversy amongst academics, politicians, popular writers and journalists alike. [ . . . ]
[O]n the one hand, we have the view that we do, indeed, live in a new – *globalized* – world economy in which our lives are dominated by global forces. On the other hand, we have the view that not all that much has changed; that we still inhabit an *international*, rather than a globalized, world economy in which national forces remain highly significant. The truth, it seems to me, lies in neither of these two polarized positions. Although in quantitative terms the world economy was perhaps at least as integrated economically before 1913 as it is today – in some respects, even more so – the nature of that integration was *qualitatively* very different (UNCTAD 1993: 113):

- International economic integration before 1913 – and, in fact, until only about three decades ago – was essentially *shallow integration* manifested largely through arm's length *trade* in goods and services between independent firms and through international movements of portfolio capital.

- Today, we live in a world in which *deep integration*, organized primarily by transnational corporations (TNCs), is becoming increasingly pervasive. ' "Deep" integration extends to the level of the *production* of goods and services and, in addition, increases visible and invisible trade. Linkages between national economies are therefore increasingly influenced by the cross-border value adding activities within . . . TNCs and within networks established by TNCs' (UNCTAD 1993: 113).

However, although there are undoubtedly global*izing* forces at work we do not have a fully global*ized* world economy. Globalization tendencies can be at work without this resulting in the all-encompassing end-state – the globalized economy – in which all unevenness and difference are ironed out, market forces are rampant and uncontrollable, and the nation-state merely passive and supine. [ . . . ] The position taken in this [article] is that globalization is a complex of inter-related *processes*, rather than an end-state. Such tendencies are highly uneven in time and space. In taking such a process-oriented approach it is important to distinguish between processes of *internationalization* and processes of *globalization*:

- *Internationalization processes* involve the simple extension of economic activities across national boundaries. It is, essentially, a *quantitative* process which leads to a more extensive geographical pattern of economic activity.
- *Globalization processes* are *qualitatively* different from internationalization processes. They involve not merely the geographical extension of economic activity across national boundaries but also – and more importantly – the *functional integration* of such internationally dispersed activities.

Both processes – internationalization and globalization – coexist. In some cases, what we are seeing is no more than the continuation of long-established international dispersion of activities. In others, however, we are undoubtedly seeing an increasing dispersion and integration of activities across national boundaries. The pervasive internationalization, and growing globalization, of economic life ensure that changes originating in one part of the world are rapidly diffused to others. We live in a world of increasing complexity, interconnectedness and volatility; a world in which the lives and livelihoods of every one of us are bound up with processes operating at a global scale.
[ . . . ]

## A New Geo-economy: Unravelling the Complexity

We *are* witnessing the emergence of a new geo-economy which is qualitatively different from the past but in which both processes of internationalization and globalization and of shallow and deep integration continue to coexist. However, they do so in ways which are highly uneven in space, in time and across economic sectors. Very few industries are truly and completely global although many display some globalizing tendencies. The question is: how can we begin to unravel the dynamic, kaleidoscopic complexity of this geo-economy?

The conventional unit of analysis in studies of the world economy is the nation-state. Virtually all the statistical data on production, trade, investment and the like are aggregated into national 'boxes'. Such a level of aggregation is less and less useful, given the nature of the changes occurring in the organization of economic activity. This is not to imply that the national level is unimportant. On the contrary, one of the major themes of this book is that nation-states continue to be key players in the contemporary global economy [ ... ]. In any case, we shall have to rely heavily on national level data to explore the changing maps of production trade and investment [ ... ]. But, as we noted earlier, national boundaries no longer 'contain' production processes in the way they once did. Such processes slice through national boundaries and transcend them in a bewildering array of relationships that operate at different geographical and organizational scales. We need to be able to get both below and above the national scale to understand what is going on.

## Production chains: a basic building block

One especially useful conceptual point of entry is the *production chain* [ ... ] which can be defined as

> *a transactionally linked sequence of functions in which each stage adds value to the process of production of goods or services.*

[ ... ]
Two aspects of production chains are especially important from our point of view [ ... ]:

- their *co-ordination and regulation*
- their *geographical configuration*.

## Co-ordination and regulation of production chains

Production chains are co-ordinated and regulated at two levels. First and foremost, they are co-ordinated by business firms, through the multifarious forms of intra- and interorganizational relationships that make up an economic system. [ ... ] [E]conomies are made up of different types of business organization – transnational and domestic, large and small, public and private – in varying combinations and inter-relationships. [F]irms [ ... ] operate over widely varying geographical ranges and perform rather different roles in the economic system.

One of the major themes of this book is that it is increasingly the *transnational corporation* (TNC) which plays the key role in co-ordinating production chains and, therefore, in shaping the new geo-economy [ ... ]. However, we need to use a broad definition of the TNC – one which goes beyond the conventional definition based upon levels of ownership of internationally based assets – to capture the diversity and complexity of transnational networks. Thus, a TNC will be defined as

> *a firm which has the power to co-ordinate and control operations in more than one country, even if it does not own them.*

This definition implies that it is not essential for a firm to *own* productive assets in different countries in order to be able to control how such assets are used. TNCs generally do own such assets but they are also typically involved in a spider's web of collaborative relationships with other legally independent firms across the globe. [ . . . ]

In this regard, Gereffi [ . . . ] makes a useful distinction between two types of 'driver':

- *Producer-driven chains*:

    refer to those industries in which transnational corporations (TNCs) or other large integrated industrial enterprises play the central role in controlling the production system (including its backward and forward linkages). This is most characteristic of capital- and technology-intensive industries like automobiles, computers, aircraft, and electrical machinery . . . What distinguishes 'producer-driven' production systems is the control exercised by the administrative headquarters of the TNCs.

- *Buyer-driven chains*:

    'refer to those industries in which large retailers, brand-named merchandisers, and trading companies play the pivotal role in setting up decentralized production networks in a variety of exporting countries.' (It is important to emphasize that, in terms of the definition introduced above, such firms are also TNCs.) [Gereffi and Korzeniewicz 1994: 97]

[ . . . ]

The second level at which production chains are regulated is that of the *state*. Contrary to those who argue that the state is either dead or dying as a viable force in the contemporary global economy, the position taken here is that the state remains a fundamentally significant influence. All the elements in the production chain are regulated within some kind of political structure whose basic unit is the nation-state but which also includes such supranational institutions as the International Monetary Fund or the World Trade Organization, as well as regional economic groupings such as the European Union or the North American Free Trade Agreement. All markets are socially constructed. Even supposedly 'deregulated' markets are still subject to some kind of political regulation. All states operate a battery of economic policies whose objective is to enhance national welfare. However, the particular policy orientation and policy mix varies according to the political, social and cultural complexion of the individual state. Hence, just as there is great diversity in TNC behaviour so, too, states vary in their behaviour depending upon their position along the ideological spectrum.

Consequently, all business organizations – even the most global TNC – have to operate within national and international regulatory systems. They have to conform to national business legislation. It is true, of course, that TNCs attempt to take advantage of national differences in regulatory regimes while states attempt to minimize such 'regulatory arbitrage'. The result is a very complex situation in which firms and states are engaged in various kinds of power play; what Stopford and Strange [1991] call a *triangular nexus* of interactions comprising firm–firm, state–state and firm–state relationships [ . . . ] In other words, the new geo-economy is essentially being structured and restructured not by the actions of either firms or states alone but by complex, dynamic interactions between the two sets of institutions [ . . . ].

## Geographical configuration of production chains

[ ... ] Just as we can identify a spectrum of organizational arrangements for co-ordinating a particular production chain so, too, we can identify a geographical spectrum of possibilities. [ ... ] [P]roduction functions may be *geographically dispersed* at one end of the spectrum or *geographically concentrated* at the other along a continuum from the global through to the local scale. One obvious influence on the geographical configuration of production chains is technological – primarily the technologies of transport and communications which transform the meaning of geographical distance. In general, therefore, there has been a tendency for the geographical extensiveness of virtually all production chains to increase. However, different types of production chain may be configured geographically in very different ways.

## Even in a Globalizing World, All Economic Activities are Geographically Localized

'The end of geography'; 'the death of distance'. These two phrases resonate, either explicitly or implicitly, throughout much of the globalization literature. According to this view, dramatic developments in the technologies of transport and communication have made capital – and the firms controlling it – 'hyper-mobile', freed from the 'tyranny of distance' and no longer tied to 'place'. In other words, it implies that economic activity is becoming 'deterritorialized'. The sociologist Manuel Castells argues that the forces of globalization, especially those driven by the new information technologies, are replacing this 'space of places' with a 'space of flows' [Castells 1989, 1996]. Anything can be located anywhere and, if that does not work out, can be moved somewhere else with ease [ ... ]. Seductive as such ideas might be, a moment's thought will show just how misleading they are. Although transport and communications technologies have indeed been revolutionized [ ... ] both geographical distance and, especially, *place* remain fundamental. Every component in the production chain, every firm, every economic activity is, quite literally, 'grounded' in specific locations. Such grounding is both physical, in the form of sunk costs [ ... ] and less tangible in the form of localized social relationships.

## Geographical clustering of economic activities is the norm

Not only does every economic activity have to be located somewhere; more significantly, there is also a very strong propensity for economic activities to form *localized geographical clusters* or *agglomerations*. In fact, the geographical concentration of economic activities, at a local or subnational scale, is the norm not the exception. The pervasiveness and the significance of geographical clustering has recently been recognized – and has come to occupy a central position – in the writings of some leading economists and management theorists, notably Paul Krugman, Michael Porter and Kenichi Ohmae. [ ... ] However, economic geographers and location theorists have been pointing to the pervasiveness of this phenomenon of geographical concentration for decades.

[ . . . ]

In a whole variety of ways, therefore, once established a localized economic cluster or agglomeration will tend to grow through a process of cumulative, self-reinforcing development [ . . . ].

The cumulative nature of these processes of localized economic development emphasizes the significance of historical trajectory. It has become common to use terminology from evolutionary economics [ . . . ] to describe the process as being *path dependent.* Thus, a region's (or a nation's) economy becomes 'locked in' to a pattern which is strongly influenced by its particular history. This may be either a source of continued strength or, if it embodies too much organizational rigidity, a source of weakness. However, even for 'successful' regions, such path dependency does not imply the absolute inevitability of continued success. [ . . . ] A central argument, then, is that *place* matters; that 'territorialization' remains a significant component in the organization of economic activity.

## Scales of Activity; Scales of Analysis

The geo-economy, therefore, can be pictured as a geographically uneven, highly complex and dynamic web of production chains, economic spaces and places connected together through threads of flows. But the spatial *scale* at which these processes operate is, itself, variable. So, too, is the meaning which different scales have for different actors within the global economic system. The tendency is to collapse the scale dimension to just two: the global and the local, and much has been written about the *global–local tension* at the interface between the two. Firms, states, local communities, it is argued, are each faced with the problem of resolving that tension.

There is no doubt that this is a real problem. However, it is not always the case that the terms 'global' and, especially, 'local' mean the same thing in different contexts. In the international business literature, for example, the term 'local' generally refers to the national, or even the larger regional, scale (i.e. at the level of Europe, Asia, North America). But for most people, 'local' refers to a very much smaller spatial scale: that of the local community in which they live. However, it is a mistake to focus only on the two extremes of the scale – the global and the local – at which economic activities occur. It is more realistic to think in terms of inter-related scales of activity and of analysis: for example, the local, the national, the regional (i.e. supra-national) and the global. These have meaning both as activity spaces in which economic and political actors operate and also as analytical categories which more accurately capture some of the complexity of the real world.

However, we need to bear in mind that the scales are not independent entities. [ . . . ] Individual industries (production/commodity chains) can be regarded as vertically organized structures which operate across increasingly extensive geographical scales. Cutting across these vertical structures are the territorially defined political-economic systems which, again, are manifested at different geographical scales. It is at the points of intersection of these dimensions in 'real' geographical space where specific outcomes occur, where the problems of existing within a globalizing economy – whether as a business firm, a government, a local community or as an individual – have to be resolved.

# References

Bairoch, P. (1982) International industrialization levels from 1750 to 1980. *Journal of European Economic History* 11.

Bairoch, P. (1993) *Economics and World History*. Brighton: Wheatsheaf.

Braudel, F. (1984) *Civilization and Capitalism*. 3 vols, London: Collins.

Castells, M. (ed.) (1989) *The Informational City*. Oxford: Blackwell.

Castells, M. (1996) *The Rise of the Network Society*, vol. 1 of *The Information Age*. Oxford: Blackwell.

Dunning, J. H. (1983) Changes in the level and structure of international production: the last hundred years. In M. Casson (ed.), *The Growth of International Business*, London: Allen and Unwin.

Dunning, J. H. (1993) *Multinational Enterprises and the Global Economy*. Reading, Mass.: Addison-Wesley.

Gereffi, G. and Korzeniewicz, M. (eds) (1994) *Commodity Chains and Global Capitalism*. Westport: Praeger.

Hobsbawm, E. (1979) The development of the world economy. *Cambridge Journal of Economics* 3.

Kennedy, P. (1987) *The Rise and Fall of the Great Powers*. New York: Random House.

Kitson, M. and Michie, J. (1995) Trade and growth: a historical perspective. In J. Michie and J. Grieve-Smith (eds), *Managing the Global Economy*, Oxford: Oxford University Press.

Kozul-Wright, R. (1995) Transnational corporations and the nation-state. In J. Michie and J. Grieve-Smith (eds), *Managing the Global Economy*, Oxford: Oxford University Press.

Krugman, P. (1991) *Geography and Trade*. Leuven: Leuven University Press.

Krugman, P. (1995) *Development, Geography and Economic Theory*. Cambridge, Mass.: MIT Press.

Krugman, P. (1996) *Pop Internationalism*. Cambridge, Mass.: MIT Press.

MacBean, A. I. and Snowden, P. N. (1981) *International Institutions in Trade and Finance*. London: Allen and Unwin.

McGrew, A. G. (1992) Conceptualising global politics. In A. G. McGrew and P. G. Lewis (eds), *Global Politics: Globalization and the Nation-State*, Cambridge: Polity Press.

Ohmae, E. (1995) *The End of the Nation-State: The Rise of Regional Economies*. New York: Free Press.

Porter, M. E. (1990) *The Competitive Advantage of Nations*. London: Macmillan.

Stopford, J. M. and Strange, S. (1991) *Rival States, Rival Firms: Competition for World Market Shares*. Cambridge: Cambridge University Press.

Stubbs, R. and Underhill, G. R. D. (eds) (1994) *Political Economy and the Changing Global Order*. London: Macmillan.

UNCTAD (1993) *World Investment Report 1993: Transnational Corporations and Integrated International Production*. New York: United Nations Conference on Trade and Development.

# 27

# Global Informational Capitalism

## *Manuel Castells*

The informational economy is global. A global economy is an historically new reality, distinct from a world economy.[1] A world economy – that is, an economy in which capital accumulation proceeds throughout the world – has existed in the West at least since the sixteenth century, as Fernand Braudel and Immanuel Wallerstein have taught us.[2] A global economy is something different: it is an economy with the capacity to work as a unit in real time, or chosen time, on a planetary scale. While capitalism is characterized by its relentless expansion, always trying to overcome limits of time and space, it was only in the late twentieth century that the world economy was able to become truly global on the basis of the new infrastructure provided by information and communication technologies, and with the decisive help of deregulation and liberalization policies implemented by governments and international institutions. Yet, not everything is global in the economy: in fact, most production, employment, and firms are, and will remain, local and regional. In the last two decades of the twentieth century, international trade grew faster than production, but the domestic sector of the economy still accounts for the large majority of GDP in most economies. Foreign direct investment grew even faster than trade in the 1990s, but still is a fraction of total direct investment. Yet, we can assert that there is a global economy because economies around the world depend on the performance of their globalized core. This globalized core includes financial markets, international trade, transnational production, and, to some extent, science and technology, and specialty labor. It is through these globalized, strategic components of the economy that the economic system is globally interconnected. Thus, I will define more precisely *the global economy as an economy whose core components have the institutional, organizational, and technological capacity to work as a unit in real time, or in chosen time, on a planetary scale*. I shall review succinctly the key features of this globality.

## Global Financial Markets

Capital markets are globally interdependent, and this is not a small matter in a capitalist economy.[3] Capital is managed around the clock in globally integrated financial markets working in real time for the first time in history: billion dollars worth of transactions take place in seconds in the electronic circuits throughout the globe. New information systems and communication technologies allow capital to be shuttled back and forth between economies in very short time, so that capital, and therefore savings and investment, are interconnected worldwide, from banks to pension funds, stock exchange markets, and currency exchange. Thus, global financial flows have increased dramatically in their volume, in their velocity, in their complexity, and in their connectedness. [ . . . ]

A critical development in financial globalization is the staggering volume of currency trading, which conditions the exchange rate between national currencies, decisively undermining governments' autonomy in monetary and fiscal policies. The daily turnover of currency markets around the world in 1998 reached 1.5 trillion US dollars, equivalent to more than 110 percent of the UK's GDP in 1998. This volume of currency trade represented an increase in the value of global currency trading by a factor of 8 between 1986 and 1998. This extraordinary increase was, by and large, unrelated to international trade. The ratio between the annual turnover of foreign exchange and the volume of world exports increased from 12:1 in 1979 to 60:1 in 1996, thus revealing the predominantly speculative nature of currency exchange.
[ . . . ]

Since capital markets and currencies are interdependent, so are monetary policies and interest rates. And so are economies everywhere. Although major corporate centers provide the human resources and facilities necessary to manage an increasingly complex global financial network,[4] it is in the information networks connecting such centers that the actual operations of capital take place. Capital flows become at the same time global and increasingly autonomous *vis-à-vis* the actual performance of economies.[5] Ultimately, it is the performance of capital in the globally interdependent financial markets that largely shapes the fate of economies at large. This performance is not entirely dependent on economic rules. Financial markets are markets, but so imperfect that they only partly respond to laws of supply and demand. Movements in financial markets are the result of a complex combination of market rules, business strategies, politically motivated policies, central banks' machinations, technocrats' ideology, crowd psychology, speculative maneuvering, and information turbulences of various origins.[6] The ensuing flows of capital, in and out of specific securities, and specific markets, are transmitted throughout the world at the speed of light, although the impact of these movements is processed specifically (and unpredictably) by each market. Daring financial investors try to ride the tiger, anticipating trends in their computer models, and betting on a variety of scenarios. So doing, they create capital out of capital, and increase nominal value exponentially (while periodically destroying some of this value during "market corrections"). The outcome of the process is the increasing concentration of value, and of value making, in the financial sphere, in a global network of capital flows managed by networks of information systems, and their ancillary services. The globalization of financial markets is the backbone of the new global economy.

## Globalization of Markets for Goods and Services: Growth and Transformation of International Trade

International trade was, historically, the main link between national economies. However, its relative importance in the current process of globalization is less than that of financial integration, and that of internationalization of foreign direct investment and production. Yet trade is still a fundamental component of the new global economy.[7] International trade increased substantially in the last third of the twentieth century, both in volume, and as a percentage of GDP, for developed as well as for developing countries [ ... ]. For developed countries, the percentage of exports over GDP grew from 11.2 percent in 1913 to 23.1 percent in 1985, while the respective figure for imports was 12.4 percent in 1880–1900 to 21.7 percent in 1985. For non-oil exporting developing countries, the value of exports over GDP, in the late 1990s, amounted to about 20 percent. Focusing on specific countries, and comparing the value of exports over GDP in 1913 and in 1997, the US shows an increase from 4.1 to 11.4 percent, the UK, from 14.7 to 21 percent, Japan from 2.1 to 11 percent, France from 6.0 to 21.1 percent, and Germany from 12.2 to 23.7 percent. Overall, estimates of the proportion of world exports over world output in 1997 varied between 18.6 and 21.8 percent. In the United States, from the mid-1980s to the late 1990s, the share of exports plus imports in the gross domestic product increased from 18 to 24 percent.

The evolution of international trade in the last quarter of the twentieth century was characterized by four major trends: its sectoral transformation; its relative diversification, with a growing proportion of trade shifting to developing countries, albeit with great differences among developing countries; the interaction between liberalization of global trade and regionalization of the world economy; and the formation of a network of trade relations between firms, cutting across regions and countries. Together, these trends configure the trading dimension of the new global economy. Let us review each one of them.

Trade of manufactured goods represents the bulk of non-energy international trade, in sharp contrast to the predominance of primary commodities in earlier patterns of international trade. Since the 1960s, trade in manufactures has accounted for the majority of world trade, comprising three-quarters of all trade in the late 1990s. This sectoral transformation continues, with the growing importance of services in international trade, favored by international agreements liberalizing this trade. The construction of a transportation and telecommunications infrastructure is aiding the globalization of business services. By the mid-1990s the value of services trade was estimated at over 20 percent of total world trade.

There is a deeper transformation in the structure of trade: the knowledge component of goods and services becomes decisive in terms of value added. Thus, to the traditional trade imbalance between developed and developing economies, resulting from unequal exchange between valued manufactures and less valued primary commodities, a new form of imbalance is superimposed. This is the trade between high-technology and low-technology goods, and between high-knowledge and low-knowledge services, characterized by a pattern of uneven distribution of knowledge and technology between countries and regions around the world. From 1976 to 1996 the share of high- and medium-technology goods in global trade increased from about one-third to well above one-half [ ... ]. It follows that the outward orientation of an economy does not guarantee its development. It all depends on the value of what the economy is able to export. Thus, in one of the greatest paradoxes of new patterns of growth, Sub-Saharan Africa has a higher export/GDP ratio than that of developed economies: 29 percent of GDP in the 1990s. However, since these exports are concentrated in low-value primary commodities, the process of unequal exchange keeps African economies in their poverty, while small elites profit personally from a nationally unprofitable trade. Technological capacity, technological infrastructure, access to knowledge, and highly skilled human resources become critical sources of competitiveness in the new international division of labor.[8]

Alongside the worldwide expansion of international trade, there has been a trend toward relative diversification of the areas of trade [ . . . ]. In 1965 exports between developed economies accounted for 59 percent of the total, but in 1995, the proportion had been reduced to 47 percent, while the corresponding figure for exports between developing economies increased from 3.8 to 14.1 percent. This broadening of the geographical basis of international trade must be qualified, however, by several considerations. First, developed economies continue to be the overwhelming partners in international trade: they have expanded their trade pattern toward newly industrializing economies, rather than being displaced by competition. Second, while the share of developing countries in manufacturing exports has substantially increased, from 6 percent in 1965 to 20 percent in 1995, this still leaves 80 percent for developed countries. Third, trade in high-value, high-technology products is overwhelmingly dominated by developed economies, and concentrated in intra-industry trade among developed economies. Fourth, the increasingly important trade in services is also skewed in favor of developed economies: in 1997, OECD countries accounted for 70.1 percent of total services exports, and for 66.8 percent of services imports. Fifth, manufacturing exports from developing countries are concentrated in a handful of newly industrialized and industrializing countries, mainly in East Asia, while, during the 1990s, shares of world trade for Africa and the Middle East have stagnated, and Latin America's share has remained the same. However, China is not accounted for in the calculations [ . . . ] and its exports have increased substantially, at an annual average of about 10 percent between 1970 and 1997, so contributing to an increase in the overall share of developing countries in world exports well over the 20 percent mark. This still left OECD economies with 71 percent of the world's total exports of goods and services at the end of the twentieth century, while accounting for only 19 percent of the world's population.[9]

Thus, the new international division of labor, on the one hand, maintains the trade dominance of OECD countries, particularly in high-value trade, through technological deepening and trade in services. On the other hand, it opens up new channels of integration of newly industrializing economies in the patterns of international trade, but this integration is extremely uneven, and highly selective. It introduces a fundamental cleavage among countries, and regions, that were traditionally grouped under the vague notion of "the South."

## Globalization versus Regionalization?

In the 1980s and 1990s, the evolution of international trade was marked by the tension between two apparently contradictory trends: on the one hand, the growing liberalization of trade; on the other, a variety of governments' projects to set up trading blocs. The most important of these trading areas is the European Union, but the apparent trend toward regionalization of the world economy was present in other areas of the world, as exemplified by the North American Free Trade Agreement (NAFTA), MERCOSUR, and the Asian Pacific Economic Council (APEC). These trends, together with persistent protectionist practices throughout the world, mainly in East and South Asia, led a number of observers, including myself, to propose the notion of a regionalized global economy.[10] That is, a global system of trade between trading areas, with increasing homogenization of customs within the area, while maintaining trade barriers *vis-à-vis* the rest of the world. However, a closer look at the evidence, in the light of developments in the late 1990s, calls into question the regionalization thesis. Held and colleagues, after reviewing a number of studies, conclude that "the evidence suggests that trade regionalization is complementary, and has grown alongside, interregional trade."[11] Indeed, a study by Anderson and Norheim on world trade patterns since the 1930s shows an equally strong growth of trade both between and within regions. The intensity of intra-regional trade is in fact lower in Western Europe than in America or Asia, undermining the importance of institutionalization in reinforcing intra-regional trade.[12] Other studies suggest a rising propensity for extra-regional trade in America and Asia, and a fluctuating propensity in Europe.[13]

[ ... ]

While the projects of trading blocs either faded or evolved into full economic integration in the 1990s, the openness of global trade was boosted by a number of institutional steps toward its liberalization. After the successful conclusion of GATT's Uruguay Round by the Marrakesh Agreement in 1994, leading to a significant reduction of tariffs around the world, a new World Trade Organization (WTO) was created to act as watchdog of a liberal trade order and a mediator of trade disputes between trading partners. Multilateral agreements sponsored by the WTO have created a new framework for international trade, furthering global integration. In the late 1990s, on the initiative of the United States government, the WTO focused its activity on liberalizing trade in services, and on reaching an agreement on trade-related aspects of intellectual property rights (TRIPS). On both grounds, it signaled the strategic connection between the new stage of globalization and the informational economy.

So, on close examination, the configuration of the global economy at the turn of the century sharply departs from the regionalized structure that was hypothesized in the early 1990s. The European Union is one economy, not one region. Eastern Europe is in the process of becoming part of the European Union, and, for some time, it will be, essentially, an appendage of the EU. Russia will take a long time to recover from its devastating transition to wild capitalism, and when it will be finally able to trade with the global economy (beyond its current role of provider of primary commodities) will do so on its own terms. NAFTA and Central America are, in fact, extensions of the US economy. MERCOSUR is, for the time being, a work in progress, always in danger from the latest presidential mood in Brazil and Argentina. Chilean exports diversify all over the world. So probably do Colombian, Bolivian, and Peruvian exports, particularly if we were able to assess the value of their main export good (which is not coffee). Under these conditions, the traditional dependency of South American trade *vis-à-vis* the United States seems to be increasingly called into question. Consequently, a "region of the Americas" does not seem to exist, although there is a US/NAFTA entity, and, evolving independently, the project of MERCOSUR. There is no Asian Pacific region, although there is substantial trans-Pacific trade (with the US being at one end of it). China and India assert themselves as stand-alone, continental economies, establishing their own, independent connections with the networks of international trade. The Middle East continues to be kept in its limited role as oil supplier, with little diversification of its domestic economies. Northern Africa is in the process of being made a satellite of the European Union, as a deterrent against uncontrollable and undesired immigration from impoverished countries. And Sub-Saharan Africa, with the important exception of South Africa, is being increasingly marginalized in the world economy [ ... ]. Thus, after all, it seems that there is little regionalization of the global economy, beyond the customary pattern of trade agreements, and disputes, between the European Union, Japan, and the United States. Besides, the areas of influence of these three economic superpowers increasingly overlap. Japan and Europe make substantial in-roads into Latin America. The US intensifies its trade with both Asia and Europe. Japan expands its trade with Europe. And China and India are forcefully entering the global economy with a multiplicity of trade partners. In sum, the process of regionalization of the global economy has largely dissolved, in favor of a multi-layered, multi-networked structure of trade patterns, which cannot be apprehended by using the categories of countries as units of trade and competition.

Indeed, markets for goods and services are becoming increasingly globalized. But the actual trading units are not countries, but firms, and networks of firms. This does not mean that all firms sell worldwide. But it does mean that the strategic aim of firms, large and small, is to sell wherever they can throughout the world, either directly or via their linkage with networks that operate in the world market. And there are indeed, to a large extent thanks to new communication and transportation technologies, channels and opportunities to sell everywhere. This statement must be qualified, however, by the fact that domestic markets account for the largest share of GDP in most countries, and that in developing countries, informal economies, mainly aimed at local markets, constitute the bulk of urban employment. Also, some major economies, for instance Japan, still have important segments (for example, public works, retail trade) sheltered from worldwide competition by government protection and by cultural/institutional insulation.[14] And public services and government institutions throughout the world, accounting for between one-third and over a half of jobs in each country, are, and will be, by and large removed from international competition. Yet, the dominant segments and firms, the strategic cores of all economies, are deeply connected to the world market, and their fate is a function of their performance in such a market. Sectors and firms producing non-tradable goods and services cannot be understood in isolation from tradable sectors. The dynamism of domestic markets depends ultimately on the capacity of domestic firms and networks of firms to compete globally.[15] Furthermore, international trade can no longer be separated from transnational production processes in goods and services. Thus, intra-firm international trade may account for over one-third of total international trade.[16] And the internationalization of production, and finance, are among the most important sources of growth in the international trade of services.[17]

The debate over the regionalization of the global economy denotes, however, a very important matter: the role of governments and international institutions in the process of globalization. Networks of firms, trading in the global market, are only one part of the story. Equally important are the actions of public institutions in fostering, restraining, and shaping free trade, and in positioning governments to support those economic players whose interests they represent. Yet the complexity of interaction between government strategies and trade competition cannot be understood under the simplistic notions of regionalization and trading blocs. I shall propose some hints on this political-economic approach to globalization after reviewing another layer of its complexity: the networked internationalization of the core of the production process.

## The Internationalization of Production: Multinational Corporations and International Production Networks

During the 1990s there was an accelerated process of internationalization of production, distribution, and management of goods and services. This process comprised three interrelated aspects: the growth of foreign direct investment, the decisive role of multinational corporations as producers in the global economy, and the formation of international production networks.

Foreign direct investment (FDI) increased by a factor of 4 in 1980–95, considerably faster than world output, and world trade [ . . . ]. FDI doubled its share of world capital formation from 2 percent in the 1980s to 4 percent in the mid-1990s. In the late 1990s, FDI continued to increase at about the same rate as in the early 1990s. Most of FDI originates in a few OECD countries, although US domination in FDI outflows is on the decline (in spite of its much higher volume): US share of global FDI fell from about 50 percent in the 1960s to about 25 percent in the 1990s. Other major investors are headquartered in Japan, Germany, the UK, France, The Netherlands, Sweden, and Switzerland. Most FDI stocks are concentrated in developed economies, in contrast with earlier historical periods, and this concentration grew over time: in 1960, developed economies accounted for two-thirds of FDI stocks; in the late 1990s, their share had grown to three-quarters. However, the pattern of FDI flows (as opposed to stocks) is increasingly diversified, with developing countries receiving a growing share of this investment, although still significantly less than developed economies [ . . . ]. Some studies show that FDI flows, in the late 1980s, were less concentrated than international trade. In the 1990s developing countries increased their share of outward FDI flows, although they still accounted for less than 10 percent of FDI stocks. However, a smaller share of world FDI still represents a significant share of total direct investment for developing economies. Thus, overall, patterns of FDI in the 1990s showed, on the one hand, the persistence of the concentration of wealth in the developed economies; on the other hand, the increasing diversification of productive investment following the internationalization of production.[18]

FDI is associated with the expansion of multinational corporations as major producers of the global economy. FDI frequently takes the form of mergers and acquisitions in the developed economies and, increasingly, in the developing world as well. Annual cross-borders of mergers and acquisitions jumped from 42 percent of total FDI in 1992 to 59 percent of FDI in 1997, reaching a total value of US$ 236 billion [ . . . ]. Multinational corporations (MNCs) are the main source of FDI. But FDI accounts for only 25 percent of investment in international production. MNCs' foreign subsidiaries finance their investments from a variety of sources, including borrowing in local and international markets, subsidies from governments, and co-financing from local firms. MNCs, and their linked production networks, are the vector of internationalization of production, of which the expansion of FDI is just one manifestation. Indeed, the expansion of world trade is, by and large, the result of MNCs' production, since they account for about two-thirds of total world trade, including about one-third of world trade which takes place between branches of the same corporation. If networks of firms linked to a given MNC were included in the calculation, the proportion of intra-networked firm trade would considerably increase. Thus, a large share of what we measure as international trade is, in fact, a measure of cross-border production within the same production unit. In 1998, there were about 53,000 MNCs, with 450,000 foreign subsidiaries, and global sales of $9.5 trillion dollars (which exceeded the volume of world trade). They accounted for 20–30 percent of total world output, and between 66 and 70 percent of world trade (depending on various estimates) [ . . . ]. The sectoral composition of MNCs experienced a substantial transformation in the second half of the twentieth century. Until the 1950s, most FDI was concentrated in the primary sector. But by 1970, FDI in the primary sector accounted for only 22.7 percent of total FDI, in contrast to 45.2 percent in the secondary sector, and 31.4 percent in the tertiary sector. In 1994, a new structure of investment could be perceived, as FDI in services accounted for the majority of FDI (53.6 percent), while the primary sector was down to 8.7 percent, and manufacturing's share had shrunk to 37.4 percent. Even so, MNCs account for the majority of world manufacturing exports. With the liberalization of trade in services, and the conclusion of the TRIPS agreement protecting intellectual property rights, MNCs' dominance in the international trade of services, and particularly of advanced business services, seems to be guaranteed.[19] As with manufacturing, increase in trade in services in fact reflects the expansion of international production of goods and services, since multinationals and their subsidiaries need the infrastructure of services required to operate globally.

While there is no doubt that multinationals constitute the core of internationalized production, and thus a fundamental dimension of the globalization process, it is less clear what they exactly are.[20] A number of analysts question their multinational character, arguing that they are nation-based corporations with a global reach. Multinational corporations are overwhelmingly based in OECD countries. Yet, on the other hand, in 1997 there were 7,932 multinational corporations based in developing countries, up from 3,800 in the late 1980s, thus representing about 18 percent of the total number for 1997 (which was 44,508). Furthermore, if we calculate, [ . . . ] for 1997 values, a simple ratio between parent corporations located in a given area of the world and foreign affiliates located in this area, we obtain some interesting observations. To be sure, the ratio is 38.9 for developed economies in contrast to 6.1 for developing countries, illustrating the asymmetrical distribution of global productive power, a rough measure of economic dependency. But most revealing is the comparison of ratios between different developed areas. Japan (with a whopping 116.5 ratio) shows its asymmetrical integration in global production networks. On the other hand, the US, with an 18.7 ratio, appears to be deeply penetrated by foreign companies. Western Europe is in between these two marks, with a 40.3 ratio, displaying the highest number of home-based parent corporations, but, at the same time, being also the location of 61,900 foreign affiliates (in contrast to 18,600 for the US). This reciprocal penetration of advanced economies is confirmed by the fact that inward stocks of foreign direct investment in the most advanced economies grew substantially in the 1990s. In other words, the US and Western European companies have increasing numbers of subsidiaries in each other's territories; Japanese companies have extended their multilocational pattern around the world, while Japan remains much less permeable to foreign subsidiaries than other areas of the world; multinationals based in developing countries are making inroads into the global production system, as yet on a limited scale. OECD-based corporations are present all over the developing world: in the late 1990s, MNCs accounted for about 30 percent of domestic manufacturing in Latin America, between 20 and 30 percent of total private output in China, 40 percent of value added in manufacturing in Malaysia, and 70 percent in Singapore – but only 10 percent of Korean, 15 percent of Hong Kong, and 20 percent of Taiwanese manufacturing output.

How national are these multinational corporations? There is a persistent mark of their national matrix in their top personnel, in the company's culture, and in the privileged relationship to the government of their original birthplace.[21] However, a number of factors work toward the increasingly multinational character of these corporations. Sales and earnings of foreign affiliates account for a substantial proportion of total earnings for each corporation, particularly for US companies. High-level personnel are often recruited with their familiarity with each specific environment in mind. And the best talent is promoted within the corporate chain of command, regardless of national origin, thus contributing to an increasingly multicultural mix in the higher echelons. Business and political contacts are still crucial, but they are specific to the national context where the corporation operates. Thus, the greater the extent of a company's globalization, the greater the spectrum of its business contacts and political connections, according to conditions in each country. In this sense, they are multinational rather than transnational corporations. That is, they have multiple national allegiances, rather than being indifferent to nationality and national contexts.[22]

However, the critical trend in the evolution of global production in the 1990s is the organizational transformation of the production process, including the transformation of multinational corporations themselves. Global production of goods and services, increasingly, is not performed by multinational corporations, but by transnational production networks, of which multinational corporations are an essential component, yet a component which could not operate without the rest of the network.[23] [ ... ]

Besides multinational corporations, small and medium firms in many countries – with the US (e.g. Silicon Valley), Hong Kong, Taiwan, and northern Italy hosting the most prominent examples – have formed cooperative networks, enabling themselves to be competitive in the globalized production system. These networks have connected with multinational corporations, becoming reciprocal subcontractors. Most often, networks of small/medium businesses become subcontractors of one or several large corporations. But there are also frequent cases of these networks setting up agreements with multinational companies to obtain market access, technology, management skills, or brand name. Many of these networks of small and medium businesses are transnational themselves, through agreements that operate across borders, as exemplified by the Taiwanese and Israeli computer industries extending their networks to Silicon Valley.[24]

Furthermore, [ ... ] multinational corporations are increasingly decentralized internal networks, organized in semi-autonomous units, according to countries, markets, processes, and products. Each one of these units links up with other semi-autonomous units of other multinationals, in the form of *ad hoc* strategic alliances. And each one of these alliances (in fact, networks) is a node of ancillary networks of small and medium firms. These networks of production networks have a transnational geography, which is not undifferentiated: each productive function finds the proper location (in terms of resources, cost, quality, and market access) and/or links up with a new firm in the network which happens to be in the proper location.

Thus, dominant segments of most production sectors (either for goods or for services) are organized worldwide in their actual operating procedures, forming what Robert Reich labeled "the global web."[25] The production process incorporates components produced in many different locations by different firms, and assembled for specific purposes and specific markets in a new form of production and commercialization: high-volume, flexible, customized production. Such a web does not correspond to the simplistic notion of a global corporation obtaining its supplies from different units around the world. The new production system relies on a combination of strategic alliances and *ad hoc* cooperation projects between corporations, decentralized units of each major corporation, and networks of small and medium enterprises connecting among themselves and/or with large corporations or networks of corporations. These trans-border production networks operate under two main configurations: in Gereffi's terminology, producer-driven commodity chains (in industries such as automobiles, computers, aircraft, electrical machinery), and buyer-driven commodity chains (in industries such as garment, footwear, toys, housewares).[26] What is fundamental in this web-like industrial structure is that it is territorially spread throughout the world, and its geometry keeps changing, as a whole and for each individual unit. In such a structure, the most important element for a successful managerial strategy is to position a firm (or a given industrial project) in the web in such a way as to gain competitive advantage for its relative position. Thus, the structure tends to reproduce itself and to keep expanding as competition goes on, so deepening the global character of the economy. [ ... ] Thus, the new international division of labor is increasingly intra-firm, or, more precisely, intra-networks of firms. These transnational production networks, anchored by multinational corporations, unevenly distributed across the planet, shape the pattern of global production, and, ultimately, the pattern of international trade.

## Informational Production and Selective Globalization of Science and Technology

Productivity and competitiveness in informational production are based on the generation of knowledge and information processing. Knowledge generation and technological capacity are key tools for competition between firms, organizations of all kinds, and, ultimately, countries.[27] Thus, the geography of science and technology should have a major impact on the sites and networks of the global economy. Indeed, we observe an extraordinary concentration of science and technology in a small number of OECD countries. In 1993, ten countries accounted for 84 percent of global R&D, and controlled 95 percent of the US patents of the past two decades. By the late 1990s, the fifth of the world's people living in the high-income countries had at their disposal 74 percent of telephone lines, and accounted for over 93 percent of Internet users.[28] This technological domination would run against the idea of a knowledge-based global economy, except under the form of a hierarchical division of labor between knowledge-based producers, located in a few "global cities and regions," and the rest of the world, made up of technologically dependent economies. Yet patterns of technological interdependence are more complex than the statistics of geographical inequality would suggest.

First of all, basic research, the ultimate source of knowledge, is located, in overwhelming proportion, in research universities and in the public research system around the world (such as Germany's Max Planck; France's CNRS; Russia's Academy of Sciences; China's Academia Sinica, and in the US, institutions such as the

National Institute of Health, major hospitals, and research programs sponsored by institutions such as the National Science Foundation, and the Defense Department's DARPA). This means that, with the important exception of military-related research, the basic research system is open and accessible. Indeed, in the US, in the 1990s, over 50 percent of PhD degrees in science and engineering were conferred upon foreign nationals. About 47 percent of these foreign PhD holders ended up staying in the US, but this is a matter of the inability of their countries of origin to attract them, rather than an indication of the closed nature of the science system (thus, 88 percent of PhD students from China and 79 percent from India stayed in the US, but only 13 percent from Japan and 11 percent from South Korea).[29] Furthermore, the academic research system is global. It relies on relentless communication between scientists around the world. The scientific community has always been to a large extent an international, if not global, community of scholars, in the West since the times of European scholasticism. Science is organized in specific fields of research, structured around networks of researchers who interact through publications, conferences, seminars, and academic associations. But, in addition, contemporary science is characterized by on-line communication as a permanent feature of its endeavor. Indeed, the Internet was born from the perverse coupling of the military and "big science," and its development until the early 1980s was, by and large, confined to networks of scientific communication. With the spread of the Internet in the 1990s, and the acceleration of the speed and scope of scientific discovery, the Internet and electronic mail have contributed to the formation of a global scientific system. In this scientific community there is certainly a bias in favor of dominant countries and institutions, as English is the international language, and US and Western European science institutions overwhelmingly dominate access to publications, research funds, and prestigious appointments. However, within these limits, there is a global network of science, which, albeit asymmetrical, ensures communication, and diffusion of findings and knowledge. Indeed, those academic systems, such as the Soviet Union, which forbade communication in some fields of research (e.g. information technology) paid the heavy penalty of insurmountable retardation. Scientific research in our time is either global or ceases to be scientific. Yet, while science is global, the practice of science is skewed toward issues defined by advanced countries, as Jeffrey Sachs has pointed out.[30] Most research findings end up diffusing throughout planetary networks of scientific interaction, but there is a fundamental asymmetry in the kind of issues taken up by research. Problems which are critical for developing countries, but offer little general, scientific interest, or do not have a promising, solvent market, are neglected in research programs of dominant countries. For instance, an effective malaria vaccine could save the lives of tens of millions of people, particularly children, but there have been few resources dedicated to a sustained effort toward finding it, or to diffuse worldwide the results of promising treatments, usually sponsored by the World Health Organization. AIDS medicines developed in the West are too expensive to be used in Africa, while about 95 percent of HIV cases are in the developing world. The business strategies of multinational pharmaceutical companies have repeatedly blocked attempts to produce some of these drugs cheaply, or to find alternative drugs, as they control the patents on which most research is based. Therefore, science is global, but it also reproduces in its internal dynamics the process of exclusion of a significant proportion of people, by not treating their specific problems, or by not treating them in terms which could yield results leading to improvement in their living conditions.

[ . . . ]

To understand how and why technology diffuses in the global economy it is important to consider the character of new, information-based technologies. Because they are essentially based in knowledge stored/developed in human minds, they have extraordinary potential for diffusion beyond their source, provided that they find the technological infrastructure, organizational environment, and human resources to be assimilated and developed through the process of learning by doing.[31] These are quite demanding conditions. However, they do not preclude catch-up processes for latecomers, if these "latecomers" quickly develop the proper environment. This is exactly what happened in the 1960s and 1970s in Japan, in the 1980s in the Asian Pacific, and, to a lesser extent, in the 1990s in Brazil and Chile. But the global experience of the 1990s suggests a different path of technological development. As soon as firms and individuals around the world accessed the new technological system (be it by technology transfer or endogenous adoption of technological know-how), they hooked up with producers and markets where they could use their knowledge and market their products. Their projection went beyond their national base, thus reinforcing the multinational corporations-based production networks, while, at the same time, these firms and individuals learned through their connections with these networks, and developed their own competitive strategies. So, there has been, at the same time, a process of concentration of technological know-how in transnational production networks, and a much broader diffusion of this know-how around the world, as the geography of trans-border production networks becomes increasingly complex.

[ . . . ]

In sum, while there is still a concentration of the stock of science and technology in a few countries, and regions, the flows of technological know-how increasingly diffuse around the world, albeit in a highly selective pattern. They are concentrated in decentralized, multidirectional production networks, which link up with university and research resources around the world. This pattern of technology generation and technology transfer contributes decisively to globalization, as it closely mirrors the structure and dynamics of transnational production networks, adding new nodes to these networks. The uneven development of science and technology de-localizes the logic of informational production from its country basis, and shifts it to multilocational, global networks.[32]

## Global Labor?

If labor is the decisive production factor in the informational economy, and if production and distribution are increasingly organized on a global basis, it would seem that we should witness a parallel process of globalization of labor. However, matters are far more complicated. [ . . . ]

There is, increasingly, a process of globalization of specialty labor. That is, not only highly skilled labor, but labor which becomes in exceptionally high demand around the world and, therefore, will not follow the usual rules in terms of immigration laws, wages, or working conditions. This is the case for high-level professional labor: top business managers, financial analysts, advanced services consultants, scientists and engineers, computer programmers, biotechnologists, and the like. But it is also the case for artists, designers, performers, sports stars, spiritual gurus, political consultants, and professional criminals. Anyone with the capacity to generate exceptional value added in any market enjoys the chance to shop around the globe – and to be shopped around, as well. This fraction of specialty labor does not add up to tens of millions of people, but it is decisive for the performance of business networks, of media networks, and of political networks, so that, overall, the market for most valuable labor is indeed becoming globalized.

On the other hand, for the huddled masses of the world, for those without exceptional skills, but with the stamina, or the desperation, to improve their living conditions, and to fight for their children's future, the record is mixed. By the end of the twentieth century an estimated 130–145 million people were living outside their countries, up from 84 million in 1975. Since these figures refer to legally recorded migration, the high number of undocumented immigrants would probably add many millions. Still, the total number of immigrants amounts to only a small fraction of the global labor force. A significant proportion of these migrants were in Africa and in the Middle East (some calculations put it at about 40 million migrants in 1993). In the 1990s there was a substantial increase of immigration in the United States, in Canada, in Australia, and, to a lesser extent, in Western Europe. There were also hundreds of thousands of new immigrants in countries which had little immigration until recently, as in the case of Japan.[33] A substantial proportion of this immigration is undocumented. However, the level of immigration in most Western countries does not exceed historical levels, in proportion to the native population. Thus, it seems that, together with increasing flows of immigration, what is really happening, and triggering xenophobic reactions, is the transformation of the ethnic make-up of Western societies. This is particularly the case in Western Europe, where many of the so-called immigrants were in fact born in their country of "immigration," but were being kept, in the late 1990s, as second-class citizens by barriers to naturalization: the situation of Turks in Germany, and of Koreans in Japan are examples of the use of the "immigrant" label as a code word for discriminated minorities. This trend toward multi-ethnicity in both North America and Western Europe will accelerate in the twenty-first century as a result of the lower birth rate of the native population, and as new waves of immigration are triggered by the growing imbalance between rich and poor countries.

A significant proportion of international migration is the result of wars and catastrophes, which displaced about 24 million refugees in the 1990s, particularly in Africa. While this trend is not necessarily related to globalization of labor, it does move millions of people around the world, in the wake of the globalization of human misery. Thus, as the 1999 United Nations *Human Development Report* states, "the global labour market is increasingly integrated for the highly skilled – corporate executives, scientists, entertainers, and the many others who form the global professional elite – with high mobility and wages. But the market for unskilled labour is highly restricted by national barriers."[34] While capital is global, and core production networks are increasingly globalized, the bulk of labor is local. Only an elite specialty labor force, of great strategic importance, is truly globalized.

However, beyond the actual movements of people across borders, there is a growing interconnection between workers in the country where they work, and the rest of the world, through global flows of production, money (remittances), information, and culture. The establishment of global production networks affects workers around the world. Migrants send their money home. Lucky entrepreneurs in their country of immigration often become middlemen between their country of origin and their country of residence. Networks of family, friends, and acquaintances grow over time, and advanced communication and transportation systems allow millions to live in-between countries. Thus, the study of "transnationalism from below," in the terminology of the leading researchers in this area, Michael P. Smith and Luis E. Guarnizo,[35] reveals a global networking of labor that goes beyond the simplistic notion of a global labor force – which, in a strict analytical sense, does not exist. In sum, while most labor is not globalized, throughout the world, there is increasing migration, increasing multi-ethnicity in most developed societies, increasing international population displacement, and the emergence of a multilayered set of connections between millions of people across borders and across cultures.

## The Geometry of the Global Economy: Segments and Networks

An additional qualification is essential in defining the contours of the global economy: it is not a planetary economy, albeit it has a planetary reach. In other words, the global economy does not embrace all economic processes in the planet, it does not include all territories, and it does not include all people in its workings, although it does affect directly or indirectly the livelihood of all humankind. While its effects reach out to the whole planet, its actual operation and structure concern only segments of economic sectors, countries, and regions, in proportions that vary according to the particular position of a sector, country, or region in the international division of labor.

In the midst of a substantial expansion of international trade, the share of less-developed countries in the value of world exports fell from 31.1 percent in 1950 to 21.2 percent in 1990. While the share of OECD countries in world exports of goods and services declined between the 1970s and 1996, it still counted for over two-thirds of total exports in the late 1990s [ ... ]. Most international trade takes place within the OECD area. Foreign direct investment follows a similar pattern. While the share of OECD countries over total FDI is significantly lower than in the 1970s, it still accounts for almost 60 percent. In 1997, FDI reached $400 billion, a seven-fold increase over the level of 1970, but 58 percent went to advanced industrial economies, 37 percent to developing countries, and 5 percent to the transition economies of Eastern Europe. Furthermore, FDI in developing countries, while rising substantially in the 1990s, is heavily concentrated in a few markets: 80 percent went to 20 countries, with the lion's share belonging to China, and, far behind, Brazil and Mexico. A similar pattern of selective globalization emerges in financial markets. In 1996, 94 percent of the portfolio and other short-term capital flow to developing countries and transitional economies went to just 20 countries. Only 25 developing countries have access to private markets for bonds, commercial bank loans, and equity. In spite of all the talk about emergent markets in global finance, in 1998 they only accounted for 7 percent of total market capitalization value, while representing 85 percent of the world's population.[36] As for production, in 1988, OECD countries, together with the four Asian tigers, accounted for 72.8 percent of world manufactures, a proportion that declined only slightly in the 1990s. The concentration is even greater in high-value production: in 1990, the G-7 countries accounted for 90 percent of high-technology manufacturing, and were holding 80.4 percent of global computing power.[37] Data collected by

UNESCO in 1990 indicated that scientific and technical manpower resources, in proportion to the population, were 15 times higher in North America than the average level for developing countries. R&D expenditures in North America represented over 42 percent of the world's total, while expenditures in Latin America and Africa together amounted to less than 1 percent of the same total.[38]

In sum, the global economy is characterized by a fundamental asymmetry between countries, in terms of their level of integration, competitive potential, and share of benefits from economic growth. This differentiation extends to regions within each country, as shown by Allen Scott in his investigation of new patterns of uneven regional development.[39] The consequence of this concentration of resources, dynamism, and wealth in certain territories is the increasing segmentation of the world population, following the segmentation of the global economy, and ultimately leading to global trends of increasing inequality and social exclusion.

This pattern of segmentation is characterized by a double movement: on the one hand, valuable segments of territories and people are linked in the global networks of value making and wealth appropriation. On the other hand, everything, and everyone, which does not have value, according to what is valued in the networks, or ceases to have value, is switched off the networks, and ultimately discarded. Positions in the networks can be transformed over time, by revaluation or devaluation. This places countries, regions, and populations constantly on the move, which is tantamount to structurally induced instability. For instance, in the late 1980s and throughout the 1990s, the dynamic centers of developing Asian economies, such as Thailand, the Philippines, and Indonesia, were connected to multinational production/trade networks, and global financial markets. The financial crisis of 1997–8 destroyed much of the newly acquired wealth of these countries. By the end of 1999, the Asian economies seemed to be on their path to recovery. But a substantial part of manufacturing, of the property market, and of the banking industry of these countries, and a large proportion of formal employment, had been wiped out by the crisis. Poverty and unemployment sky-rocketed. In Indonesia a process of de-industrialization and de-urbanization took place, as millions of people returned to the countryside, looking for survival [ . . . ]. The fall-out of the Asian crisis, of the Mexican crisis, of the Brazilian crisis, of the Russian crisis, shows the destructive power of volatility in the global economy. The new economic system is at the same time highly dynamic, highly selective, highly exclusionary, and highly unstable in its boundaries. Powered by new communication and information technologies, networks of capital, production, and trade are able to identify sources of value making anywhere in the world, and link them up. However, while dominant segments of all national economies are linked into the global web, segments of countries, regions, economic sectors, and local societies are disconnected from the processes of accumulation and consumption that characterize the informational, global economy. I do not pretend that these "marginal" sectors are not socially connected to the rest of the system, since there is no such thing as a social vacuum. But their social and economic logic is based upon mechanisms clearly distinct from those of the informational economy. While the informational economy shapes the entire planet, and in this sense it is indeed global, most people in the planet do not work for or buy from the informational, global economy. Yet all economic and social processes do relate to the structurally dominant logic of such an economy. How and why such a connection is operated, and who and what is connected and disconnected over time, are fundamental features of our societies which require specific, careful analysis [ . . . ].

## The Political Economy of Globalization: Capitalist Restructuring, Information Technology, and State Policies

A global economy, in the precise sense defined [here], emerged in the last years of the twentieth century.[40] It resulted from the restructuring of firms and financial markets in the wake of the 1970s' crisis. It expanded by using new information and communication technologies. It was made possible, and by and large induced, by deliberate government policies. The global economy was not created by markets, but by the interaction between markets and governments and international financial institutions acting on behalf of markets – or of their notion of what markets ought to be. [ . . . ]

Why did governments engage in this dramatic push for globalization, thus undermining their own sovereign power? If we reject dogmatic interpretations that would reduce governments to the role of being "the executive committee of the bourgeoisie," the matter is rather complex. It requires differentiating between four levels of explanation: the perceived strategic interests of a given nation-state; the ideological context; the political interests of the leadership; and the personal interests of people in office.

Concerning the interests of the state, the answer varies for each state. The answer is clear for the main globalizer, the US government: an open, integrated global economy works to the advantage of American firms, and American-based firms, thus of the American economy. This is because of the technological advantage, and superior managerial flexibility, that the US enjoys *vis-à-vis* the rest of the world. Together with the long-time presence of American multinationals around the world, and with American hegemonic presence in the international institutions of trade and finance, globalization is tantamount to increased economic prosperity for the US, although certainly not for all firms, and not for all people on American soil. This American economic interest is something that Clinton and his economic team, particularly Rubin, Summers, and Tyson, understood well. They worked hard to bring the liberal trade gospel to the world, applying US economic and political muscle when necessary.

For European governments, the Maastricht Treaty, committing them to economic convergence, and true unification by 1999, was their specific form of adopting globalization. It was perceived as the only way for each government to compete in a world increasingly dominated by American technology, Asian manufacturing, and global financial flows which had wiped out European monetary stability in 1992. Engaging global competition from the strength of the European Union appeared to be the only chance of saving European autonomy, while prospering in the new world. Japan adapted only reluctantly, but, forced by a serious, lasting recession, and a deep financial crisis, by the late 1990s introduced a series of reforms that would gradually open up the Japanese economy, and would align its financial rules on global standards [ . . . ]. China and India saw in the opening of world trade the opportunity to engage in a development process, and to build the technological and economic basis for renewed national power. The price to pay was a cautious opening to foreign trade and investment, thus linking their fate to global capitalism. For industrializing countries around the world, most of them with recent experience of economic crisis and hyperinflation, the new model of public policy held the promise of a new departure, and the significant incentive of support from major world powers. For the reformers who came to power in the transition economies in Eastern Europe, liberalization was tantamount to a definitive break with the communist past. And for many developing countries around the world, they did not even have to figure out their strategic interests: the IMF and the World Bank decided for them, as the price to repair their run down economies.

States' interests are always perceived within an ideological framework. And the framework of the 1990s was constituted around the collapse of statism, and the crisis of legitimacy suffered by welfarism and government control during the 1980s. Even in the Asian Pacific countries the developmental state suffered a crisis of legitimacy when it became an obstacle for democracy. Neo-liberal ideologues (called "neo-conservatives" in the US) came out of their closet around the world, and were joined in their crusade by new converts, striving to deny their Marxist past, from French *nouveaux philosophes* to brilliant Latin American novelists. When neo-liberalism, as the new ideology came to be known, spilled over its narrow-minded Reagan/Thatcher mold, to cast itself in a variety of expressions adapted to specific cultures, it quickly established a new ideological hegemony. In the early 1990s it came to constitute what Ignacio Ramonet labeled as "*la pensée unique*" ("the only thinking"). While the actual ideological debate was considerably richer, on the surface it did appear as if political establishments around the world had adopted a common intellectual ground: an intellectual current not necessarily inspired by Von Hayek and Fukuyama, but certainly a tributary of Adam Smith and Stuart Mill. In this context, free markets were expected to operate economic and institutional miracles, particularly when coupled with the new technological wonders promised by futurologists.

The political interest of new leaders coming to government in the late 1980s and early 1990s favored the globalization option. By political interest, I mean to be elected to government, and to stay in it. In most instances, new leaders were elected as a result of a declining, or sometimes collapsing, economy, and they consolidated their power by substantially improving the country's economic performance. This was the case for Clinton in 1992 (or, at least, so said flawed economic statistics, to George Bush's dismay). His successful presidential campaign was built around the motto "It's the economy, stupid!", and the key strategy of Clinton's economic policy was for further deregulation and liberalization, domestically and internationally, as exemplified by the approval of NAFTA in 1993. While Clinton's policy cannot really be credited as the cause of the outstanding performance of the US economy in the 1990s, Clinton and his team helped the dynamism of the new economy by getting out of the way of private business, and by using US influence to open markets around the world.

Cardoso was unexpectedly elected president of Brazil in 1994, on the basis of his successful monetary stabilization Plan Real, which he implemented as Finance Minister, breaking the back of inflation for the first time ever. To keep inflation under control he had to integrate Brazil into the global economy, facilitating the competitiveness of Brazilian firms. This goal, in turn, required financial stabilization. Similar developments took place in Mexico, with Salinas and Zedillo, economic reformers within the PRI; with Menem in Argentina, reversing the traditional nationalism of his Peronist party; with Fujimori in Peru, out of nowhere; with the new democratic government in Chile; and, much earlier, with Rajiv Gandhi in India, with Deng Xiao Ping, and later Jiang Zemin and Zhu-Rongji in China, and with Felipe Gonzalez in Spain.

In Russia, Yeltsin and his endless succession of economic teams played as their only card the integration of Russia into global capitalism, and they surrendered their economic sovereignty to the IMF, and to Western governments. In Western Europe, in the 1990s, the adjustment policies imposed by the Maastricht Treaty exhausted the political capital of incumbent governments, and opened the way for a new wave of economic reform. Blair in Britain, Romano Prodi and the Partito Democratico di Sinistra in Italy, and Schroeder in Germany, all betted on improving the economy, and fighting unemployment, by furthering liberal economic policies, tempered with innovative social policies. Jospin in France followed a pragmatic policy, without the ideological themes of liberalism, but with a *de facto* convergence with market-oriented European Union policies. The ironic twist of political history is that the reformers who enacted globalization, all over the world, came mostly from the left, breaking with their past as supporters of government control of the economy. It would be a mistake to consider this a proof of political opportunism. It was, rather, realism about new economic and technological developments, and a sense of the quickest way to take economies out of their relative stagnation.

Once the option for the liberalization/globalization of the economy was taken, political leaders were compelled to find the appropriate personnel to manage these post-Keynesian economic policies, often far removed from the traditional orientations of pro-government, left-wing policies. Thus, Felipe Gonzalez, coming to power in October 1982, in the midst of a grave economic and social crisis, appointed as Super-Minister of Economy one of the few socialists with personal entry into the conservative circles of Spanish high finance. The subsequent appointments of the appointee configured an entirely new class of neo-liberal technocrats throughout the Spanish socialist government, some of them recruited from IMF circles. In another example of this process, Brazil's President Cardoso, when faced by a monetary crisis running out of control in January 1999, fired two different presidents of Brazil's Central Bank in two weeks, and ended up appointing the Brazilian financier who used to manage the Soros hedge fund for Brazil, counting on his ability to deal with speculators in global financial markets. He in fact succeeded in calming down the financial turmoil, at least for a while. My argument is not that the financial world controls governments. It is in fact the contrary. For governments to manage economies in the new global context, they need personnel embodying the knowledge of daily survival in this brave new economic world. To do their job, these economic experts need additional personnel, who share similar skills, language, and values. Because they have the access codes to the management of the new economy, their power grows disproportionately to their actual political appeal. Therefore, they establish a symbiotic relationship with political leaders who come to power because of their appeal to voters. Together they work to improve their fate through their performance in global competition – in the hope that this will also benefit their shareholders, as citizens have come to be known.

There is a fourth layer of explanation concerning the fatal attraction of governments to economic globalization: the personal interests of people in positions of decision-making power. In general, this is not, by any means, the most important factor in explaining government policies toward globalization. And it is a negligible factor in some instances of high levels of government that I have been able to observe personally – for instance, in the Brazilian presidency in 1994–9. Yet, the personal vested interests of political leaders and/or their high-ranking personnel in the globalization process have exercised considerable influence in the speed and shape of globalization. These personal interests take, primarily, the form of increasing personal wealth obtained by two main channels. The first consists of the financial rewards, and lucrative appointments on leaving office, gained as a result of the network of contacts they have established and/or as appreciation of decisions which helped business deals. The second channel is, more blatantly, corruption in its different forms: bribes, taking advantage of insider knowledge on financial deals and real-estate acquisitions, participation in business ventures in exchange for political favors, and the like. Certainly, the personal business interests of political personnel (legal or illegal) are a very old story, probably a constant of politics in recorded history. Yet, my argument here is more specific: it favors pro-globalization policies because it opens up a whole new world of opportunity. In many developing countries, it is in fact the only game in town, since access to the country is the main asset controlled by the political elites, enabling them to participate in the global networks of wealth. For instance, the catastrophic management of the Russian economic transition cannot be understood without considering its overarching logic: the formation of a government-protected financial oligarchy, which rewarded personally many of the leading Russian liberal reformers (and decisively helped to re-elect Yeltsin in 1996), in exchange for the privilege of being the intermediaries between the Russian riches and global trade and investment – while the IMF was blinding itself to the matter, and using Western taxpayers' money to feed this liberal oligarchy with billions of dollars. Similar stories can be documented throughout Asia, Africa, and Latin America. But they are not absent either in North America and Western Europe. For instance, in 1999 a few weeks after the entire European Commission was forced to resign by the European Parliament, under strong suspicion of petty wrong-doing, the still-acting Commissioner for Telecommunications, Mr Bangemann, was appointed by Spanish Telefonica to a special consultant position in the company. While there were no explicit accusations of corruption, European public opinion was shocked to learn of the appointment of Mr Bangemann by a company which had greatly benefited from the deregulation of European telecommunications accomplished under Bangemann's tenure. These examples simply illustrate an important analytical point: political decisions cannot be understood in a personal and social vacuum. They are made by people who, besides representing governments, and holding political interests, have a personal interest in a process of globalization that has become an extraordinary source of potential wealth for the world's elites.

So, the global economy was politically constituted. Restructuring of business firms, and new information technologies, while being at the source of globalizing trends, could not have evolved, by themselves, toward a networked, global economy without policies of de-regulation, privatization, and liberalization of trade and investment. These policies were decided and enacted by governments around the world, and by international economic institutions. A political economy perspective is necessary to understand the triumph of markets over governments: governments themselves called for such a victory, in a historic death-wish. They did so to preserve/enhance the interests of their states, within the context of the emergence of a new economy, and in the new ideological environment that resulted from the collapse of statism, the crisis of welfarism, and the contradictions of the developmental state. In acting resolutely for globalization (sometimes hoping for a human face) political leaders also pursued their political interests, and often their personal interests, within various degrees of decency. Yet, the fact that the global economy was politically induced at its onset does not mean that it can be politically undone, in its main tenets. At least, not that easily. This is because the global economy is now a network of interconnected segments of economies, which play, together, a decisive role in the economy of each country – and of many people. Once such a network is constituted, any node that disconnects itself is simply bypassed, and resources (capital, information, technology, goods, services, skilled labor) continue to flow in the rest of the network. Any individual decoupling from the global economy implies a staggering cost: the devastation of the economy in the short term, and the closing of access to sources of growth. Thus, within the value system of productivism/consumerism, there is no individual alternative for countries, firms, or people. Barring a catastrophic meltdown of the financial market, or opting out by people following completely different values, the process of globalization is set, and it accelerates over time. Once the global economy has been constituted, it is a fundamental feature of the new economy.

[ … ]

## Notes

1  The best, and most comprehensive, analysis of globalization is Held et al. (1999). A key source of data and ideas is the 1999 United Nations' *Human Development Report* elaborated by UNDP (1999). A well-documented, journalistic report is *The New York Times* series "Global Contagion," published in February 1999: Kristoff (1999); Kristoff and Sanger (1999); Kristoff and WuDunn (1999); Kristoff and Wyatt (1999). Most data used in my analysis of economic globalization come from international institutions, such as the United Nations, the IMF, the World Bank, the World Trade Organization, and the OECD. Many of them are reported in the above-cited publications. For the sake of simplicity, I will not refer each figure to its specific source. This note should be considered to be a generic reference to data sources. I have also used in the general analysis underlying this section: Chesnais (1994); Eichengreen (1996); Estefania (1996); Hoogvelt (1997); Sachs (1998a, b); Schoettle and Grant (1998); Soros (1998); Friedmann (1999); Schiller (1999); Giddens and Hutton (2000).
2  Braudel (1967); Wallerstein (1974).
3  See Khoury and Ghosh (1987); Chesnais (1994); Heavey (1994); Shirref (1994); *The Economist* (1995); Canals (1997); Sachs (1998b, c); Soros (1998); Kristoff (1999); Kristoff and Wyatt (1999); Picciotto and Mayne (1999); Giddens and Hutton (2000); Zaloom (forthcoming).
4  Sassen (1991).
5  Chesnais (1994); Lee et al. (1994).
6  Soros (1998); Zaloom (forthcoming).
7  Tyson (1992); Hockman and Kostecki (1995); Krugman (1995); Held et al. (1999: 476–92).
8  World Bank (1998).
9  UNDP (1999).
10  Castells (1993); Cohen (1993).
11  Held et al. (1999: 168).
12  Anderson and Norheim (1993).
13  Held et al. (1999: 168).
14  Tyson (1992).
15  Cohen (1990); BRIE (1992); Sandholtz et al. (1992); World Trade Organization (1997, 1998).
16  UNCTAD (1995).
17  Daniels (1993).
18  IMF (1997); UNDP (1999).
19  UNDP (1999).
20  Reich (1991); Carnoy (1993); Dunning (1993); UNCTAD (1993, 1994, 1995, 1997); Graham (1996); Dicken (1998); Held et al. (1999: 236–82).

21  Cohen (1990); Porter (1990).
22  Imai (1990a, b); Dunning (1993); Howell and Woods (1993); Strange (1996); Dicken (1998).
23  Henderson (1989); Coriat (1990); Gereffi and Wyman (1990); Sengenberger and Campbell (1992); Gereffi (1993); Borrus and Zysman (1997); Dunning (1997); Ernst (1997); Held et al. (1999: 259–70).
24  Adler (1999); Saxenian (1999).
25  Reich (1991).
26  Gereffi (1999).
27  Freeman (1982); Dosi et al. (1988); Foray and Freeman (1992); World Bank (1998).
28  Sachs (1999); UNDP (1999).
29  Saxenian (1999).
30  Sachs (1999).
31  Mowery and Rosenberg (1998).
32  The analysis of global networks of innovative milieux, as exemplified by Silicon Valley, was pioneered by the late Richard Gordon; see Gordon (1994). For a collective discussion of Gordon's important intellectual insights, see the special issue "Competition and Change" of the *Journal of Global Political Economy* (May, 1998).
33  Campbell (1994); Stalker (1994, 1997); Massey et al. (1999); UNDP (1999).
34  UNDP (1999: 2).
35  Smith and Guarnizo (1998).
36  Data are from UNDP (1999); see also Sengenberger and Campbell (1994); Hoogvelt (1997); Duarte (1998); PNUD (1998a, b); UNISDR (1998); World Bank (1998); Dupas (1999).
37  CEPII (1992).
38  US National Science Board (1991).
39  Scott (1998).
40  For an empirical account of the process of globalization in different areas of the world during the 1980s and early 1990s, I refer the reader to the first edition of [my] *The Rise of the Network Society* (1996), chapter 2, section on "The Newest International Division of Labor", pp. 106–50. [ ... ]

## References

Adler, G. (1999) *Relationships between Israel and Silicon Valley in the software industry.* Berkeley, CA: University of California Press.

Anderson, K. and Norheim, H. (1993) Is world trade becoming more regionalised? *Review of International Economics* 1.

Borrus, M. G. and Zysman, J. (1997) Wintelism and the changing terms of global competition: prototype of the future. *BRIE working paper.* University of California, Berkeley, CA.

Braudel, F. (1967) *Civilisation materielle et capitalisme. XV–XVII siècle.* Paris: Armand Colin.

BRIE (1992) Globalization and Production. *BRIE working paper 45.* University of California.

Canals, J. (1997) *Universal Banking: International Comparisons and Theoretical Perspectives.* Oxford: Oxford University Press.

Carnoy, M. et al. (eds) (1993) *The New Global Economy in the Information Age.* University Park, PA: Penn State University Press.

Castells, M. (1993) The informational economy and the new international division of labour. In M. Carnoy et al., *The New Global Economy*, pp. 15–45.

CEPII (Centre d'Etudes Prospectives et d'Informations Internationales) (1992) *L'Economie mondiale 1990–2000: l'impératif de la croissance.* Paris: Economica.

Chesnais, F. (1994) *La Mondialisation du capital.* Paris: Syros.

Cohen, S. (1993) Geo-economics: lessons from America's mistakes. In M. Carnoy et al., *The New Global Economy*, pp. 97–147.

Cohen, S. (1990) Corporate nationality can matter a lot. Testimony before the US Congress Joint Economic Committee (September).

Coriat, B. (1990) *L'Atelier et le robot*. Paris: Christian Bourgois Editeur.

Daniels, P. W. (1993) *Service Industries in the World Economy*. Oxford: Blackwell.

Dicken, P. (1998) *Global Shift*. London: Chapman.

Dosi, G., Pavitt, K., et al. (eds) (1988) *The Economics of Technical Change and International Trade*. Brighton, Sussex: Wheatsheaf.

Duarte, F. (1998) *Global e local no mundo contemporaneo*. Sao Paulo: Editora Moderna.

Dunning, J. (1993) *Multinational Enterprises and the Global Economy*. Reading, MA: Addison-Wesley.

Dunning, J. (1997) *Alliance Capitalism and Global Business*. London: Routledge.

Dupas, G. (1999) *Economia global e exclusao social*. Sao Paulo: Paz e Terra.

Eichengreen, B. (1996) *Globalizing Capital: A History of the International Monetary System*. Princeton, NJ: Princeton University Press.

Ernst, D. (1997) From partial to systemic globalization: international production networks in the electronic industry. *BRIE working paper*. Berkeley, University of California.

Estefania, J. (1996) La nueva economía: La globalización. *Editorial Debate*. Madrid.

Foray, D. and Freeman, C. (1992) *Technologie et richesse des nations*. Paris: Economica.

Freeman, C. (1982) *The Economics of Industrial Innovation*. London: Pinter.

Friedmann, T. L. (1999) *The Lexus and the Olive Tree*. New York: Times Books.

Gereffi, G. (1993) Global Production Systems and Third World Development. *Global Studies Research Program, working paper series*. University of Wisconsin.

Gereffi, G. (1999) International trade and industrial upgrading in the apparel commodity chain. *Journal of International Economics* 48: 37–70.

Gereffi, G. and Wyman, D. (eds) (1990) *Manufacturing Miracles: Paths of Industrialization in Latin America and East Asia*. Princeton, NJ: Princeton University Press.

Giddens, A. and Hutton, W. (2000) *On the Edge*. London: Jonathan Cape.

Gordon, R. (1994) Internationalization, multinationalization, globalization: Contradictory world economies and new spatial divisions of labour. *Working paper 94*. University of California Center for the Study of Global Transformations.

Graham, E. (1996) *Global Corporations and National Governments*. Washington, DC: Institute for International Economics.

Heavey, L. (1994) Global integration. *Pension World* 30(7): 24–7.

Held, D., McGrew, A., et al. (1999) *Global Transformations: Politics, Economics and Culture*. Stanford, CA: Stanford University Press.

Henderson, J. (1989) *The Globalisation of High Technology Production: Society, Space and Semiconductors in the Restructuring of the Modern World*. London: Routledge.

Hockman, E. and Kostecki, G. (1995) *The Political Economy of the World Trading System: From GATT to WTO*. Oxford: Oxford University Press.

Hoogvelt, A. (1997) *Globalisation and the Postcolonial World: The New Political Economy of Development*. London: Macmillan.

Howell, J. and Woods, M. (1993) *The Globalization of Production and Technology*. London: Belhaven Press.

Imai, K. I. (1990a) *Joho netto waku shakai no tenbo [The information network society]*. Tokyo: Chikuma Shobo.

Imai, K. I. (1990b) *Jouhon Network Shakai no Tenkai [The development of information network society]*. Tokyo: Tikuma Shobou.

IMF (1997) *International Capital Markets*. Washington, DC: IMF.

Khoury, S. and Ghosh, A. (1987) *Recent Developments in International Banking and Finance*. Lexington, MA: D. C. Heath.

Kristoff, N. (1999) World ills are obvious, the cures much less so. *New York Times*: 1, 14–15.

Kristoff, N. and Sanger, D. E. (1999) How US wooed Asia to let cash flow in. *New York Times*: 1, 10–11.

Kristoff, N. and WuDunn, S. (1999) Of world markets, none an island. *New York Times*: 1, 8–9.

Kristoff, N. and Wyatt, E. (1999) Who went under in the world's sea of cash. *New York Times*: 1, 10–11.

Krugman, P. (1995) Growing world trade: causes and consequences. *Brookings Papers on Economic Activity*: 327–62.

Lee, P., King, P., et al. (1994) All change. *Euromoney* (June): 89–101.

Maddison, A. (1995) *Monitoring the World Economy, 1820–1992*. Paris: OECD Development Centre Studies.

Massey, D. R. et al. (eds) (1999) *Worlds in Motion: Understanding International Migration at the End of the Millennium*. Oxford: Clarendon Press.

Minigione, E. (ed.) (1996) *Urban Poverty and the Underclass*. Oxford: Blackwell.

Mowery, D. and Rosenberg, N. (1998) *Paths of Innovation: Technological Change in 20th-Century America*. Cambridge: Cambridge University Press.

Picciotto, S. and Mayne, R. (eds) (1999) *Regulating International Business: Beyond the MAI*. Oxford: Oxfam.

PNUD (Programa de Naciones Unidas para el Desarrollo) (1998a) *Desarrollo humano en Chile*. Santiago de Chile: Naciones Unidas.

PNUD (Programa de Naciones Unidas para el Desarrollo) (1998b) *Desarrollo humano en Bolivia*. La Paz: Naciones Unidas.

Porter, M. (1990) *The Competitive Advantage of Nations*. New York: Free Press.

Pritchett, L. (1995) Divergence, big time. *Policy Research Working Paper 1522*. Washington, DC: The World Bank.

Reich, R. (1991) *The Work of Nations*. New York: Random House.

Sachs, J. (1998a) International economics: Unlocking the mysteries of globalization. *Foreign Policy* (Spring): 97–111.

Sachs, J. (1998b) Proposals for reform of the global financial architecture. Paper prepared for the United Nations Development Programme meeting on the reform of global financial architecture, New York.

Sachs, J. (1998c) The IMF and the Asian Flu. *The American Prospect* (March–April): 16–21.

Sachs, J. (1999) Helping the world's poorest. *The Economist* (August 14): 17–20.

Sandholtz, W. et al. (1992) *The Highest Stakes: The Economic Foundations of the Next Security System*. New York: Oxford University Press.

Sassen, S. (1991) *The Global City: New York, London, Tokyo*. Princeton, NJ: Princeton University Press.

Saxenian, A. L. (1999) *Silicon Valley's New Immigrant Entrepreneurs*. San Francisco: Public Policy Institute of California.

Schiller, D. (1999) *Digital Capitalism: Networking in the Global Market System*. Cambridge, MA: MIT Press.

Schoettle, E. C. B. and Grant, K. (1998) Globalisation: A Discussion Paper. New York: The Rockefeller Foundation.

Scott, A. (1998) *Regions in the World Economy*. Oxford: Oxford University Press.

Sengenberger, W. and Campbell, D. (eds) (1992) *Is the Single Firm Vanishing? Inter-enterprise Networks, Labour, and Labour Institutions*. Geneva: International Institute of Labour Studies.

Sengenberger, W. and Campbell, D. (eds) (1994) *International Labour Standards and Economic Interdependence*. Geneva: International Institute for Labour Studies.

Shirref, D. (1994) The metamorphosis of finance. *Euromoney* (June): 36–42.

Smith, M. P. and Guarnizo, L. E. (eds) (1998) *Transnationalism from Below*. Brunswick, NJ: Transaction Books.

Soros, G. (1998) *The Crisis of Global Capitalism: Open Society Endangered*. New York: Perseus.

Stalker, P. (1994) *The Work of Strangers: a Survey of International Labour Migration*. Geneva: International Labour Organization.

Stalker, P. (1997) *Global Nations: The Impact of Globalization on International Migration*. Geneva: International Labour Office, Employment and Training Department.

Strange, S. (1996) *The Retreat of the State: The Diffusion of Power in the World Economy*. Cambridge: Cambridge University Press.

The Economist (1995) Currencies in a spin. *The Economist*: 69–70.

Tyson, L. d'A. (1992) *Who's Bashing Whom? Trade Conflict in High Technology Industries*. Washington, DC: Institute of International Economics.

UNISDR (United Nations Institute for Social Development Research) (1998) *Proceedings of the International Conference on Globalization and Inequality*. Geneva: published on-line.

United Nations Conference on Trade and Development (1993) World Investment Report 1993: Transnational Corporations and Integrated International Production. New York: UNCTAD.

United Nations Conference on Trade and Development (1994) World Investment Report 1994: Transnational Corporations, Employment and the Workplace. New York: UNCTAD.

United Nations Conference on Trade and Development (1995) World Investment Report 1995: Transnational Corporations and Competitiveness. New York: United Nations.

United Nations Conference on Trade and Development (1997) World Investment Report 1997: Transnational Corporations, Market Structure and Competition Policy. New York: United Nations.

United Nations Development Programme (1999) *Human Development Report 1999: Globalization with a Human Face*. New York: Oxford University Press.

US National Science Board (1991) *Science and Engineering Indicators: 1991*. Washington, DC: US Government Printing Office.

Wallerstein, I. (1974) *The Modern World System*. New York: Academic Press.

World Bank (1998) *World Development Report, 1998/99: Knowledge and Development*. Washington, DC: The World Bank.

World Trade Organization (1997) *Annual Report*. Geneva: WTO.

World Trade Organization (1998) *Annual Report*. Geneva: WTO.

Zaloom, C. (forthcoming) Risk, rationality and technology: prediction and calculative rationality in global financial markets. Berkeley, CA: University of California.

# 28

# The Limits to Economic Globalization

## Paul Hirst and Grahame Thompson

The 'globalization' of economic activity and the governance issues it raises are often thought to have appeared only after the Second World War, and particularly during the 1960s. The post-1960s era saw the emergence of MNC activity on the one hand and the rapid growth of international trade on the other. Subsequently, with the collapse of the Bretton Woods semi-fixed exchange rate regime in the 1971–3 period, the expansion of international securities investment and bank lending began in earnest as capital and particularly money markets rapidly internationalized, adding to the complexity of international economic relations and heralding what is often thought to be the genuine globalization of an integrated and interdependent world economy. In this chapter we scrutinize this popular history and trace the main periods of the internationalization of economic activity, which will be shown to have developed in a cyclical and uneven fashion. The key issue at stake in our assessment is the changing autonomy of national economies in the conduct of their economic activity.[1]

## MNCs, TNCs and International Business

The history of the internationalization of business enterprises is a long one, in no way confined just to the period since 1960. Trading activities, for instance, date from the earliest civilizations, but it was the Middle Ages in Europe that marked the initiation of systematic cross-border trading operations carried out by institutions of a private corporate nature (though often with strong state backing and support).
[ ... ]

However, it is the development of international manufacturing as the industrial revolution took hold that presents the closest precursor to the modern-day MNC. Here the early pre-eminence of British firms as multinational producers becomes apparent. Initially North and South America presented the most favourable investment opportunities, but these were soon followed by Africa and Australasia. There is some dispute as to whether 'colonial investments' should be considered a true precursor of foreign direct investment, but production abroad for the local market began in this way. Technical and organizational developments after the 1870s allowed a wider variety of similar products to be produced domestically and abroad within the boundaries of the same firm, while the exploration and development of minerals and other raw material products also attracted large amounts of FDI (Dunning 1993: ch. 5).
[ ... ]

[It] is generally agreed that manufacturing multinationals appeared in the world economy after the mid-nineteenth century and that they were well established by the First World War. International business activity grew vigorously in the 1920s as the truly diversified and integrated MNC matured, but it slowed down during the depressed 1930s and war-torn 1940s, and began a fluctuating expansion again after 1950. [ . . . ]

## Trade and International Integration

A better statistical base is available for exploring the trends in international trade. Again the history of this part of international economic activity goes back a long way. [ . . . ] A similar pattern emerges here as in the case of FDI, though perhaps more pronounced in its features. The volume of world foreign trade expanded at about 3.4 per cent per annum between 1870 and 1913. After 1913 trade was adversely affected by the growth of tariffs, quantitative restrictions, exchange controls and then war, and it expanded by less than 1 per cent per annum on average between 1913 and 1950. After 1950, however, trade really took off to grow at over 9 per cent per annum until 1973. Between 1973 and the mid-1980s the growth rate fell back to nearer the late nineteenth-century levels, with expansion at a rate of only 3.6 per cent [ . . . ].
[ . . . ]

The relationship between growth in output and in trade is a central one for international economics analysis. It is not our intention to explore the theoretical links between these here (see Kitson and Michie 1995). However, trade growth from 1853 to 1872 was already faster than the growth in world production, while from 1872 to 1911 it grew at about the same rate. Between 1913 and 1950 there was a devastating decline in both the rate of growth of trade (0.5 per cent per annum) and of output growth (1.9 per cent per annum). Only since 1950 has there been a consistent expansion of trade relative to production, even during the cyclical downturn after 1973 [ . . . ].

## Migration and the International Labour Market

A third broad area of analysis in the context of the history of the international economy concerns migration and its consequences for the integration of the global labour market. It is generally agreed that migration is becoming (or has become) a 'global phenomenon' (see, for instance, Serow et al. 1990: 159; Segal 1993: ch. 7; Castles and Miller 1993: ch. 4). However, by global these authors mean that, since the mid-1970s in particular, many more countries have been affected by migration, that there has been a growing diversity of areas of origin for migrants, and that migrants are of a wider range of socioeconomic statuses than ever before. Thus for these authors globalization registers a quantitative change in the extent and scope of migration rather than a feature of a potentially different socioeconomic order.

There are a number of different kinds of migrants. Clearly the early slave trade was a form of 'involuntary' migration (it is estimated that 15 million slaves were moved from Africa to the Americas before 1850: Castles and Miller 1993: 48). Refugees and asylum seekers can also be considered as migrants. But for the purposes of our analysis we focus on 'voluntary' migration. The period considered extends from the 'mass migration' after 1815 (mainly from Europe) to the emergence and extension of labour migration of the 'guest worker' variety after the Second World War.

It is difficult to judge exactly how many migrants there have been since 1815, so all the following numbers should be treated with some caution. Castles and Miller (1993) report that there could have been as many as 100 million migrants of all kinds in 1992 (including some 20 million refugees and asylum seekers, and 30 million overseas workers). They point out, however, that this represented only about 1.7 per cent of the world population. Thus the vast majority of the world's population remain in their country of origin.

The greatest era for recorded voluntary mass migration was the century after 1815 [ . . . ]. Around 60 million people left Europe for the Americas, Oceania, and South and East Africa. An estimated 10 million voluntarily migrated from Russia to Central Asia and Siberia. A million went from Southern Europe to North Africa. About 12 million Chinese and 6 million Japanese left their homelands and emigrated to East and South Asia. One and a half million left India for South East Asia and South and West Africa (Segal 1993: 16 – the statistics for Indian migration are probably severely underestimated here).

Between the two world wars international migration decreased sharply. To a large extent this was in response to the depressed economic conditions during much of the interwar period, but it was also due to restrictive immigration policies instigated in many of the traditional recipient countries, particularly the United States.

An upsurge in international migration began in the post-1945 period, particularly involving Europe and the United States once again (Livi-Bacci 1993). This was the period, however, of the relative growth of migration from the developing countries to the developed ones [ . . . ] and the introduction of the 'guest worker' phenomenon. During the 1970s and 1980s global trends favoured the controlled movements of temporary workers on a 'guest' basis, with entry for immigrants restricted to the highly skilled or those with family already in the country of destination.
[ . . . ]

## The Relative Openness and Interdependence of the International System

A key question posed by the preceding analysis is whether the integration of the international system has dramatically changed since the Second World War. Clearly, there has been considerable international economic activity ever since the 1850s, but can we compare different periods in terms of their openness and integration?

One way of doing this is to compare trade to GDP ratios. Table 1 provides information on these for a range of countries. Apart from the dramatic differences in the openness to trade of different economies demonstrated by these figures (compare the US and the Netherlands), the startling feature is that trade to GDP ratios were consistently higher in 1913 than they were in 1973 (with the slight exception of Germany where they were near enough equal). Even in 1995, Japan, the Netherlands and the UK were still less open than they were in 1913, with France and Germany only slightly more open. The US was the only country that was considerably more open than it was in 1913. [ . . . ]

**Table 1**  Ratio of merchandise trade to GDP at current prices (exports and imports combined), 1913, 1950, 1973 and 1995

|             | 1913  | 1950 | 1973 | 1995  |
|-------------|-------|------|------|-------|
| France      | 35.4  | 21.2 | 29.0 | 36.6  |
| Germany     | 35.1  | 20.1 | 35.2 | 38.7  |
| Japan       | 31.4  | 16.9 | 18.3 | 14.1  |
| Netherlands | 103.6 | 70.2 | 80.1 | 83.4  |
| UK          | 44.7  | 36.0 | 39.3 | 42.6[a] |
| US          | 11.2  | 7.0  | 10.5 | 19.0  |

[a] 1994.
*Sources*: Figures from 1913 to 1973 derived from Maddison 1987, table A-23, p. 695; figures for 1995 derived from *OECD National Accounts, 1997*, country tables

[...] [C]oncentrating on just the period after the Second World War shows a steady growth in trade openness, with a particularly dramatic entry of the East Asian economies into the international trading system.

Getting back to the longer-term trends, however, the evidence also suggests greater openness to capital flows in the pre-First World War period compared to more recent years. Grassman (1980), measuring 'financial openness' in terms of current account balance to GNP ratios, finds no increase in openness between 1875 and 1975: indeed there is a decline in capital movements for his leading six countries (Great Britain, Italy, Sweden, Norway, Denmark and the US). This is even the case for the post-Second World War period, though from the mid-1970s there is some sign of an increasing trend in financial openness. [...]

In addition, Lewis reports that capital exports rose substantially over the thirty years before the First World War, though they were subject to wide fluctuations. But when a comparison is made with the years 1953–73, the order of magnitude of capital exports was much lower in the latter period (Lewis 1981: 21). Finally, in a comprehensive comparison of the pre-1914 Gold Standard period with the 1980s, Turner (1991) also concludes that current account imbalances and capital flows, measured in relation to GNP, were larger before 1914 than in the 1980s.

Thus, using gross figures for ratios of trade and capital flows relative to output confirms that 'openness' was greater during the Gold Standard period than even in the 1990s. But these gross figures could disguise important differences between the periods. [...] [The] composition of output might be important in judging the real extent of interdependence. In the case of financial flows we should also recognize the change in their character and the significance of the financial regimes under which they took place. In the high Gold Standard period long-term capital dominated international capital flows. In the recent period there has been a switch to shorter-term capital. In addition, a wider range of countries have now been included under the international capital movement umbrella. [...]

Moving away from trade and capital flows for the moment, we can now look at the implications of the trends in international migration. First, it must be emphasized that these are contained within the twin considerations of the labour market and governmental policy. A world market for labour just does not exist in the same way that it does for goods and services. Most labour markets continue to be nationally regulated and only marginally accessible to outsiders, whether legal or illegal migrants or professional recruitment. Moving goods and services is infinitely easier than moving labour. Even a rapid and sustained expansion of the world economy is unlikely to significantly reduce the multiple barriers to the movement of labour. Other than in the context of regionally developing free trade agreements of the EU type, freedom of labour movement still remains heavily circumscribed. Even the NAFTA explicitly excludes freedom of movement of persons, though there is *de facto* freedom between Canada and the US, and enormous illegal flows between Mexico and the US. Extraregional migration of all kinds is a small percentage of global labour movements. Most migration is of the country next door variety. During the nineteenth century the mass movement of workers to the sources of capital was accepted and encouraged; now it is rejected except as a temporary expedient.

In as much as there is global international migration for employment, it is concentrated on the Gulf states, North America and Western Europe. A crude estimate of this category gives a figure of about 20 million in 1990 (prior to the Gulf War, which saw a massive return home, particularly of Third World migrant workers, from the Gulf states). This form of international labour force reached its peak in the early 1970s. The worldwide recession and subsequent developments like the Gulf War interrupted the growth of temporary migrant employment. A large proportion of these workers are illegally residing and working abroad. Legal expatriate workers tend to be in the managerial, skilled and technical employment categories.

[ . . . ]

Two sets of more general points are worth making in the light of these remarks. The first is that there have been phases of massive international migration over many centuries and there seems nothing unprecedented about movements in the post-Second World War period, or those in more recent decades. The second related point is that in many ways the situation between 1815 and 1914 was much more open than it is today. The supposed era of 'globalization' has not seen the rise of a new unregulated and internationalized market in labour migration. In many ways, the world's underprivileged and poor have fewer international migratory possibilities nowadays than they had in the past. At least in the period of mass migration there was the option to uproot the whole family and move in the quest for better conditions, a possibility that seems to be rapidly shrinking for equivalent sections of the world's population today. They have little choice but to remain in poverty and stick it out. The 'empty lands' available to European and other settlers in the US and Canada, South America, southern Africa and Australia and New Zealand just do not exist today, with a concomitant loss of 'freedom' for the world's poor.

Things look different for the well off and privileged, however. Those with professional qualifications and technical skills still have greater room for manoeuvre and retain the option to move if they wish. The 'club class' with managerial expertise, though relatively few in number in terms of the global population, are the most obvious manifestation of this inequity in long-term migratory opportunities.

Another strong contemporary feature of the international system that is often invoked as an indicator of 'globalization' is the emergence of large discriminatory regional trading blocs like the EU, NAFTA and APEC (Asia-Pacific Economic Cooperation). [ . . . ] [H]ere it is worth pointing to the historical precedents for these kinds of bodies. A marked discrimination in trade and investment patterns was produced during the colonial empire period in the nineteenth century. For the French and British empires the biases to trade between the colonial power and its colonies were between two and four times greater than would have been expected given the 'natural' economic fundamentals that determine trade, such as the size of the countries involved, GDP per capita, proximity and common borders. The biases were even higher for Belgium, Italy and Portugal and their overseas dependencies. In fact, the concentration of trade with the countries that made up British and French empires did not peak until 1938; it declined steadily following the independence movements after the Second World War, but did not reach unity until as late as 1984 (Frankel 1997: 126). Trade within the Austro-Hungarian Empire, before it broke up at the end of the First World War, was also four or five times what it would have been if determined simply by the natural fundamentals (Frankel 1997: 119). [ ... ]

Thus it was in the 1930s that regionalism was probably at its height. There was a definite discriminatory sterling bloc, overlapping imperfectly with the British Empire/Commonwealth. Then there was a group of countries that remained on the Gold Standard, and a subsection of central and south-eastern European countries that gravitated towards Germany. The US erected trade barriers, and formed a partial dollar bloc with the Spanish-speaking countries adjacent to North America. According to Frankel, all these were heavily discriminatory – though some more than others – except for the partial dollar bloc (Frankel 1997: 127–8). The differences between the blocs have, however, been emphasized by Eichengreen and Irwin (1995, 1997). Sterling bloc countries traded disproportionately among themselves, and discrimination increased during the 1930s, while those remaining on the Gold Standard were more disparate. In as much as they erected barriers between themselves, this reduced trade discrimination.

There have thus been several earlier periods of regionalization, some of which were more intense than the present period. What is distinctive about the present situation, however, is the formation of larger formal *de jure* free trade area (FTA) blocs, and the extension of their *de facto* influence over a wider range of countries and areas. For the first time there are three almost continent-wide blocs (that is the EU, NAFTA, and Japan plus some of East Asia) either firmly established or in proto-existence.

As a preliminary conclusion, then, we can say that the international economy was in many ways more open in the pre-1914 period than at any time since, including from the late 1970s onwards. International trade and capital flows, both between the rapidly industrializing economies themselves and between these and their various colonial territories, were more important relative to GDP levels before the First World War than they probably are today. Add to this the issue of international migration just explored and we have an extraordinarily developed, open and integrated international economy at the beginning of this century. Thus the present position is by no means unprecedented.

[ ... ]

## Openness and Integration: What is at Stake?

Returning to the broad issue of integration preliminarily discussed above, the actual measurement of the degree of integration in financial markets is difficult both theoretically and empirically. Economic analysis in this area tends to be driven by the idea of 'efficient (international) financial market' theory; that is, that capital markets operate competitively to allocate (international) savings and investment so as to equalize returns on capital. Thus key indicators of the degree of integration would be measures such as interest rates as between countries or the value of the same shares on domestic and international stock markets: the nearer these are to equality as between different national financial markets, the more integrated the international economy has become. With a fully integrated capital market there would be single international rates of interest on short-term and long-term loans, and a single share or bond price, other things remaining equal.

Of course, the key constraint here is the 'other things remaining equal' one. In reality they just do not, so the task of empirical analysis from within this dominant perspective is to account for, and then adjust for, these 'imperfections' so as to arrive at a proxy measure of the degree of 'true' integration. [ . . . ] As might be expected, all this requires some formidable assumptions to be made, ones that few other than the truly converted *cognoscenti* might either appreciate or accept. However, despite some scepticism about this underlying approach, it is worth considering its main results. [ . . . ]

The degree of international financial integration could be analysed in a number of forms and at a number of levels (Frankel 1992; Herring and Litan 1995; Harris 1995). These can be grouped under three overlapping headings: those associated with interest rate differentials; those associated with differential prices of securities; and those associated with real resource flows and capital mobility. We deal with each of these in turn, beginning with a discussion of the relationships between interest rates and exchange rates.

One of the most straightforward indicators of financial integration concerns offshore markets like that for Eurocurrencies. Formally, measures of offshore financial market integration can be established in terms of covered interest rate parities. This implies that depositors can receive the same return on whatever Eurocurrency they hold, taking into account the cost involved in protecting against possible exchange rate changes. Such interest rate parity seems to hold in the Eurocurrency markets. A more developed form of integration would be when offshore and onshore markets are closely linked, but it is here that difficulties begin to arise. Banking regulations and capital controls establish a separation between these two spheres, and these have often been introduced and maintained for public policy reasons. But with the progressive harmonization of banking regulations and the abandonment of capital controls this form of integration was effectively established between the advanced countries by 1993: thus covered interest rate parity between national rates has now also been more or less achieved.

Deeper forms of integration would be signalled by first uncovered interest rate parity and then real interest rate parity between deposits in different currencies. [ . . . ] While tests to measure the presence of these latter two forms of integration are complex and controversial, real interest rate parity seemed far from established by the mid-1990s, so that the level of international financial integration fell short of what would prevail in a truly integrated system. By contrast, the Gold Standard period was one where short-term interest rates were closely correlated, and there was a strong tendency for real rates of return to be equalized internationally (Turner 1991: 16–17).

The second broad approach is to focus on asset prices in different national financial systems. Here one problem is to distinguish domestic influences on prices from international ones, but there is a *prima facie* case that stock markets are closely linked, with disruption in one being quickly transmitted to others (so-called 'contagion'). In this context it is changes in the 'volatility' of price movements that would represent an indicator of increased globalization, not the existence of links as such, and the evidence on this score remains at best ambiguous (Harris 1995: 204–6). In fact, historically based studies have reinforced the impression of greater financial integration, measured in these terms, in the pre-First World War period. [ . . . ] Zevin [1992], in his survey of a wide range of the financial integration literature, reports on a number of measures supporting the highly integrated nature of the pre-First World War international economy. [ . . . ] The Gold Standard period was thus also the one displaying the most interdependent and integrated international economy in terms of security markets, the extent of which seems yet to have been repeated.

How did the international financial system adjust so rapidly when technological developments were so primitive? In fact, the idea that the contemporary era of communications technology is unprecedented again needs to be challenged. The coming of the electronic telegraph system after 1870 in effect established more or less instantaneous information communications between all the major international financial and business centres (Standage 1998). By the turn of the century a system of international communications had been established that linked parties together much in the way that the contemporary Internet does. Although the networks were not so developed in terms of individual subscribers, corporate and institutional linkages were dense and extensive. Compared to a reliance on the sailing ship (and even steam propulsion), the telegraph marked a real qualitative leap in communications technology, in many ways more important than the shift into computer technology and telematics after 1970.

A third important related approach in trying to identify the extent of financial integration involves measuring real resource flows: can increased financial integration be implied from increased capital mobility? In this case it is the relationship between national savings and investment that becomes the object of analysis. This approach has generated the most extensive literature, but its results remain controversial.

The more integrated the capital markets, the more mobile capital will become internationally and the more likely it is that domestic savings and investment will diverge. If there were a completely integrated global financial system, domestic investment would not be fundamentally constrained by domestic savings, and the correlation between savings and investment would be broken. Thus national economies will lose their ability to 'regulate' or 'determine' domestic investment. In fact, this is just another way of pointing to the key role of interest rate differentials as a measure of integration and as the determinant of investment. As openness increases, domestic savings become irrelevant to domestic investment since interest rates converge and savings and investment adjust accordingly.

But national savings–investment correlations have not unambiguously declined in the 1980s and 1990s, during the period of capital market liberalization and floating exchange rates. Careful analysis by Bosworth (1993: 98–102) and by Obstfeld (1993, e.g. p. 50) shows this not to be the case [ . . . ]. The persistence of the correlation between national savings and investment, first established in 1980 (Feldstein and Horioka 1980), well into a period of financial liberalization, deregulation and supposed global integration, testifies to the continued robust relative autonomy of financial systems, and this despite the (sometimes desperate) attempts by conventional economic analysts to prove otherwise (e.g. Bayoumi 1990).

[ . . . ]

So long as governments continue to target their current accounts, retain some sovereignty within their borders (so that at least the threat of government intervention in cross-border capital movements remains) and differentially regulate their financial systems, investors cannot think about domestic and foreign assets in the same way. Different national financial systems are made up of different institutions and arrangements, with different conceptions of the future and assessments of past experience, and thus operate with different modalities of calculation. All these features factor into a continued diversity of expectations and outlooks which cannot all be reduced to a single global marketplace or logic. What is more, even the most committed of the integrationists who have looked at national savings–investment correlations tend to conclude that the less developed countries (LDCs) and most NICs remain largely out of the frame as far as this form of financial integration is concerned. Thus, even for the integration enthusiasts, there are limits to the extent of the 'globalization' of financial markets.[2]

[ . . . ]

The importance of this assessment of openness and integration is obvious. It has to do with the ability of distinct national economies to devise and regulate their own economic policies. The fact that the degree of constraint on national economies in the Gold Standard period seems to have been consistently greater than at any time since should not blind us to the problems and issues facing economies because of the level of integration at the present time. It is certainly the case that, on the basis of some of the measures discussed above, the level of economic integration has increased since 1960 – though this is not obvious on just the savings–investment measure, except perhaps for the most recent period. In addition, it would be difficult to accept that the qualitative dimension has been constant over the entire period since 1870. The number and range of financial instruments has changed dramatically since 1960, for instance, and with them new problems of management and regulation have arisen (Turner 1991; Cosh et al. 1992). Before we look at the internationalization of money and short-term capital markets, however, we need to look to the more mundane areas of financial integration to see whether the underlying framework for the operation of capital markets has radically changed in the recent period. Money markets are probably more highly integrated than are capital markets. But it is capital markets that most immediately affect the economic prospects for the long-term growth of national economies.

## Recent Developments in International Financial Market Activity

These issues can be first approached by investigating the cross-border transactions and holdings of bonds and equities between countries and in various domestic financial institutions. As a percent of GDP the cross-border *transactions* in bonds and equities have escalated since the mid-1970s [ . . . ]. But if this is looked at from a slightly different angle, changes may not appear quite so dramatic.

[ . . . ]

What the figures [ . . . ] demonstrate, however, is the enormous variation between countries in terms of the importance of foreign holdings. Some financial systems are

clearly much more 'open' than others on this measure. Of the G5 countries, the UK and Japan are much more 'open' than are the US, Germany and France.
[ . . . ]

[W]hat is clear is that there is no obvious convergence of all the advanced countries to a common openness position. By and large the differences between them seem to have been maintained, indicating continued variation in the characteristics and structures of their domestic financial systems. Thus, up to the mid-1990s at least, the operation of 'globalization' did not seem to have forced the domestic financial institutions of the advanced countries to have fundamentally broken with the historical variation in their character, though there had been some increase in their overall internationalization.

[ . . . ]

Similar comments could be made about the operation of commercial banks. An increase in the importance of foreign assets and liabilities in their balance sheets is [ . . . ] mainly attributable to a growth between 1960 and 1980, since when the positions have tended to stabilize. [ . . . ] But there remains a great variation between [ . . . ] economies [ . . . ] largely based on entrenched historical differences.

The final point to make here is to look at the 'bottom line', as it were, of the internationalization of financial systems by assessing the importance of foreign assets ultimately owned by households as a proportion of their total financial assets. Thus we are still concentrating on the holdings only of financial assets, but looking at their importance in household wealth. The problem with the figures presented so far is that they do not cover the entire financial system. [ . . . ]

[ . . . ] A variation between countries similar to the patterns outlined above emerges, and with great diversity among them. But only two countries show a foreign proportion of over 15 per cent. Around 10 per cent and below is the norm. Broadly speaking, then, people's financial wealth still remains a domestic affair: it stays at home.

[ . . . ]

## Short-term Lending

Broadly speaking, the period since the liberalization moves of the 1970s has seen an upsurge in international financial activity associated with three developments: increased extent of international lending, financial innovation and financial agglomeration. [ . . . ]

[ . . . ] In 1998 it was anticipated that total loans would be over US$2,000 billion – a 2,000-fold increase on the late 1970s position. A key development is the growth of 'securitization': the displacement of conventional loan business (traditionally conducted by banks) by the issue of marketable bonds and other securities. [ . . . ]

[ . . . ] Since most of these are derivative of the move towards security lending – they provide borrowers and lenders with the possibility of hedging against the risk of interest rate and exchange rate movements – they are collectively termed 'derivatives'.

[ . . . ]

[ . . . ] By 1991 their worth was larger than that of exchange-traded instruments and was more than 50 per cent that of the total of foreign currency claims of all banks reporting to the Bank for International Settlements (BIS). They have shown spectacular growth during the 1990s. Such instruments are often traded 'off-balance sheet' – they earn a fee income rather than constituting part of a financial institution's asset or liability structure. These developments provide opportunities for intermediaries to engage in risk arbitrage in a lower-cost and less regulated environment, but they thereby raise important new problems of systemic exposure to risk. [ . . . ]

Financial innovation continues apace. The latest developments represent a resurgence of bond instruments with so-called 'dragon bonds' and 'global bonds'. 'Dragon bonds' are issued and traded simultaneously just on East Asian markets, while their 'global' counterparts are issued and traded in all major international financial centres on a round-the-clock basis. After the first global bond was marketed by the World Bank in 1989, this market expanded to over US$100 billion by mid-1994, capturing 8 per cent of total external bond issue in that year (OECD 1994: 57, table 1).

This latest development in bond markets testifies to the strength of the trend towards internationalization in the world's financial systems. But as mentioned above, the penetration of foreign assets into domestic institutional investment markets is still relatively light. The US, in particular, remains highly undiversified and autonomous on this score. In as much as global trading of securities and derivatives exists, it still tends to remain within a single region (North America, Europe or Asia-Pacific).

But again there is a trend in the government bond market towards further openness. The average foreign penetration of national government bond markets in advanced countries increased from 10 per cent in 1983 to 15 per cent in 1989 (Turner 1991); for the EU countries, it increased only from 19 per cent in 1987 to 26 per cent in 1993 (European Union 1997: 14, table 13).

The final issue to discuss in this subsection is the development of financial conglomerates. The international financial services industry is increasingly characterized by a small number of highly capitalized securities and banking houses which are global players with diversified activities. In part this is the result of the continuing trend towards predominantly institutional investment. 'Collective saving' is a strengthening feature of all OECD countries, so the institutions managing these funds could become key international players.

Broadly speaking, there is worldwide excess capacity in this industry, leading to intense competitive pressures to which cost-cutting and diversification are the strategic commercial responses. As a result, the financial conglomerates operate through very complex and often opaque corporate structures. Attempts at risk transfer between a shrinking number of players are legion, and even between the different components of the companies themselves. Thus contagion risk, market risk and systemic risk have all increased, presenting new and important regulatory problems for governments and international bodies [ . . . ].

An important point to note about the present era as compared with the Gold Standard period is that the recent growth of international lending has not just dramatically increased the range of financial instruments: it has changed the whole character of capital flows. As mentioned above, late nineteenth-century lending was mainly long term in nature, going to finance investment in real assets. Even that part of total flows consisting of investment in financial assets was mainly used to finance real investment. This is no longer so. The explosion of aggregate lending had until very recently been made up almost exclusively of financial assets. Only since the mid-1980s has substantial real investment reappeared with the growth of FDI [ . . . ].

[ . . . ]

# Conclusion

We have striven to argue a number of points [here]. First, that the level of integration, interdependence, openness, or however one wishes to describe it, of national economies in the present era is not unprecedented. Indeed, the level of autonomy under the Gold Standard in the period up to the First World War was much lower for the advanced economies than it is today. This is not to minimize the level of integration now, or to ignore the problems of regulation and management it throws up, but merely to register a certain scepticism over whether we have entered a radically new phase in the internationalization of economic activity.

The second point has been to argue that governance mechanisms for the international economy have been in place over almost the entire twentieth century, in one form or another. This is just as much the case today as it was at the turn of the century. We may not like the particular mechanisms that are established now and how they work, but they are there all the same. The issue then becomes how to devise better or more appropriate ones.

Thirdly, we have argued that there are some new and different issues of economic interdependence in the present era which are particular to it. Our argument is not that things have remained unchanged: quite fundamental reorganizations are going on in the international economy to which an imaginative response is desperately needed. [...]

Finally, we have traced the trajectory of 'national economic autonomy' through the various regimes of governance operating over the twentieth century. This has shown that such autonomy has oscillated between periods of strong and then weak forces, and that it has operated with various degrees of effectiveness. Perhaps the overall trajectory of this assessment is to point to the impossibility of complete national economic autonomy as the twentieth century has progressed. The debacle of the floating rates regime of 1974–85 seems, if nothing else, to have confirmed the demise of this form of governance as a viable long-term objective in the present era. [...]

## Notes

1  By the term 'autonomy' we mean the ability of the authorities in a national economy to determine their own economic policy and implement that policy. This is obviously a matter of degree. Autonomy is closely linked to 'openness', 'interdependence' and 'integration', three other categories used [here]. Openness implies the degree to which national economies are subject to the actions of economic agents located outside their borders and the extent to which their own economic agents are orientated towards external economic activity. This is in turn linked to the degree of interdependence of the economic system in which these agents operate. Thus interdependence expresses the systemic links between all economic activity within a system or regime. Integration is the process by which interdependence is established.

2  Of course this emphasis on the relationship between domestic savings and domestic investment might seem to reinforce the neoclassical view of investment determination. The critique of this from an essentially post-Keynesian perspective is that the constraint on investment is not savings but the ability to raise finance for investment. In an advanced industrial economy with a developed financial system, credit creation is the key to investment; it is the access to 'liquidity' that determines economic activity, and this is endogenously created.

Formally we would agree with this analysis for mature advanced economies with a developed banking system operating efficiently in an essentially stable financial environment. However, we would emphasize that there are two exceptions to this image. The first is for those societies that remain less developed, that have an *underdeveloped* banking system in particular. The second is for those economies that have an *overdeveloped* financial system typified by speculation and instability. In both these cases, the 'normal' financing system for investment either just does not exist, or breaks down in the face of speculative pressures. In addition, we would argue that it is this second case that increasingly typifies the position faced in the advanced industrial countries. In both of these cases, however, we are thrown back on to a more 'primitive' conception of what determines investment, namely the brute fact of national savings.

# References

Banuri, T. and Schor, J. B. (eds) (1992) *Financial Openness and National Autonomy*. Oxford: Clarendon Press.

Bayoumi, T. (1990) Saving–investment correlations: immobile capital, government policy or endogenous behaviour? *IMF Staff Papers* 37(2): 360–87.

Bosworth, B. P. (1993) *Saving and Investment in a Global Economy*. Washington DC: Brookings Institution.

Castles, S. and Miller, M. J. (1993) *The Age of Mass Migration*. Basingstoke: Macmillan.

Cosh, A. D., Hughes, A. and Singh, A. (1992) Openness, financial innovation, changing patterns of ownership, and the structure of financial markets. In Banuri and Schor 1992.

Dunning, J. H. (1993) *Multinational Enterprises and the Global Economy*. Wokingham: Addison-Wesley.

Eichengreen, B. and Irwin, D. A. (1995) Trade blocs, currency blocs and the reorientation of world trade in the 1930s. *Journal of International Economics* 38: 1–24.

Eichengreen, B. and Irwin, D. A. (1997) The role of history in bilateral trade flows. In J. A. Frankel (ed.), *The Regionalization of the World Economy*, Chicago: University of Chicago Press.

European Union (1997) Advancing financial integration. In *European Economy, Supplement A: Economic Trends* 12 (Dec.), EU, Brussels.

Feldstein, M. and Horioka, C. (1980) Domestic savings and international capital flows. *Economic Journal* 90 (June): 314–29.

Frankel, J. A. (1992) Measuring international capital mobility: a review. *American Economic Review* 82(2): 197–202.

Frankel, J. A. (1997) *Regional Trading Blocs in the World Economic System*. Washington DC: Institute for International Economics.

Grassman, S. (1980) Long-term trends in openness of national economies. *Oxford Economic Papers* 32(1): 123–33.

Harris, L. (1995) International financial markets and national transmission mechanisms. In J. Michie and J. Grieve Smith (eds), *Managing the Global Economy*, Oxford: Oxford University Press.

Herring, R. J. and Litan, R. E. (1995) *Financial Regulation in the Global Economy*. Washington DC: Brookings Institution.

Kitson, M. and Michie, J. (1995) Trade and growth: a historical perspective. In J. Michie and J. Grieve Smith (eds), *Managing the Global Economy*, Oxford: Oxford University Press.

Lewis, A. (1981) The rate of growth of world trade, 1830–1973. In S. Grassman and E. Lundberg (eds), *The World Economic Order: Past and Prospects*, Basingstoke: Macmillan.

Livi-Bacci, M. (1993) South–North migration: a comparative approach to North American and European experiences. In *The Changing Course of Migration*, Paris: OECD.

Maddison, A. (1987) Growth and slowdown in advanced capitalist economies: techniques of quantitative assessment. *Journal of Economic Literature* 25(2): 649–98.

Obstfeld, M. (1993) International capital mobility in the 1990s. NBER Working Paper 4534, National Bureau of Economic Research, Cambridge, Mass.

OECD (1992) *International Direct Investment: Policies and Trends in the 1980s*. Paris: OECD.

OECD (1994) *Financial Market Trends*. Paris: OECD.

Segal, A. (1993) *Atlas of International Migration*. London: Hans Zell.

Serow, W. J. et al. (eds) (1990) *Handbook on International Migration*. New York: Greenwood Press.

Standage, T. (1998) *The Victorian Internet: The Remarkable Story of the Telegraph and the Nineteenth Century Online Pioneers*. London: Weidenfeld and Nicolson.

Turner, P. (1991) Capital flows in the 1980s: a survey of major trends. *BIS Economic Papers*, no. 30, Bank for International Settlements, Geneva.

Zevin, R. (1992) Are world financial markets more open? If so, why and with what effects? In Banuri and Schor 1992.

# 29

# The Nation-State in the Global Economy

## *Robert Gilpin*

The idea that the nation-state has been undermined by the transnational forces of economic globalization has appeared in writings on the international system and on the international economy. Many writings have argued that international organizations (IOs) and nongovernmental actors are replacing nation-states as the dominant actors in the international system. Books that have made this claim include those with such dramatic titles as *The Retreat of the State*, *The End of Geography*, and the *End of Sovereignty?*[1] Daniel Yergin and Joseph Stanislaw maintain that the market has wrested control from the state over the commanding heights of the economy and that the economic role of the nation-state is just about at an end.[2] Other writers believe a global economy has emerged or is emerging in which distinct national economies no longer exist and national economic policies are no longer possible.[3] This chapter disagrees with such views and argues that the nation-state continues to be the major actor in both domestic and international affairs.

At the beginning of the twenty-first century, the nation-state is clearly under serious attack from both above and below, and there is no doubt that there have been very important changes. Within many nations, the politics of identity and ethnic conflict is challenging the integrity of states, as ethnic and regional groups seek independence or at least greater autonomy.[4] Yet it is important to understand that the Kurds, Palestinians, and many other groups all want nation-states of their own; they do not wish to eliminate nation-states but to divide present nation-states into units that they themselves can control. It is also accurate to say that economic globalization and transnational economic forces are eroding economic sovereignty in important ways. Nevertheless, both the extent of globalization and the consequences of economic globalization for the nation-state have been considerably exaggerated. For better or for worse, this is still a state-dominated world.

As Vincent Cable of the Royal Institute of International Affairs (London) has noted, it is not easy to assess globalization's implications for the nation-state.[5] Although the economic role of the state has declined in certain significant ways, it has expanded in others and, therefore, it is inaccurate to conclude that the nation-state has become redundant or anachronistic. As Cable says, the situation is "much messier" than that. The impact of the global economy on individual nations is highly uneven, and its impact varies from issue to issue; finance is much more globalized than are services and industrial production. While globalization has reduced some policy options, the degree of reduction is highly dependent on national size and economic power; the United States and Western Europe, for example, are much less vulnerable to destabilizing financial flows than are small economies. Indeed, the importance of the state has even actually increased in some areas, certainly with respect to promoting international competitiveness through support for R&D, for technology policy, and for other assistance to domestic firms.

Economic globalization is much more limited than many realize, and consequently, its overall impact on the economic role of the state is similarly limited. Moreover, although economic globalization has been a factor in whatever diminishment of the state may have occurred, ideological, technological, and international political changes have had an even more powerful influence. Furthermore, many and perhaps most of the social, economic, and other problems ascribed to globalization are actually due to technological and other developments that have little or nothing to do with globalization. Even though its role may have diminished somewhat, the nation-state remains preeminent in both domestic and international economic affairs. To borrow a phrase from the American humorist Mark Twain, I would like to report that the rumors of the death of the state "have been greatly exaggerated."[6]

## The Limited Nature of Economic Globalization

In one sense, globalization has been taking place for centuries whenever improvements in transportation and communications have brought formerly separated peoples into contact with one another. The domestication of the horse and camel, the invention of the sailing ship, and the development of the telegraph all proved powerful instruments for uniting people, although not always to their liking. For thousands of years, ideas, artistic styles, and other artifacts have diffused from one society to another and have given rise to fears similar to those associated with economic globalization today. Nevertheless, it is important to discuss the economic globalization that has resulted from the rapid economic and technological integration of national societies that took place in the final decades of the twentieth century, especially after the end of the Cold War. This recent global economic integration has been the result of major changes in trade flows, of the activities of multinational corporations, and of developments in international finance.

Despite the increasing significance of economic globalization, the integration of the world economy has been highly uneven, restricted to particular economic sectors, and not nearly as extensive as many believe. As a number of commentators have pointed out, there are many ways in which the world is less integrated today than it was in the late nineteenth century. This should remind us that although the technology leading to increased globalization may be irreversible, national policies that have been responsible for the process of economic globalization have been reversed in the past and could be reversed again in the future.

As the twenty-first century opens, the world is not as well integrated as it was in a number of respects prior to World War I. Under the gold standard and the influential doctrine of laissez-faire, for example, the decades prior to World War I were an era when markets were truly supreme and governments had little power over economic affairs. Trade, investment, and financial flows were actually greater in the late 1800s, at least relative to the size of national economies and the international economy, than they are today. Twentieth-century changes appear primarily in the form of the greatly increased speed and absolute magnitude of economic flows across national borders and in the inclusion of more and more countries in the global economy. Yet, economic globalization is largely confined to North America, Western Europe, and Pacific Asia. And even though these industrial economies have become much more open, imports and investments from abroad are still small compared to the size of the domestic economies. For example, American imports rose from 5 percent of the total U.S. production in 1970 to just 13 percent in 1995, even though the United States was the most globalized economy.

Although trade has grown enormously during the past half century, trade still accounts for a relatively small portion of most economies; moreover, even though the number of "tradables" has been increasing, trade is still confined to a limited number of economic sectors. The principal competitors for most firms (with important exceptions in such areas as motor vehicles and electronics) are other national firms. The largest portions of foreign direct investment flows are invested in the United States, Western Europe, and China; a very small portion of the investment in sectors other than raw materials and resources has been invested in most less developed countries. International finance alone can be accurately described as a global phenomenon. Yet, even the globalization of finance must be qualified, as much of international finance is confined to short-term and speculative investment.

The most important measure of the economic integration and interdependence of distinct economies is what economists call the "law of one price." If identical goods and services in different economies have the same or nearly equal prices, then economists consider these economies to be closely integrated with one another. However, evidence indicates that the prices of identical goods around the world differ considerably whether measured by *The Economist* magazine's Big Mac index or by more formal economic measures.[7] When the law of one price is applied to the United States, it is clear that American prices differ greatly from those of other countries, especially Japan's. Price differentials in the cost of labor around the world are particularly notable, and there are large disparities in wages. All of this clearly suggests that the world is not as integrated as many proclaim.

The significant and sizable decline in migration is one of the major differences between late-nineteenth-century globalization and globalization of the early twenty-first century. During the past half century, the United States has been the only country to welcome large numbers of new citizens. Although Western Europe has accepted a flood of refugees and "guest workers," the situation in those countries has been and remains tenuous; few have been or will be offered citizenship. The globalization of labor was considerably more advanced prior to World War I than afterward. In the late nineteenth century, millions of Europeans crossed the Atlantic to settle as permanent residents in North America; West Europeans also migrated in significant numbers to such "lands of recent settlement" as Australia, Argentina, and other temperate-zone regions. There were large migrations of Indians and Chinese to Southeast Asia, Africa, and other tropical regions. All these streams of migration became powerful determinants of the structure of the world economy.[8] In the early twenty-first century, labor migration is no longer a major feature of the world economy, and even within the European Union, migration from one member nation to another is relatively low.

Barriers to labor migration are built by policies intended to protect the real wages and social welfare of the nation's citizens, and the modern welfare state is based on the assumption that its benefits will be available only to its own citizens.[9] Some reformers in industrialized countries have constructed an ethical case that national wealth should be shared with the destitute around the world, but to my knowledge, even they have not advocated elimination of the barriers to international migration in order to enable the poor to move to more wealthy countries and thus decrease international income disparities. I find it remarkable that in the debate over globalization, little attention has been given to the most important factor of production; namely, labor and labor migration. For the billions of people in poor countries, national borders certainly remain an important feature of the global economy.

## Alleged Consequences of Economic Globalization

The conjuncture of globalization with a number of other political, economic, and technological developments transforming the world makes it very difficult to understand economic globalization and its consequences. Among far-reaching economic changes at the end of the twentieth century have been a shift in industrialized countries from manufacturing to services and several revolutionary technological developments associated with the computer, including the emergence of the Internet and information economy. The skills and education required by jobs in the computer age place unskilled labor in the industrialized countries at a severe disadvantage in their wages and job security.

Although some economic and technological developments associated with the computer, including the rapid advances in telecommunications, have certainly contributed to the process of globalization, and globalization in some cases has accentuated these economic and technological changes, the two developments are not synonymous. In fact, the contemporary technological "revolution" has been a far more pervasive and, in many ways, a much more profound development than is globalization, at least thus far. For example, the most important development currently altering individual lives is the incredible revolution in the biological sciences, such as biological engineering. Yet this important development in human affairs has nothing whatsoever to do with globalization as it is commonly conceived.

Many of the problems alleged to be the result of economic globalization are really the consequence of unfortunate national policies and government decisions. Environmentalists rage against globalization and its evils; yet, most environmental damage is the result of the policies and behaviors of national governments. Air, water, and soil pollution result primarily from the lax policies of individual nations and/or from their poor enforcement procedures. The destruction of the Amazon forest has been caused principally by the Brazilian government's national development policies; in the United States, forest clear-cutting is actually promoted by generous government subsidies to logging companies. Land-hungry peasants in Southeast Asia are permitted to destroy forests to acquire cultivable land. Small farmers in France, the United States, and elsewhere blame globalization for their economic plight, but small farms are victims of economic/technological changes that have increased the importance of economies of scale in agriculture. Unfortunately, large farms and agribusinesses are now best suited to take full advantage of such economic/technological changes. The American agricultural sector, especially the large farms, even benefit from generous government subsidies. It would be easy to expand the list of problems generally attributed to globalization that have really been caused by technological changes, by national government policies, or by other wholly domestic factors.

In Western Europe, globalization is frequently blamed for many of the problems that have emerged from the economic and political integration of the region. Both globalization and regionalism are characterized by lowered economic barriers, restructuring of business, and other economic/social changes; it is easy, therefore, to see why some have conflated the two developments into one. Yet, globalization and regionalism are different, especially in the goals that each is seeking to achieve.

The tendency to blame globalization for many vexing problems of modern life is due in part to nationalistic and xenophobic attitudes on the political right and an anti-capitalist mentality on the political left. Nationalistic attitudes have been expressed by Ross Perot, Patrick Buchanan, and American organized labor; the latter long ago gave up the slogan "workers of the world unite" in favor of their own parochial interests. The leftist criticism of capitalism runs deep in some peoples and countries and within advanced capitalist economies, most notably France. The antagonism toward capitalism is directed at the principal representatives of the capitalist system in the modern world: the United States, large multinational firms, and such international economic institutions as the International Monetary Fund and World Trade Organization. When I note these criticisms, I myself do not intend to endorse such excesses of capitalism as rampant commercialism, enormous disparities in wealth and privilege, advertising's creation of "wants," or the worship of wealth as the measure of all things. Capitalism is a system based on self-interest that is too frequently made manifest in outright greed. Despite capitalism's serious flaws, the evils of today's world will not be solved by attacks on globalization. One may say about capitalism what Winston Churchill is reputed to have said about democracy, that it is the worst of all social systems except for all the others.

[ . . . ] [I]n another of my books, *The Challenge of Global Capitalism*, I have addressed many of the negative consequences alleged to have been caused by globalization and have argued that most of the charges against globalization are wrong, misleading, or exaggerated.[10] Domestic and international income disparities, the problems of unskilled workers, and the alleged "race to the bottom" in modern welfare states in general should not be attributed to economic globalization. In almost all cases, such other factors as technological changes, national policies, or the triumph of conservative economic ideologies carry primary responsibility for these developments. Those particularly concerned about income inequalities among national societies should recognize that globalization in the form of exports from industrializing to industrialized countries has actually greatly benefited the industrializing countries; furthermore, very few countries have developed in this century without active participation in the global economy.

## Effectiveness of Macroeconomic Policy

Since the end of World War II, and especially since governments accepted Keynesian economics in the early postwar era, national governments in the advanced industrialized economies have been held responsible for national economic performance. States were assigned the tasks of promoting national economic stability and steering their economies between the undesirable conditions of recession and inflation. Through macroeconomic policies, the state has been able to control, at least to some extent, the troubling vicissitudes of the market. However, the argument that the power of the state over economic affairs has significantly declined implies that national governments can no longer manage their economies. While it is true that macroeconomic policy has become more complicated in the highly integrated world economy of the twenty-first century, these policies do still work and can achieve their goals at least as well as in the past. What better example than the Federal Reserve's very successful management of the American economy in the mid-to-late 1990s! Moreover, today as in the past, the principal constraints on macroeconomic policy are to be found at the domestic rather than at the international level.

Macroeconomic policy consists of two basic tools for managing a national economy: fiscal policies and monetary policies. The principal instruments of fiscal policy are taxation and government expenditures. Through lowering or raising taxes and/or increasing or decreasing national expenditures, the federal government (Congress and the Executive) can affect the national level of economic activities. Whereas a federal budget deficit (spending more than tax receipts) will stimulate the economy, a budget surplus (spending less than tax receipts) will decrease economic activities. Monetary policy works through its determination of the size and velocity of a nation's money supply. The Federal Reserve can stimulate or depress the level of economic activities by increasing or restricting the supply of dollars available to consumers and producers. The principal method employed by the Federal Reserve to achieve this goal is to determine the national level of interest rates; whereas a low interest rate stimulates economic growth, a high rate depresses it.

Many commentators argue that the effectiveness of monetary policy has been significantly reduced by increased international financial flows. If, for example, a central bank lowers interest rates to stimulate the economy, investors will transfer their capital to other economies with higher interest rates and thus counter the intended stimulus of lower rates. Similarly, if a central bank increases interest rates in order to slow the economy, investment capital will flow into the economy, counter the intended deflationary effects of higher rates, and stimulate economic activities. In all these ways, economic globalization is believed to have undermined the efficacy of fiscal and monetary policy. Therefore, some consider national governments no longer able to manage their economies.

To examine this contention, it is helpful to apply the logic of the "trilemma" or "irreconcilable trinity" [ . . . ]. Every nation is confronted by an inevitable trade-off among the following three desirable goals of economic policy: fixed exchange rates, national autonomy in macroeconomic policy, and international capital mobility. A nation might want a stable exchange rate in order to reduce economic uncertainty and stabilize the economy. Or it might desire discretionary monetary policy to avoid high unemployment and steer the economy between recession and inflation. Or a government might want freedom of capital movements to facilitate the conduct of trade, foreign investment, and other international business activities. Unfortunately, a government cannot achieve all three of these goals simultaneously. It can obtain at most two. For example, choosing a fixed and stable exchange rate along with some latitude for independent monetary policies would mean forgoing freedom of capital movements, because international capital flows could undermine both exchange rate stability and independent monetary policies. On the other hand, a country might choose to pursue macroeconomic policies to promote full employment, but it then would have to sacrifice either a fixed exchange rate or freedom of capital movement.

Such an analysis tells us that although economic globalization does constrain government policy options, it does not impose a financial straitjacket on national macroeconomic policies. Whether an individual nation does or does not have the capacity for an independent macroeconomic policy is itself a policy choice. If a nation wants the capability to pursue an independent macroeconomic policy, it can achieve that goal by abandoning either fixed exchange rates or capital mobility. Different countries do, in fact, make different choices. The United States, for example, prefers independent monetary policy and freedom of capital movements and therefore sacrifices exchange rate stability; members of the European Economic Monetary Union (EMU), on the other hand, prefer fixed exchange rates and have created a common currency to achieve this goal. Some other countries that place a high value on macroeconomic independence – China, for example – have imposed controls on capital movements.

Different domestic economic interests also have differing preferences. Whereas export businesses have a strong interest in the exchange rate, domestic-oriented businesses place a higher priority on national policy autonomy. Investors prefer freedom of capital movement, whereas labor tends to be opposed to such movement, unless the movement should mean increased investment in their own nation. Economic globalization in itself does not prevent a nation from using macroeconomic policies for managing its economy.

The mechanisms employed to conduct monetary policy have not been seriously affected by globalization. Although various central banks operate differently from one another, an examination of the ways in which the American Federal Reserve (the Fed) steers the American economy is instructive and reveals that, at least in the American case, globalization has had only minimal effects.

Through its power to increase or decrease the number of dollars available to consumers and producers (liquidity), the Fed is able to steer the overall economy. The level of national economic activity is strongly influenced by the size of the nation's money supply; an increase in the money supply stimulates economic activities and a decrease slows down economic activity. The Fed has three basic instruments to influence the nation's supply of money. The first directly affects the money supply; the other tools work indirectly through the banking system.

The Fed's primary means for management of the economy is "open market operations," conducted through the Open Market Desk of the Federal Reserve Bank of New York. Through sale or purchase of US Government bonds directly to the public, the Fed can influence the overall level of national economic activity. If, for example, the Fed wants to slow the economy, it sells US Government bonds. This takes money or liquidity out of the economy. If, on the other hand, the Fed wants to stimulate the economy, it uses dollars to purchase US Government bonds and thus increases the money or liquidity in the economy.

The Fed can also change the discount rate, which is the interest rate on loans that the Fed makes directly to the nation's commercial banks. The Fed, for example, loans money to banks whose reserves fall below the Fed's reserve requirements (see below); this may happen if a bank has made too many loans or is experiencing too many withdrawals. By lending to private banks and increasing the reserves of those banks, the Fed enables banks to make more loans and thus to increase the nation's money supply. Whereas raising the discount rate decreases loans and money creation, lowering of the discount rate increases loans and money creation. These changes in turn have a powerful influence on the overall level of economic activity.

Another tool that the Fed has available is its authority to determine the reserve requirements of the nation's banks. Reserve requirements specify the minimal size of the monetary reserves that a bank must hold against deposits subject to withdrawal. Reserve requirements thus determine the amount of money that a bank is permitted to lend and, thereby, how much money the bank can place in circulation. Through raising or lowering reserve requirements, the Fed sets a limit on how much money the nation's banks can inject into the economy. However, this method of changing the money supply is used infrequently because changed reserve requirements can be very disruptive to the banking system.

Globalization and a more open world economy have had only minimal impact on the Fed's ability to manage the economy. Yet the effectiveness of open market operations has probably been somewhat reduced by growth of the international financial market, and the purchase or sale of US securities by foreigners certainly affects the national money supply. In the late 1990s, it was estimated that approximately $150 billion was held overseas. However, the effect of that large amount is minimized by the size of the more than $8 trillion domestic economy. Also, the American financial system (like that of other industrialized countries) exhibits a "home bias"; that is to say, most individuals keep their financial assets in their own currency. It is possible, however, that central banks in smaller and weaker economies find that their ability to manage their own money supply has been decreased, as was exemplified by the 1997 Asian financial crisis.

One should note that the continuing power of the Fed over the banks and the money supply through control of the interest rate has been challenged by the development of the credit card and other new forms of money. These credit instruments have decreased, at least somewhat, the effectiveness of the Fed's use of this instrument to control the economy. Still more problematic for the Fed is the increasing use of e-money in Internet commerce. In effect, these developments mean that the monopoly of money creation once held by the Fed and the banking system is being diluted. Through use of a credit card and/or participation in e-commerce, an individual or business can create money. Yet, at some point e-money and other novel forms of money must be converted into "real" or legal tender, and at that point the Fed retains control of the creation of real money. Thus, although the monetary system has become much more complex, the Fed still has ultimate control over that system and through it, the overall economy.

Although the power of central banks over interest rates and the money supply has been somewhat diminished, as long as cash and bank reserves remain the ultimate means of exchange and of settlement of accounts, central banks can still retain control over the money supply and hence of the economy. In fact, even if everyone switched to electronic means of payment but credit issuers still settled their balances with merchants through the banking system (as happens with credit cards now), central banks would still retain overall control. However, one day, e-money could displace other forms of money. If and when this develops, financial settlements could be carried out without going through commercial banks, and central banks would lose their ability to control the economy through interest rates. Such a development could lead to the "denationalization" of money. However, it seems reasonable to believe that some public authority would still be needed to control inflation and monitor the integrity of the computer system used for payments settlements.

With respect to *reserve requirements*, intense competition among international banks has induced some central banks to reduce reserve requirements in order to make the domestic banking industry more competitive internationally. Japanese banks, for example, have long been permitted by the government to keep much smaller reserves than American banks. One of the major purposes of the Basle Agreement (1988) was to make reserve requirements more uniform throughout the world. Rumor has it that this agreement was engineered by the Fed to decrease the international competit- iveness of Japanese and other foreign banks vis-à-vis American international banks. Whatever the underlying motive, the agreement has been described as a response to financial globalization, and the establishment of uniform international reserve requirements has largely reestablished their effectiveness as instruments of policy.

The most important constraints on macroeconomic policy are found at the domestic level. If an economy were isolated from the international economy, fiscal policy would be constrained by the cost of borrowing. If a national government were to use deficit spending to stimulate its economy, the resulting budget deficit would have to be financed by domestic lenders. In that situation, an upper limit would be placed on government borrowing, because as the budget deficit and the costs of servicing that deficit rose, bond purchasers would become more and more fearful that the government might default on its debt and/or use monetary policy to inflate the money supply and thus reduce the real value of the debt. Increased risk as debt rises causes lenders to stop lending and/or to charge higher and higher interest rates; this then discourages fur- ther borrowing by the government. Also, another important constraint on monetary policy in a domestic economy is the threat of inflation; this threat places an upper limit on the ability of a central bank to stimulate the economy by increasing the money supply and/or lowering the interest rate. At some point, the threat of inflation will discourage economic activity. In short, there are limits on macroeconomic policy that have nothing whatsoever to do with the international economy – and these domestic constraints existed long before anyone had heard the term "globalization."

Economic globalization has made the task of managing an economy easier in some ways and more difficult in others. On the one hand, globalization has enabled govern- ments to borrow more freely; the United States in the 1980s and 1990s borrowed heavily from Japanese and other foreign investors in order to finance a federal bud- get deficit and a high rate of economic growth. However, this debt-financed growth strategy, as Susan Strange pointed out first in *Casino Capitalism* (1986) and again in *Mad Money* (1998), is extraordinarily risky and can not continue forever. Fearing collapse of the dollar, investors could one day flee dollar-denominated assets for safer assets denominated in other currencies.[11] The consequences of such flight could be devastating for the United States and for the rest of the world economy. Thus, although economic globalization has increased the latitude of governments to pursue expansionary economic policies through borrowing excessively abroad, such serious financial crises of the postwar era as the Mexican crisis in 1994–1995, the 1997 East Asian financial crisis, and the disturbing collapse of the Russian ruble in August 1998 demonstrate the huge and widespread risks associated with such a practice.

Economic globalization and the greater openness of domestic economies have also modified the rules of economic policy. Certainly, the increasing openness of national economies has made the exercise of macroeconomic policy more complex and difficult. This does not mean that a national government can no longer guide the economy around the dangerous shoals of inflation and recession, but it does mean that the risk of shipwreck has grown.

[ ... ]

## Notes

1 Richard O'Brien, *Global Financial Integration: The End of Geography* (London: Pinter Publishers, 1991); Walter B. Wriston, *The Twilight of Sovereignty: How the Information Revolution Is Transforming Our World* (New York: Scribner's, 1992); Joseph A. Camilleri and Jim Falk, *End of Sovereignty? The Politics of a Shrinking and Fragmenting World* (Brookfield, Vt.: Elgar, 1992); Susan Strange, *The Retreat of the State: The Diffusion of Power in the World Economy* (New York: Cambridge University Press, 1996).

2 Daniel Yergin and Joseph Stanislaw, *The Commanding Heights: The Battle Between Government and the Marketplace That is Remaking the Modern World* (New York: Simon and Schuster, 1998).

3 Paul Hirst and Grahame Thompson, *Globalization in Question: The International Economy and the Possibility of Governance* (London: Polity Press, 1996), 1.

4 Vincent Cable, "The Diminished Nation-State: A Study in the Loss of Economic Power," in *What Future for the State? Daedalus* 124, no. 2 (spring 1995): 44–6.

5 Ibid., 38.

6 Mark Twain was a nineteenth-century American author whose obituary was mistakenly published before his death, leading Twain to comment that rumors of his death were greatly exaggerated.

7 Charles Engel and John H. Rogers, "Regional Patterns in the Law of One Price: The Roles of Geography versus Currencies," in Jeffrey A. Frankel (ed.), *The Regionalization of the World Economy* (Chicago: University of Chicago Press, 1998), 153.

8 W. Arthur Lewis, *The Evolution of the International Economic Order* (Princeton: Princeton University Press, 1978).

9 James Mayall, *Nationalism and International Society* (Cambridge: Cambridge University Press, 1990), Chapter 5.

10 A very effective critique of the antiglobalist position is found in Geoffrey Garrett, "Global Markets and National Politics," *International Organization* 52, no. 4 (autumn 1998): 787–824.

11 Susan Strange, *Casino Capitalism* (Oxford: Blackwell, 1986); and *Mad Money: From the Author of Casino Capitalism* (Manchester, UK: Manchester University Press, 1998).

# 30

# Global Market versus the New Regionalism

## *Björn Hettne*

An economic system presupposes some kind of social order. A social order is a coherent system of rules which is accepted by the actors constituting the system. The concept can contain both coercive and consensual dimensions. The market system of exchange is not in itself an order, but is confined by a particular order that expresses its underlying value system, or normative content. Therefore, market systems differ to the extent that their underlying social orders differ. If, as in the case of the post-communist world, there is a transition between different orders, the market can only reflect the confusion and turbulence of this transition, but it will not by itself create order.

In Europe the concept of 'social market' is commonly used to designate a market system which is mildly regulated to maintain a reasonable degree of social justice in society. In the context of the EC/EU, the so called 'social dimension' of the integration process fulfils a similar role, although it is uncertain how to implement it in a transnational context where states differ in their commitments to the goal of social justice.

The problem of social order and what is often called 'economic freedom', meaning non-regulation of economic activities and flows, has been thoroughly analysed and discussed primarily in national contexts. This essay deals with the problem of how, on a world scale and in a context where no formal political authority exists, 'economic freedom' can be made compatible with social order. The basic issue is the relationship between forces of globalisation and forces of regionalisation. Regionalism is one possible approach to 'a new multilateralism'.

[ ... ]

[The material below] explores the potentials and possibilities of a regionalised world order; that is the territorial logic of the state applied to the emerging regional systems (neo-mercantilism). It should be remembered, however, that real developments depend on the dialectical relationship between the two logics, the forces of market expansion and the need for political control. Globalisation and regionalisation can be seen as complementary processes, modifying each other, in the formation of a new world order. World regions rather than nation-states may in fact constitute basic units in a future multilateral world order.

## Regionalism: Some Conceptual Clarifications

Regionalism is looked upon as a threat by some and as a promise by others. Since various meanings are attached to it, some conceptual clarifications may be in order.

First of all, what is a region? It is not a very homogeneous phenomenon, even if we limit ourselves to world regions (macroregions) and forget about different sub-national regions or microregions. Three contrasting, although not necessarily contradict-ing, models should be underlined: trading blocs or 'megamarkets' resulting from the possible breaking up of the free trade regime; the geo-political division of the world into sometimes competing, sometimes aligned military-political power blocs; and the process of regionalisation from below resulting largely from internal transformations within emerging regions. Here we are mainly concerned with regions in the third sense, that is transnational formations which express a regional identity rather similar to nation-alism. This 'extended nationalism'[1] is the 'new' regionalism.

Second, one has to make a distinction between a *normative* and a *positive* under-standing of regionalism. In what follows, I suggest a normative meaning: regional integration as a political project. I use substitutes such as 'regional cooperation' or 'regional initiatives' in a more positive or descriptive context.

Third, one should also distinguish *hegemonic regionalism*, brought about by pressure from a hegemonic power, exemplified by SEATO (South East Asia Treaty Organiza-tion), CENTO (Central Treaty Organization) and so on, from *autonomous regionalism*, which essentially is regionalism from below.[2] It is the latter which is relevant in dis-cussing the new regionalism. The hegemonic regional arrangements led to few if any links among its members and were of little use in intra-regional and intra-state conflict resolution.

Fourth, regionalism can refer exclusively to a particular region, or it can be a world order concept. One can argue in favour of or against, for instance, ASEAN (Association of South East Asian Nations) regionalism without bothering about other regions. One can even deplore the formation of rival regions. However, one can also be primarily concerned with advantages or disadvantages of a regionalised world, that is a world order consisting of regional groupings as the defining element. The first meaning of regionalism, as a form of 'extended nationalism' with a potential aggress-iveness towards other regions, can perhaps be called *particularistic regionalism*, the second meaning, as a potential world order, *universalistic regionalism*. The positive and normative approaches apply in both cases. As far as universalistic regionalism is concerned, the normative approach would indicate a preferred world order, charac-terised by a 'concertation' of distinct regional cultures.

It must, finally, be emphasised that world regions as distinct political actors are evol-ving through a dialectical historical process, and that they, consequently, differ a lot in their *capacity as actor*. We could perhaps speak of degrees of *regionness* in analogy with concepts such as 'stateness' and 'nationness'. A higher degree of regionness implies a higher degree of economic independence, communication, cultural homogeneity, coher-ence, capacity to act and, in particular, capacity to resolve conflicts. Regionalisation is the process of increasing regionness, and the concept can refer to a single region as well as to the world system.

We can distinguish *five levels of regional complexity, of 'regionness'*. They express a certain evolutionary logic, but the idea is not to suggest a stage theory but rather a framework for comparative analysis.

The first level is region as a *geographical and ecological unit*, delimited by natural geographical barriers: 'Europe from the Atlantic to the Urals', 'Africa south of the Sahara', or 'the Indian subcontinent'. In order to further regionalise, this particular territory must, necessarily, be inhabited by human beings.

The second level is, thus, region as *social system*, which implies translocal relations of social, political, cultural and economic nature between human groups. These relations may be positive or negative, but, either way, they constitute some kind of regional complex. For instance, they can form a security complex, in which the constituent units (normally states) are dependent on each other as well as the overall political stability of the regional system, as far as their own security is concerned.[3] The region, like the international system of which it forms part, is anarchic. The classic case is nineteenth-century Europe. At this low level of organisation, power balance or some kind of 'concert' is the sole security guarantee. From a regionalist perspective (in the normative sense) this is a rather primitive security mechanism.

The third level is region as *organised cooperation* in any of the cultural, economic, political or military fields. In this case, region is defined by the membership of the regional organisation in question. The point to be stressed here is the unidimensionality which characterises this stage of regional cooperation. The creation of a regional organisation is a crucial step towards multilateralism in a regional context. In the absence of any organised regional cooperation, the concept of regionalism does not make much sense. But it is also important that the organised cooperation covers the whole relevant region. It should not be any group of countries in more or less temporary coalitions pursuing purely national interests. It should be possible to relate the 'formal region' (defined by organisational membership) to the 'real region' (which has to be defined through less precise criteria) in order to assess the relevance and future potential of a particular regional organisation.

Regional cooperation through a formal organisation is sometimes rather superficial, but at least a framework for cooperation is created. This can be of great value, if and when an objective need for cooperation should arise. An example is the South Asian Association for Regional Cooperation (SAARC). Of particular importance in this case is that the 'organisational region' corresponds to the regional security complex. This is, for instance, not the case with ASEAN, which organised the capitalist community of countries in the South East Asian region, in contradistinction to the communist or post-communist grouping. As this particular division is losing its relevance, prerequisites for a more authentic regionalism are emerging.

The fourth level is region as *regional civil society*, which takes shape when the organisational framework promotes social communication and convergence of values throughout the region. Of course the pre-existence of a shared cultural tradition throughout the region is of crucial importance here, but culture is not only a given but continuously created and recreated. However, the defining element here is the multidimensional quality of regional cooperation.

The fifth level of regionness is region as *acting subject* with a distinct identity, actor capability, legitimacy, and structure of decision-making. Crucial areas for regional intervention are conflict resolution (between and within former 'states') and welfare (in terms of social security and regional balance). The organisational expression of this level of complexity naturally also tends to become more complex, as the current transformation of the European Community into a European Union shows. The ultimate outcome of this comprehensive level of regionalism (which is something for the future) could be a 'region-state', which in terms of scope can be compared to the classical empires, but in terms of political order constitutes a voluntary evolution of sovereign national political units into a supranational community to which certain functions are transferred.

The higher degrees of regionness define what I mean by *the new regionalism*. It differs from the 'old' regionalism in the following respects:

(a)   Whereas the old regionalism was formed in a bipolar Cold War context, the new is taking shape in a more multipolar world order.
(b)   Whereas the old regionalism was created 'from above' (that is by the superpowers), the new is a more spontaneous process 'from within' (in the sense that the constituent states themselves are main actors).
(c)   Whereas the old regionalism was specific with regard to objectives, the new is a more comprehensive, multidimensional process.

Europe represents the most advanced regional arrangement the world has seen, and it will consequently serve as our paradigm for the new regionalism in the sense that its conceptualisation draws on empirical observations of the European process. Furthermore, Europe is also a concrete model often referred to as an example to follow by other regional organisations. In more negative terms, the integration process in Europe is seen as a threat to the global trade system, the so-called Fortress Europe, and therefore a pretext for organising regional trade systems, such as NAFTA or the East Asian Economic Caucus (EAEC). Thus, the emphasis on the new regionalism as a process 'from within' does not mean that it is purely endogenous to the respective region. Even if the initiatives are taken within the region, the factors which make these initiatives necessary are global.

## The Dimensions of Regionalisation

The process of regionalisation implies a change from relative heterogeneity to increased homogeneity with regard to different dimensions, the most important being *culture, security, economic policies and political regime*.

*Cultural homogeneity* is formed very slowly. Normally, regionalisation necessitates a certain degree of cultural homogeneity to start with, what we can call an 'inherent regional civil society'. The Nordic countries, for instance, are and have always been culturally very similar, and this made it possible for them to adopt very different solutions to their security problems and yet constitute what has been called a security community. In contrast, the fundamental cultural similarity among South Asian states has not prevented inter-state hostilities which are due to differences in other dimensions, made manifest especially by the break-up of European empires into a number of more or less realistic nation-state projects. Cultural homogenisation also has its limits and in order not to become conflictive it must be countered by cultural pluralism.

*Security* is a crucial dimension, and security divisions therefore imply economic divisions, as was very clearly shown in the pattern of regional economic cooperation in Europe during the Cold War. Consequently, a fundamental change of the security order paves the way for a new pattern of regional economic cooperation as well.[4] It should therefore be expected that the dismantling of the Cold War system dramatically changes the preconditions for regional cooperation globally. A greater South East Asian region (ASEAN plus the Indochina region) and a reunification of the two Koreas are such possibilities. The Indo-Pakistan conflict, although largely indigenous to the region, also had its Cold War dimension, which further complicated the issue. Similarly, post-apartheid Southern Africa will be a quite different political entity compared with the situation that prevailed before.

A common security order is a necessary, albeit not sufficient, precondition for regional integration. Of equal importance is the compatibility of economic policies. An autarkic ambition of a certain state, particularly if it happens to be the regional power (like India in South Asia), will effectively prevent a process of regionalisation from taking place to the extent that the rest of the states are outward-oriented. Regional integration based on a shared commitment to the market principle is the normal case, but history has shown that free trade areas, in which unequal countries participate, regularly generate tensions which ultimately erode the regional arrangement. The new regionalism could avoid this trap by a commitment to 'developmental regionalism', which would imply regional economic regulation without going to the extent of delinking from the world economy. There is, however, so far very little empirical experience of this strategy.

The homogenisation of *economic policies* may pave the way for further regionalisation, as when similar regimes are voted to power simultaneously, but it may also be a conscious political decision, as when the economic and political union was decided in Maastricht. This decision was obviously premature in view of the real differences among the twelve, not to speak of some of the candidates for future membership. Nevertheless, the decision should lead to a further harmonisation of economic policies in order to avoid or not to prolong two or more camps within the European Union.

On the global level, the IMF and the World Bank exercise a near-monopoly over credit, as far as weaker clients are concerned. The conditions of access to this credit system, the economic conditionalities, are such as to homogenise the rules of the economic game throughout the world. Similarly, there are strong global forces favouring democratisation of national political regimes. In 1991 the number of democratic states for the first time in world history exceeded the number of non-democratic states.[5] To some extent this is the result of new political conditionalities in development aid. It goes without saying that the democratic reforms 'imposed' by these measures are in harmony with Western conceptions of democracy, whereas, as the Algerian aborted election showed, radical popular influences in Third World societies are not necessarily welcomed by the guardians of the world order.

## The Dynamics of Regionalisation

Regionalisation is a complex process of change taking place simultaneously at three levels: the structures of the world system as a whole, the level of interregional relations, and the internal pattern of the single region. Changes on the three levels interact, and the relative importance of them differs from one region to another.

What I call the '*new regionalism*' was not consistent with the bipolar Cold War system, since the 'quasi-regions' in this system tended to reproduce the global division within their own respective regions. This pattern of hegemonic regionalism was of course evident in Europe, but it was more or less discernible in all world regions at the height of the Cold War. The end of it could lead either to a multipolar system or to a reinforcement of US hegemony.

Moving to the level of interregional relations, European regionalism is the trigger of global regionalisation, at least in two different ways: one positive (promoting regionalism), the other negative (provoking regionalism). In the *positive* way, the European Community has been seen as the model to emulate. This was explicitly stated in the Colombo meeting of the SAARC (December 1991). Similarly the Abuja summit (July 1991) of the OAU called for an African Economic Community on the lines of the EC, and the SADCC (renaming itself SADC) upgraded its supranational competence. The EC is, furthermore, actively encouraging regional formations in the Third World through its 'regional dialogue' or 'group-to-group diplomacy'. This is quite different from the entrenched US bilateralism with the more or less explicit purpose of discouraging regionalism.

The *negative* aspect referred to is of course the infamous European Fortress – the threat of regional protectionism which will provoke rather than promote other regional bloc formations. After the break-down in the GATT negotiations in late 1991, for which European agricultural protectionism was blamed, the Malaysian prime minister referred to the European Fortress as an established fact. He consequently invited Japan to act as a leader of an East Asian Economic Grouping – later to be called Caucus – which implied an East and South East Asian superbloc with a Sino-Japanese core. This would be a formidable response to potential European and North American fortresses. The Japanese response was silence, but there are reasons to believe that the option is kept open. Thus, even in regions where there is a strong commitment to multilateralism, preparations for regional groupings are being made, perhaps in secret.

Will the EU become a Fortress Europe? No one knows, and the point to be made here is that the future pattern of interregional relations depends on which of several possible scenarios for internal change and external relations will come about. What could be more unpredictable than the fall of the Berlin Wall in 1989? And the consequences are still hard to grasp. Will the Commonwealth of Independent States (CIS) become a region? Or will Ukraine and Belorus turn to the West, while Russia 'goes Pacific'? Where will Central Asia belong? Will it remain in the CIS or will it be 'divided' between Turkey and Iran?

Finally, on the level of 'the region in the process of taking shape', the basic dimension is homogenisation, and the elimination of extremes, in terms of culture, security, economic policies and political systems.

Some further comments on the dynamics of regionalisation must be made. The process of regionalisation is itself multidimensional at least at higher levels of 'regionness'. For instance, the security system influences the pattern of economic relations between the states of the region. In Europe, the EC, EFTA, and COMECON were clearly reflections of the Cold War order. The end of this order created a completely new situation, as far as regional economic cooperation was concerned. In South Asia, the security order has created a very strange situation with an introverted India – while all other states maximise their external economic relations in order to minimise their dependence on the regional great power. Again, a transformation of the South Asian regional security complex into a regional security community would also completely change the basis for regional economic cooperation. Another example, which few would consider a likely candidate for a coherent region, is the post-Soviet region organised in the CIS. The formation of a regional political structure, more or less like the formation of nation-states, implies a major transformation of power structures on different levels of society, and this is hardly conceivable without a major crisis.

## The 'Black-Hole Syndrome'

The actual process of regionalisation is triggered by events, the importance of which can be understood only in retrospect. However, one type of event, relevant for regionalisation, which seems to turn up frequently is the 'black-hole syndrome'.

'Black hole' (a metaphor coined by Richard Falk) is a 'pretheoretic' way of accounting for the disintegration of nation-states, or rather 'nation-state projects', in the context of global change. The earlier examples of break-down of states are few, and tended rather to confirm the basic persistence of the inter-state, or Westphalian, system. The division of Pakistan was explained by the geopolitical peculiarity of that particular state-formation. Biafra proved the impossibility of separatism, and Lebanon did revert to a generalised state of conflict rather than breaking up.

Today, the situation is different, and the reason is that the structure of the world order is changing, thus lifting the 'overlay' of stabilising controls which formed part of the old order, that is the Cold War. The peripheral tendencies characterising a number of state-formations that contain great socio-economic and cultural differences will likely take the upper hand as the geopolitical environment becomes transformed and creates new possible alignments and a direct approach to the world economy for emerging microregions.

Yugoslavia provides the paradigm, now more or less repeated all over the post-Soviet region. The collapse of political authority at one level opens up a previously latent power struggle at a lower level, and the process may go on almost indefinitely in a complex multi-ethnic polity. If there is not even an embryonic regional structure the process of disintegration may go on until the 'international community' is forced to take action. Somalia provides one example. To the extent that there is a regional institutional framework which can be used for purposes of conflict resolution, the tendency is for the region to intervene.[6] Thus, the eruption of 'black holes' under certain conditions promotes the process of regionalisation.

'Black holes', or the threat of them, lead to regional security crises, as we can see: Yugoslavia in Europe, Sri Lanka in South Asia, Afghanistan in Central Asia, Lebanon in the Middle East, Liberia in West Africa, Somalia and Ethiopia in East Africa, Cambodia in South East Asia, and Nagorno-Karabakh and Moldova in the latest 'region': the CIS. These security crises form part of regionalisation processes – but there is of course no uniform outcome. Rather, one could say that 'black holes' can make or break regions, depending on the viability of the regional arrangement.

For obvious reasons, 'black holes' are seen as critical problems within the concerned region, while they look less threatening at a long distance, particularly if there are several of them erupting at the same time. Europeans worry more about Yugoslavia than about Liberia, Japanese more about Cambodia than Somalia. Thus one has reasons to believe that a regional engagement in regional conflict resolution is preferable to a global [one]. Even the small steps which have been taken towards humanitarian intervention, overruling state sovereignty, are quite dramatic in terms of yesterday's praxis of international law.[7]

## Hegemonism and Regionalism

As was noted in my opening paragraph, a market, in order to function, presupposes some kind of social order. The premise holds for the past as well as for the present. It was the historical function of mercantilism to create 'national economies' out of localised 'natural economies'. The nation-state was then the protector and promoter of the economy situated within the boundaries of the state. This meant a dramatic expansion of the market system.

The crucial issue now is how economic exchange and even cooperation can take place under the conditions of anarchy supposedly characterising the international system or, differently put, how the 'anarchy' becomes orderly enough to permit 'free', that is largely unregulated, economic transactions of different types.

Theoretically at least, this problem can be solved in more than one way. Recent debate, however, has focused on the importance of hegemonic stability for the functioning of the international economy and thus also on the implications of hegemonic decline. These are, on the economic level, a fragmentation of the world economy, and, on the political level, an increased rivalry between leading capitalist countries, or possibly between carriers of the predominant model and a project to replace it with some qualitatively different model.

The theory of hegemonic stability, which explains the persistence of a global liberal trade regime by the backing from a hegemonic power, assumes a free-trade orientation of the hegemon, as well as a willingness to pay the necessary costs for keeping the world economy open. The hegemon guarantees the liberal world economy. Deviation from required hegemonic behaviour implied in the definition (for instance exploiting its position for short-run benefits) already by itself indicates hegemonic decline. Thus, it is necessary to distinguish between being *dominant* in the international system and performing a *functional* role for its orderly functioning.

Hegemony is a special kind of power, based on different but mutually supportive dimensions, fulfilling certain functions (providing international collective goods) in a larger system which lacks a formal authority structure and, consequently, is more or less voluntarily accepted by other actors. A hegemony is primarily a consensual order, such as was analysed by Gramsci in a national (Italian) context.[8] This implies that hegemony can decline simply as a consequence of a legitimacy deficit, even if the coercive power resources as such should remain intact. It also implies that a reduction in military capability is compatible with the maintenance of a hegemonic position – to the extent that the leadership role of the hegemon for various pragmatic reasons continues to be accepted. Since a social order is necessary, any order is preferable to anarchy, or what Polanyi called the utopian project of the rule of the market.[9]

Theorising about hegemony is highly abstract, since there is little empirical evidence to draw on. A specific hegemony is a historical structure. A historical structure is *sui generis*. British hegemony developed in a power vacuum, and the resources devoted to military power were therefore marginal.[10] In contrast, the US hegemony evolved in the context of a superpower conflict which involved competing socio-economic systems, engaged in a Cold War and planning for an 'imaginary war'.[11] This added a radically new dimension to the post-war hegemonic rivalry, a systemic conflict.

Thus, the Cold War order was dualistic, in the sense that a socialist subsystem existed as a challenge to the capitalist world order, providing rebellious states with a safe haven.

Regionalism was subsumed under the Cold-War logic, which implied a linkage between regional organisations and the fundamental cleavage of the system (hegemonic regionalism). The New World Order proclaimed by US President George Bush during the Gulf War can be seen as a counter strategy of the declining hegemon against the challenges of 'regional hegemonism', the Iraqs to come. Regional hegemonism is the 'malign' form of neo-mercantilism. The New Regionalism is the 'benign' form. The great task in creating a post-hegemonic future is to promote 'benign' rather than 'malign' neo-mercantilism.

[ . . . ]

## The Neo-mercantilist Position

Let us now try to draw the threads together. The 'new regionalism' can be defined as a multidimensional process of regional integration which includes economic, political, social and cultural aspects. It is both a positive concept, summarising certain tendencies in the world system, and a normative position, arguing in favour of such tendencies as a potential new world order. Here I am particularly concerned with the second meaning, which I have called the neo-mercantilist position.[12] It is a package rather than a single policy, whether concerned with economics or foreign policy. The concept thus goes beyond the free trade idea, that is the interlinking of several previously more or less secluded national markets into one functional economic unit. Rather, the political ambition of creating territorial identity and regional coherence is the primary neo-mercantilist goal. In this observation other differences between 'old' and 'new' regionalism are implied. New regionalism is spontaneous and 'from below', or rather 'from within', whereas the old type often was imposed on a group of countries in the interest of superpower strategy. The new regionalism belongs to a new global situation characterised by multipolarity.

What we could call neo-mercantilism is thus a transnational phenomenon. Its spokesmen do not believe in the viability of closed national economies in the present stage of the development of the world economy. On the other hand, neither do they believe in the viability of an unregulated world economy. Nor do they – in contrast with the Trilateralists – put much faith in the possibility of managing such a world economy. Rather, neo-mercantilists believe in the regionalisation of the world into more or less self-sufficient blocs, where political stability and social welfare are major concerns. Ultimately, this will lead to region-states, replacing nation-states and thereby restoring stability and control.

This is the 'benign' view of mercantilism, contrasted to a 'malevolent' view by Barry Buzan as follows:

> The benign view sees a mercantilist system of large, inward-looking blocs, where protectionism is predominantly motivated by considerations of domestic welfare and internal political stability. Such a system potentially avoids many of the organizational problems of trying to run a global or quasi-global liberal economy in the absence of political institutions on a similar scale. The malevolent view sees a rerun of the mercantilist dynamic of the past, in which protectionism is motivated primarily by considerations of state power.[13]

Karl Polanyi, critic of the market utopia and early neo-mercantilist, warned against the 'hazards of planetary interdependence' associated with global market expansion.[14]

This sceptical view corresponds to the one taken by contemporary neo-mercantilists who conceive a market system as a fragile arrangement. The post-war world economy is seen as a historic compromise between international economic *laissez-faire* and a certain level of domestic control.

This essentially Keynesian approach was gradually abandoned during the crisis of the 1970s, and in the subsequent decade purist liberal principles were becoming increasingly dominant, a trend that culminated when the socialist world began to disintegrate towards the end of the decade. The conclusion of the Cold War led to a hegemonic position for the market, which would indicate that the stage is set for the second phase of Polanyi's double movement, that is when the self-protection of society is activated.

This leads up to the argument for a regionalised world system as the form that today's protectionism could take. It is different from the classical Listian argument in favour of a coherent national economy. Keynes essentially repeated List's argument when he, in a now classic article written before the war, questioned the value of free trade.[15] He saw a certain degree of national self-sufficiency as a precondition for international political stability, denouncing the 'decadent international capitalism' of his time.

A decade later, when international peace had been fundamentally disturbed, Karl Polanyi developed a regionalist scenario, posed against what he at the time feared was going to be a new fruitless attempt to reshape the hegemonic world order or 'universal capitalism', this time under the leadership of the United States. Like Keynes earlier, he was concerned with the crucial question in international political economy: what kind of international economic structure and pattern of development was most conducive to peace and long term stability. Both warned against an unregulated liberal world order, but while Keynes emphasised the need for national self-sufficiency, Polanyi saw the solution to the world order problem in an emerging pattern of regionalism.[16] Polanyi, however, underestimated the post-war hegemonic potential of the United States, calling it 'an attempt doomed to failure'.

The post-war hegemonic world order is now in a process of transformation towards some kind of 'post-hegemonic', or 'post-Cold-War' world order. Hence the concept of region again assumes a new importance as a possible mode of organising the world. The world system logic is pointing towards further regionalisation, at least in the shorter perspective. Ultimately, the two processes of globalisation and regionalisation may prove complementary.

There is a difference between this new form of protectionism and the traditional mercantilist concern with state-building and national power. Neo-mercantilists argue in favour of the regionalisation of the world into more or less self-sufficient blocs. These blocs would be introverted and maintain symmetric relations among themselves. This is the 'benign' type. The 'malign' type is offensive and aggressive, an 'extended economic nationalism'. The 'benign view' of mercantilism coincides with what I call 'the new regionalism'.

[ . . . ]

## Notes

1   D. Seers, *The Political Economy of Nationalism* (Oxford: Oxford University Press, 1983).
2   A. Acharya, 'Regional military-security cooperation in the Third World: a conceptual analysis of the relevance and limitations of ASEAN', *Journal of Peace Research* 29(1) (1992);

and S. D. Muni, 'Changing global order and cooperative regionalism: the case of southern Asia', in Helena Lindolm (ed.), *Approaches to the Study of International Political Economy* (Göteborg: Padrigu, 1992).

3   B. Buzan, *People, States and Fear: An Agenda for International Security Studies in the Post-Cold War Era* (Brighton: Harvester Wheatsheaf, 1991).

4   Björn Hettne, 'The concept of mercantilism', in L. Magnusson (ed.), *Mercantilist Economies* (Boston: Kluwer, 1993).

5   H.-H. Holm and G. Sørensen, 'A new world order: the withering away of anarchy and the triumph of individualism? Consequences for IR theory', IPRA General Conference, Kyoto, 1992.

6   In the summer of 1990, in the shadow of the Kuwait crisis, ECOWAS (Economic Organization of West African States) intervened in the Liberian civil war. Although not fully backed by the whole region, it was unprecedented in the history of African regional cooperation. The Liberian crisis can be said to have speeded up the process of regional cooperation. The shared view in the region was that 'the ECOWAS states cannot stand idly by and watch a member state slide into anarchy' (WA, 1–7 July 1991).

7   The point is well taken by Flora Lewis (*International Herald Tribune*, Friday, 17 July 1992): The words of Helsinki do represent a striking advance in formal international relations. They assert the 'collective conscience of our community' that insistence on human and democratic rights does not 'belong exclusively to the internal affairs of the state concerned. This propounds both a serious limitation on the thesis of absolute national sovereignty and a new responsibility as my brother's keeper.'

8   R. W. Cox, 'Gramsci, hegemony and international relations: an essay in method', *Millennium: Journal of International Studies* 12(2) (1983).

9   'To allow the market mechanism to be the sole director of the fate of human beings and their natural environment . . . would result in the demolition of society' (K. Polanyi, *The Great Transformation* (Boston: Beacon Press, 1957), pp. 71–3).

10   P. Kennedy, *The Rise and Fall of the Great Powers* (New York: Random House, 1987), p. 151.

11   M. Kaldor, *The Baroque Arsenal* (London: Deutsch, 1982).

12   Hettne, 'The concept of mercantilism'.

13   B. Buzan, 'Economic structure and international security: the limits of the liberal case', *International Organization* 38(4) (1984), p. 608.

14   Polanyi, *The Great Transformation*, p. 181.

15   J. M. Keynes, 'National self-sufficiency', *Yale Review* 22(4) (1933), pp. 755–69.

16   Karl Polanyi, 'Universal capitalism or regional planning', *London Quarterly of World Affairs* (Jan. 1945).

# 31

# Globalization and the Political Economy of Capitalist Democracies

## *Fritz Scharpf*

[ ... ] Even during the early post-war decades, when national problem-solving capabilities had reached their apex, policy choices were always constrained by internal and
external factors beyond the control of democratically accountable office holders.
Internally, constitutions with a bill of rights and institutional checks and balances,
enforced by judicial review, are the most important legal constraints; in addition there
are always resource constraints and, less obviously, there is the need to respect a good
deal of autonomy of functional subsystems – like the economy, science, education,
health care, or the arts – with whose internal logic and professional criteria the democratic state would, with good reason, hesitate to interfere (Willke 1983). Externally,
the 'sovereignty' of the nation state is territorially limited, yet many of the problems
that will be of concern to its citizens are affected by factors crossing national boundaries. For military security, that has always been obvious, but it has also become
true for international terrorism and organized crime, for transnational and global
environmental pollution, for transnational migration, and for global communication.
All of these border-crossing effects have significantly increased by comparison to the
early post-war decades, and all of these challenge the capacity of the democratic nation
state autonomously to shape the collective fate of its citizens. However, the major
constraint on democratic self-determination within national boundaries arises from
the reintegration of global capital markets and transnational markets for goods and
services.

## Capitalist Democracy: A Precarious Symbiosis

The democratic state and the capitalist economy coexist in symbiotic interdependence.
On the one hand, the productivity and profitability of advanced capitalist economies
depends not only on the definition and protection of property rights and contractual
obligations by the legal and police systems of the state, but also on the provision of
public infrastructure, including education and basic research, and a wide variety of
public services. Conversely, the political viability of the democratic state has come to
depend crucially on the performance of national economies, which directly determines
the incomes and employment opportunities of citizens and voters, and which generates
the tax revenues to finance public services and welfare spending. At the same time,
however, this symbiotic relationship is characterized by fundamental tensions: the
sovereignty of the state is territorially limited, while the capitalist economy tends toward

global interaction. The logic of capitalist accumulation and of market competition compels enterprises to exploit all factors of production, natural as well as human, and to externalize the social and the environmental costs of this exploitation. The capitalist economy, moreover, will not only generate material abundance for consumers, jobs for workers, and tax revenue for governments, but also highly unequal income distributions, regional and sectoral winners and losers, and cyclical and structural crises which may result in mass unemployment and mass poverty. The democratic state, by contrast, derives its claim to legitimacy from a commitment to the public interest and to distributive justice, and governments are constrained, through the mechanisms of electoral accountability, to orient their policies toward the interests of the broad majority of its voters. They are therefore under political pressure to protect groups in the electorate against the losses caused by structural change, to prevent mass unemployment, to regulate labour markets and production processes in the interest of the workers affected, and to achieve a normatively defensible distribution of incomes.

In following their own logic, therefore, democratic governments will want to inhibit the 'creative destruction' associated with dynamic capitalism, and they will tend to reduce the income differentials between winners and losers in the market. In doing so, however, they run into two basic difficulties, one informational and one structural. With regard to the former, the collapse of communist systems is also taken to have confirmed the Hayekian thesis that there is no way in which governments could efficiently coordinate the demands of tens or hundreds of millions of consumers for millions of products produced by hundreds of thousands of firms using thousands of different types of resources. Instead, the efficiency of the capitalist economy depends on the ability of profit-oriented investors and of competing firms to seek out and use local information about consumer demands and production possibilities that could never be centralized to begin with and which, if centralized, would lead to unmanageable information overload at the centre. Thus, if the state intervenes in the economy, it is likely to interfere with, and potentially to disable, the intelligence of decentralized information processing and, ultimately, to paralyse the dynamism of the capitalist economy (Hayek 1944; 1945; Streit 1993). Moreover, if state intervention is considered a political option at all, it may also be instrumentalized by well-organized and well-informed pressure groups in the economy itself for purposes that will serve the rent-seeking interests of 'distributive coalitions', rather than the public interest which, from the normative perspective of welfare economics, might perhaps justify state intervention under conditions that could be analytically characterized as market failures (Olson 1982).

The second difficulty of political intervention arises from a structural asymmetry: political interest focuses on the output side of the economic process, on products that increase general welfare, on the employment opportunities, and on the externalities associated with processes of production. The capitalist economy, however, is controlled from the side of capital inputs: capital owners must be motivated to invest in production capacities which, together with the necessary labour inputs, will ultimately result in marketable products. But whereas the investment decisions that drive the economic process are motivated by the anticipation of future profits, government intervention (and the collective-bargaining strategies of powerful unions) will generally have the effect of reducing the post-tax incomes from capital investments.

On the face of it, this may appear as a symmetric constellation of mutual dependence: capital owners must invest and create jobs in order to achieve a profit, whereas unions and governments must allow capital owners to achieve a profit in order to benefit from employment, wage income, and tax revenues. But that is a spurious symmetry. While governments and workers are indeed without alternatives, *capital owners do have a choice*. If they find it unattractive to invest in job-creating productive assets, they may instead opt for speculative or interest-bearing financial assets, they may buy gold and other value-conserving assets, or they might simply consume, rather than invest, their savings. In other words, in a capitalist economy governments and unions combined do not have the power to reduce the rate of return on productive investments below that of the next-best alternative available to capital owners,[1] and they never have the power to reduce the rate of return below zero, and still expect production and employment to continue. Moreover, since from the point of view of the investor it is the *cumulative* effect of taxes, regulations, and collective-bargaining agreements which affects profitability, all of the political actors involved – local, regional, and national governments with their functional subdivisions, and labour unions – must be extremely cautious in their dealings with the economy, lest they reduce the incentives for productive investments on which they all depend.

In the political-economy literature of the 1970s, these tensions were elevated to the status of self-destructive 'contradictions' of capitalist democracies. On the left, theories of 'late capitalism' predicted an imminent and inevitable 'legitimacy crisis' of the state – which was compelled to instrumentalize its democratically based power in order to fulfil the ever more demanding functional requisites of the capitalist economy, and to respect capital interests which could not, themselves, be normatively justified under the criterion of 'generalizability' (Offe 1972; 1984; Habermas 1973; 1976). On the conservative side, by contrast, theories of 'overloaded government' predicted an inflation of political demands in competitive mass democracies which would force governments to intensify taxation and economic regulation to an extent that would eventually destroy the viability of capitalist economies (Crozier et al. 1975; Hennis et al. 1977; 1979). From either perspective, therefore, the precarious symbiosis of the democratic state and the capitalist economy could not last.

Against these predictions of inevitable collapse, it seems necessary to remind oneself of the fact that capitalist democracies have in fact worked very well during *les trente glorieuses* after the Second World War. They succeeded, by and large, in exploiting the capitalist capacity for technical progress and dynamic growth; they learned to dampen the cycles of economic booms and recessions, and to avoid mass unemployment; they were able to impose regulatory constraints on the capitalist exploitation of human and natural resources; and they developed welfare-state correctives for the injustices of capitalist distribution – and they managed to do all this without going down the Hayekian 'Road to Serfdom' (Hayek 1944). But it is even more important to realize that this 'democratic civilization' of dynamic capitalism occurred under exceptional, and perhaps historically unique, conditions regarding the relationship between the state and the economy.

## The 'Great Transformation': A Brief Respite?

By their own logic, profit-oriented economic interactions tend to ignore national boundaries and to evolve toward global integration; by contrast, political interventions are constrained by the boundaries of the territorial state. Thus, unless the nation state is able and willing to control border-crossing transactions, the attempt to control economic processes within national boundaries can always be counteracted by external influences – capital inflows or outflows, import competition or foreign buyouts, mass immigration or tax flight and brain drain.

The period between 1870 and the First World War was indeed characterized by open capital markets, free trade, and free migration. Under the gold standard, all currencies were convertible at fixed exchange rates, and in the absence of capital export controls, money could freely flow to the most profitable uses throughout the capitalist world. Before 1914, in fact, foreign direct investment had reached levels that were only again surpassed in the 1980s (Hirst and Thompson 1995). Similarly, under British leadership, free trade became the general rule on the markets for industrial goods; and protectionism, where it was still practised at all, was generally limited to markets for agricultural goods. In short, the capitalist world of that period (though of course much smaller than now) could indeed be described as an integrated market for capital and industrial goods – and to a lesser degree for services and labour as well. It was in fact not under the control either of national governments or of an international regulatory regime – and it was, by and large, the world which Marx and Engels had described: with rapid technological progress and great gains in material wealth, but also with great inequality, exploitation, deep cyclical crises and crashes of financial markets (Kindleberger 1978), and misery for the masses. But since most governments were not yet democratically accountable to the masses, it also was a world without major legitimacy crises.

After the First World War, the gold standard and free trade were re-established, but the mobilization of the masses for the war effort had generally been accompanied not only by the spread of universal suffrage and democratic accountability, but also by the removal of legal restrictions on trade union activity, and by the introduction or expansion of at least some minimal forms of social security for conditions of unemployment, disability, sickness, and old-age poverty. Thus, when the crisis proneness of international capitalism reasserted itself with a vengeance at the end of the 1920s, the minimal welfare state was directly involved: mass unemployment destroyed the financial viability of the new social-security systems, and the political protest of the impoverished masses not only affected the survival of governments of the day, but it threatened, and in the case of Weimar Germany destroyed, the legitimacy of democratic government as such. For that reason, governments everywhere were forced to react in one way or another to the Great Depression. They did so by reasserting control over their economic boundaries and, in the process, destroying the integrated world economy.

In the early 1930s, the major industrial nations in fact responded to the Great Depression with protectionist, or even autarkist, strategies of competitive devaluation, rigid controls of capital transfers, protective tariffs, quantitative import restrictions, and subsidized exports (Kindleberger 1973; Rothermund 1993). As a result, the world economy collapsed with disastrous consequences for output and employment (Kindleberger 1995). Nevertheless, as a consequence of this 'Great Transformation' (Polanyi 1957), the boundaries of the territorial state had for a time become coextensive with the effective boundaries of markets for capital, goods, services, and labour (Winkel 1985). Moreover, behind these protectionist barriers, national policy makers also learned to use the Keynesian techniques of macro-economic intervention in the capitalist economy without pre-empting micro-economic choices of producers and consumers.

The boundaries of national economies were, of course, not impermeable. What mattered was that transactions across them were under the *potential* control of national governments, and that they continued to be impeded by significant tariff and non-tariff barriers and other transaction costs. As a consequence, capital owners were largely restricted to investment opportunities within the national economy, and firms were mainly confronted by domestic competitors. The relative importance of international trade increased only gradually; and since governments could control imports and exchange rates, the international competitiveness of national producers was not a major issue.

While these conditions lasted, government interest rate policy was able to define the minimal rate of return on financial investments and thus the relative attractiveness of financial and real investments. If interest rates were lowered, job-creating real investments became relatively more attractive, and vice versa. At the same time, government policy on taxation and deficit spending had a direct and undiluted impact on aggregate domestic demand. Thus, Keynesian demand management was generally able to smooth the business cycle and to maintain full employment and steady economic growth,[2] which then permitted the expansion of mass incomes, public services, and welfare transfers. Equally important: within national boundaries, government regulations and nation-wide collective-bargaining agreements were able to control the conditions of production without undercutting the viability of capitalist accumulation. Since the external boundaries could be controlled, all relevant competitors were producing under the same regime – with the consequence that the costs of regulation could be passed on to consumers. Hence the rate of return on investment was not necessarily affected by high levels of regulation and union power.

During the same period, world markets for goods, services, and capital were gradually liberalized and integrated again within the framework of American-led international economic regimes (Keohane 1984). But these regimes were meant to, and did, establish a form of 'embedded liberalism' that still allowed national governments to protect the welfare of their citizens against external disruptions (Ruggie 1982). Within that framework, the industrial nations of Western Europe developed distinctly national versions of the capitalist welfare state. Despite the considerable differences between the 'Social-Democratic', 'Corporatist', or 'Liberal' variants (Esping-Andersen 1990), however, all of them were remarkably successful in maintaining and promoting a vigorous capitalist economy, while also controlling, in different ways and to different degrees, the destructive tendencies of unfettered capitalism in the interest of specific social, cultural, and/or ecological values (Scharpf 1991; Merkel 1993).

## Boundary Control Lost Again

Things changed radically, however, when the breakdown of the Bretton Woods regime of fixed, but adjustable, exchange rates, combined with the oil-price crises of the 1970s, unleashed an explosive growth of 'offshore' financial markets in places that were not under the effective control of any of the major central banks (Kapstein 1994). At the same time, technological innovations and the increasing importance of multinational firms undercut the effectiveness of national controls over capital transfers (Cerny 1994). As a consequence, financial assets are now mobile around the globe, and the minimal rate of return that investors can expect is again determined by global financial markets,[3] rather than by national monetary policy. Moreover, real interest rates were generally about twice as high after the early 1980s as they used to be in the 1960s.[4] So if a government should now try to reduce interest rates below the international level, this would no longer stimulate job-creating real investment in the national economy, but would drive capital out of the country, causing devaluation and a rising rate of inflation.[5] More generally, any national policy that would unilaterally raise taxes on capital incomes or reduce the expected rate of return on investments would now be punished by capital flight (Sinn 1993).[6]

At the same time, the liberalization of markets for goods and services was pushed forward by the progress of GATT and WTO negotiations in reducing tariffs and quantitative restrictions world-wide (Hoekman and Kostecki 1995) and by the spread of deregulation and privatization policies from the United States and Britain to the rest of the OECD world. Within the European Community, finally, even the remaining legal barriers protecting national economies were being abolished by the successful drive to complete the 'internal market' by the end of 1992. In short, the territorial state again lost control over its economic boundaries. Once the transnational reintegration of the markets for capital, goods, and services had surpassed a certain threshold, some observers concluded that, regretfully, 'Polanyi's Great Transformation was over' (Cerny 1994: 339), while others hailed the arrival of the 'century of globalization', in which public policy would no longer be able to counteract market forces (Giersch 1997).

At any rate, interventionist policies have become more difficult and costly at the national level – which is not to say that they are now impossible. For a while, at any rate, the 'power resources of the labour movement' (Korpi 1983), and, more generally, the political forces supporting the post-war class compromise, were, and may still be, strong enough to defend existing entitlements and to resist the dismantling of the welfare state (Pierson 1994; Garrett 1995; 1998). But even under the most auspicious political circumstances, resistance comes at considerable economic cost. Once the territorial state has lost, or given up, the capacity to control capital transfers, attempts to increase taxes on capital incomes and business profits are likely to reduce the tax base; and once the state has given up control over the boundaries of markets for goods and services, it can no longer make sure that all competing suppliers will be subject to the same regulatory regime. Thus, if now the costs of regulation or of collective bargaining are increased unilaterally within a member state, they can no longer be passed on to consumers, who are now free to turn to foreign sources. Instead, and *ceteris paribus*, imports will increase in that state, exports decrease, profits will fall, investment decline, and firms will go bankrupt or move production to more benign locations.

Moreover, since the exit options of national firms, and the competitiveness of foreign suppliers, are also affected by the regulatory and tax policies of other governments, and by the strategies of unions in other countries, national governments and unions now must compete with other locations for mobile factors of production. This 'competition among systems of regulation' seems to have the characteristics of a Prisoner's Dilemma in which all competing countries are tempted to make larger concessions to capital and business interests than they would otherwise have preferred. If the existing level of social protection is nevertheless to be maintained, a greater share of the cost must be borne by workers and consumers. Thus, the need to retain or attract mobile capital and business, and to maintain the international competitiveness of the national economy, has obvious and significant consequences for distribution. Capital incomes have risen, and income from labour has fallen behind, while governments everywhere had to shift the tax burden from mobile to relatively immobile factors – i.e. primarily onto wage incomes and consumer spending (Sinn 1993; Steinmo 1994). In short, the post-war politico-economic regimes and the welfare state are under siege even where they are still being defended (Canova 1994; Freeman 1995; Pierson 1996).

In principle, this is a general problem that is felt not only in Western Europe, but in all industrialized countries – in the United States as well as in Japan or in South Korea – and which is usually discussed as a consequence of economic 'globalization'. It is particularly acute, however, within the European Union where economic integration has progressed much further, and where firms are now legally and effectively free to shop for the most attractive location of production without any constraints on their access to the former home market, and without any fear that, at some time in the future, their calculations could be upset by the imposition of 'anti-dumping levies' or by varieties of non-tariff barriers that may still be employed under the free-trade regime of the World Trade Organization (WTO). Thus, as EU member states have completely lost the option of discriminating in favour of domestic producers (Kapteyn 1996), their capacity to defend existing patterns of national policy is reduced to a much greater degree than is generally implied by the pressures of global economic competition. [...]

## Notes

1  From a left-of-centre political perspective, the secular rise of government indebtedness after the mid-1970s should therefore appear as an unmitigated disaster: it has provided capital owners with perfectly secure and reasonably profitable alternatives to employment-creating real investments, and it must use general tax revenues that are increasingly collected from wage earners to pay for the debt service to capital owners. Under the lure of Keynesian economics, unfortunately, left-wing political parties and labour unions have come to ignore these redistributive consequences of deficit spending.

2  During the 'stagflation' crisis of the early and mid-1970s, it became obvious that Keynesian demand management of the Anglo-American variety was unable to deal with inflationary pressures and rising unemployment at the same time. Where stagflation was in fact overcome, success depended on neo-corporatist institutional conditions that allowed unions to assume responsibility for containing wage-push inflation while demand-side fiscal and monetary strategies continued to assure full employment (Scharpf 1991).

3  The empirical evidence that capital is still not in fact perfectly mobile, and that differences in real interest rates remain, is explained by information asymmetries, rather than by state policies impeding mobility (Gordon and Bovenberg 1996).

4  The reasons for this secular rise of real interest rates are not well understood, but it seems clear that the dramatic rise of government indebtedness after the oil-price crises of the 1970s as well as the 'monetarist' shift of central bank priorities, from assuring full employment to the fight against inflation, must be part of any explanation.

5  Keynesian full-employment policy could thus no longer rely on the support of national monetary policy. If it was still applied at all, its full burden had to be carried by fiscal policy – which was not only less effective in economic terms but would, at high real interest rates, soon become prohibitively expensive.

6  Conversely, national monetary policy does have the power to attract capital, by setting national interest rates above the international level. But in doing so, it will raise the exchange rate, which decreases the international competitiveness of the national economy.

# References

Canova, T. (1994) The Swedish model betrayed. *Challenge* 37(3): 36–40.

Cerny, P. G. (1994) The dynamics of financial globalization: Technology, market structure, and policy response. *Policy Sciences* 27: 319–42.

Crozier, M., Huntington, S. P., et al. (1975) *The Crisis of Democracy: Report on the Governability of Democracies to the Trilateral Commission.* New York: New York University Press.

Esping-Andersen, G. (1990) *The Three Worlds of Welfare Capitalism.* Cambridge: Polity Press.

Freeman, R. B. (1995) The limits of wage flexibility in curing unemployment. *Oxford Review of Economic Policy* 11: 63–72.

Garrett, G. (1995) Capital mobility, trade, and the domestic politics of economic policy. *International Organization* 49: 171–81.

Garrett, G. (1998) *Partisan Politics in the Global Economy.* Cambridge: Cambridge University Press.

Giersch, H. (1997) Das Jahrhundert der Globalisierung: Der Standortwettbewerb bringt nicht das Ende der Wirtschaftspolitik: Aber am Ende ist eine Politik, die den Marktkraften entgegenwirken will. *Frankfurter Allgemeine Zeitung* (11 Jan.): 13.

Gordon, R. H. and Bovenberg, L. A. (1996) Why is capital so immobile internationally? Possible explanations and implications for capital income taxation. *American Economic Review* 86: 1057–75.

Habermas, J. (1973) *Legitimationsprobleme im Spatkapitalismus.* Frankfurt am Main: Suhrkamp.

Habermas, J. (1976) *Legitimation Crisis.* London: Heinemann.

Hayek, F. A. (1944) *The Road to Serfdom.* Chicago: University of Chicago Press.

Hayek, F. A. (1945) The use of knowledge in society. *American Economic Review* 35: 519–30.

Hennis, W., et al. (1977) *Regierbarkeit: Studien zu ihrer Problematisierung.* Stuttgart: Klett.

Hennis, W., et al. (1979) *Regierbarkeit: Studien zu ihrer Problematisierung.* Stuttgart: Klett.

Hirst, P. and Thompson, G. (1995) Globalization and the future of the nation state. *Economy and Society* 24: 408–42.

Hoekman, B. M. and Kostecki, M. (1995) *The Political Economy of the World Trading System: From GATT to the WTO.* Oxford: Oxford University Press.

Kapstein, E. B. (1994) *Governing the World Economy: International Finance and the State.* Cambridge, Mass.: Harvard University Press.

Keohane, R. O. (1984) *After Hegemony: Cooperation and Discord in the World Political Economy.* Princeton: Princeton University Press.

Kindleberger, C. P. (1973) *The World in Depression 1929–1939.* London: Allen Lane.

Kindleberger, C. P. (1978) *Manias, Panics, and Crashes: A History of Financial Crisis.* New York: Basic Books.

Kindleberger, C. P. (1995) *The World Economy and National Finance in Historical Perspective.* Ann Arbor: University of Michigan Press.

Korpi, W. (1983) *The Democratic Class Struggle.* London: Routledge and Kegan Paul.

Merkel, W. (1993) *Ende der Sozialdemokratie? Machtressourcen und Regierungspolitik im internationalen Vergleich.* Frankfurt am Main: Campus.

Offe, C. (1972) *Strukturprobleme des kapitalistischen Staates.* Frankfurt am Main: Suhrkamp.

Offe, C. (1984) *Contradictions of the Welfare State.* London: Hutchinson.

Olson, M. (1982) *The Rise and Decline of Nations: Economic Growth, Stagflation, and Social Rigidities.* New Haven: Yale University Press.

Pierson, P. (1994) *Dismantling the Welfare State? Reagan, Thatcher, and the Politics of Retrenchment.* Cambridge: Cambridge University Press.

Pierson, P. (1996) The new politics of the welfare state. *World Politics* 48: 147–79.

Polanyi, K. (1957) *The Great Transformation: The Political and Economic Origins of Our Time.* Boston: Beacon Press.

Rothermund, D. (1993) *Die Welt in der Wirtschaftskrise 1929–1939*. Munster: Lit.

Ruggie, J. G. (1982) International regimes, transactions, and change: Embedded liberalism in the postwar economic order. *International Organization* 36: 379–415.

Scharpf, F. W. (1991) *Crisis and Choice in European Social Democracy*. Ithaca, NY: Cornell University Press.

Sinn, S. (1993) The taming of Leviathan: Competition among governments. *Constitutional Political Economy* 3: 177–221.

Steinmo, S. (1994) The end of redistribution? International pressures and domestic policy choices. *Challenge* 37(6): 9–17.

Streit, M. E. (1993) Cognition, competition, and catallaxy: In memory of Friedrich August von Hayek. *Constitutional Political Economy* 4: 223–62.

Willke, H. (1983) *Entzauberung des Staates: Uberlegungen zu einer sozietalen Steuerungstheorie*. Konigstein: Athenaum.

Winkel, H. (1985) Der Glaube an die Beherrschbarkeit von Wirtschaftskrisen (1933–1970): Lehren aus der Weltwirtschaftskrise. *Die Groze Krise der dreiziger Jahre: Vom Niedergang der Weltwirtschaft zum Zweiten Weltkrieg*. G. Schulz. Gottingen: Vandenhoeck and Ruprecht: 17–43.

# 32

# Has Globalization Gone Too Far?

## Dani Rodrik

[ . . . ]

The process that has come to be called "globalization" is exposing a deep fault line between groups who have the skills and mobility to flourish in global markets and those who either don't have these advantages or perceive the expansion of unregulated markets as inimical to social stability and deeply held norms. The result is severe tension between the market and social groups such as workers, pensioners, and environmentalists, with governments stuck in the middle.[1]

This [chapter] argues that the most serious challenge for the world economy in the years ahead lies in making globalization compatible with domestic social and political stability – or to put it even more directly, in ensuring that international economic integration does not contribute to domestic social *dis*integration.

[ . . . ]

## Sources of Tension

I focus on three sources of tension between the global market and social stability and offer a brief overview of them here.

First, reduced barriers to trade and investment accentuate the asymmetry between groups that can cross international borders (either directly or indirectly, say through outsourcing[2]) and those that cannot. In the first category are owners of capital, highly skilled workers, and many professionals, who are free to take their resources where they are most in demand. Unskilled and semiskilled workers and most middle managers belong in the second category. Putting the same point in more technical terms, globalization makes the demand for the services of individuals in the second category *more elastic* – that is, the services of large segments of the working population can be more easily substituted by the services of other people across national boundaries. Globalization therefore fundamentally transforms the employment relationship.

The fact that "workers" can be more easily substituted for each other across national boundaries undermines what many conceive to be a postwar social bargain between workers and employers, under which the former would receive a steady increase in wages and benefits in return for labor peace. This is because increased substitutability results in the following concrete consequences:

- Workers now have to pay a larger share of the cost of improvements in work conditions and benefits (that is, they bear a greater incidence of nonwage costs).
- They have to incur greater instability in earnings and hours worked in response to shocks to labor demand or labor productivity (that is, volatility and insecurity increase).

- Their bargaining power erodes, so they receive lower wages and benefits whenever bargaining is an element in setting the terms of employment.

These considerations have received insufficient attention in the recent academic literature on trade and wages, which has focused on the downward shift in demand for unskilled workers rather than the increase in the elasticity of that demand.

Second, globalization engenders conflicts within and between nations over domestic norms and the social institutions that embody them. As the technology for manufactured goods becomes standardized and diffused internationally, nations with very different sets of values, norms, institutions, and collective preferences begin to compete head on in markets for similar goods. And the spread of globalization creates opportunities for trade between countries at very different levels of development.

This is of no consequence under the traditional multilateral trade policy of the WTO and the General Agreement on Tariffs and Trade (GATT): the "process" or "technology" through which goods are produced is immaterial, and so are the social institutions of the trading partners. Differences in national practices are treated just like differences in factor endowments or any other determinant of comparative advantage. However, introspection and empirical evidence both reveal that most people attach values to processes as well as outcomes. This is reflected in the norms that shape and constrain the domestic environment in which goods and services are produced – for example, workplace practices, legal rules, and social safety nets.

Trade becomes contentious when it unleashes forces that undermine the norms implicit in domestic practices. Many residents of advanced industrial countries are uncomfortable with the weakening of domestic institutions through the forces of trade, as when, for example, child labor in Honduras displaces workers in South Carolina or when pension benefits are cut in Europe in response to the requirements of the Maastricht treaty. This sense of unease is one way of interpreting the demands for "fair trade." Much of the discussion surrounding the "new" issues in trade policy – that is, labor standards, environment, competition policy, corruption – can be cast in this light of procedural fairness.

We cannot understand what is happening in these new areas until we take individual preferences for processes and the social arrangements that embody them seriously. In particular, by doing so we can start to make sense of people's uneasiness about the consequences of international economic integration and avoid the trap of automatically branding all concerned groups as self-interested protectionists. Indeed, since trade policy almost always has redistributive consequences (among sectors, income groups, and individuals), one cannot produce a principled defense of free trade without confronting the question of the fairness and legitimacy of the practices that generate these consequences. By the same token, one should not expect broad popular support for trade when trade involves exchanges that clash with (and erode) prevailing domestic social arrangements.

Third, globalization has made it exceedingly difficult for governments to provide social insurance – one of their central functions and one that has helped maintain social cohesion and domestic political support for ongoing liberalization throughout the postwar period. In essence, governments have used their fiscal powers to insulate domestic groups from excessive market risks, particularly those having an external origin. In fact, there is a striking correlation between an economy's exposure to foreign trade and the size of its welfare state. It is in the most open countries, such as Sweden,

Denmark, and the Netherlands, that spending on income transfers has expanded the most. This is not to say that the government is the sole, or the best, provider of social insurance. The extended family, religious groups, and local communities often play similar roles. My point is that it is a hallmark of the postwar period that governments in the advanced countries have been expected to provide such insurance.

At the present, however, international economic integration is taking place against the background of receding governments and diminished social obligations. The welfare state has been under attack for two decades. Moreover, the increasing mobility of capital has rendered an important segment of the tax base footloose, leaving governments with the unappetizing option of increasing tax rates disproportionately on labor income. Yet the need for social insurance for the vast majority of the population that remains internationally immobile has not diminished. If anything, this need has become greater as a consequence of increased integration. The question therefore is how the tension between globalization and the pressures for socialization of risk can be eased. If the tension is not managed intelligently and creatively, the danger is that the domestic consensus in favor of open markets will ultimately erode to the point where a generalized resurgence of protectionism becomes a serious possibility.

Each of these arguments points to an important weakness in the manner in which advanced societies are handling – or are equipped to handle – the consequences of globalization. Collectively, they point to what is perhaps the greatest risk of all, namely that the cumulative consequence of the tensions mentioned above will be the solidifying of a new set of class divisions – between those who prosper in the globalized economy and those who do not, between those who share its values and those who would rather not, and between those who can diversify away its risks and those who cannot. This is not a pleasing prospect, even for individuals on the winning side of the divide who have little empathy for the other side. Social disintegration is not a spectator sport – those on the sidelines also get splashed with mud from the field. Ultimately, the deepening of social fissures can harm all.

## Globalization: Now and Then

This is not the first time we have experienced a truly global market. By many measures, the world economy was possibly even more integrated at the height of the gold standard in the late 19th century than it is now. [ . . . ] In the United States and Europe, trade volumes peaked before World War I and then collapsed during the interwar years. Trade surged again after 1950, but none of the three regions is significantly more open by this measure now than it was under the late gold standard. Japan, in fact, has a lower share of exports in GDP now than it did during the interwar period.

Other measures of global economic integration tell a similar story. As railways and steamships lowered transport costs and Europe moved toward free trade during the late 19th century, a dramatic convergence in commodity prices took place (Williamson 1996). Labor flows were considerably higher then as well, as millions of immigrants made their way from the old world to the new. In the United States, immigration was responsible for 24 percent of the expansion of the labor force during the 40 years before World War I (Williamson 1996: appendix table 1). As for capital mobility, the share of net capital outflows in GNP was much higher in the United Kingdom during the classical gold standard than it has been since.

Does this earlier period of globalization hold any lessons for our current situation? It well might. There is some evidence, for example, that trade and migration had significant consequences for income distribution. According to Jeffrey Williamson, "[G]lobalization . . . accounted for more than half of the rising inequality in rich, labor-scarce countries [e.g., the United States, Argentina, and Australia] and for a little more than a quarter of the falling inequality in poor, labor-abundant countries [e.g., Sweden, Denmark, and Ireland]" in the period before World War I (1996: 19). Equally to the point are the political consequences of these changes:

> There is a literature almost a century old that argues that immigration hurt American labor and accounted for much of the rise in inequality from the 1890s to World War I, so much so that a labor-sympathetic Congress passed immigration quotas. There is a literature even older that argues that a New World grain invasion eroded land rents in Europe, so much so that landowner-dominated Continental Parliaments raised tariffs to help protect them from the impact of globalization. (Williamson 1996: 1)

Williamson (1996: 20) concludes that "the inequality trends which globalization produced are at least partly responsible for the interwar retreat from globalization [which appeared] first in the rich industrial trading partners."

Moreover, there are some key differences that make today's global economy more contentious. First, restrictions on immigration were not as common during the 19th century, and consequently labor's international mobility was more comparable to that of capital. Consequently, the asymmetry between mobile capital (physical and human) and immobile "natural" labor, which characterizes the present situation, is a relatively recent phenomenon. Second, there was little head-on international competition in identical or similar products during the previous century, and most trade consisted of the exchange of noncompeting products, such as primary products for manufactured goods. The aggregate trade ratios do not reflect the "vast increase in the exposure of tradable goods industries to international competition" that is now taking place compared with the situation in the 1890s (Irwin 1996: 42). Third, and perhaps most important, governments had not yet been called on to perform social-welfare functions on a large scale, such as ensuring adequate levels of employment, establishing social safety nets, providing medical and social insurance, and caring for the poor. This shift in the perceived role of government is also a relatively recent transformation, one that makes life in an interdependent economy considerably more difficult for today's policymakers.

At any rate, the lesson from history seems to be that continued globalization cannot be taken for granted. If its consequences are not managed wisely and creatively, a retreat from openness becomes a distinct possibility.

## Implications

[ . . . ]

We need to be upfront about the irreversibility of the many changes that have occurred in the global economy. Advances in communications and transportation mean that large segments of national economies are much more exposed to international trade and capital flows than they have ever been, regardless of what policymakers choose to do. There is only limited scope for government policy to make a difference. In addition, a serious retreat into protectionism would hurt the many groups that benefit from trade and would result in the same kind of social conflicts that globalization itself generates. We have to recognize that erecting trade barriers will help in only a limited set of circumstances and that trade policies will rarely be the best response to the problems that will be discussed here. Transfer and social insurance programs will generally dominate. In short, the genie cannot be stuffed back into the bottle, even if it were desirable to do so. We will need more imaginative and more subtle responses. [ . . . ]

## Notes

1   See also Kapstein (1996) and Vernon (n.d.). Kapstein argues that a backlash from labor is likely unless policymakers take a more active role in managing their economies. Vernon argues that we might be at the threshold of a global reaction against the pervasive role of multinational enterprises.
2   Outsourcing refers to companies' practice of subcontracting part of the production process – typically the most labor-intensive and least skill-intensive parts – to firms in other countries with lower costs.

## References

Irwin, Douglas (1996) The US in a New Global Economy? A Century's Perspective. *American Economic Review, Papers and Proceedings* 86(2) (May).

Kapstein, Ethan (1996) Workers and the World Economy. *Foreign Affairs* 75(3) (May–June).

Vernon, Raymond (n.d.) In the Hurricane's Eye: Multinational Enterprises in the Next Century. MS, Harvard University.

Williamson, Jeffrey (1996) Globalization and Inequality Then and Now: The Late Nineteenth and Late Twentieth Centuries Compared. NBER Working Paper 5491, National Bureau of Economic Research, Cambridge, Mass.

# 33

# Global Markets and National Politics

*Geoffrey Garrett*

[ ... ]

This article puts under the analytic microscope the proposition that global markets trump national politics as social forces. I focus on the relationships between three dimensions of integration into international markets – trade in goods and services, the multinationalization of production, and financial capital mobility – and the macroeconomic policy choices of the advanced industrial countries up until the mid-1990s.

One can certainly point to examples where globalization constraints on national policy choices are readily apparent. The mobility of financial capital, for example, has tended to put downward pressure on budget deficits because of the interest rate premiums the capital markets attach to them. But it is hard to make the case that globalization constraints are pervasive, or even the norm. Indeed, there are numerous instances in which various facets of market integration have been associated with both more interventionist government policies and greater divergence in national trajectories over a range of policy areas – without precipitating damaging capital flight in countries that have eschewed the neoliberal path.

Trade and government spending is the classic relationship that goes against simplistic conceptions of the lowest common denominator effects of market integration – not only in the Organization for Economic Cooperation and Development (OECD)[1] but also in the developing world.[2] Other globalization myths, however, should also be exposed. For example, increasing liquid capital mobility has been associated with faster growth in government spending and even with increases in effective rates of capital taxation – without resulting in capital flight or higher interest rates. Moreover, there is no evidence that the multinationalization of production has reduced macroeconomic policy autonomy.

There are two basic reasons why globalization constraints on policy choice are weaker than much contemporary rhetoric suggests. First, market integration has not only increased the exit options of producers and investors; it has also heightened feelings of economic insecurity among broader segments of society. This situation has strengthened political incentives for governments to use the policy instruments of the state to mitigate market dislocations by redistributing wealth and risk.

Second, although there are costs associated with interventionist government (the familiar refrain of neoclassical economics about tax distortions, crowding out, and regulatory rigidities), numerous government programs generate economic benefits that are attractive to mobile finance and production. Today it is not controversial to argue that good government entails protecting property rights and increasing human capital and physical infrastructure. But the logic should be extended further. Some economists have argued that reducing inequality stimulates growth by increasing social stability.[3] Prominent political scientists contend that economic policies redistributing wealth and risk also maintain popular support for the market.[4]

It should be a central objective of globalization research to see how these two sets of dynamics – capital's exit threats versus popular demands for redistribution, and the economic costs and benefits of interventionist government – play out in different contexts. In this article I point to two sources of variation. The first concerns differences among various facets of market integration and aspects of government policy choice (see the preceding examples). The second source of variation concerns domestic political conditions. Countries in which the balance of political power is tilted to the left continue to be more responsive to redistributive demands than those dominated by center-right parties. The existence of strong and centralized organizations of labor and business that coordinate economic activity reduces the economic costs of interventionist government by mitigating free-rider problems.

In summary, I do not believe that "collision course" is the correct metaphor to apply to the panoply of relationships between interventionist national economic policies and global markets. Peaceful coexistence is probably a better general image, as all agree it was during the golden age of capitalist democracy after World War II. One might go further to argue that, even in a world of capital mobility, there is still a virtuous circle between activist government and international openness. The government interventions emblematic of the modern welfare state provide buffers against the kinds of social and political backlashes that undermined openness in the first half of the twentieth century – protectionism, nationalism, and international conflict. At a time when Ethan Kapstein and others voice fears of the 1930s all over again [Kapstein 1996: 37], it is important that the economic benefits of government activism be better understood.

[ . . . ]

## Globalization Constraints

### Three globalization mechanisms

Market integration is thought to affect national policy autonomy through three basic mechanisms. These are trade competitiveness pressures, the multinationalization of production, and the integration of financial markets.

Increasing trade competition is the first component of the conventional globalization thesis. According to this view, big government is by definition uncompetitive.[5] Government spending crowds out private investment, is less efficient than market allocations, and cushions market disciplines on prices and wages. In turn, spending must be funded either by borrowing or by higher taxes. Taxes cut into firms' profits and depress entrepreneurial activity. Government borrowing increases interest rates. As a result of these effects, output and employment suffer from public sector expansion. Since no government can afford these consequences, trade competition must result in a rolling back of the public economy.

The second globalization mechanism concerns the multinationalization of production and the attendant credibility of firms' threats to move production from one country to another in search of higher rates of return. This was the "giant sucking sound" Ross Perot predicted the North American Free Trade Agreement would produce. Multinational exit has also been at the forefront of European debates in the 1990s. Indeed, for some, software engineers telecommuting from Bangalore to Seattle and Silicon Valley are the harbingers of the New World of the twenty-first century.[6] Robert Reich, for example, proclaimed in influential articles in the *Harvard Business Review* that the distinction between "us" and "them" in the global economy is not between countries, but rather between a nation's citizens and multinational firms operating in it, irrespective of where they are owned.[7]

As with trade, conventional arguments about the policy consequences of the multinationalization of production focus on the costs to business of interventionist government. The difference is that firms with production facilities in more than one country can evade these costs by exiting the national economy. Governments must thus embrace the free market if they are to compete for the investment and jobs provided by multinational firms.

The final argument made about globalization constraints focuses on the international integration of financial markets. Traders operating twenty-four hours a day can move mind-boggling amounts of money around the globe more or less instantaneously in ceaseless efforts to arbitrage profits. The potential for massive capital flight acts as the ultimate discipline on governments. In an already infamous aside, Clinton political strategist James Carville is said to have uttered "I used to think that if there was reincarnation, I wanted to come back as the president or the pope. But now I want to be the bond market: you can intimidate everyone."[8]

Scholarly analyses of the domestic effects of the integration of financial markets often are almost as strident, replete with evocative images such as "casino capitalism,"[9] "quicksilver capital,"[10] and "who elected the bankers?"[11] The central logic underpinning this research program is the power conferred on financial capital by the credibility of its exit threats. Governments are held to ransom by the markets, the price is high, and punishment for noncompliance is swift.[12] If the policies and institutions of which the markets approve are not found in a country, money will hemorrhage until they are. [ . . . ]

## Reassessing the Policy Consequences of Globalization

### Trade, compensation, and embedded liberalism

Arguments about the constraining effects of market integration on economic policy choice have a long and distinguished history. There is, however, a very different approach to the globalization–domestic politics relationship that also has an impressive pedigree. Karl Polanyi's analysis of the emergence of industrial democracy in the nineteenth century emphasized a "double movement" with two components.

> One component was the principle of economic liberalism, aiming at the establishment of a self-regulating market, relying on the support of the trading classes, and using largely laissez faire and free trade as its methods; the other was the principle of social protection, aiming at the conservation of man and nature as well as productive organization, relying on the varying support of those most immediately affected by the deleterious action of the market, and using instruments of intervention as its methods.[13]

Forty years later, John Gerard Ruggie made a similar argument about the post-World War II reconstruction of open markets and democratic politics.[14] He characterized the Bretton Woods system as sustaining an "embedded liberalism" compromise that coupled trade liberalization with domestic policies that cushioned market dislocations. At about the same time, Peter Katzenstein argued that the distinctive feature of the small European democracies was their willingness to adjust and adapt to international markets while compensating those adversely affected by this process.[15] Most recently, Dani Rodrik showed that the trade openness–domestic compensation nexus continues to hold throughout the world, not just in the industrial democracies.[16]

The embedded liberalism perspective did not question the core proposition of trade theory that liberalization, in the long run, is good for all segments of society. The distinctive feature of this scholarship was the recognition that the short-run political dynamics of exposure to trade (and to other international markets) are very different. Openness increases social dislocations and inequality and hence heightens political pressures for dampening these effects. If protectionism (and the disastrous spiral of economic decline, nationalism, and conflict with which it was associated in the 1930s) is to be averted, government must redistribute market allocations of wealth and risk.

Bretton Woods facilitated the twin goals of trade liberalization and domestic compensation by combining fixed exchange rates with capital controls.[17] Fixed rates promoted trade by stabilizing expectations about future price movements. Capital controls gave governments the macroeconomic autonomy to smooth business cycles through countercyclical demand management.

[ ... ]

Strategies of domestic compensation in response to trade liberalization, however, were not limited to demand management. Rather, analysts describe the domestic policy regimes that emerged during the Bretton Woods era as the "Keynesian welfare state." In addition to the Keynesianism described earlier, the term also implied the public provision of social insurance (through pensions, unemployment benefits, and other income transfer programs) and social services (most notably education and health care), all paid for by relatively high and progressive systems of taxation.[18]

It is easy to see why the welfare state component served the political purposes of embedded liberalism. Social insurance directly supports those adversely affected by market risk. The public provision of social services not only provides benefits to consumers irrespective of their ability to pay but also generates a source of employment that is less vulnerable to the vicissitudes of market competition. Progressive taxes take into account the ability of different segments of society to pay for government programs. The welfare state redistributes wealth and risk, thereby dampening popular opposition to free markets.

But what about the economic effects of the welfare state (that is, assuming spending and taxation are in balance)? [ ... ] The contending arguments mirror closed economy analyses from public finance, made all the more important by trade liberalization, which renders national economies price takers in international markets. Claims about the uncompetitiveness of the welfare state concentrate on the costs of government provision of social insurance and social services. The welfare state lessens market disciplines and crowds out private sector entrepreneurship; taxes distort investment decisions in ways that reduce efficiency.

On the other hand, many people argue that interventionist government generates numerous economic benefits that may at least offset these costs. The key notion here is the public provision of collective goods that are undersupplied by markets. Even economists in the Chicago school tradition consider some government services to be essential to capitalism: the rule of law and securing of property rights.[19] For new growth theorists, public education and the government provision of human capital and physical infrastructure are also important drivers of development.[20]

The logic of politically correctable market failures can, however, be applied more broadly. For example, it is well established in development economics that material inequality is bad for growth. Alberto Alesina and Roberto Perotti have argued that this is because inequality leads to social conflict, which stability-seeking investors do not like.[21] Since the welfare state mitigates conflict by reducing market-generated inequalities of risk and wealth, it may have beneficial rather than deleterious consequences for business.[22] Government spending may thus stimulate investment via two channels – increasing productivity through improvements in human and physical capital and increasing stability through maintaining support for market openness.

In summary, the embedded liberalism compromise of the Bretton Woods period combined an international regime of trade openness, fixed exchange rates, and capital controls with the domestic political economy of the Keynesian welfare state. The final observation that should be made about this combination is that many analysts believe that embedded liberalism was most prominent and worked best in countries characterized by strong and centralized (corporatist) labor movements and powerful social democratic parties. Center-left parties are more likely to be sensitive to the political demands of short-term market losers. Corporatist labor movements have incentives to tailor wage growth to benefit the economy as a whole and hence not to take advantage of government compensation (in the form either of Keynesian demand management or welfare state expansion) with demands for less work at higher pay.[23]

## The crisis of embedded liberalism?

Notwithstanding the manifest successes of embedded liberalism in the Bretton Woods period, it is widely believed today that the open markets–domestic compensation compromise is no longer viable. The most prominent causal agent in its purported demise is heightened mobility of productive and financial capital and the decline of restrictions on international flows with which it has been associated.[24] No one suggests that political demands for compensation or the need for government to mitigate anti-international pressures have declined.[25] Rather, the conventional view is that the ability of government to deliver its side of the embedded liberalism compromise has been dramatically reduced.

There are two different mechanisms by which increased capital mobility is thought to render domestic compensation infeasible.[26] The first concerns financial market integration and traditional Keynesianism. Ruggie and others argue that financial integration makes fixed exchange rates imperative, to increase the markets' confidence about the stability of national economic policy.[27] But [ ... ] fixing the exchange rate under capital mobility vitiates macroeconomic policy autonomy.

The second mechanism concerns the multinationalization of production and the nature of the public economy. Rodrik argues that governments can no longer maintain, let alone expand, the generous welfare state–progressive taxation mix.[28] Mobile firms are deemed unwilling to pay the taxes to fund government programs. Rodrik claims that the future of the welfare state can only be secured by shifting the tax burden from mobile (firms and financiers) to immobile (labor) asset holders, emasculating its redistributive effects.

Thus, two of the most perceptive students of the contemporary international political economy both accept the core proposition of the conventional wisdom on globalization. A quantum leap in the exit threats of mobile producers and investors has tilted the balance of power strongly in favor of the market over politics at the national level. The following two subsections question this argument by exploring in more detail the domestic effects of the multinationalization of production and financial market integration.

## The multinationalization of production and the collective goods of government

Embedded liberalism, Bretton Woods style, comprised three elements – fixed exchange rates and capital controls, Keynesian demand management, and extensive government spending and redistributive taxation. How might we expect these to be affected by the multinationalization of production?

One could argue that multinationals favor fixed exchange rates because these lessen uncertainty about the consequences of internationally diversified production regimes.[29] If this were the case in a world of liquid capital mobility, governments that acceded to the demands of multinationals would also be giving up their monetary autonomy. But today there is arguably a better way than pressing for fixed exchange rates for multinational producers to insure against international price movements: hedging using financial instruments. The range of derivatives options available to investors is limited only by the imagination of market makers. And multinationals would probably prefer to control their own risk portfolios than to cede this right to governments. This is all the more likely given the difficulty of running stable pegged exchange rates in the contemporary era (see the next subsection). As a result, it seems unlikely that the multinationalization of production should significantly increase the incentives for governments to fix their exchange rates and hence tie their hands with respect to monetary policy.

The primary concern of the globalization literature with respect to the multinationalization of production, however, is the reaction of mobile producers to high levels of government spending and taxation (and to other production costs, most notably wages). The conventional view is that the decisional calculus of multinationals is simple: produce in the lowest cost location. If this were correct, increased exit options for firms would put considerable downward pressures on the size and scope of the public economy.

For those who study FDI decisions and corporate alliance strategies for a living, however, the behavior of multinational producers is more complex. First, the right metric of costs controls for productivity, and on this score small government–low-wage economies do not look nearly so attractive.[30] Second, the literature on international corporate strategy focuses primarily on accessing new technology, new distribution channels, and new markets as the drivers of FDI and strategic alliances.[31] Third, if a firm opens, acquires, or allies with a production facility in a foreign country, this does not necessarily imply that it reduces activity in its home country. Under many circumstances new foreign activities will go hand in hand with increased activity and employment at home – "upstream" – in portions of the productive, marketing, and distributive processes where more of the final value is added. Finally, international diversification provides another way for firms to hedge against currency risk. Taken together, these considerations belie the notion of a lowest cost mantra in the location decisions of multinational producers.[32]

Why might multinationalized producers be willing to locate in countries with large public economies and high taxes? My answer is the same as that for trade. Multinational producers care about the real economy, and factors such as productivity and stability heavily influence their investment decisions. Activist governments can do something positive to influence these decisions, by increasing human and physical capital stocks and by promoting public support for open markets. Indeed, these collective goods may be even more important than was the case for trade as a result of the heightened feelings of economic insecurity among citizens generated by multinationalization.

There is an important objection to my argument, however, that was not germane to the trade discussion – tax competition among governments for mobile producers. Rodrik rightly argues that even if multinational producers benefit from government interventionism in the ways I have suggested, they nonetheless have incentives to try to free ride on these collective goods by not paying the taxes to fund them.[33] Multinationals can use threats of exit to force governments to shift the tax burden away from capital and onto labor. But before making such threats, firms must weight the costs and benefits of helping finance the provision of collective goods from which they benefit in one country versus paying lower taxes but receiving fewer benefits in another.[34] It is an empirical, not a theoretical, matter whether the costs of big government outweigh the benefits I have outlined and hence whether multinationalization should put downward pressures on capital taxation.

In summary, there is little reason to expect that the multinationalization of production produces strong pressures for fixed exchange rates or constrains macroeconomic policy autonomy in the classical Keynesian sense. A better argument can be made about constraints on the spending, and particularly the taxing, policies of governments. But these constraints will be much less apparent if, as I argue in this case, large public economies generate numerous outcomes that are attractive to multinationals.

## The mobility of financial capital, exchange-rate regimes, and fiscal policy

Even if I am right to question common assumptions about the behavior of multinationalized producers, the debate could simply shift to policy constraints generated by the integration of financial markets. Here again, I wish to argue that the strictures imposed by global capital are not nearly so tight as is often presumed. Unpacking the likely policy effects of the international integration of financial markets should begin with its implications for the choice of exchange-rate regimes.

There is only one clear case where financial integration vitiates macroeconomic policy autonomy – monetary policy where there are no barriers to cross-border capital movements and where a country's exchange rate is fixed.[35] But this only raises the questions: Why do countries choose to fix their exchange rates? How important is globalization to this choice?[36] European Union officials in the context of the monetary union debate have revived old arguments from Bretton Woods about the importance of currency stability to trade.[37] Empirical work, however, fails to show any strong positive impact of fixed rates on trade expansion, presumably because of the effectiveness of currency-hedging instruments under floating rate regimes.[38] The more common argument these days concerns the policy credibility of governments with the financial markets. By fixing the exchange rate, governments are supposed to be able to mitigate the damaging effects of capital flight or other policies that would be required to stop it.

Unlike exporters and multinational producers, financial market actors care much less about productivity and the real economy than they do about monetary phenomena that affect day-to-day returns on financial transactions. Inflation is the key variable. If the markets expect inflation to increase in the future, the price they are willing to pay for a national currency will decrease, and the interest rates they charge on loans will be higher. Thus, governments have incentives to establish reputations for price stability because inflationary expectations lead the financial markets to behave in ways that harm the real economy.

Few economists dispute the argument that inflation-fighting credibility is important to macroeconomic performance.[39] There is much less support, however, for the notion that fixing the exchange rate is a good way to achieve credibility under conditions of financial integration. The evidence is at best mixed as to whether participation in fixed exchange-rate regimes lowers inflation rates.[40] There may be better domestic ways to gain credibility with the financial markets, such as making the central bank more independent or enacting balanced budget laws.[41] Moreover, one should expect financial market actors to prefer floating exchange rates to fixed ones since they make money from arbitrage and commissions.[42]

On the other side of the equation, the costs of fixed exchange rates are often high. Although fiscal policy may be quite effective in a country that pegs its exchange rate, it cannot use monetary policy to adjust to any economic shock that affects it differently from the object of the peg (gold, a single currency, or a basket of currencies). Depreciating the nominal value of a currency remains a very effective way to increase the real competitiveness of an economy in recession – because domestic prices do not rise immediately in response to nominal depreciations.[43] But smooth depreciations are not possible for countries seeking to defend currency pegs. Rather, governments typically engage in desperate efforts to maintain a given exchange rate and are often vanquished by the markets in damaging waves of speculative attacks. In this context it should be noted that the headline currency crises of the 1990s – in Europe, Mexico, and East Asia – all involved countries seeking to sustain pegs that the markets deemed untenable.

For these reasons many economists today recommend that fixed exchange-rate regimes under conditions of financial integration should only extend to countries that constitute optimal currency areas. These areas comprise only those countries for whom there is little need to maintain domestic monetary autonomy – because their business cycles move together, wages adjust quickly to asymmetric shocks, labor is mobile across national borders, or fiscal arrangements transfer funds from boom to bust regions.

In the headline case of European monetary union, for example, most analysts believe that Europe's optimal currency area extends only to Austria, the Benelux countries, Germany, and perhaps France – but certainly not to Italy.[44] [ ... ]

In summary, the arguments in favor of the common globalization proposition that the integration of financial markets creates irresistible pressures for government to fix their exchange rates to increase market credibility are far from convincing. Fixed exchange rates may make sense for some highly interdependent economies. Countries that cannot gain market credibility with domestic policies (for example, some unstable developing nations) may have little choice but to fix their exchange rates. But for many countries, and probably the bulk of the OECD, floating the exchange rate makes more sense under conditions of financial capital mobility.

Moving to fiscal policy, increasing public sector deficits clearly puts upward pressure on interest rates in a world of capital mobility (particularly if the exchange rate floats). But how large is this interest-rate premium? Financial integration reduces the costs of fiscal expansion by making available an immense size of potential lenders.[45] At some point, of course, higher debt burdens may trigger fears of governments' defaulting on their loans – resulting in dramatic reductions in the availability of credit and skyrocketing interest rates. This was the case during the Latin American debt crises of the 1980s, but this limit seems not yet to have been reached in any industrial democracy.[46]

Belgium is the clearest instance of the weakness of fiscal constraints under capital mobility. The Belgian franc has long been stably pegged against the deutsche mark, with very small interest-rate differentials between the two countries. This is despite the fact that Belgian public debt has been the highest in the OECD for most of the last decade, and more than twice as large as Germany's. To take a harder European case, public debt is also very high in Italy. Italian interest rates have sometimes during the past twenty years been as much as three or four points higher than German rates. But if this is the most brutal fiscal repression wrought by global finance among the industrial countries, the proclamations of many commentators would seem somewhat hyperbolic.

I have now discussed two conventional parts of macroeconomic policy – exchange-rate regime choice and the running of fiscal deficits – in the context of global finance. What about constraints on the size of government itself? Here a distinction should be drawn between the preferences of financial markets actors and those of multinationalized producers. The latter can and should pay predominant attention to the effect of government policy on productivity and real aggregates – and hence ask whether the costs of big government outweigh the benefits (as discussed in the previous subsection). Financial market participants, in contrast, focus almost exclusively on the effect of government policy on the supply of and demand for money.

The financial markets must ask a simple question: will a government raise new taxes to pay for higher spending, or will it seek to borrow money? If the answer is "tax," one should expect the markets to be relatively unconcerned – even if some of these revenues are raised by capital taxation. But if the answer is "borrow," the markets know that the government will have an incentive to inflate in the future to try to reduce the real cost of their debt. Higher interest rates must be charged if bond yields are to be maintained, the currency must depreciate if real exchange rates are to remain stable. Thus, the financial markets care much less about the size and scope of government interventions than about how they are paid for.

[ ... ]

# Macroeconomic Policy

In this section I examine the relationships between market integration and macroeconomic policy. I concentrate on three policy indicators: total government spending, public sector deficits, and capital taxation. Spending is a simple summary indicator of government involvement in the economy. Deficits measure overall budgetary stances. Capital taxation is the single part of tax systems that many believe to be most vulnerable to globalization constraints.[47]

# Over-time trends

[ . . . ] Average [OECD] government spending basically doubled as a portion of GDP from 1960 to the mid-1990s, when it comprised over half of total output. As might be expected, spending increased most during the deep recessions of the mid-1970s, early 1980s, and early 1990s. But the size of the public economy only decreased as a portion of GDP during one upturn in the business cycle – the mid-1980s. Given that this is the period on which many influential analyses of globalization constraints are based, this may explain the prominence of assertions about public sector rollback. Nonetheless, the history of government spending in the postwar OECD is predominantly one of sustained growth.

The expansion of the public economy has not been wholly matched by increased taxes. Budget deficits increased by about seven points from 1960 to 1994. It is often assumed that this revenue shortfall reflects the declining ability of governments to tax increasingly mobile capital. Changes in marginal rates of corporate income taxation are consistent with this view – they have declined considerably in most OECD countries in the past fifteen years.[48] But from the perspective of revenue-hungry governments, these marginal rates are not the whole story. Governments certainly have incentives to reduce taxes that impede growth-creating investment, of which marginal corporate tax rates are a clear example. But most cuts in marginal rates in the OECD have been accompanied by other reforms that have increased the tax base – reductions in investment incentives, depreciation allowances, and other loopholes that pertain to capital taxation.[49]

[ . . . ] [T]he overall trend in effective rates of capital taxation has been upward, quite strongly so. Rates in the early 1990s averaged almost 40 percent, up from around 30 percent in the early 1970s. This is a long way from predictions of a free fall in capital taxation resulting from the exit threats of multinational firms and financial speculators.

In summary, the trends [ . . . ] are hard to square with the notion of pervasive globalization constraints on national economic policy autonomy. Does one get a different picture by examining economic policy data on a country-by-country basis?

# Variations across countries and market segments

In this subsection I explore cross-national variations in economic policy and their relationships with globalization. Three indicators of market integration are used – total trade (a simple proxy for competitiveness pressures),[50] FDI flows (for the multina-tionalization of production),[51] and the financial openness index and covered interest-rate differentials (the integration of financial markets). These relationships are also compared with the associations between economic policy and a simple partisan poli-tics variable (the combined power of left-wing parties and organized labor movements) that historically has had a marked impact on economic policy choice.

[...]

The coefficient of variation for total government spending since 1985 is quite small. One could debate whether OECD public economies have become "about the same size." After all, Switzerland's public economy is still only half the size of Sweden's. What is more interesting, however, is that national trajectories diverged considerably from historical averages (1960–84) to the post-1985 period. Taking the extreme cases, spending grew six times as much in Spain as in the United Kingdom. This divergence is precisely the opposite of the conventional wisdom about the effects of globalized markets.

The deficits data are even less supportive of the conventional view. There was con-siderable dispersion in budgetary stances in the post-1985 period as well as in terms of changes from historical averages. Some of the cross-national differences are dra-matic. Switzerland ran surpluses of over 2 percent of GDP after the 1985 period, whereas deficits in neighboring Italy were over 10 percent. Deficits in Greece increased by more than six points from the pre- to post-1985 periods, but they declined by almost two points in Japan.

Perhaps most surprisingly of all, the capital tax coefficients of variation do not look much different from the spending and deficits numbers. In the post-1985 period, con-siderable dispersion in capital tax rates remained. But the divergence from pre- to post-1985 rates of capital taxation was even more marked. Capital tax rates declined by 2.7 points in the United States, but they increased by more than 10 points in Finland, Japan, and Sweden.

These descriptive data can only support one conclusion: fiscal policies among the OECD countries have not converged in recent years. Is there any more evidence of global-ization constraints when one breaks market integration down into its components?

[...]

On the one hand, and consistent with my arguments, exposure to trade, FDI flows, and left-labor power were all associated with greater spending after 1985. On the other hand, the covered interest rate–spending correlation implies a constraining effect of capital mobility on the public economy. One way to reconcile these findings would be to endogenize capital mobility, hypothesizing that strong left-labor regimes have chosen to protect their public economies by retaining significant controls on the mobility of capital.[52] This may have been the case in the past, but the correlation between the power of the left and the strength of trade unions and capital mobility all but evaporated by the latter half of the 1980s.[53]

An alternative explanation is that countries have reacted in very different ways to increasing capital mobility, based on the balance of partisan power within their borders. I have presented elsewhere more sophisticated analyses – using panel regres-sions with multiplicative interactions between globalization and partisan politics – that support this view.[54] Strong left-labor regimes responded to financial market integra-tion with ever-higher levels of public spending, whereas governments in countries with much weaker left parties and trade unions cut back the public economy.

Now consider the correlations for public sector deficits after 1985. Contra standard assumptions about left-labor power, deficits historically have been smaller in strong left-labor regimes than elsewhere.[55] Nonetheless, one should expect globalization – especially financial market integration – to have put downward pressures on deficits. The bivariate correlations do not strongly support this expectation. Financial openness and total trade were somewhat correlated with smaller deficits. But this was not the case for FDI or interest-rate differentials.

Finally and perhaps most surprisingly, the capital tax correlations for the post-1985 period were no more supportive of globalization conventional wisdom. Lower tax rates were correlated with greater exposure to trade, financial openness, and covered interest-rate differentials, but none of these associations was at all strong. In contrast, FDI flows were weakly associated with higher capital taxes. Finally, the association between left-labor power and capital tax rates was positive and larger than any of the globalization–taxation correlations were.

No great weight can be attached to these simple bivariate correlations. But even the most sophisticated existing research on taxation and globalization does not strongly support a race-to-the-bottom interpretation. Rodrik finds that capital mobility constrains capital taxation but only in countries with high levels of trade dependence and trade volatility.[56] Quinn and Swank report little or no relationship between capital mobility and corporate taxation.[57] Garrett argues that the effects of globalization on capital taxes, as was the case for spending, are contingent on the partisan balance of power.[58] Hallerberg and Basinger demonstrate that the number of veto players, not capital mobility, best explains changes in marginal corporate tax rates in the latter 1980s.[59]

Let us now turn to correlations based on changes in economic policy pre- and post-1985 [...]. These data are no more indicative of a policy race to the bottom. Both measures of financial integration were quite strongly associated with faster increases in government spending (as was left-labor power). The financial integration–deficit correlations were much weaker and of contradictory signs.

Consistent with the over-time analysis, the bivariate correlations presented in this subsection belie common notions about strong and pervasive globalization constraints on national autonomy. These analyses are certainly not definitive, but they should prompt further research into what are undoubtedly complicated relationships between globalization and policy choice.

## Capital Flight

If the OECD countries have not converged around a less interventionist macroeconomic policy regime in recent years, have countries with larger public economies or bigger budget deficits suffered from debilitating capital flight? If the answer is "yes," one might reasonably suspect that globalization-induced convergence would soon become the norm. If not, continuing cross-national variations in policy regimes would seem more likely. This section examines the policy–capital flight relationship with respect to multinational exit, interest rate premiums, and currency depreciation.

[...] Larger public sector deficits were associated with smaller, not larger, net outflows of FDI – reflecting the need for domestic debt to be funded by infusions of foreign capital. These correlations should give pause to purveyors of conventional globalization parables, for whom the loss of multinational investment as a result of interventionist government is a central theme.

Things were different, however, with respect to the behavior of the financial markets, measured by the long-term interest rates charged on government debt and the strength of currencies in foreign exchange markets. There was a clear correlation between a country's budgetary stance and the reaction of the financial markets. Bigger deficits were associated with higher interest rates and with greater depreciations against the dollar. Furthermore, interest rates were higher in countries with larger public economies, and depreciations were associated with higher rates of capital taxation. [ ... ]

In summary, there is some evidence supporting the view that governments that have persisted with activist fiscal stances in recent years have paid a price in global capital markets. The causal pathways between fiscal policy and the propensity for capital flight, however, are quite diffuse. It is possible, of course, that the absence of globalization constraints on government spending and taxation only shows that financial markets are not yet sufficiently integrated for these effects to be apparent. There may be a threshold – not yet reached in the OECD – beyond which the policy race to the bottom will ensue. One preliminary way to test this argument is to examine the political economy of fiscally decentralized countries, where there are effectively no barriers to movement across state lines. The United States is a good example.

[ ... ] The relevant comparison with respect to the OECD is not overall tax rates (given the size of the federal government in the United States), but rather the dispersion of tax rates. The coefficient of variation for state taxes is .32. This is higher than the comparable OECD-wide coefficients for both capital taxation and government spending [ ... ]. The complete integration of the US market has not resulted in convergence of tax rates around a minimal mean. Nor is it the case that the low-tax states are the best macroeconomic performers – Louisiana, North Dakota, and Wyoming are quite poor. Texas and Alaska can afford low taxes because of their wealth of natural resources. The data should give pause to those who believe that it is only a matter of time before market pressures force fiscal convergence on the OECD.

## Governing in the Global Economy

In this article I have sought to paint in broad brush strokes the relationship between the globalization of markets and national autonomy in the OECD. I have made two basic points. First, there are strong parallels between recent arguments about the constraining effects of globalization on national autonomy and those all the way back to the eighteenth century about the domestic effects of market integration. With hindsight, we know that past predictions of the effective demise of the nation-state were unfounded. Are there signs that things will be different in the contemporary epoch?

My second point is that, up until the mid-1990s, globalization has not prompted a pervasive policy race to the neoliberal bottom among the OECD countries, nor have governments that have persisted with interventionist policies invariably been hamstrung by damaging capital flight. Governments wishing to expand the public economy for political reasons may do so (including increasing taxes on capital to pay for new spending) without adversely affecting their trade competitiveness or prompting multinational producers to exit. The reason is that governments provide economically important collective goods – ranging from the accumulation of human and physical capital, to social stability under conditions of high market uncertainty, to popular support for the market economy itself – that are undersupplied by markets and valued by actors who are interested in productivity. This is particularly the case in corporatist political economies where the potential costs of interventionist government are mitigated by coordination among business, government, and labor.

This is not to say, however, that no facet of globalization significantly constrains national policy options. In particular, the integration of financial markets is more constraining than either trade or the multinationalization of production. But even here, one must be very careful to differentiate among various potential causal mechanisms.

Talk of lost monetary autonomy only makes sense if one believes that the integration of financial markets forces governments to peg their exchange rates to external anchors of stability. On recent evidence, the credibility gains of doing so are far from overwhelming; indeed, noncredible pegs (that is, those not consistent with other political and economic conditions) have promoted the most debilitating cases of financial speculation and instability. On the other hand, the costs of giving up the exchange rate as a tool of economic adjustment are great, and economies that allow their currencies to float freely seem to benefit as a result. Governments simply should not feel any compunction to give up monetary autonomy in the era of global financial markets.

But even if countries float their exchange rates, the financial markets – fearing inflation – do impose interest-rate premiums on governments that persistently run large budget deficits. Some governments have been willing to pay this price in the name of other objectives. Others have sought domestic solutions to credibility problems in the markets, such as central banking reforms. Still others (especially in the developing world) apparently have been unable to attain reputations for fiscal responsibility. For these countries, fixing the exchange rate may be the only option, but there can be no guarantee that this will not just fuel even more financial speculation.

Finally, there is no evidence that the financial markets attach interest-rate premiums to the expansion of the public economy per se – that is, provided new tax revenues balance increased spending. This is even true if the taxation of capital is one source of new revenues. Moreover, the empirical connections between expansion of the public economy and deficits are quite weak and heavily mediated by domestic political conditions. Strong left-labor regimes, for example, have historically been able to increase government spending without incurring large debts. The financial markets are essentially disinterested in the size and scope of government. Their primary concern is whether the government balances its books.

My analysis is thus considerably more bullish about the future of the embedded liberalism compromise than some of its earlier advocates suggest. As a result, I do not believe that supporters of interventionist government must call for a dose of protectionism or the reimposition of capital controls to maintain the domestic balance between equity and efficiency. Nor must advocates look to international cooperation and institutions as the only attractive option for the future. As has been the case for more than two hundred years, the coupling of openness with domestic compensation remains a robust and desirable solution to the problem of reaping the efficiency benefits of capitalism while mitigating its costs in terms of social dislocations and inequality.

## Notes

1　Cameron 1978.
2　Rodrik 1997.
3　Alesina and Perotti 1996.
4　See Katzenstein 1985; Przeworski and Wallerstein 1982; and Ruggie 1983.
5　See C. Pierson 1991; and Pfaller et al. 1991.
6　Greider 1997.
7　Reich 1990 and 1991.
8　"A Survey of the World Economy: Who's in the Driving Seat?" *The Economist*, Oct. 7, 1995, p. 3.
9　Strange 1986.
10　McKenzie and Lee 1991.
11　Pauly 1997.
12　For review article, see Cohen 1996.
13　Polanyi [1944] 1957: 132.
14　Ruggie 1983.
15　Katzenstein 1985.
16　Rodrik 1997.
17　The Bretton Woods system also allowed for consensually agreed adjustments in exchange-rate parities to correct fundamental disequilibrium in the balance of payments and IMF lending to support exchange rates during temporary crises. For an excellent analytic history of Bretton Woods, see Eichengreen 1996.
18　The seminal study is Shonfield 1965. Other important examples include Esping-Andersen 1985; Goldthorpe 1984; and Lindberg and Maier 1985.
19　[ . . . ] It has also become a central component of official development policy; World Bank 1997.
20　See Aschauer 1991; and Barro and Sala-I-Martin 1995.
21　Alesina and Perotti 1996.
22　Garrett 1998a. For an alternative view, see Persson and Tabellini 1994.
23　See Alvarez et al. 1991; Garrett 1998a; and Lange and Garrett 1985. Some scholars argue that the successes of this regime type had as much to do with the organization of business as the organization of labor; see Soskice 1990; and Swenson 1991.
24　Some scholars suggest that financial integration has been driven by developments in information technology over which governments have had little control; see Bryant 1987; and Goodman and Pauly 1993. Others argue that the removal of capital controls was an ideological choice that could be reversed; see Sobel 1994; and Banuri and Schor 1992. I take the intermediate position of Frieden and Rogowski that, even if theoretically still effective, the opportunities costs associated with capital controls have increased greatly in recent decades; Frieden and Rogowski 1996.
25　P. Pierson 1996.
26　Scholars often argue that corporatist labor market institutions have eroded over time, particularly in Scandinavia. Iversen 1996; and Pontusson and Swenson 1996. But more broadly based studies suggest that the structure of organized labor movements has been remarkably stable; see Golden 1998; Lange and Scruggs 1997; and Lange et al. 1995.
27　Ruggie 1996. See also Scharpf 1991.
28　Rodrik 1997. For a similar argument, see Steinmo 1993.
29　Moravcsik makes this argument, for example, with respect to European efforts to fix exchange rates since the end of Bretton Woods; Moravcsik 1998.
30　Krugman 1996. Nonetheless, many fear that the rapid dissemination of technology will soon dramatically reduce productivity differences among countries.
31　See Cantwell 1989; Caves 1996; Dunning 1988; and IMF 1991.

32  This is not to claim, however, that production costs are irrelevant. There are some sectors, such as textiles and apparel, where labor costs have a large bearing on location decisions; Leamer 1996. Moreover, there are temptations for governments to try to attract FDI by offering specific tax concessions and other monetary inducements; see Hines 1997.

33  Rodrik 1997.

34  Of course, multinational firms could still try to free ride on government services through tax evasion or accounting tricks.

35  Mundell 1962.

36  For a good precis of the various arguments about the determinants of exchange-rate regime choice, see Eichengreen 1994.

37  Commission of the European Communities 1990.

38  IMF 1983.

39  This is the core of the rational expectations revolution in macroeconomics. See Friedman 1968; and Lucas 1972.

40  Collins was the first to question the inflation-fighting properties of the EMS; Collins 1988.

41  Fratianni and von Hagen 1992.

42  Frieden 1991.

43  Obstfeld 1997.

44  If this is correct, why would Germany want irrevocably to fix its exchange rate against Italy? Analyses of Germany's EMU position typically involve politics, specifically Helmut Kohl's ambitions concerning political union in Europe. For an accessible survey of the contending arguments and evidence, see Garrett 1998b.

45  Corsetti and Roubini 1995.

46  Corsetti and Roubini 1991.

47  These indicators exclude important facets of microeconomic reform that arguably have been driven by globalization in recent decades – deregulation and privatization, for example. The qualitative evidence on microeconomic reform, however, is not conclusive. For insightful analyses, see Berger and Dore 1996; and Vogel 1995.

48  Cummins et al. 1995.

49  Swank 1998.

50  Garrett and Mitchell show that the effects of total trade on welfare state expenditures are not significantly different from those of trade volatility or imports from low-wage economies; Garrett and Mitchell 1998.

51  Note that these flow numbers do not take into account the stock of foreign investment in a country, nor strategic alliances among multinational firms from different countries.

52  Quinn and Inclan 1997.

53  Garrett 1998a.

54  Garrett 1995.

55  Garrett and Lange 1991.

56  Rodrik 1997.

57  See Quinn 1997; and Swank 1998.

58  Garrett 1998c.

59  Hallerberg and Basinger 1998.

## References

Alesina, A. and Perotti, R. (1996) Income Distribution, Political Instability and Investment. *Quarterly Journal of Economics* 94.

Alvarez, R., Garrett, G., and Lange, P. (1991) Government Partisanship, Labor Organization and Macroeconomic Performance. *American Political Science Review* 85.

Aschauer, D. (1991) *Public Investment and Private Sector Growth*. Washington DC: Economic Policy Institute.

Banuri, T. and Schor, J. (1992) *Financial Openness and National Autonomy*. New York: Oxford University Press.

Barro, R. and Sala-I-Martin, X. (1995) *Economic Growth*. New York: Macmillan.

Berger, S. and Dore, R. (1996) *National Diversity and Global Capitalism*. Ithaca: Cornell University Press.

Bryant, R. (1987) *International Financial Integration*. Washington DC: Brookings Institution.

Cameron, D. R. (1978) The Expansion of the Public Economy. *American Political Science Review* 72.

Cantwell, J. (1989) *Technical Innovations in MNCs*. Oxford: Blackwell.

Caves, R. (1996) *Multinational Enterprise and Economic Analysis*, 2nd edn. New York: Cambridge University Press.

Cohen, B. J. (1996) Phoenix risen: the resurrection of global finance. *World Politics* 48: 268–96.

Collins, S. (1988) Inflation and the European Monetary System. In F. Giavazzi, S. Milosia, and M. Miller (eds), *The European Monetary System*, New York: Cambridge University Press.

Commission of the European Communities (1990) One Market, One Money. *European Economy* 44.

Corsetti, G. and Roubini, N. (1991) Fiscal Deficits, Public Debt and Government Insolvency. *Journal of Japanese and International Economies* 5.

Corsetti, G. and Roubini, M. (1995) Political Biases in Fiscal Policy. In B. Eichengreen, J. Frieden, and J. Von Hagen (eds), *Monetary and Fiscal Policy in an Integrated Europe*, New York: Springer.

Cummins, J., Hassett, K., and Hubbard, R. (1995) Tax Reforms and Investment: A Cross-Country Comparison. NBER Working Paper 5232, National Bureau of Economic Research, Cambridge, Mass.

Dunning, J. (1988) *Multinationals, Technology and Competitiveness*. Boston: Unwin Hyman.

Eichengreen, B. (1994) The Endogeneity of Exchange Rate Regimes. In P. Kenen (ed.), *Understanding Interdependence*, Princeton: Princeton University Press.

Eichengreen, B. (1996) *Globalizing Capital: A History of the International Monetary System*. Princeton: Princeton University Press.

Esping-Andersen, G. (1985) *States against Markets*. Princeton: Princeton University Press.

Fratianni, M. and Von Hagen, J. (1992) *The European Monetary System and European Monetary Union*. Boulder: Westview Press.

Frieden, J. (1991) Invested Interests: The Politics of National Economic Policies in a World of Global Finance. *International Organization* 45.

Frieden, J. and Rogowski, R. (1996) The Impact of the International Economy on National Policies in Internationalization and Domestic Policies. In R. Keohane and H. Milner (eds), *Internationalization and Domestic Politics*, New York: Cambridge University Press.

Friedman, M. (1968) The Role of Monetary Policy. *American Economic Review* 58: 1–17.

Garrett, G. (1995) Capital Mobility, Trade and the Domestic Politics of Economic Policy. *International Organization* 49.

Garrett, G. (1998a) *Partisan Politics in the Global Economy*. New York: Cambridge University Press.

Garrett, G. (1998b) The Transition to Economic and Monetary Union. In B. Eichengreen and J. Frieden (eds), *Forging an Integrated Europe*, Ann Arbor: University of Michigan Press.

Garrett, G. (1998c) Capital Flows, Capital Mobility and Capital Taxation. MS, Yale University.

Garrett, G. and Lange, P. (1991) Political Responses to Interdependence, What's Left for the Left? *International Organization* 45.

Garrett, G. and Mitchell, D. (1998) External Risk and Social Insurance: Reassessing the Globalization–Welfare State Nexus. MS, Yale University.

Golden, M. (1998) Economic Integration and Industrial Relations. MS, University of California at Los Angeles.

Goldthorpe, J. (1984) *Order and Conflict in Contemporary Capitalism*. New York: Oxford University Press.

Goodman, J. and Pauly, L. (1993) The Obsolescence of Capital Controls. *World Politics* 46.

Greider, W. (1997) *One World, Ready or Not*. New York: Simon and Schuster.

Hallerberg, M. and Basinger, S. (1998) Internationalization and Changes in Tax Policy in OECD Countries. *Comparative Political Studies* 31.

Hines, J. (1997) Altered States: Taxes and the Location of FDI in America. *American Economic Review* 87.

IMF (1983) Exchange Rate Volatility and World Trade. MS, IMF, Washington DC.

IMF (1991) Determinants and Systemic Consequences of International Capital Flows. MS, IMF, Washington DC.

Iverson, T. (1996) Power Flexibility and the Breakdown of Centralized Wage Bargaining. *Comparative Politics* 28.

Kapstein, E. B. (1996) Workers and the World Economy? *Foreign Affairs* 75: 16–37.

Katzenstein, P. (1985) *Small States in World Markets: Industrial Policy in Europe*. Ithaca: Cornell University Press.

Krugman, P. (1996) *Pop Internationalism*. Cambridge, Mass.: MIT Press.

Lange, P. and Garrett, G. (1985) The Politics of Growth. *Journal of Politics* 47.

Lange, P. and Scruggs, L. (1997) Where Have All the Members Gone? Paper presented at the 93rd Annual Meeting of the American Political Science Association, Washington DC, Aug.

Lange, P., Wallerstein, M., and Golden, M. (1995) The End of Corporatism? Wage Setting in the Nordic and Germanic Countries. In S. Jacoby (ed.), *The Workers of Nations*, New York: Oxford University Press.

Leamer, E. (1996) Wage Inequality from International Competition and Technological Change. *American Economic Review* 86.

Lindberg, L. and Maier, C. (1985) *The Politics of Inflation and Economic Stagnation*. Washington DC: Brookings Institution.

Lucas, R. (1972) Expectations and the Neutrality of Money. *Journal of Economic Theory* 4.

McKenzie, R. and Lee, D. (1991) *Quicksilver Capital: How the Rapid Movement of Wealth Has Changed the World*. New York: Free Press.

Moravcsik, A. (1998) *The Choice for Europe: Social Purpose and State Power From Messina to Maastricht*. Ithaca: Cornell University Press.

Mundell, R. (1962) A Theory of Optimal Currency Areas. *American Economic Review* 51.

Obstfeld, M. (1997) Open Economy, Macroeconomics, Developments in Theory and Policy. NBER Working Paper 6319, National Bureau of Economic Research, Cambridge, Mass.

Pauly, L. (1997) *Who Elected the Bankers?* Ithaca: Cornell University Press.

Persson, T. and Tabellini, G. (1994) Is Inequality Harmful for Growth? *American Economic Review* 86.

Pfaller, A. et al. (1991) *Can the Welfare State Compete?* London: Macmillan.

Pierson, C. (1991) *Beyond the Welfare State?* Cambridge: Polity Press.

Pierson, P. (1996) The Politics of the Welfare State. *World Politics* 48.

Polanyi, K. (1957) *The Great Transformation*, first publ. 1944. New York: Farrar and Rinehart.

Pontusson, J. and Swenson, P. (1996) Labor Markets, Production Strategies and Wage Bargaining Institutions. *Comparative Political Studies* 29.

Przeworski, A. and Wallerstein, M. (1982) The Structure of Class Conflict in Democratic Capitalist Societies. *American Political Science Review* 76.

Quinn, D. (1997) The Correlation of Changes in International Financial Regulation. *American Political Science Review* 91.

Quinn, D. and Inclan, L. (1997) The Origins of Financial Openness. *American Journal of Political Science* 41.

Reich, R. (1990) Who Is Us? *Harvard Business Review* 68.

Reich, R. (1991) Who Is Them? *Harvard Business Review* 69.

Rodrik, D. (1997) *Has Globalization Gone Too Far?* Washington DC: Institute for International Economics.

Ruggie, J. (1983) International Regimes, Transactions and Change: Embedded Liberalism in the New Post War Economic Order. In S. Krasner (ed.), *International Regimes*, Ithaca: Cornell University Press.

Ruggie, J. (1996) Globalization and the Embedded Liberalism Compromise. Working Paper 97/1, Max Planck Institute for Gesellschaftforschung, Cologne.

Scharpf, F. (1991) *Crisis and Choice in European Social Democracy*. Ithaca: Cornell University Press.

Shonfield, A. (1965) *Modern Capitalism*. New York: Oxford University Press.

Sobel, A. (1994) *Domestic Choices, International Markets*. Ann Arbor: University of Michigan Press.

Soskice, D. (1990) Wage Determination: The Changing Role of Institutions in Advanced Industrialised Countries. *Oxford Review of Economic Policy* 6.

Steinmo, S. (1993) *Taxation and Democracy*. New Haven: Yale University Press.

Strange, S. (1986) *States versus Markets*. Cambridge: Cambridge University Press.

Swank, D. (1998) Funding the Welfare State. *Political Studies* 46(4).

Swenson, P. (1991) Bringing Capital Back In, or Social Democracy Reconsidered. *World Politics* 45.

Vogel, D. (1995) *Trading Up: Consumer and Environmental Regulation in a Global Economy*. Cambridge, Mass.: Harvard University Press.

World Bank (1997) *World Development Report 1997*. New York: Oxford University Press.

# 34

# The Effect of Globalization on Taxation, Institutions, and Control of the Macroeconomy

## Duane Swank

Despite the evidence against conventional globalization theory [ ... ], it may still be the case that increases in international capital mobility and financial integration contribute indirectly to rollbacks in social protection and otherwise constrain democratically elected governments from pursuing their social policy goals. Specifically, international capital mobility may contribute to the retrenchment of the welfare state through its impacts on the funding basis of the welfare state, the strength of political institutions that support the welfare state – most notably social corporatism – and the efficacy of macroeconomic policy to control unemployment and promote economic growth (and hence prevent fiscal stress that can lead to retrenchment). [ ... ]

## International Capital Mobility and Taxation

Much of the writing on internationalization and domestic politics and policy has highlighted the impact of international capital mobility on taxation. This is a particularly important relationship because, of course, the ability of the governments in advanced democratic polities to pursue social protection and other democratically determined goals inevitably hinges on (often) substantial taxation on a variety of economic activities and resource bases. It is also important because, if conventional propositions about capital mobility-induced tax competition and reduction in redistributive taxes are correct, not only will the revenue base of the welfare state be reduced as capital mobility increases, but egalitarian effects of the welfare state will be diminished by the movement toward less progressive tax structures.
[ ... ]

### An overview of theory and evidence

Scholars have long argued that capital mobility constrains the fiscal capacities of the state to tax mobile assets. The basic notion dates at least to Adam Smith who states the argument succinctly (1976 [1776]: 848–9):

> The . . . proprietor of stock is properly a citizen of the world, and is not necessarily attached to any particular country. He would be apt to abandon the country in which he is exposed to a vexatious inquisition, in order to be assessed a burdensome tax, and would remove his stock to some country where he could, either carry on his business, or enjoy his fortune at his ease. A tax that tended to drive away stock from a particular country, would so far tend to dry up every source of revenue, both to the sovereign and to the society. Not only the profits of stock, but the rent of land and the wages of labour, would necessarily be more or less diminished by its removal.

Many contemporary economists concur with the implicit policy recommendations of Smith. That is, in theoretical models of taxation in small economies with fully mobile capital, the optimal rate of tax on income from capital is thought to be zero; short-falls of revenue are offset by shifting the tax burden to relatively less mobile factors, such as labor and land (e.g., Gordon (1986); Razin and Sadka (1991); Gordon and Mackie-Mason (1995)).

Several contemporary scholars have made the direct linkage between capital mob-ility and actual tax policy change more explicit, arguing that internationalization is empirically associated with specific tax policies and reforms that shift revenue from capital to less mobile factors and otherwise undercut the revenue base of governments. Taking a historical perspective, Bates and Lien (1985) suggest that revenue-dependent governments have generally imposed lower rates on mobile assets and incorporated the preferences of these asset holders into policies and even institutions. Steinmo (1993, 1994) and McKenzie and Lee (1991), among other contemporary observers, have argued that capital mobility has effectively led governments to reduce tax burdens on corporate profits and high income-earners, substantially reducing tax-based income redistribution and the revenue-raising capacities of the state. Vito Tanzi (1995) has argued that transfer pricing and other mobility-related tax avoidance strategies have led to tax policy change: the risk of capital flight and the absence of new foreign invest-ment, as well as new difficulties in tax collection associated with capital mobility, lead to tax competition among national governments; this, in turn, reduces taxes on mobile assets, generates reforms not dictated by efficiency or democracy (e.g., creation of tax havens), and generally threatens the revenue base of national governments.

However, there are several reasons to believe that rises in international capital move-ments may not necessarily result in significant reductions in the tax burdens on capital or in overall government revenues. First, most research on foreign direct and portfolio capital investment has shown that, while important in determining the rate of return on capital investment and ultimately the decisions of international enterprises, tax policy constitutes only one of several important factors shaping investment decisions (e.g., Giovannini, Hubbard, and Slemrod (1993); IMF (1991); OECD (1990, 1991)).[1] Second, some formal analysis in political economy questions the globalization-taxation link-age. Importantly, Wallerstein and Przeworski (1995) extend their well-known work on "structural dependence" to the case of internationally mobile capital. They find that as long as the cost of investment is fully deductible (i.e., through depreciation), governments can collect substantial revenues from a stable tax on uninvested profits even when capital is fully mobile. In their analysis, Wallerstein and Przeworski find that capital investment by business will only decline during the period between the announcement and implementation of new taxes on profits. Third, international investors may value certain public goods such as political stability, human capital, and modern infrastructure (Garrett (1998b)). In the presence of fiscal stability (i.e., the absence of large budget deficits, low inflation), the benefits of these public goods may well offset the costs of the taxes required to finance them.

A number of new studies have addressed the question of the actual impacts of capital mobility on tax policy.[2] Specifically, Geoffrey Garrett (1996, 1998a, 1998b) has reported evidence that the liberalization of capital controls is largely unrelated to total revenues, general categories of taxation (as shares of GDP), or the effective tax rate on capital in the developed democracies. Similar findings are reported by Dennis Quinn (1997): in samples of developed and developing nations, Quinn finds substantively small and positive relationships between liberalization of capital flows and corporate taxes (as percentage shares of GDP and of total taxation) at both levels of economic development. Hallerberg and Basinger (1998) study 1986–90 changes in corporate and personal income tax rates in a sample of advanced democracies and find that changes in tax rates are, at best, only indirectly related to the liberalization of capital markets. Generally, the number of veto players who may slow tax policy reform is an important determinant of the pace of 1986–90 changes in tax rates. In my own study of business taxation (Swank 1998), I show that corporate income taxes and employer social security and payroll taxes (both standardized by aggregate operating income) are positively associated with rises in actual capital flows and liberalization; however, the increases in business taxes associated with rises in capital mobility are small. On the other hand, Dani Rodrik (1997) reports results that support conventional theory: he finds that trade openness and, at high levels of trade openness, capital control liberalization are negatively associated with effective tax rates on capital; increasing trade openness is also associated with increases in taxes on labor. While Rodrik's findings represent an important exception to the pattern, the weight of the evidence leads to the unanticipated impression that international capital mobility may be unrelated (or even positively related) to capital taxation.

In previous work (Swank 1998), I drew on theory, the policy record of individual nations, and the secondary literature to offer an interpretation for the absence of systematic, downward pressure on overall tax burdens on business from internationalization. I argued that one should focus on the policy "rules" governing business taxation, how these have changed in the contemporary era, and the general political and economic context of tax policy reform. That is, one should focus on the set of assumptions, beliefs, and prescriptions about relationships between taxes, investment, and economic performance that cohere and persist among partisan policy makers and specialists across time and countries. Ample evidence exists to suggest that there was a shift in tax policy orientations during the period of expansion of capital mobility in the developed democracies. However, the empirical record indicates that, while heavily influenced by the ascendance of neoliberal economic orthodoxy – a change that complements and is reinforced by rises in internationalization – the shift in tax policies did not produce the outcomes predicted by the structural dependence–diminished democracy theory.[3]

As to tax policy change in the 1980s and 1990s, comparative case studies of national experiences (e.g., Boskin and McClure (1990); Pechman (1988)) and detailed surveys of national and aggregate directions of reform (e.g., OECD (1989, 1991, 1993)) paint a clear picture of policy change that involved a shift from market-regulating to market-conforming policy "rules." Specifically, beginning most notably with the tax reform of 1984 in Britain, and closely followed by the tax legislation of 1986 in the

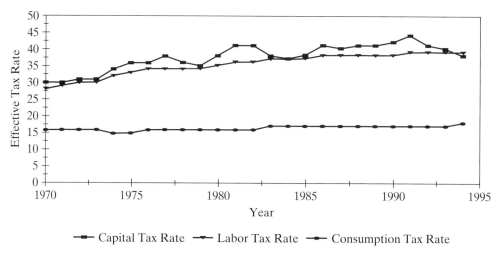

**Figure [1]**   Trends in effective tax rates averages – 13 developed democracies

United States, national policy makers have cut tax rates on corporate profits in a majority of advanced democracies: the maximum marginal tax rate on corporate profits fell on average from 49 to 37 percent between 1981 and 1992, and a large majority of nations experienced appreciable declines in corporate income tax rates. However, policy makers have simultaneously emphasized base-broadening. This has primarily involved, in a majority of nations, elimination of investment reliefs that had theretofore effectively lowered taxes paid by capital substantially. Some nations (e.g., Australia, and the pioneers of the policy reform, the United Kingdom and the United States) have done away with investment allowances, credits, and grants entirely, while others (e.g., Austria and Finland) have lowered them substantially.[4]

As previously cited studies and publications of the Fiscal Affairs Secretariat of the OECD make clear (see particularly OECD (1987, 1993)), tax policy makers in Ministries of Finance and throughout OECD governments have been influenced by two principles in the adoption of these reforms. First, while business income tax rate cuts were viewed as economically advantageous, policy makers emphasized the need to make overall changes in revenue neutral, or otherwise protect the revenue needs of the state (OECD 1987: 25). Thus, rate cuts should be offset, in particular, by the elimination of allowances, credits, exemptions, and other special business tax provisions for regional or sectoral development. In fact, as Figure [1] makes clear, the effective tax burden on capital has not fallen notably between the early 1970s and 1990s.[5] Second, tax-based investment incentives, once believed to be essential for encouraging investment, were now viewed as inefficient. As an OECD (1993: 56–7) report indicates, investment reliefs have become associated with inefficient allocation of investment, tax avoidance, lost tax revenue and, interestingly, ineffective outcomes in that they do not apparently produce the investment they were designed to promote. Thus, the emphasis in business income tax policy has become the creation of a level playing field where the market will presumably allocate investment in the most efficient manner.

The upshot of the trends in the taxation of business income is that both the conscious redistributive and economic management roles of corporate taxation are being reduced. That is, while increases in the taxation of capital to fund new social policy initiatives are unlikely, so too is the systematic use of investment reliefs in corporate taxes to target and spur domestic investment and to engineer favorable climates for international investors. Indeed, there appears to have been a rejection of this policy strategy in most market-oriented democracies. As Slemrod (1990) has pointed out, a strategy of mixing a low tax rate with few investment reliefs makes sense for many nations in an internationally interdependent economy. This is so because low rates retain taxable income that would otherwise be shifted through transfer-pricing to low-tax nations. That is, low rates "defend the treasury" in an international economy. Moreover, increasing the tax burden on investment (that is, on profits that are invested) also "defends the treasury" in the sense that more revenues from foreign investment are collected if that investment comes from countries with tax credits for foreign taxes paid and with ample rates of investment taxes themselves. Slemrod believes that the "low tax rate/no investment break" strategy certainly makes sense for countries like the United States and probably many more advanced market-oriented democracies in a world with globally integrated markets.

Moreover, similar trends toward lower nominal rates, a broader tax base, and little change in overall revenue collection can be seen in changes in the taxation of personal income. In fact, between the mid-1980s and mid-1990s, the highest (central government) marginal rate on personal income has fallen on average from 56 to 43 percent in the advanced democracies. However, as in the case of corporate income taxes, governments have eliminated a variety of deductions, exemptions, and allowances; in addition, citizens in the typical advanced democratic nation have experienced some increase in social security contributions.[6] Figure [1] highlights the fact that, after increasing from the early 1970s to mid-1980s, the overall effective tax rate on labor income has actually remained relatively stable. In addition, despite some notable exceptions, near universal reductions in marginal personal income tax rates (with fewer tax brackets) have not produced a trend toward substantially lower effective tax rates for higher income-earners.[7]

The effective tax rate on consumption and the tax share of domestic product are also relatively stable. As Figure [1] illustrates, the effective tax rate on consumption has held steady at about 17 percent.[8] If anything, total tax burdens have inched up slightly between the early 1980s and mid-1990s as capital mobility and financial integration increased rapidly: the OECD average for total tax shares of GDP was 38 percent in 1980 and 41 percent in 1994. Overall, while the shift in tax policy toward market-conforming orientations is clear (i.e., lower rates with fewer exemptions, allowances, and deductions), there does not appear to be a notable redistribution of tax burdens from capital to labor and consumption (within relatively constant levels of total taxation).

Certainly, part of the explanation of this relative stability in taxation, in the context of the shift to more market-conforming orientations in tax policy, is related to public expenditure pressures. Concomitant with downward pressures on taxes associated with neoliberal macroeconomic orthodoxy and internationalization, governments have simultaneously faced significant political pressures to maintain extant programmatic commitments, as well as meet rises in needs and demands for additional social spending (e.g., such as those that come from the "crisis of aging"). Given that upper limits on debt and deficits had in all likelihood been reached in the 1980s and early 1990s in most nations, spending pressures have probably made it much more difficult for many governments to substantially reduce the aggregate volume of tax collections from levies on capital or other relatively mobile factors, such as skilled labor. Given the difficulty in retrenching the welfare state and public sector as a whole, these pressures contribute to policy maker emphases on revenue neutrality of tax reforms.

However, it is quite difficult to draw any firm conclusions about the myriad forces shaping tax policy from a perusal of descriptive data. The extant studies reviewed above, including my own, provide evidence about the tax effects of only one or two dimensions of capital mobility (primarily liberalization of capital controls) and, with a few exceptions, use relatively imprecise measures of tax burdens. [ . . . ]

## Assessing the tax impacts of international capital mobility

To examine the actual consequences of capital mobility for the levels and distribution of tax burdens, I utilize the measures of effective tax rates on capital, labor, and consumption developed by Mendoza, Razin, and Tesar (1994) and defined above. I also extend the models of taxation that I developed in my earlier research on tax policy (Swank 1992, 1998). In that work, I hypothesized that business (and other) tax burdens are functions of past levels of taxation, the funding requirements of programmatic outlays, macroeconomic factors (inflation, economic growth), and partisan politics: Left and Christian Democratic parties will generally favor higher levels of taxes. Tax burdens on capital may also be influenced by specific domestic business conditions, such as recent investment and profit rates. Following Cameron's (1978) seminal study (and contra the globalization thesis), I also hypothesized that tax burdens would be higher in economies more open to international trade. Personal income and social security levies on labor, as well as general taxation, should also be influenced by the unemployment rate. I directly extend these hypotheses to the present case.[9]

[ . . . ]

[ . . . ] [The] conventional academic wisdom about internationalization and taxation does not seem to be accurate. [ . . . ] [R]ises in international capital mobility are not generally related to the effective tax rate on capital. [ . . . ] Moreover, and contrary to conventional theory, the relationship between the liberalization of capital controls and the effective tax rate on capital is positive and statistically significant. This result suggests that as capital controls were lifted, concomitant changes in tax policy (e.g., cuts in rates, base broadening, and related tax policy reforms) produced moderate increases in tax revenues from capital; there is no evidence that rises in international capital mobility produce significantly lower profits (i.e., a lower denominator) and in turn a higher effective average tax rate.[10]

Turning to the effects of capital mobility on labor, consumption, and overall taxation, [ . . . ] there is little evidence that tax burdens have shifted away from capital or that internationalization has produced a general reduction in taxation. [ . . . ] The one exception to the overall pattern of findings occurs in the case of the relationship between direct foreign investment and total taxation (as a percentage of GDP). Here, analysis indicates that, net of other forces, increases in direct foreign investment are associated with small declines in the overall tax share of GDP. However, this finding is not reproduced in the alternative econometric analyses: when controlling for all country and time points, or when examining the impact of changes in direct investment on changes in total tax burdens (in the context of general error correction models), this relationship disappears.

One might also highlight other results that bear on the focal questions of this study. First, trade openness is not generally related to taxes on capital or labor; it is positively associated with consumption taxes and total taxation.[11] Cameron's (1978) original finding of a positive and significant effect of trade openness on various measures of public sector size has also been confirmed for the contemporary period in other studies: trade openness and associated measures such as volatility in terms of trade are positively related to various measures of public sector intervention in markets (e.g., Garrett (1998a); Rodrik (1997); c.f. Iversen (2001)). Second, [...] partisan governments have clear effects on taxation. Left governments levy higher tax burdens on capital and produce higher overall tax burdens, while Christian Democratic governments prefer higher taxes on labor (income and social security taxes relative to wages and salaries). Finally, it is important to note that these partisan effects on taxation are not generally diminished as capital mobility increases. That is, on balance, the effects of Left governments on capital and total taxation and of Christian Democratic governments on labor tax rates hold at low and high levels of international financial integration.[12]

Generally, it seems clear that the dramatic rises in international capital mobility have not produced significant changes in the distribution of tax burdens across capital, labor, and consumption or in the overall level of taxation. That is, there is no evidence for the period from the 1960s through the mid-1990s that the economic and political pressures associated with international capital mobility have dramatically shifted tax burdens from capital to other factors of production or substantially undercut the general fiscal capacity of governments to raise revenues. Democratically elected governments can still maintain relatively extensive networks of social protections and services if they so choose. In other words, there appears to be no overriding internationally generated structural imperatives for tax reduction that force all welfare states to "run to the bottom."[13]

## Internationalization and Political Institutions: The Case of Social Corporatism

International capital mobility may shape welfare state restructuring through its effects on political institutions that support the welfare state. The impact of globalization on social corporatist interest representation is particularly salient and important. [...] [A] number of scholars have suggested that large welfare states may be weakened by the internationalization-induced decline of social corporatist institutions and practices (e.g., Huber and Stephens (1998); Kurzer (1993); Mishra (1993); Moses (2000)). This proposition is especially important because, as demonstrated in the preceding analysis, social corporatism is positively related to an array of features of social welfare protection and a principal institutional mechanism that blunts the potentially negative welfare state impacts of internationalization.

Rises in capital mobility are commonly thought to engender a shift of power resources away from labor and government to capital (e.g., Huber and Stephens (1998); Kurzer (1993); Moses (2000)). In turn, this shift of power to capital may well contribute to the weakening of core features of social corporatism, such as centralized wage bargaining and union density.[14] A number of mechanisms linking capital mobility to the decline of social corporatism have been highlighted in the literature. The relative gains from bargaining for wage restraint (and engagement in tripartite social pacts) to increasingly mobile enterprises may be diminished because capital mobility may present relatively more advantageous options for employers (e.g., Kurzer (1993)); even if centralized collective bargains are struck, mobile enterprises may choose subsequently to invest internationally, thereby weakening the prospects of future corporatist exchange (Moses 2000). Internationally mobile employers may seek more flexibility in work organization and this, in turn, may diminish the attractiveness of unions (e.g., Scruggs and Lange (1999); Western (1997)). From the perspective of Hecksher-Ohlin-Samuelson trade theory [ . . . ], globalization creates declining incomes and employment prospects among often unionized semi- and unskilled workers (while increasing the income of skilled workers); potential increases in wage inequality fragment trade union movements, and declining jobs and income among lower skilled workers may diminish the attractiveness of unions (see Golden and Londregan (1998), for theorizing along these lines).

In sum, scholars have emphasized that international capital mobility may simultaneously weaken unions and strengthen employers. Moreover, according to some observers, domestic political economic changes are pushing the actual preferences of increasingly mobile capital in the direction of decentralization and deregulation of labor and industrial relations systems. Huber and Stephens (1998), building on the work of Iversen (1996), Pontusson and Swenson (1996), and others, have suggested that in moderate to very strong social corporatist systems (most notably Sweden), post-Fordist flexible, specialized production of high quality goods and the compression of wage differentials (an outcome of past corporatist exchange) have created strong incentives for employers to press for decentralization of collective bargaining; the exit option enhances the power of employers to press for such change. Is there evidence to support these views?

## Globalization and social corporatism: empirical evidence

An examination of trends in major elements of social corporatism over the last three decades might initially appear to support the globalization thesis. Figure [2] displays annual 15-nation averages for two major features of social corporatism highlighted in the literature [ . . . ]: union density and the level of wage bargaining.[15] As the figure suggests, both union density and the level of collective wage bargaining have declined from the late 1970s or early 1980s; the timing of these decreases generally corresponds with the acceleration of international financial integration.

[ . . . ]

Is globalization systematically associated with a decline in corporatism, as theory and some country-specific evidence suggest? Or, alternatively, have countries followed divergent paths during the era of increasing internationalization of markets?[16] Two recent studies shed light on this question. First, Golden and Londregan (1998) examine the effects of the liberalization of financial flows, as well as trade openness and trade volatility, on a battery of dimensions of the labor and industrial relations system: union density, the share of union members in confederations, the intraconfederal concentration of members, and confederal and government involvement in wage

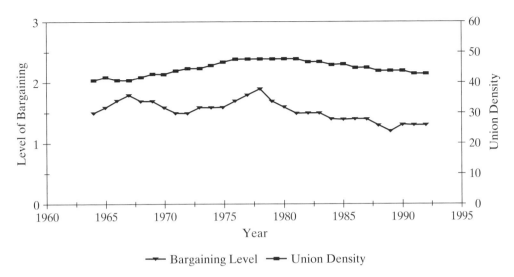

**Figure [2]**   Trends in social corporatism

setting. Employing pooled–time series analysis of 1950–92 data for 16 nations (the 15 focal nations of the present study plus Switzerland), they find no evidence of any relationship between liberalization of international finance (or trade openness) and variations in labor and industrial relations systems. The only statistically significant relationships occur between trade volatility and union density (a negative relationship) and trade volatility and the share of union members in confederations (a positive relationship). In sum, the authors produce little evidence to support the conventional globalization thesis.

The second study adopts similar methodology and explores the impact of financial liberalization, flows of foreign direct investment (FDI), and trade openness on union density in the same 16 nations between 1960 and 1995 (Scruggs and Lange 1999). In pooled–time series models of union density rates, the authors find no direct and systematic relationships between liberalization of capital controls, FDI, and trade openness on the one hand, and variations in union density on the other. This set of findings lends weight to the conclusions generated by Golden and Londregan. However, the authors also examine the effects of international capital mobility across different institutional contexts. They find that where labor market institutions are strong (e.g., the presence of the Ghent unemployment system), liberalization of capital markets is not related to variations in union density; where such institutions are weak, liberalization is negatively associated with density.[17] As such, these findings converge with predictions from Western's (1997) theory and suggest that the impact of capital mobility on unions might be contingent on broader institutions in much the same way as globalization's impacts on the welfare state are determined by national political institutions.

To further assess the possibility that capital mobility may negatively affect social corporatism, I estimated the impacts of the liberalization of capital controls, total capital flows, and flows of FDI on the strength of social corporatism using the focal measure of corporatism employed in the present study (a factor score index of density, confederal power, and the level of bargaining).[18] Tests for the effects of FDI are especially important, as much of the theorizing and debate over globalization's impacts on unions and corporatist institutions directly or indirectly stresses the importance of the ability of enterprises to move production or create jobs internationally through direct investment.

[ . . . ]

Overall, while far from conclusive, [ . . . ] preliminary tests tend to confirm findings and reinforce conclusions from recent empirical assessments of the impacts of globalization on unions and social corporatist institutions. First, there is no evidence of systematic and direct effects of rises in international capital mobility on core features of social corporatism. Second, international financial integration may be associated with decreases in union density, (further) decentralization of wage bargaining, and weakening in other features of social corporatism in more liberal political economies. This proposition, however tentative, is certainly consistent with the results reported here, the implications of Western's (1997) theory, and findings reported by Scruggs and Lange (1999). At the same time, these two preliminary conclusions do not rule out the possibility that international capital mobility may have enhanced the ability of employers to pursue decentralization in a small number of cases (e.g., Sweden), while in other cases social corporatist institutions might have been maintained (e.g., Norway), reconstituted (e.g., the Netherlands), or developed (e.g., Italy). With regard to the central focus of this inquiry, it appears to be the case that international capital mobility has not shaped welfare state restructuring indirectly through systematic downward pressures on social corporatism. While some features of social corporatism have certainly weakened in the 1980s and 1990s, there is no evidence for the common claim that globalization is substantially responsible for the decline.

## Globalization and Control of the Macroeconomy

While a thorough examination of the impact of globalization on macroeconomic policy is beyond the parameters of this study, it may be useful to consider the argument that capital mobility creates pressure for welfare state retrenchment primarily through its impact on macroeconomic policy autonomy and, in turn, economic performance pressures on the welfare state. Specifically, according to some analysts, rises in international capital mobility result in the loss of crucial economic instruments for maintaining low unemployment in larger welfare states; rises in unemployment create substantial fiscal stress or even crisis and, in turn, force rollbacks in the welfare state. While variations of this argument appear regularly in debates about the domestic impacts of globalization, I will focus on two important studies of globalization and economic policy and performance in large welfare states to explicate the proposition.[19]

[ . . . ]

Together, the analyses of Huber and Stephen and Moses suggest that the exogenous pressures of internationalization of production and financial markets stripped policy makers of key supply-side and monetary policy instruments that had been crucial in sustaining full or near-full employment in the 1970s and 1980s. In turn, the absence of these instruments in the late 1980s and especially 1990s left social democratic political economies vulnerable to the unemployment consequences of external shocks (e.g., the collapse of Soviet markets for Finland's exports) and business cycles (e.g., the early-1990s economic downturn across the developed democracies). The resultant "unemployment crises" engendered "welfare state crises" and social welfare protection was retrenched. Does this argument identify a key (albeit indirect) linkage between globalization and welfare state reform?

First, while the argument is plausible for the Nordic cases (although see below), there are clear limits on its generalizability as a systematic explanation of how capital mobility shapes welfare state retrenchment. [ . . . ] [T]he argument is at least partly applicable to France, but much less so for Germany or Italy. In the case of France, increased international competitiveness and short-term currency market pressures on the franc interacted with inflationary pressures, expanding fiscal deficits, and declining investment in the early 1980s to produce a shift in national economic policy from "Keynesianism in one country" to restrictive fiscal and monetary policies, a stable currency position, and subsequent financial liberalization. As a result, key French economic policy instruments, especially the state credit control in what Loriaux (1991) calls the "overdraft economy" and the flexibility for supportive exchange rate devaluations, were lost. Arguably, the abandonment of these economic policy instruments can be cited as one cause of the inability of French policy makers to abate rises in unemployment rates in the 1980s and 1990s. [ . . . ]

On the other hand, in the cases of Germany and Italy, one finds it difficult to link rises in international capital mobility to notable reforms in economic policy strategy and, subsequently, sharp upturns in unemployment and welfare state retrenchment. [ . . . ] [T]he German political economy has long been oriented to production for export markets and has long maintained high levels of formal liberalization of capital controls. German adaptation to post-1960s economic performance problems and rises in internationalization has played on the strengths of the German model. From the late 1970s to early 1990s, economic modernization to bolster exports of diversified, high-quality manufactured goods has been facilitated by the educational and vocational training system, consensual industrial relations system, industry-finance linkages, and a framework of supportive state policies. Macroeconomic policy has been characterized by the late adoption of the principles of Keynesian countercyclical demand management and the early-1970s embrace of monetarist orthodoxy by the Bundesbank. Although the expansion of international capital markets and movements has reinforced the restrictive monetary policies of the Bundesbank at times (e.g., in the late 1970s and early 1980s), increases in capital mobility did not result in significant losses of economic policy instruments or institutional reforms during the era from the late 1970s to early 1990s.

In the case of Italy, one can argue that there is a similar absence of linkages between international capital mobility, significant loss of key economic policy instruments, and unemployment and welfare state crises. While domestic economic performance problems (including unemployment) contributed to the fiscal crisis of the early 1990s and the initiation of significant welfare state restructuring, adaptation to economic performance problems and higher levels of international economic integration from the late 1970s to the early 1990s involved reforms in the Italian economic model that actually contributed to welfare state expansion (e.g., compensation for structural adjustment) and, on some dimensions, better economic policy performance [ . . . ]. The early-1990s crisis involved the interaction of excessive general government deficit and debt, dramatic political system change, and the impetus of Maastricht Treaty convergence criteria and, as such, extended far beyond the unemployment crises emphasized by the theory discussed here.

A second problem with the macroeconomic autonomy argument is that losses in key policy instruments may well be due to other forces (especially where governments consciously abandon instruments for the neoliberal policies of financial deregulation, hard currency, and so forth). In fact, although Huber and Stephens (1998), Moses (2000), and others generally assume that loss of key instruments is in large part the result of internationalization, other scholars have offered alternative interpretations of the causes of the shift to the neoliberal economic policies described above. They have also explicitly questioned any overriding, independent effect of international financial integration. Two recent, complementary sets of work are representative of a broader literature on the origins of 1980s shifts toward neoliberal policy orientations. First, Notermans (1993) and Forsyth and Notermans (1997) have argued that the early to mid-1980s shift to more restrictive monetary and fiscal policies, a formally or informally fixed currency, and associated neoliberal reforms (e.g., central bank independence, deregulation of international and domestic financial controls) was a conscious response of national policy makers to the inability of extant Keynesian policy prescriptions and instruments and domestic political economic institutions (e.g., corporatist wage setting) to adequately control post-1960s inflationary pressures. Thus, the desire to establish the credibility for commitments to price stability (and not ineluctable pressures from capital mobility) was the principal impetus behind the initiation of reforms that eliminated or weakened the use of a variety of monetary and supply-side instruments.[20]

In addition, McNamara's (1998) analysis of the causes of the development of the European Monetary Union sheds additional light on the origins of the shift to restrictive policies, fixed exchange rates, and related reforms. For McNamara, these policy changes represent an emergent neoliberal consensus among national policy makers in Europe around the desirability to control inflation generally, and to pursue hard currency policies specifically. In fact, McNamara explicitly rejects the argument that the neoliberal consensus was directly driven by the imperatives of international capital mobility and financial integration. Instead, she argues that the development of the neoliberal consensus across the larger welfare states of Europe – a system of shared beliefs and redefined common interests among national policy makers – was caused by three sets of additional forces. First, in McNamara's view, the emergence of neoliberal consensus was assisted by the common experiences of the weakness of Keynesian prescriptions and policies in the face of post-1960s economic performance problems. Second, the monetarist macroeconomic paradigm offered explanations and policy prescriptions for 1970s and early-1980s performance problems and policy failures and, in turn, was diffused through the economic and national policy communities of the developed democracies. Finally, the German experience of inflation control through restrictive monetary policy by an independent central bank and hard currency policies created an example for emulation across Europe. Overall, McNamara's and Notermans's arguments highlight the roles of long-term patterns in economic performance, macroeconomic ideas, political interests, and their interaction in shaping the conscious choices of governments to change economic policy regimes; the imperatives of international financial integration, alone, play a small role in the views of these authors.

In addition, a number of scholars have suggested that alternative economic policies and institutions have been developed by governments of large welfare states that, in the intermediate to long run, mitigate unemployment and general economic performance problems (and hence weaken pressures to retrench the welfare state). Other scholars have emphasized the continuity of (relatively successful) features of interventionist economic policies in large welfare states and the limited effects on national policy autonomy of globalization.

[ ... ]

As Boix (1998) points out, internationalization does not constrain these latter policies, which operate to enhance the productivity of human and physical capital. According to Boix, Left parties in particular have, in the 1980s and 1990s, continued to pursue activist supply-side policies that entail substantial government intervention. In empirical analyses of fiscal policy instruments and the scope of the public economy, Garrett (1998a, 1998b) highlights the finding that the principal costs of significant intervention to governments in a world of international finance involve the high interest premiums that accompany fiscal deficits. Overall, the central implication of Garrett's, Boix's, and related work is straightforward: while some governments have largely lost autonomy in exchange rate and domestic monetary policy – and faced new constraints on other instruments – significant policy options still remain for the active promotion of employment and general economic performance in the presence of global markets.

## Summing Up

Does international capital mobility create pressures for significant welfare state retrenchment through its negative impacts on the revenue-raising capacities of the state, social corporatism, and macroeconomic policy autonomy? Generally, the answer is "no". As the preceding analyses have demonstrated, internationalization is not systematically related to reductions of tax burdens on capital, the shift of tax burdens to relatively immobile factors, or cuts in overall tax shares of GDP. Furthermore, there is no clear systematic relationship between international capital mobility and core elements of social corporatist systems of interest representation across the developed capitalist democracies during the last three decades or so. In addition, there is little evidence that globalization, itself, has systematically eliminated all of the economic policy tools necessary to promote low unemployment and, in turn, a sustainable welfare state of generous and comprehensive proportions.

However, while the preceding sections of this chapter have offered ample theory and evidence in support of these conclusions, it is also necessary to point out that internationalization of markets generally, and international capital mobility specifically, may have had limited, adverse effects on the welfare state through these indirect channels of influence. First, the shift to market-conforming tax policy regimes – which itself involves a loss of tax-based policy instruments and potentially less redistribution, if not lower revenues – occurred concomitantly with internationalization. Policy-maker perceptions about the benefits of lower nominal rates and broader tax bases (and the limits on tax increases) were certainly shaped by the economic and political logics of international financial integration. Second, while there is no systematic negative relationship between international capital mobility and elements of social corporatism, case evidence and quantitative analysis suggest that, under some political economic conditions and in some institutional contexts, globalization may have contributed to decentralization and other reforms of social corporatist institutions. Finally, although policy makers have been influenced by a variety of forces in shifting to more neoliberal macroeconomic policy orientations (and although instruments for inter-ventionist economic guidance remain), the promotion of economic growth and employment through targeting of domestic credit (i.e., through tax, interest rate, and industrial policy), efficacious domestic monetary policy, and selective exchange rate policy is highly constrained in smaller, more open economies at 1990s levels of inter-national financial integration. In sum, while the arguments assessed above strongly overstate the indirect consequences of internationalization for the welfare state, glob-alization has certainly not been irrelevant for taxation, trends in social corporatism, and macroeconomic control.

## Notes

1  The actual relationship between taxation and international investment is complex. Jun (1990) has argued that tax-related aspects of investment decisions depend on (1) the tax treat-ment of foreign income; (2) the tax treatment of profits generated from domestic invest-ment (i.e., the relative return between domestic and foreign investment); and (3) the tax treatment of external funds across different countries (also see Slemrod (1990)).

2  I do not explicitly analyze the tax policy impacts of European economic integration in the present work. For an overview of theory and research and an interesting analysis of tax competition and efforts at coordination of corporate tax policy within the EU, see Radaelli (1997).

3  The sources of this shift in tax policy rules (in the context of the broader liberalization of domestic and international markets) is largely beyond the scope of the present inquiry. I might note, however, that it in all likelihood stems from the interaction between ideas, ideology, and interests – societal and state-centered – in the context of 1970s and 1980s economic performance problems and structural change. (See C. J. Martin (1991) for a particularly interesting and insightful analysis of U.S. tax policy changes of the sort discussed here.)

4  I should note that standard depreciation for most capital investment has been maintained in all of the advanced democracies. See OECD (1991, 1993) for a detailed, comparative review of depreciation methods and remaining investment reliefs.

5  For instance, between 1980 and 1993, the effective tax rate on capital income has hovered within a percentage point or two of 40 per cent. The effective tax rate on capital income equals taxes on property income and immovable property plus taxes on capital and finan-cial transactions, all as a percentage of operating surplus, as suggested by Mendoza, Razin, and Tesar (1994). [ . . . ]

6  While many countries have added new tax reliefs, the majority of developed democracies have broadened the tax base by eliminating allowances, exemptions, and credits (e.g., OECD (1993)). Employee social security taxes have increased steadily in the majority of nations over the last 25 years. For instance, between 1970 and 1994, employee social security col-lections in the average OECD country rose from 1.8 per cent to 3.2 per cent of GDP (OECD, 1995). Averages for the OECD or developed democracies pertain to the 15 focal nations of this study.

7  Effective taxes on higher income-earners refer to the percentage of income paid in taxes by workers at 200 and 400 percentage of the gross earnings of the average production worker. Effective taxes on labor income is computed as: taxes paid on wages and salaries plus total social security contributions and payroll taxes as a percentage of total wages and salaries plus employers' social security taxes, as suggested by Mendoza, Razin, and Tesar (1994). As the OECD (1997) illustrates, only in the United States, the United Kingdom, and in Sweden were average taxes significantly lowered in the middle and high ends of the income distribution; small declines in effective tax rates at the high end of the income distribution were recorded for Australia and Germany, as well.

8   The effective consumption tax rate is computed as: general goods and services taxes plus excise taxes as a percentage of private and government consumption spending minus consumption by producers of government services, goods and services taxes, and excise tax payments, as suggested by Mendoza, Razin, and Tesar (1994).

9   I discuss rationales for the inclusion and specific operationalization of political and economic variables in my earlier papers on tax policy (Swank 1992; 1998). There, as well as in the present analysis, I use the following control variables in a general model of taxation: the lagged tax rate; present levels of government outlays (as a percentage of GDP); lagged levels of trade openness; the proportion of cabinet portfolios held by parties of a particular ideological type (here, Left and Christian Democratic parties); lagged levels of inflation, unemployment, and economic growth; and lagged percentage changes in real investment in machinery and equipment and in total real business profits. All lags are one year.
    [ . . . ]

10  In complementary work (Swank and Steinmo, 2000), I find in systematic empirical analysis that, if anything, rises in capital mobility (and trade openness) are associated with higher profits.

11  Flat-rate general consumption taxes (value added and sales taxes) are often touted as efficient alternatives to graduated income and capital taxes in that they are the least intrusive in the efficient operation of markets. As such, they may be the preferred alternative in an economy relatively open to competitive international markets. I also tested for the prospect that, following Rodrik's (1997) finding, increases in international capital mobility would produce downward pressure on the tax burdens on capital at high levels of trade openness. Examining the capital tax effects of individual measures of flows, liberalization, and interest rate convergence across levels of trade openness, I found no support for this hypothesis.

12  Examining the interaction of parties and international capital mobility in Table [1] models (results not shown), only 3 of the 15 possible interactions – party variables in the capital, labor, and total tax equations with the 5 measures of capital markets – are significant. That is, partisan effects are not contingent on the level of capital mobility.

13  Two points are in order. First, the shift toward market-conforming policies in the areas of business and personal income taxation eliminates some tools governments have used to achieve social and economic policy objectives (Steinmo, 1998). Second, many nations have begun to rely more heavily on taxes of a regressive nature; the 1990s reforms initiating new employee social security taxes in Sweden and higher employee social security taxes in post-1990 Germany are just two examples of this trend. While these reforms do not suggest that redistributive taxes are a thing of the past, they do point to the prospect that a cumulative process of tax reform may produce less egalitarian tax structures in a large majority of developed nations in the not-so-distant future. As such, the redistributive impacts of the contemporary welfare state will be reduced.

14  As commonly understood, social corporatism is construed as a system of densely and well-organized trade unions, well-organized employers' associations, centralized collective bargaining, and associated incorporation of unions (and employers) in bipartite and tripartite concertation over major economic and social policies.

15  The 15 nations are the same countries utilized in analyses throughout this study. Union density is computed as the percentage of employed wage and salary workers belonging to unions and the level of bargaining is a 0.0–3.0 scale ranging from enterprise-level bargaining (0.0) to economy-wide bargaining with sanctions (3.0).

16  Of course a number of rival hypotheses on the origins of corporatist decline exist. For instance, the direct effects of technological change and the shift to post-Fordist flexible manufacturing of diversified high-quality products (Pontusson and Swenson, 1996); employers' desire to reduce wage compression in some social corporatist systems (Huber and Stephens, 1998; Wallerstein, Golden, and Lange, 1997); the deregulatory impetus of neoliberal orthodoxy

and governments (e.g., Streeck (1993)) and the rise in white-collar or public-sector unions within trade union movements (e.g., Garrett and Way (1999)) may all play roles in corporatist decline.

17  With somewhat contradictory implications, Scruggs and Lange also report that under strong labor market institutions – especially central bargaining and corporatist interest intermediation – FDI actually has a larger negative effect on density than under weak labor market institutions.

18  All variables are operationalized as above. I also estimated the effects of the broader 0–14-point scale of financial liberalization developed by Quinn, borrowing on international capital markets, and covered interest rate divergence. However, the effects of these dimensions of capital mobility on social corporatism are insignificant (or in one case significant and positive).

19  At a general level, the specific argument considered here is based on the common Mundell-Flemming model of monetary policy in open economies. At its most elemental level, the model asserts that national policy makers can only achieve two of three goals among the set of fixed exchange rates, capital mobility, and monetary policy autonomy. For a nontechnical overview, see Cohen (1996); for an accessible yet rigorous presentation of a variety of models in this theoretical perspective, see Shepherd (1994). A related argument that I do not consider here is that globalization – both international financial integration and trade openness – directly increases unemployment in the developed capitalist democracies, and hence precipitates welfare state fiscal stress. For a review of the literature on globalization effects on unemployment, see Martin (1996).

20  In addition, [ . . . ] much of the expansion in most areas of capital mobility and financial integration often occurred after the shift to more neoliberal policy orientations.

## References

Bates, R. and Lien, D.-H. D. (1985) A note on taxation, development and representative government. *Politics and Society* 14(1): 53–70.

Boix, C. (1998) *Political Parties, Growth, and Inequality: Conservative and Social Democratic Party Strategies in the World Economy*. New York: Cambridge University Press.

Boskin, M. and McClure, C. (1990) *World Tax Reform*. San Francisco: International Centre for Economic Growth.

Cameron, D. (1978) The expansion of the public economy: A comparative analysis. *American Political Science Review* 72(4): 1243–61.

Cohen, B. (1996) Phoenix risen: The resurrection of global finance. *World Politics* 48 (January): 268–90.

Forsyth, D. and Notermans, T. (1997) *Regime Changes: Macroeconomic Policy and Financial Regulation from the 1930s to the 1990s*. Providence: Berghahn Books.

Garrett, G. (1996) Capital mobility, trade, and the domestic politics of economic policy. In R. Keohane and H. Milner (eds), *Internationalization and Domestic Politics*. New York: Cambridge University Press.

Garrett, G. (1998a) *Partisan Politics in a Global Economy*. New York: Cambridge University Press.

Garrett, G. (1998b) Global markets and national policies: Collision course or virtuous circle? *International Organization* 52(4): 787–824.

Garrett, G. and Way, C. (1999) Public sector unions, corporatism, and macroeconomic performance. *Comparative Political Studies* 32(4): 411–34.

Giovannini, A., Hubbard, R. G., and Slemrod, J. (1993) *Studies in International Taxation*. Chicago: University of Chicago Press.

Golden, M. and Londregan, J. (1998) *Globalization and Industrial Relations*. Department of Political Science, UCLA.

Gordon, R. H. (1986) Taxation of investment and savings in a world economy. *American Economic Review* 76(5): 1086–102.

Gordon, R. H. and Mackie-Mason, J. K. (1995) Why is there corporate taxation in a small open economy? In Martin Feldstein, et al. (eds), *The Effects of Taxation on Multinational Corporations*, Chicago: University of Chicago Press.

Hallerberg, M. and Basinger, S. (1998) Internationalization and changes in tax policy in OECD countries: the importance of domestic veto players. *Comparative Political Studies* 31(3): 321–53.

Huber, E. and Stephens, J. D. (1998) Internationalization and the social democratic welfare model: crises and future prospects. *Comparative Political Studies* 33 (June): 353–97.

IMF (1991) *Determinants and Consequences of International Capital Flows*. Washington DC: International Monetary Fund.

Iversen, T. (1996) Power, flexibility, and the breakdown of central wage bargaining: Denmark and Sweden in comparative perspective. *Comparative Politics* 28(4): 399–436.

Iversen, T. (2001) The dynamics of welfare state expansion: trade openness, deindustrialization, and partisan politics. In P. Pierson (ed.), *The New Politics of the Welfare State*. New York: Oxford University Press.

Kurzer, P. (1993) *Business and Banking: Political Change and Economic Integration in Western Europe*. Ithaca: Cornell University Press.

Loriaux, M. (1991) *France After Hegemony: International Change and Financial Reform*. Ithaca: Cornell University Press.

Martin, C. J. (1991) *Shifting the Burden: The Struggle Over Growth and Corporate Taxation*. Chicago: University of Chicago Press.

Martin, A. (1996) What does globalization have to do with the erosion of welfare states? Sorting out the issues. Center for European Studies, Harvard University.

McKenzie, R. and Lee, D. (1991) *Quicksilver Capital: How the Rapid Movement of Wealth Has Changed the World*. New York: Free Press.

McNamara, K. R. (1998) *The Currency of Ideas: Monetary Politics in the European Union*. Ithaca: Cornell University Press.

Mendoza, E. G., Razin, A., and Tesar, L. L. (1994) Effective tax rates in macroeconomics: cross-country estimates of tax rates in factor incomes and consumption. *Journal of Monetary Economics* 34: 297–323.

Mishra, R. (1993) Social policy in the post-modern world. In C. Jones (ed.), *New Perspectives on the Welfare State in Europe*, New York: Routledge.

Moses, J. (2000) Floating fortunes: Scandinavian full employment in the tumultuous 1970s and 1980s. In R. Geyer, C. Ingrebritsen, and J. Moses (eds), *Globalization, Europeanization, and the End of Scandinavian Social Democracy?* New York and London: St Martin's Press, Macmillan.

Notermans, T. (1993) The abdication of national policy autonomy: why the macroeconomic policy regime has become so unfavorable to labor. *Politics and Society* 21(2): 133–67.

OECD (1987) *Taxation in Developed Countries*. Paris: Organization for Economic Cooperation and Development.

OECD (1989) *Economies in Transition*. Paris: Organization for Economic Cooperation and Development.

OECD (1990) *Taxation and International Capital Flows*. Paris: Organization for Economic Cooperation and Development.

OECD (1991) *Taxation in a Global Economy: Domestic and International Issues*. Paris: Organization for Economic Cooperation and Development.

OECD (1993) *Taxation in OECD Countries*. Paris: Organization for Economic Cooperation and Development.

OECD (1995) *The Jobs Study: Taxation, Employment, and Unemployment*. Paris: Organization for Economic Cooperation and Development.

OECD (1997) *Taxing International Business: Emerging Trends in APE and OECD Countries*. Paris: Organization for Economic Cooperation and Development.

Pechman, J. A. (1988) *World Tax Reform: A Progress Report*. Washington DC: Brookings Institution.

Pontusson, J. and Swenson, P. (1996) Labor markets, production strategies and wage bargaining institutions: the Swedish employer offensive in comparative perspective. *Comparative Political Studies* 29(2): 223–50.

Quinn, D. (1997) The correlates of change in international financial regulation. *American Political Science Review* 91(3): 531–52.

Radaelli, C. (1997) *The Politics of Corporate Taxation in the European Union: Knowledge and International Policy Agendas*. New York: Routledge.

Razin, A. and Sadka, E. (1991) International tax competition and gains from tax harmonization. *Economic Letters* 37(1): 69–76.

Rodrik, D. (1997) *Has Globalization Gone Too Far?* Washington DC: Institute for International Economics.

Scruggs, L. and Lange, P. (1999) *Where Have All the Members Gone? Union Density in an Era of Globalization*. Revised version of a paper presented at the 1997 Annual Meeting of the American Political Science Association. TS, Departments of Political Science, University of Connecticut and Duke University.

Shepherd, W. F. (1994) *International Financial Integration: History, Theory, and Applications in OECD Countries*. Brookfield, VT: Ashgate.

Slemrod, J. (1990) Tax principles in an international economy. In M. Boskin and J. Charles McClure (eds), *World Tax Reform*, San Francisco: International Centre for Economic Growth.

Smith, A. (1976 [1776]) *An Inquiry into the Nature and Causes of the Wealth of Nations*. Oxford: Clarendon Press.

Steinmo, S. (1993) *Democracy and Taxation*. New Haven: Yale University Press.

Steinmo, S. (1994) The end of redistributive taxation: tax reform in a global world economy. *Challenge* 37(6) (Nov–Dec): 9–17.

Steinmo, S. (1998) *The New Political Economy of Taxation: International Pressures and Domestic Policy Choices*. Boulder: University of Colorado.

Streeck, W. (1993) The rise and decline of neocorporatism. In L. Ulman, B. Eichengreen, and W. T. Dickens (eds), *Labor and an Integrated Europe*, Washington DC: Brookings Institution.

Swank, D. (1992) Politics and the structural dependence of the state in democratic capitalist nations. *American Political Science Review* 86(1): 38–54.

Swank, D. (1998) Funding the welfare state: globalization and the taxation of business in advanced market economies. *Political Studies* 46(4): 671–92.

Swank, D. and Steinmo, S. (2000) The new political economy of taxation in advanced capitalist democracies. Annual Meeting of the Midwest Political Science Association, Chicago, IL.

Tanzi, V. (1995) *Taxation in an Integrating World*. Washington DC: Brookings Institution.

Wallerstein, M. and Przeworski, A. (1995) Capital taxation with open borders. *Review of International Political Economy* 2 (Summer): 425–45.

Wallerstein, M., Golden, M., and Lange, P. (1997) Unions, employers' associations, and wage-setting institutions in Northern and Central Europe, 1950–1992. *Industrial and Labor Relations Review* 50(3) (April): 379–401.

Western, B. (1997) *Between Class and Market: Postwar Unionization in the Capitalist Democracies*. Princeton, NJ: Princeton University Press.

# Part V
## Divided World, Divided Nations?

Global inequality is perhaps the most critical issue on the contemporary global agenda. Not surprisingly, the debate about its causes and remedies is complex. The principal division is between those who argue that globalization is creating a more unequal and impoverished world and those who argue that it is spreading wealth and reducing poverty. This divide cuts across the categories of sceptics and globalists, producing a complicated and nuanced debate.

Amongst the most powerful statements to be found linking globalization to inequality is the extract from the 1999 United Nations Development Programme Human Development Report. This extract describes the various dimensions of global poverty, and the forms of inequality associated with globalization. It highlights the causal mechanisms by which global economic integration creates a more unequal and divided world. Although the specific causes of the growing gap between rich and poor in the world economy remain subject to dispute, the UNDP extract produces evidence to show that the numbers of people living in absolute poverty, according to some estimates, have increased over the last decades of the twentieth century. Moreover, it asserts that the gap between richest and poorest in the world is now at historic levels. Redressing such inequality, according to the UNDP, will require concerted global action to manage globalization in the interests of the poor, and not just the world's most affluent citizens.

In the subsequent extract, Manuel Castells develops a more analytical account of the relationship between globalization and world inequality. Castells examines the causal links between the dynamics of the new 'global informational capitalism' and growing inequality, poverty, social exclusion and immiseration on a world scale. He argues that the new global division of labour has created distinctive patterns of exclusion, marginalization and poverty, which cut across national boundaries. In effect, the uneven nature of globalization is creating a new social division of the world that transcends the old geographic core-periphery organization of the world economy. Although the OECD countries in general benefit most from globalization, all nations are being divided by the forces of global capitalism into communities of winners and losers. For Castells, global informational capitalism, with its associated neoliberal economic orthodoxy, is the principal cause of growing world inequality.

By contrast, the debate between Robert Wade and Martin Wolf, in the next extract, highlights the principal areas of disagreement concerning the thesis of growing global impoverishment. This exchange pinpoints significant disagreements concerning both the interpretations of the available empirical evidence and the underlying causal analysis. Whereas Wade is careful not to identify globalization as the sole culprit behind growing inequality, Wolf is largely dismissive of the conventional radical analysis. The main sources of disagreement revolve around several issues: the empirical evidence; matters of interpretation; and the causal status of globalization. Wolf disputes much of the conventional evidence regarding increasing levels of world poverty and inequality. For the most part, standards of living across the globe have been on the increase, such that many more of the world's peoples have better standards of living than fifty or a hundred years ago. He contests the interpretation that globalization, as opposed to national policies and domestic factors, is creating a more unequal world, highlighting the disparities in national economic performance within the South. Furthermore, he argues that globalization produces economic growth and spreads wealth. In this respect, inequality and poverty are endemic amongst the least globalized national economies.

Developing this analysis further, the study by David Dollar and Aart Kraay contends that globalization is associated with a narrowing of the gap between rich and poor in the world economy and the erosion of absolute poverty. As they conclude, 'the current wave of globalization . . . has actually promoted economic equality and reduced poverty'. This conclusion derives from an historical analysis of patterns of world income inequality which indicates that over the period 1820–1995 worldwide income inequality has declined from its peak in 1970. This is reinforced by other data which indicate that both the absolute numbers and the proportion of the world's population living in poverty have steadily declined since 1980. The explanation for these trends, they argue, can be linked to the intensification of globalization, which has enabled more of the world's poorest nations to choose a route out of poverty through trade and foreign investment. Integration into the world economy, rather than autarky, is the key to poverty reduction.

It is, however, precisely this integration into the world economy which Jill Steans contends has had such a profound impact on gender inequalities, especially in the South. Steans argues that the particular form taken by economic globalization in the last two decades – neoliberal economic globalization – has not transformed the old North–South division of the world but superimposed on it new kinds of division along gender lines. Thus, whilst for some groups the world may appear increasingly as a shared social space, for many women globalization is experienced as a new form of impoverishment, social exclusion and inequality. In other words, our shared planet is marked by the creation of rapidly diverging social worlds and life chances.

Some of the implications of these trends for global stability and world order, and the current trajectory of neoliberal economic globalization, are considered by Ngaire Woods. In this extract, she questions whether the existing structures of global governance, with their inbuilt hierarchies, can confront effectively the problems of a globalizing world, most especially poverty and inequality. Woods concludes that to be effective in the twenty-first century, global governance institutions need to become both more representative of the world community and more accountable to it. Without institutional reform, the prospects for making globalization work for the poor appear decidedly limited; but equally, without reform, the prospects for the globalization project itself are under threat.

In the final extract, Joseph Stiglitz reflects on the failure of global governance institutions to deliver on the promises of globalization. In a controversial assessment of the key economic institutions, namely the IMF, World Bank and WTO, he concludes that these bodies require reform if they are to contribute to the alleviation, rather than the aggravation, of global poverty and inequality. Such reform requires the rewriting of some of the principal rules of the world economic order and, as Woods notes, broadening participation in global decision-making. Only then can globalization be 'reshaped' and begin to deliver on the promise of a more just and sustainable global economy.

# 35
# Patterns of Global Inequality

## *UNDP Report 1999*

[ ... ]

Globalization is not new. Recall the early sixteenth century and the late nineteenth. But this era is different:

- *New markets* – foreign exchange and capital markets linked globally, operating 24 hours a day, with dealings at a distance in real time.
- *New tools* – Internet links, cellular phones, media networks.
- *New actors* – the World Trade Organization (WTO) with authority over national governments, the multinational corporations with more economic power than many states, the global networks of non-governmental organizations (NGOs) and other groups that transcend national boundaries.
- *New rules* – multilateral agreements on trade, services and intellectual property, backed by strong enforcement mechanisms and more binding for national governments, reducing the scope for national policy.

**Globalization offers great opportunities for human advance – but only with stronger governance.**

This era of globalization is opening many opportunities for millions of people around the world. Increased trade, new technologies, foreign investments, expanding media and Internet connections are fuelling economic growth and human advance. All this offers enormous potential to eradicate poverty in the twenty-first century – to continue the unprecedented progress in the twentieth century. We have more wealth and technology – and more commitment to a global community – than ever before.

Global markets, global technology, global ideas and global solidarity can enrich the lives of people everywhere, greatly expanding their choices. The growing interdependence of people's lives calls for shared values and a shared commitment to the human development of all people.

The post-cold war world of the 1990s has sped progress in defining such values – in adopting human rights and in setting development goals in the United Nations conferences on environment, population, social development, women and human settlements.

But today's globalization is being driven by market expansion – opening national borders to trade, capital, information – outpacing governance of these markets and their repercussions for people. More progress has been made in norms, standards, policies and institutions for open global markets than for people and their rights. And a new commitment is needed to the ethics of universalism set out in the Universal Declaration of Human Rights.

[ ... ]

When the market goes too far in dominating social and political outcomes, the opportunities and rewards of globalization spread unequally and inequitably – concentrating power and wealth in a select group of people, nations and corporations, marginalizing the others. When the market gets out of hand, the instabilities show up in boom and bust economies, as in the financial crisis in East Asia and its worldwide repercussions, cutting global output by an estimated $2 trillion in 1998–2000. When the profit motives of market players get out of hand, they challenge people's ethics – and sacrifice respect for justice and human rights.

The challenge of globalization in the new century is not to stop the expansion of global markets. The challenge is to find the rules and institutions for stronger governance – local, national, regional and global – to preserve the advantages of global markets and competition, but also to provide enough space for human, community and environmental resources to ensure that globalization works for people – not just for profits. Globalization with:

- *Ethics* – less violation of human rights, not more.
- *Equity* – less disparity within and between nations, not more.
- *Inclusion* – less marginalization of people and countries, not more.
- *Human security* – less instability of societies and less vulnerability of people, not more.
- *Sustainability* – less environmental destruction, not more.
- *Development* – less poverty and deprivation, not more.

## The opportunities and benefits of globalization need to be shared much more widely.

Since the 1980s many countries have seized the opportunities of economic and technological globalization. Beyond the industrial countries, the newly industrializing East Asian tigers are joined by Chile, the Dominican Republic, India, Mauritius, Poland, Turkey and many others linking into global markets, attracting foreign investment and taking advantage of technological advance. Their export growth has averaged more than 5 per cent a year, diversifying into manufactures.

At the other extreme are the many countries benefiting little from expanding markets and advancing technology – Madagascar, Niger, the Russian Federation, Tajikistan and Venezuela among them.

These countries are becoming even more marginal – ironic, since many of them are highly "integrated", with exports nearly 30 per cent of GDP for Sub-Saharan Africa and only 19 per cent for the OECD. But these countries hang on the vagaries of global markets, with the prices of primary commodities having fallen to their lowest in a century and a half. They have shown little growth in exports and attracted virtually no foreign investment. In sum, today, global opportunities are unevenly distributed – between countries and people [ . . . ].

If global opportunities are not shared better, the failed growth of the last decades will continue. More than 80 countries still have per capita incomes lower than they were a decade or more ago. While 40 countries have sustained average per capita income growth of more than 3 per cent a year since 1990, 55 countries, mostly in Sub-Saharan Africa and Eastern Europe and the Commonwealth of Independent States (CIS), have had declining per capita incomes.

Many people are also missing out on employment opportunities. The global labour market is increasingly integrated for the highly skilled – corporate executives, scientists, entertainers and the many others who form the global professional elite – with high mobility and wages. But the market for unskilled labour is highly restricted by national barriers.

Inequality has been rising in many countries since the early 1980s. In China disparities are widening between the export-oriented regions of the coast and the interior: the human poverty index is just under 20 per cent in coastal provinces, but more than 50 per cent in inland Guizhou. The countries of Eastern Europe and the CIS have registered some of the largest increases ever in the Gini coefficient, a measure of income inequality. OECD countries also registered big increases in inequality after the 1980s – especially Sweden, the United Kingdom and the United States.

Inequality between countries has also increased. The income gap between the fifth of the world's people living in the richest countries and the fifth in the poorest was 74 to 1 in 1997, up from 60 to 1 in 1990 and 30 to 1 in 1960. In the nineteenth century, too, inequality grew rapidly during the last three decades, in an era of rapid global integration: the income gap between the top and bottom countries increased from 3 to 1 in 1820 to 7 to 1 in 1870 and 11 to 1 in 1913.

By the late 1990s the fifth of the world's people living in the highest-income countries had:

- 86 per cent of world GDP – the bottom fifth just 1 per cent.
- 82 per cent of world export markets – the bottom fifth just 1 per cent.
- 68 per cent of foreign direct investment – the bottom fifth just 1 per cent.
- 74 per cent of world telephone lines, today's basic means of communication – the bottom fifth just 1.5 per cent.

Some have predicted convergence. Yet the past decade has shown increasing concentration of income, resources and wealth among people, corporations and countries:

- OECD countries, with 19 per cent of the global population, have 71 per cent of global trade in goods and services, 58 per cent of foreign direct investment and 91 per cent of all Internet users.
- The world's 200 richest people more than doubled their net worth in the four years to 1998, to more than $1 trillion. The assets of the top three billionaires are more than the combined GNP of all least developed countries and their 600 million people.
- The recent wave of mergers and acquisitions is concentrating industrial power in megacorporations – at the risk of eroding competition. By 1998 the top 10 companies in pesticides controlled 85 per cent of a $31 billion global market – and the top 10 in telecommunications, 86 per cent of a $262 billion market.
- In 1993 just 10 countries accounted for 84 per cent of global research and development expenditures and controlled 95 per cent of the US patents of the past two decades. Moreover, more than 80 per cent of patents granted in developing countries belong to residents of industrial countries.

All these trends are not the inevitable consequences of global economic integration – but they have run ahead of global governance to share the benefits.

UNDP Report 1999

**Globalization is creating new threats to human security – in rich countries and poor.**

One achievement of recent decades has been greater security for people in many countries – more political freedom and stability in Chile, peace in Central America, safer streets in the United States. But in the globalizing world of shrinking time, shrinking space and disappearing borders, people are confronting new threats to human security – sudden and hurtful disruptions in the pattern of daily life.

## Financial volatility and economic insecurity

The financial turmoil in East Asia in 1997–99 demonstrates the risks of global financial markets. [ ... ] Two important lessons come out of this experience.

First, the human impacts are severe and are likely to persist long after economic recovery.

[ ... ]

Second, far from being isolated incidents, financial crises have become increasingly common with the spread and growth of global capital flows. They result from rapid buildups and reversals of short-term capital flows and are likely to recur. More likely when national institutions regulating financial markets are not well developed, they are now recognized as systemic features of global capital markets. No single country can withstand their whims, and global action is needed to prevent and manage them.

## Job and income insecurity

In both poor and rich countries dislocations from economic and corporate restructuring, and from dismantling the institutions of social protection, have meant greater insecurity in jobs and incomes. The pressures of global competition have led countries and employers to adopt more flexible labour policies with more precarious work arrangements. Workers without contracts or with new, less secure contracts make up 30 per cent of the total in Chile, 39 per cent in Colombia.

France, Germany, the United Kingdom and other countries have weakened worker dismissal laws. Mergers and acquisitions have come with corporate restructuring and massive layoffs. Sustained economic growth has not reduced unemployment in Europe – leaving it at 11 per cent for a decade, affecting 35 million. In Latin America growth has created jobs, but 85 per cent of them are in the informal sector.

## Health insecurity

Growing travel and migration have helped spread HIV/AIDS. More than 33 million people were living with HIV/AIDS in 1998, with almost 6 million new infections in that year. And the epidemic is now spreading rapidly to new locations, such as rural India and Eastern Europe and the CIS. With 95 per cent of the 16,000 infected each day living in developing countries, AIDS has become a poor person's disease, taking a heavy toll on life expectancy, reversing the gains of recent decades. For nine countries in Africa, a loss of 17 years in life expectancy is projected by 2010, back to the level of the 1960s.

## Cultural insecurity

Globalization opens people's lives to culture and all its creativity – and to the flow of ideas and knowledge. But the new culture carried by expanding global markets is disquieting. As Mahatma Gandhi expressed so eloquently earlier in the century, "I do not want my house to be walled in on all sides and my windows to be stuffed. I want the cultures of all the lands to be blown about my house as freely as possible. But I refuse to be blown off my feet by any." Today's flow of culture is unbalanced, heavily weighted in one direction, from rich countries to poor.
[ ... ]

## Personal insecurity

Criminals are reaping the benefits of globalization. Deregulated capital markets, advances in information and communications technology and cheaper transport make flows easier, faster and less restricted not just for medical knowledge but for heroin – not just for books and seeds but for dirty money and weapons.

Illicit trade – in drugs, women, weapons and laundered money – is contributing to the violence and crime that threaten neighbourhoods around the world. Drug-related crimes increased from 4 per 100,000 people in Belarus in 1990 to 28 in 1997, and from 1 per 100,000 to 8 in Estonia. The weapons trade feeds street crime as well as civil strife. In South Africa machine guns are pouring in from Angola and Mozambique. The traffic in women and girls for sexual exploitation – 500,000 a year to Western Europe alone – is one of the most heinous violations of human rights, estimated to be a $7 billion business.
[ ... ]

At the root of all this is the growing influence of organized crime, estimated to gross $1.5 trillion a year, rivalling multinational corporations as an economic power. Global crime groups have the power to criminalize politics, business and the police, developing efficient networks, extending their reach deep and wide.

## Environmental insecurity

Chronic environmental degradation – today's silent emergency – threatens people worldwide and undercuts the livelihoods of at least half a billion people. Poor people themselves, having little choice, put pressure on the environment, but so does the consumption of the rich. The growing export markets for fish, shrimp, paper and many other products mean depleted stocks, less biodiversity and fewer forests. Most of the costs are borne by the poor – though it is the world's rich who benefit most. The fifth of the world's people living in the richest countries consume 84 per cent of the world's paper.

## Political and community insecurity

Closely related to many other forms of insecurity is the rise of social tensions that threaten political stability and community cohesion. Of the 61 major armed conflicts fought between 1989 and 1998, only three were between states – the rest were civil.

Globalization has given new characteristics to conflicts. Feeding these conflicts is the global traffic in weapons, involving new actors and blurring political and business interests. In the power vacuum of the post-cold war era, military companies and mercenary armies began offering training to governments – and corporations. Accountable only to those who pay them, these hired military services pose a severe threat to human security.

**New information and communications technologies are driving globalization – but polarizing the world into the connected and the isolated.**

With the costs of communications plummeting and innovative tools easier to use, people around the world have burst into conversation using the Internet, mobile phones and fax machines. The fastest-growing communications tool ever, the Internet had more than 140 million users in mid-1998, a number expected to pass 700 million by 2001.

Communications networks can foster great advances in health and education. They can also empower small players. The previously unheard voices of NGOs helped halt the secretive OECD negotiations for the Multilateral Agreement on Investment, called for corporate accountability and created support for marginal communities. Barriers of size, time and distance are coming down for small businesses, for governments of poor countries, for remote academics and specialists.

Information and communications technology can also open a fast track to knowledge-based growth – a track followed by India's software exports, Ireland's computing services and the Eastern Caribbean's data processing.

Despite the potential for development, the Internet poses severe problems of access and exclusion. Who was in the loop in 1998?

- *Geography divides.* Thailand has more cellular phones than Africa. South Asia, home to 23 per cent of the world's people, has less than 1 per cent of Internet users.
- *Education is a ticket to the network high society.* Globally, 30 per cent of users had at least one university degree.
- *Income buys access.* To purchase a computer would cost the average Bangladeshi more than eight years' income, the average American, just one month's wage.
- *Men and youth dominate.* Women make up just 17 per cent of the Internet users in Japan, only 7 per cent in China. Most users in China and the United Kingdom are under 30.
- *English talks.* English prevails in almost 80 per cent of all Websites, yet less than one in 10 people worldwide speaks it.

This exclusivity is creating parallel worlds. Those with income, education and – literally – connections have cheap and instantaneous access to information. The rest are left with uncertain, slow and costly access. When people in these two worlds live and compete side by side, the advantage of being connected will overpower the marginal and impoverished, cutting off their voices and concerns from the global conversation.
[ ... ]

**National and global governance have to be reinvented – with human development and equity at their core.**

None of these pernicious trends – growing marginalization, growing human insecurity, growing inequality – is inevitable. With political will and commitment in the global community, they can all be reversed. With stronger governance – local, national, regional and global – the benefits of competitive markets can be preserved with clear rules and boundaries, and stronger action can be taken to meet the needs of human development.

Governance does not mean mere government. It means the framework of rules, institutions and established practices that set limits and give incentives for the behaviour of individuals, organizations and firms. Without strong governance, the dangers of global conflicts could be a reality of the 21st century – trade wars promoting national and corporate interests, uncontrolled financial volatility setting off civil conflicts, untamed global crime infecting safe neighbourhoods and criminalizing politics, business and the police.

[ . . . ]

# 36

# The Rise of the Fourth World

## Manuel Castells

The rise of informationalism at the turn of the millennium is intertwined with rising inequality and social exclusion throughout the world. In this [article] I shall try to explain why and how this is so, while displaying some snapshots of the new faces of human suffering. The process of capitalist restructuring, with its hardened logic of economic competitiveness, has much to do with it. But new technological and organizational conditions of the Information Age [ . . . ] provide a new, powerful twist to the old pattern of profit-seeking taking over soul-searching.

However, there is contradictory evidence, fueling an ideologically charged debate, on the actual plight of people around the world. After all, the last quarter of the twentieth century saw access to development, industrialization, and consumption for tens of millions of Chinese, Koreans, Indians, Malaysians, Thais, Indonesians, Chileans, Brazilians, Mexicans, Argentinians, and smaller numbers in a variety of countries – even allowing for the reversal of fortune for some of these millions as a consequence of the Asian financial crisis of 1997–8, and its aftershocks in other areas of the world. The bulk of the population in Western Europe still enjoys the highest living standards in the world, and in the world's history. And in the United States, while average real wages for male workers stagnated or declined for over two decades, until 1996, with the exception of the top of the scale of college graduates, the massive incorporation of women into paid labor, relatively closing their wage gap with men, has maintained decent standards of living, overall, on the condition of being stable enough to keep a two-wage household, and agreeing to put up with increased working time. Health, education, and income statistics around the world show, on average, considerable improvement over historical standards.[1] In fact, for the population as a whole, only the former Soviet Union, after the collapse of statism, and Sub-Saharan Africa, after its marginalization from capitalism, have experienced a decline in living conditions, and for some countries in vital statistics, in the past ten years (although most of Latin America regressed in the 1980s). Yet, as Stephen Gould entitled a wonderful article years ago, "the median isn't the message."[2] Even without entering into a full discussion of the meaning of the quality of life, including the environmental consequences of the latest round of industrialization, the apparently mixed record of development at the dawn of the Information Age conveys ideologically manipulated bewilderment in the absence of analytical clarity.

This is why it is necessary, in assessing the social dynamics of informationalism, to establish a distinction between several processes of social differentiation: on the one hand, *inequality, polarization, poverty*, and *misery* all pertain to the domain of relationships of distribution/consumption or differential appropriation of the wealth generated by collective effort. On the other hand, *individualization of work, over-exploitation of workers*, *social exclusion*, and *perverse integration* are characteristic of four specific processes *vis-à-vis* relations of production.[3]

*Inequality* refers to the differential appropriation of wealth (income and assets) by different individuals and social groups, relative to each other. *Polarization* is a specific process of inequality that occurs when both the top and the bottom of the scale of income or wealth distribution grow faster than the middle, thus shrinking the middle, and sharpening social differences between two extreme segments of the population. *Poverty* is an institutionally defined norm concerning a level of resources below which it is not possible to reach the living standards considered to be the minimum norm in a given society at a given time (usually, a level of income per a given number of members of a household, as defined by governments or authoritative institutions). *Misery*, a term I propose, refers to what social statisticians call "extreme poverty," that is the bottom of the distribution of income/assets, or what some experts conceptualize as "deprivation," introducing a wider range of social/economic disadvantages. In the United States, for instance, extreme poverty refers to those households whose income falls below 50 percent of the income that defines the poverty line. It is obvious that all these definitions (with powerful effects in categorizing populations, and defining social policies and resource allocation) are statistically relative and culturally defined, besides being politically manipulated. Yet, they at least allow us to be precise about what we say when describing/analyzing social differentiation under informational capitalism.

The second set of processes, and their categorization, pertains to the analysis of relations of production. Thus, when observers criticize "precarious" labor relations, they are usually referring to the process of individualization of work, and to its induced instability on employment patterns. Or else the discourse on social exclusion denotes the observed tendency to permanently exclude from formal labor markets certain categories of the population. These processes do have fundamental consequences for inequality, polarization, poverty, and misery. But the two planes must be analytically and empirically differentiated in order to establish their causal relationships, thus paving the way for understanding the dynamics of social differentiation, exploitation, and exclusion in the network society.

By *individualization of labor* I mean the process by which labor contribution to production is defined specifically for each worker, and for each of his/her contributions, either under the form of self-employment or under individually contracted, largely unregulated, salaried labor. [ . . . ]

I use the term *over-exploitation*[4] to indicate working arrangements that allow capital to systematically withhold payment/resource allocation, or impose harsher working conditions, on certain types of workers, below what is the norm/regulation in a given formal labor market in a given time and space. This refers to discrimination against immigrants, minorities, women, young people, children, or other categories of discriminated workers, as tolerated, or sanctioned, by regulatory agencies. A particularly meaningful trend in this context is the resurgence of child paid labor throughout the world, in conditions of extreme exploitation, defenselessness, and abuse, reversing the historical pattern of social protection of children existing under late industrial capitalism, as well as in industrial statism and traditional agricultural societies.[5]

*Social exclusion* is a concept proposed by the social policy think-tanks of the European Union's Commission, and adopted by the United Nations' International Labour Office.[6] According to the European Commission's Observatory on National

Policies to Combat Social Exclusion, it refers to "the social rights of citizens . . . to a certain basic standard of living and to participation in the major social and occupational opportunities of the society."[7] Trying to be more precise, I define *social exclusion as the process by which certain individuals and groups are systemically barred from access to positions that would enable them to an autonomous livelihood within the social standards framed by institutions and values in a given context.*[8] Under normal circumstances, in informational capitalism, *such a position is usually associated with the possibility of access to relatively regular, paid labor, for at least one member of a stable household.* Social exclusion is, in fact, the process that disfranchises a person as labor in the context of capitalism. In countries with a well-developed welfare state, inclusion may also encompass generous compensations in case of long-term unemployment or disability, although these conditions are increasingly exceptional. I would consider among the socially excluded the mass of people on long-term welfare assistance under institutionally punitive conditions, such as is the case in the United States. To be sure, among the English gentry, and among the oil sheiks, there are still a few independently wealthy individuals who could not care less about being demoted to non-labor: I do not consider them to be socially excluded.

Social exclusion is a process, not a condition. Thus, its boundaries shift, and who is excluded and included may vary over time, depending on education, demographic characteristics, social prejudices, business practices, and public policies. Furthermore, although the lack of regular work as a source of income is ultimately the key mechanism in social exclusion, how and why individuals and groups are placed under structural difficulty/impossibility to provide for themselves follows a wide array of avenues of destitution. It is not only a matter of lacking skills or not being able to find a job. It may be that illness strikes in a society without health coverage for a substantial proportion of its members (for example, the United States). Or else drug addiction or alcoholism destroys humanity in a person. Or the culture of prisons and the stigma of being an ex-convict closes ways out of crime on return to freedom. Or the injuries of mental illness, or of a nervous breakdown, placing a person between the alternatives of psychiatric repression and irresponsible de-institutionalization, paralyze the soul and cancel the will. Or, more simply, functional illiteracy, illegal status, inability to pay the rent, thus inducing homelessness, or sheer bad luck with a boss or a cop, trigger a chain of events that sends a person (and his/her family very often) drifting toward the outer regions of society, inhabited by the wreckage of failed humanity.

Moreover, the process of social exclusion in the network society concerns both people and territories. So that, under certain conditions, entire countries, regions, cities, and neighborhoods become excluded, embracing in this exclusion most, or all, of their populations. This is different from the traditional process of spatial segregation, as I shall try to show when examining the new features of American inner-city ghettos. Under the new, dominant logic of the space of flows [ . . . ], areas that are non-valuable from the perspective of informational capitalism, and that do not have significant political interest for the powers that be, are bypassed by flows of wealth and information, and ultimately deprived of the basic technological infrastructure that allows us to communicate, innovate, produce, consume, and even live, in today's world. This process induces an extremely uneven geography of social/territorial exclusion and inclusion, which disables large segments of people while linking up trans-territorially, through information technology, whatever and whoever may offer value in the global networks accumulating wealth, information, and power.

The process of social exclusion, and the insufficiency of remedial policies of social integration, lead to a fourth, key process characterizing some specific forms of relations of production in informational capitalism: I call it *perverse integration*. It refers to the labor process in the criminal economy. By criminal economy, I mean income-generating activities that are normatively declared to be crime, and accordingly prosecuted, in a given institutional context. There is no value judgment in the labeling, not because I condone drug trafficking, but because I do not condone either a number of institutionally respectable activities that inflict tremendous damage on people's lives. Yet, what a given society considers to be criminal is so, and it has substantial consequences for whoever engages in such activities. [ . . . ] [I]nformational capitalism is characterized by the formation of a global criminal economy, and by its growing interdependence with the formal economy and political institutions. Segments of the socially excluded population, along with individuals who choose far more profitable, if risky, ways to make a living, constitute an increasingly populated underworld which is becoming an essential feature of social dynamics in most of the planet.

There are systemic relationships between informational capitalism, capitalist restructuring, trends in the relationships of production, and new trends in the relationships of distribution. Or, in a nutshell, between the dynamics of the network society, inequality, and social exclusion. I shall try to advance some hypotheses on the nature and shape of these relationships. [ . . . ] Beforehand, let me briefly overview the state of the world concerning inequality, poverty, and social exclusion.

## Toward a Polarized World? A Global Overview

"Divergence in output per person across countries is perhaps *the* dominant feature of modern economic history. The ratio of per capita income in the richest versus the poorest country [between 1870 and 1989] has increased by a factor of 6 and the standard deviation of GDP per capita has increased between 60 and 100 percent," writes Pritchett, summarizing the findings of his econometric study for the World Bank.[9] In much of the world, this geographical disparity in the creation/appropriation of wealth has increased in the past two decades, while the differential between OECD countries and the rest of the planet, representing the overwhelming proportion of the population, is still abysmal. Thus, using the historical economic statistics elaborated by Maddison,[10] Benner and I have [ . . . ] represented graphically in figure [1] [ . . . ] the evolution of GDP per capita [ . . . ] for a group of selected countries, ranked by the relative value of their index *vis-à-vis* the United States, between 1950, 1973, and 1992. Japan has succeeded in almost catching up in the past four decades, while Western Europe has improved its relative position, but still trails the US by a considerable margin. During the 1973–92 period, the sample of Latin American, African, and Eastern European countries studied by Maddison have fallen behind even further. As for ten Asian countries, including the economic miracles of South Korea, China, and Taiwan, they have substantially improved their relative position, but in absolute levels, in 1992, they were still poorer than any other region of the world except Africa, representing, as a whole, only 18 percent of the US level of wealth, although this is mainly due to China's population.

However, if the distribution of wealth between countries continues to diverge, overall the average living conditions of the world's population, as measured by the

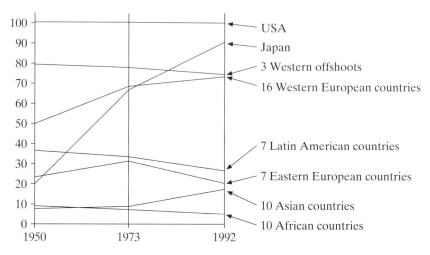

**Figure [1]**   GDP per capita index in a 55-country sample (USA = 100)

United Nations Human Development Index, have improved steadily over the past three decades. This is due, primarily, to better educational opportunities, and improved health standards, which translate into a dramatic increase in life expectancy, which in developing countries went up from 46 years in the 1960s to 62 years in 1993, and to 64.4 years in 1997, particularly for women.[11]

The evolution of income inequality presents a different profile if we take a global view, or if we look at its evolution within specific countries in a comparative perspective. In a global approach, there has been, over the past three decades, increasing inequality and polarization in the distribution of wealth. According to UNDP's 1996/1999 Human Development Reports, in 1993 only US$5 trillion of the US$23 trillion global GDP were from the developing countries even if they accounted for nearly 80 percent of total population. The poorest 20 percent of the world's people have seen their share of global income decline from 2.3 percent to 1.4 percent in the past 30 years. Meanwhile, the share of the richest 20 percent has risen from 70 percent to 85 percent. The ratio of the income of the 20 percent richest people in the world over the poorest 20 percent increased – from 30 : 1 in 1960 to 74 : 1 in 1997. In 1994 the assets of the world's 358 billionaires (in US dollars) exceeded the combined annual incomes of countries with 45 percent of the world's population. The concentration of wealth at the very top accelerated in the second half of the 1990s: the net worth of the world's 200 richest people increased from US$440 billion to more than US$1 trillion between 1994 and 1998. Thus, in 1998, the assets of the three richest people in the world were more than the combined GNP of the 48 least developed countries, comprising 600 million people.[12] The gap in per capita income between the industrial and the developing worlds tripled, from US$5,700 in 1960 to US$15,000 in 1993.[13] "Between 1960 and 1991, all but the richest quintile [of the world's people] saw their income share fall, so that by 1991 more than 85 percent of the world's population received only 15 percent of its income – yet another indication of an even more polarized world."[14]

On the other hand, there is considerable disparity in the evolution of *intra-country inequality* in different areas of the world. In the past two decades, income inequality has increased in the United States,[15] United Kingdom,[16] Brazil, Argentina, Venezuela,

**Table [1]**    Change in income inequality after 1979 in OECD countries

| Country | Period | Annual change in Gini coefficient[1] | |
|---|---|---|---|
| | | Relative (%) | Absolute (point change) |
| United Kingdom | 1979–95 | 1.80 | 0.22 |
| Sweden | 1979–94 | 1.68 | 0.38 |
| Denmark | 1981–90 | 1.20 | – |
| Australia | 1981–89 | 1.16 | 0.34 |
| Netherlands | 1979–94 | 1.07 | 0.25 |
| Japan | 1979–93 | 0.84 | 0.25 |
| United States | 1979–95 | 0.79 | 0.35 |
| Germany[2] | 1979–95 | 0.50 | 0.13 |
| France | 1979–89 | 0.40 | 0.12 |
| Norway | 1979–92 | 0.22 | 0.05 |
| Canada | 1979–95 | −0.02 | 0.00 |
| Finland | 1979–94 | −0.10 | −0.02 |
| Italy | 1980–91 | −0.64 | −0.58 |

[1] Measured as the relative change in the Gini coefficient, where growth reflects more inequality.
[2] Western Germany.
*Source*: Gottschalk and Smeeding (1997) elaborated by Mishel et al. (1999: 374)

Bolivia, Peru, Thailand, and Russia;[17] and, in the 1980s, in Japan,[18] Canada, Sweden, Australia, Germany,[19] and in Mexico,[20] just to cite a few relevant countries. But income inequality *decreased* in the 1960–90 period in India, Malaysia, Hong Kong, Singapore, Taiwan, and South Korea.[21] Also, according to data elaborated by Deininger and Squire, if we compare the level of income inequality, measured by Gini coefficient, by major regions of the world, between the 1990s and the 1970s, in 1990 it was much higher in Eastern Europe, somewhat higher in Latin America, but lower in all other regions, when analyzed at a highly aggregate level.[22] The Gini coefficient remained for Latin America as a whole at about 0.58 throughout the 1990s, thus reflecting the highest level of inequality among major regions in the world.[23]

Yet, while allowing for a certain range of variation of trends in different countries, table [1] shows a predominant trend toward increasing inequality, as measured by the annual change in Gini coefficient, for most OECD countries between the late 1970s and the mid-1990s. The United Kingdom is the country where inequality increased the fastest. But what is particularly striking is that the two other countries with rapidly increasing inequality are Sweden and Denmark, which were until recently egalitarian societies. If we add Japan to the same category of fast-growing inequality in societies with low levels of inequality, this observation would suggest the hypothesis of a structural trend toward increasing inequality in the network society. On the other hand, Finland, a very advanced network society, did not follow the trend of its Scandinavian neighbors, and Italy significantly reduced inequality. If Spanish and Portuguese data were included in the table they would show a pattern of stable, moderate inequality. Transition economies in Eastern Europe and the CIS experienced, in the 1990s, the fastest rise in inequality ever. By the end of the twentieth century, in Russia the income share of the richer 20 percent was 11 times that of the poorer 20 percent.[24]

If the evolution of intra-country inequality varies, *what appears to be a global phenomenon (albeit with some important exceptions, particularly China) is the growth of poverty, and particularly of extreme poverty*. Indeed, the acceleration of uneven development, and the simultaneous inclusion and exclusion of people in the growth process, which I consider to be a feature of informational capitalism, translates into polarization, and the spread of misery among a growing number of people. Thus, according to UNDP:

> Since 1980, there has been a dramatic surge in economic growth in some 15 countries, bringing rapidly rising incomes to many of their 1.5 billion people, more than a quarter of the world's population. Over much of this period, however, economic decline or stagnation has affected 100 countries, reducing the incomes of 1.6 billion people, again more than a quarter of the world's population. In 70 of these countries average incomes are less than they were in 1980 – and in 43 countries less than they were in 1970. [Furthermore], during 1970–85 global GNP increased by 40 percent, yet the number of poor increased by 17 percent. While 200 million people saw their per capita incomes fall during 1965–80, more than one billion people did in 1980–93.[25]

In the mid-1990s, taking as the extreme poverty line a consumption equivalent to one US dollar a day, 1.3 billion people, accounting for 33 percent of the developing world's population, were in misery. Of these poor people, 550 million lived in South Asia, 215 million in Sub-Saharan Africa, and 150 million in Latin America.[26] In a similar estimate, using the one dollar a day dividing line for extreme poverty, ILO estimated that the percentage of the population below this line increased from 53.5 percent in 1985 to 54.4 percent in 1990 in Sub-Saharan Africa; from 23 percent to 27.8 percent in Latin America; and decreased from 61.1 percent to 59 percent in South Asia, and from 15.7 percent to 14.7 percent in East/South-East Asia (without China). According to UNDP, between 1987 and 1993 the number of people with incomes of less than one dollar a day increased by 100 million to reach 1.3 billion. If we consider the level of income of less than two dollars a day, another billion people should be added. Thus, at the turn of the millennium well over one third of humankind was living at subsistence or below subsistence level. In addition to income poverty, other dimensions of poverty are even more striking: in the mid-1990s about 840 million people were illiterate, more than 1.2 billion lacked access to safe water, 800 million lacked access to health services, and more than 800 million suffered hunger. Nearly a third of the people in the least developed countries – mainly in Sub-Saharan Africa – were not expected to survive to the age of 40. Women and children suffer most from poverty: 160 million children under five were malnourished, and the maternal mortality rate was about 500 women per 100,000 live births.[27] The largest concentration of poverty was, by far, in the rural areas: in 1990, the proportion of poor among the rural population was 66 percent in Brazil, 72 percent in Peru, 43 percent in Mexico, 49 percent in India, and 54 percent in the Philippines.[28] As for Russia, the CIS countries, and Eastern Europe, a report issued by the World Bank in April 1999 calculated that there were 147 million people living below the poverty line of four dollars a day. The equivalent figure for 1989 was 14 million.

On the other hand, some countries, and particularly China and Chile, reduced substantially their poverty level during the 1990s. In the case of China this was due to high economic growth, coupled with rural–urban migration. In the case of Chile it was the result of deliberate policies by the first Chilean democratic administration, after Pinochet's "miracle" had reduced to poverty about 43 percent of the Chilean population.[29] Thus structural trends notwithstanding, poverty is also a function of public policies. The issue is that during the 1980s and 1990s most governments gave priority to techno-economic restructuring over social welfare. As a result, poverty also increased during the 1980s and early 1990s in most developed countries. The number of families below the poverty line increased by 60 percent in the UK, and by 40 percent in The Netherlands. Overall, by the mid-1990s, there were over 100 million people below the poverty level in industrialized countries, including five million homeless people.[30]

To the structural persistence of poverty in all areas of the world must be added the sudden inducement of poverty by economic crises linked to volatility in global financial markets. Thus, the Asian crisis of 1997–8 plunged into poverty in Indonesia an additional 40 million people, or 20 percent of the population, and brought below the poverty level 5.5 million people in Korea and 6.7 million in Thailand. Indeed, while markets and exports may recover in a relatively short time (about two years in most Asian economies affected by the 1997–8 crisis), employment, income, and social benefits are curtailed for a much longer period. An analysis of over 300 economic crises in more than 80 countries since 1973 showed that output growth recovered to the level prior to the crisis in one year on average. But real wage growth took about four years to recover and employment growth five years. Income distribution worsened on average for three years, improving over pre-crisis levels by the fifth year.[31] And this is counting on the fact that, during this three to five year period, there is no further crisis.

Thus, overall, *the ascent of informational, global capitalism is indeed characterized by simultaneous economic development and underdevelopment, social inclusion and social exclusion*, in a process very roughly reflected in comparative statistics. There is polarization in the distribution of wealth at the global level, differential evolution of intra-country income inequality, albeit with a predominantly upward trend toward increasing inequality, and substantial growth of poverty and misery in the world at large and in most – but not all – countries, both developed and developing. [ . . . ]

## Notes

1   UNDP (1996).
2   Gould (1985).
3   For an informed discussion on analyzing poverty and social exclusion in a comparative perspective, see Rodgers et al. (1995); Mingione (1996).
4   I use the term "over-exploitation" to distinguish it from the concept of exploitation in the Marxian tradition, that, in strict Marxist economics, would be applicable to all salaried labor. Since this categorization would imply accepting the labor theory of value, a matter of belief rather than of research, I prefer to bypass the debate altogether, but avoid creating further confusion by using "exploitation," as I would like to do for cases of systematic discrimination such as the ones I am referring to in my categorization.
5   ILO (1996).
6   Rodgers et al. (1995).
7   Room (1992: 14).
8   By "autonomy," in this context, I mean the average margin of individual autonomy/social heteronomy as constructed by society. It is obvious that a worker, or even a self-employed person, is not autonomous *vis-à-vis* his/her employer, or network of clients. I refer to social

conditions that represent the social norm, in contrast with people's inability to organize their own lives even under the constraints of social structure, because of their lack of access to resources that social structure mandates as necessary to construct their limited autonomy. This discussion of socially constrained autonomy is what underlies the conceptualization of inclusion/exclusion as the differential expression of people's social rights.

 9  Pritchett (1995: 2–3).
10  Maddison (1995).
11  UNDP (1996: 18–19).
12  UNDP (1999: 37).
13  UNDP (1996: 2–3).
14  UNDP (1996: 13).
15  Fischer et al. (1996).
16  Townsend (1993).
17  UNDP (1996).
18  Bauer and Mason (1992).
19  Green et al. (1992).
20  Skezely (1995).
21  UNDP (1996).
22  Deininger and Squire (1996: 584).
23  UNDP (1999: 39).
24  UNDP (1999: 36).
25  UNDP (1996: 1–2).
26  UNDP (1996: 27).
27  ILO (1995: table 13).
28  ILO (1994).
29  UNDP – Chile (1998).
30  UNDP (1997: 24; 1999: 37).
31  UNDP (1999: 40).

# References

Bauer, J. and Mason, A. (1992) The distribution of income and wealth in Japan. *Review of Income and Wealth* 38(4): 403–28.

Deininger, K. and Squire, L. (1996) A new data set measuring income inequality. *The World Bank Economic Review* 10(3): 565–91.

Fischer, C. et al. (1996). *Inequality by Design*. Princeton, NJ: Princeton University Press.

Gottschalk, P. and Smeeding, T. M. (1997) Empirical Evidence on Income Inequality in Industrialized Countries. Luxembourg Income Study Working Paper, no. 154.

Gould, S. J. (1985) The median isn't the message. *Discover* (June): 40–2.

Green, G. et al. (1992) International comparisons of earnings inequality for men in the 1980s. *Review of Income and Wealth* 38(1): 1–15.

ILO (International Labour Office) (1994) *World Labour Report 1994*. Geneva: ILO.

ILO (International Labour Office) (1995) *World Employment Report 1995*. Geneva: ILO.

ILO (International Labour Office) (1996) *Child Labour: Targeting the Intolerable*. Geneva: ILO.

Maddison, A. (1995) *Monitoring the World Economy, 1820–1992*. Paris: OECD Development Centre Studies.

Minigione, E. (ed.) (1996) *Urban Poverty and the Underclass*. Oxford: Blackwell.

Mishel, L. et al. (1999) *The State of Working America 1998/99*. Ithaca and London: Cornell University Press.

Pritchett, L. (1995) Divergence, big time. Policy Research Working Paper, no. 1522. Washington, DC: The World Bank.

Rodgers, G., Gore, C. et al. (eds) (1995) *Social Exclusion: Rhetoric, Reality, Responses*. Geneva: International Institute of Labour Studies.

Room, G. (1992) *Observatory on National Policies to Combat Social Exclusion: Second Annual Report*. Brussels: Commission of the European Community.

Skezely, M. (1995) Poverty in Mexico during adjustment. *Review of Income and Wealth* 41(3): 331–48.

Townsend, P. (1993) *The International Analysis of Poverty*. London: Harvester/Wheatsheaf.

UNDP (United Nations Development Programme) (1996) *Human Development Report 1996*. New York: Oxford University Press.

UNDP (United Nations Development Programme) (1997) *Human Development Report 1997*. New York: Oxford University Press.

UNDP (United Nations Development Programme) (1999) *Human Development Report 1999: Globalization with a Human Face*. New York: Oxford University Press.

UNDP (United Nations Development Programme) – Chile (1998) *El desarrollo humano en Chile*. Santiago de Chile: Naciones Unidas.

# 37

# Are Global Poverty and Inequality Getting Worse?

*'Yes'*          *'No'*

*Robert Wade*     *Martin Wolf*

**Dear Martin**

*22nd January 2002*

You have written eloquently in the *Financial Times* about globalisation. You make three main points. (1) Poverty and inequality on a world scale have both fallen over the past two decades for the first time in more than 150 years. (2) These falls are due to greater global economic integration. (3) The anti-globalisation movement encourages countries to adopt policies that will in fact only intensify their poverty and inequality.

Let us take the first point about trends in poverty and inequality. If you are wrong here, the rest of your argument begins to wobble and, in fact, there are reasons to doubt what you say. On poverty, the World Bank is the main source of numbers. Bank researchers have found that the number of people in absolute poverty (with incomes less than about $1 per day) was roughly constant in 1987 and 1998, at around 1.2 billion. Since world population increased, the *proportion* of the world's population in absolute poverty fell sharply from around 28 per cent to 24 per cent in only 11 years. This is good news.

But recent research on where the Bank got the 1.2 billion suggests that the method for calculating the numbers is questionable. The effect is probably to understate the true numbers in poverty. How much higher than 1.2 billion we do not yet know.

So what is happening to global inequality? It is widening rapidly, if we compare the average incomes for each country and treat each one as a unit (China = Uganda). Yet income inequality among countries has become more equal, since around 1980, if we compare the average incomes for each country and weight each one by its population. However, this result comes from fast growth in China and India. If they are excluded this measure of inequality shows no obvious trend since 1980.

In any case, this measure – using the average income of each country weighted by population – is interesting only as an approximation to what we are really interested in, which is the income distribution among all the world's people or households, regardless of where they live. The problem is that we do not have good data for the incomes of all the world's people. You say that global inequality amongst households has probably fallen. But the most comprehensive data on world incomes, based on household income and expenditure surveys, find a sharp increase in inequality over as short a time as 1988 to 1993. Some of this may be statistical error; but the results do mean that the balance of probability falls in the direction of increasing global inequality among households.

This conclusion is strengthened by the trends in industrial pay inequality *within* countries. Pay inequality within countries was stable or declining from the early 1960s to 1982, then sharply increased from 1982 to the present. The year 1982 was a dramatic turning point towards greater inequality within the world's countries.

Doesn't the fast growth of populous China and India create a presumption that world income distribution is becoming more equal? No. At low levels of income, growth has to be fast for a long time before the absolute gap with slow-growing, high income countries begins to fall. The absolute income gap between a developing country with an average income of $1,000 a year, growing at 6 per cent, and a developed country with average income of $30,000, growing at 1 per cent, continues to widen until after the 40th year. China and India are not reducing the gap between their average incomes and the averages of the countries of western Europe, North America and Japan. They are, though, closing the gap with the faltering, middle-income states like Mexico, Brazil, Russia and Argentina, which is why average inequality among countries has become more equal since around 1980. But this reduction in the gap between China and India and the middle-income states is probably offset by widening income inequality *within* the two giants.

Perhaps all the thunder and lightning about the trends diverts attention from the main issue: the sheer magnitude of poverty and inequality on a world scale. The magnitude is unacceptable, regardless of the trend, and the world development agenda should make inequality reduction (not only poverty reduction) a high priority. Roughly 85 per cent of world income goes to 20 per cent of the world's population and 6 per cent to 60 per cent of the world's population. Can this meet any plausible test of legitimacy? It is difficult to see how it could meet the Rawlsian principle that a given degree of inequality is acceptable if it is necessary for the worst off to become better off.

Integration/globalisation is nothing like the engine of development you say it is. The engine is the advance of technology and the diffusion of technical capacities of people, firms and governments. Some forms of integration may help this, others may hinder it, depending partly on a country's stage of development.

*Regards*
Robert


## Dear Robert

*25th January 2002*

All data on incomes and income distribution are questionable, above all those generated in developing countries. But, contrary to what you say, World Bank researchers have calculated the numbers in extreme poverty – less than $1 a day – on a consistent basis, in recent studies.

The data shows a decline since 1980 of 200m people in the category of the absolutely poor. This is a fall from 31 per cent of the world's population to 20 per cent (not 24 per cent, which is the proportion in developing countries alone). That is a spectacularly rapid fall in poverty by historical standards. It makes a nonsense of the idea that poverty alleviation has been blighted by globalisation.

Now turn to the even murkier area of inequality. Here you argue that if we exclude China and India, there is no obvious trend in inequality. But why would one want to exclude two countries that contained about 60 per cent of the world's poorest people two decades ago and still contain almost 40 per cent of the world's population today? To fail to give these giants their due weight in a discussion of global poverty alleviation or income distribution would be *Hamlet* without the prince.

You then write that changes in relative average incomes across countries are not what we are really interested in, "which is the income distribution among all the world's people or households." This is wrong in itself. If a country's average income rises rapidly, it does also possess greater means for improving the lot of the poor. Maybe the government refuses to use the opportunity, but a successor government could.

In any case, we do possess data on relative household incomes. In a *Foreign Affairs* article, David Dollar and Aart Kraay of the World Bank report a big decline in worldwide income inequality since its peak in about 1970 [see below, chapter 38]. The study builds on work that goes back to 1820. The underlying method is to calculate the percentage gap between a randomly selected individual and the world average. The more unequal the distribution of world income, the bigger that gap becomes. They report that this gap peaked at 88 per cent of world average income in 1970, before falling to 78 per cent in 1995, roughly where it was in 1950.

The chief driver of changes in inequality among households is changes between countries, not within them. This was also the finding of Branko Milanovic's study of global household income distribution between 1988 and 1993, which you cite approvingly. You rely on this study to support the thesis of rising household inequality. But it contains at least four defects. First, there are well-known inconsistencies between data on household expenditures and national accounts. Second, the methods used generate no increase in rural real incomes in China, which is inconsistent with most views of what actually happened. Third, the period of five years is very short. Fourth and most important, this was an atypical period, because India had an economic upheaval in 1991, while China's growth was temporarily slowed by the Tiananmen crisis.

My conclusion is that the last two decades saw a decline not just in absolute poverty but also in world-wide inequality among households. The chief explanation for this was the fast growth of China and, to a lesser extent, of India. This progress was not offset by rising inequality within them. In the case of India there was no such rise. In China there has been a rise in inequality in the more recent period of its growth, largely because of controls on the movement of people from the hinterland to the coastal regions.

Unfortunately, you muddy the waters on inequality by raising the question of growing absolute gaps in incomes between rich and poor countries. If the income of the poor rises faster than the income of the rich, inequality falls, even if absolute gaps rise, since the standard measures of inequality describe relative, not absolute, differences in incomes.

This is vastly more than just a question of definition. China's average incomes per head are only a tenth of those of the US. They would have to grow at around 20 per cent a year to match the absolute increases now prevailing in the US. I see no point in bemoaning the failure to achieve what is impossible. Unless you are suggesting implausibly huge income transfers from taxpayers in rich countries to the world's poor, or complete freedom of migration, absolute gaps in living standards will rise for many decades, even if poor countries now grow very quickly. This is the tyranny of history: we can only start from where we are.

The trends in pay inequality you bring in to support your arguments further cloud the issue. Few of the world's poor earn wages that anybody reports. They work as subsistence farmers or do casual work in informal activities. Almost all reported wage earners are in the upper half of the global income distribution.

Yet this debate is, as you say, not just about measuring poverty and inequality, but about what these trends mean. You write that the magnitude of poverty and inequality are unacceptable. I agree on the former. That is why raising average incomes in poor countries and of poor people in both poor and less poor countries is an urgent goal of public policy.

But your position on the unacceptability of inequality also amounts to saying that the world would be a better place if the rich countries of today had never started rapid development in the 19th and 20th centuries. Maybe you do think this. But almost all citizens of advanced countries do not. They have no intention of doing without what they now have. So bemoaning the magnitude of global inequality, as opposed to the low standards of living of large parts of the world, is just empty rhetoric. It has no significance for action.

Today's global inequality and continuing, though also declining, mass poverty are the outcome of deep-seated historic processes that can be reversed only with vast and sustained improvements in poor countries, supported by rich ones. A start was made in the 1980s and 1990s. But the huge worry concerns those poor countries where there is now no sustained rise in living standards.

*Yours*
Martin


### Dear Martin

*29th January 2002*

On absolute poverty, you take the World Bank figures at face value, I say that they cannot be so taken. On inequality, you cite the work of World Bank economist David Dollar as the main evidence that world income inequality has declined over the past 20–25 years. But his method gives too much weight to what happens in the middle swathe of world population and too little weight to what happens towards the lower and upper ends of the distribution.

Contrary to what you say, inequality in India – rural-urban, intra-urban, intra-rural – increased over the past two decades. And everyone agrees inequality in China has risen rapidly. In a recent year, the ratio of the richest to poorest state or province was 1.9 for the US, 4.2 for India and for China, 7 in the early 1990s, 11 in the late 1990s.

You place too much trust not only in David Dollar's methodology, but also in the Bank's data set on inequality to which it is applied. Anyone applying the "laugh test" would have grounds for doubt: according to the Bank, Spain is the most equal country in Europe; France is much more unequal than Germany; India and Indonesia are in the same equality league as Norway. The data is based on uncoordinated sample surveys, separated in time and space, often conducted by unofficial researchers, in countries with differing concepts of income and differing attitudes towards revealing income to strangers. The Milanovic data based on household income and expenditure surveys around the world also has its problems, as you say, but is not obviously inferior to the Bank's national income data; and it suggests sharply rising inequality.

You say that "bemoaning the magnitude of global inequality, as opposed to the low standards of living of large parts of the world, is just empty rhetoric." No. If the magnitude of inequality is as large and difficult to justify as it seems to be, this greatly fortifies the case for public policy actions – some national, some international – to "tilt the playing field" in favour of the lagging regions. A significantly more equal world is likely to be more stable, peaceful and possibly more prosperous. Also, there's no reason for you to reject measures of absolute income gaps just because these are not relevant to the standard measures of inequality. We should be concerned with both absolute and relative gaps, for both relate to important ethical values, both are relevant to feelings of disempowerment and deprivation. Absolute gaps between, say, the top quintile and the bottom quintile of the world's population, you have to agree, are rising sharply.

So far, all this has been about your first point to do with trends in poverty and inequality. Your second point is about globalisation (or increased economic integration) as the world's best means of reducing poverty and inequality. I doubt it. The most powerful engine of development is the diffusion of technical capacities. This is proceeding at a furious rate in China, more sedately in India, at a snail's pace in most of Latin America, and slower, if at all, in sub-Saharan Africa and much of the Middle East. China and India are likely to experience a shift towards more income equality when they come near to full employment, five to ten decades from now. But any such shift in Latin America, sub-Saharan Africa and the Middle East will be even further away.

The World Bank studies on which you rely for your conclusions about the benign impacts of globalisation are shot through with problems. They distinguish "globalising" countries from "non-globalising" countries, and find that the former have much better economic performance than the latter. They measure globalising by changes in the ratio of trade to GDP. So globalising countries are ones that had a big rise in their trade/GDP ratio.

Let us accept that the countries the Bank calls globalisers did, indeed, have fast economic growth. The question is: why? At best, the Bank studies show that countries that start being closed, with very low trade/GDP, can have fast growth if they take policy steps that yield more trade/GDP. This sounds plausible, and it matches the experience of South Korea and Taiwan in the 1950s. But the finding does not support the policy prescription that all developing countries should liberalise their trade regimes in order to experience faster growth.

For two decades, the Bank's official view about development has been: adopt a liberal trade policy (low tariff and non-tariff barriers), deregulate markets, privatise state enterprises, welcome foreign firms, maintain fiscal balance and low inflation. The trouble is that there is no evidence that opening to trade does generally result in subsequently faster growth, holding other things like macroeconomic conditions constant.

The best examples of globalising countries are China and India, which are hardly poster-children for globalisation. They have certainly both had fast rises in trade/GDP in the recent period, and also fast economic growth. But the onset of fast growth occurred about a decade prior to their liberalising trade reforms. And the Bank would now be denouncing their trade policies and internal market-restricting policies as growth and efficiency-inhibiting – if they had not been growing so fast. Their policies remain far from those that the Bank seeks to get its borrowers to adopt; in fact, their trade barriers remain amongst the highest in the world. Their experience, and that of Japan, South Korea and Taiwan earlier, shows that countries do not have to have liberal trade policies in order to grow fast. It shows only that as countries become richer they tend to liberalise trade, which is not the same thing. The sensible ones liberalise in line with the growth of domestic capacities – they try to expose domestic producers to enough competition to make them more efficient, but not enough to kill them. China and India suggest a policy regime that is not close to what the Bank says, but nor is it "anti-globalisation."

The China-WTO agreement shows the dangers of pressing free trade upon developing countries. The agreement makes it difficult for China to adopt one of the most powerful inequality-mitigating measures: agricultural subsidies. In Japan, South Korea, Taiwan and, of course, Europe and the US, agricultural subsidies have been an important means of redistributing the fruits of industrialisation. China has had to sign away its rights to all but very low subsidies, with consequences that, given the degree of regional inequality, could be quite explosive. Likewise, China's agreement to give equal access to foreign companies will mean that it cannot protect "inefficient" labour-intensive industries that serve to equalise incomes. It is worrying for the whole world that the Chinese government itself now seems to think it can maintain an urban-rural apartheid state by means of the pass laws, while opening the economy at a pace so fast that unemployment will shoot upwards from its already high levels.

The point is more general. Under WTO rules, developing countries face constraints which prevent them from adopting the measures that already-developed countries (including East Asian ones) deployed to nurture their technological learning. This is outrageous. WTO rules and the Bank's official view need to be revised, soon, in the self-interest of the west, as well as the bulk of the world's population.
*Regards*
Robert


## Dear Robert

*3rd February 2002*

A significant decline has occurred in the proportion of the world population in absolute poverty over the past two decades. I think we agree on this. Whether there has been a fall in absolute numbers is less certain, though also, in my view, highly plausible. Your denial of this latter proposition rests on the view that any data or analyses from the World Bank must be tainted. Yet you rely on another Bank study for the proposition that inequality increased between 1988 and 1993. Your position is that any study which comes to a conclusion you dislike must be rejected (and vice versa).

You stress that absolute gaps between the world's richest and poorest people are rising. I agree. But so what? Even if poor countries grew far faster than rich ones, absolute gaps in living standards would rise for many years. This is the result of two centuries of differential growth. Why bemoan what cannot be helped?

What is needed, you then suggest, is "to tilt the playing field" in favour of lagging regions. There have been many attempts to do this, from *carte blanche* for protection to substantial aid. None has been notably successful. So what are *you* proposing? Huge transfers to the world's poor, free migration into rich countries, or a permanent depression in the north? I look forward to your attempts to sell any of these. Yet the very notion that impoverishment of the north might be a good thing shows the absurdity of your obsession with equality in itself. World income distribution was far less unequal two centuries ago, when perhaps 80 per cent of its population lived in extreme poverty. Did this make 1800 better than today?

The only sensible goal must be to raise the standards of living of the world's poorest people as quickly as we can. What is needed for this is faster growth. Look at China and India's own data. Indian data gives a decline of about 100m in absolute poverty between 1980 and 2000. China uses a lower poverty line but reports that the number of extreme poor in China declined from 250m in 1978 to 34m in 1999. Unfortunately, these successes have been offset by calamitous failures elsewhere, notably in sub-Saharan Africa.

I assume you support the need for faster growth in poor countries. Presumably, you also endorse the need for open markets in the north. After all, Taiwan and South Korea developed through exploitation of access to world markets. Yet many in the anti-globalisation movement are against trade liberalisation by the north. Many of them also say that foreign direct investment (FDI) impoverishes the poor. You say that China is not a "poster-child for globalisation." But China has been the biggest recipient of FDI in the developing world. Malaysia, to take another example, has received roughly as much inward FDI as the whole of sub-Saharan Africa.

The causes of developing country growth are complex. But your technological determinism is even more simple-minded than your caricature of the so-called Washington consensus. Many countries devoted much effort to upgrading technological capacity, but have failed to sustain rapid development: the Soviet Union was one and India another. One cannot separate technology from the context in which it is applied.

Among the essential pre-conditions for growth are: a stable state; security of the person and of property; widespread literacy and numeracy; basic health; adequate infrastructure; the ability to develop businesses without suffocation by red tape or corruption; broad acceptance of market forces; macro-economic stability, and a financial system capable of transferring savings to effective uses. In successful countries, these conditions emerge in a mutually reinforcing cycle. There is also evidence, I accept, that some initial equality in income and asset distribution helps.

The tragedy of Africa is that so few of these pre-conditions exist. Do I believe that trade liberalisation would fix this? No. But trade is the handmaiden of growth. There is no country that set out to reduce its reliance on trade, as anti-globalisers propose, and subsequently secured sustained growth. Even in the inauspicious soil of Africa, countries such as Uganda, which tried to exploit market opportunities, have achieved faster growth and poverty reduction.

Finally, you argue that, under WTO rules, developing countries are being forced to forgo their ability to adopt inequality-alleviating or growth-promoting policies. You assume that, in the absence of external constraints on their policy discretion, these countries would choose well-targeted trade policy interventions. This proposition does fail your laugh test. In any case, developing countries *can* use tariffs if they wish. China could have remained outside the WTO. But the Chinese authorities believed their country would do even better inside. I suspect this judgement will be proved right.

I would invite you to subscribe to the following three propositions. First, the biggest policy challenge is to accelerate economic growth in poor countries. Second, open markets in the north and FDI make an important contribution to such growth. Third, self-sufficiency is a foolish development strategy. If you accept these points, you are on my side of the policy argument [ ... ], like it or not.
*Yours*
Martin

# 38
# Spreading the Wealth

## David Dollar and Aart Kraay

## A Rising Tide

One of the main claims of the antiglobalization movement is that globalization is widening the gap between the haves and the have-nots. It benefits the rich and does little for the poor, perhaps even making their lot harder. As union leader Jay Mazur put it in [*Foreign Affairs*], "globalization has dramatically increased inequality between and within nations" ("Labor's New Internationalism," January/February 2000). The problem with this new conventional wisdom is that the best evidence available shows the exact opposite to be true. So far, the current wave of globalization, which started around 1980, has actually promoted economic equality and reduced poverty.

Global economic integration has complex effects on income, culture, society, and the environment. But in the debate over globalization's merits, its impact on poverty is particularly important. If international trade and investment primarily benefit the rich, many people will feel that restricting trade to protect jobs, culture, or the environment is worth the costs. But if restricting trade imposes further hardship on poor people in the developing world, many of the same people will think otherwise.

Three facts bear on this question. First, a long-term global trend toward greater inequality prevailed for at least 200 years; it peaked around 1975. But since then, it has stabilized and possibly even reversed. The chief reason for the change has been the accelerated growth of two large and initially poor countries: China and India.

Second, a strong correlation links increased participation in international trade and investment on the one hand and faster growth on the other. The developing world can be divided into a "globalizing" group of countries that have seen rapid increases in trade and foreign investment over the last two decades – well above the rates for rich countries – and a "nonglobalizing" group that trades even less of its income today than it did 20 years ago. The aggregate annual per capita growth rate of the globalizing group accelerated steadily from one percent in the 1960s to five percent in the 1990s. During that latter decade, in contrast, rich countries grew at two percent and nonglobalizers at only one percent. Economists are cautious about drawing conclusions concerning causality, but they largely agree that openness to foreign trade and investment (along with complementary reforms) explains the faster growth of the globalizers.

Third, and contrary to popular perception, globalization has not resulted in higher inequality within economies. Inequality has indeed gone up in some countries (such as China) and down in others (such as the Philippines). But those changes are not systematically linked to globalization measures such as trade and investment flows, tariff rates, and the presence of capital controls. Instead, shifts in inequality stem more from domestic education, taxes, and social policies. In general, higher growth rates in globalizing developing countries have translated into higher incomes for the poor. Even with its increased inequality, for example, China has seen the most spectacular reduction of poverty in world history – which was supported by opening its economy to foreign trade and investment.

Although globalization can be a powerful force for poverty reduction, its beneficial results are not inevitable. If policymakers hope to tap the full potential of economic integration and sustain its benefits, they must address three critical challenges. A growing protectionist movement in rich countries that aims to limit integration with poor ones must be stopped in its tracks. Developing countries need to acquire the kinds of institutions and policies that will allow them to prosper under globalization, both of which may be different from place to place. And more migration, both domestic and international, must be permitted when geography limits the potential for development.

## The Great Divide

Over the past 200 years, different local economies around the world have become more integrated while the growth rate of the global economy has accelerated dramatically. Although it is impossible to prove causal linkage between the two developments – since there are no other world economies to be tested against – evidence suggests the arrows run in both directions. As Adam Smith argued, a larger market permits a finer division of labor, which in turn facilitates innovation and learning by doing. Some of that innovation involves transportation and communications technologies that lower costs and increase integration. So it is easy to see how integration and innovation can be mutually supportive.
[ . . . ]

As economic integration has progressed, the annual growth rate of the world economy has accelerated, from 1 percent in the mid-nineteenth century to 3.5 percent in 1960–2000. Sustained over many years, such a jump in growth makes a huge difference in real living standards. It now takes only two to three years, for example, for the world economy to produce the same amount of goods and services that it did during the entire nineteenth century. Such a comparison is arguably a serious understatement of the true difference. since most of what is consumed today – airline travel, cars, televisions, synthetic fibers, life-extending drugs – did not exist 200 years ago. For any of these goods or services, therefore, the growth rate of output since 1820 is infinite. Human productivity has increased almost unimaginably.

All this tremendous growth in wealth was distributed very unequally up to about 1975, but since then growing equality has taken hold. One good measure of inequality among individuals worldwide is the mean log deviation – a measure of the gap between the income of any randomly selected person and a general average. It takes into account the fact that income distributions everywhere are skewed in favor of the rich, so that the typical person is poorer than the group average; the more skewed the distribution, the larger the gap. Per capita income in the world today, for example, is around $5,000, whereas a randomly selected person would most likely be living on close to $1,000 – 80 percent less. That gap translates into a mean log deviation of 0.8.

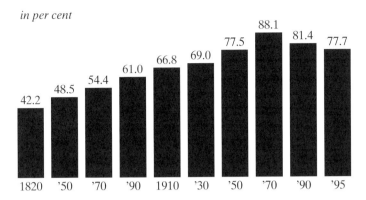

*in per cent*

[Figure 1]   Worldwide income inequality, 1820–1995
*Note*: Figures represent the mean log deviation between a typical individual income and the average per capita income
*Sources*: F. Bourguignon and C. Morrisson, "Inequality Among World Citizens, 1820–1992," working paper 2001–25 (Paris: Department and Laboratory of Applied and Theoretical Economics, 2001); and David Dollar, "Globalization, Inequality, and Poverty Since 1980," World Bank background paper, available at http://www.worldbank.org/research/global

Taking this approach, an estimate of the world distribution of income among individuals shows rising inequality between 1820 and 1975 [see figure 1]. In that period, the gap between the typical person and world per capita income increased from about 40 percent to about 80 percent. Since changes in income inequality within countries were small, the increase in inequality was driven mostly by differences in growth rates across countries. Areas that were already relatively rich in 1820 (notably, Europe and the United States) grew faster than poor areas (notably, China and India). Global inequality peaked sometime in the 1970s, but it then stabilized and even began to decline, largely because growth in China and India began to accelerate.

Another way of looking at global inequality is to examine what is happening to the extreme poor – those people living on less than $1 per day. Although the percentage of the world's population living in poverty has declined over time, the absolute number rose fairly steadily until 1980. During the Great Depression and World War II, the number of poor increased particularly sharply, and it declined somewhat immediately thereafter. The world economy grew strongly between 1960 and 1980, but the number of poor rose because growth did not occur in the places where the worst-off live. But since then, the most rapid growth has occurred in poor locations. Consequently the number of poor has declined by 200 million since 1980. Again, this trend is explained primarily by the rapid income growth in China and India, which together in 1980 accounted for about one-third of the world's population and more than 60 percent of the world's extreme poor.

## Upward Bound

The shift in the trend in global inequality coincides with the shift in the economic strategies of several large developing countries. Following World War II, most developing regions chose strategies that focused inward and discouraged integration with the global economy. But these approaches were not particularly successful, and throughout the 1960s and 1970s developing countries on the whole grew less rapidly than industrialized ones. The oil shocks and U.S. inflation of the 1970s created severe problems for them, contributing to negative growth, high inflation, and debt crises over the next several years. Faced with these disappointing results, several developing countries began to alter their strategies starting in the 1980s.

For example, China had an extremely closed economy until the mid-1970s. Although Beijing's initial economic reform focused on agriculture, a key part of its approach since the 1980s has involved opening up foreign trade and investment, including a drop in its tariff rates by two-thirds and its nontariff barriers by even more. These reforms have led to unprecedented economic growth in the country's coastal provinces and more moderate growth in the interior. From 1978 to 1994 the Chinese economy grew annually by 9 percent, while exports grew by 14 percent and imports by 13 percent. Of course, China and other globalizing developing countries have pursued a wide range of reforms, not just economic openness. Beijing has strengthened property rights through land reform and moved from a planned economy toward a market-oriented one, and these measures have contributed to its integration as well as to its growth.

Other developing countries have also opened up as a part of broader reform programs. During the 1990s, India liberalized foreign trade and investment with good results; its annual per capita income growth now tops four percent. It too has pursued a broad agenda of reform and has moved away from a highly regulated, planned system. Meanwhile, Uganda and Vietnam are the best examples of very low-income countries that have increased their participation in trade and investment and prospered as a result. And in the western hemisphere, Mexico is noteworthy both for signing its free-trade agreement with the United States and Canada in 1993 and for its rapid growth since then, especially in the northern regions near the US border.

These cases illustrate how openness to foreign trade and investment, coupled with complementary reforms, typically leads to faster growth. India, China, Vietnam, Uganda, and Mexico are not isolated examples; in general, countries that have become more open have grown faster. The best way to illustrate this trend is to rank developing countries in order of their increases in trade relative to national income over the past 20 years. The top third of this list can be thought of as the "globalizing" camp, and the bottom two-thirds as the "nonglobalizing" camp. The globalizers have increased their trade relative to income by 104 percent over the past two decades, compared to 71 percent for rich countries. The nonglobalizers, meanwhile, actually trade less today than they did 20 years ago. The globalizers have also cut their import tariffs by 22 percentage points on average, compared to only 11 percentage points for the nonglobalizers.

How have the globalizers fared in terms of growth? Their average annual growth rates accelerated from 1 percent in the 1960s to 3 percent in the 1970s, 4 percent in the 1980s, and 5 percent in the 1990s. Rich countries' annual growth rates, by comparison, slowed to about 2 percent in the 1990s, and the nonglobalizers saw their growth rates decline from 3 percent in the 1970s to 1 percent in the 1980s and 1990s.

The same pattern can be observed on a local level. Within both China and India, the locations that are integrating with the global economy are growing much more rapidly than the disconnected regions. Indian states, for example, vary significantly in the quality of their investment climates as measured by government efficiency, corruption, and infrastructure. Those states with better investment climates have integrated themselves more closely with outside markets and have experienced more investment (domestic and foreign) than their less-integrated counterparts. Moreover, states that were initially poor and then created good investment climates had stronger poverty reduction in the 1990s than those not integrating with the global economy. Such internal comparisons are important because, by holding national trade and macroeconomic policies constant, they reveal how important it is to complement trade liberalization with institutional reform so that integration can actually occur.

The accelerated growth rates of globalizing countries such as China, India, and Vietnam are consistent with cross-country comparisons that find openness going hand in hand with faster growth. The most that these studies can establish is that more trade and investment is highly correlated with higher growth, so one needs to be careful about drawing conclusions about causality. Still, the overall evidence from individual cases and cross-country correlation is persuasive. As economists Peter Lindert and Jeffrey Williamson have written, "even though no one study can establish that openness to trade has unambiguously helped the representative Third World economy, the preponderance of evidence supports this conclusion." They go on to note that "there are no antiglobal victories to report for the postwar Third World."

Contrary to the claims of the antiglobalization movement, therefore, greater openness to international trade and investment has in fact helped narrow the gap between rich and poor countries rather than widen it. During the 1990s, the economies of the globalizers, with a combined population of about 3 billion, grew more than twice as fast as the rich countries. The nonglobalizers, in contrast, grew only half as fast and nowadays lag further and further behind. Much of the discussion of global inequality assumes that there is growing divergence between the developing world and the rich world, but this is simply not true. The most important development in global inequality in recent decades is the growing divergence within the developing world, and it is directly related to whether countries take advantage of the economic benefits that globalization can offer.

## The Path out of Poverty

The antiglobalization movement also claims that economic integration is worsening inequality within countries as well as between them. Until the mid-1980s, there was insufficient evidence to support strong conclusions on this important topic. But now more and more developing countries have begun to conduct household income and consumption surveys of reasonable quality. (In low-income countries, these surveys typically track what households actually consume because so much of their real income is self-produced and not part of the money economy.) Good surveys now exist for 137 countries, and many go back far enough to measure changes in inequality over time.

One way of looking at inequality within countries is to focus on what happens to the bottom 20 percent of households as globalization and growth proceed apace. Across all countries, incomes of the poor grow at around the same rate as GDP. Of course, there is a great deal of variation around that average relationship. In some countries, income distribution has shifted in favor of the poor; in others, against them. But these shifts cannot be explained by any globalization-related variable. So it simply cannot be said that inequality necessarily rises with more trade, more foreign investment, and lower tariffs. For many globalizers, the overall change in distribution was small, and in some cases (such as the Philippines and Malaysia) it was even in favor of the poor. What changes in inequality do reflect are country-specific policies on education, taxes, and social protection.

It is important not to misunderstand this finding. China is an important example of a country that has had a large increase in inequality in the past decade, when the income of the bottom 20 percent has risen much less rapidly than per capita income. This trend may be related to greater openness, although domestic liberalization is a more likely cause. China started out in the 1970s with a highly equal distribution of income, and part of its reform has deliberately aimed at increasing the returns on education, which financially reward the better schooled. But the Chinese case is not typical; inequality has not increased in most of the developing countries that have opened up to foreign trade and investment. Furthermore, income distribution in China may have become more unequal, but the income of the poor in China has still risen rapidly. In fact, the country's progress in reducing poverty has been one of the most dramatic successes in history.

Because increased trade usually accompanies more rapid growth and does not systematically change household-income distribution, it generally is associated with improved well-being of the poor. Vietnam nicely illustrates this finding. As the nation has opened up, it has experienced a large increase in per capita income and no significant change in inequality. Thus the income of the poor has risen dramatically, and the number of Vietnamese living in absolute poverty dropped sharply from 75 percent of the population in 1988 to 37 percent in 1998. Of the poorest 5 percent of households in 1992, 98 percent were better off six years later. And the improved well-being is not just a matter of income. Child labor has declined, and school enrollment has increased. It should be no surprise that the vast majority of poor households in Vietnam benefited immediately from a more liberalized trading system, since the country's opening has resulted in exports of rice (produced by most of the poor farmers) and labor-intensive products such as footwear. But the experience of China and Vietnam is not unique. India and Uganda also enjoyed rapid poverty reduction as they grew along with their integration into the global economy [see figure 2].

## The Open Societies

These findings have important implications for developing countries, for rich countries such as the United States, and for those who care about global poverty. All parties should recognize that the most recent wave of globalization has been a powerful force for equality and poverty reduction, and they should commit themselves to seeing that it continues despite the obstacles lying ahead.

[ . . . ]

If globalization proceeds, its potential to be an equalizing force will depend on whether poor countries manage to integrate themselves into the global economic system. True integration requires not just trade liberalization but wide-ranging institutional reform. Many of the nonglobalizing developing countries, such as Myanmar, Nigeria, Ukraine, and Pakistan, offer an unattractive investment climate. Even if they decide to open themselves up to trade, not much is likely to happen unless other reforms are also pursued. It is not easy to predict the reform paths of these countries; some of the

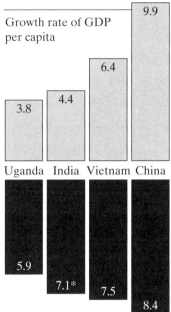

Growth rate of GDP per capita

Uganda  India  Vietnam  China

Rate of poverty reduction

**[Figure 2]**  GDP growth and poverty reduction in Uganda, India, Vietnam, and China, 1992–98, in percent per year

* India poverty reduction figure is for 1993–99
*Source*: David Dollar, "Globalization, Inequality, and Poverty Since 1980," World Bank background paper, available at http://www.worldbank.org/research/global

relative successes in recent years, such as China, India, Uganda, and Vietnam, have come as quite a surprise. But as long as a location has weak institutions and policies, people living there are going to fall further behind the rest of the world.

Through their trade policies, rich countries can make it easier for those developing countries that do choose to open up and join the global trading club. But in recent years, the rich countries have been doing just the opposite. GATT was originally built around agreements concerning trade practices. Now, institutional harmonization, such as agreement on policies toward intellectual property rights, is a requirement for joining the WTO. Any sort of regulation of labor and environmental standards made under the threat of WTO sanctions would take this requirement for harmonization much further. Such measures would be neoprotectionist in effect, because they would thwart the integration of developing countries into the world economy and discourage trade between poor countries and rich ones. [ . . . ]

A final potential obstacle to successful and equitable globalization relates to geography. There is no inherent reason why coastal China should be poor; the same goes for southern India, northern Mexico, and Vietnam. All of these locations are near important markets or trade routes but were long held back by misguided policies. Now, with appropriate reforms, they are starting to grow rapidly and take their natural place in the world. But the same cannot be said for Mali, Chad, or other countries or regions cursed with "poor geography" – i.e., distance from markets, inherently high transport costs, and challenging health and agricultural problems. It would be naive to think that trade and investment alone can alleviate poverty in all locations. In fact, for those locations with poor geography, trade liberalization is less important than developing proper health care systems or providing basic infrastructure – or letting people move elsewhere.

Migration from poor locations is the missing factor in the current wave of globalization that could make a large contribution to reducing poverty. Each year, 83 million people are added to the world's population, 82 million of them in the developing world. In Europe and Japan, moreover, the population is aging and the labor force is set to shrink. Migration of relatively unskilled workers from South to North would thus offer clear economic benefits to both. Most migration from South to North is economically motivated, and it raises the living standard of the migrant while benefiting the sending country in three ways. First, it reduces the South's labor force and thus raises wages for those who remain behind. Second, migrants send remittances of hard currency back home. Finally, migration bolsters transnational trade and investment networks. In the case of Mexico, for example, ten percent of its citizens live and work in the United States, taking pressure off its own labor market and raising wages there. India gets six times as much in remittances from its workers overseas as it gets in foreign aid.

Unlike trade, however, migration remains highly restricted and controversial. Some critics perceive a disruptive impact on society and culture and fear downward pressure on wages and rising unemployment in the richer countries. Yet anti-immigration lobbies ignore the fact that geographical economic disparities are so strong that illegal immigration is growing rapidly anyway, despite restrictive policies. In a perverse irony, some of the worst abuses of globalization occur because there is not enough of it in key economic areas such as labor flows. Human traffic, for example, has become a highly lucrative, unregulated business in which illegal migrants are easy prey for exploitation.

Realistically, none of the industrialized countries is going to adopt open migration. But they should reconsider their migration policies. Some, for example, have a strong bias in their immigration rules toward highly skilled workers, which in fact spurs a "brain drain" from the developing world. Such policies do little to stop the flow of unskilled workers and instead push many of these people into the illegal category. If rich countries would legally accept more unskilled workers, they could address their own looming labor shortages, improve living standards in developing countries, and reduce illegal human traffic and its abuses.

In sum, the integration of poor economies with richer ones over the past two decades has provided many opportunities for poor people to improve their lives. Examples of the beneficiaries of globalization can be found among Mexican migrants, Chinese factory workers, Vietnamese peasants, and Ugandan farmers. Many of the better-off in developing and rich countries alike also benefit. After all the rhetoric about globalization is stripped away, many of the policy questions come down to whether the rich world will make integrating with the world economy easy for those poor communities that want to do so. The world's poor have a large stake in how the rich countries answer.

# 39
# Globalization and Gendered Inequality

*Jill Steans*

[ ... ]

## Global Political Economy

### Critical interventions

The study of global political economy has become a dynamic and expanding area within the study of International Relations in recent years. From an initial narrow focus on the relationship between state power and decision-making in the context of the constraints imposed by the economic environment, global political economy has expanded to include the activities of multinational corporations, the influence on state policy of 'military industrial complexes', the role of international organizations in the global economy and the problems of debt and development.

In part the conceptual shift from *international* to *global* political economy is a response to the phenomenon of *globalization*. Global 'restructuring', the increasing influence of transnational corporations, the complex global division of labour, and the intimate relationship between debt, 'development' and environmental degradation, are all integral parts of the ongoing process of interconnectedness characteristic of globalization.[1] While the nature of globalization has been disputed, and its impact is undoubtedly uneven, it can nevertheless be usefully understood as a reordering of time and distance in our lives.[2] Critical approaches to [global political economy] recognize that global processes shape and transform economic activity and that a number of 'actors', both governmental and non-governmental, are agents of economic, social and political change. Political economy can no longer be viewed as an entirely 'internal affair'; it is necessary, therefore, to explore its global dimension while recognizing the specificity of some areas. Furthermore [ ... ] globalization has encouraged new forms of identification and expressions of solidarity which cut across state boundaries. This concern with the global dimension of social and economic activity has led to considerable criticism of the state-centric assumptions of the orthodoxy in *international* political economy.
[ ... ]

## Gender and global restructuring

Since the 1970s, the global economy has been undergoing a process of restructuring. The first phase of global restructuring can be traced to the 1973 oil crisis when big companies in the West resorted to international subcontracting to survive. Initially the knowledge-intensive parts of the production process went to the West, while trans-national corporations shifted the labour-intensive parts of the production process to developing countries where cheap female labour was abundant. In the 1980s as big business emphasized the importance of managerial flexibility and decentralized production, corporate strategies in the West sought a more flexible workforce to under-mine the power of trade unions.[3]

Global restructuring and the many resistances that it has generated have given rise to profound challenges to the orthodoxy, notably its statecentric predilections. However, neither neorealist, liberal interdependence, nor Marxist-inspired dependency models seem to be able fully to capture this phenomenon, and none are able to elucid-ate the gender-specific effects of restructuring. Mitter claims that restructuring in the 1980s had a profound effect on the composition of the workforce.[4] The process encouraged the growth of a 'new proletariat' in both the North and South, with women ghettoized in assembly-line work with poor pay and prospects. The 'feminization' of the workforce was a significant phenomenon in many regions of the North previ-ously characterized by heavy industry. Mitter argues that in areas where traditionally unionized industries such as coal and steel had previously thrived, the male workforce frequently had a reputation for radicalism. Employers in growth industries thus pre-ferred to employ the wives and daughters of, for example, ex-miners and ex-steelworkers.

In the 1980s big business also invested more and more in hitech research, auto-mation and computer-integrated manufacturing systems. This investment was aimed at replacing skilled labour. However, where labour-intensive and skilled-work aspects of production predominated, it was not always cost-effective to invest heavily in machin-ery. This was particularly the case where there was a supply of cheap female labour, because women made the most flexible robots of all.[5] In both Europe and North America, in the garment industry, for example, employers who felt threatened by the restruc-turing of the global economy but who could not relocate abroad moved to feminize their workforce and this resulted in the re-emergence of sweatshops and home-working.[6] This phenomenon was replicated in a number of other industries, including electronics, toy-manufacturing and food-processing. In the West, the official reasons given for preferring women were similar to those offered in the Third World. Employers stressed the 'natural dexterity' and 'nimble fingers' of women workers. However, because women's skills were thus defined in an ideologically biased way – that is, as natural rather than learnt – they were not rewarded.

Furthermore, 'masculinity' continued to be identified with the claims of 'bread-winner' status, and this also provided a justification for paying women less, even though male unemployment was actually increasing. Women were frequently paid between 20 and 50 per cent less than men in comparable jobs.[7] This was justified both by the idea that women and men had innate capabilities and personality traits and on the grounds that men needed to support families but women did not. A further significant aspect of global restructuring in the 1980s was the increasing numbers of part-time and home-workers. The rise in home-working in the West was also a direct manifesta-tion of 'flexible-manning' business strategies. Mitter and van Luijken claim that women constituted and continue to constitute the majority of home-workers, because every-where women constitute the poorest sections of society.[8] They claim that there is a marked similarity between home-work and housework – both are done by women and both remain invisible. Calling home-working the 'informal sector' of the economy misrepresents the numbers involved. It is not outside or parallel to the formal sector. It is an integral part of the global market economy.[9]

As the least unionized and poorest paid of all workers, women have been particularly vulnerable to the market policies which have continued to characterize global economic restructuring in the 1990s. Where women are encouraged to take up roles in the paid sector – and women now make up some 41 per cent of paid workers in developed countries and 34 per cent worldwide[10] – it is still the case that on average they earn 30–40 per cent less than men for comparable work. Women in general work longer hours than men and make up a disproportionate number of those working in the informal sector, though much of this work is unrecorded and so invisible. Women are concentrated in low-paid jobs. In the developing world, women are still heavily concentrated in Export Production Zones. The centrepiece of recent IMF strategies in the 1980s and 1990s has been export-led growth and structural adjustment. Indebted governments set aside territory specifically for the use of factories producing goods for the global market. In Asia, in the 1980s, women made up 85 per cent of workers in Export Production Zones. In other areas, the figure for women workers was typically around 75 per cent.[11] While there is some evidence that the 1990s have seen a 'remasculinization' of the workplace, women remain concentrated in the lowest-paid jobs.

Elson and Pearson claimed that the provision of women into such jobs was encouraged because it could be viewed as a way of involving women in the development process.[12] World-market factories producing components for the electronics industry, for example, are usually owned or partially owned by subsidiaries of Japanese, North American and European multinationals. These have been particularly important in the development of the global trade in consumer goods. A number of large US and European retailing firms are continuing to place large contracts with world-market factories. When deciding where to locate, a crucial factor remains the availability of a suitable labour force, which is defined in terms of low cost and high productivity. It seems that, as in the 1980s, in the 1990s women remain the cheapest and most productive of all workers. Women's attempts to translate paid employment into financial independence, however, are often thwarted by lack of access to capital, inadequate education and training and because women carry an unequal burden of family responsibilities.

A further aspect of global political economy which has attracted the interest of feminist scholars is the rapid growth of sex tourism, or prostitution, which is linked to the expansion of the tourist industry. In a number of countries tourism has become an important earner of foreign currency. In Thailand, the Philippines, the Caribbean, West Africa and Brazil, the growing sex industry is linked closely with the expansion of tourism and is inextricably linked to the problems of debt and development strategies.[13] Sex tourism does not just involve women, although it is overwhelmingly women who are drawn into this particular form of prostitution – frequently women who have been displaced as a direct consequence of 'development' strategies. Nor can prostitution be viewed solely from the perspective of tourism. Nevertheless it is conditioned by the demands of a stratified global market and the impact of development policies which are themselves conditioned by global economic processes.[14] Thahn Dan has suggested that prostitution is itself becoming a globally traded commodity. The growing integration of the tourist industry which links countries, hotel chains and package-holiday firms is a crucial enabling factor which allows spare capacity in airline seats and hotel beds to be matched with the demand for esoteric sexual services. With the growing globalization of capital, one finds the spread of prostitution. It is, Thahn Dan claims, no accident that Bangkok and Manila, both major cities which have experienced massive growth in prostitution in recent years, are also both major centres for multinational corporations and regional centres for global organizations. Increasingly the issue of prostitution needs a global analysis.[15] Enloe argues that sex tourism is both a part of the global political system and the global economy and the fact 'that it is not taken seriously says more about the ideological construction of seriousness than the politics of tourism'.[16]

[ . . . ]

## The UN Decade for Women

From its inception, the United Nations (UN) has seen itself as having a role to play in promoting development. Similarly the UN has a long history of promoting the status of women throughout the world. Until quite recently most of the UN's work in this area had concentrated on promoting women's status through the development process. In 1973 the United States Foreign Assistance Act led to the setting up of USAID. This act required women to be involved in decision-making bodies which dealt with aid and development issues. This measure prompted UN agencies, including the International Bank for Reconstruction and Development, UNESCO, the ILO and FAO, to set up special offices that concentrated on women's role in the development process. Shortly afterwards, in 1975, the First United Nations Conference on Women was held in Mexico to mark the beginning of International Women's Year. At the Mexico conference, delegates adopted a Plan of Action which aimed to improve the status of women, and 1976–85 was duly designated as the United Nations Decade for the Advancement of Women. In 1976 INSTRAW[17] and the Voluntary Fund for the UN Decade for Women (UNIFEM) were set up. The midway point in the UN Decade for Women was marked by the Second United Nations Conference on Women, held in Copenhagen in 1980.

In some respects the very existence of the UN Decade for Women was an important step forward. Up until that point, women had not really figured in debates about development at all. For the first time attempts were made to assess women's contribution to development, particularly in the crucial area of subsistence agriculture. The UN initiative required the attention of governments and gave women some access to policy-making by insisting that women's offices were set up within development agencies. It also led to the first real attempts to look at how technologies could be developed and applied which would help to reduce the drudgery characteristic of much women's work. In addition, it also helped to legitimize the women's movement as an international actor.[18] The so-called 'Women in Development' (WID) approach that underpinned various initiatives was also important in terms of facilitating the inclusion of women in workshops and seminars, by facilitating networking amongst women and by disseminating information through the WIDlink newsletter. The WID literature produced in the 1970s put the issue of women firmly on the political agenda, highlighted the inequalities of opportunity and the disproportionate contribution which women made to the development process. Furthermore, while the special offices set up to deal with women and development were often poorly funded, they did at least allow women to travel and meet and challenged the idea that men were the bread-winners in all societies.[19]

However, since 1985, the WID approach has been subjected to considerable criticism. At the end of the UN Decade for Women, surveys suggested the relative status and position of women throughout the world had declined in the previous ten years.[20] To some extent, the failure of the UN Decade can be explained by the failure on the part of many states to implement UN recommendations. In the 1980s a survey conducted by INSTRAW found that out of ninety-six countries, only six included women's issues as central issues in their development plans.[21] However, the failure was also attributed to the underlying assumptions of the WID approach. During the UN Decade, development policies were based on the underlying belief that the problems of Third World women were related to insufficient participation in the process of development. It has been argued that WID rested on a liberal feminist view that the problems of sexual inequality could be largely overcome if women were integrated into the public sphere. The aim of WID was to 'bring in' women, but women were already involved in the development process. According to Ashworth and Allison, the WID idea also contained the seeds of its own failure, because it recognized as visible producers only those whose commodities could be traded. The economic role of women as subsistence farmers, providers and full-time carers, which is the cornerstone of economic life, remained uncounted and unrewarded.[22]

Furthermore, the possibility that increasing poverty amongst women, and the relative decline of women to men during the decade, were the direct result of previous development policies was not considered. However [...] many development strategies which made reform and restructuring of agriculture production a priority had led directly to the displacement of women from the land that they had traditionally farmed. Critics argued that WID policy documents avoided and obscured issues of inequalities and power by presenting the issue of assistance to women as a purely technical exercise. It did not address the broader redistributional issues that assisting women raised. The WID approach ignored the broader context in which women-specific projects were inscribed. Increases in the productivity of women were not matched by relief from reproductive tasks. Women were too often regarded as 'victims' in need of assistance, rather than farmers, workers, investors and trade unionists. Ashworth, Allison and Redcliffe have argued that the central issue of gender inequalities in development policies ignored the fact that men and women could not benefit equally from aid and development initiatives if they had different political rights, burdens of time, and expectations and if the laws of inheritance and ownership discriminated against women and they could not get access to credit.[23]

Criticisms of the assumptions that guided the WID approach led to widespread calls for a different approach, which placed less emphasis on access and more on recognition of the degree to which women were already involved in the development process. The term 'gender and development' (GAD) was coined to describe an approach which was sensitive to the specificity of gender relations in particular countries and localities, rather than simply centred on women. Here 'the technical project of access, as numerical inclusion' was seen as insufficient to challenge the unequal allocation of values which sustained oppressive gender relations.[24] The stress on gender, rather than women, was a reminder that men must also be the target of attempts to redress gender inequalities and that their interests are also socially constructed and amenable to change.[25]

Gender and development approaches also highlighted the degree to which the neutrality and autonomy of the state, the focus of the liberal feminist strategies typical of WID, could not simply be taken for granted. As feminists have long argued, 'part of the definition of the state and the delimitation of the state's proper sphere involves the active codification and policing of the boundaries of the public and the private'.[26] Furthermore, in many states those boundaries also 'delineate gendered spheres of activity, where the paradigmatic subject of the public and economic arena is male and that of the private and domestic is female'.[27] In this way, according to Goetz, by confirming and institutionalizing the arrangements that distinguish the public from the private, states are involved in the social and political institutionalization of gendered power differences. For example, states set the parameters for women's structurally unequal position in families and markets by condoning gender-differential terms in inheritance rights and legal adulthood, by tacitly condoning domestic and sexual violence, or by sanctioning differential wages for equal or comparable work.[28]
[ . . . ]

## 'Mainstreaming' gender issues

Since the UN Decade for Women, there have been calls to 'mainstream' gender issues in development strategies. Mainstreaming means incorporating gender concerns into development strategies and policies as a matter of course rather than as 'add ons'. Although, as debates about gender and development have shifted from an emphasis on bringing women in, to an analysis of gender relations, to understanding the gender dimension of environmental concerns, 'mainstreaming' in common usage has also come to mean highlighting gender issues in other areas within the remit of the UN, such as human rights provision.

The Third UN Conference on Women, held in Nairobi in 1985 at the end of the UN Decade for Women, produced an important document called *Forward Looking Strategies for the Advancement of Women to the Year 2000* (FLSAW). The strategies outlined in the document aimed to promote women's interests in health, employment, family life, political life, and also promote women's human rights. Since the UN Decade for Women in 1976, UN development agencies have included sections that are specifically charged to advance the interests of women. These sections have pushed for a greater degree of gender sensitivity in government policies, for awareness of the problems of women's double burden, for equal access to and control over land and property, and for equal access to credit. The United Nations has long recognized the need to include the contribution which women make to the economy in order to undertake effective planning and estimate potential output. More accurate data enables more effective policies to be formulated in areas ranging from employment and income distribution to social security provision and welfare. Thus, the FLSAW document pressed for the inclusion of unpaid work in national accounts and in social and economic indicators. It also pressed for the allocation of social and economic benefits to take into account this broader definition of work. Redefining work in the global economy effectively means recognizing both waged and unwaged work as essential to the social and economic well-being of countries.

The Fourth UN Conference on Women, held in Beijing in 1995, took place after the Commission on the Status of Women had met in 1990 to review the progress of the FLSAW since 1985. The Commission decided that not enough progress had been made. The Fourth UN Conference on Women was the largest UN conference to date. The Draft Platform for Action which was negotiated at Beijing echoed many of the key themes and objectives of the FLSAW, identifying eleven specific areas of concern: poverty, access to education, inequality in health-care provision, violence against women, the needs of women refugees, access to participation in economic decision-making structures, greater participation in public life and the political process, improvements in monitoring mechanisms, improvements in the awareness on the part of women of the commitments made by member states, the representation of women in the media, and, finally, women's contribution to managing natural resources and safeguarding the environment. The conference 'Platform of Action' made explicit linkages between the empowerment of women, access to reproductive health care, equality and women's human rights.

[ . . . ]

## Gender issues in global perspective

[ . . . ]

   In much contemporary feminist analysis the still striking disparities between North and South, rural and urban and rich and poor are emphasized. Western feminists acknowledge explicitly that concern with gender inequalities has to be seen in the context of broad inequalities not only between states and regions, but between women of colour and women of different social groups. For example, the 'expert report' on the ECE region, in preparation for Beijing,[29] explicitly recognized that issues of women's rights and sustainable development could not be seriously addressed unless the consumption and production patterns in the ECE region changed. Significantly European feminists have also cited the problems of racism in Europe, noting that women of colour in the region are particularly affected by global restructuring processes and make a particular contribution to unwaged and low-waged work. Women in Europe have, therefore, joined women in Latin America and in the Asia Pacific region in rejecting dominant economic paradigms and arguing that the deep contradictions in economic policies of restructuring and globalization are resulting in economic and social policies which are detrimental to the rights of women.

[ . . . ]

### Notes

1   A. Giddens, *The Consequences of Modernity* (Cambridge: Polity Press, 1990).
2   Ibid.
3   S. Mitter, *Common Fate, Common Bond: Women in the Global Economy* (London: Pluto, 1986).
4   Ibid.
5   Ibid.
6   S. Mitter and A. Luijken, *The Unseen Phenomenon: The Rise of Homeworking* (London: Change Publications, 1989).
7   See discussion in G. Ashworth and N. May, *Of Conjuring and Caring* (London: Change Publications, 1990).
8   Mitter and Luijken, *The Unseen Phenomenon*.

9 Ibid.
10 E. Hooper, *Report on the UN ECE Regional Preparatory Meeting for the Fourth World Conference on Women* (Geneva, 1994).
11 See Mitter, *Common Fate*, and D. Elson and R. Pearson, 'The situation of women and the internationalisation of factory production', in K. Young, C. Wolkowitz and R. McCullagh, *Of Marriage and the Market: The Subordination of Women Internationally and its Lessons* (London: Routledge, 1991).
12 Elson and Pearson, 'Situation of women'.
13 M. Umfreville, *$£XONOMIC$: An Introduction to the Political Economy of Sex, Time and Gender* (London: Change Publications, 1990).
14 T. Thahn Dan, 'The dynamics of sex tourism: the case of South East Asia', *Development and Change*, 14: 533–53.
15 Ibid.
16 C. Enloe, *Bananas, Beaches and Bases: Making Feminist Sense of International Politics* (London: Pandora, 1989), p. 40.
17 The United Nations' international research and training institute for the advancement of women.
18 For a fuller discussion see I. Tinker and J. Jaquette, 'UN Decade for Women: its impact and legacy', *World Development*, 15(3) (1987): 419–27; J. Vickers, *Women in the World Economic Crisis* (London: Zed Books, 1991).
19 Tinker and Jaquette, 'UN Decade'.
20 Ibid.
21 Ibid.
22 E. Boserup, *Women's Role in Economic Development* (London: Earthscan, 1989).
23 H. Allison, G. Ashworth and N. Redcliffe, *Hardcash: Man Made Development and its Consequences: A Feminist Perspective on Aid* (London: Change Publications, 1980).
24 Ibid.
25 Ibid.
26 A. M. Goetz, *The Politics of Integrating Gender to State Development Processes: Trends, Opportunities and Constraints in Bangladesh, Chile, Jamaica, Mali, Morocco and Uganda* (Geneva: United Nations Research Institute for Social Development, 1995), p. 8.
27 Ibid.
28 Ibid., p. 3.
29 E. Hooper, *Report on the UN ECE Regional Preparatory Meeting for the Fourth World Conference on Women* (Geneva, 1994).

# 40

# Order, Globalization and Inequality in World Politics

*Ngaire Woods*

## Why Investigate Inequality?

Traditional investigations into world order have tended to neglect the issue of inequality. They have confined themselves to questions such as: how relations are ordered among states?; who comprises the 'society of states'?; who makes the rules?; and what kinds of leverage and coercion are available to enforce the rules? In other words, they have eschewed investigating the role that equality and inequality have played in promulgating and influencing international order.[1] Yet there are powerful reasons for investigating inequality in any discussion of order in international relations today. Although traditionally great powers or super-powers have provided stability and order through leadership or the balance of power, today these rudimentary institutions will not suffice. Processes of globalization are challenging the bases of order in profound ways: first, [ . . . ] by exacerbating inequalities both within and among states; and second, by eroding the capacity of traditional institutions to manage the new threats.

[ . . . ] Globalization [ . . . ] transforms the processes, the actors and capabilities, and the agenda of world politics, necessitating more effective international institutions of management. Today institutions need to probe deeply into domestic politics, ensuring compliance with agreements on issues ranging from the environment to trade and arms control. To do this effectively, they need full participation and commitment from a wide range of members. Yet [ . . . ] existing multilateral organizations are still hierarchically arranged. Their authority and effectiveness depends upon the will and actions of their most powerful members and, as the most powerful states balance up the advantages of stronger and more effective institutions against possible losses in their own control and sovereignty, they repeatedly come down on the side of the latter. This means [ . . . ] that international institutions are committing themselves to maintaining the old hierarchical order, even in the face of its ineffectiveness in dealing with new challenges and problems.

## Inequality and the Traditional View of International Order

Order in international relations carries many meanings and many interpretations. At a conference on 'Conditions of World Order' thirty years ago, several leading academic lights in international relations were brought together in Bellagio, Italy. They defined 'order' as 'the minimum conditions for coexistence',[2] eschewing any wider definition of order which would open up discussions of necessary conditions for a 'good life' or any other set of deeper values. And indeed, this is a traditional vision of international order. It begins with a European conception of the 'Westphalian system',[3] the key actors within which are sovereign states who are in a formal sense equal – each is accorded an equal 'formal' sovereignty. However, order among these states is traditionally understood to be a product of *hierarchy*. A balance of power among the major states, such as that prescribed in the Treaty of Utrecht (1713), prevents any one state from predominating or extinguishing the sovereignty of all others.

Inequality within the traditional conception of world order is a positive, restraining, and ordering force. It permits the operation of a balance of power as a substitute for the centralized authority of a Hobbesian Leviathan in domestic politics. At the same time, hierarchy in the international system, or the imbalance of power, has never meant a strict imposition of the absolute will of the most powerful state or states. Rather, within the hierarchical system institutions have emerged which permit limited accommodation and change. The Concert of Europe, for example, or the League of Nations, were institutions which reflected the need of the most powerful to accommodate those directly beneath them – to ensure that they have a stake in the system so that they will assist in preserving the status quo. However, the scope of this type of accommodation within traditional realist views of international relations has been strictly limited.[4]

Similarly, in contemporary accounts of international relations the comfortable relationship between power and accommodation is continued in theories that assume that 'hierarchy' breeds order. In the realist tradition, inequality simply describes the status quo in international relations and not a deeper set of normative concerns.[5] Order is provided by a powerful state which sets up institutions and rules in the international system.[6] The real debate within the recent literature has been about whether or not a hegemon is required to maintain and enforce the rules. It has certainly not focused on the degree to which a particular regime will cement or alleviate inequalities. Neo-realists argue that a hegemon is essential.[7] The institutionalist critics of neo-realism argue that a hegemon is not required for the institutions to acquire a driving force of their own.[8] However, even within the institutionalist view, the role of norms and institutions can only be explained *after* a power-political framework has been ascertained.[9] Hierarchy and inequality are thus asserted as a precondition for subsequent kinds of order.

[ ... ]

Yet the experience of the 1990s suggests that traditional hierarchy does not maintain order in the face of new challenges. Although immediately after the end of the Cold War there was a brief euphoric period during which a 'New World Order' led by the United States was trumpeted,[10] the idea was short-lived. The United States and its close allies soon found that a global agenda of democratization, liberalization, peace, and self-determination would often be self-contradictory. In transition or democratizing countries, difficult choices had to be made between either economic liberalization or democratization, with governments often forced to give priority to one or the other.[11] Self-determination, on the other hand, often seemed to lead to civil war and conflict, nowhere as starkly as in the former Yugoslavia.[12] A clearer hierarchy of power in the international system – the new 'leadership' of the United States – did not offer solutions to these problems. Rather, a second wave of policy since the end of the Cold War has highlighted the shortcomings of existing international institutions [ ... ].

Today, in order for countries to achieve the myriad goals of wealth, environmental protection, and a wide range of forms of security [...] a more sophisticated order is required. Yet while the most powerful states in the system resist any reform of the institutions they dominate, it is difficult to imagine any such new order evolving. [...]

## The Impact of Globalization

In the market-based economists' account, globalization opens up opportunities and advantages to all states. Yet the existing evidence highlights that the process is a much more uneven one than the theory suggests. Globalization describes dramatic changes in the transactions and interactions taking place among states, firms, and peoples in the world. It describes both an increase in cross-border transactions of goods and services, and an increase in the flow of images, ideas, people, and behaviour. Economistic views treat the process as technologically driven. Yet globalization has also been driven by deregulation, privatization, and political choices made by governments. Whilst flows of goods, services, people, and capital are increasing, they are, at the same time, often barred or blocked by regulations. In other words, the impact of globalization has been strongly shaped by those with the power to make and enforce the rules of the global economy.[13] At the same time, however, to create rules which are enforceable, rule-makers are increasingly having to rely upon a wider group of actors and a wider range of institutions. This creates a real tension between increases in inequality caused by processes of globalization and the necessary increase in participation required to regulate the processes. In this section, the key elements of globalization are analysed to highlight these tensions.

A first core aspect of globalization is technological change, which has transformed the possibilities of global economic activity. Firms can now organize production globally using new means of communication, and new, more flexible techniques of production. This has led to what Charles Oman [...] calls 'global localization'. Increasingly, multinational firms (MNCs) produce goods as close to their markets as they can. This means they have a presence in several regions or areas of the world economy. The political implications are manifold and, importantly for our purposes, they do not all point to deregulation and an opening up of possibilities. Rather, those who benefited first (and most) from technological change have also been very quick in seeking to protect their position, pushing for international rules which may well hinder others wishing to emulate them.

Where once MNCs were a force for liberalization and the opening up of trade barriers (so that they could trade into regions and countries), today, having situated themselves within regions or countries in which they wish to trade, they no longer need to press for the opening up of borders. Life inside a 'fortress' Europe or NAFTA might be quite comfortable. Furthermore, rather than diffusing technological advances worldwide, leading companies have pushed for increasingly strict international rules on intellectual property.[14] Competition today is not just for a competitive edge in technological or economic terms. Rather, firms also compete for control of the rules of the game at international and at regional levels. Yet, for the rules to have an impact they must be enforced by governments not all of whom firms can influence. Globalization is cementing old economic inequalities between 'haves' and 'have-nots'

– not just in the sense of having technology or not, but also in the sense of having the capacity to make rules or not. Yet at the same time, globalization is creating a new set of requirements for regulation and enforcement which requires the cooperation of the so-called 'have-nots'. This cannot be achieved through the hierarchical arrangements of old.

International trade is another aspect of globalization which has had highly uneven consequences. While there is a dispute as to how much world trade has increased,[15] there is clear evidence that high levels of trade in today's world economy are strongly concentrated in trade among industrialized countries.[16] For this reason, although globalization suggests that world markets are opened up and the flow of transactions among all states is thereby increased, in fact we find that the effects of change are vastly unequal. Although many developing countries have liberalized their trade policies, some are being marginalized. [ ... ] In brief, trade liberalization has cemented inequalities among states. Yet it has also resulted in increasing demands for regulation, for example from industrialized countries who argue that where countries flout international labour, environmental, and safety standards, they present 'unfair' competition. The demand for an 'even playing field' requires greater regulation and enforcement at a global level.

Yet greater demands for regulation do not translate solely into efforts to strengthen global institutions. On the contrary, globalization has been accompanied by a surge of new regional and bilateral arrangements.[17] In some ways regionalism cements the old hierarchy, yet in others it loosens it. In theory, regional organizations offer small and less powerful states a way to unite and exercise more influence in setting trade rules and in enjoying open access to a wider market than their national market.[18] Furthermore, the prospect of regional trade arrangements and integration offers a useful lever to governments who need to dismantle powerful domestic vested interests: new policies offer both the carrot of wider markets and the stick of stiffer regional competition.[19] In these ways, the 'new regionalism' could well be seen as an even and powerful way of opening up trade. However, increasing regionalism may also cement inequalities by marginalizing less powerful states – for example, by excluding developing countries from the 'fortresses' mentioned above. Furthermore, regional institutions can provide powerful states with excuses for not using global institutions: they might, for example, choose to take their disputes to the forum in which they feel they have the most power to ensure a particular outcome.[20]

International finance is a further arena of globalization which has powerful implications for traditional notions of hierarchy and order. Technology and US policies in the post-war period[21] have unleashed powerful forces in financial markets, as international banks and investment funds expand their global operations. Today financial markets and investment funds shift capital so fast that governments in both industrialized and developing countries fear capital flight and speculative attacks by the market. In some ways this has a levelling effect: all governments live in some fear of the markets and all are susceptible to a speculative attack. Yet the tendency of capital markets to punish governments occurs in an uneven way which highlights both weaknesses and vulnerabilities in developing countries as well as in the institutions upon which they rely for assistance.[22] Industrialized countries in the more global economy can borrow to ease the monetary costs of fiscal expansion[23] and the evidence suggests that this does not necessarily heighten the risks of capital flight and market fear of default.[24] By contrast, in developing countries, high public debt, and indeed even high private debt (as in Mexico in 1994, and South Korea in 1997) can trigger markets into withdrawing, leading to a run on both investment and the currency.[25] Yet paradoxically, the threat of this kind of crisis means that previously less significant countries can now pose a systemic threat to international economic stability: the tail can now wag the dog. So whilst financial globalization reinforces old inequalities, at the same time it creates new challenges and crises which the old unequal order cannot deal with particularly effectively.

Finally, globalization has included the spread of policy ideas. Global economic order is not founded on state power and rules alone, but also on sets of policy ideas and beliefs. These are promulgated both formally through international organizations [ . . . ] and informally through networks of education and research which 'globalize' particular orthodoxies. Both the 1980s and the 1990s provide powerful examples of this. In the 1980s 'structural adjustment' was urged on developing countries the world over,[26] and in the 1990s a similar set of liberalizing policies were urged on the former Eastern bloc countries – the so-called 'transition economies'. The impact of these policy changes was mostly to increase income inequality within these countries.[27] In the late 1990s, there have been some changes in the prescriptions being written in Washington. The reform of the economy is now being followed up with second and third phases of reform, described as 'modernizing the state'. Good governance, transparency, accountability, and participation are now being advocated by the international financial institutions.[28] In theory, of course, if these ideas were applied to these institutions themselves, the result might well be a more egalitarian and participatory international economic order.[29] In reality, however, their application is being strictly limited.[30] Nevertheless, for the international institutions the new agenda reflects a recognition that to succeed, their reforms need greater commitment and participation by recipient governments – a top-down model of incentives and leverage exercised from Washington will not succeed.

Globalization, it has been argued, is changing both competition among, and policies within, countries. It is also affecting the nature of actors and institutions in world politics. In a system created for 51 countries, 193 states now enjoy a sovereignty which is becoming ever more diffuse. Control over policy in certain areas is increasingly passing either 'down' to local bodies, or 'up' to regional or international bodies.[31] Alongside states, new actors are striding the stage of world politics: the 'stateless' multinational in the 'borderless world';[32] national groups without a state (such as Quebec, Scotland, Chiapas, Palestine, and Chechnya); rebels and terrorists enjoying a greater capacity to publicize themselves and gain an audience.[33] These new actors cut across the traditional structures of state sovereignty and inter-state order, challenging governments and demanding access to the inter-state organizations charged with global governance.[34] Indeed, the very principles on which sovereignty is recognized and respected are changing, so that, in the words of an international law scholar, we are faced with an 'impossibility of reconciling the notions of sovereignty which prevailed even as recently as fifty or sixty years ago with the contemporary state of global interdependence'.[35] [ . . . ]

Particularly noticeable in their demands for a status in international organizations are the non-governmental organizations (NGOs) claiming a transnational or sub-national constituency.[36] NGOs have carved out a role for themselves in many multilateral organizations,[37] not to mention taken a lead in international relations on some issues such as the environment.[38] It is now the case that NGOs can participate within some international fora, such as the World Bank's Panel of Inspection hearings on environmental issues.[39] Yet, before heralding the rise of a 'transnational civil society', the limitations on NGO claims to greater legitimacy or accountability must also be recognized.[40]

Traditional conceptions of order not only fail to take new actors into account in portraying international order, they also fail to explain how and why these actors have emerged onto the stage of world politics. It is assumed that actors change as the configuration of power changes. Yet the new actors and the changing authority of old actors also reflects a shift in beliefs and understandings about representation and legitimacy, as we will see in the following section.

In summary, globalization is challenging the traditional state-centred and hierarchical world order.[41] Yet few of the forces analysed here have altered the structure of institutions of management. Rather, technological change, trade liberalization, regionalism, the globalization of international finance, and policy ideas are all proceeding within the rules and institutions which reflect the traditional hierarchy of power. However, that hierarchical order is becoming less effective as new 'global' issues, such as environmental problems, trade rules, and concerns about transnational crime or movements of people, demand greater levels of cooperation among states.

## International Institutions and the Management of Order

The above discussion of globalization underlines that inequality is not just about starting positions and outcomes in international relations. It is also, crucially, about 'meta-power' or who gets to make the rules within which international relations proceed and who decides how and where to enforce them. During the 1970s North–South debate, the South pressed for more of a say in the rules governing international economic order and, for the most part, they failed. The rules governing trade, investment, finance, and monetary order continued largely to be written by Northern countries. Today, this top-down approach to making and enforcing rules is being questioned even within the North. The question being posed is: what makes international institutions effective?

[ . . . ]

## International trade

Until 1992, international trade was regulated globally under the auspices of the GATT, a very loose institution whose rules and procedures were developed in an ad hoc way.[42] Within this arrangement there was a clear inequality of power, with the 'Quad' (the US, the European Union, Japan, and Canada) able to work behind the scenes to shape most decisions. The results were trading rules which had a very uneven impact on countries [ . . . ]. Importantly, these results reflected a process which magnified inequalities among members. The GATT operated as a club with a core membership empowered to decide who to admit and on what conditions.[43] Several attempts were made to change the structure of representation and decision-making within the GATT: developing countries tried unsuccessfully in the 1970s to create a powerful Executive Committee within which they would have a voice; and in the other direction, the United States tried to push the idea of an IMF-style Executive Board with weighted voting during the Uruguay Round.

Yet the unequal 'club' approach of the GATT has become unsatisfactory as globalization, or more specifically trade liberalization, proceeds apace. Trading nations both large and small require an institution which can regulate in areas such as non-tariff barriers and domestic practices, and which can deal with a raft of new issues, including services, intellectual property, trade-related investment, and labour and environmental standards.[44] For these reasons, even the United States needs a multilateral organization, for its strongest regional arrangement – NAFTA – accounts for less than a third of its trade.[45] In a globalizing world, compliance with an international trade regime requires a high level of participation, commitment, and confidence from all members. Hence, the decentralized framework of the GATT was inadequate: the resolution of disputes, for example, was held hostage to the consensus required of panels making decisions. Yet the replacement for the GATT, the World Trade Organization (WTO), has not resolved the problem of participation and compliance.[46]

The new organization has a structure and enforcement mechanisms which transform it into a more powerful international institution. The WTO is now the administrator of all multilateral trade agreements, an overseer of national trade policies, and has a disputes settlement procedure which, unlike that of the GATT, can make rulings on disputes which are automatically accepted by the organization unless there is a consensus *against* acceptance. At least in theory, developing countries are better served by this step towards more legalized and institutionalized procedures, since it restrains the capacity of large trading countries to veto Panel decisions. Certainly, developing countries seem already to be using the new WTO processes more: whereas the GATT mechanisms tended to be used mainly by the 'Quad', about half the requests before the WTO in mid-1996 were from developing countries.[47]

However, for the WTO to be effective in upholding an international rule of law, it needs compliance from its largest and most powerful member. Yet the United States had the worst record of compliance with GATT panel judgements of any country,[48] and further 'retreated from multilateralism' in the 1980s, adopting policies which were 'increasingly aggressive and bilateral'.[49] The trend towards unilateral trade policy was reflected in Congress during its debate on ratifying the Uruguay Round results (and the new WTO),[50] and yet more obviously since then, as the US has boycotted the WTO dispute settlement proceedings triggered by the Helms–Burton Act's penalties on other countries' dealings with Cuba.[51] [ . . . ]

The World Trade Organization has been created in recognition of the need for powerful rule-based institutions to facilitate global trade. Yet alongside the WTO, unilateral and bilateral actions are continuing, such as those of the US. This means that the credibility and effectiveness of the new system is being constantly undermined by assertions of the old power-political hierarchy as the basis for order in international trade. Yet that power-political order, which had been so clearly reflected in the GATT, simply cannot deal effectively with the new issues mentioned above. The tension is a simple one. Although a strong rule-based international regime is increasingly in the interests of the US in a global world economy, it remains to be seen whether the US is prepared to give up the rights of its special position as *primus inter pares* in order to reap the benefits of a multilateral regime.

# The international financial system

The international financial and monetary system has changed dramatically with the emergence of ever-larger global capital markets, investment funds, and floating exchange rates. From the end of the Second World War, the rules of the system were very much set by the United States, conferring at various stages with Western Europe and Japan.[52] The fora within which decisions have been taken include the G7, the Bank for International Settlements (BIS), and the IMF (within which the United States is the largest voter and shareholder). During the 1970s developing countries made repeated attempts to increase their voice on the international financial and monetary system, with very limited success.[53] However, over the past two decades, the success and ongoing stability of the international financial and monetary system had come to rely much more heavily on the behaviour of less powerful countries, who have traditionally been marginalized.

Recent crises show the vulnerabilities of an increasingly globalized international financial and monetary system. At the end of 1994, the Mexican currency collapsed, sending reverberations through the system which have been dwarfed by the more recent crises in East Asia 1996–7 and in Russia 1998. Overall, all actors now agree that international financial and monetary stability requires a much deeper and broader level of cooperation than ever before – in order to deal with issues of capital account liberalization, financial sector reforms, exchange rate policies, and sound banking regulation and supervision. The costs of inadequate cooperation are clear. When financial crisis erupted in East Asia, the International Monetary Fund provided some US$36 billion in financial support, and mobilized a further US$77 billion from multilateral and bilateral sources. In Russia, the IMF provided US$11.2 billion in financial support and likewise coordinated an even larger relief package. The policies associated with both 'resources' have subsequently been heavily criticized.[54]

[ . . . ]

Politically, the depth of conditions being required of East Asian countries has caused many commentators to ask fundamental questions about how legitimate it is for the IMF to do this. For example, Marty Feldstein recently wrote in *Foreign Affairs*: 'The legitimate political institutions of the country should determine the nation's economic structure and the nature of its institutions. A nation's desperate need for short-term financial help does not give the IMF the moral right to substitute its technical judgements for the outcomes of the nation's political process.'[55]

The issue here is a difficult one. The IMF is charged with the role of safeguarding the stability of the international monetary system. Yet in a globalizing world, this is difficult to do without incursion into the domestic policies of countries. An alternative approach is to accept that stability requires deeper international standards and to ask how the Fund might bolster its legitimacy in entering into this new terrain. The answer here surely lies in rethinking the representation and participation of those whose compliance is required – so as to lessen the sense of unequal 'imposition' or the impingement on democratic processes.[56] Already the IMF has made some effort to open up its way of working, such as by publishing an increasing number of background papers to bilateral negotiations, by rethinking the role 'external evaluation' might play in its work, and by opening up the issue of 'governance' in its dealings with member countries. These changes, however, do not alter the representation and ownership structure which underpins the Board of the organization, and as a result do not imbue the organization with any greater degree of legitimacy in propounding 'deep' interventions and reforms such as we have seen in East Asia.

[...]

International financial institutions have been undergoing some changes in the 1990s. However, for the most part, these have been refinements on 'work as usual' in these organizations. It is doubtless useful for the institutions to open themselves up to greater scrutiny and wider membership. However, decision-making processes have remained the same and rely on a hierarchy which reflects fifty-year-old inequalities. Yet the evidence suggests that effectively to manage a globalizing world economy, these institutions need greater legitimacy, and a greater degree of representation and participation. This requires change of a more fundamental kind, which is unlikely given the persistence of the old hierarchy.

## The United Nations Security Council

Finally, the United Nations Security Council has sprung into action since the end of the Cold War.[57] Yet its membership today seems anachronistic with respect to the work it is trying to do. The victors of the Second World War took permanent seats on the Council in an attempt to institute a system of collective security managed by the Great Powers. Those original five members still have permanent seats, and their concurring vote is still required for the Council to pass any substantive resolution. This gives each of China, Russia, the US, France, and the UK a veto over Security Council decisions. The other ten seats on the Council rotate around different groupings of countries. Like other institutions this chapter has analysed, the Security Council institutionalized a hierarchy of states which existed at the end of the Second World War. Yet the Council remained virtually inactive during the Cold War, marginalized by balance-of-power politics between the super-powers. This has now changed.

Between August 1990 and May 1995 the Council adopted 325 resolutions (as well as some 82 'Presidential statements'), giving an average of 80 resolutions per year. This compares with an average of 14 per year over the preceding 44 years. The new high level of Security Council activity brings prominently to the fore several issues of governance. Developing countries have been quick to point out that the Council's new level of activity involves intervention in an unprecedented way into the affairs of (almost exclusively) developing countries. This has focused attention sharply on the core inequality of the institution. The power inequality was amply demonstrated in the 1980s, when the United States bullied the UN as a whole into de facto altering its Constitution so as to give the US a veto over critical budget decisions.[58]

In the 1990s, some very modest changes have occurred in the United Nations Security Council.[59] Beyond this, many members have accepted that the membership of the Council should be enlarged, to include at least Germany and Japan as permanent members and probably also representatives of developing countries.[60] However, there is great unwillingness on the part of the existing permanent members to permit any dilution of their rights in the institution. Leading the opposition but not alone is the United States.[61] [...]

# Concluding Thoughts

## Inequality and effective institutions in a globalizing world

Although the traditional view of international order placed great weight on the hierarchy of power, when modern international institutions were created fifty years ago it was appreciated that a balance had to be struck between 'efficiency' wrought through great-power management, and 'legitimacy', which was necessary to ensure the cooperation of the rest. The latter required that some basic notion of 'equality' be respected. Within the United Nations the balance was felt to be struck by a General Assembly in which all states would have an equal vote, and a Security Council in which the most powerful states would have a veto. Even in the IMF, where most voting power was apportioned according to economic power, 'basic votes' were apportioned to symbolize the equality of member states. As Joseph Gold explains, 'the authors of the plans for the Fund and the negotiators felt that the bold step of weighting the voting power . . . should be combined with the political consideration of the traditional equality of states in international law. The basic votes were to serve the function of recognizing the doctrine of the equality of states.'[62] What theorists have referred to as the 'trappings of universality'[63] have been vital to the place and role of international organizations.

In the 1990s, for international institutions to be effective they will have to reflect more than ever a wide range of members and to embody commitments that all members are prepared to implement. On some issues, this has already been recognized. Although many believed the era of global summitry to be over at the end of the 1970s, in fact the 1990s has seen North–South Summits on issues including: the environment and development (Rio de Janeiro 1992); population and development (Cairo 1994); women (Beijing 1995); and global climate change (Kyoto 1997). These summits reflect a recognition that effective action in these areas will depend vitally upon commitments from a range of governments – rich, poor, weak, and strong – and that compliance is unlikely to be forthcoming unless parties each have a stake in the final agreement and a clear stake in abiding by it. Yet outside of these summits, in the organizations and institutions which are needed to regulate and facilitate international issues, there is little indication that powerful member states have any intention of altering the hierarchical basis on which order has traditionally been maintained, even though that hierarchy will not serve to meet the more complex challenges of order in a globalizing world.

## Notes

1  Stanley Hoffmann (ed.), *Conditions of World Order* (New York, 1968).
2  Raymond Aron, chairing the meeting, argued that world order could mean any one of five things: an arrangement of reality; relations among the parts of world politics; the minimum conditions for existence; the minimum conditions for *co*existence; or the conditions for the good life. Yet Stanley Hoffmann notes that the fifth meaning was instantly ruled out on the grounds that it could lead members only 'to platitudes or to an acrimonious reproduction of the conflicts of values that exist in the world' (ibid., p. 2). Instead, the Conference chose to focus on the fourth definition, defining order as the 'conditions under which men might live together relatively well in one planet' (ibid.).

3 Although one might equally quote a plethora of other non-European systems – Asian, African, and pre-Columbian American – each of which were also ordered by hierarchically structured suzerain systems of considerable longevity.

4 Hedley Bull, *The Anarchical Society: A Study of Order in World Politics*, 2nd edn (London, 1995); Martin Wight, *Power Politics*, 2nd edn, ed. Hedley Bull and Carsten Holbraad (London, 1986); Hans J. Morgenthau, *Politics among Nations: The Struggle for Power and Peace* (New York, 1985).

5 Kenneth N. Waltz, *Theory of International Politics* (New York, 1979); and see the critiques by Robert Cox and Richard Ashley in Robert O. Keohane (ed.), *Neorealism and its Critics* (New York, 1986).

6 Barry Buzan, Charles Jones and Richard Little, *The Logic of Anarchy: Neorealism to Structural Realism* (New York, 1993); David A. Baldwin, *Neorealism and Neoliberalism: The Contemporary Debate* (New York, 1993).

7 Joseph M. Grieco, *Cooperation among Nations: Europe, America, and Non-tariff Barriers to Trade* (Ithaca, 1990).

8 Robert O. Keohane, *After Hegemony: Cooperation and Discord in the World Political Economy* (Princeton, 1984).

9 Robert Keohane, Joseph Nye and Stanley Hoffmann, *After the Cold War: International Institutions and State Strategies in Europe, 1989–1991* (Cambridge, Mass., 1993).

10 George Bush, 'New World Order', in *Public Papers of the Presidents, Administration of George Bush*, vol. 2 (1990), pp. 1218–22.

11 B. Grosh and S. Orvis, 'Democracy, confusion, or chaos: political conditionality in Kenya', *Studies in Comparative International Development* 31(4) (1997): 46–65; Luiz Carlos Bresser Pereira, Adam Przeworski and José María Maravall, *Economic Reforms in New Democracies: A Social-Democratic Approach* (Cambridge, 1993); Stephan Haggard and Robert R. Kaufman, *The Political Economy of Democratic Transitions* (Princeton, 1995); Laurence Whitehead, *Economic Liberalization and Democratization: Explorations of the Linkages* (London, 1993); Adam Przeworski, *Democracy and the Market: Political and Economic Reforms in Eastern Europe and Latin America* (Cambridge, 1991).

12 Michael Ignatieff, *Blood and Belonging: Journeys into the New Nationalism* (London, 1994).

13 Thomas Franck, *Fairness in International Law and Institutions* (Oxford, 1995).

14 Frederick Abbott and David Gerber, *Public Policy and Global Technological Integration* (The Hague, 1997); Michael Blakeney, *Trade-Related Aspects of Intellectual Property Rights: A Concise Guide to the TRIPs Agreement* (London, 1996); Carlos Correa, *Intellectual Property Rights and Foreign Direct Investment* (New York, 1993).

15 UNDP, *Human Development Report* (New York, 1997) takes 17 countries for which there are data and shows that exports as a share of GDP in 1913 were 12.9 percent compared to 14.5 percent in 1993.

16 Indeed, the least developed countries, which account for 10 percent of the world's people, have seen their share of world trade drop to 0.3 percent – half of what it was two decades ago: UNDP, *Human Development Report*, p. 84.

17 See Diana Tussie, 'From multilateralism to regionalism', in *Oxford Development Studies Special Issue on Globalization* (Oxford, 1998).

18 Vincent Cable (ed.), *Trade Blocs? The Future of Regional Integration* (London, 1994); Till Geiger, *Regional Trade Blocs, Multilateralism and the GATT: Complementary Paths to Free Trade?* (London, 1996); Andrew Gamble and Anthony Payne, *Regionalism and World Order* (London, 1996).

19 John Whalley, *Why Do Countries Seek Regional Trade Agreements?* (Cambridge, 1996); Haggard and Kaufman, *The Political Economy of Democratic Transitions*; Joan Nelson (ed.), *Economic Crisis and Policy Choice: The Politics of Adjustment in the Third World* (Princeton, 1990).

20 Robert Z. Lawrence and Charles Oman, *Scenarios for the World Trading System and their Implications for Developing Countries* (Paris, 1991). For a more general statement about

international institutions, see Stephen Krasner, *Structural Conflict: The Third World against Global Liberalism* (Berkeley, 1985).

21  Eric Helleiner, *States and the Reemergence of Global Finance: From Bretton Woods to the 1990s* (Ithaca, 1994).

22  Ricardo Ffrench-Davis, 'The Tequila effect: its origins and its widespread impact', *Desarrollo Económico: Revista de Ciencias Sociales* 37 (1997): 195–214.

23  G. Corsetti and N. Roubini, 'Political biases in fiscal policy', in Barry Eichengreen, Jeffrey Frieden and J. von Hagen (eds), *Monetary and Fiscal Policy in an Integrated Europe* (New York, 1995).

24  Geoffrey Garrett, 'Shrinking states? Globalization and national autonomy in the OECD', in *Oxford Development Studies Special Issue on Globalization*; G. Corsetti and N. Roubini, 'Fiscal deficits, public debt and government insolvency', *Journal of Japanese and International Economies* 5 (1991): 354–80.

25  Ffrench-Davis, 'The Tequila effect'.

26  John Williamson (ed.), *Latin American Adjustment: How Much Has Happened?* (Washington DC, 1990).

27  See A. Hurrell and N. Woods (eds), *Inequality, Globalization and World Politics* (Oxford, 1999), ch. 6, and A. B. Atkinson and John Micklewright, *Economic Transformation in Eastern Europe and the Distribution of Income* (Cambridge, 1992).

28  World Bank, *Governance: The World Bank's Experience* (Washington DC, 1994); IMF, *Good Governance: The IMF's Role* (Washington DC, 1997).

29  Ngaire Woods, 'Governance in international organizations: the case for reform in the Bretton Woods institutions', in UNCTAD (ed.), *International Monetary and Financial Issues for the 1990s*, vol. 9 (New York, 1998), pp. 81–106.

30  For critiques of this agenda, see P. Blunt, 'Cultural relativism, good governance, and sustainable human development', *Public Administration and Development* 15 (1995): 1–9; A. Goetz and D. O'Brien, 'Governing for the common wealth: the World Bank's approach to poverty and governance', *IDS Bulletin* 26 (1995): 17–26.

31  Thomas J. Biersteker and Cynthia Weber, *State Sovereignty as Social Construct* (Cambridge, 1996); Joseph Camilleri and Jim Falk, *The End of Sovereignty? The Politics of a Shrinking and Fragmenting World* (Aldershot, 1992).

32  Kenichi Ohmae, *The Borderless World: Power and Strategy in the Interlinked Economy* (London, 1994).

33  Adrian Guelke, *The Age of Terrorism and the International Political System* (London, 1995).

34  Thomas George Weiss and Leon Gordenker, *NGOs, the UN and Global Governance* (Boulder, 1996).

35  Franck, *Fairness in International Law*, p. 4.

36  L. MacDonald, 'Globalizing civil society: interpreting international NGOs in Central America', *Millennium* 23(2) (1994): 267–85; Thomas Princen, *Environmental NGOs in World Politics: Linking the Local and the Global* (London, 1994).

37  Weiss and Gordenker, *NGOs, the UN and Global Governance*; Nick Wheeler, 'Guardian angel or global gangster: a review of the ethical claims of international society', *Political Studies* 44 (1996): 123–35.

38  John Meyer, David Frank, Ann Hironaka, Evan Schoefer and Nancy Tuma, 'The structuring of a world environmental regime 1870–1990', *International Organization* 51 (1997): 623–52.

39  R. Bisell, 'Recent practice of the Inspection Panel of the World Bank', *American Journal of International Law* 91 (1997): 741–4; Ibrahim Shihata, *The World Bank Inspection Panel* (Oxford, 1994).

40  See the views expressed by IMF Executive Directors as to the non-accountability of NGOs, reported in Anne Bichsel, 'The World Bank and the International Monetary Fund from the perspective of the Executive Directors from developing countries', *Journal of World*

*Trade* 28 (1994): 141–67; and M. Edwards and D. Hulme, 'Too close for comfort: the impact of official aid on non-governmental organizations', *World Development* 24 (1996): 961–73.

41   This point is not new to the 1990s. See Richard N. Cooper, *The Economics of Inter-dependence: Economic Policy in the Atlantic Community* (New York, 1968); Robert O. Keohane and Joseph S. Nye, *Power and Interdependence*, 2nd edn (London, 1989); Joseph Nye, *Bound to Lead: The Changing Nature of American Power* (New York, 1990); James N. Rosenau and Ernst-Otto Czempiel (eds), *Governance without Government: Order and Change in World Politics* (Cambridge, 1992).

42   The GATT was originally a temporary measure and little provision was made for procedures, voting structure, and decision-making rules. These arose subsequently by evolution – the Council, for example, was created by a resolution of GATT contracting parties in 1960.

43   Vincent Cable, 'The new trade agenda: universal rules amid cultural diversity', *International Affairs* 72 (1996): 227–46, at 232.

44   Jeffrey Schott and John Buurman, *The Uruguay Round: An Assessment* (Washington DC, 1994); Carl Hamilton and John Whalley, 'Evaluation of the Uruguay Round results on developing countries', *World Economy* 18 (1995): 31–49; World Bank, *The Uruguay Round: Winners and Winners* (Washington DC, 1995).

45   John Odell and Barry Eichengreen, 'The United States, the ITO, and the WTO: exit options, agent slack and presidential leadership', in Anne Krueger (ed.), *The WTO as an International Organization* (Chicago, 1998), pp. 181–209, at p. 206.

46   On the background to this, see John Jackson, *Restructuring the GATT System* (London, 1990).

47   Information from the WTO Legal Office.

48   Robert Hudec, *Enforcing International Trade Law: The Evolution of the Modern GATT Legal System* (Salem, Mass., 1993).

49   Anne Krueger, 'Introduction', in Krueger, *The WTO as an International Organization*.

50   John Jackson, 'The great 1994 sovereignty debate: US acceptance and implementation of the Uruguay Round results', *Columbia Journal of Transnational Law* 36 (1997): 157–88.

51   Odell and Eichengreen, 'The United States, the ITO, and the WTO'.

52   Benjamin Cohen, *In Whose Interest? International Banking and American Foreign Policy* (New Haven, 1986); Andrew Walter, *World Power and World Money: The Role of Hegemony and International Monetary Order* (New York, 1993); Helleiner, *States and the Reemergence of Global Finance*.

53   C. Randall Henning, 'The Group of Twenty-Four: two decades of monetary and financial cooperation among developing countries', in UNCTAD (ed.), *International Monetary and Financial Issues for the 1990s*, vol. 1 (New York, 1992), pp. 137–54.

54   A Supplemental Reserve Facility has been created.

55   Marty Feldstein, 'Refocusing the IMF', *Foreign Affairs* 77 (1998): 20–33; Nigel Gould-Davies and Ngaire Woods, 'Russia and the IMF', *International Affairs* 75 (Jan. 1999): 23–42.

56   See Woods, 'Governance in international organizations'.

57   James Mayall (ed.), *The New Interventionism 1991–1994: United Nations Experience in Cambodia, Former Yugoslavia and Somalia* (Cambridge, 1996).

58   Articles 17(1) and 18(2) of the UN Charter require that the UN budget be approved by a two-thirds majority of the General Assembly. US demands for a change in this requirement led to a compromise whereby critical budget decisions would be adopted by consensus at the stage of the Committee for Programme and Coordination – hence giving the United States a de facto veto over the UN budget: Gene M. Lyons, 'Competing visions: proposals for UN reform', in Chadwick Alger et al. (eds), *The United Nations System: The Policies of Member States* (Tokyo, 1995).

59   Michael Wood, 'Security Council: procedural developments', *International and Comparative Law Quarterly* 45 (1996): 150–61.

60 Bruce Russett, Barry O'Neill and James Sutterlin, 'Breaking the Security Council restructuring logjam', *Global Governance* 2 (1996): 65–80. Note that among the developing countries' regions there are competing contenders for a permanent seat: India vs Pakistan or Indonesia; Brazil vs Mexico or Argentina; Nigeria vs South Africa or Egypt.
61 Benjamin Rivlin, 'UN reform from the standpoint of the United States', in *UN University Lectures: 11* (Tokyo, 1996).
62 Joseph Gold, *Voting and Decisions in the International Monetary Fund* (Washington DC, 1972), p. 18; and William N. Gianaris, 'Weighted voting in the International Monetary Fund and the World Bank', *Fordham International Law Journal* 14 (1990–1): 910–45, at 919.
63 Friedrich Kratochwil and John Gerard Ruggie, 'International organization: a state of the art on an art of the state', *International Organization* 40 (1986): 753–5.

# 41

# The Promise of Global Institutions

## Joseph Stiglitz

[ . . . ]

Why has globalization – a force that has brought so much good – become so controversial? Opening up to international trade has helped many countries grow far more quickly than they would otherwise have done. International trade helps economic development when a country's exports drive its economic growth. Export-led growth was the centerpiece of the industrial policy that enriched much of Asia and left millions of people there far better off. Because of globalization many people in the world now live longer than before and their standard of living is far better. People in the West may regard low-paying jobs at Nike as exploitation, but for many people in the developing world, working in a factory is a far better option than staying down on the farm and growing rice.

[ . . . ]

Those who vilify globalization too often overlook its benefits. But the proponents of globalization have been, if anything, even more unbalanced. To them, globalization (which typically is associated with accepting triumphant capitalism, American style) *is* progress; developing countries must accept it, if they are to grow and to fight poverty effectively. But to many in the developing world, globalization has not brought the promised economic benefits.

[ . . . ]

To understand what went wrong, it's important to look at the three main institutions that govern globalization: the IMF, the World Bank, and the WTO. There are, in addition, a host of other institutions that play a role in the international economic system – a number of regional banks, smaller and younger sisters to the World Bank, and a large number of UN organizations, such as the UN Development Program or the UN Conference on Trade and Development (UNCTAD). These organizations often have views that are markedly different from the IMF and the World Bank. [ . . . ]

[Here] I focus mostly on the IMF and the World Bank, largely because they have been at the center of the major economic issues of the last two decades, including the financial crises and the transition of the former Communist countries to market economies. The IMF and the World Bank both originated in World War II as a result of the UN Monetary and Financial Conference at Bretton Woods, New Hampshire, in July 1944, part of a concerted effort to finance the rebuilding of Europe after the devastation of World War II and to save the world from future economic depressions. The proper name of the World Bank – the International Bank for Reconstruction and Development – reflects its original mission; the last part, "Development," was added almost as an afterthought. At the time, most of the countries in the developing world were still colonies, and what meager economic development efforts could or would be undertaken were considered the responsibility of their European masters. [ . . . ]

The International Monetary Fund was charged with preventing another global depression. It would do this by putting international pressure on countries that were not doing their fair share to maintain global aggregate demand, by allowing their own economies to go into a slump. When necessary it would also provide liquidity in the form of loans to those countries facing an economic downturn and unable to stimulate aggregate demand with their own resources.

In its original conception, then, the IMF was based on a recognition that markets often did not work well – that they could result in massive unemployment and might fail to make needed funds available to countries to help them restore their economies. The IMF was founded on the belief that there was a need for *collective action at the global level* for economic stability, just as the United Nations had been founded on the belief that there was a need for collective action at the global level for political stability. The IMF is a *public* institution, established with money provided by taxpayers around the world. This is important to remember because it does not report directly to either the citizens who finance it or those whose lives it affects. Rather, it reports to the ministries of finance and the central banks of the governments of the world. They assert their control through a complicated voting arrangement based largely on the economic power of the countries at the end of World War II. There have been some minor adjustments since, but the major developed countries run the show, with only one country, the United States, having effective veto. (In this sense, it is similar to the UN, where a historical anachronism determines who holds the veto – the victorious powers of World War II – but at least there the veto power is shared among five countries.)

Over the years since its inception, the IMF has changed markedly. Founded on the belief that markets often worked badly, it now champions market supremacy with ideological fervor [the Washington Consensus]. Founded on the belief that there is a need for international pressure on countries to have more expansionary economic policies – such as increasing expenditures, reducing taxes, or lowering interest rates to stimulate the economy – today the IMF typically provides funds only if countries engage in policies like cutting deficits, raising taxes, or raising interest rates that lead to a contraction of the economy. Keynes would be rolling over in his grave were he to see what has happened to his child.

[ . . . ]

A half century after its founding, it is clear that the IMF has failed in its mission. It has not done what it was supposed to do – provide funds for countries facing an economic downturn, to enable the country to restore itself to close to full employment. In spite of the fact that our understanding of economic processes has increased enormously during the last fifty years, and in spite of IMF's efforts during the past quarter century, crises around the world have been more frequent and (with the exception of the Great Depression) deeper. By some reckonings, close to a hundred countries have faced crises.[1] Worse, many of the policies that the IMF pushed, in particular, premature capital market liberalization, have contributed to global instability. And once a country was in crisis, IMF funds and programs not only failed to stabilize the situation but in many cases actually made matters worse, especially for the poor. The IMF failed in its original mission of promoting global stability; it has also

been no more successful in the new missions that it has undertaken, such as guiding the transition of countries from communism to a market economy.
[ . . . ]

The result for many people has been poverty and for many countries social and political chaos. The IMF has made mistakes in all the areas it has been involved in: development, crisis management, and in countries making the transition from communism to capitalism. Structural adjustment programs did not bring sustained growth even to those, like Bolivia, that adhered to its strictures; in many countries, excessive austerity stifled growth; successful economic programs require extreme care in *sequencing* – the order in which reforms occur – and pacing. If, for instance, markets are opened up for competition too rapidly, before strong financial institutions are established, then jobs will be destroyed faster than new jobs are created. In many countries, mistakes in sequencing and pacing led to rising unemployment and increased poverty. After the 1997 Asian crisis, IMF policies exacerbated the crises in Indonesia and Thailand. Free market reforms in Latin America have had one or two successes – Chile is repeatedly cited – but much of the rest of the continent has still to make up for the lost decade of growth following the so-called successful IMF bailouts of the early 1980s, and many today have persistently high rates of unemployment – in Argentina, for instance, at double-digit levels since 1995 – even as inflation has been brought down. The collapse in Argentina in 2001 is one of the most recent of a series of failures over the past few years. Given the high unemployment rate for almost seven years, the wonder is not that the citizens eventually rioted, but that they suffered quietly so much for so long. Even those countries that have experienced some limited growth have seen the benefits accrue to the well-off, and especially the *very* well-off – the top 10 percent – while poverty has remained high, and in some cases the income of those at the bottom has even fallen.

Underlying the problems of the IMF and the other international economic institutions is the problem of governance: who decides what they do. The institutions are dominated not just by the wealthiest industrial countries but by commercial and financial interests in those countries, and the policies of the institutions naturally reflect this. The choice [of] heads for these institutions symbolizes the institutions' problem, and too often has contributed to their dysfunction. While almost all of the activities of the IMF and the World Bank today are in the developing world (certainly, all of their lending), they are led by representatives from the industrialized nations. (By custom or tacit agreement the head of the IMF is always a European, that of the World Bank an American.) They are chosen behind closed doors, and it has never even been viewed as a prerequisite that the head should have any experience in the developing world. The institutions are not representative of the nations they serve.

The problems also arise from who *speaks* for the country. At the IMF, it is the finance ministers and the central bank governors. At the WTO, it is the trade ministers. Each of these ministers is closely aligned with particular constituencies *within* their countries. The trade ministries reflect the concerns of the business community – both exporters who want to see new markets opened up for their products and producers of goods which compete with new imports. These constituencies, of course, want to maintain as many barriers to trade as they can and keep whatever subsidies they can persuade Congress (or their parliament) to give them. The fact that the trade barriers raise the prices consumers pay or that the subsidies impose burdens on taxpayers is of less concern than the profits of the producers – and environmental and labor issues are of even less concern, other than as obstacles that have to be overcome. The finance ministers and central bank governors typically are closely tied to the financial community; they come from financial firms, and after their period of government service, that is where they return. Robert Rubin, the treasury secretary during much of the period described in this book, came from the largest investment bank, Goldman Sachs, and returned to the firm, Citigroup, that controlled the largest commercial bank, Citibank. The number-two person at the IMF during this period, Stan Fischer, went straight from the IMF to Citigroup. These individuals naturally see the world through the eyes of the financial community. The decisions of any institution naturally reflect the perspectives and interests of those who make the decisions; not surprisingly [ ... ], the policies of the international economic institutions are all too often closely aligned with the commercial and financial interests of those in the advanced industrial countries.

For the peasants in developing countries who toil to pay off their countries' IMF debts or the businessmen who suffer from higher value-added taxes upon the insistence of the IMF, the current system run by the IMF is one of taxation without representation. Disillusion with the international system of globalization under the aegis of the IMF grows as the poor in Indonesia, Morocco, or Papua New Guinea have fuel and food subsidies cut, as those in Thailand see AIDS increase as a result of IMF-forced cutbacks in health expenditures, and as families in many developing countries, having to pay for their children's education under so-called cost recovery programs, make the painful choice not to send their daughters to school.

Left with no alternatives, no way to express their concern, to press for change, people riot. The streets, of course, are not the place where issues are discussed, policies formulated, or compromises forged. But the protests have made government officials and economists around the world think about alternatives to these Washington Consensus policies as the one and true way for growth and development. It has become increasingly clear not to just ordinary citizens but to policy makers as well, and not just those in the developing countries but those in the developed countries as well, that globalization as it has been practiced has not lived up to what its advocates promised it would accomplish – or to what it can and should do. In some cases it has not even resulted in growth, but when it has, it has not brought benefits to all; the net effect of the policies set by the Washington Consensus has all too often been to benefit the few at the expense of the many, the well-off at the expense of the poor. In many cases commercial interests and values have superseded concern for the environment, democracy, human rights, and social justice.

Globalization itself is neither good nor bad. It has the *power* to do enormous good, and for the countries of East Asia, who have embraced globalization *under their own terms*, at their own pace, it has been an enormous benefit, in spite of the setback of the 1997 crisis. But in much of the world it has not brought comparable benefits. For many, it seems closer to an unmitigated disaster.

[ ... ]

Unfortunately, we have no world government, accountable to the people of every country, to oversee the globalization process in a fashion comparable to the way national governments guided the nationalization process. Instead, we have a system that might be called *global governance without global government*, one in which a few institutions – the World Bank, the IMF, the WTO – and a few players – the finance, commerce, and trade ministries, closely linked to certain financial and commercial interests – dominate the scene, but in which many of those affected by their decisions are left almost voiceless. It's time to change some of the rules governing the international economic order, to think once again about how decisions get made at the international level – and in whose interests – and to place less emphasis on ideology and to look more at what works. It is crucial that the successful development we have seen in East Asia be achieved elsewhere. There is an enormous cost to continuing global instability. Globalization can be reshaped, and when it is, when it is properly, fairly run, with all countries having a voice in policies affecting them, there is a possibility that it will help create a new global economy in which growth is not only more sustainable and less volatile but the fruits of this growth are more equitably shared.

## Note

1  While there have been a host of critiques of the structural adjustment program, even the IMF's review of the program noted its many faults. This review includes three parts: internal review by the IMF staff (IMF Staff, *The ESAF at Ten Years: Economic Adjustment and Reform in Low Income Countries. Occasional Papers #156, February 12, 1998*); external review by an independent reviewer (K. Botchwey et al., *Report by a Group of Independent Experts Review: External Evaluation of the ESAF* (Washington, DC: IMF, 1998)); and a report from IMF staff to the Board of Directors of the IMF, distilling the lessons from the two reviews (IMF Staff, *Distilling the Lessons from the ESAF Reviews* (Washington, DC: IMF, July 1998)).

# Part VI
## World Orders, Normative Choices

The debate between globalists and sceptics involves fundamental considerations about the nature of world order – as it is and as it might be. Disagreements can range over at least three separate dimensions: first, the philosophical – concerned, above all, with conceptual and normative tools for analysing world order; second, the empirical-analytical – concerned, above all, with the problems of understanding and explaining world order; and, third, the strategic – concerned, above all, with an assessment of the feasibility of moving from where we are to where we might like to be.

On the one hand, globalists take the view that the progressive emergence of a global economy, the expansion of transnational links which generate new forms of collective decision-making, the development of intergovernmental and quasi-supranational institutions, the intensification of transnational communication systems and the development of new regional and global military orders all raise fundamental questions about the fate of the modern state and about the appropriate locus for the articulation of the political good. Globalists seek to rethink the nature and meaning of the modern polity in its global setting. They reject the assumption that one can understand the nature and possibilities of political life by referring primarily to national structures and processes.

The transnational and global scale of contemporary economic and social problems presents, globalists contend, a unique challenge to the modern state. This challenge involves, in the first instance, the recognition of the way globalization generates a serious 'political deficit' – a deficit which encompasses democracy, regulation and justice. As regional and global forces escape the reach of territorially based polities, they erode the capacity of national states to pursue programmes of regulation, accountability and social justice in many spheres. Second, re-examining the changing context of the modern state entails recognizing the way globalization stimulates new political energies and forces which are providing an impetus to the reconfiguration of political power. These include the numerous transnational movements, agencies and NGOs pursuing greater coordination and accountability in regional and global settings. Third, globalists affirm that a shift is, and ought to be, taking place between political and ethical frameworks based on the national political community and those based on a wider set of considerations. In this account, national viewpoints are highly partial and particular and can be juxtaposed with a cosmopolitan outlook. Such an outlook is preoccupied with the claims of each person as an individual or as a member of humanity as a whole. It defends the idea that human beings are in a fundamental sense equal, and that they deserve impartial political treatment – that is, treatment based on principles upon which all people could act. Cosmopolitanism is a moral frame of reference for specifying principles that can be universally shared; and, concomitantly, it rejects as unjust all those practices, rules and institutions anchored in principles not all could adopt. Weighing the claims of each person equally and considering principles which each person could accept implies that the particular boundaries between states and other communities have no deep (overriding) moral significance.

Globalists often link their moral cosmopolitanism to a fourth consideration: the advocacy of institutional cosmopolitanism; that is, the extension of global governance and the creation of political institutions and mechanisms which would provide a framework of political regulation across the globe. Although globalists often differ with each other over the precise form and nature of such a framework, they are generally committed to the view that a cosmopolitan institutional framework means that states should have a somewhat, if not markedly, diminished role in comparison with institutions and organizations of regional and global governance. Accordingly, states would no longer be regarded as the sole centre of legitimate power within their own borders. States would need to be rearticulated with, and relocated within, an overarching political framework which would strip away the idea of sovereignty from fixed borders and territories, and redefine it as a form of legitimate political authority which could be embedded or entrenched in diverse realms, from local associations and cities to states, regions and, eventually, the global order.

In stark contrast, sceptics hold that the modern theory of the state presupposes a community which rightly governs itself. The modern theory of the sovereign democratic state, they contend, upholds the idea of a national community of fate – a community which properly governs itself and determines its own future. This idea is not challenged by the nature of the pattern of global interconnections and the issues that have to be confronted by a modern state. For the sceptics, particularly those who subscribe to a communitarian outlook, the values of the community take precedence over all universal requirements. The national political good trumps universal principles of right. The boundaries of political community stipulate the proper boundaries for theories of democracy and justice. The modern political community remains the fundamental unit of world order, the key basis of contemporary politics, the proper locus of rights and duties, and the key focus for all regulatory activity. Even if particular regional or global problems escape the immediate capacities of states, it is only by states collaborating together, that is, through various forms of intergovernmentalism, that such issues and problems can be actually – and legitimately – tackled.

In the first contribution to this part of the book, Fred Halliday focuses on the prospects and problems posed by the development of global governance. He accepts that the task of promoting global governance is very important, but he also wants to stress that it is immensely difficult. For beyond the identification and evaluation of problems, and the elaboration of hypothetical solutions to them, the pursuit of global governance today 'involves confronting some deep resistances in the international system and some obstacles that have arisen in the very process of global change over recent years'. Testing this thesis, Halliday explores five contentious issues around which arguments about global governance have developed – these include the nature and role of the great powers; dilemmas of peacekeeping (the Yugoslav case); economic nationalism; the changing nature and loss of innocence of non-governmental organizations; and the role of global values. He accepts that without the development and expansion of the institutions of global governance, international political order or prosperity will be hard to sustain, but he also recognizes that the modern state has had an essential role in managing and regulating the economy and promoting welfare within and between countries over the last one hundred years. Arguments about global governance should not be carried to the point where the essential role of the state in regulating order and prosperity is eclipsed from view. Nor should arguments in favour of global governance ignore the role that most central institutions of the state can play, and that no other institutions are able to play at the present time – for no other political institution has the resources, capabilities and legitimacy of the modern state. Arguments for cosmopolitanism would be all the stronger if they understood this better, and grasped the sheer complexity of many of the issues they must confront.

In the next extract, by Anthony McGrew, the main lines of contention in the debate about transnational democracy are elaborated and evaluated. McGrew distinguishes four principal accounts of transnational democracy – namely, liberal-internationalism, radical democratic pluralism (or global civic republicanism), cosmopolitan democracy and deliberative democracy. He assesses the normative arguments and justifications that underpin each of these, while also identifying major points of criticism. This leads him to a serious engagement with the sceptical case, which considers the very idea of, and arguments for, transnational democracy to be profoundly naive and intellectually flawed. Responding to this scepticism, McGrew presents a powerful case for both the desirability and feasibility of transnational democracy – irrespective of its specific form – as an essential element in the construction of a more just world order.

In the following chapter David Held explores some of the ethical and political implications of living with global forces and processes that increasingly enmesh us in 'overlapping communities of fate'. Not only are we 'unavoidably side by side' (as Kant put it), but the degrees of mutual interconnectedness and vulnerability are rapidly growing. These new circumstances, Held argues (in a vein similar to McGrew), give us little choice but to establish a 'common framework of political action' given shape and form by a common framework of law and regulation. He finds the resources for this choice in the cosmopolitan tradition, which stretches from the Stoics to contemporary political philosophy. Held defends a number of core principles at the heart of cosmopolitanism today and examines how they could be entrenched in legal and political terms. At the centre of his approach is an account of the political authority of states as 'but one moment in a complex, overlapping regime of political authority'. Within this framework, the laws and rules of the nation-state are one focus for legal development, political reflection and mobilization, alongside cities, supranational regions and global authority centres. This overlapping 'cosmopolitan polity', Held contends, would be one that in form and substance reflected and embraced the diverse forms of power and authority that operate – that already operate – within and across borders. Cosmopolitanism provides the tools and resources for the 'taming of globalization'.

In his chapter, Robert Dahl argues that democracy is likely to remain coterminous with the borders of national political communities, despite cosmopolitan attempts (such as Held's) to extend it. The idea of democracy requires, at a minimum, that people enjoy a measure of popular control over decision-making. In general, the smaller the political community, the more likely it is that there will be a positive relationship between effective popular control over decision-making and consequential decisions. The larger the political community, the more difficult it is for popular control to be effective and for decision-making to be democratically accountable. It is already the case, Dahl argues, that large nation-states make meaningful democratic control very difficult, even though they secure this in some policy domains. Accordingly, it is hard to imagine how democracy could ever be usefully and effectively extended to the domain of international organizations. For Dahl, democracy is simply the wrong model for the accountability of international organizations. He notes that foreign policy itself is one of the most problematic areas at the national level for the achievement of democratic control. Although there are moments when citizens are extremely interested and even committed to foreign policy questions, by and large foreign policy is a matter for elites, and inevitably so. International organizations have an important role, but they should be made to work as bureaucratic bargaining systems and not be assessed by democratic criteria. There is much work to be done in elaborating the appropriate criteria for assessing the legitimacy of IGOs.

In the extract of his work printed here, 'The Postnational Constellation', Jürgen Habermas argues that globalization heralds the end of the dominance of the nation-state as the proper model for political organization. The globalization of markets and economic processes erode the secure bases of sovereign power once enjoyed by the classical nation-state. The grave difficulty is that while this is happening, there is no guarantee that anything better will replace the modern state. Habermas's chapter looks critically at the idea of a cosmopolitan alternative to the nation-state, engaging particularly with the notion of cosmopolitan democracy (see chapters 43 and 44 in this volume). He argues that 'the ethical-political self-understanding of citizens' of a particular democratic polity is missing in the global order and in any currently imaginable inclusive community of world citizens. Habermas doubts that even a worldwide consensus on human rights could serve as an alternative basis for the traditions of civic solidarity that emerged with the development of nation-states. He is unconvinced that the cultural and ethical resources exist for the 'institutionalization of procedures for creating, generalizing and coordinating global interests' within anything that resembles the organizational structure of a world polity. In his view, the present complex and diffuse empirical picture suggests that we need to search for a political model not of multilevel politics within a world organization, but, rather, for a model of interactions between political processes that persist at national, international and global levels. He unfolds what this might mean by thinking of how to extend the general accessibility of 'a deliberative process whose structure grounds an expectation of rationally acceptable results', but warns that this could only be achieved if global powers build institutions for transnational will-formation that address the current extremes of social inequalities. Elaborating a deliberative model for global governance, Habermas argues in favour of a broadening of national perspectives into a viewpoint of 'global governance'. Whether this will ever arise, he concedes, is a matter for future political development – not simply theoretical reflection.

Why have the affluent states done so little to eradicate global poverty? Why isn't the amelioration of life-threatening poverty a priority of justice for the world's most developed and powerful states? What are the central moral issues arising from the present global order and what are the responsibilities of the strongest societies? Thomas Pogge responds to these questions directly in his chapter. After setting out salient facts about global poverty and inequality, he shows that there are morally significant connections between the global poor and the global rich, which may make the failure 'to make a serious effort toward poverty reduction . . . not merely a lack of beneficence, but an active impoverishing, starving, and killing of millions of innocent people by economic means'. Alternative ways of organizing global economic cooperation with different distributional consequences are within our grasp, many of which only require quite modest changes in the form and scope of economic policy. If we are not to allow further tens of millions of people to die, we need to pursue these. Pogge concludes that death through poverty and the underfulfilment of human rights in many developing countries 'is not a home-grown problem [of those countries], but one we greatly contribute to through the policies we pursue and the international order we impose'. Accordingly, 'the reduction of severe global poverty should be our foremost moral priority'.

In the past few decades, new regional and global transnational actors have emerged, contesting the terms of globalization – not just corporations but new social movements such as the environmental movement, the women's movement and the anti-globalization movement. These are the 'new' voices of an emergent transnational public domain heard, for instance, at the Rio Conference on the Environment, the Cairo Conference on Population Control, the Beijing Conference on Women, the Johannesburg Conference on Sustainable Development, and on the streets in Seattle, Prague and Genoa. Some hold that these developments indicate the beginnings of 'globalization from below' – the 'coming out' of global activism and global civil society. What is global civil society? In her chapter, Mary Kaldor seeks to address this question and to explore different meanings of the term. 'Global civil society' emerged against the backdrop of the spread of demands for democratization around the world and the intensifying process of global interconnectedness. It reflects a demand for greater personal autonomy and self-organization in highly complex and uncertain societies, where power and decision-making increasingly escape national boundaries. Kaldor interprets this as a call not to abolish states or the states system, but, rather, as an aspiration to extend the impact and efficacy of human rights, to deepen the international rule of law guaranteed by a range of interlocking institutions and to develop citizen networks which might monitor, contest and put pressure on these institutions. She summarizes the point thus: 'what we might describe as global civil society would be the interaction of those groups, networks and movements who provide a voice for individuals in global arenas and who act as . . . the transmission belts between the individual and global institutions'. Kaldor does not see global civil society as a model or as a blueprint, but as 'a contested process, in which different views about the world's future can be expressed'.

Quoting Bob Dylan, 'strange things are happening like never before', Chris Brown starts his chapter by reflecting on the huge scale of protests, and the diverse range of interests and positions represented, in the recent struggles over globalization. He notes that 'there is today a widespread sense that we live in a world gone wrong'; but, he bluntly asks, 'has it?' Brown is extremely sceptical of much of the anti-globalization rhetoric and argues that its key feature 'is that it is backward-looking, apparently intent on creating a better yesterday, a sanitized version of the past'. He defends many changes associated with the growing strength of global capitalism which have been 'enormously positive' for many of the world's peoples. In addition, he attacks the idea that there is a straightforward practical alternative to the states order that would deliver higher levels of social justice. Brown supports, in principle, the market economy, the free trade system and the world of states which allows for a diversity of communities and values. But he is not complacent about any of these. The rich are excessively protectionist about their markets; too many states are weak and vulnerable to corruption and in-fighting; and the poor frequently suffer from inadequate infrastructural resources and capacities. There are serious transnational public problems that need addressing, above all global environmental degradation. He is not optimistic about the immediate future and especially about what might be learnt from the anti-globalization movement. However, he does not think this leaves us conceptually or politically powerless: the 'real agenda of world politics' must not be confused by misleading and false criticism and a failure to weigh up carefully the strengths and weaknesses of the current system.

Finally, in the closing piece Hedley Bull explores various arguments about developmental tendencies which might take one beyond the states system. His contribution appraises different forms of universal political organization which might arise. Bull focuses on some of the classical arguments for world government; and finds that they rest on an assumed priority of order over liberty or human justice. He defends the idea of a states system as a better prospect than world government. But there are other tendencies that he explores, notably the tendency to what he has called 'a new mediaevalism'. A new medieval order would be one in which individuals were no longer simply loyal to one centre of political authority. Political life would be marked by overlapping authority and criss-crossing loyalties, without necessary allegiance to one form of concentrated political power. Bull concedes that such a development is not beyond our imagination, and might already exist in germ in communities such as the European Union, but he doubts it would prove more durable than the states system. However, his essential contention is that the states order has, despite its many limitations, served us well, and that the most likely alternatives to it carry not only serious risks of failure but also questions about their desirability and feasibility. He warns against the proliferation of alternative schemes to the states system which do not take account of our inability to transcend past experience, and of the limits of our knowledge and political imagination.

# 42

# Global Governance: Prospects and Problems

## *Fred Halliday*

## Introduction: Global Governance

In the 1990s special attention is being paid to the question of 'global governance'. This is a term almost no one used a decade ago, but which is now generally held to refer to the institutions for managing relations between states across a range of issues, from security to human rights and the environment. 'Governance' in its simplest sense refers to the art of governing, to ensuring that it is morally defensible and efficient.[1] It does not imply that there should be any one institution, but rather, in the present context, refers to a set of interlocking but separate bodies which share a common purpose. Thus it covers the activities of states, but also those of inter-governmental organisations, most notably the UN, and the role of non-governmental organisations (NGOs) and transnational movements: all of these combine, not least through influencing each other, to produce the system of global governance. The argument is not whether such a system is desirable or not: we already have a many-layered global governance system, and indeed one of the central issues is to overcome, through reform, the defaults of a system that has been up and running for several decades. The question is how to make this governance system more effective, more just, and more responsive to the changing international situation.

[ . . . ]

   The discussion on global governance has [ . . . ] acquired an importance and an urgency [ . . . ]. The case being made is clear and powerful: that the problems facing the contemporary world cannot be solved either by leaving everything to the actions of individual states, or to the workings of the market, and that the existing mechanisms are insufficient to deal with them. Some proposals do suggest that existing institutions be wound up: the Economic and Social Council of the UN (ECOSOC), and the UN Conference on Trade and Development (UNCTAD), being favourite candidates. But the majority of proposals speak of developing existing institutions and, where appropriate, adding on new ones. [ . . . ]

   The proposals for reform also tend to reflect ways in which the philosophies of global governance, and the concerns uppermost in the minds of the drafters, have shifted over the past fifty years [since the UN was established]. This is evident above all in three respects: first, there is much greater awareness of the importance of unspecific, 'global', problems, of which defence of the environment, an issue almost ignored up to the mid-1980s, is one; secondly, many recognise the importance, for social and economic reasons as much as for reasons of equity, of promoting the interests of women;

thirdly, there is a shift from the overwhelmingly state-centred approach of the UN Charter to a recognition of the rights of individuals and communities who may be in conflict with states [ . . . ].

## Contentious Issues: Five Examples

These [points] present a powerful case [ . . . ]. What is more difficult is to match these calls for change, in institutions but also in values, against the world as we know it, and to come up with approaches that meet the challenge, and also have a chance of being implemented. That such reforms can work should not be doubted: few, before they were set up, could have believed that either the UN or the European Union would get as far as they did.

Yet assertion of the need for strengthening governance may not be sufficient: the difficulties involve not only the obstacles that currently exist to such a process, but also something less often discussed, the very inherent complexity of these questions, the conflicts that are necessarily tied up with managing the world and building institutions of governance. These conflicts are not the products of chance or political ill-will, but are also inherent ones, and will require difficult choices. Some obvious examples of such inherent problems are raised in the current public debate – that between the worldwide demand for economic growth and the need to protect the environment is an obvious one, as is that between human rights and the sovereignty of states. In what follows here I want to take five such issues pertaining to global governance and address their implications for the growth of global governance. These are intended both to illustrate the possibilities of global governance, and to underline the need for realistic thinking in regard to it.

## (i) The role of the great powers

It is the assumption of most writing on global governance, and on growing international cooperation, that this will take place on a shared, multilateral, basis. Proposals for the reform of the Security Council embody such a perspective. Yet international relations has rarely been conducted on this basis, but rather on a mixture of such shared policy-making and of leadership by the more powerful members. In the UN system, for example, the General Assembly is counterposed to the, much more effective, Security Council, in which powerful states have a special place. In the field of security one could contrast the international response to the Kuwait crisis, in which one power did play a leading role, and that to the Yugoslav crisis, in which, until the NATO bombing attacks of late August 1995, this spectacularly failed to occur. In the literature on managing the world economy there is a strong current that argues for 'hegemonic stability', i.e. for the view that unless one country is willing and able to play a leading role, to set the rules and punish wrong-doers, the system will not work. The classic case is the collapse of 1929.[2] More recently the argument is that the Bretton Woods system did not 'fail' – it was destroyed by Richard Nixon in 1971. The lack of any such hegemonic system thereafter has been the source of the world's financial and economic instability. In the ecological debate, there is little point in having agreements if the richest, and most pollution-producing, states do not sign and observe them. The argument can, therefore, be made that the pursuit of international goals – peace, prosperity, safety from ecological collapse, etc. – requires that some states play a leading role and ensure that others follow the rules. This need not necessarily take the form of traditional, imperial, coercion, but can involve a range of pressures and inducements. Indeed, the evidence suggests that as prosperity is diffused, and as democratic institutions grow, then the room for peaceful, negotiated, agreements between states increases and the need for coercion and enforcement decreases.

The difficulties with this argument are many. The most obvious is that it is unjust and that the awareness of this injustice will provoke revolt: any such system will go the way of the colonial empires.[3] It is not easy to argue in favour of a hegemonic system of global governance and few of this year's sets of proposals try to do so. Even when the UN does act effectively this issue tends to be avoided: one of the most repeated arguments *against* the UN role in Kuwait was that the Security Council was 'manipulated' by the USA into taking military action, the assumption being that this in itself was sufficient reason to invalidate the result. Yet one can argue that this is the only way in which such institutions can, realistically, be supposed to operate and that it is better to recognise this. The same would apply, with obvious variations, to the international economic system: the US no doubt gains from having its currency used for three-quarters of world trade, but if this leads the US to maintain a relatively free trading system and to support some stability in world financial and currency systems, it is, arguably, a price worth paying.

There is, however, another problem with this argument, and that is that it presupposes that the great powers, their governments and populations, *actively want* to play an appropriate international role, to reap the benefits and to assume the burdens. It can be argued that a major challenge facing the international system today is that the one power capable of playing such a role shows very little interest in so doing: the US has been the dominant power in the world economy since 1945 and was handed victory in the political and military conflict with the USSR in 1991 – its response has been to draw back from those victories. Many in the USA seem to doubt whether, in any meaningful sense, they won the cold war at all, and there is scant enthusiasm in Congress for an activist US foreign policy, be this in the economic or security fields. If there is little enthusiasm for the advantages, there is, less surprisingly, little enthusiasm for paying the costs. US foreign economic aid is much smaller, as a percentage of GNP, than that of most other developed countries. When it comes to the ecological issue, the US is a reluctant participant in any policy that inhibits its own population: no one will run for office proposing that US taxes on gasoline prices, currently a third or less of European levels, are raised to international levels. The US is, as Secretary-Generals have not tired of telling us, the largest debtor to the UN. One might conclude that the one significant obstacle to the development of global governance is the reluctance of the world's leading power to assume the role that the consolidation and development of that system requires. Yet there is no obvious reason why the US 'ought' to perform these roles, whatever the rest of the world may think.

## (ii) Dilemmas of peace-keeping: the Yugoslav case

Reform of peace-keeping activities is, along with reform of the Security Council and Secretariat itself, a favoured theme of writers on the UN and global governance. The current sets of proposals are no exception: while few favour a revival of the Charter's own mechanism as originally conceived, the Military Staff Committee, composed of senior officers of the permanent members' armed forces, many see a stronger peace-keeping role as desirable and possible. Suggestions are many: more effort should go into anticipating crises and into pre-emptive diplomacy; there should be a permanent UN force, capable of rapid reaction and intervention; the member states should put up more money for peace-keeping; all should contribute forces; mandates should be clear; the 'integrity' of the UN command should be respected.

Yet of all the shadows cast over the fiftieth anniversary of the UN, that of the war in ex-Yugoslavia was perhaps the greatest.[4] Here is a war in which the UN played an active role, in the humanitarian, diplomatic and peace-keeping fields, in which the Security Council maintained an active involvement, passing many resolutions, and yet where the organisation's ability to reduce conflict was apparently little. Yugoslavia represented a crisis not just of the UN itself, not least in the organisation's failure to deliver on threats or protect those who sought refuge with it in the 'safe havens', but of international institutions and internationalist values in general: far from the 'integrity' of the UN command being respected, it is an open secret that interested states time and again sought to influence the activities of UN officials, military and civilian, in the field. At times it was unclear which international body – the UN or NATO – was in charge: certainly the bombing of Serb positions in late August 1995 was ordered by NATO, not the UN. Yugoslavia has involved a crisis for the many other organisations – NATO, EU – that have tried to play a role, for the many non-governmental organisations involved, for any belief in restraint in the conduct of war towards combatants and non-combatants alike and, not least, for any idea that the world is moving away from a situation in which ethnic communities resort to hatred and killing to resolve problems that could, on any objective calculation, be settled by peaceful means. Whatever else can be said of the period before war broke out, it cannot be claimed that pre-emptive diplomacy was not tried. The wars of former Yugoslavia seem therefore to defy much that is subsumed in the term 'global governance'.

There are, of course, some very important qualifications to be made to this judgement. In the first place, it is pure coincidence, if an unhappy one, that this conflict should have flared up in the fiftieth year of the UN: in a broader perspective, the UN's record in peace-keeping is a quite substantial one, and above all in the years since the end of the cold war. In a range of countries – El Salvador, Namibia, Cambodia to name but some – the UN has been central to the attainment of peace. In many other parts of the world – South Africa, the Israel/Palestine conflict, Ireland, Russo-Ukrainian relations – diplomatic breakthroughs have taken place, in which the UN may have been secondary, but where the institutions of global governance, NGOs included, played an important role. There is much in that achievement to build on, and for the UN to be proud of. Secondly, much of the criticism of the UN in former Yugoslavia ignores what it did achieve: the saving of hundreds of thousands of lives, the insulation of Macedonia. Above all, criticism of the UN rests upon an illusion, namely that the UN can in some way impose peace. In fact, as the UN learnt long ago, you cannot keep peace in a situation where the combatants do not want peace, and where, as they have done so spectacularly in former Yugoslavia, they use and abuse the UN, manipulating cease-fires, diplomatic initiatives and humanitarian issues for their own purposes. The first result of what has happened to the UN in the Balkans should be not to criticise it, but to identify those in every camp who have prevented peace, and, at the same time, to *reduce our expectations* of what the UN can actually do. There have certainly been failures in the UN operation, and not a little mismanagement and corruption too:[5] but the main responsibility for what has occurred there does not lie with the UN.

Beyond these qualifications, there are, however, other issues of a more general kind, that are inherent in the present debate on global governance and which pertain to peace-keeping in general. Three of these can be mentioned here. The first concerns that of recognition of states, and of the right of groups to secede from existing states: the fighting in Yugoslavia was precipitated by the decisions of Slovenia, Croatia and Bosnia to leave the Yugoslav federation, and by the decision of key states in the international community to recognise them. The argument for this course of action is clear enough: the leaderships who declared independence had the support of the majority of their peoples, they were exercising their right to self-determination under the UN Charter, and those who recognise them were acting in accordance with international law and practice. But this is to ignore the contrary arguments, concerning the rights of the ethnic minorities within Croatia and Bosnia and, more broadly, the predictable international consequences of such an action. For all that the text of the UN Charter allows secession, the international community has, until the collapse of Soviet communism, been very cautious about recognising it, for obvious reasons.[6] Yet some resolution of this issue, some sense of when secession is and is not possible, is a necessary part of any system of global equity and security.

The second issue underlying the Balkan case is the relation between different forms of intervention: human rights, humanitarian, diplomatic, peace-keeping, peace-enforcement (i.e. coercive). The UN has been involved in all of these, yet they are, in many respects, incompatible: humanitarian intervention (i.e. saving lives) can conflict with the human rights approach (i.e. identifying and prosecuting war criminals) and with enforcement; diplomatic efforts may involve working with those responsible for ethnic cleansing, and may, at times, lead negotiators to accept the results of such forcible expulsions; most obviously of all, peace-keeping, with white vehicles and with a presumption of neutrality, conflicts with peace-enforcement, which involves bombing violators of cease-fires and safe havens. Behind all of these problems, and indeed behind the whole Yugoslav story, lies another problem, namely that of the international response: if there has been an international failure, including a failure of global governance, it lies not in external manipulation of one party or the other, or in the indecisiveness of Boutros-Ghali, his representative Yasuko Akashi and others, but in the lack of support *from public opinion in the developed world* for a stronger military commitment. The question of *why* the armies of France, Britain, the US or anywhere else should be actively involved with the risk of serious casualties has not been resolved: in the actions of late August 1995 NATO forces intervened, but with air power and long-range artillery. There was no commitment of combat troops on the ground, and not a little suspicion that this show of force was a prelude to a withdrawal of forces in the event of negotiations breaking down. The subsequent Dayton agreement did lead to deployment of a Stabilisation Force on the ground, but it set a timetable for withdrawal and remained restrained, to say the least, in implementing contentious parts of the Dayton programme. The issue of weak public support for peace-enforcement is the one that is most avoided, yet it is the central one in the wars of former Yugoslavia, if not in the whole future of global governance.

## (iii) Economic nationalism

This discussion of the challenges to international peace and security is parallel to another issue, one that both underlies the need for global governance but also highlights the difficulties involved, namely what is termed 'globalisation'. By 'globalisation' is meant the breaking down of national barriers and the creation of a new single, world-wide, entity: this is most obviously the case in the field of finance, with the spread of a global currency market, and the attendant mobility of investment capital. But it is increasingly so with regard to trade, as national barriers come down, and production, with the rise of multinational corporations. In other areas too – in culture, fashion, information technology – globalisation is on the increase.

The globalisation issue itself has provoked an enormous amount of controversy, both as to what is actually occurring and as to what is desirable. Each of these arguments has implications for the debate on global governance. Those who argue that globalisation *is* indeed occurring would conclude that the nation state, as historically constituted, is increasingly unable to fulfil its traditional roles – of managing the economy, defending the living standards of its population, ensuring equity within its own frontiers, and even of defending security interests. The conclusion they would draw is that these functions have to be transferred to international bodies that can now manage the world economy and international welfare across frontiers: some existing institutions can be developed for this purpose – the World Bank, the IMF, the Bank of International Settlements, the Group of Seven Economic Summits, the OECD, the General Agreement on Tariffs and Trade and now the World Trade Organization, founded on 1 January 1995 – but, they would argue, more are needed. Yet there are two obvious problems with this line of argument: the first, long made by critics from the Third World, is that international bodies reflect not the general interest of their members, but the interests of the powerful minority of rich states, and that any proposals for extending their powers or creating a new UN Economic Council would serve to protect the privileges of the rich; the second, inherent in the globalisation argument itself, is that these bodies can only function if their constituent members, nation states, are themselves strong – yet the very reason for having such bodies is said to be that nation states are now in a weaker situation than hitherto.

There is little doubt that such globalisation has produced a growing process of global economic interdependence. While the EU states have decided at their Intergovernmental Conference to take further steps towards integration (whatever the British may decide to do or not do), the other two global trading blocs – NAFTA and a yen bloc in the Far East – are being consolidated, while in South America a range of countries have created MERCOSUR. *Our Global Neighbourhood*, the report of the Commission on Global Governance, suggests a range of ways in which the promotion of interdependence and the management of the world economy may be enhanced, including the setting up of an Economic Security Council, a renewed effort to get donor states to meet the target of 0.7 per cent of GDP for official development assistance, co-operation on migration and the financing of 'global purposes' through charges on the use of common global resources.[7] The Ford Foundation proposes that the Economic Council become, in effect, a global equivalent of the European Union: it 'would promote the harmonisation of the fiscal, monetary and trade policies of the Member States and encourage international cooperation on issues such as transfers of technology and resources, indebtedness, and the functioning of commodity markets'.[8] Here the two distinct currents of thought – global governance in the institutional sense and globalisation in the economic and financial spheres – seem to meet.

There are, however, questions that can be raised about this line of argument. They suggest that all may not go as expected in this sphere, and that matters could indeed go into reverse: universities could, in a decade or two, be offering courses on the break-up of trading blocs, just as they now study decolonisation or the end of the cold war, two equally unanticipated transformations. Equally, and even if we do not see an outright retreat from interdependence and multilateralism, there are difficult, and inevitable, choices that will have to be made and which cannot be resolved by good-will and political effort alone.

In the first place, it is far from obvious that all countries, or even the richer OECD states, would really be prepared to cede their economic sovereignty to a world body. There are tensions enough in the EU, and the kind of global planning body proposed by Ford may be a long way off. In the same vein, it is not clear that even the major states are committed to a full system of free trade. Within months of the establishment of the WTO we have seen conflicts involving the USA and Japan over automobile imports, and over US reluctance to extend the WTO's multilateral regime to cover banking, insurance and securities. The EU is committed to freeing trade within its frontiers, but has institutionalised a set of barriers to free trade in agricultural and industrial goods between its members and the rest of the world: the Common Agricultural Policy is a protectionist policy on a grandiose scale. When it comes to less developed countries, not least those with strong state sectors, then the record is even more mixed.

This reluctance on free trade reflects a growing concern in the developed world with employment levels: this is as true in Europe as it is in the USA and has led to a growing respectability for what is broadly termed 'protectionism'. Since this can take many forms – tariffs, but also a range of obstacles politely termed 'non-tariff barriers' – it remains within the range of options open to many countries. What is striking is that over the past year or two calls for protectionism have become more common in the developed world, a response both to the opening of markets and to the enduring effects of the recession. We heard a lot about it in the French elections of 1995, and more, not least from Pat Buchanan, in the US elections of 1996. At the same time, this has been as much a concern of the traditional parties of the left, influenced by trade unions, as of the right.

Interlocked with this issue is a topic that is becoming of greater and greater concern throughout the developed world, namely migration. At a time when other factors of production – capital, technology, productive capacity – are becoming more mobile, the most traditional factor of production, labour, is becoming less so. In many countries a combination of trade union defence of jobs and the rise of new right-wing parties is pushing towards a strong nationalist restriction of immigration. The old liberal regime, assuming relatively free movement of labour across frontiers, one that lasted from the early nineteenth century through to the 1960s, has collapsed: yet no one is sure what can, or should, replace it. Many individuals still hold to a presumption in favour of free movement, but no government in the world is willing to implement it. There are obvious conflicts here of economic need and political sensitivity, of universalist moral obligation and nationalist interest. One only has to look at the passions aroused in Germany by limits on the admission of refugees, or in French debates on the Muslim immigrant population, to see how difficult it is to discuss this question in a reasonable way. Is there some means of managing, even planning, migration through instruments of global governance? This issue is not going to go away. *Our Global Neighbourhood* talks of the need to respect international conventions on migrant workers, and of the need 'to develop more comprehensive institutionalised co-operation regarding migration'. These are, of course, different things: the former is relatively easy to envisage, involving the proper treatment of people who have already migrated; the latter involves the much thornier question of freedom of movement and open labour markets.

## (iv) The loss of innocence of NGOs

One of the distinguishing features of the current debate on global governance is the emphasis put on the role of non-governmental organisations. They are seen as part of a growing international civil society, and are, in various ways, incorporated into the formal, state-to-state, processes of the UN. On many issues – political prisoners, the environment, landmines, to name but three – it is NGOs which have, within countries and internationally, developed the policies of global institutions.

This growth of NGOs and of the recognition of their work is in broad terms posit-ive, but it is accompanied by several difficulties, ones that have become clearer as the initial, first, generation of NGO activity has given way to the more complex world of the 1990s. In the first place, it is often an illusion to see NGOs as an alternative to, or substitute for, states. What NGOs seek to do is, in many cases, to influence states, to get them to keep their promises or conform in greater degree to international norms. NGOs are, moreover, often working not to fill a role but to get the state to do so – be this in the realm of welfare provision, or providing food, or maintaining order. In this sense NGOs are not a replacement for states, or a solution to attempts to reduce the role of the state: they are part of the broader support *for* the role of states. In some cases, of course, states deliberately support NGOs in work that the state itself supports but would prefer not to organise directly: British aid agencies, for example, acquire a considerable percentage of their income from the state, in the form of 'matching funds' that combine with monies received from private sources. Increasingly, moreover, and very much parallel with the growth in awareness of NGOs, states have come to influence or even control NGOs: many of the supposedly 'independent' bodies that attend international conferences on particular issues are what are termed 'GONGOs' – government-controlled NGOs, sponsored, more or less overtly, by states. They use the appearance of independence to promote the goals of their state.

This loss of innocence of NGOs has, however, been compounded by two other develop-ments which qualify, even if they do not contradict, the initial liberal view of such bodies as constituents of international civil society. On the one hand, there is the very diversity of the programmes of NGOs themselves: some, arguably most, are particip-ants in 'international civil society' and can be said, in broad terms, to reinforce the system of global governance; but some most certainly are not – be this in movements against immigration in developed countries, fundamentalist religious groups in north and south, or criminal and terrorist organisations. Not all that is 'non-governmental' is civil. On the other hand, NGOs are themselves becoming increasingly involved in controversy and becoming the objects of political hostility: in the 1980s this involved, for example, disputes on the provision of humanitarian aid to guerrilla movements in Ethiopia or South Africa; in the 1990s NGO representatives have become targets of attack – murder, kidnapping and extortion, while the issue of humanitarian aid to refugees becoming embroiled with assistance to armed, criminal, groups was highlighted in the case of eastern Zaire. The killing of six Red Cross nurses in Chechnya in December 1996 and the kidnapping of NGO officials in Cambodia are examples of this trend.

For NGOs themselves the shifting contours of global governance, and the changed circumstances of the post-cold war world, have also involved questioning of their role, general and specific, that has affected their morale and performance. The Director of Amnesty International, for example, shocked many of his fellow workers in saying that Amnesty was a creation of the cold war: what this meant, in terms of mission, the focus on political prisoners and the commitment to universality, was less clear. The Red Cross has found its role, of mediating between states in war, made far more complex by the spreading of wars in which states are not the main actors, and in which traditional conceptions of military discipline, and indeed the military/civilian distinction, are less relevant.[9] The largest British aid-giving NGO, Oxfam, has been confronted with a shift in public attitudes away from charitable North–South transfers, and a questioning, by public and specialist alike, of the earlier conception of aid. At the same time it has come under increasing pressure to promote its activities in support of the needy not only in the Third World, but in developed countries. For NGOs in general, this loss of certainty and clarity from within has compounded the increase in pressures from without.

## (v) Global values

Much is made, in the literature on 'globalisation' and in the report of the Commission on Global Governance, of the emergence of 'global' values, of a commitment to humanity as a whole rather than to individual states and/or nations. The Report talks of a 'Global Civic Ethic' and, in particular, argues for a strengthened interpretation of the right of humanitarian intervention, undercutting where necessary the traditional concept of state sovereignty. There is much validity in these arguments: the lawyers have made considerable headway in showing how we can talk of values that transcend individual states or peoples; there are plenty of areas – international law, signature of human rights conventions, the very language and practice of international relations – where such a common culture exists. There is also evidence to suggest that amongst younger elites the world over there is a more shared culture, of value and aspiration, and an easier interaction than would have been the case in earlier times: a brief tour of the student cafeteria at LSE will illustrate this. *Le Monde Diplomatique* has talked of the new 'cosmocratie' produced by globalised educational opportunity.

There are, however, reasons to be cautious about this perspective of continued progress towards a common humanity. First of all, the philosophers, for all their progress on some issues, are very much not of one mind about the existence of universal, or global, values. On the one hand, in contrast to the lawyers, many doubt whether it is ever possible to talk of a common, or universal, interest – differences of interest will almost always prevail, and cannot be dissolved by identifying some chimerical, harmonious, shared concern. Secondly, the main trend in moral philosophy today is away from belief in universal, rationally justified, values towards a stress on the inevitable link between values and particular, historically formed and separate, 'communities'. These communities may debate with each other, and engage in more or less civilised interaction, but they cannot dissolve their differences.[10]

Outside the world of philosophy the picture is even less sanguine. For a variety of reasons, there has, over the past two decades or so, been an explosion in nationalist movements, proclamations of new identities, and demands for the recognition of new ethnic and communal rights. This long predated the collapse of communism but has, most spectacularly in former Yugoslavia, been stimulated by the disintegration of multi-ethnic communist states. Within many societies, not least those of western Europe and the USA, there has also been a growing assertion of diversity, of difference, in rejection of hitherto prevailing common norms. Among the majority populations of developed countries there has also, as already noted in regard to hostility to migration, been a growing resort to nationalism and intolerance. For many regions of the world, the trend is towards more difference, and more rejection of universal or common values. At the same time, with the rise of movements of both ethnic and religious character, there has been a growing rejection of the universal aspirations associated with the west – in the rhetoric of non-western states, be they China or Iran, and in that of many movements, there is a denial that any values, especially those associated with the former imperialist countries, can have universal application. One of the most common terms of derogation is to say that something is 'ethnocentric' or 'eurocentric', as if this origin is, in itself, a source of invalidity. This goes, among other things, for any attempt to establish common norms on human rights, on the position of women, or on democracy. Even amongst educated and much-travelled elites it is an open question how deep the new internationalism goes: people who work in multi-national corporations or international institutions may feel some commitment to international values, but they can, at the same time, remain very much committed to their own countries of origin. More and more people may speak English, but they do not cease to speak their own languages, and they may resent the way in which globalisation of communications, through the media and information technology, has been dominated by one language. If there is much truth in the saying that 'Travel broadens the mind', the opposite has also been known to occur.

## Conclusion: Democracy and Global Governance

The task of promoting global governance is, therefore, both a necessary and a daunting one: beyond the identification or evaluation of problems, and the elaboration of proposals, it involves confronting some deep resistances in the international system and some obstacles that have arisen in the very process of global change over recent years. We can see this in a range of contexts: the success of peace-keeping, for example, continues to run up against the reluctance of sovereign states to commit their forces to combat, and of states criticised by the international community to yield to UN pressure; growing awareness of the ecological crisis threatening us goes together with contention and evasion, in north and south; the rising recognition of the importance of women's position in society has produced outright rejection of change in some states, in the name of sovereignty and national tradition, and adaptive manipulation in others – there was lots of this at Beijing; a greater stress on the rights of individuals produces denunciation of international, and specifically 'western', interference from others.

[ . . . ]

For much of the middle of this century it was held that the state had a necessary role to play in managing the economy and promoting welfare within countries: the concept of 'global governance' is, broadly speaking, a translation to the international sphere of this argument. The Commission on Global Governance and Ford Foundation reports are, although they avoid saying so too explicitly, Keynesianism on a global scale. Despite the success of neo-liberal thinking over the past decade or two, the argument is much more evenly balanced than might at first sight appear. There are many, not least the governments of the successful countries of the Far East, who insist that without state direction there can be no attainment of order or prosperity. That is, in a nutshell, the argument for global governance, an argument that may be made all the more forcefully if the obstacles, and difficult choices involved, are clearly recognised.

## Notes

1  *The Shorter Oxford English Dictionary* (1973) defines 'governance' as 'the action or manner of government . . . the office, function or power of governing . . . method of management, system of regulations'.

2  Charles Kindleberger, *The World in Depression, 1929–39* (Berkeley: University of California Press, 1980).

3  This is, in essence, the argument of Robert Harvey's *The Return of the Strong: The Drift to Global Disorder* (London: Macmillan, 1995).

4  On the record of post-1989 peace-keeping see James Mayall (ed.), *The New Interventionism 1991–1994* (Cambridge: Cambridge University Press, 1996).

5  One of the less publicised downsides of global governance is the opportunities it provides for making money through fraud. The means favoured by UN division commanders in the Balkans peace-keeping operations has been to sell off fuel to the combatants and present UN headquarters with fake invoices: it is reckoned that this could earn the commanders several million dollars a year.

6  The collapse of Soviet communism has produced the fragmentation of four multi-ethnic states (the USSR, Yugoslavia, Czechoslovakia, Ethiopia) and has led to the emergence of twenty-two new sovereign states. Yet from 1945 to 1989 only one state, Bangladesh, was created through secession.

7  *Our Global Neighbourhood*, Report of the Commission on Global Governance (Oxford: Oxford University Press, 1995).

8  Ford Foundation, *The United Nations in its Second Half-Century* (New York: Ford Foundation, 1995).

9  The ICRC is, technically, *not* an NGO but an intergovernmental organisation. It is included here because of its independent status.

10  Note e.g. Michael Walzer, *Thick and Thin: Moral Argument at Home and Abroad* (London: University of Notre Dame Press, 1994).

# 43
# Models of Transnational Democracy

## Anthony McGrew

Democratic theory (and practice), notes Shapiro, has always appeared 'impotent when faced with questions about its own scope'.[1] Binary oppositions between the public and the private, the national and the international have been central to controversies concerning the proper limits to the democratic project. Radical critiques of modern liberal democracy, for instance, have advocated both the widening and deepening of the democratic order to embrace the private spheres of the household and the workplace. Yet, until comparatively recently, democratic theorists rarely ventured beyond the state, since prevailing orthodoxy presumed a categorical difference between the moral realm of the sovereign political community and the amoral realm of the anarchical society between states; the domestic and international arenas respectively.[2] In effect, theorists of modern democracy tended to take no account of the anarchical society, whilst theorists of international relations tended to set aside democracy. It is only in the post-cold war era that the historically estranged literatures of international relations theory and democratic theory have begun to exhibit a shared fascination with the idea of democracy beyond borders, that is, transnational (or global) democracy.[3] This 'transnational turn' articulates a profound shift in thinking about the modern democratic project that deserves serious critical scrutiny.
[ . . . ]

## Theorizing Transnational Democracy

Within the burgeoning literature on transnational democracy, four distinctive normative theories can be discerned, namely, liberal-internationalism, radical pluralist democracy, cosmopolitan democracy and deliberative democracy. [ . . . ]

## Liberal-internationalism

In its earliest manifestations liberal-internationalism presented a radical challenge to the prevailing *Realpolitik* vision of world order. The goal of liberal theorists from the eighteenth to the twentieth centuries has generally been to construct an international order based on economic interdependence through trade, the rule of law, cooperation between states and arbitration of disputes. Some liberals like Woodrow Wilson have also envisaged a role for international organizations. As Long argues, however, contemporary variants of liberal-internationalism have lost this radical edge, promoting the reform, rather than transformation, of world order.[4] Although a liberal radicalism of a kind survives, in the guise of orthodox economic neo-liberalism, it is deeply antagonistic to notions of global governance and transnational democracy, advocating instead a world of unfettered global markets.

Liberal institutionalism within international relations theory is primarily concerned with illuminating the rational calculus of international cooperation, so the question of transnational democracy tends to be conceived principally in procedural terms, such as creating more representative, transparent and accountable international institutions.[5] Keohane, for instance, understands democracy at the international level as a form of 'voluntary pluralism under conditions of maximum transparency'.[6] A more pluralistic world order, in this view, is also a more democratic world order. It involves the reconstruction of aspects of liberal-pluralist democracy at the international level, shorn of the requirements of electoral politics. In place of parties competing for votes, a vibrant transnational civil society channels its demands to the decision-makers, whilst also making them accountable for their actions. International institutions thus become arenas within which the interests of both states and the agencies of civil society are articulated. Furthermore, they function as key political structures through which consensus is negotiated and collective decisions are legitimated.

There are other significant contributions to liberal-internationalism, notably the report of the Commission on Global Governance. But they share a common commitment to more representative, responsive and accountable international governance. Such ideas also tend to dominate current thinking about the reform of global institutions, from the IMF to the World Trade Organization (WTO). This is not surprising given that liberal-internationalism reflects the aspirations and values of the western states and elites that dominate the institutions of global governance. But, as Falk argues, it is a philosophy that offers a restricted and somewhat technocratic view of transnational democracy.[7] It also fails to acknowledge that inequalities of power tend to make democracy the captive of powerful vested interests. Critiques of classical pluralism, from those of Dahl to Lindblom, have recognized how corporate power distorts the democratic process.[8] But the insights of neo-pluralism find little expression in the liberal-internationalist literature, which tends to overlook structural inequalities of power in the global system and, in particular, the power imbalances between the agencies of transnational civil society and global capital. Advocating transparency and accountability is insufficient by itself to combat such inequalities of access and influence. Institutional tinkering is unlikely to resolve the democratic deficit that afflicts global governance. Despite acknowledging the significance of transnational civil society, the liberal-internationalist account remains singularly western and state-centric, stressing the transparency and accountability of international institutions to national governments.

## Radical democratic pluralism

Radical democratic pluralism eschews the reformism of liberal-internationalism in favour of direct forms of democracy and self-governance. It means, therefore, the creation of alternative forums from the global to the local levels.[9] It rejects vigorously the liberal reformist position, because existing structures of global governance privilege the interests of a wealthy and powerful cosmocracy whilst excluding the needs and interests of much of humanity. Advocates of radical pluralist democracy, who include Burnheim, Connolly, Patomaki and Walker, are therefore concerned with the normative foundations of a 'new politics', which would empower individuals and communities.[10] Its advocates are concerned with the creation of 'good communities' based upon equality, active citizenship, promotion of the public good, humane governance and harmony with the natural environment. Radical pluralist democracy, Hutchings argues, 'represents something of a cocktail of elements of post-modernist, Marxist and civic republican democratic theory'.[11]

Radical democratic pluralism is essentially a 'bottom-up' theory of the democratization of world order, focusing upon environmental, feminist, peace and other social movements. These challenge the authority of states, multinational corporations and international organizations that uphold neo-liberalism. They also challenge liberal conceptions of the 'political' and the conventional divisions between foreign/domestic, public/private, society/nature. Therefore, a radical politics builds on the experiences of critical social movements, which demonstrate that one of the 'great fallacies of political theory is the assumption that a centralized management of power . . . is necessary to assure political order'.[12] 'Real' democracy, therefore, is to be found in the juxtaposition of a multiplicity of self-governing and self-organizing collectivities constituted on diverse spatial scales – from the local to the global.

Radical democratic pluralism reflects a strong attachment to theories of direct democracy and participatory democracy. It also draws upon neo-Marxist critiques of liberal democracy, claiming that effective participation and self-governance require social and economic equality. Furthermore, it connects to the civic republican tradition in so far as its exponents believe that individual freedom can only be realized in the context of a strong sense of political community and an understanding of the common good.[13]

To the extent that radical pluralist democracy requires the construction of alternative forms of global governance, it is a threat to the existing principles of world order. Its critics argue that it is precisely this rejection of the constitution of world order that is problematic. Without, for instance, some conception of sovereignty, it is difficult to envisage how the competing claims of a plurality of communities, even within the same borders, might be reconciled short of force. Furthermore, in the absence of the present rather imperfect liberal world order – embodying (to varying degrees) the principles of the rule of law and normative constraints on the exercise of organized violence – it might be argued there is no secure basis for constructing and nurturing transnational democracy. Territorial democracy, history suggests, has only thrived in circumstances where the rule of law exists and political violence is absent. A compelling critique of the radical pluralist argument might therefore be found in its ambivalence towards the very conditions – the rule of law and sovereignty – which make democracy (at whatever level) possible.

## Cosmopolitan democracy

By comparison with the radical pluralist account, cosmopolitan democracy pays particular attention to the institutional and political conditions that are necessary to effective democratic governance within, between and across states. Held develops a sophisticated account of cosmopolitan democracy, which builds upon the existing principles of the liberal international order (e.g. the rule of law and human rights), to construct a new global constitutional settlement.[14] Advocating a 'double democratization' of political life, the advocates of cosmopolitan democracy seek to reinvigorate democracy within states by extending it to the public realm between and across states. Transnational democracy and territorial democracy are conceived as mutually reinforcing, rather than conflicting, principles of political rule. Cosmopolitan democracy seeks 'a political order of democratic associations, cities and nations as well as of regions and global networks'.[15]

Central to this model is the principle of autonomy for both individuals and collectivities, to be upheld through development of a cosmopolitan democratic law. This law establishes 'powers and constraints, and rights and duties, which transcend the claims of nation-states'.[16] Accordingly, the principle of democratic autonomy depends upon 'the establishment of an international community of democratic states and societies committed to upholding a democratic public law both within and across their own boundaries: a cosmopolitan democratic community'.[17] The aim is not to establish a world government, but rather 'a global and divided authority system – a system of diverse and overlapping power centres shaped and delimited by democratic law'.[18] Rather than a hierarchy of political authority, from the local to the global, cosmopolitan democracy involves a heterarchical arrangement. Conceptually, this lies between federalism and the much looser arrangements implied by the notion of confederalism. For it requires 'the subordination of regional, national and local "sovereignties" to an overarching legal framework, but within this framework associations may be self-governing at diverse levels'.[19] The entrenchment of cosmopolitan democracy therefore involves a process of *reconstructing* the existing framework of global governance.

This democratic reconstruction requires that democratic practices be embedded more comprehensively 'within communities and civil associations by elaborating and reinforcing democracy from "outside" through a network of regional and international agencies and assemblies that cut across spatially delimited locales'.[20] Such mechanisms could promote accountability over forms of global power, which at present escape effective democratic control.

Cosmopolitan democracy represents an enormously ambitious agenda for reconfiguring the constitution of global governance and world order. Whilst it draws considerable inspiration from modern theories of liberal democracy, it is also influenced by critical theory, theories of participatory democracy and civic republicanism. It is distinguished from liberal-internationalism by its radical agenda and a scepticism towards the primacy of state-centric and procedural notions of democracy. Whilst accepting the important role of progressive transnational social forces it nevertheless differentiates itself from radical pluralist democracy through its attachment to the centrality of the rule of law and constitutionalism as necessary conditions for the establishment of a more democratic world order.

But the idea of cosmopolitan democracy is not without its critics. Sandel considers the ethic that informs notions of cosmopolitan democracy to be 'flawed, both as a moral ideal and as a public philosophy for self-government in our time'.[21] This, he argues, is because at the core of cosmopolitanism is a liberal conception of the individual, which neglects the ways in which individuals, their interests and values, are 'constructed' by the communities of which they are members. Accordingly, democracy can only thrive by first creating a democratic community with a common civic identity. Whilst globalization does create a sense of universal connectedness, it does not, in Brown's view, generate an equivalent sense of community based upon shared values and beliefs.[22] Nor, it can be argued, do theorists of cosmopolitan democracy deliver a convincing account of how the ethical and cultural resources necessary for its effective realization are to be generated. It can also be criticized for a top-down approach, in which reconstructing the constitution of global governance along more democratic lines is taken as the key to realizing transnational democracy. Such faith in a new constitution for global governance, however, overlooks the inherent tensions that exist between the democratic impulse and the logic of constitutional constraints upon what the demos may do.[23] Nor, as Thompson identifies, is it necessarily clear how, within this multi-layered system of global governance, jurisdictional conflicts between different layers of political authority are to be reconciled or adjudicated by democratic means, let alone how accountability in such a system can be made more effective.[24] This raises important issues of consent and legitimacy. The problem, Thompson argues, is one of 'many majorities' such that 'no majority has an exclusive and overarching claim to democratic legitimacy'.[25] Furthermore, he claims that cosmopolitan democracy will only serve to intensify the enduring tensions between democracy and the protection of individual rights, since rights claims may be pursued through international authorities, thus challenging the legitimacy of democratically sanctioned local policies or decisions. Finally, as both Patomaki and Hutchings suggest, in presuming the universal validity of western democratic values, the cosmopolitan democracy project becomes vulnerable to charges of legitimizing a new mode of imperialism.[26]

## Deliberative (discursive) democracy[27]

One sympathetic attempt to address some of the criticisms inherent in both the cosmopolitan and radical democratic pluralist projects is to be found in the work on deliberative democracy and related conceptions of stakeholder democracy.[28] Rather than proposing a new constitutional settlement for the global polity, or the creation of alternative structures of global governance, advocates of deliberative democracy are concerned with elucidating 'the possibilities for democratizing the governance that does exist in the international system rather than the government that might'.[29] Deliberative democrats are interested in the discursive sources of existing systems of global governance and the role of transnational civil society 'in establishing deliberative democratic control over the terms of political discourse and so the operation of governance in the international system'.[30] In effect, they are concerned with the principles and necessary conditions for the creation of a genuine transnational public sphere of democratic deliberation. Such principles include non-domination, participation, public deliberation, responsive governance and the right of all affected to a voice in public decisions that impinge on their welfare or interests.[31] As Dryzek argues, the realization of transnational democracy depends upon a recognition that 'the essence of democratic legitimacy is to be found not in voting or representation . . . but rather in deliberation'.[32]

   While advocates of deliberative democracy do not discount totally the value of a liberal attachment to institutional reform of global governance, nor the cosmopolitan requirement for a democratic constitution for world order, both visions are regarded as insufficient in themselves for the grounding of transnational democracy. Instead, the deliberative ideal looks to the creation of 'an association whose affairs are governed by the public deliberation of its members'.[33] This involves, its advocates argue, the cultivation of transnational public spheres in which there can be genuine dialogue between the agencies of public governance and those affected by their decisions and actions. Rational and informed deliberation amongst all those affected, rather than simply those with a declaratory interest in the matter in question, is ultimately tied to realizing the common good. This is to be distinguished from a liberal pluralist conception of democracy, in which the achievement of consensus amongst the expressed interests and preferences of citizens or organized interests is taken to have primacy in public decision-making. Furthermore, public authorities are expected to justify their actions, whilst those affected must have the right to contest these policies, since governance is regarded as democratic only 'to the extent that the people individually and collectively enjoy a permanent possibility of contesting what government decides'.[34] Accordingly, deliberative democracy requires informed and active citizens, as well as the vigorous promotion of those rights and conditions necessary to their empowerment. Given the significance of the all-affected principle, the criteria and procedures for inclusion within the deliberative political process become critical.

Central to the deliberative argument is the principle of stakeholding: that all those affected by, or with a stake in, the decisions of public authorities have the right to a voice in the governance of those matters.[35] Membership of the relevant deliberative community is therefore contingent upon the specific configuration of stakeholders involved on any issue, that is, those whose interests or material conditions are directly or indirectly implicated in the exercise of public power. The process of deliberation itself becomes constitutive of the relevant deliberative community. This reflexivity, argue its advocates, makes deliberative democracy admirably suited to a world in which there are overlapping communities of fate and in which the organization and exercise of power no longer coincide with the bounded territorial political community. Unlike liberal representative democracy, in which the demos is defined in relation to fixed territorial boundaries, deliberative democracy presumes a largely functional or systemic conception of the demos uninhibited by pre-existing territorial, cultural or human boundaries. As Dryzek notes: 'Deliberation . . . can cope with fluid boundaries, and the production of outcomes across boundaries. For we can look for democracy in the character of political interaction . . . without worrying about whether or not it is confined to particular territorial entities.'[36]

Advocates of deliberative democracy argue that it offers a set of principles upon which inclusive, responsive and responsible transnational democracy can be constructed. Its more orthodox variants tend to emphasize its reformist ambitions: deliberation is conceived as a mechanism for enhancing the democratic legitimacy of public decision-making, from the local to the global level.[37] By contrast, more radical manifestations highlight its transformative potential to the extent that it is concerned with the contestation of global institutional agendas, challenging unaccountable sites of transnational power and empowering the progressive forces of transnational civil society.[38] This tension between a procedural, as opposed to substantive, interpretation of deliberative democracy arises from its rather eclectic philosophical origins, which embrace the traditions of critical theory, discourse analysis, republicanism, participatory and direct democracy.

Critics of deliberative democracy argue that it is not a discrete model of democracy so much as a mechanism for resolving and legitimizing public decisions. So it only has value in the context of an established democratic framework. This criticism is valid whether the focus is transnational, local or national democracy. Furthermore, despite its emphasis upon discourse, it tends to overlook the problems which language and cultural diversity present to the construction of a genuine transnational deliberative public sphere. This problem cannot simply be wished away as a technical matter of translation, but raises serious issues about the role of language and culture in defining the conditions of possibility of genuine political deliberation.[39] In arguing too that the deliberative communities are essentially constituted through the all-affected principle, the basis upon which stakeholders are to be incorporated – whether as direct participants or through representatives – is never clearly specified. Indeed, the emphasis upon self-organization tends to ensure that the procedural requirements and institutional conditions of effective deliberation remain somewhat vaguely stipulated. Finally, there is significant silence about how intractable conflicts of interests or values can be resolved deliberatively without recourse to some authoritatively imposed solution. Therefore, deliberative democracy may be of marginal value in dealing with many of the most pressing global distributional or security issues – from debt relief to humanitarian intervention – which figure on the world political agenda. Deliberative democracy, like other theories of transnational democracy, is also vulnerable to a more fundamental critique.

## Transnational Democracy: Plausible or Desirable?

Whatever the intellectual merits of any particular design for transnational democracy, serious doubts have been raised about the very plausibility and desirability of the idea. Communitarian, realist and some radical critiques take issue with the advocates of transnational democracy on theoretical, institutional, historical and ethical grounds.

Political communitarians, such as Kymlicka, are unconvinced by the cosmopolitan premises that inform theories of transnational democracy. Democracy, argues Kymlicka, has to be rooted in a shared history, language or political culture: the constitutive features of modern territorial political communities. These features are all more or less absent at the transnational level. Despite the way globalization binds the fate of communities together, the reality is that 'the only forum within which genuine democracy occurs is within national boundaries'.[40] Even within the European Union (EU) transnational democracy is little more than an elite phenomenon. If there is no effective moral community beyond the state, there can be, in this view, no true demos. Of course, advocates of transnational democracy argue that political communities are being transformed by globalization, therefore the idea of the demos as a fixed, territorially delimited unit is no longer tenable.[41] But the sceptics pose the critical question of who or what agency decides how the demos is to be constituted, and upon what basis? Without some unequivocal specification of the principles by which the demos is to be constituted, it is difficult to envisage either how transnational democracy could be institutionalized or how it would necessarily provide the basis for more representative, legitimate and accountable global governance. By failing to respond to this question with a theoretically rigorous or convincing argument, suggest the sceptics, the advocates of transnational democracy fatally undermine the plausibility of their project.[42]

For political realists, state sovereignty and international anarchy present the most insuperable barriers to the realization of democracy beyond borders. Even though elements of an international society of states may exist, in which there is an acceptance of the rule of law and compliance with international norms, order at the global level, suggest realists, remains contingent rather than enduring. Conflict and force are ever present and a daily reality in many regions of the world. These are not the conditions in which any substantive democratic experiment is likely to prosper, since a properly functioning democracy requires the absence of political violence and the rule of law. In relations between sovereign states organized violence is always a possibility and the rule of law largely an expression of *Realpolitik*. International order is always order established by and for the most powerful states. Global governance therefore is merely a synonym for western hegemony, whilst international institutions remain the captives of dominant powers. States act strategically to encourage international governance only where it enhances their autonomy, or circumvents domestic scrutiny of sensitive issues, so generating a political imperative prejudicial to the democratization of global governance.[43] Short of a democratic hegemon, or alternatively some form of world federation of democratic states, imposing or cultivating transnational democracy, the conditions for its realization must accordingly appear theoretically and practically implausible. Few sovereign democratic states are likely to trade national self-governance for a more democratic world order, whilst no authoritarian state would ever conceivably entertain the prospect. Transnational democracy remains, for realists, a utopian ideal.

Even if transnational democracy were possible, it remains, many sceptics conclude, a politically and ethically undesirable [aspiration].[44] At the heart of theories of transnational democracy is an intractable conflict between a normative commitment to effective national democracy and the desire for democracy beyond the state. This dilemma arises from the fact that the democratic practices and decisions of one have enormous potential to override or negate the democratic credentials and requirements of the other. In most mature democracies this dilemma is resolved through constitutional mechanisms, but these are signally absent in the international arena. A telling illustration of this dilemma concerns the EU's 'democratically mandated' intervention in Austrian politics following the electoral success of the far right in early 2000. Collectively, the EU threatened to withhold official recognition of any coalition government in which Mr Haider, the leader of the main far right party, played a role, despite the democratically expressed preferences of the Austrian electorate. Whatever the ethics of this particular case, the general point is that transnational democracy has the potential to extinguish effective self-governance at local or national levels.[45] Without effective safeguards – which, in the absence of a global constitution, cannot be institutionally grounded – the danger of transnational democracy is that it is susceptible to crude majoritarian impulses, which have the potential to negate the legitimate democratic rights and wishes of (national) minorities. Conversely, without the institutional capacity to enforce the democratic will of the majority against the entrenched interests of the Great Powers of the day, transnational democracy simply becomes hostage to the interests of the most powerful geo-political forces. Herein lies what might be referred to as the paradox of transnational democracy. Without a capacity to enforce the transnational democratic will on the most powerful geo-political and transnational social forces, democracy beyond the state is necessarily ineffective, yet the very existence of such a capability creates the real possibility of tyranny.

It is partly for such reasons that even those of a more radical persuasion query the desirability of transnational democracy. Amongst some radical critics the very idea of transnational democracy conceals a new instrument of western hegemony.[46] As with the philosophy of 'good governance' promulgated by G7 governments and multilateral agencies, it is considered primarily a western preoccupation.[47] For most of humanity it is a distraction from global problems such as AIDS, famine, desertification and poverty. As the United Nations Development Programme puts it, the most pressing issue for humankind is whether globalization can be given a human face.[48] In this context transnational democracy may be an entirely inappropriate and irrelevant response, given that the critical problem is how to ensure that global markets and global capital work in the interests of the majority of the world's peoples without destroying the natural environment.[49] Democratizing global governance, even if it were feasible, may be more likely to strengthen and legitimize the hegemony of global capital than it is to challenge its grip on the levers of global power.[50] The historical record of advanced capitalist societies, argue the sceptics, demonstrates how the imperatives of capitalism take precedence over the workings of democracy. Therein lies the prospective fate of transnational democracy. Accelerating global inequality and looming environmental catastrophe simply cannot be resolved by a dose of transnational democracy. On the contrary, as Hirst suggests, what is required are powerful and effective, rather than democratic, global bodies which can override the entrenched interests of global capital by promoting the common welfare – social democracy at the global level.[51] Alternatively, the deconstruction of global governance and the devolution of power to self-governing, sustainable local communities is a strategy favoured by radicals of a green persuasion.[52] The ethical preference of many radical critics is for strengthening existing systems of social democratic governance and new forms of participatory democracy below the state.[53] Real democracy is always local (national) democracy.

What the various sceptical arguments share is a sense that transnational democracy is neither necessarily an appropriate response to globalization nor a project that is as ethically and theoretically persuasive as its advocates suppose. On the contrary, it is fraught with theoretical shortcomings and practical dangers. Not the least amongst these, suggests Dahl, is the danger of popular control in respect of vital matters of economic and military security.[54] Furthermore, the development of national (territorial) democracy has been strongly associated with force and violence, whilst the history of modern democracy illustrates how, even within the context of a shared political culture, it remains a distinctly fragile system of rule. In a world of cultural diversity and growing inequality, the possibility of realizing transnational democracy must therefore be judged to be negligible, unless it is imposed either by a concert of democratic states or a benign democratic hegemon. Not surprisingly, for most sceptics, self-governance within states, whether democratic or not, is considered ethically preferable to the likely tyranny of a more democratic global polity.

## Can Transnational Democracy be Dismissed?

In response, advocates of transnational democracy accuse the sceptics of a too hasty dismissal of the theoretical, ethical and empirical arguments that inform their designs for democracy beyond borders. More specifically, they argue that by discounting the significant political transformations being brought about by intensifying globalization and regionalization, the sceptics seriously misread the possibilities for significant political change towards a more democratic world order.[55] These transformations irrevocably alter the conditions which made sovereign, territorial, self-governing political communities possible, for in a world of global flows the local and the global, the domestic and the foreign, are largely indistinguishable.[56]

Modern political communities are historical and social constructions. Their particular form, coinciding with the territorial reach of the 'imagined community' of the nation, is a product of particular conditions and forces. Historically, the state has been the primary incubator of modern democratic life. But, as Linklater observes, political communities have never been static, fixed creations, but have always been in the process of construction and reconstruction.[57] As globalization and regionalization have intensified, modern political communities have begun to experience a significant transformation, whilst new forms of political community are emerging. According to Held, national political communities coexist today alongside 'overlapping communities of fate' defined by the spatial reach of transnational networks, systems, allegiances and problems.[58] In Walzer's terms these may be conceived as 'thin' communities, as opposed to the 'thick' communities of the locale and nation-state. Nevertheless, they constitute necessary ethical and political preconditions for the cultivation of transnational democracy.[59] [ . . . ]

Moreover, political communities beyond the state are being created by what some argue is the growing constitutionalization of world order.[60] The accumulation of multilateral, regional and transnational arrangements (which have evolved in the last fifty years) has created a tacit global constitution. In seeking to manage and regulate transborder issues, states have codified their respective powers and authority, and institutionalized an elaborate system of rules, rights and responsibilities for the conduct of their joint affairs. This has gone furthest in the EU, where effectively a quasi-federal constitution has emerged. But in other contexts, such as the WTO, the authority of national governments is being redefined, as the management of trade disputes becomes subject to a rule of law.[61]

Associated with this institutionalization has been the elaboration and entrenchment of some significant democratic principles within the society of states.[62] Thus, self-determination, popular sovereignty, democratic legitimacy and the legal equality of states have become orthodox principles of international society. As Mayall comments, there has been an entrenchment of 'democratic values, as the standard of legitimacy within international society'.[63] This democratization of international society also appears to have accelerated in recent years, in response to processes of globalization, the activities of transnational civil society and the socializing dynamic of an expanding community of democratic states. Despite its unevenness and fragility, it represents, combined with the constitutionalization of world order, the forging of the necessary historical conditions – the creation of 'zones of peace' and the rule of law – for the cultivation of transnational democracy.[64]

Further evidence of this process of democratization is to be found in the political response of many governments and agencies of transnational civil society to the consequences of economic globalization.[65] A common aspiration amongst progressive political forces is a system of global governance that is accountable, responsive and transparent. The growing perception that power is leaking away from democratic states and electorates to unelected and effectively unaccountable global bodies, such as the

WTO, has prompted increased political pressure, on G8 governments especially, to bring good governance to global governance.[66] Of course, democracy involves more than simply transparent and accountable decision-making. It is interesting to note that the debate about reform draws significantly upon liberal-internationalism and the deliberative, radical and cosmopolitan discourses of transnational democracy discussed above. In the context of the WTO, for instance, the language of stakeholding has been much in evidence, somewhat curiously in both US official government and civil society proposals for its reform.[67]

Of course, for sceptics such as Dahl these developments do not invalidate the normative argument that international institutions cannot be truly democratic.[68] Yet, as advocates of transnational democracy point out, this overlooks completely the significant examples of international or suprastate bodies, from the EU to the International Labour Organization (ILO), whose institutional designs reflect novel combinations of traditional inter-governmental and democratic principles.[69] While the EU represents a remarkable institutionalization of a distinctive form of democracy beyond borders, it is by no means unique. The ILO, for instance, has institutionalized a restricted form of 'stakeholding' through a tripartite system of representation corresponding to states, business and labour organizations respectively. Newer international functional bodies, such as the International Fund for Agricultural Development and the Global Environmental Facility, also embody stakeholding principles as a means to ensure representative decision-making. Furthermore, virtually all major international institutions have opened themselves up to formal or informal participation by the representatives of civil society.[70] Even the WTO has created a civil society forum. In certain respects, therefore, basic democratic principles are constitutive of existing global and regional systems of governance.

Finally, in questioning the value of transnational democracy, socialists raise the serious issue of whether democracy can be trusted to deliver greater global social justice. In regard to liberal democracy in the national context, the historical record appears somewhat mixed. By contrast, advocates of transnational democracy commence from a rather different reading (historical and conceptual) of the relationship between capitalism – as a primary engine of global inequality and injustice – and democracy. This reading recognizes the inevitable contradictions between the logic of capitalism and the logic of democracy. It departs from the fatalism of many structural Marxist and radical critiques in arguing, on both theoretical and historical grounds, that transnational democracy is a necessary requirement for the realization of global social justice. The history of European social democracy, in mitigating the inequalities of market capitalism, is taken as an important case in point. Accordingly, the case for transnational democracy is inseparable from the argument for global social justice. Indeed, the value of transnational democracy, suggest its most passionate advocates, lies precisely in its capacity to provide legitimate mechanisms and grounds for taming the power of global capital, thereby promoting and realizing the conditions for greater global social justice. That existing institutions of global governance fail in this task should be no surprise, since they are the captives of dominant economic interests.[71] Nonetheless, for the advocates of transnational democracy this is not a valid reason for abandoning the project, but, on the contrary, for advocating it more vigorously.

[ . . . ]

## Notes

1   I. Shapiro, 'Democracy's edges: Introduction', in I. Shapiro and C. Hacker-Cordón (eds), *Democracy's Edges* (Cambridge, Cambridge University Press, 1999), p. 1.

2   W. E. Connolly, 'Democracy and territoriality', *Millennium* 20, 3 (1991): 463–84; R. B. J. Walker, 'On the spatio-temporal conditions of democratic practice', *Alternatives* 16, 2 (1991): 243–62.

3   I. Clark, *Globalization and International Relations Theory* (Oxford, Oxford University Press, 1999); D. Held, *Democracy and the Global Order* (Cambridge, Polity, 1995).

4   P. Long, 'The Harvard school of liberal international theory: the case for closure', *Millennium* 24, 3 (1995): 489–505.

5   R. Falk, 'Liberalism at the global level: the last of the independent commissions?', *Millennium* 24, 3 (1995): 563–78.

6   R. Keohane, 'International institutions: can interdependence work?' *Foreign Policy* Spring (1988): 82–96.

7   Falk, 'Liberalism at the global level'.

8   G. McLennan, *Marxism, Pluralism and Beyond* (Cambridge, Polity, 1989).

9   K. Hutchings, *International Political Theory* (London, Sage, 1999), pp. 166ff.

10  See Connolly, 'Democracy and territoriality'; Walker, 'On the spatio-temporal conditions of democratic practice'; J. Burnheim, *Is Democracy Possible?* (Cambridge, Cambridge University Press, 1985); J. Burnheim, 'Democracy, nation-states, and the world system', in D. Held and C. Pollitt (eds), *New Forms of Democracy* (London, Sage, 1986), pp. 218–39; J. Burnheim, 'Power-trading and the environment', *Environmental Politics* 4, 4 (1995): 49–65; R. B. J. Walker, 'International relations and the concept of the political', in K. Booth and S. Smith (eds), *International Relations Theory Today* (Cambridge, Polity, 1995), pp. 306–27; H. Patomaki, 'Republican public sphere and the governance of globalizing political economy', in M. Lensu and J.-S. Fritz (eds), *Value Pluralism, Normative Theory and International Relations* (London, Macmillan, 2000), pp. 160–95.

11  Hutchings, *International Political Theory*, pp. 166–7.

12  Burnheim, 'Democracy, nation-states, and the world system', pp. 220–1.

13  I. Barns, 'Environment, democracy and community', *Environment and Politics* 4, 4 (1995): 101–33.

14  Held, *Democracy and the Global Order*.

15  Held, *Democracy and the Global Order*, p. 234.

16  D. Held et al., *Global Transformations: Politics, Economics and Culture* (Cambridge, Polity Press, 1999), p. 70.

17  Held, *Democracy and the Global Order*, p. 229.

18  Ibid., p. 234.

19  Ibid.

20  Ibid., p. 237.

21  M. Sandel, *Democracy's Discontent* (Harvard, Harvard University Press, 1996), p. 342.

22  C. Brown, 'International political theory and the idea of world community', in Booth and Smith (eds), *International Relations Theory Today*, pp. 90–109.

23  M. Saward, *The Terms of Democracy* (Cambridge, Polity, 1998).

24  D. Thompson, 'Democratic theory and global society', *Journal of Political Philosophy* 7, 2 (1999): 111–25.

25  Ibid., p. 112.

26  Hutchings, *International Political Theory*, p. 177; Patomaki, 'Republican public sphere and the governance of globalizing political economy'.

27 Dryzek makes a distinction between deliberative and discursive democracy. The latter represents a more radical conception of deliberative democracy that seeks to move beyond its origins in liberal and critical theory. For simplicity, however, both versions are used interchangeably here. See J. S. Dryzek, *Deliberative Democracy and Beyond* (Oxford, Oxford University Press, 2000), ch. 1.

28 See e.g. J. S. Dryzek, *Discursive Democracy* (Cambridge, Cambridge University Press, 1990); D. Deudney, 'Global village sovereignty', in K. T. Litfin (ed.), *The Greening of Sovereignty* (Cambridge, MA, MIT Press, 1998), pp. 299–325; Thompson, 'Democratic theory and global society'; Dryzek, *Deliberative Democracy and Beyond*.

29 Dryzek, *Deliberative Democracy and Beyond*, p. 120.

30 Ibid., p. 138.

31 See Dryzek, *Discursive Democracy*; Saward, *The Terms of Democracy*, pp. 64–5; and P. Pettit, *Republicanism: A Theory of Freedom and Government* (Oxford, Oxford University Press, 1997).

32 J. S. Dryzek, 'Transnational democracy', *Journal of Political Philosophy* 7, 1 (1999): 44.

33 Cohen, quoted in Saward, *The Terms of Democracy*, p. 64.

34 Pettit, *Republicanism*, p. 185.

35 See Burnheim, 'Democracy, nation-states, and the world system'; Deudney, 'Global village sovereignty'; R. Eckersley, 'Deliberative democracy, ecological representation and risk: towards a democracy of the affected', mimeo (2000); and M. Saward, 'A critique of Held', in B. Holden (ed.), *Global Democracy: Key Debates* (London, Routledge, 2000), pp. 32–46.

36 Dryzek, *Deliberative Democracy and Beyond*, p. 129.

37 E.g., Saward, *The Terms of Democracy*.

38 E.g., Dryzek, 'Transnational democracy'; Eckersley, 'Deliberative democracy, ecological representation and risk'.

39 W. Kymlicka, 'Citizenship in an era of globalization', in Shapiro and Hacker-Cordón (eds), *Democracy's Edges*, pp. 112–26.

40 Ibid., p. 124.

41 A. Linklater, *The Transformation of Political Community* (Cambridge, Polity, 1998).

42 See, e.g., C. Gorg and J. Hirsch, 'Is international democracy possible?', *Review of International Political Economy* 5, 4 (1998): 585–615; R. A. Dahl, 'Can international organizations be democratic?', in Shapiro and Hacker-Cordón (eds), *Democracy's Edges*, pp. 19–36; Kymlicka, 'Citizenship in an era of globalization'; Saward, 'A critique of Held'.

43 K. D. Wolf, 'The new raison d'état as a problem for democracy in world society', *European Journal of International Relations* 5, 3 (1999): 333–63.

44 See e.g. D. Zolo, *Cosmopolis: Prospects for World Government* (Cambridge, Polity, 1997); Gorg and Hirsch, 'Is international democracy possible?'; Dahl, 'Can international organizations be democratic?'; P. Hirst, 'Between the local and the global: democracy in the twenty-first century', in R. Axtmann (ed.), *Balancing Democracy* (London, Continuum, 2001), pp. 255–75; and J. Mayall, 'Democracy and international society', *International Affairs* 76, 1 (2000): 61–75.

45 Hutchings, *International Political Theory*, p. 166.

46 See R. Burbach, O. Nunez and B. Kagarlistsky, *Globalization and its Discontents* (London, Pluto, 1996); M. Elmandrjra, 'The need for the deglobalization of globalization', in C. Pierson and S. Tormey (eds), *Politics at the Edge* (London, Macmillan, 2000), pp. 29–40.

47 The seven most advanced industrial countries – the USA, Germany, Japan, the UK, France, Canada and Italy – hold periodical G7 (Group of Seven) summits to review the state of the international economy. When joined by Russia, the G7 becomes the G8.

48 UNDP, *Globalization With a Human Face – UN Human Development Report 1999* (Oxford, UNDP/Oxford University Press, 1999).

49 See R. Cox, 'Globalization, multilateralism and democracy', in R. Cox (ed.), *Approaches to World Order* (Cambridge, Cambridge University Press, 1996), pp. 524–37; Burbach, Nunez and Kagarlistsky, *Globalization and its Discontents*.

50  S. Gill, 'Globalization, market civilization, and disciplinary neo-liberalism', *Millennium* 24, 3 (1995): 399–424; Burbach, Nunez and Kagarlistsky, *Globalization and its Discontents*.

51  P. Hirst and G. Thompson, *Globalization in Question* (Cambridge, Polity, 1999); Hirst, 'Between the local and the global: democracy in the twenty-first century'.

52  See J. Dryzek, *The Politics of the Earth* (Oxford, Oxford University Press, 1997); E. Laferriere and P. J. Stoett, *International Relations and Ecological Thought* (London, Routledge, 1999).

53  J. H. Mittleman, *The Globalization Syndrome* (Princeton, Princeton University Press, 2000).

54  Dahl, 'Can international organizations be democratic?'.

55  See D. J. Elkins, *Beyond Sovereignty: Territory and Political Economy in the Twenty First Century* (Toronto, University of Toronto Press, 1995); M. Castells, *End of the Millennium* (Oxford, Blackwell, 1998); Clark, *Globalization and International Relations Theory*; Held et al., *Global Transformations: Politics, Economics and Culture*; Mittleman, *The Globalization Syndrome*.

56  See R. Devetak, 'Incomplete states: theories and practices of statecraft', in J. MacMillan and A. Linklater (eds), *Boundaries in Question* (London, Frances Pinter, 1995), pp. 19–39; Linklater, *The Transformation of Political Community*.

57  Linklater, *The Transformation of Political Community*.

58  D. Held, 'The changing contours of political community', in B. Holden (ed.), *Global Democracy: Key Debates* (London, Routledge, 2000), pp. 17–31.

59  See M. Walzer, *Thick and Thin: Moral Argument at Home and Abroad* (London, University of Notre Dame Press, 1994).

60  See Gill, 'Globalization, market civilization, and disciplinary neo-liberalism'; D. J. Elazar, *Constitutionalizing Globalization* (Boston, Rowman and Littlefield, 1998).

61  G. R. Shell, 'Trade legalism and international relations theory: an analysis of the WTO', *Duke Law Journal* 44, 5 (1995): 829–927.

62  J. Crawford, *Democracy in International Law* (Cambridge, Cambridge University Press, 1994).

63  Mayall, 'Democracy and international society', p. 64.

64  Held, *Democracy and the Global Order*.

65  See R. O'Brien et al., *Contesting Global Governance: Multilateral Economic Institutions and Global Social Movements* (Cambridge, Cambridge University Press, 2000); J. A. Scholte, *Globalization: A Critical Introduction* (London, Macmillan, 2000).

66  N. Woods, 'Good governance in international organization', *Global Governance*, 5 (1999): 39–61.

67  See Shell, 'Trade legalism and international relations theory'; and A. McGrew, 'The WTO: technocracy or banana republic?', in A. Taylor and C. Thomas (eds), *Global Trade and Global Social Issues* (London, Routledge, 1999), pp. 197–216.

68  Dahl, 'Can international organizations be democratic?'.

69  Woods, 'Good governance in international organization'.

70  T. G. Weiss and L. Gordenker (eds), *NGOs, the UN, and Global Governance* (London, Lynne Rienner, 1996).

71  S. Gill, 'Economic globalization and the internationalization of authority: limits and contradictions', *GeoForum* 23, 3 (1992): 269–83; and Cox, 'Globalization, multilateralism and democracy'.

# 44

# Cosmopolitanism: Taming Globalization

## David Held

[ . . . ]

How should cosmopolitanism be understood [in a global age]? In the first instance, cosmopolitanism can be taken as those basic values that set down standards or boundaries that no agent, whether a representative of a government, state, or civil association, should be able to cross. Focused on the claims of each person as an individual or as a member of humanity as a whole, these values espouse the idea that human beings are in a fundamental sense equal and that they deserve equal political treatment; that is, treatment based upon the equal care and consideration of their agency irrespective of the community in which they were born or brought up. After over two hundred years of nationalism and sustained nation-state formation, such values could be thought of as out of place. But such values are already enshrined in, and central to, the laws of war, human rights law, and the statute of the ICC, among many other international rules and legal arrangements [see chapter 14 in this volume].

There is a second, important sense in which cosmopolitanism defines a set of norms and legal frameworks in the here and now and not in some remote utopia. This is the sense in which cosmopolitanism defines forms of political regulation and law-making that create powers, rights, and constraints that transcend the claims of nation-states and have far-reaching consequences in principle. This is the domain between national and global law and regulation – the space between domestic law, which regulates the relations between a state and its citizens, and traditional international law, which applies primarily to states and interstate relations (Eleftheriadis 2000). This space is already filled by a host of legal regulations, from the plethora of legal instruments of the EU and the international human rights regime as a global framework for promoting rights, to the diverse agreements of the arms control system and environmental regimes. Cosmopolitanism is not, thus, made up of political ideals for another age but embedded in rule systems and institutions that have already transformed state sovereignty in many ways.

Yet the precise sense in which these developments constitute a form of "cosmopolitanism" remains to be clarified, especially given that the ideas of cosmopolitanism have a complex history from the Stoics to contemporary political philosophy. For my purposes here, cosmopolitanism can be taken as the moral and political outlook that offers the best prospects of overcoming the problems and limits of classic and liberal sovereignty [see chapters 42 and 43 in this volume]. It builds upon some of the strengths of the liberal international order, particularly its commitment to universal standards, human rights, and democratic values that apply, in principle, to each and all. It specifies, in addition, a set of general principles upon which all could act (O'Neill 1991, 1996); for these are principles that can be universally shared and can form the basis for the protection and nurturing of each person's equal interest in the determination of the institutions that govern his or her life.

## Cosmopolitan Principles

What are these principles? Seven are paramount. They are the principles of:

1   equal worth and dignity;
2   active agency;
3   personal responsibility and accountability;
4   consent;
5   reflexive deliberation and collective decision-making through voting procedures;
6   inclusiveness and subsidiarity;
7   avoidance of serious harm and the amelioration of urgent need.

The meaning of these principles needs unpacking in order that their implications can be clarified for the nature and form of political community today. An account of each will be built up, explaining its core concerns and setting out elements of its justification. Inevitably, given the length of an article, this will not amount to a definitive exposition. It will, however, offer an elucidation of what cosmopolitanism should mean in contemporary circumstances.

The first principle recognizes simply that everyone has an equal moral status in the world. It might seem a weak principle as it is currently formulated, in that it does not generate much specific content. But it is a basic constitutive principle specifying that all people are of equal moral significance and should enjoy, in principle, equal consideration of their interests. Without the acknowledgment of this principle, there would be no basis for a cosmopolitan outlook.

It should be acknowledged from the outset that this formulation of "moral personality" is intertwined with liberalism and the Enlightenment, although its roots stretch back much further (see Nussbaum 1997). Its origins are clearly tied to particular traditions and places. But this fact alone does not invalidate the egalitarian conception of the moral worth of persons. To conceive of people as having equal moral value is to make a general claim about the basic units of the world comprising persons as free and equal beings (see Kuper 2000). This broad position runs counter to the common view that the world comprises fundamentally contested conceptions of the moral worth of the individual and the nature of autonomy. It does so because, to paraphrase (and adapt) Bruce Ackerman, there is no Islamic nation without a woman who insists on equal liberties, no Confucian society without a man who denies the need for deference, and no developing country without a person who yearns for a predictable pattern of meals to help sustain his or her life projects (see Ackerman 1994, 382–3). Principle 1 is the basis for articulating the equal worth and liberty of all humans, wherever they were born or brought up. It is the basis of underwriting the liberty of others, not of obliterating it. Its concern is with the irreducible moral status of each and every person – the acknowledgment of which links directly to the possibility of self-determination and the capacity to make independent choices. Or, as Nussbaum put it, "one should always behave so as to treat with equal respect the dignity of reason and moral choice in each and every human being" (1997, 31).

The second principle recognizes that, if principle 1 is to be universally recognized and accepted, then human agency cannot be understood merely as the product of coercive forces or as the passive embodiment of fate; rather, human agency must be conceived as the ability to act otherwise – the ability not just to accept but to shape human community in the context of the choices of others. Active agency connotes the capacity of human beings to reason self-consciously, to be self-reflective, and to be self-determining. It involves the ability to deliberate, judge, choose, and act upon different possible courses of action in private as well as public life. It places at its center the capability of persons to choose freely, to enter into self-chosen obligations, and to enjoy the underlying conditions for the reflexive constitution of their activities.[1]

The active agency of each must recognize and coexist with the active agency of all others. Principle 2 affirms that all human beings must be able to enjoy the pursuit of activity without the risk of arbitrary or unjust interference while recognizing that this liberty applies to everyone. The principle of active agency bestows both opportunities and duties – opportunities to act (or not as the case may be) and duties to ensure that independent action does not curtail and infringe upon the action possibilities of others (unless, of course, sanctioned by negotiation or consent: see below). Active agency is a capacity both to make and pursue claims and to have such claims made and pursued in relation to oneself. Each person has an equal interest in active agency or self-determination.

The connotations of principles 1 and 2 cannot be grasped fully unless supplemented by principle 3: the principle of personal responsibility and accountability. At its most basic, this principle can be understood to mean that it is inevitable that people will choose different cultural, social, and economic projects and that such differences need to be both recognized and accepted. People develop their skills and talents differently and enjoy different forms of ability and specialized competency. That they fare differently, and that many of these differences arise from a voluntary choice on their part, should be welcomed and accepted (see Barry 1998, 147–9). These prima facie legitimate differences of choice and outcome have to be distinguished from unacceptable structures of difference that reflect conditions that prevent or partially prevent the pursuit of self-chosen activities for some (Held 1995, 201–6). In particular, actors have to be aware of and accountable for the consequences of actions, direct or indirect, intended or unintended, that may restrict or delimit the choices of others – choices that may become highly constrained for certain groups who have had no role in or responsibility for this outcome. In other words, it is important to recognize that actors (and social processes) may shape and determine the autonomy of others without their participation, agreement, or consent.

Under such circumstances, there is an obligation to ensure that those who are "choice-determining" for some people (who, in turn, risk becoming "choice-takers") are fully accountable for their activities. If people's equal interest in principles 1 and 2 is to be safeguarded, it means giving close attention to those groups of people who become vulnerable or disabled by social institutions from fully participating in the determination of their own lives. Individuals, thus, have both personal responsibility rights as well as personal responsibility obligations. The freedom of action of each person must be one of accommodation to the liberties (and potential liberties) of others. The obligations taken on in this context cannot all be fulfilled with the same types of initiative (personal, social, or political) or at the same level (local, national, or global), but whatever their mode of realization, all such efforts can be related to one common denominator: the concern to discharge obligations we all take on by virtue of the claims we make for the recognition of personal responsibility rights (cf. Raz 1986, chs. 14, 15, esp. 407–8, 415–17).

Principle 4 recognizes that a commitment to equal worth and personal responsibility requires a noncoercive process in and through which people can pursue and negotiate their interconnections, interdependence, and difference. Interlocking lives, projects, and communities require forms of deliberative procedures and decision-making that take account of each person's equal interest in such processes. The principle of consent constitutes the basis of collective agreement and governance. When coercion and force take the place of deliberative and consensual mechanisms, discussion is halted and conflict settlements are typically made in favor of sectional interests. Against this, the idea of self-determining agency must acknowledge that, if it is to be equally effective for all, people should be able to participate on a free and equal basis in a process in which their consent (or lack of it) can be registered in the government of their collective affairs.

Participation in a process of consent requires that all people enjoy an equality of status with respect to the basic decision-making institutions of relevant political communities. Agreed judgment about rules, laws, and policies should ideally follow from public debate and the "force of the better argument" – not from the intrusive outcome of nondiscursive elements and forces (Habermas 1973; Held 1995, ch. 7). It might seem that, ideally, collective decisions should follow from the "will of all." However, principles 4 and 5 must be interpreted together. For principle 5 acknowledges that while a legitimate public decision is one that results from "the deliberation of all," this needs to be linked with voting at the decisive stage of collective decision-making and with the procedures and mechanisms of majority rule (see Manin 1987). The will of all is too strong a requirement of collective decision-making and the basis on which minorities (of even one) can block or forestall public responses to key issues. The deliberation of all recognizes the importance of inclusiveness in the process of consent, as required by principle 4, while interpreting this to mean that an inclusive process of participation can coexist with a decision-making procedure that allows outcomes that accrue the greatest support (Dahl 1989).[2] If people are marginalized or fall outside this framework, they are disadvantaged not primarily because they have less than others in this instance, but because they can participate less in the processes and institutions that govern their lives. It is their "impaired agency" that becomes the focus of concern and the proper target for compensatory measures (Doyal and Gough 1991, 95–6; see Raz 1986, 227–40).

Principles 4 and 5 depend for their efficacy on their entrenchment in a political community or communities. During the period in which nation-states were being forged – and the territorially bound conception of democracy was consolidated – the idea of a close mesh between geography, political power, and democracy could be assumed. It seemed compelling that political power, sovereignty, democracy, and citizenship were simply and appropriately bounded by a delimited territorial space. These links were by and large taken for granted and generally unexplicated (Held 1995). Principle 6 raises issues concerning the proper scope of democracy, or democratic jurisdiction, given that the relation between decision-makers and decision-takers is not necessarily symmetrical or congruent with respect to territory [ . . . ].

The principle of inclusiveness and subsidiarity seeks to clarify the fundamental criterion for drawing proper boundaries around those who should be involved in particular domains, those who should be accountable to a particular group of people, and why. At its simplest, it states that those significantly (i.e., nontrivially) affected by public decisions, issues, or processes should, *ceteris paribus*, have an equal opportunity, directly or indirectly through elected delegates or representatives, to influence and shape them. Those affected by public decisions ought to have a say in their making (see Whelan 1983; Saward 2000). Accordingly, democracy is best located when it is closest to and involves those whose life chances and opportunities are determined by significant social processes and forces.

Principle 6 points to the necessity of both the decentralization and centralization of political power. If decision-making is decentralized as much as possible, it maximizes the opportunity of each person to influence the social conditions that shape his or her life. But if the decisions at issue are translocal, transnational, or transregional, then political institutions need not only to be locally based but also to have a wider scope and framework of operation. In this context, the creation of diverse sites and levels of democratic fora may be unavoidable. it may be unavoidable, paradoxically, for the very same reasons as decentralization is desirable: it creates the possibility of including people who are significantly affected by a political issue in the public (in this case, transcommunity public) sphere. If diverse peoples beyond borders are, for example, effectively stakeholders in the operation of select regional and global forces, their de facto status as members of diverse communities would need to be matched by a de jure political status, if the mechanisms and institutions that govern these political spaces are to be brought under the rubric of principle 6. Stakeholders in de facto communities and networks of local, national, regional, and global processes will be politically empowered only if they achieve the necessary complementary de jure status.

Properly understood, principle 6 should be taken to entail that decision-making should be decentralized as much as possible, maximizing each person's opportunity to influence the social conditions that shape his or her life. Concomitantly, centralization is favored if, and only if, it is the necessary basis for avoiding the exclusion of persons who are significantly affected by a political decision or outcome (Pogge 1994a, 106–9). These considerations yield, as Pogge has written, "the result that the authority to make decisions of some particular kind should rest with the democratic political process of a unit that (1) is as small as possible but still (2) includes as equals all persons significantly . . . affected by decisions of this kind" (1994a, 109).

Elsewhere, I have proposed three tests to help filter policy issues to the different levels of democratic governance: the tests of extensity, intensity, and comparative efficiency (Held 1995, ch. 10). The test of extensity assesses the range of people within and across borders who are significantly affected by a collective problem and policy question. The test of intensity examines the degree to which the latter impinges on a group of people(s) and, therefore, the degree to which regional or global initiatives are warranted. The third test – the test of comparative efficiency – is concerned to provide a means of examining whether any proposed regional or global initiative is necessary insofar as the objectives it seeks to meet cannot be realized satisfactorily by those working at "lower" levels of local or national decision-making.[3] Accordingly, the principle of inclusiveness and subsidiarity may require diverse and multiple democratic public fora for its suitable enactment. It yields the possibility of multilevel democratic governance. The ideal number of appropriate democratic jurisdictions cannot be assumed to be embraced by just one level – as it is in the theory of the liberal democratic nation-state (Held 1996, pt. 2).

Finally, principle 7 needs to be explicated: the avoidance of harm and the amelioration of urgent need. This is a principle for allocating priority to the most vital cases of need and, where possible, trumping other, less urgent public priorities until such a time as all human beings, de facto and de jure, are covered by the first six principles; that is to say, until they enjoy the moral status of universal recognition and have the means to participate in their respective political communities and in the overlapping communities of fate that shape their needs and welfare. Put more abstractly, this "participative" definition of the active agent can be defined as the necessary level of intermediate need-satisfaction required to produce the optimum use of human capacities, where the optimum is conceived in terms of the actual ability of individuals and groups to best utilize their capacities within the context of the communities that determine their life chances. "Intermediate needs" are those things that have "universal satisfier characteristics"; that is, properties, whether of goods, services, or activities, that enhance autonomy in all cultures (Doyal and Gough 1991, 162, 157). Examples of the latter are drinking water, nutritional food, appropriate housing, health care, adequate education, and economic security. If people's intermediate needs are unmet and they cannot fully participate in the sociopolitical processes that structure their opportunities, their potential for involvement in public and private life will remain unfulfilled. Their ability to make (or not make) choices and to form the course of their life projects will have been impaired, irrespective of the choices they would have made about the extent of their actual engagement.

A social provision which falls short of the potential for active agency can be referred to as a situation of manifest "harm" in that the participatory potential of individuals and groups will not have been achieved; that is to say, people would not have adequate access to effectively resourced capacities which they might make use of in particular circumstances (Sen 1999). This "participative" conception of agency denotes an "attainable" target – because the measure of optimum participation and the related conception of harm can be conceived directly in terms of the "best resource mix" or "highest standard" presently achieved in a political community (see Doyal and Gough 1991, 169). But attainable participative levels are not the same thing as the most pressing levels of vulnerability, defined by the most urgent need. It is abundantly clear that within many, if not all, communities and countries, certain needs, particularly concerning health, education, and welfare, are not universally met. The "harm" that follows from a failure to meet such needs can be denoted as "serious harm," marked as it often is by immediate, life-and-death consequences. This harm constitutes a domain of need and suffering that is both systematic and wholly unnecessary. As it is understood here, serious harm is directly avoidable harm. To maintain such a position is to take the view that capabilities and resources exist, even within the current frameworks of power and wealth, to mitigate and solve such problems. In the most basic sense, the challenges posed by avoidable suffering are "political and ethical, and possibly psychological, but do not arise from any absolute scarcity or from an absence of resources and technical capabilities" (Falk 1995, 56–7). Accordingly, if the requirements of principle 7 are to be met, law and public policies ought to be focused, in the first instance, on the prevention of serious harm; that is, the eradication of harm inflicted on people "against their will" and "without their consent" (Barry 1998, 231,

207). Such a stance would constrain the rightful range of public policy, directing the latter to those who are victims of harm, whether this be the intended or unintended outcome of social forces and relations.

The seven principles can best be thought of as falling into three clusters. The first cluster, comprising what can be called "constituting principles" (principles 1–3), sets down the fundamental organizational features of the cosmopolitan moral universe. Its crux is that each person is a subject of equal moral concern; that each person is capable of acting autonomously with respect to the range of choices before him or her; and that, in deciding how to act or which institutions to create, the claims of each person affected should be taken equally into account. Personal responsibility means in this context that actors and agents have to be aware of, and accountable for, the consequences of their actions, direct or indirect, intended or unintended, that may restrict and delimit the choices of others. The second cluster, "legitimating principles" (principles 4–6), forms the basis of translating individually initiated activity, or privately determined activities more broadly, into collectively agreed or collectively sanctioned frameworks of action or regulatory regimes. Legitimating principles are self-binding principles that make voluntariness and self-determination possible for each and all (cf. Holmes 1988). Public power can be conceived as legitimate to the degree to which principles 4, 5, and 6 are upheld. The final principle (7) lays down a framework for prioritizing need; in distinguishing vital from nonvital needs, it creates an unambiguous starting point and guiding orientation for public decisions. While this "prioritizing commitment" does not, of course, create a decision procedure to resolve all clashes of priority in politics, it clearly creates a moral framework for focusing public policy on those who are most vulnerable (see Held, *Cosmopolitanism: A Debate*, forthcoming 2004, for an elaboration of these themes).

I take cosmopolitanism ultimately to denote the ethical and political space occupied by the seven principles. It lays down the universal or organizing principles that delimit and govern the range of diversity and difference that ought to be found in public life. It discloses the proper basis or framework for the pursuit of argument, discussion, and negotiation about particular spheres of value, spheres in which local, national, and regional affiliations will inevitably be weighed.[4] However, it should not be concluded from this that the meaning of the seven principles can simply be specified once and for all. For while cosmopolitanism affirms principles that are universal in their scope, it recognizes, in addition, that the precise meaning of these is always fleshed out in situated discussions; in other words, that there is an inescapable hermeneutic complexity in moral and political affairs that will affect how the seven principles are actually interpreted, and the weight granted to special ties and other practical-political issues. I call this mix of regulative principles and interpretative activity "framed pluralism" or a "layered" cosmopolitan position (cf. Tully 1995). This cosmopolitan point of view builds on principles that all could reasonably assent to, while recognizing the irreducible plurality of forms of life (Habermas 1996). Thus, on the one hand, the position upholds certain basic egalitarian ideas – those that emphasize equal worth, equal respect, equal consideration, and so on – and, on the other, it acknowledges that the elucidation of their meaning cannot be pursued independently of an ongoing dialogue in public life. Hence there can be no adequate institutionalization of equal rights and duties without a corresponding institutionalization of national and transnational forms of public debate, democratic participation, and accountability

(McCarthy 1999; and see below). The institutionalization of cosmopolitan principles requires the entrenchment of democratic public realms.

## Cosmopolitan Law and Authority

Against this background, the nature and form of cosmopolitan law can begin to be addressed. In the first instance, cosmopolitan law can be understood as a form of law that entrenches the seven principles. If these principles were to be systematically entrenched as the foundation of law, the conditions for the possibility of the cosmopolitan regulation of public life could initially be set down. For the principles specify the organizational basis of legitimate public power. Political power becomes legitimate power in the cosmopolitan doctrine when, and only when, it is entrenched and constituted by these cosmopolitan elements.

Within the framework of cosmopolitan law, the idea of rightful authority, which has been so often connected to the state and particular geographical domains, has to be reconceived and recast. Sovereignty can be stripped away from the idea of fixed borders and territories and thought of as, in principle, an attribute of basic cosmopolitan democratic law which can be drawn upon and enacted in diverse realms, from local associations and cities to states and wider global networks. Cosmopolitan law demands the subordination of regional, national, and local "sovereignties" to an overarching legal framework, but within this framework associations may be self-governing at diverse levels (Held 1995, 234).

Clear contrasts with the classic and liberal regimes of sovereignty follow [see chapter 14 in this volume]. Within the terms of classic sovereignty, the idea of the modern polity is associated directly with the idea of the state – the supreme power operating in a delimited geographic realm. The state has preeminent jurisdiction over a unified territorial area – a jurisdiction supervised and implemented by territorially anchored institutions. While the notion of the state within the frame of classic sovereignty is associated with an unchecked and overarching supreme power, in the liberal conception a legitimate political power is one marked by an impersonal, legally circumscribed structure of power, delimited nationally and (increasingly) internationally. The geopolitics and geo-economics of the liberal international sovereign order are fierce, but they are locked, at least in principle, into the universal human rights regime and the growing standards of democratic governance. Within the cosmopolitan framework, by contrast, the political authority of states is but one moment in a complex, overlapping regime of political authority; legitimate political power in this framework embeds states in a complex network of authority relations, where networks are regularized or patterned interactions between independent but interconnected political agents, nodes of activity, or sites of political power (Modelski 1972; Mann 1986; Castells 1996). Cosmopolitan sovereignty comprises networked realms of public authority shaped and delimited by cosmopolitan law. Cosmopolitan sovereignty is sovereignty stripped away from the idea of fixed borders and territories governed by states alone, and is instead thought of as frameworks of political regulatory relations and activities, shaped and formed by an overarching cosmopolitan legal framework.

In this conception, the nation-state "withers away." But this is *not* to suggest that states and national democratic polities become redundant. Rather, states would no longer be regarded as the sole centers of legitimate power within their borders, as is already the case in diverse settings (see Held et al. 1999, "Conclusion"). States need to be articulated with and relocated within an overarching cosmopolitan framework. Within this framework, the laws and rules of the nation-state would become but one focus for legal development, political reflection, and mobilization.

Under these conditions, people would in principle come to enjoy multiple citizenships – political membership, that is, in the diverse political communities that significantly affect them. In a world of overlapping communities of fate, individuals would be citizens of their immediate political communities and of the wider regional and global networks that impact upon their lives. This overlapping cosmopolitan polity would be one that in form and substance reflects and embraces the diverse forms of power and authority that operate within and across borders.

## Institutional Requirements

The institutional requirements of a cosmopolitan polity are many and various. In thinking about the pertinence and efficacy of cosmopolitanism to international legal and political arrangements, it is helpful to break down these requirements into a number of different dimensions. All relate to the idea of cosmopolitanism but function analytically and substantively at different levels, ranging from the legal and the political to the economic and the sociocultural. Four institutional dimensions of cosmopolitanism will be set out below and related to the key recurring problems embedded in the liberal international order (see [chapter 14 in this volume]). Each of the different dimensions can contribute to an expansion of the resources necessary to move beyond these problems and, eventually, to produce a satisfactory elucidation of cosmopolitan sovereignty.

## Legal cosmopolitanism

Legal cosmopolitanism explores the tension between legal claims made on behalf of the states systems and those made on behalf of an alternative organizing principle of world order in which all persons have equivalent rights and duties (Pogge 1994a, 90ff.). It posits an ideal of a global legal order in which people can enjoy an equality of status with respect to the fundamental institutions of the legal system. At the center of legal cosmopolitanism is *legalis homo*, someone free to act by law, free to ask for and expect the law's protection, free to sue and be sued in certain courts, but who does not directly make or determine the law (Pocock 1995, 36ff.). The focus of *legalis homo* is equal legal standing and personal rights.

Legal cosmopolitanism is universalizing and potentially inclusive. It is not, as one commentator usefully put it, "tied to a particular collective identity, or membership of a demos" (Cohen 1999, 249). It can be deployed to create the basis for the equal treatment of all, the entrenchment of a universal set of rights and obligations, and the impartial delimitation of individual and collective action within the organizations and associations of state, economy, and civil society (Held 1995, ch. 12). As such, it is a resource to help resolve the challenges posed by asymmetries of power, national policy spillovers, and overlapping communities of fate.

The institutional requirements of legal cosmopolitanism include:

> The entrenchment of cosmopolitan democratic law; a new "thick" charter of rights and obligations embracing political, social, and economic power.
>
> An interconnected global legal system, embracing elements of criminal, commercial, and civil law.
>
> Submission to ICJ and ICC jurisdiction; creation of a new international human rights court, and further development of regional human rights institutions.

## Political cosmopolitanism

Without complementary forms of law-making and enforcement, however, there is no reason to think that the agenda of *legalis homo* will automatically mesh with that of the protection of equal membership in the public realm and the requirements of active citizenship. For this, legal cosmopolitanism needs to be related to political cosmopolitanism. Political cosmopolitanism involves advocacy of regional and global governance and the creation of political organizations and mechanisms that would provide a framework of regulation and law enforcement across the globe. Although cosmopolitan positions often differ on the precise nature and form of such a framework, they are generally committed to the view that political cosmopolitanism entails that states should have a somewhat, and in some areas a markedly, diminished role in comparison with institutions and organizations of regional and global governance.

From this perspective, the rights and duties of individuals can be nurtured adequately only if, in addition to their proper articulation in national constitutions, they are underwritten by regional and global regimes, laws, and institutions. The promotion of the political good and of principles of egalitarian political participation and justice are rightly pursued at regional and global levels. Their conditions of possibility are inextricably linked to the establishment and development of transnational organizations and institutions of regional and global governance. The latter are a necessary basis of cooperative relations and just conduct.

Political cosmopolitanism, accordingly, takes as its starting point a world of "overlapping communities of fate." In the classic and liberal regimes of sovereignty, nation-states largely dealt with issues that spilled over boundaries by pursuing "reasons of state," backed ultimately by coercive means. But this power logic is singularly inappropriate to resolve the many complex issues, from economic regulation to resource depletion and environmental degradation, that engender an intermeshing of national fortunes. Recognizing the complex structures of an interconnected world, political cosmopolitanism views certain issues as appropriate for delimited (spatially demarcated) political spheres (the city, state, or region), while it sees others – such as the environment, world health, and economic regulation – as needing new, more extensive institutions to address them. Deliberative and decision-making centers beyond national territories are appropriately situated (see principle 6, p. 530) when the cosmopolitan principles of equal worth, impartial treatment, and so on can be properly redeemed only in a transnational context; when those significantly affected by a public matter constitute a cross-border or transnational grouping; and when "lower" levels of decision-making cannot manage and discharge satisfactorily transnational or international policy questions. Only a cosmopolitan political outlook can ultimately accommodate itself to the political challenges of a more global era, marked by policy spillovers, overlapping communities of fate, and growing global inequalities.

The institutional requirements of political cosmopolitanism include:

Multilayered governance, diffused authority.
A network of democratic fora from the local to the global.
Enhanced political regionalization.
Establishment of an effective, accountable, international military force for last-resort use of coercive power in defense of cosmopolitan law.

## Economic cosmopolitanism

Economic cosmopolitanism enters an important proviso about the prospects of political cosmopolitanism, for unless the disjuncture between economic and political power is addressed, resources will remain too skewed to ensure that formally proclaimed liberties and rights can be enjoyed in practice by many; in short, "nautonomy" will prevail – the asymmetrical production and distribution of life-chances, eroding the possibilities of equal participative opportunities and placing artificial limits on the creation of a common structure of political action (Held 1995, ch. 8). At issue is what was earlier referred to as the tangential impact of the liberal international order on the regulation of economic power and market mechanisms and on the flourishing socio-economic inequalities that exist side by side with the spread of liberal democracy. A bridge has to be built between human rights law and international economic law, between a formal commitment to the impartial treatment of all and a geopolitics driven too often by sectional economic interests, and between cosmopolitan principles and cosmopolitan practices.

This understanding provides a rationale for a politics of intervention in economic life – not to control and regulate markets per se, but to provide the basis for self-determination and active agency. Economic cosmopolitanism connotes the enhancement of people's economic capacities to pursue their own projects – individual and collective – within the constraints of community and overlapping communities of fate, that is, within the constraints created by taking each human being's interest in declared liberties equally seriously. It thus specifies good reasons for being committed to reforming and regulating all those forms of economic power that compromise the possibility of equal worth and active agency. It aims to establish fair conditions for economic competition and cooperation as the background context of the particular choices of human agents (see Pogge 1994b).

It follows from this that political intervention in the economy is warranted when it is driven by the objective of ensuring that the basic requirements of individual autonomy are met within and outside economic organizations. Moreover, it is warranted when it is driven by the need to overcome those consequences of economic interaction, whether intended or unintended, that generate damaging externalities such as environmental pollution threatening to health. The roots of such intervention lie in the indeterminacy of the market system itself (see Sen 1985, 19). Market economies can function in a manner commensurate with self-determination and equal freedom only if this indeterminacy is addressed systematically and if the conditions of the possibility of self-governance are met.

In addition, a transfer system has to be established within and across communities to allow resources to be generated to alleviate the most pressing cases of avoidable economic suffering and harm. If such measures involved the creation of new forms of regional and global taxation – for instance, a consumption tax on energy use, or a tax on carbon emissions, or a global tax on the extraction of resources within national territories, or a tax on the GNP of countries above a certain level of development, or a transaction tax on the volume of financial turnover in foreign exchange markets – independent (nonnational) funds could be established to meet the most extreme cases of need. Sustained social framework investments in the conditions of autonomy (sanitation, health, housing, education, and so on) could then follow. Moreover, the raising of such funds could also be the basis for a critical step in the realization of political cosmopolitanism: the creation of an independent flow of economic resources to fund regional and global governance, a vital move in removing the latter's dependency on leading democratic princes and the most powerful countries.

The institutional requirements of economic cosmopolitanism embrace:

Reframing market mechanisms and leading sites of economic power.
Global taxation mechanisms.
Transfer of resources to the most economically vulnerable in order to protect and enhance their agency.

## Cultural cosmopolitanism

Cultural cosmopolitanism is the capacity to mediate between national traditions, communities of fate, and alternative styles of life. It encompasses the possibility of dialogue with the traditions and discourses of others with the aim of expanding the horizons of one's own framework of meaning and prejudice. Political agents who can "reason from the point of view of others" are likely to be better equipped to resolve, and resolve fairly, the new and challenging transboundary issues and processes that create overlapping communities of fate. The development of this kind of cultural cosmopolitanism depends on the recognition by growing numbers of peoples of the increasing interconnectedness of political communities in diverse domains, including the economic, cultural, and environmental; and on the development of an understanding of overlapping "collective fortunes" that require collective solutions – locally, nationally, regionally, and globally.

The formation of cultural cosmopolitanism has been given an enormous impetus by the sheer scale, intensity, speed, and volume of global cultural communication, which today has reached unsurpassed levels (see Held et al. 1999, ch. 7). Global communication systems are transforming relations between physical locales and social circumstances, altering the "situational geography" of political and social life (Meyrowitz 1985). In these circumstances, the traditional link between "physical setting" and "social situation" is broken. Geographical boundaries can be overcome as individuals and groups experience events and developments far afield. Moreover, new understandings, commonalties, and frames of meaning can be elaborated without direct contact between people. As such, they can serve to detach, or disembed, identities from particular times, places, and traditions, and can have a "pluralizing impact" on identity formation, producing a variety of options that are "less fixed or unified" (Hall 1992).

While everyone has a local life, the ways people make sense of the world are now increasingly interpenetrated by developments and processes from diverse settings. Hybrid cultures and transnational media organizations have made significant inroads into national cultures and national identities. The cultural context of national traditions is transformed as a result.

Cultural cosmopolitanism emphasizes "the fluidity of individual identity, people's remarkable capacity to forge new identities using materials from diverse cultural sources, and to flourish while so doing" (Scheffler 1999, 257). It celebrates, as Rushdie put it, "hybridity, impurity, intermingling, the transformation that comes of new and unexpected combinations of human beings, cultures, ideas, politics, movies, songs" (quoted in Waldron 1992, 751). But it is the ability to stand outside a singular cultural location (the location of birth, land, upbringing, conversion) and to mediate traditions that lies at its core. However, there are no guarantees about the extent to which such an outlook will prevail. For it has to survive and jostle for recognition alongside often deeply held national, ethnic, and religious traditions (see Held and McGrew 2000, 13–18 and pt. 3). It is a cultural and cognitive orientation, not an inevitability of history.

The institutional requirements of cultural cosmopolitanism include:

> Recognition of increasing interconnectedness of political communities in diverse domains, including the social, economic, and environmental.
>
> Development of an understanding of overlapping "collective fortunes" that require collective solutions – locally, nationally, regionally, and globally.
>
> The celebration of difference, diversity, and hybridity while learning how to "reason from the point of view of others" and mediate traditions.

## Concluding Reflections

The core of the cosmopolitan project involves reconceiving legitimate political authority in a manner that disconnects it from its traditional anchor in fixed territories and instead articulates it as an attribute of basic cosmopolitan democratic arrangements or basic cosmopolitan law which can, in principle, be entrenched and drawn upon in diverse associations. Significantly, this process of disconnection has already begun, as political authority and forms of governance are diffused "below," "above," and "alongside" the nation-state.

Recent history embraces many different forms of globalization. There is the rise of neoliberal deregulation so much emphasized from the mid-1970s. But there is also the growth of major global and regional institutions, from the UN to the EU. The latter are remarkable political innovations in the context of state history. The UN remains a creature of the interstate system; however, it has, despite all its limitations, developed an innovative system of global governance which delivers significant international public goods – from air-traffic control and the management of telecommunications to the control of contagious diseases, humanitarian relief for refugees, and some protection of the environmental commons. The EU, in remarkably little time, has taken Europe from the disarray of the post-Second World War era to a world in which sovereignty is pooled across a growing number of areas of common concern. Again, despite its many limitations, the EU represents a highly innovative form of governance that creates a framework of collaboration for addressing transborder issues.

In addition, it is important to reflect upon the growth in recent times of the scope and content of international law. Twentieth-century forms of international law have [ ... ] taken the first steps toward a framework of universal law, law that circumscribes and delimits the political power of individual states. In principle, states are no longer able to treat their citizens as they think fit. Moreover, the twentieth century saw the beginnings of significant efforts to reframe markets – to use legislation to alter the background conditions and operations of firms in the marketplace. While efforts in this direction failed in respect of the North Atlantic Free Trade Agreement, the "Social Chapter" of the Maastricht Agreement, for instance, embodies principles and rules that are compatible with the idea of restructuring aspects of markets. While the provisions of this agreement fall far short of what is ultimately necessary if judged by the standards of a cosmopolitan conception of law and regulation, they set down new forms of regulation that can be built upon.

Furthermore, there are, of course, new regional and global transnational actors contesting the terms of globalization – not just corporations but new social movements. These are the "new" voices of an emergent "transnational civil society," heard, for instance, at the Rio Conference on the Environment, the Cairo Conference on Population Control, the Beijing Conference on Women, and at the "battles" of Seattle, Washington, Genoa, and elsewhere. In short, there are tendencies at work seeking to create new forms of public life and new ways of debating regional and global issues.

These changes are all in early stages of development, and there are no guarantees that the balance of political interests will allow them to develop. Nor are there any guarantees that those who push for change will accept the necessity of deliberation with all key stakeholders and will recognize the time it takes to develop or create institutions. But the changes under way point in the direction of establishing new modes of holding transnational power systems to account – that is, they help open up the possibility of a cosmopolitan order. Together, they form an anchor on which a more accountable form of globalization can be established.

## Notes

1  The principle of active agency does not make any assumption about the extent of self-knowledge or reflexivity. Clearly, this varies and can be shaped by both unacknowledged conditions and unintended consequences of action (see Giddens 1984). It does, however, assume that the course of agency is a course that includes choice and that agency itself is, in essence, defined by the capacity to act otherwise.

2  Minorities clearly need to be protected in this process. The rights and obligations entailed by principles 4 and 5 have to be compatible with the protection of each person's equal interest in principles 1, 2, and 3 – an interest which follows from each person's recognition as being of equal worth, with an equal capacity to act and to account for his or her actions. Majorities ought not to be able to impose themselves arbitrarily upon others; there must always be institutional arrangements to safeguard the individuals' or minorities' position, that is, protective rules and procedures. The principles of consent and reflexive deliberation have, in this context, to be understood against the background specified by the first three principles; the latter frame the basis of their operation. Together, these principles can form the essential ingredients – the constitutive and self-binding rules and mechanisms – of public life, allowing it to function and reproduce over time.

3  The criteria that can be used to pursue an inquiry into comparative efficacy include the availability of alternative local and national legislative or administrative means, the cost of

a proposed action, and the possible consequences of such action for the constituent parts of an area (see Neunreither 1993).

4 Contemporary cosmopolitans, it should be acknowledged, are divided about the demands that cosmopolitanism lays upon the individual and, accordingly, upon the appropriate framing of the necessary background conditions for a "common" or "basic" structure of individual action and social activity. Among them there is agreement that in deciding how to act or which rules or regulations ought to be established, the claims of each person affected should be weighed equally – "no matter where they live, which society they belong to, or how they are connected to us" (Miller 1998, 165). The principle of egalitarian individualism is regarded as axiomatic. But the moral weight granted to this principle depends heavily upon the precise modes of interpretation of other principles (see Nussbaum 1996; Barry 1998; Miller 1998; Scheffler 1999).

## References

Ackerman, B. (1994) Political Liberalism. *Journal of Philosophy* 91: 364–86.

Barry, B. (1998) International Society from a Cosmopolitan Perspective. In D. Mapel and T. Nardin (eds), *International Society: Diverse Ethical Perspectives*, Princeton, NJ: Princeton University Press.

Castells, M. (1996) *The Rise of the Network Society*. Oxford: Blackwell.

Cohen, Jean (1999) Changing Paradigms of Citizenship and the Exclusiveness of the *Demos*. *International Sociology* 14: 245–68.

Dahl, R. A. (1989) *Democracy and Its Critics*. New Haven, CT: Yale University Press.

Doyal, L., and Gough, I. (1991) *A Theory of Human Need*. London: Macmillan.

Eleftheriadis, P. (2000) The European Constitution and Cosmopolitan Ideals. *Columbia Journal of European Law* 7: 21–39.

Falk, R. (1995) *On Humane Governance: Toward a New Global Politics*. Cambridge: Polity Press.

Giddens, A. (1984) *The Constitution of Society*. Cambridge: Polity Press.

Habermas, J. (1973) Wahrheitstheorien. In H. Fahrenbach (ed.), *Wirklichkeit und Reflexion*, Pfüllingen, Germany: Neske.

Habermas, J. (1996) *Between Facts and Norms: Contributions to a Discourse Theory of Law and Democracy*. Cambridge: Polity Press.

Hall, S. (1992) The Question of Cultural Identity. In S. Hall, D. Held, and A. McGrew (eds), *Modernity and its Futures*, Cambridge: Polity Press.

Held, D. (1995) *Democracy and the Global Order: From the Modern State to Cosmopolitan Governance*. Cambridge: Polity Press.

Held, D. (1996) *Models of Democracy*, 2nd edn. Cambridge: Polity Press.

Held, D. (forthcoming) *Cosmopolitanism* (Cambridge: Polity Press).

Held, D., and McGrew, A. (eds) (2000) *The Global Transformations Reader*. Cambridge: Polity Press.

Held, D., and McGrew, A., Goldblatt, D., and Perraton, J. (1999) *Global Transformations: Politics, Economics and Culture*. Cambridge: Polity Press.

Holmes, S. (1988) Precommitment and the Paradox of Democracy. In J. Elster and R. Slagstad (eds), *Constitutionalism and Democracy*, Cambridge: Cambridge University Press.

Kuper, A. (2000) Rawlsian Global Justice: Beyond *The Law of Peoples* to a Cosmopolitan Law of Persons. *Political Theory* 28: 640–74.

McCarthy, T. (1999) On Reconciling Cosmopolitan Unity and National Diversity. *Public Culture* 11: 1, 175–208.

Manin, B. (1987) On Legitimacy and Political Deliberation. *Political Theory* 15: 3.

Mann, M. (1986) *The Sources of Social Power*, vol. 1. Cambridge: Cambridge University Press.

Meyrowitz, J. (1985) *No Sense of Place*. Oxford: Oxford University Press.

Miller, D. (1998) The Limits of Cosmopolitan Justice. In D. Mapel and T. Nardin (eds), *International Society: Diverse Ethical Perspectives*, Princeton, NJ: Princeton University Press.

Modelski, G. (1972) *Principles of World Politics*. New York: Free Press.

Neunreither, K. (1993) Subsidiarity as a Guiding Principle for European Community Activities. *Government and Opposition* 28: 2.

Nussbaum, M. C. (1996) Patriotism and Cosmopolitanism. In J. Cohen (ed.), *For Love of Country: Debating the Limits of Patriotism*, Boston: Beacon Press.

Nussbaum, M. C. (1997) Kant and Cosmopolitanism. In J. Bohman and M. Lutz-Bachmann (eds), *Perpetual Peace: Essays on Kant's Cosmopolitan Ideal*, Cambridge, MA: MIT Press.

O'Neill, O. (1991) Transnational Justice. In D. Held (ed.), *Political Theory Today*, Cambridge: Polity Press.

O'Neill, O. (1996) *Towards Justice as Virtue*. Cambridge: Cambridge University Press.

Pocock, J. G. A. (1995) The Ideal of Citizenship since Classical Times. In R. Beiner (ed.), *Theorizing Citizenship*, Albany, NY: State University of New York Press.

Pogge, T. (1994a) Cosmopolitanism and Sovereignty. In C. Brown (ed.), *Political Restructuring in Europe: Ethical Perspectives*, London: Routledge.

Pogge, T. (1994b) An Egalitarian Law of Peoples. *Philosophy and Public Affairs* 23: 195–224.

Raz, J. (1986) *The Morality of Freedom*. Oxford: Oxford University Press.

Rushdie, S. (1990) In Good Faith. In *The Independent* (February 11).

Saward, M. (2000) A Critique of Held. In B. Holden (ed.), *Global Democracy*, London: Routledge.

Scheffler, S. (1999) Conceptions of Cosmopolitanism. *Utilitas* 11: 255–76.

Sen, A. (1985) The Moral Standing of the Market. *Social Philosophy and Policy* 2: 2.

Sen, A. (1999) *Development as Freedom*. Oxford: Oxford University Press.

Tully, J. (1995) *Strange Multiplicity: Constitutionalism in an Age of Diversity*. Cambridge: Cambridge University Press.

Waldron, J. (1992) Minority Cultures and the Cosmopolitan Alternative. *University of Michigan Journal of Law Reform* 25: 751–92.

Whelan, F. (1983) Prologue: Democratic Theory and the Boundary Problem. In J. R. Pennock and R. W. Chapman (eds), *Nomos XXV: Liberal Democracy*, New York and London: New York University Press.

# 45

# Can International Organizations be Democratic? A Skeptic's View

*Robert A. Dahl*

Can international organizations, institutions, or processes be democratic? I argue that they cannot be. Any argument along these lines raises the question, "What is democracy?" or, better, "What do I mean by democracy?" If I can say what democracy is, presumably I can also say what democracy is not, or to put it another way, what is not a democracy. In brief: an international organization is not and probably cannot be a democracy.[1]

## Democracy

Yet to say what democracy is and is not is far more difficult than we would like. This is so for many reasons, of which I will offer three.

First, as we all know, the term democracy has been and continues to be used indiscriminately. Although the word may be applied most frequently to a form of government, it is not restricted to forms of government. What is more, government itself is a protean term. Not only do states have governments; so also do economic enterprises, trade unions, universities, churches, voluntary associations, and other human organizations of infinite variety, from families and tribes to international organizations, economic, military, legal, criminal, and the rest. Even when the word democracy is applied to governments, and further restricted to the government of a state, the concept unfolds into several complex dimensions.[2] In usage, then, the meaning of the term is virtually unbounded – indeed so unrestricted that it has even been used to signify dictatorship.[3]

To explain why international institutions and processes will be non-democratic, I intend to consider just two of the innumerable aspects of democracy. These are democracy as a system of popular control over governmental policies and decisions, and democracy as a system of fundamental rights.

When we consider democracy from the first and probably the most familiar point of view, we interpret it as consisting of rule by the people, or rather the demos, with a government of the state that is responsive and accountable to the demos, a sovereign authority that decides important political matters either directly in popular assemblies or indirectly through its representatives, chosen by lot or, in modern democracies, by means of elections. Viewing democracy from the second point of view, we interpret it as providing an extensive body of rights. These are of at least two kinds. One consists of rights, freedoms, and opportunities that are essential to popular control and the functioning of the democratic institutions themselves, such as freedom of speech and assembly. The other consists of a broad array of rights, freedoms, and opportunities that, though arguably not strictly essential to the functioning of democratic institutions, tend to develop among a people who govern themselves democratically, such as rights to privacy, property, a minimum wage, non-discrimination in employment, and the like.

One may value democracy from either point of view, or, more likely, from both, and of course for other reasons as well. However that may be, I am going to focus mainly on the first perspective, democracy as a system of popular control over governmental policies and decisions, and I will offer several reasons for believing that whatever kind of government may prevail in international organizations it will not be recognizably democratic in that sense. The famous democratic deficit that has been so much discussed with respect to the European Union is not likely to be greatly reduced in the EU; elsewhere the deficit is likely to be far greater.

The second problem in saying what democracy is and is not is to determine how and where to locate the threshold or cut-off. It is not very useful to treat democracy as if we could specify a sharp, clear line between democracy and non-democracy. Imagine that we had two scales for democracy rather like scales for measuring temperatures. One would run from a theoretical system that is perfectly or ideally democratic to a theoretical system that is completely non-democratic; the other would run from actual or real-world systems that sufficiently meet ideal democratic criteria to be called democracies to the most extreme non-democratic systems that we actually observe in human experience. An analogy might be a thermometer used for weather and one going from absolute zero to the boiling point of water. If we were to place the two democracy scales alongside one another, systems at the top of the scale for measuring actual democracy would surely fall considerably short of the top of the scale on which we would locate an ideal democracy – and so too, no doubt, at the bottom. At what point on the scale of actual political systems are we justified in designating a political system as democratic or non-democratic? Unfortunately the transition from democracy to non-democracy is not like the freezing point of water. None the less, even if the threshold is pretty hazy, I want to argue that international systems will lie below any reasonable threshold of democracy.

A third difficulty in defining democracy arises because, in practice, all democratic systems, with the exception perhaps of a few tiny committees, allow for, indeed depend on, delegation of power and authority; the citizen body delegates some decisions to others. Size and complexity make delegation essential. Despite all their concern for maintaining the authority of the assembly, even Athenians could not avoid delegation. In modern representative democracies, or what I sometimes call polyarchies, the extent of delegation is enormous, in theory running from the demos to its elected representatives to higher executives to top administrators and on down the lengthy bureaucratic hierarchy. To what extent the demos effectively controls important final decisions has been, of course, a much disputed empirical question, not to say a crucial ideological issue. But we would agree, I think, that, in practice, delegation might be so extensive as to move a political system beyond the democratic threshold.

I believe this is very likely to be true with international organizations and institutions, including the European Union (hereafter, the EU).

## The Problem

If that judgment were shown to be justified, a democrat might say, we cannot in good conscience support such delegation of power and authority by democratic countries to international organizations and institutions. Yet this answer will not do. In both democratic theory and practice a fundamental dilemma lurks half hidden, ordinarily just out of view. Other things being more or less equal, a smaller democratic unit provides an ordinary citizen with greater opportunities to participate in governing than a larger unit. But the smaller the unit the more likely that some matters of importance to the citizen are beyond the capacity of the government to deal with effectively. To handle these broader matters, the democratic unit might be enlarged; but in doing so the capacity of the citizen to participate effectively in governing would be diminished. To put it loosely, one might say that although your government gains more control over the problem, your capacity to influence that government is diminished.

At the extreme limit, a democratic unit of, say, twenty people, could provide every member with unlimited opportunities to participate in its decisions and little or no delegation would be necessary. Yet the government would have no capacity to deal effectively with most matters that were important to the members. At the other extreme, a world government might be created in order to deal with problems of universal scope, such as poverty, hunger, health, education, and the environment. But the opportunities available to the ordinary citizen to participate effectively in the decisions of a world government would diminish to the vanishing point. To speak in this case of "delegating authority" would simply be a misleading fiction useful only to the rulers.[4]

## Optimists and Skeptics

In the latter half of the twentieth century this dilemma has reappeared because of the increasing use of international organizations, institutions, and processes to deal with matters that are beyond the effective capacities of the government of a single country. So the question arises: to what extent can the ideas and practices of democratic government be applied to international organizations, institutions, and processes? Those who believe that democracy can be extended to the international realm offer an optimistic answer. International institutions not only should be democratized but actually can be (Archibugi and Held 1995; Held 1995). An opposing view is offered by skeptics such as Philippe Schmitter (1996), who argues that even within "the emerging Europolity" (which is surely the most promising international site for democratization) a recognizably democratic political system is unlikely to develop. For reasons I am going to present here, I share Schmitter's skepticism, although I take a somewhat different path to reach a similar conclusion.

My skepticism applies not just to the European Union but even more to international organizations in general. I do not mean to say that we should reject the benefits of international organizations and institutions. The benefits may sometimes even include assistance in fostering democratization in non-democratic countries. But I believe we should openly recognize that international decision-making will not be democratic. Whether the costs as measured in democratic values are outweighed by gains as measured in other values, and perhaps even by gains in the democratization of non-democratic countries, obviously depends, among other things, on how much one values democracy. Overarching judgments are likely to be either vacuous or highly controversial. The only point I wish to press here, however, is that international policy decisions will not ordinarily be made democratically.

My argument is simple and straightforward. In democratic countries where democratic institutions and practices have been long and well established and where, as best we can tell, a fairly strong democratic political culture exists, it is notoriously difficult for citizens to exercise effective control over many key decisions on foreign affairs. What grounds have we for thinking, then, that citizens in different countries engaged in international systems can ever attain the degree of influence and control over decisions that they now exercise within their own countries?

## Foreign Affairs and Popular Control: The Standard Version

Scholars and other commentators have observed for many years that exercising popular control over foreign policy decisions is a formidable problem. Consider the United States. In the standard version[5] foreign affairs are remote from the lives, experiences, and familiar knowledge of ordinary citizens. Although a small "attentive public" may exist "before whom elite discussion and controversy takes place" (Almond 1950: 139), a great many citizens lack knowledge of foreign affairs, certainly in depth.[6] Concrete experience, personal familiarity, social and professional ties, knowledge of relevant histories, data, and trends are weak or entirely lacking and are replaced, if at all, by flickering images drawn from radio, television, or newspaper accounts. In addition, the sheer complexity of many international matters often puts them beyond the immediate capacities of many, probably most, citizens to appraise. The upshot is that crucial foreign policy decisions are generally made by policy elites without much input from or accountability to the majority of citizens.

The US decision in late 1993 to adopt NAFTA closely fits the pattern. A week before the vote on NAFTA in the House of Representatives, 79 percent of those surveyed in a CBS/*New York Times* poll were unsure or did not know whether their Congressional representative favored or opposed NAFTA. "Some Americans felt strongly about NAFTA. But the vast majority neither understood it nor cared enough about it to become well informed. As a result, public opinion was effectively neutralized on the issue and had little effect on the final outcome" (Newhouse and Mathews 1994: 31–2; see also Molyneux 1994: 28–30).

Americans are not unique. Is it realistic, for example, to expect citizens in European countries to develop informed judgments about European Monetary Union and its desirability? The editors of *The Economist* recently observed that "public debate on the subject has been dismally poor right across Europe . . . Far from engaging in argument, the pro and anti tribes ignore each other resolutely" (*The Economist* 1996: 17).

One response to the standard account might be: So what? If the average citizen is uninterested in foreign affairs and not fully competent to make informed judgments, is it not better to leave the matter to the political leaders and activists?

We can take it as axiomatic that virtually all decisions by any government, including a democratic government, are disadvantageous to some people. If they produce gains, they also result in costs. If the trade-offs in advantages and disadvantages were identical for everyone, judgments involved in making collective decisions would be roughly equivalent to those involved in making individual decisions; but the trade-offs are not the same for everyone. Typically costs and benefits are distributed unevenly among those subject to a decision. So the perennial questions arise: What is the best decision? Who can best decide? How?

A part of the perennial answer is that the proper criterion for government decisions is the public good, the general interest, the collective good, and other similar, though perhaps not strictly equivalent, formulations. But as we all know, how to define the public good and how to achieve it are formidable problems.

Proposed solutions to the problem of the public good seem to fall into two rough categories: substantive and procedural. Substantive solutions offer a criterion, such as happiness, welfare, well-being, utility, or whatever; a metric or measure that can be summed or aggregated over the persons concerned; and a distributive principle for determining what constitutes a just or justifiable allocation of the good among persons. Procedural solutions offer a process for determining and validating decisions, such as majority rule, or a full-blown democratic process, or guardianship, or judicial determination, and so on. On closer examination, however, neither substantive nor procedural solutions are sufficient; each requires the other. Because substantive solutions are not self-enacting, they require procedures for determining the substantively best outcomes; and because procedures, including democratic procedures, are means to ends, not ends in themselves, their justification depends on more than purely procedural values.

In practice all substantive solutions are contested, indeed highly contested; none commands general acceptability, except perhaps in a purely formulaic way, such as Pareto optimality or the greatest good of the greatest number. In the absence of full agreement on substantive criteria, many people in democratic countries tend to accept procedural solutions as sufficient, at least most of the time. When we disagree, they might say, then let the majority decide, if not directly then through our representatives; though to be acceptable, the majority decision must not only follow proper procedures but must also lie within some generally agreed on boundaries as to rights, liberties, minimal standards of justice, and so on.[7]

As a practical matter, the problem of determining the general good would be easier to solve in a political unit containing a highly homogeneous population. At the limit of complete homogeneity, differences in the impact of collective decisions would vanish, but of course that limit is rarely if ever reached, even in a unit as small as a family. In any case, an increase in the size of a political unit is usually accompanied by an increase in the diversity of interests, goals, and values among the people in the unit. Thus when a democratic unit is enlarged to include new territory and people, the demos is likely to become more heterogeneous. Diversity in turn tends to increase the number of possible political interests and cleavages based on differences in economic position, language, religion, region, ethnic or racial identity, culture, national affiliation, historical memories, organizational attachments, and others.

As the number of persons and the diversity of interests increase, the idea of a common good or general interest becomes ever more problematic. Earlier I mentioned some of the cognitive and emotional obstacles to popular control over foreign policy decisions. These make it harder for citizens to perceive and understand the situations, conditions, needs, wants, aims, and ends of other citizens who are distant and different from themselves in crucial respects. Even if they acquire some grasp on these matters, their incentives to act for the benefit of the distant others when it may be to their own cost or disadvantage are weak or non-existent. Beyond the boundaries of one's own intimate attachments, altruism is uncommon, and as a steady state among many people it is too feeble to be counted on. In sum, among a large group of persons with varied and conflicting ends, goals, interests, and purposes, unanimity is unattainable, disagreement on the best policy is to be expected, and civic virtue is too weak a force to override individual and group interests.[8]

If the public good on foreign affairs were rationally demonstrable, if in fine Platonic fashion the elites possessed the necessary rationality and sufficient virtue to act on their knowledge of the public good, and if ordinary citizens had no opinions or held views that demonstrably contradicted their own best interests, then a defensible argument might be made that the political leaders and activists should be entrusted with decisions on foreign affairs. But on international issues the public good is as rationally contestable as it is on domestic questions and we have no reason to believe that the views of elites are in some demonstrable sense objectively correct. Yet the weight of elite consensus and the weakness of other citizens' views means that the interests and perspectives of some, possibly a majority, are inadequately represented in decisions. Views that might be strengthened among ordinary citizens if these views were more effectively brought to their attention in political discussion and debate remain dormant. The alternatives are poorly explored among ordinary citizens, if not among the policy elites. Yet if citizens had gained a better understanding of their interests and if their views had then been more fully developed, expressed, and mobilized, the decisions might have gone another way.

These conditions probably exist more often on foreign affairs than on domestic issues. Sometimes elites predominantly favor one of the major alternatives; many citizens are confused, hold weak opinions, or have no opinions at all; and those who do have opinions may favor an alternative that the political leaders and activists oppose. So public debate is one-sided and incomplete, and in the end the views and interests of the political leaders and activists prevail.

To provide a satisfactory account of the empirical evidence bearing on this conjecture would be a large undertaking, all the more so if one attempted to compare the experiences of several democratic countries. The best I can offer are several scattered pieces of evidence:

- As I have already indicated, the US decision about NAFTA appears to fit the pattern pretty well.
- Support for European unification was markedly higher among "opinion leaders" than among non-leaders in twelve European countries from 1973–91 (Wessels 1995: 143–4, tables 7.2 and 7.3). From evidence for changes in support over time, one author concludes that:

> a system of internationalized governance such as the EC could not expect support if there were no political leaders and activists, political parties, and attentive publics who care about it. That does not turn the European integration process into a process independent of mass opinion. Quite the contrary: because support and legitimacy are necessary, élites and political actors have to work to secure them. (Wessels 1995: 162)

## The Revised Standard Version: Occasional Activation

In the standard version, the views of elites tend to prevail, particularly when they pretty much agree. But suppose that the policy on which they agree is seen to cause or threatens to cause great harm to the interests, goals, and well-being of a large number of citizens. We need only recall the Vietnam War, in which US policy was initially made almost exclusively by "the best and the brightest," the elite of the elites, until the human waste and futility of the war became so evident as to create intense public opposition *and* a broadening split among the political leaders and activists. On such occasions, political leaders and activists are sharply divided, ordinary citizens are activated, mass publics develop strong views about foreign affairs, and public opinion becomes highly influential in key foreign policy decisions (Aldrich, Sullivan, and Bordiga 1989).

It is misleading to say, for example, that Americans never become involved in foreign affairs. Answering the standard Gallup question, "What do you think is the most important problem facing this country today?" in about one-third of the 150 surveys from 1935 to 1985 Americans ranked foreign affairs highest. At least once in each of eighteen years during that fifty-year interval Americans put foreign affairs highest. Not surprisingly, the importance of foreign affairs soared during wars: World War II, Korea, Vietnam. In short, their responses were appropriate to the circumstances.[9] While support for the war effort during World War II was widespread among elites and the general public, during the wars in Korea and Vietnam elite opinion, at least in some highly influential quarters, lagged behind general public opinion.

In Europe, questions about a country's relations with the EU and its predecessor, the European Community, have led to the political activation of a large part of the electorate,[10] aroused intense passions, and produced sharp divisions within the general population, sometimes in opposition to the predominant views of the political leaders and activists. Political activation and sharp divisions were particularly visible in the referendum in Norway in 1972 on membership in the EC, in France in 1992 on ratifying the Maastricht Treaty, and in Norway and Sweden in 1994 on membership in the EU. In all four referenda, citizens disagreed as sharply in their views of what would be best for themselves and their country as they would on divisive domestic issues. Voters in the French referendum on Maastricht split almost evenly (51 percent yes to 49 percent no) along class and occupational lines.[11] By small majorities Norwegians rejected membership in the EC in a referendum in 1972 and again in the EU in 1994. In public argument, advocates of the economic, security, and cultural advantages of the EU were in conflict with opponents who tended to stress such values as democracy, absence of red-tape Brussels bureaucracy, environmental protection, welfare state values and policies, counter-culture as well as gender equality. Analysis of the vote reveals significant differences among Norwegians. "No" votes were concentrated more heavily in the northern and western periphery; in fishing and farming communities; among church members, women, and those working in primary industries or in the public sector, particularly in social and public health services. "Yes" votes were concentrated more in urbanized areas, particularly in the area around Oslo, and among voters with university education or higher incomes. Voters who identified themselves as supporters of the Christian, Agrarian, or Left Socialist parties preponderantly opposed EU membership, while both Labor and Conservative voters strongly supported it.[12] The referendum in Sweden appears to have divided voters in a somewhat similar fashion. It is worth noting, by the way, that Swedish surveys revealed that within a year the majority in favor had declined to a minority, though by then the die was cast.

The revised standard version of the influence of public opinion on foreign policy, then, would read something like this: although citizens in democratic countries are usually less interested in foreign affairs than in domestic issues, in some circumstances they can become activated and play an influential or even decisive role in key foreign policy decisions. A policy is likely to activate citizens if it causes or threatens to cause such severe harm to the interests, goals, and well-being of a large minority, or even a majority, of citizens that they become aroused in opposition, political activists arise to champion their cause, and political leaders are themselves split. The question then begins to look very much like a hard-fought domestic issue. If the threatened costs of the policy are fairly obvious, concrete, and immediate, while the promised gains are abstract, theoretical, and distant, leaders in favor of the policy may ultimately lose.

Yet even in the revised standard version, such issues are rare: in Vietnam, casualties brought the costs home while the promised gains, like preventing the dominoes of South and Southeast Asia from falling, were to most Americans remote, uncertain, and highly theoretical. So, too, joining the EU pits assurances of long-run and somewhat abstract gains for some Europeans against more specific and understandable losses perceived by others.

But foreign policy decisions like these are uncommon. Even NAFTA did not activate many voters, despite the efforts of its opponents to generate fears of its consequences. As a result, most Americans gave it scant attention. In effect, the decision was made by political leaders and activists without much influence by ordinary citizens.

## International Organizations and Processes

If popular control is formidably difficult within democratic countries, surely the problem will be even harder to solve in international institutions. If Norway had joined the EU, would its citizens be able to exercise anything like the degree of influence and control over the decisions in Brussels and Strasbourg that they have over the decisions of their own parliament and cabinet? Swedish citizens may now have more influence on the policy decisions of the EU than Norwegians, but would anyone contend that they exercise as much influence in the European Parliament as they do in their own? Or Danes? That these are small and relatively homogeneous countries only reinforces the point. Scale and heterogeneity matter. But the same question might be asked about a larger country such as Britain.

To achieve a level of popular control that is anywhere near the level already existing within democratic countries, international organizations would have to solve several problems about as well as they are now dealt with in democratic countries. Political leaders would have to create political institutions that would provide citizens with opportunities for political participation, influence, and control roughly equivalent in effectiveness to those already existing in democratic countries. To take advantage of these opportunities, citizens would need to be about as concerned and informed about the policy decisions of international organizations as they now are about government decisions in their own countries. In order for citizens to be informed, political and communication elites would need to engage in public debate and discussion of the alternatives in ways that would engage the attention and emotions of the public. To insure public debate, it would be necessary to create an international equivalent to national political competition by parties and individuals seeking office.[13] Elected representatives, or functional equivalents to them (whatever they might be), would need to exercise control over important international bureaucracies about as well as legislatures and executives now do in democratic countries.

How the representatives of a hypothetical international demos would be distributed among the people of different countries poses an additional problem. Given huge differences in the magnitude of the populations of different countries, no system of representation could give equal weight to the vote of each citizen and yet prevent small countries from being steadily outvoted by large countries; thus all solutions acceptable to the smaller democracies will deny political equality among the members of the larger demos. As with the United States and other federal systems, acceptable solutions may be cobbled together as one has been for the EU. But whatever compromise is reached, it could easily be a source of internal strain, particularly in the absence of a strong common identity.

Strain is all the more likely because, as I have already said, just as in national democracies most decisions are bound to be seen as harming the interests of some people, so too in international organizations. The heaviest burden of some decisions might be borne by particular groups, regions, or countries. To survive these strains, a political culture supportive of the specific institutions would help – might indeed be necessary. But developing a political culture takes time, perhaps many generations. In addition, if policy decisions are to be widely acceptable and enforceable among the losers, then it is probable that some common identity, equivalent to that in existing democratic countries, would have to develop. On present evidence, even Europeans do not now possess a common identity.[14] How then can we reasonably expect one to grow elsewhere?

In sum: if it is difficult enough for ordinary citizens to exercise much influence over decisions about foreign affairs in their own countries, should we not conclude that the obstacles will be far greater in international organizations? Just as many important policy decisions in democratic countries are in effect delegated by citizens to the political elites, will not the citizens of countries engaged in an international association delegate effective control to the international policy elites? And will not the extent of delegation in international organizations go well beyond any acceptable threshold of democracy?

## Conclusions

To say that international organizations are not and are not likely to be democratic is not to say that they are undesirable. It seems evident that they are necessary to many of the same human needs and goals that advocates of democracy contend are best served by democratic governments, and, as I said at the beginning, they can sometimes assist a non-democratic country to make the difficult transition from a highly undemocratic to a more democratic government. In addition, international organizations can help to expand human rights and the rule of law, the other important aspect of democracy that I emphasized earlier. Even measured against some loss in democratic control, these are important potential gains.

Despite these possible advantages I see no reason to clothe international organizations in the mantle of democracy simply in order to provide them with greater legitimacy.

[ . . . ]

## Notes

1   I am indebted to Martin Gilens for polling data on American opinion and to Bernt Hagtvet and Rune Premfors for providing me with articles, published and unpublished, on the referenda on membership in the European Union in the Nordic countries and Austria.

2   In my own work, for example, a minimally coherent and adequate assessment seems to me to require descriptions of ideal criteria, their moral justifications, different forms of actual political institutions that we call democratic (which is to say, more or less democratic by ideal standards), chiefly democratic polyarchy, and some conditions favorable or unfavorable for the emergence and stability of actual democratic political systems.

3   "The most explicit occurrence," according to Christophersen, "is Babeuf's statement that the terms 'democracy' and 'Robespierrism' were identical, and the latter term signified a revolutionary dictatorship, or a strict and merciless emergency rule, which was to crush anything that barred the victory of revolution" (Christopherson 1966: 304). Lenin and his followers also equated dictatorship of the proletariat with democracy, or proletarian democracy.

4   For my earlier explorations of this dilemma, see Dahl 1967: 953–70, 1989: 317ff and 1994, and Dahl and Tufte 1973: 13ff.

5   The classic and still highly relevant study is Almond 1950.

6   In surveys in the US from the 1930s to 1994, 553 questions concerned foreign affairs. Of these, "14 percent were answered correctly by at least three-quarters of survey respondents . . . An additional 28 percent of the items were correctly answered by between half and three-quarters of those asked . . . [M]ore than half could be answered by less than half the general public. 36 percent of the questions were known by only one-quarter to one-half of those asked. In the 1940s, this included knowledge about the forms of government of Sweden and Yugoslavia . . . and that the United States was sending military aid to Greece. Finally, nearly a quarter of the items could be answered by fewer than one-fourth of those asked. These little known facts included knowing that the United States was sharing information about the atomic bomb with England and Canada in the 1940s . . . knowing about how many soldiers had been killed in Vietnam in the 1960s, knowing how much of the federal budget goes to defense or foreign aid in the 1970s . . ." (Delli Carpini and Keeter 1996: 82–6).

7   The process of deliberation in democratic decision-making, to which democratic theorists have been giving increased attention, can be seen as a crucial procedural stage necessary if democratic decisions are to be substantively justifiable. See Guttman and Thompson 1996 and Fishkin 1991.

8   I have elaborated on this question in Dahl 1987 and 1995.

9   Thus, in 1939, the public concerns of Americans began to shift from domestic to foreign affairs, moved to first place after Hitler invaded Poland, were replaced at the end of World War II by domestic matters, which in turn were replaced by Cold War worries in the late 1940s. "From that point until the early 1960s, foreign affairs dominated public concern, ranking first in 48 of 56 surveys and often commanding over 50 percent of the public . . . In 1963 the hegemony of foreign affairs was interrupted by the emergence of the civil rights movement . . . until foreign affairs, boosted by the Vietnam War, regained the top position in 1965. From 1960 to 1970 Vietnam and other international issues dominated public concern. The only exception occurred in August 1967, when race riots pushed social control to the forefront . . . With minor exceptions, economics has completely dominated public

concerns for the last 10 years [1974–84], often capturing 60 percent of the public" (Smith 1985).

10   The turnout on the EU referendum in Austria was 82 per cent, which exceeded the general election of 1994; in Finland, 74 percent, about the same as in the election of 1991; in Sweden, 83.3 percent, about 3.5 percent lower than in the immediately preceding general election; in Norway, 89 percent, which exceeded turnout in all previous elections (Jahn and Storsved 1995).

11   The "no" vote was 70 percent among farm laborers, 62 percent among farmers, and 60 percent among urban manual workers. Lower white collar workers and persons in crafts and small business split almost evenly. People in big business, management, professions, academics, scientists, teachers, and health and social workers voted in favor by substantial majorities (Brulé 1992).

12   Cf. Petterson, Jenssen, and Listhaug 1996; Hansen 1996; Bjorklund (n.d.). Although the various factors tend to overlap, multiple regression analysis indicates that those listed had significant independent effects.

13   Although his conclusions are somewhat more hopeful than mine, Ramón Vargas-Machuca 1994 addresses some of the problems.

14   "As an economic, political, and administrative construction, Europe evidently elicits evaluative attitudes, but not a real community of belonging of the kind experienced in nation states. If the European Union is able, in the future, to generate a new system of belonging, it is difficult to imagine, from what we know, what it will be like. . . . For the present, a European identity is a vanguard phenomenon" (Duchesne and Frognier 1995: 223).

# References

Aldrich, John H., Sullivan, John L., and Bordiga, Eugene (1989) Foreign affairs and issue voting: do presidential candidates "waltz before a blind audience"? *American Political Science Review* 83(1): 124–41.

Almond, Gabriel (1950) *The American People and Foreign Policy*. New York: Harcourt Brace.

Archibugi, Daniele and Held, David (eds) (1995) *Cosmopolitan Democracy, An Agenda for a New World Order*. Cambridge: Polity Press.

Bjorklund, Tor (n.d.) Change and continuity: the "no" majority in the 1972 and 1994 referendum concerning Norwegian membership in the EU (MS).

Brulé, Michel (1992) France after Maastricht. *The Public Perspective* 4(1): 28–30.

Christophersen, Jens A. (1966) *The Meaning of Democracy*. Oslo: Universitetsvorlaget.

Dahl, Robert A. (1967) The city in the future of democracy. *American Political Science Review* 61: 953–70.

Dahl, Robert A. (1987) Dilemmas of pluralist democracy: the public good of which public? In Peter Koslowski (ed.), *Individual Liberty and Democratic Decision-making*, Tübingen: J. C. B. Mohr, pp. 201–14.

Dahl, Robert A. (1989) *Democracy and its Critics*. New Haven: Yale University Press.

Dahl, Robert A. (1994) Democratic dilemma: system effectiveness versus citizen participation. *Political Science Quarterly* 109: 23–34.

Dahl, Robert A. (1995) Is civic virtue a relevant ideal in a pluralist democracy? In Susan Dunn and Gary Jacobsohn (eds), *Diversity and Citizenship*, Lanham, MD: Rowman and Littlefield, pp. 1–16.

Dahl, Robert A. and Tufte, Edward R. (1973) *Size and Democracy*. Stanford: Stanford University Press.

Delli Carpini, Michael X. and Keeter, Scott (1996) *What Americans Know About Politics and Why It Matters*. New Haven: Yale University Press.

Duchesne, Sophie and Frognier, André-Paul (1995) Is there a European identity? In Oskar Niedermayer and Richard Sinnott (eds), *Public Opinion and International Governance*, New York: Oxford University Press, pp. 193–226.

*The Economist* (1996) The wrong design. 14 December, p. 17.

Fishkin, James (1991) *Democracy and Deliberation*. New Haven: Yale University Press.

Guttman, Amy and Thompson, Dennis (1996) *Democracy and Disagreement*. Cambridge, MA: Harvard University Press.

Hansen, Tore (1996) The regional basis of Norwegian EU-resistance (MS).

Held, David (1995) *Democracy and the Global Order, From the Modern State to Cosmopolitan Governance*. Stanford: Stanford University Press.

Jahn, Detlef and Storsved, Ann-Sofie (1995) Legitimacy through referendum? The nearly successful domino-strategy of the EU referendums in Austria, Finland, Sweden and Norway. *West European Politics* 18: 18–37.

Molyneux, Guy (1994) NAFTA revisited: unified "opinion leaders" best a reluctant public. *The Public Perspective, A Roper Center Review of Public Opinion and Polling* (January/February): 28–30.

Newhouse, Neil S. and Mathews, Christine L. (1994) NAFTA revisited: most Americans just weren't deeply engaged. *The Public Perspective, A Roper Center Review of Public Opinion and Polling* (January/February): 31–2.

Pettersen, Per Arnt, Jenssen, Anders Todal, and Listhaug, Ola (1996) The 1994 EU referendum in Norway: continuity and change. *Scandinavian Political Studies* 19(3): 257–81.

Schmitter, Philippe C. (1996) Is it really possible to democratize the Euro-polity? Unpublished.

Smith, Tom W. (1985) The polls: America's most important problems, Part I: National and international. *Public Opinion Quarterly* 49: 264–74.

Vargas-Machuca, Ramón (1994) How to be larger and more accountable: the paradoxical challenge of European political parties. Paper presented at the Center for Advanced Study in the Social Sciences of the Juan March Institute, Madrid, 15–17 December.

Wessels, Bernhard (1995) Support for integration: elite or mass driven? In Oskar Niedermayer and Richard Sinnott (eds), *Public Opinion and International Governance*, Oxford: Oxford University Press, pp. 137–62.

# 46

# The Postnational Constellation

## Jürgen Habermas

[ ... ]

If based on nothing more than an expanded economic foundation and a unified currency, a European Federation could at best aim for limited effects [ ... ], for example creating advantages for global competition. But the creation of larger political unities in itself changes nothing about the mode of locational competition as such; that is, the model of defensive alliances against the rest of the world. On the other hand, such supranational agreements at least meet a necessary condition for politics to catch up with globalized markets. Thus at the very least, a group of globally competent actors might emerge, which in principle would be capable not just of broad agreements but also of their implementation. [ ... ] I would like to go into the question of whether such political actors, acting within the framework of the United Nations, can strengthen an initially very loose network of transnational agreements sufficiently to make a change of course toward a world domestic policy possible without a world government.

At the global level, coordination problems that are already difficult enough at the European level grow still sharper. Because a negative coordination – refraining from taking measures – has the lowest possible implementation costs, the liberalization of the world market (under the hegemonic pressure of the United States) and the emergence of an international economic regime were ultimately successful in dismantling trade barriers. The external effects of toxic waste production, and the border-crossing risks of high technology, have even led to organizations and practices that take over some regulatory tasks. But the hurdles are still too high for the introduction of global regulation, which would require not just a positive coordination of the actions of different governments, but an intervention in existing patterns of distribution as well.

In light of the most recent crises in Mexico and Asia, there is naturally a growing interest in warding off stock market crashes, and in strengthening regulations for credit transactions and currency speculation. Critical events in the international financial markets point to the need for institutionalization. Moreover, globalized market commerce demands legal certainty, i.e. transnationally effective equivalents to the familiar guarantees of the private rights of citizens, which states grant to investors and trading partners within the national framework. "Deregulation can be seen as negotiating on the one hand the fact of globalization, and, on the other, the ongoing need for guarantees of contracts and property rights for which the state remains as the guarantor of last instance."[1] But just wishing for the regulatory powers of the state, whether for global financial markets or for the urban infrastructures and services that transnational businesses depend on, doesn't make the state either willing or able to undertake market-correcting regulations of this kind.[2] Under the conditions of global competition, national governments, incapable of macro-steering to influence the cycles of their increasingly de-nationalized "popular economies," have to limit themselves to improving the relative attractiveness of their local position, i.e. local conditions for capital valuation.

Influencing the mode of locational competition itself would be an entirely different matter. As things stand now, when it is not even possible to reach an agreement for a worldwide transaction tax on speculation profits, it is very hard to imagine any organization, standing conference, or indeed any procedure that the OECD states could agree to, for example, to serve as a framework for national taxation legislation. An international negotiating system that could place limits on the "race to the bottom" – the cost-cutting deregulatory race that reduces the capacities for social-political action and damages social standards – would need to enact and enforce redistributive regulations. Within a European Union that has assumed the character of a state, regardless of its multinational composition and the central roles of national governments, decisive policies of this sort would at least be conceivable. On the global level, however, both the competence for political action of a world government and a corresponding basis of legitimation are lacking. The United Nations is a loose community of states. It lacks the quality of a community of world citizens, who can legitimate their political decisions – and can make the consequences of those decisions into reasonable burdens for those affected – on the basis of a democratic opinion- and will-formation. Reflections on an order of world peace have occupied philosophers since the famous proposal of the Abbé Saint-Pierre (1729) until our own times, and they usually conclude with a warning about a despotic world rule.[3] But a look at the condition, the function, and the constitution of world organizations shows this worry to be groundless.

Today the United Nations unites member states that exhibit extreme differences in terms of population size and density, legitimation status, and level of economic development. In the UN General Assembly every member state has its own voice, while the composition of the Security Council and the voting rights of members take actual power relations into account. The United Nations' articles require national governments to observe human rights, to respect one another's sovereignty, and to refrain from the use of military force. With the criminalization of wars of aggression and crimes against humanity, nations, as the subjects of international law, have forfeited a general presumption of innocence. Of course, the United Nations has neither a standing international court of criminal justice (now in its planning stages in Rome) nor its own military forces at its disposal. But it can impose sanctions, and grant mandates for humanitarian interventions.

After the Second World War, the newly founded United Nations assumed the specific goal of preventing future wars. Its peacekeeping function was from the very beginning bound up with the task of the political enforcement of human rights. Since then, questions of environmental security have been added to this basic task of the prevention of war. But both the normative foundations of the UN Declaration on Human Rights, as well as the concentration on questions of security in the broadest sense, reveal the clearly limited functional responsibilities that the world organization, with no monopoly of violence, is charged with: controlling wars, civil wars and state-sponsored criminality on the one hand, and preventing humanitarian catastrophes and worldwide risks on the other. In view of this restriction to the basic services of maintaining order, even the most ambitious reforms of existing institutions would not lead in the direction of a world government.

The advocates of a "cosmopolitan democracy"[4] pursue three goals: first, the creation of a new political status of "world citizens," whose membership in world organizations would no longer be mediated through their nationality, but who would instead have popular representation in a world parliament through direct elections above the national level; second, the construction of a court of criminal justice with the usual competencies, whose decisions would be binding for national governments as well; finally, dismantling the UN Security Council in favor of a competent executive branch.[5] But even a world organization that has been expanded along these lines, and is operating on a broad basis of legitimacy, would be more or less effective only in restricted areas of competence, including reactive security and human rights policies, and preventive environmental policies.

The restriction to elementary services for maintaining order is a response not just to the pacifistic motivations that gave rise to the United Nations as a world organization in the first place. The world organization also lacks a basis of legitimacy on structural grounds. It is distinguished from state-organized communities by the principle of complete inclusion – it may exclude nobody, because it cannot permit any social boundaries between inside and outside. Any political community that wants to understand itself as a democracy must at least distinguish between members and non-members. The self-referential concept of collective self-determination demarcates a logical space for democratically united citizens who are members of a particular political community. Even if such a community is grounded in the universalist principles of a democratic constitutional state, it still forms a collective identity, in the sense that it interprets and realizes these principles in light of its own history and in the context of its own particular form of life. This ethical-political self-understanding of citizens of a particular democratic life is missing in the inclusive community of world citizens.[6]

Even if, despite this, world citizens were to organize themselves on a global level, and even if they created a form of democratically elected political representation, they would not be able to generate any normative cohesion from an ethical-political self-understanding that drew on other traditions and value orientations, but only from a legal-moral form of self-understanding. The normative model for a community that exists without any possible exclusions is the universe of moral persons – Kant's "kingdom of ends." It is thus no coincidence that "human rights," i.e. legal norms with an exclusively moral content,[7] make up the entire normative framework for a cosmopolitan community. This fact still doesn't predict whether the UN Declaration on Human Rights, whose wording was agreed on by the comparatively small number of founding members of the United Nations in 1946, could approach a unanimous interpretation and application in today's multi-cultural world. I cannot go into this cross-cultural discourse on human rights here.[8] But even a worldwide consensus on human rights could not serve as the basis for a strong equivalent to the *civic* solidarity that emerged in the framework of the nation-state. Civic solidarity is rooted in particular collective identities; cosmopolitan solidarity has to support itself on the moral universalism of human rights alone.

In comparison to the active solidarity among citizens, which among other things made the redistributive policies of the social welfare state tolerable, the solidarity of *world* citizens has a reactive character, insofar as it generates a kind of cosmopolitan cohesion in the first instance through feelings of indignation over the violations of rights, i.e. over repression and injuries to human rights committed by states. A legal community of world citizens that is all-inclusive yet organized in time and space certainly would be different from a universal community of moral persons, for which any such organization would be neither possible nor necessary. On the other hand, however, such a legal community of world citizens could not demand the comparatively firm levels of integration of state-organized communities with their own collective identities. I see no structural obstacles to expanding national civic solidarity and welfare-state policies to the scale of a postnational federation. But the political culture of a world society lacks the common ethical-political dimension that would be necessary for a corresponding global community – and its identity formation. At this point the objections that neo-Aristotelians have already raised against a national, let alone a European, constitutional patriotism come into play. A cosmopolitan community of world citizens can thus offer no adequate basis for a global domestic policy. The institutionalization of procedures for creating, generalizing, and coordinating global interests cannot take place within the organizational structure of a world state. Hence any plans for a "cosmopolitan democracy" will have to proceed according to another model.

A politics that can catch up with global markets, one that will be able to change the mode of locational competition, cannot simply be introduced at the top level of a multilevel politics organized into a "world state." Rather than a state, it has to find a less demanding basis of legitimacy in the organizational forms of an international negotiation system, which already exist today in other political arenas. In general, procedures and accords require a sort of compromise between independent actors who have the ability to impose sanctions to compel consideration of their respective interests. In a politically constituted community organized via a state, this compromise formation is more closely meshed with procedures of deliberative politics, so that agreements are not simply produced by an equalization of interests in terms of power politics. Within the framework of a common political culture, negotiation partners also have recourse to common value orientations and shared conceptions of justice, which make an understanding beyond instrumental-rational agreements possible. But on the international level this "thick" communicative embeddedness is missing. And a "naked" compromise formation that simply reflects back the essential features of classical power politics is an inadequate beginning for a world domestic policy. Naturally, procedures for intergovernmental accords are not dependent on given constellations of power alone. As normative framing conditions delimit the choice of rhetorical strategies, they effectively structure negotiations just as much as the influence of "epistemic communities" (which occasionally generate thoroughly normative, global background consensuses over supposedly purely scientific questions, as in the case of today's neoliberal economic regime). Global powers no longer operate in the state of nature envisioned by classical international law, but on the middle level of an emerging world politics.

This presents a diffuse picture – not the stable picture of a multilevel politics *within* a world organization, but rather the dynamic picture of interferences and interactions *between* political processes that persist at national, international, and global levels. The international negotiating systems that make agreements between state actors possible communicate on the one side with internal state processes that respective governments depend on; on the other side they also connect up with the contexts and policies of the world organization. The result is at least a prospect for a world domestic policy without a world government – provided that two problems can be clarified. The first problem is more fundamental; the second is empirical. (a) How can we envision the democratic legitimation of decisions beyond the schema of the nation-state? And (b), what are the conditions for a transformed self-understanding of global actors in which states and supranational regimes begin to see themselves as members of a community, who have no choice but to consider one another's interests mutually, and to perceive general interests?

(a) Both the liberal and the republican traditions understand the political participation of citizens in an essentially voluntaristic sense: all should have the same chance to voice their own preferences or their political will in an effective way, be it in pursuit of their private interests (Locke), or in the exercise of their political autonomy (Mill). But if we also ascribe an epistemic function to democratic will-formation, the pursuit of self-interest and the realization of political freedom are supplemented by a further dimension, the public use of reason (Kant). Accordingly, the democratic procedure no longer draws its legitimizing force only, indeed not even predominantly, from political participation and the expression of political will, but rather from the general accessibility of a deliberative process whose structure grounds an expectation of rationally acceptable results.[9] Such a discourse-theoretical understanding of democracy changes the theoretical demands placed on the legitimacy conditions for democratic politics. A functioning public sphere, the quality of discussion, accessibility, and the discursive structure of opinion- and will-formation: all of these could never entirely replace conventional procedures for decision-making and political representation. But they do tip the balance, from the concrete embodiments of sovereign will in persons, votes, and collectives to the procedural demands of communicative and decision-making processes. And this loosens the conceptual ties between democratic legitimacy and the familiar forms of state organization.

Supposedly weak forms of legitimation then appear in another light.[10] For example, the institutionalized participation of non-governmental organizations in the deliberations of international negotiating systems would strengthen the legitimacy of the procedure insofar as mid-level transnational decision-making processes could then be rendered transparent for national public spheres, and thus be reconnected with decision-making procedures at the grassroots level. And equipping the world organization with the right to demand that member states carry out referendums on important issues at any time is also an interesting suggestion under discourse-theoretical premises.[11] As in the cases of UN summit conferences on environmental threats, equal rights for women, disputed interpretations of human rights, global poverty, etc., this might at least force a discussion on how best to regulate issues that would otherwise remain invisible and would never make it onto the political agenda.

(b) Of course, a renewed political closure of an economically unmastered world society would be possible only if global powers also involve themselves in the institutionalized procedures for building a transnational will-formation regarding the preservation of social standards and the redress of extreme social inequities. They have to be willing to broaden their perspectives on what counts as the "national interest" into a viewpoint of "global governance." But this changed perspective, from "international relations" to a world domestic policy, cannot be expected from governments if their populations themselves do not reward them for it. The governing elites have to concern themselves with consensus and re-election within their own national arenas; thus they ought not to be punished for operating on the cooperative procedures of a cosmopolitan community rather than those of national independence. Innovations will not happen if the political elites cannot find any resonance with the already transformed value orientations of their electorates. But if the self-understanding of governments only changes under the pressure of an altered domestic climate, then the crucial question is whether, in the civil societies and political public spheres of increasingly interconnected regimes, whether here, in Europe and in the Federal Republic of Germany, a cosmopolitan consciousness – the consciousness of a compulsory cosmopolitan solidarity, so to speak – will arise.

The re-regulation of the world society has, until now, not even taken the shape of an exemplary project for which one could provide examples. Its first addressees are not governments but citizens, and citizens' movements. But social movements crystallize around normatively liberating perspectives for resolving conflicts that had previously appeared insoluble. The articulation of a vision is also the task of political parties that have not yet entirely withdrawn from civil society and barricaded themselves into the political system. Parties that don't simply cling to the status quo need a perspective that moves beyond it. And the status quo today is nothing other than the whirlpool of an accelerating process of modernization that has been left to its own devices. The political parties that are still able to exert any formative influence also have to muster the courage for forward thinking in other respects. Within the national sphere – the only one that they can currently operate in – they have to reach out toward a European arena of action. And this arena, in turn, has to be programmatically opened up with the dual objective of creating a social Europe that can throw its weight onto the cosmopolitan scale.

## Notes

1  S. Sassen, *Globalization and its Discontents*, New York 1998, 199.
2  Cf. Sassen (ibid. 202 f):

> A focus on place, and particularly the type of place I call "global cities," brings to the fore the fact that many of the resources necessary for global economic activities are not hypermobile and could, in principle, be brought under effective regulation . . . A refocussing of regulation onto infrastructures and production complexes in the context of globalization contributes to an analysis of the regulatory capacities of states that diverges in significant ways from understandings centered on hypermobile outputs and global telecommunications.

3  D. Archibugi, "Models of International Organization in Perpetual Peace Projects," *Review of International Studies* 18 (1992), 295–317.
4  D. Held, *Democracy and the Global Order*, Cambridge 1995, 267–87.
5  D. Archibugi, "From the United Nations to Cosmopolitan Democracy," in D. Archibugi and D. Held (eds), *Cosmopolitan Democracy: An Agenda for a New World Order*, Cambridge 1995, 121–62; D. Held, "Democracy and the New World Order," ibid. 96–120.
6  Cosmopolitan consciousness could in any case take on a more concrete form by a delimitation of the temporal dimension – a stylization of the resistance of the present to the past of the nation-state.
7  J. Habermas, *The Inclusion of the Other*, ed. C. Cronin and P. de Greif, Cambridge, MA, 1998, 220–6.
8  C. Taylor, "A World Consensus on Human Rights?" *Dissent* (Summer 1996), 15–21; J. Habermas, "Remarks on Legitimization through Human Rights," *Philosophy and Social Criticism* 24 (1998), 157–72; on this see also T. McCarthy, "On Reconciling Cosmopolitan Unity and National Diversity" (MS 1998).
9  J. Habermas, "Three Normative Models of Democracy," in Habermas, *The Inclusion of the Other*, 239–52.
10  A. Linklater, "Cosmopolitan Citizenship," *Citizenship Studies* 2 (1998), 23–41.
11  Jamie Carney, "Structure for a Democratic World Government" (MS 1998).

# 47

# Priorities of Global Justice

## *Thomas W. Pogge*

Looking back on the post-Cold-War period, the greatest surprise for me was that the affluent states have done so very little toward eradicating global poverty. This is surprising, because the conditions for a major effort were exceptionally favorable. The demise of the Soviet bloc gave the affluent states greatly enhanced opportunities to incorporate their moral values and concerns into their foreign policy and into the rapidly evolving international institutional order. It also enabled these states to cut their military expenditures as a share of gross domestic product (GDP) from 4.1 percent of their combined GDPs in 1985 to 2.2 percent in 1998 (UNDP 1998, 197; UNDP 2000, 217), and thereby to reap an annual peace dividend of roughly $477 billion.[1] Maintaining healthy economic and technological growth throughout the period, the affluent states thus had both the power and the funds to make a major effort toward poverty eradication.

However, no such effort took place. The affluent states, during the same period, actually cut their official development assistance (ODA) as a share of gross national product (GNP) by one third.[2] They have also reduced their allocations to multilateral development efforts, revised Part XI of the 1982 *United Nations Convention on the Law of the Sea* to the disadvantage of poor countries, and imposed onerous terms of trade on the latter in the context of the Uruguay Round.[3]

To be sure, the affluent states have been more willing to appeal to moral values and to use such appeals in justification of initiatives – such as the NATO bombing of Yugoslavia – that would have been unthinkable during the Cold War. But these appeals only heighten the puzzle. If it makes sense to spend billions and to endanger thousands of lives in order to rescue a million people from Serb oppression, would it not make more sense to spend similar sums, without endangering any lives, on leading many millions out of life-threatening poverty?

To appreciate the force of this question about priorities, one must know some of the salient facts about global poverty. Nearly a fifth of all human beings alive today, 1,175 million, live below $1/day, that is, their income or expenditure per day has less purchasing power than $1.08 had in the US in 1993.[4] According to this extremely low poverty line, persons need only $41 per month to count as non-poor in the US or $10 per month to avoid poverty in a typical poor country.[5]

Such severe poverty has grave consequences: 815 million persons are undernourished, 1.1 billion lack access to safe water, 2.4 billion lack access to basic sanitation, and 854 million adults are illiterate (UNDP 2002, 21, 29, 11). More than 880 million lack access to basic health services (UNDP 1999, 22). Approximately 1 billion have no adequate shelter and 2 billion no electricity (UNDP 1998, 49). "Two out of five children in the developing world are stunted, one in three is underweight and one in ten is wasted" (FAO 1999, 11). Some 250 million children between 5 and 14 do wage work outside their household – often under harsh or cruel conditions: as soldiers, prostitutes, or domestic servants, or in agriculture, construction, textile or carpet production.[6] Roughly one third of all human deaths, some 50,000 daily, are due to poverty-related causes, easily preventable through better nutrition, safe drinking water, vaccines, cheap re-hydration packs and antibiotics.[7]

Severe poverty causes not only massive underfulfillment of social and economic human rights, such as the "right to a standard of living adequate for the health and well-being of oneself and one's family, including food, clothing, housing and medical care."[8] Severe poverty and economic inequality also contribute significantly to the underfulfillment of civil and political human rights associated with democratic government and the rule of law. Desperately poor people, often stunted from infancy, illiterate, and heavily pre-occupied with the struggle to survive, can do little by way of either resisting or rewarding their local and national rulers, who are therefore likely to rule them oppressively while catering to the interests of other (often foreign) agents more capable of reciprocation. The income and staying power of such rulers often depends less on their poor subjects than on a small local elite or on a few foreign companies and governments, to whom they can sell the country's natural resources and from whom they can obtain grants and loans and weapons. Such rulers have little need for popular support and many of them use torture, restrict freedom of expression, and perpetuate their rule by force.

Severe poverty is by far the greatest source of human misery today. Deaths and harms from direct violence around the world – in Chechnya, East Timor, Congo, Bosnia, Kosovo, Ethiopia and Eritrea, Rwanda, Somalia, Iraq, Afghanistan, and so on – provoke more publicity and hand-wringing. But they are vastly outnumbered by deaths and harms due to poverty. In 2000, some 310,000 deaths were due to war; other homicides and violence caused some 520,000 more. Starvation and preventable diseases, by contrast, claimed about 18 million human lives.[9] The few years since the end of the Cold War have seen nearly 250 million deaths due to poverty-related causes.

While the data about global poverty may be daunting, it is in fact becoming more and more feasible for the affluent countries to eradicate such poverty. The reason is the dramatic long-term trend of rising global economic inequality: "The income gap between the fifth of the world's people living in the richest countries and the fifth in the poorest was 74 to 1 in 1997, up from 60 to 1 in 1990 and 30 to 1 in 1960." Earlier estimates are 11 to 1 for 1913, 7 to 1 for 1870, and 3 to 1 for 1820 (UNDP 1999, 3). Today, the 1,175 million persons below $1/day together live on about $99 billion annually, with an aggregate gap of about $42 billion to the $1/day poverty line.[10] This aggregate gap is only 0.16 percent of the gross national incomes of the high-income economies (World Bank 2002, 235).[11] And even if we take a less measly poverty line, twice as high, the poverty problem looks surprisingly manageable: the 2,812 million persons below $2/day together live on about $386 billion annually, with an aggregate gap of about $289 billion to the $2/day poverty line. Even this much larger aggregate gap is only 1.13 percent of the gross national incomes of the high-income economies (World Bank 2002, 235).[12] For the first time in human history it is quite feasible, economically, to wipe out hunger and preventable diseases worldwide without real inconvenience to anyone – all the more so because the affluent countries no longer face any serious military threat.

The moral upshot of all this seems obvious: we should provide a path out of poverty to that great majority of all poor people whom we can reach without the use of force. When we can save so many millions from hunger, disease, and premature death, then the affluent states should be willing to spend one percent of our gross national incomes ($255 billion annually) specifically on poverty eradication – and even more, if we can do so effectively. We should make this effort so as to ensure that the poor, especially poor children, have secure access to food and shelter, vaccines, safe water, basic health services and sanitation, primary education, electricity, road or rail links, and will thus be able to fend for themselves in the new global economy. If we can make so huge a difference to hundreds of millions at so little cost to ourselves, we must not refuse to make this effort.

While this call for greater solidarity is plausible in what it directs us to do, it is misleading in the grounds it suggests for this directive. The account appeals to a positive duty to protect persons from great harms and risks if one can do so at little cost.[13] I have no doubt that we have such a moral duty and that this duty requires us to make a serious effort toward poverty reduction. And yet, it would be misleading to characterize our present and (quite predictable) future failure to make such an effort as a lack of beneficence. We are not bystanders who find ourselves confronted with foreign deprivations whose origins are wholly unconnected to ourselves. In fact, there are at least three morally significant connections between us and the global poor: first, their social starting positions and ours have emerged from a single historical process that was pervaded by massive grievous wrongs. The same historical injustices, including genocide, colonialism, and slavery, play a role in explaining both their poverty and our affluence. Second, they and we depend on a single natural resource base from the benefits of which they are largely, and without compensation, excluded. The affluent countries and the elites of the developing world divide these resources on mutually agreeable terms without leaving "enough and as good" for the remaining majority of humankind. Third, they and we coexist within a single global economic order that has a strong tendency to perpetuate and even to aggravate global economic inequality.[14]

Given these connections, our failure to make a serious effort toward poverty reduction may constitute not merely a lack of beneficence, but our active impoverishing, starving, and killing millions of innocent people by economic means. To be sure, we do not intend these harms, and we are thus not on a par with Stalin, who used economic policies and institutions specifically in order to impoverish and kill segments of the population he deemed hostile to the Soviet regime. We may not even have foreseen these harms when, beginning in the late 1980s, we constructed today's freer, more global economic architecture. Now that we do know, our moral situation is more akin to that of Mao Tse-Tung in 1959. Mao did not foresee that his Great Leap Forward, begun in 1958, would acutely aggravate poverty in China. But when the catastrophic effects of these policies became evident, he continued his policies and declined foreign help. Some 20–30 million Chinese perished in 1959–62 as a direct consequence of this moral failure. Continuing our current global economic structures and policies unmodified would manifest a similar moral failure. Perhaps we had reason to believe our own persistent pronouncements that the new global economic architecture would cease the reproduction of poverty. So perhaps we just made an innocent and blameless mistake. But it is *our* mistake nonetheless, and we must not allow it to kill yet further tens of millions in the developing world.

The call for greater beneficence in the face of world hunger is one that politicians, diplomats, international bankers, and economists are willing to entertain. Most of them will even agree with it, blaming our failure to do more on other politicians, diplomats, bankers, economists, or the voting public. The idea that our economic policies and the global economic institutions we impose make us causally and morally responsible for the perpetuation – even aggravation – of world hunger, by contrast, is an idea rarely taken seriously by established intellectuals and politicians in the developed world. But this subversive idea nonetheless plays an important role, in that theorists of poverty and justice, consciously and unconsciously, expend much intellectual energy on making invisible this idea and the three connections that support it. Focusing on the third of these connections, let me briefly indicate some of the distortions arising from our interest in obscuring the role that the design of the global economic order plays in perpetuating and aggravating poverty.

A good example of such distortion in philosophical work is provided by John Rawls. When discussing the economic order of a single society, Rawls pays great attention to the fact that economic cooperation can be structured in many ways and that such structural alternatives have diverse distributional effects (cf. Rawls 1996, 265–7). In response to this fact, he not only insists that the shaping and reshaping of a national economic order should be controlled by all adult participants through a democratic political process, but also argues that justice requires citizens to aim for a national economic order that satisfies the difference principle, i.e., allows social and economic inequalities to arise only insofar as they tend to optimize the lowest socio-economic position (Rawls 1999a, §§11, 12, 17).

What is true of a domestic economic order is clearly true of the international economic order as well: Alternative ways of organizing global economic cooperation have diverse distributional effects and differ, in particular, in how supportive or obstructive they are of economic development in the poorest countries and areas. In his recent treatment of international justice, Rawls seems briefly to acknowledge this point when he calls for correction of any "unjustified distributive effects" of cooperative organizations (Rawls 1999b, 43). But how is this vague demand to be specified? Rawls endorses "fair standards of trade to keep the market free and competitive" (Rawls 1999b, 43) – but, as he stresses himself (Rawls 1996, 267), free and competitive markets are quite compatible with huge and ever increasing inequality. What is needed is a principle that assesses alternative global economic orders in terms of their distributive effects as his difference principle assesses alternative ways of structuring a national economy. Yet in the international case Rawls specifically rejects any such principle without "a target and a cutoff point" (Rawls 1999b, 115–19). He also rejects any international analogue to a democratic process which, at least in theory, allows a majority of citizens in a liberal society to restructure its economic order if it favors the rich too much.

Like the existing global economic order, that of Rawls's Society of Peoples is then shaped by free bargaining.[15] There is one crucial constraint, however, as Rawls insists on a universal minimum: "Peoples have a duty to assist other peoples living under unfavorable conditions that prevent their having a just or decent political and social regime" (Rawls 1999b, 37). This duty is unobjectionable and hugely important. If existing affluent societies honored it, malnutrition and preventable diseases would be much less common. And yet, making this duty the only distributive constraint on global economic institutions is nonetheless implausible. Imposition by affluent and powerful societies of a skewed global economic order that hampers the economic growth of poor societies and further weakens their bargaining power – such imposition is not made right by the fact that the former societies also keep the latter from falling below the minimum. Moreover, making this duty the only distributive constraint also misleads us to perceive the injustice of the status quo as insufficient assistance to the poorer societies, when it really consists in the imposition of a skewed global order that aggravates international inequalities and makes it exceedingly hard for the weaker and poorer populations to secure a proportional share of global economic growth. Rawls obscures then the important causal role that the global economic order plays in the reproduction of poverty and inequality, suggesting that each society bears sole responsibility for its own place in the economic rank-order: "The causes of the wealth of a people and the forms it takes lie in their political culture and in the religious, philosophical, and moral traditions that support the basic structure, as well as in the industriousness and cooperative talents of its members, all supported by their political virtues. . . . Crucial also is the country's population policy" (Rawls 1999b, 108). Thus, he goes on, a society may be poor because of high population growth or low investment (Rawls 1999b, 117–18) and, in any case, "if it is not satisfied, it can continue to increase savings, or, if this is not feasible, borrow from other members of the Society of Peoples" (Rawls 1999b, 114). In these ways, Rawls's account of international justice renders all but invisible the question whether the global economic order we currently impose, by creating a headwind against economic development in the poorest areas, is harming the poor and therefore unjust.

We find similar distortions in economic work. Our international bankers and economists tell us that our global economic order is fine and that protests against it (in Seattle and Washington) are actually harming the poor. The same bankers and economists also dutifully tell us about the horrendous conditions among the poor and about the lack of progress, lest anyone suspect them of not knowing or not caring enough.[16] So why does a global economic order designed with so much tender loving concern for the global poor not improve their condition? The official answer in unison: because their own governments in the developing countries are not pursuing optimal policies. Our bankers and economists differ on what the optimal policies are and hence on how their common claim should be elaborated. The more libertarian types on the right tell the story of the Asian tigers – Hong Kong, Taiwan, Singapore, and South Korea – as showing how misery disappears under governments that allow free enterprise to flourish with a minimum in taxes and regulations. The more social-democratic types tell the story of Kerala, a state in India with a traditionally socialist government, as showing how misery can be abolished even at low income levels if only governments make a serious effort to this end.[17] The stories vary, but the lesson is the same: with the right policies, any poor state can over time meet the basic needs of its people; so there is nothing wrong with the global economic order as it is.

These stories have the familiar ring of the Horatio Alger stories often appealed to in celebration of the unbridled American capitalism before the New Deal: in America, even a farm boy can become rich.[18] Left aside in such celebrations is the crucial question why nearly all the relevant agents fail even while (supposedly) they can succeed. Once this question is asked, there are two obvious and complementary answers. First, what is possible for each may not be possible for all. Even if each farm boy could have become a millionaire in the world of Alger's stories, it was still quite impossible for more than a few to succeed. So we can indeed say that each farm boy who failed had himself to blame, for he could have succeeded. But we cannot blame the fact that over 99 percent failed on the farm boys themselves. In the system as it was, they could not have changed this fact, either individually or collectively. Similarly with unemployment: it does not follow from the fact that *each* person willing to work can find work that *all* such persons can. And similarly also for poor countries. There was indeed a profitable niche in the world economy (better technology than other poor countries and lower labor costs than more affluent countries), which the Asian tigers exploited, but this niche would not have been so profitable if many poor states had scrambled to occupy it all at once.

Second, there may be systemic reasons for why many of the relevant agents do not make the necessary effort. Most farm boys may have lacked stamina and initiative because, having grown up in grinding poverty, they were suffering the lasting effects of childhood malnutrition and disease or of primitive schools stifling ambition. With the governments of poor countries, the problem most often is not merely inability, but also unwillingness to reduce domestic poverty. Yet this unwillingness, the corruption endemic to many of these governments, does not show that such poverty cannot be traced back to the existing global economic order. To the contrary, the prevalence of official corruption may itself be a consequence of our economic policies, of the global economic order we impose and of the extreme international inequalities that have accumulated over two centuries. Let me develop this point a bit further.

A paradigm case of corruption is bribery. Bribes are a major factor in the awarding of public contracts in the developing countries, which suffer staggering losses as a result. These losses arise in part from the fact that bribes are "priced in": bidders on contracts must raise their price in order to get paid enough to pay the bribes. Additional losses arise as bidders can afford to be noncompetitive, knowing that the success of their bid will depend on their bribes more than on the price they offer. The greatest losses probably arise from the fact that officials focused on bribes pay little attention to whether the goods and services they purchase on their country's behalf are of good quality or even needed at all. Much of what developing countries have imported over the years has been of no use to them – or even harmful, by promoting environmental degradation or violence (bribery is especially pervasive in the arms trade). May we then conclude that poverty in developing societies is the fault of their own tolerance of corruption and of their own leaders' venality?

This comfortable conclusion is upset by the fact that the developed states have permitted their companies not merely to pay bribes, but even to deduct these from their taxes. By providing financial inducements and moral support, these states have made a vital contribution to promoting and entrenching a culture of corruption in developing societies. Fortunately, this contribution is now being phased out. The first major step was the US Foreign Corrupt Practices Act of 1977, enacted after the Lockheed Corporation was found to have paid a $2 million bribe not to a Third-World potentate, but to the Japanese Prime Minister Kakuei Tanaka. It took another 20 years until 32 affluent states, under OECD auspices and under public pressure generated by a new NGO (Transparency International), signed a *Convention on Combating Bribery of Foreign Officials in International Business Transactions*, which requires them to criminalize the bribery of foreign officials.[19] It remains to be seen whether this Convention will produce serious enforcement efforts and thus will reduce bribery and undermine the now deeply entrenched culture of corruption in many developing countries.[20]

Surveying the ruling elites of many developing countries, one may well surmise that they would have done their best to enrich themselves, and done little for the eradication of poverty in their countries, even if they had not been bribed by foreigners. Many of these countries have not managed to become genuinely democratic, and their rulers can therefore hang on by force even if opposed by the vast majority of the population. Does this support the view that poverty in the developing societies is their own fault after all?

To see how this conclusion is problematic, consider a very central feature of the current global institutional order. Any group controlling a preponderance of the means of coercion within a country is internationally recognized as the legitimate government of this country's territory and people – regardless of how that group came to power, of how it exercises power, and of the extent to which it may be supported or opposed by the population it rules. That such a group exercising effective power receives international recognition means not merely that we engage it in negotiations. It means also that we accept this group's right to act for the people it rules, that we, most significantly, confer upon it the privileges freely to borrow in the country's name (international borrowing privilege) and freely to dispose of the country's natural resources (international resource privilege).

The international borrowing privilege includes the power to impose internationally valid legal obligations upon the country at large. Any successor government that refuses to honor debts incurred by an ever so corrupt, brutal, undemocratic, unconstitutional, repressive, unpopular predecessor will be severely punished by the banks and governments of other countries; at minimum it will lose its own borrowing privilege by being excluded from the international financial markets. Such refusals are therefore quite rare, as governments, even when newly elected after a dramatic break with the past, are compelled to pay the debts of their ever so awful predecessors.

The international borrowing privilege has three important negative effects on human rights fulfillment in the developing countries. First, this privilege facilitates borrowing by destructive governments. Such governments can borrow more money and can do so more cheaply than they could do if they alone, rather than the entire country, were obliged to repay. In this way, the borrowing privilege helps such governments stay in power even against near-universal popular discontent and opposition. Second, the international borrowing privilege imposes upon democratic successor regimes the often huge debts of their corrupt predecessors. It thereby saps the capacity of such democratic governments to implement structural reforms and other political programs, thus rendering such governments less successful and less stable than they would otherwise be.[21] Third, the international borrowing privilege provides incentives toward coup attempts: whoever succeeds in bringing a preponderance of the means of coercion under his control gets the borrowing privilege as an additional reward.

The international resource privilege enjoyed by a group in power is much more than our mere acquiescence in its effective control over the natural resources of the country in question. This privilege includes the power to effect legally valid transfers of ownership rights in such resources. Thus a corporation that has purchased resources from the Saudi or Suharto families, or from Mobuto or Sani Abacha, has thereby become entitled to be – and actually *is* – recognized anywhere in the world as the legitimate owner of these resources. This is a remarkable feature of our global institutional order. A group that overpowers the guards and takes control of a warehouse may be able to give some of the merchandise to others, accepting money in exchange. But the fence who pays them becomes merely the possessor, not the owner, of the loot. Contrast this with a group that overpowers an elected government and takes control of a country. Such a group, too, can give away some of the country's natural resources, accepting money in exchange. In this case, however, the purchaser acquires not merely possession, but all the rights and liberties of ownership, which are supposed to be – and actually *are* – protected and enforced by all other states' courts and police forces. The international resource privilege, then, is the power to confer globally valid ownership rights in the country's resources.

The international resource privilege has disastrous effects in many poor countries, whose resource sector often constitutes a large segment of the national economy. Whoever can take power in such a country by whatever means can maintain his rule, even against widespread popular opposition, by buying the arms and soldiers he needs with revenues from the export of natural resources (and funds borrowed abroad in the country's name). This fact in turn provides a strong incentive toward the undemocratic acquisition and unresponsive exercise of political power in these countries. The international resources privilege also gives foreigners strong incentives to corrupt the officials of such countries who, no matter how badly they rule, continue to have resources to sell and money to spend. We see here how the local causal chain – persistent poverty caused by corrupt government caused by natural resource wealth – can itself be traced back to the international resource privilege, which renders resource-rich developing countries more likely to experience coup attempts and civil wars and more likely also to be ruled by corrupt elites, so that – despite considerable natural wealth – poverty in these countries tends to decline only slowly, if at all.[22]

These brief remarks on bribery and on the international borrowing and resource privileges show at least in outline how the current global order we uphold shapes the national culture and policies of the poorer and weaker countries. It does so in four main ways. It crucially affects what sorts of persons exercise political power in these countries, what incentives these persons face, what options they have, and what impact the implementation of any of their options would have on their most disadvantaged compatriots. In many ways, our global order is disadvantageous to the global poor by sustaining oppression, corruption, and hence poverty, in the developing world. It is hardly surprising that this order reflects the interests of the wealthy and powerful states. Their governments, dependent on our votes and taxes, work hard on shaping the rules for our benefit. To be sure, the global poor have their own governments. But almost all of them are too weak to exert real influence on the organization of the global economy. More importantly, these governments have little incentive to attend to the needs of their poor compatriots, as their continuation in power depends on the local elite and on foreign governments and corporations. Such rulers – able to sell the country's resources, to buy arms and soldiers to maintain their rule, and to amass personal fortunes – like the global order just the way it is. And so do we. If ownership rights in natural resources could not be acquired from tyrannical rulers, for example, the resources we need to import would be scarcer and hence more expensive.

The conclusion is once again that the underfulfillment of human rights in the developing countries is not a homegrown problem, but one we greatly contribute to through the policies we pursue and the international order we impose. We have then not merely a positive responsibility with regard to global poverty, like Rawls's "duty of assistance," but a negative responsibility to stop imposing (i.e., to reform) the existing global order[23] and to prevent and mitigate the harms it continually causes for the world's poorest populations. Because our responsibility is negative and because so much harm can be prevented at so little cost to ourselves, the reduction of severe global poverty should be our foremost moral priority.

## Notes

1  This is 1.9 percent of their combined GDPs of $25,104 billion in 2001 (World Bank 2002, 239).

2  From 0.33 percent of their combined GNPs in 1990 (UNDP 2002, 202) to 0.22 percent in 2001 (www.oecd.org/EN/document/0,,EN-document-15-nodirectorate-no-12-29438-15,00.html). Aggregate ODA in 2001 was $51.4 billion (ibid.), down from $53.7 billion in 2000 (UNDP 2002, 202) and $56.4 billion in 1999 (UNDP 2001, 190). The US has led the decline by reducing ODA from 0.21 to 0.10 percent of GNP in a time of great prosperity, culminating in enormous budget surpluses. In coming years, the US is set to increase its ODA in the aftermath of September 11 – the figure for 2001 already includes a special $600 million US disbursement toward stabilizing Pakistan.

3  For details, see Pogge 2002, introduction and chapter 5.

4  Chen and Ravallion 2001, 290, and World Bank 2000, 23. (Martin Ravallion and Shaohua Chen have managed the World Bank's income poverty assessments for well over a decade. These latest data are for 1998.) Because life expectancy among the very poor is much lower than average, far more than a fifth of all human lives – and deaths – occur within the poorest quintile. Conventional methods of measuring the extent of poverty may thus distort what is morally significant by assigning lower weight to the poor in proportion to their lower life expectancy. Suppose, for example, as is approximately true, that the poor live, on average, half as long as the non-poor. The number of lives and deaths in the poorest quintile would then be twice the average number of lives and deaths in the other four quintiles: one third versus two thirds. 33 percent of all human lives and deaths would occur among the poor, even while these poor, at any given time, make up only 20 percent of the world's population. This distortion affects most conventional statistics I cite in this essay, though not of course the statement that one third of all human deaths are due to poverty-related causes.

5  To assess the incomes of poor people in poor countries, the World Bank uses official purchasing power parities (PPPs). These are typically three to seven times higher than market exchange rates: India's per capita gross national income of $460 is equated to $2,450 PPP, China's $890 to $4,260 PPP, Nigeria's $290 to $830 PPP, Pakistan's $420 to $1,920 PPP, Bangladesh's $370 to $1,680 PPP, Ethiopia's $100 to $710 PPP, Vietnam's $410 to $2,130 PPP, and so on (World Bank 2002, 234–5). Inflating the incomes of the poor according to these PPPs is deeply problematic, because PPPs are based on the prices of all goods and services worldwide, whereas the poor are compelled to concentrate their expenditures on a narrow subset of such commodities. These basic necessities are cheaper in the poor countries, but not nearly as much cheaper as general PPPs would suggest. Using general PPPs to inflate the incomes of the poor abroad thus greatly exaggerates their consumption possibilities in terms of basic necessities. See Reddy and Pogge 2002 for comprehensive evidence.

6  The UN International Labor Organization reports that "some 250 million children between the ages of 5 and 14 are working in developing countries – 120 million full time, 130 million part time" (www.ilo.org/public/english/standards/ipec/simpoc/stats/4stt.htm).

7  Cf. FAO 1999 and UNICEF 2002. For the frequency of specific causes of deaths, see WHO 2001, Annex Table 2.

8  *Universal Declaration of Human Rights*, §25.

9   The total number of human deaths in 2000 was 55.7 million, representing a death rate of 152,000 per day (WHO 2001, Annex Table 2). Among these, "worldwide 34,000 children under age five die daily from hunger and preventable diseases" (USDA 1999, iii).

10   On average, the poor live 30 percent below the $1/day poverty line. See Chen and Ravallion 2001, 290 and 293, dividing the poverty gap index by the headcount index.

11   The 53 high-income economies (World Bank 2002, 243) represent 15.57 percent of humankind and 80.97 percent of the sum of gross national incomes (ibid., 235). This means that their average income is 23 times that of the rest of the world. Disparities in wealth are much greater, still, than income disparities: "The world's 200 richest people more than doubled their net worth in the four years to 1998, to more than $1 trillion. The assets of the top three billionaires are more than the combined GNP of all least developed countries and their 600 million people" (UNDP 1999, 3). "The additional cost of achieving and maintaining universal access to basic education for all, basic health care for all, reproductive health care for all women, adequate food for all and safe water and sanitation for all is . . . less than 4 % of the combined wealth of the 225 richest people in the world" (UNDP 1998, 30).

12   Those below $2/day live, on average, 43 percent below that line. See Chen and Ravallion 2001, 290 and 293, again dividing the poverty gap index by the headcount index.

13   The problem of world hunger has often been addressed in these terms, e.g. in Singer 1972 and in Unger 1996.

14   For detailed explication of these three connections, cf. Pogge 2002, section 8.2.

15   His second and third Laws state: "Peoples are to observe treaties and undertakings. . . . Peoples are equal and are parties to the agreements that bind them" (Rawls 1999b, 37).

16   The World Bank recently interviewed 60,000 poor people in the developing countries and published snippets of their responses, "Voices of the Poor," on its website.

17   Amartya Sen has mentioned Kerala in many of his writings, and references to this state are now common in the literature (e.g., Rawls 1999b, 110).

18   Horatio Alger (1832–99) was a highly successful US writer of stories about the rise to prosperity of boys from poor backgrounds.

19   Cf. www.oecd.org/EN/about/0,,EN-about-88-3-no-no-no-88,00.html.

20   The record after the first few years is not encouraging: "Plenty of laws exist to ban bribery by companies. But big multinationals continue to sidestep them with ease" ("The Short Arm of the Law," *The Economist*, 2 March 2002, 63–5, at 63).

21   This effect is somewhat mitigated by authoritarian regimes being likewise held responsible for the debts of their democratic predecessors.

22   Economists have known for some time of the negative correlation between developing countries' resource endowments and their rates of economic growth (the so-called resource curse or Dutch Disease) – exemplified by the relatively low growth rates, over the past 40 years, of resource-rich Nigeria, Kenya, Angola, Mozambique, Zaire, Venezuela, Brazil, Saudi Arabia, Burma, and the Philippines. The causal connections accounting for this correlation, however, are only now beginning to be fully understood. Cf. Lam and Wantchekon 1999, specifically supporting the hypothesis that the causal connection between resource wealth and poor economic growth is mediated through reduced chances for democracy: "all petrostates or resource-dependent countries in Africa fail to initiate meaningful political reforms. . . . besides South Africa, transition to democracy has been successful only in resource-poor countries" (p. 31); "a one percentage increase in the size of the natural resource sector [relative to GDP] generates a decrease by half a percentage point in the probability of survival of democratic regimes" (p. 35).

23   This is suggested by §28 of the *Universal Declaration of Human Rights*: "Everyone is entitled to a social and international order in which the rights and freedoms set forth in this Declaration can be fully realized."

## References

Chen, Shaohua, and Martin Ravallion (2001) How Did the World's Poorest Fare in the 1990s? *Review of Income and Wealth* 47: 283–300.

FAO (Food and Agriculture Organization of the United Nations) (1999) *The State of Food Insecurity in the World 1999* <www.fao.org/news/1999/img/sofi99-e.pdf>.

Lam, Ricky, and Wantchekon, Leonard (1999) Dictatorships as a Political Dutch Disease. Unpublished working paper, Yale University <http://econpapers.hhs.se/paper/wopyalegr/>.

Pogge, Thomas W. (2002) *World Poverty and Human Rights*. Cambridge: Polity Press.

Rawls, John (1996) *Political Liberalism*. New York: Columbia University Press [1993].

Rawls, John (1999a) *A Theory of Justice*. Cambridge, MA: Harvard University Press [1971].

Rawls, John (1999b) *The Law of Peoples*. Cambridge, MA: Harvard University Press.

Reddy, Sanjay, and Pogge, Thomas W. (2002) How *Not* to Count the Poor. Unpublished working paper, www.socialanalysis.org.

Singer, Peter (1972) Famine, Affluence and Morality. *Philosophy and Public Affairs*, 1: 229–43.

Unger, Peter (1996) *Living High and Letting Die: Our Illusion of Innocence*. Oxford: Oxford University Press.

UNICEF (United Nations Children's Fund) (2002) *The State of the World's Children 2002*. New York: UNICEF <www.unicef.org/sowc02/pdf/sowc2002-eng-full.pdf>.

UNDP (1998) *Human Development Report 1998*. New York: Oxford University Press.

UNDP (1999) *Human Development Report 1999*. New York: Oxford University Press.

UNDP (2000) *Human Development Report 2000*. New York: Oxford University Press.

UNDP (2001) *Human Development Report 2001*. New York: Oxford University Press.

UNDP (2002) *Human Development Report 2002*. New York: Oxford University Press.

USDA (United States Department of Agriculture) (1999) *U.S. Action Plan on Food Security* <www.fas.usda.gov/icd/summit/usactplan.pdf>.

WHO (World Health Organization) (2001) *The World Health Report 2001*. Geneva: WHO Publications <www.who.int/whr/2001>.

World Bank (2000) *World Development Report 2000/2001*. New York: Oxford University Press.

World Bank (2002) *World Development Report 2003*. New York: Oxford University Press.

# 48

# Global Civil Society

## *Mary Kaldor*

[ . . . ]

The term 'global civil society' is increasingly used in both a normative and a descriptive sense. In a normative sense, it tends to refer to the aspiration for the territorial extension of civil society. The classic definition of civil society, although there have always been a range of interpretations, generally refers to a rule of law guaranteed by the state – a *Societas Civilis* to use the seventeenth century term – and the existence of independent groups of citizens able to uphold and disseminate the values and norms which underpin the rule of law and check abuses of power by the state.[1] The German sociologist Norbert Elias used the term 'the civilising process' to describe the way in which violence was removed from everyday life within the territorial confines of the state.[2]

In a descriptive sense, the term 'global civil society' tends to refer to those independent NGOs and social movements that operate across national boundaries, although there are considerable disputes about what is or is not included in the term.[3] Global civil society may be used to refer to the non-profit sector: everything that operates across national borders and between the state, the market, and the family. Alternatively, it can refer to everything between the state and the family, that is to say it can include the market. Finally, it may embody simply advocacy networks including both those that advocate a global 'civilising process' and those that take fundamentalist positions.[4]

The emergence of the term 'global civil society' can be located at the interstices of two historic developments during the 1990s: the spread of demands for democratisation and the intensifying process of global interconnectedness. The rediscovery of the term 'civil society' in Eastern Europe in the 1980s was first and foremost a response to the overbearing state and this had resonance in other parts of the world where the paternalism and rigidity of the post-war state was called into question. It reflected a new demand for personal autonomy and self-organisation in societies characterised by growing complexity and uncertainty and where traditional forms of political organisation, notably parties, were no longer the main sites of political debate.[5]

The term 'civil society' and related terms such as 'anti-politics' or 'power of the powerless' seemed to offer a discourse within which one might frame parallel concerns about the ability to control the circumstances in which individuals live, and about the substantive empowerment of citizens. While Western elites seized upon this language as evidence for the victory of actually existing democracies, the inheritors of the so-called new social movements began to use the term to express a demand for a radical extension of democracy.[6]

From the beginning, this new understanding of civil society arose in the context of intensifying global interconnectedness, which was not just economic, but political, social, and cultural as well. Global interconnectedness does not pertain only to the extended reach of multinational corporations, but it also encompasses the growth of international governmental organisations and transnational social movements.[7] During the 1990s, the process of what is known as globalisation has speeded up for various reasons including the collapse of previously closed societies, the spread of neoliberal ideas, and, above all, the dramatic developments in information technologies.

On the one hand, the process of globalisation has limited the autonomy of the state; the growing influence of international decision-making narrows the freedom of manoeuvre and the capacity to respond to democratic demands. Paradoxically, at a moment when formal democratic procedures have been extended to many new areas (Eastern Europe, Latin America, Africa), substantive democracy – the ability to participate in decisions affecting everyday life – has been eroded by the loss of autonomy of nation-states. Although nation-states remain the focus of politics, some of the key political and economic decisions are now taken in international fora and not at the level of the nation-state. On the other hand, global interconnectedness opens up new possibilities for citizens' groups and for protecting and strengthening independent political groupings in authoritarian and closed societies. After all, in Eastern Europe, it was the extension of transnational legal arrangements from above (the Helsinki Agreement), combined with various informal transnational links, that made possible the opening up of autonomous spaces.

Because of this particular historic conjuncture, it may be misleading to derive the meaning of the contemporary concepts of civil society and global civil society from the classical definitions. The rediscovery of earlier theories of civil society helped to provide a legitimating narrative, but, at the same time, these historical interpretations may have obscured the truly novel aspects of the concept. Whereas the classical definitions presupposed the existence of a state, the contemporary concept can be described as a move away from state-centred approaches, both in a societal sense – more concern with individual empowerment and personal autonomy – and in a geographical sense in respect to the territorial restructuring of social relations resulting from intensifying interconnectedness.

Some scholars, drawing on classical definitions of civil society, argue that it is not possible to talk about civil society without a state.[8] But nowadays it may no longer be possible to sustain a civil society within the territorial confines of the state. The binary distinction between civil society (the domestic) and anarchy and barbarism (the international), which was associated with the rise of the modern state with its clear territorial boundaries, is breaking down. The 'civilising process', described by Elias, depended on the concentration and centralisation of violence in the hands of the state, which resulted in the terrible totalitarianism and wars of the twentieth century.

If a global 'civilising process' is possible, it cannot be based on the establishment of a world state because this would imply an unimaginable concentration of power. Rather, it would have to mean the extension of an international rule of law guaranteed by a range of interlocking institutions, including – but not only – states, and the extension of citizens' networks who monitor, contest, and put pressure on these institutions. What we might describe as global civil society would be the interaction of those groups, networks, and movements who provide a voice for individuals in global arenas and who act as, to paraphrase a well-known dictum, the transmission belts between the individual and global institutions.

## Emerging Global Political Cleavages

In the era of the nation-state, political parties were the primary sites of political debate and the dominant political cleavage was between left and right, broadly speaking between those who favoured greater redistribution of power and material wealth and those who emphasised the importance of free markets and minimum state interference. With the collapse of the Soviet Union and the discrediting of socialist ideas, this cleavage has come to be supplanted by the division between those who emphasise parochial and particularistic concerns, often around the preservation of traditional identities, and those who could be described as cosmopolitans, who emphasise international or global principles and values and who favour tolerance and diversity.[9] All of these different positions are represented through global civil society.

It is possible to identify four relevant political groupings based on these two types of cleavages, as shown in the matrix below:

|                   | Parochial                                  | Cosmopolitan                                                              |
|-------------------|--------------------------------------------|--------------------------------------------------------------------------|
| Neoliberal        | New Right, e.g., Thatcher, Pinochet or Haider | Multinational corporations, Internationalist Liberals, e.g., Fukuyama |
| Redistributionist | Old Left, e.g., Traditional socialist parties | Global civic networks, e.g., NGOs, aid agencies                        |

The first category comprises neoliberal parochialists: those who emphasise national or religious identity and traditional values, but favour neoliberal economic policies. This type of political thinking is fairly typical of the new right who strongly favour free movements of trade and capital but oppose free movements of people. They support a strong centralised state and they make use of nationalist or fundamentalist rhetoric to mobilise popular support. The new right might take the form of traditional political parties but can also be identified in transnational networks based on religious fundamentalism or exclusive nationalism.

The second category are the old left, who favour a return to the strong state and the commitment to welfare and full employment. They believe democracy and welfare are eroded by globalisation and want to de-globalise. They are generally to be found in traditional socialist parties but they also participate in NGOs, particularly trade unions.

The third category comprises the new globalisers who predominated during the 1990s. They believe that free trade and capital movements will contribute to wealth and generate growing democratisation and political liberty. They argue that globalisation benefits developing countries because rich countries are forced to open their markets to Third World products as demonstrated by the success of the Asian Tigers. These views tend to be expressed by corporate executives, centrist politicians, and economic experts.

The final category comprises the new grouping of what I describe as 'global civic networks': those groups who aspire to a global 'civilising process' and believe that the representation of different viewpoints in global civil society is a necessary condition for this. Global civic networks include those new transnational social movements and

NGOs concerned about global issues such as the environment, war, poverty, women's rights, and so on, who often find allies within the emerging global media and within international organisations. They argue that globalisation is an uneven process; while some countries and social groups have experienced dramatic accumulation of wealth over the last two decades, other areas and individuals have experienced declining or even negative rates of economic growth, greatly increased inequalities, dislocation, war and crime. This group maintains that the present rules of global governance, such as it is, are skewed in favour of the rich countries: WTO and its predecessor GATT were successful in liberalising trade like manufacturing or financial services, which benefits rich countries, but much less successful in liberalising agriculture or older manufactures like textiles, which the rich countries want to protect. Moreover, rules established concerning patents and intellectual property rights are biased in favour of rich countries, for example, making life-giving drugs very expensive in poor countries or failing to protect traditional medicines and plants. Their concern is not to return to the era of the nation-state but to regulate the process of globalisation at a global level and to increase the access of the powerless to global institutions.

What matters in future political struggles is the kind of coalitions that are made by these different groupings. In particular, it can be argued that neither the old left nor the liberal globalisers can succeed without compromise. If I am right that a reversal of globalisation is not possible, then a reversion to the statist model of welfare is also infeasible. At the same time, given the way in which globalisation erodes substantive democracy, it is difficult to envisage a neoliberal global economic order that also guarantees political liberty since the unequal consequences of globalisation are likely to lead to demands that cannot be fulfilled through the democratic process. Karl Polanyi's argument about the authoritarian implications of neoliberalism could thus be applied at a global level.[10]

Broadly speaking, it is possible to envisage two types of successful coalitions. One is between the liberal globalisers and the new right. This would result in an unequal global system, imposed at a national level by authoritarian traditionalist governments. Nation-states would gain a new lease of life either as the enforcers of globalisation or as the authoritarian reaction to globalisation. The other is between the liberal globalisers and global civic networks, which would imply the democratisation of globalisation and the beginnings of a global civilising process. In so far as the old left have any influence, their role will depend on the kind of coalitions they choose to make. If the old left were to ally with the new right, they might help to skew the rules of globalisation in favour of their particular countries, especially in the case of powerful countries like the US. And in a few cases, for example the 'rogue states', they might succeed in building red-brown coalitions and establishing closed pockets of fundamentalism, albeit with transnational criminal links. On the other hand, if the old left were to ally with the global civic networks, they might be more successful in gaining redistributional benefits.

Essentially, these two types of coalitions could shape the public debates over the next decade about the character of globalisation. One model favours a system with minimum rules, in which increasingly authoritarian nation-states impose the free movement of trade and capital. According to this model, sustained economic growth would be accompanied by growing economic and social inequality, ethnic and racial tension, and probably increased violence and repression. Formal democratic rules might allow populist leaders using majoritarian rhetoric to win elections even though the opportunities for substantive influence are narrowed. The other model offers a system of global regulation in which the institutions responsible for setting the rules – the WTO, the IMF, the UN and so on – have a much greater degree of accountability and greater receptiveness to public debates and in which new forms of political organisations – transnational NGOs, social movements and so on – act as forms of representation of the victims of globalisation.

# Conclusion

[ . . . ]
[G]lobal civil society is not a model or a blueprint; it is a contested process, in which different views about the world's future can be expressed.

## Notes

1  See Ernest Gellner, *The Conditions of Liberty: Civil Society and its Rivals* (London: Hamish Hamilton, 1994).
2  Norbert Elias, *The Civilizing Process: State Formation and Civilization* (Oxford: Blackwell, 1982).
3  See John Keane, *Civil Society: Old Images, New Visions* (Cambridge: Polity Press, 1998).
4  Margaret E. Keck and Kathryn Sikkink, *Activists Beyond Borders* (Ithaca, NY: Cornell University Press, 1998).
5  See Ulrich Beck, *Risk Society: Towards a New Modernity* (London: Sage, 1992).
6  See Andrew Arato and Jean L. Cohen, *Civil Society and Political Theory* (Cambridge, MA: MIT Press, 1995).
7  See David Held, Anthony McGrew, David Goldblatt, and Jonathan Perraton, *Global Transformations: Politics, Economics, and Culture* (Cambridge: Polity Press, 1999).
8  Chris Brown, 'Cosmopolitanism, World Citizenship, and Global Civil Society', *Critical Review of International Social and Political Philosophy*, forthcoming.
9  Anthony Giddens, *Beyond Left and Right: The Future of Radical Politics* (Cambridge: Polity Press, 1994).
10  See Karl Polanyi, *The Great Transformation* (New York: Octagon Books, 1975).

# 49

# A World Gone Wrong?

## Chris Brown

'Strange things are happening like never before,' sang Bob Dylan, quoting the Mississippi Sheiks, in the title track of his 1993 album *World Gone Wrong*. The leaders of the world's most powerful countries who gathered at the G8 Summit in Genoa in July 2001 could only agree as they met behind a steel security wall, and retired at nights to the secure base of an ocean liner moored in the harbour, while a hard core of anarchists battled the Italian police in the streets, and some tens of thousands of peaceful demonstrators tried to make themselves heard over the din. The disturbances at Genoa followed those in Gothenburg at the US-EU Summit in May 2001; both reflected a pattern set by the Battle for Seattle at the WTO's meeting in November 1999, and what have become a series of annual events at the Davos economic summits, IMF and World Bank AGMs and on May Day. [ . . . ]

There is, of course, nothing particularly strange about the idea of demonstrations at international get-togethers, but there are several features of the current crop that are unusual. The sheer scale of the protests is pretty much unprecedented; leaving aside the street-fighting element, the number of organizations that are involved in the protests, one way or another, is large enough, but what is equally striking is the range of interests and positions represented – environmental groups, trade unions, international aid agencies, nationalist French farmers, social democrats, socialists and neo-communists. Moreover, the level of tacit popular support for the aims of the demonstrators seems quite high [ . . . ].

[ . . . ] [T]here is today a widespread sense that we live in a world gone wrong, and the aim in this [ . . . ] chapter is to investigate this mood, to ask why so many people appear to have come to this conclusion and explore some of the ways in which the world might change. There is, as yet, very little in the way of academic literature on this subject; the field is dominated by the very popular genre of anti-globalization jeremiads of which even the best, such as George Monbiot's *Captive State*, Thomas Frank's *One Market Under God*, Noreena Hertz's *The Silent Takeover*, Naomi Klein's *No Logo*, make no pretence of objectivity, no attempt to see another point of view (Monbiot, 2000; Frank, 2001; Hertz, 2001; Klein, 2001). Because of the paucity of scholarly comment, this chapter will be rather less literature-based, rather more personal, polemical even [ . . . ]. Still – old habits die hard – to start this discussion it may be helpful to examine one piece of academic writing that does do justice to the scale of the crisis faced by the current order.

## Westfailure?

Can the existing international order cope with the stresses and strains induced by globalization without some kind of transformation? If not, it could well be argued that, whatever transitional problems remain, the Westphalia System has run its course, and is now unambiguously an obstacle to the realization of a just and functioning world. Such is the argument that Susan Strange presented in a posthumously published article with a punning title, 'The Westfailure System' (Strange, 1999). Strange's argument is worth examining in its own terms, but it is also interesting because of its author – Strange was a, if not 'the', leading figure in British IR for a generation, a realist, admittedly rather unorthodox, who was resolutely opposed to normative theory, or indeed most other kinds of theory; the fact that, at the end of her life, she could draw such radical conclusions about the legitimacy of the system is, in itself, telling (C. Brown, 1999).

It should be said at the outset that while she had little sympathy for what she regarded as the 'globaloney' of globalization theory, she was convinced that the world had changed of late (Strange, 1994 and 1998). Strange was first and foremost an international political economist, and her understanding of the Westphalia System was that it grew up with the sovereign state and the market economy in symbiosis. The sovereign state provided the context for capitalism, while capitalism provided successful sovereign states with the wherewithal to prosper. Her general point, a commonplace of the literature more generally, is that the market economy has now extended itself in the world to the point where this symbiotic relationship has been broken. The territorial sovereign state is no longer capable of performing the role it once did. There are three particular points where this incapacity is most striking and damaging to human welfare.

First, a particular concern of Strange throughout her life, the global financial system is now beyond the control of any government and of the institutions that governments have created to attempt monetary management. Strange sees the creation and regulation of credit as the central international economic task. In the last resort, trade will look after itself – the giant corporations which dominate global production have an interest in world trade, and the efforts of such bodies as the WTO to regulate and control trade are of secondary importance to the motivations of these companies, who are well able to look after their own interests – but international monetary relations require supervision that a system of territorially based sovereign states can no longer supply. The destruction of Barings Bank in 1995 and the Asian collapse of 1997 are simply straws in the wind, indicators of what may be to come. On her account – and contrary to those for whom capitalism itself is the problem, who would welcome crisis on the basis that the worse the state of the world economy, the better the prospects for revolution – the economic collapse that a full-scale global financial crisis would create would be generally harmful to everyone's welfare; the potential inability of the system to manage and regulate the creation of credit means that, even in its own terms, it faces failure. However, the other two areas of 'Westfailure' she identifies are more obviously and directly disastrous.

The inability of a system of sovereign states to cope with the consequences of environmental degradation is the second such failure. Global economic growth has taken place without reference to environmental consequences such as global warming, ozone layer depletion and the loss of irreplaceable scarce resources, and the international system has proved unable to prevent the situation from getting worse in many areas, much less actually reverse these harmful consequences. The reason for this inability is clear: the system of sovereign states allows, even encourages, individual states to act selfishly. It will take a collective effort to reverse environmental degradation, but the worst polluters will have to make the biggest effort, and the present system allows them to dodge their responsibilities; the effective impossibility of sanctioning the most powerful countries – who are also the biggest polluters – means that steps to avoid catastrophe rely upon the good will of those states and their willingness to adopt an enlightened, long-term definition of their self-interest. The environmental politics of the last few years makes it clear that this cannot be relied upon. Moreover, those poorer states which are not yet polluting at the level of the US, Japan and Western Europe because of their poverty have no incentive to adopt clean but expensive technology unless a collective effort is made to compensate them for their restraint, and, again, this is not something that can be expected to happen under the present system.

Even more directly contrary to general human welfare, third, Strange points to a double failure of humanitarianism; on the one hand, the present economic order works to increase global inequality, with the least advantaged left ever further behind to face a future of malnutrition, poverty and, probably, increasingly violent civil strife, while on the other, inequalities within 'successful' states grow worse, as the possibility that domestic welfare states can protect their peoples from the restructurings forced on them by global capitalism recedes. Whatever possibility there might once have been that the state could act as an agent for social justice is being undermined by the logic of an economic system that is out of human control and serving no general interest. The only true beneficiaries of the present system are a transnational business elite who run the giant corporations that provide the driving force behind the hegemony of neo-liberalism (Van der Pijl, 1998).

This is a powerful indictment of the Westphalian order, and from a writer who could not be accused of promoting an unrealistic, utopian vision of the world. Part of the force of the indictment comes precisely from the fact that no easy solution to these ills is offered, indeed, no solution at all is on offer. [ . . . ]

## What Is To Be Done?

Once upon a time, those who opposed the capitalist world order had a clear sense of where they wanted to go. Marxists – and, for that matter, socialists more generally – knew that they wanted to replace capitalism with an economic system that was not based on the profit motive or on market forces. The ultimate goal of those who explicitly identified with Marx and Lenin was 'communism', a system where scarcity had been abolished and which would be reached via 'socialism', a fully planned industrial economy. Western social democrats focused on the establishment of a planned, mixed economy under which those capitalists who remained in business would be obliged to co-ordinate their activities under the auspices of some kind of democratically established and controlled planning body – in any event, public utilities and major industrial concerns would be under public ownership, and their decisions as to what to produce would be taken in the general interest. Both Marxists and social democrats generally favoured industrial society. Building on the paeans of praise for the world-transforming activities of the bourgeoisie that are to be found in the *Communist Manifesto*, communists anticipated the abolition of scarcity which would eventually follow once the processes of industrialization were allowed to develop free from the logic of capitalist accumulation. More prosaically, Western social democrats wished to deliver to their working-class constituencies the kinds of consumer goods that the rich took for granted and that could only be made available via mass production.

Two features of this thumbnail sketch are striking – how powerful these ideas were a generation or two ago, and how antediluvian they seem today. Of course, there are still Marxist groups around, and 'real' socialist parties abound, but the action has moved elsewhere. Whatever sympathy there might be for the remaining communist countries – North Korea, Cuba – virtually no one sees them as models for the rest of the world. Those democratic socialist parties in Europe that have survived and prospered under current conditions have largely done so by dropping virtually all of the features that would have identified them as socialist a generation ago, preferring 'third way' politics and electoral success to ideologically pure oblivion (Giddens, 2000). More to the point, few of the diverse ideologies of the campaigners against global capital draw upon the revolutionary traditions of the last two centuries. 'Subcomandante Insurgente Marcos', the leader of the Chiapas rebellion in Mexico, may have ideological roots that go back to Mao, Che Guevara and the various theories of 'people's war' of the 1960s, but it appears that the mobilization he has achieved is largely based on ethnic and traditional factors (Harvey, 1998; Marcos et al., 2001). Environmentalists can find little in the Marxist/socialist tradition to support their concerns, while trade unionists are obliged to sanitize their past in order to make contact with their new friends in the anti-globalization movement – the best example of this new consciousness being the demonstration by US steel workers at the WTO in 1999, which involved dumping imported steel into Seattle harbour for the benefit of the TV cameras; in order to preserve their environmentalist credentials, they were then obliged to undump the steel and dispose of it elsewhere.

If not an old-style revolution, then what? Different groups have their own models of the future which only rarely have any degree of ideological coherence. Labour unions are usually simply protectionist – which is one of the reasons why the governments of the newly industrializing countries (NICs) take such a jaundiced view of the anti-globalization campaigns; these governments are equally suspicious of well-meaning campaigns directed against sweatshops and child labour in the 'South'. Abolish child labour without making alternative provision for the children involved and all that will be achieved is the lowering of the competitiveness of the NICs; force Nike's subcontractors to pay North American wages in the Philippines or Vietnam and the sweatshops will indeed close, because investment in those countries will cease to be profitable. About the only anti-globalization group that does have a clear vision of the future are the 'deep green' environmentalists – but since this vision involves a dramatically reduced world population to allow the achievement of self-sufficiency and ecological balance via traditional agricultural methods, it tends not to be widely circulated outside of the websites and journals of the movement. There are, of course, consistent anti-capitalists in the anti-globalization movement, including the various anarchist groups who attend meetings such as the Genoa Summit in home-made body armour with the clear intention of taking on the police and the British 'wombles' who, in similar attire, attempt to loot and pillage. But, as these groups illustrate, there are ways of being anti-capitalist that are in no sense progressive – by their violent tactics these rioters demonstrate a closer affinity with the (equally anti-capitalist) fascist movements of contemporary Europe such as the British National Party or the French National Front than with any 'left' movement.

More representative of the general lack of ideology of the anti-globalization coalition is the slogan painted on the lead banner at one of the major demonstrations in London on May Day 2001 – 'Replace Capitalism with Something Nicer'. One profoundly hopes that this was actually meant to be funny, but, intentionally or not, it provides quite a good summary of much of the popular anti-globalization literature. Campaigners such as Naomi Klein and Noreena Hertz condemn the dominance of global brands, and the undemocratic influence of giant firms, but without providing any convincing picture of how, in the long run, this influence could be diminished. Their remedies tend to focus on effective anti-monopoly legislation to break up the corporate giants and the establishment of moves towards higher levels of local self-government and trade union rights in the workplace, along with the kind of international redistribution of income and wealth advocated by writers such as Brian Barry and Thomas Pogge [ . . . ] or, to put it differently, they support the idealized global social democracy envisaged by the *Brandt Report* at the end of the 1970s. There are practical problems here – is it actually likely that Western workers will voluntarily open up markets for Southern competitors? Can it really be envisaged that Western tax-payers will be prepared to authorize the kind of transfers of wealth that would replace the profit-oriented investments in the NICs of today's giant corporations? But more fundamental is the lack of attention to the dynamics of capitalism. The kind of locally restricted capitalism envisaged by these campaigners seems more or less guaranteed to break out of the bounds imposed upon it as soon as it can.

The French campaigners, José Bové, François Dufour and Anna de Casparis, in a similar general work, maintain that *The World is Not For Sale* (Bové et al., 2001). Bové, a French farmer who came to prominence as a result of his campaign against McDonald's in France, delivers a rhetorically powerful attack on the assumption that money is the only thing that matters, defending the importance of the preservation of local communities seen as at risk – as by Klein and Hertz – from giant corporations such as 'McDo's'. But – again as with Klein and Hertz – the French writers do not envisage an end to capitalism as such, merely the control of its global representatives. Instead, local French capitalists and socially responsible French farmers are seen as the antidote to excessive greed, not a wholly convincing vision of a better future.

As with Strange's 'Westfailure' article, these books succeed because they appear to diagnose an ill, rather than because of any positive position they advocate. There clearly is today a widespread popular sense that the 'runaway world' identified by Anthony Giddens is undermining things that are generally valued, such as a sense of community and a sense of personal security, and that many features of the contemporary world economy are manifestly unjust (Giddens, 1999). Pinning these evils on giant corporations seems to make a lot of sense, and the fact that these authors have no remedy for the disease they diagnose can in turn simply be interpreted as further evidence of the power of these corporations. In a way this is reassuring. Nothing is going to change, so it doesn't really matter that most of the readers of *No Logo* continue to buy their DKNY jeans and Nike trainers. After all, what difference can it make?

What has gone wrong here? The key feature of much of the anti-globalization literature is that it is backward-looking, apparently intent on creating a better yesterday, a sanitized version of the past in which socially responsible organic farmers, outward-looking owners of corner-shops and friendly local pubs worked together to provide the people with wholesome food and harmless entertainment – as opposed to the cheap meat and unnecessarily wide range of cheeses available in the modern supermarket, or the tawdry entertainment provided by the BBC, Channel 4, MTV and so on. The general public may be cynical about television and worried about food scares, but they are unwilling to buy into this utopia, even as they acknowledge the strength of the critique of the present upon which it is based. Perhaps what is required is a forward-looking critique of globalization – an account of the ills of the present that finds within those ills the basis for a better world, but a better world going forward not back. There are some indications that such a critique is emerging both from left-of-centre politicians – see, for example, the defence of the WTO and the G8 launched by Clare Short, the Labour Government's left-leaning International Development Minister – and from writers previously located much further to the left, such as Antonio Negri (Hardt and Negri, 2000).

## In Defence of Globalization and Some Aspects of Global Capitalism

Any morally serious defence of globalization has to be addressed primarily to the issues of rights and justice [...], that is, to the inequalities that exist in the current system – but before approaching this task a few words on some topics that are not of great moral significance but that are, nonetheless, important to the lives of the majority of ordinary people may be appropriate. The key point, hinted at above, is that a great many of the changes associated with the growing strength of global capitalism have been enormously positive for the majority of the citizens of the advanced industrial world. Even not very good supermarkets generally extend the range of goods available to lower-income groups by comparison with the council estate-based general stores they have replaced. Franchises such as McDonald's and Burger King represent an advance – certainly in hygiene and probably nutritionally – on some of the older cafes they have driven out of business in Britain, and the fact that it is now easy to buy a good cup of coffee in British cities is because of the spread of chains such as Starbucks and Coffee Republic, although, admittedly, this point may be less applicable to countries with a better-developed food culture such as France. Satellite and cable TV provides more and better mass entertainment than has been generally available in the past – and the fact that most of this entertainment is not based on high culture is hardly surprising: popular entertainment rarely, if ever, has been. The middle classes may regard package holidays in Spain with disdain, but at least the weather is usually better than Margate or Blackpool. The motor car provides ordinary people with mobility that even their immediate forefathers could not have dreamed of; the near universal spread of refrigerators and washing machines has cut out the daily drudge of shopping for perishables and washing factory-stained clothes by hand. All of these changes are the product of global capitalism, and all come with associated down-sides, but only the children of privilege – whose mothers were spared the drudgery of washing and shopping, whose parents could afford the time to have 'proper' holidays and had the cash to ensure access to high culture and the education to appreciate it – could deny that they have made things better for ordinary people.

There are also genuine issues of choice involved here. French intellectuals may deplore the fact that many of their fellow countrymen and women would rather see an American blockbuster than the latest locally produced movie but, on the assumption that they are not actually herded into the cinema by US Marines, is it actually anyone else's business how they choose to spend their leisure time? Can it really be the duty of the French state to exclude the American films that their own citizens want to see on the grounds that they are not good for them? If ordinary people wish to spend their spare cash on branded clothes, even when the latter are no different from generic items save in price, is it really Naomi Klein's business to tell them not to? Perhaps Klein would have been happier in the days of my childhood in 1950s Britain when there were far fewer logos but it was immediately obvious from the clothes they wore what class people came from, and only the middle classes and their betters were expected to be interested in fashion – the hostility of the middle classes then to 'teddy boys' was largely about telling these working-class kids not to aspire to a dress sense.

Of course, these are side-issues, and not terribly important in the wider scheme of things – most people in the world today, including many within the advanced industrial world, do not have any disposable income to speak of – but even so it is worth registering a protest against the puritanism of many in the anti-globalization movement, and, in particular, against their, perhaps unconscious, class bias against the pleasures of ordinary people. Still, the key issue is not the politics of the wearing of Calvin Klein jeans, but rather the international political economy of leisure wear in general, where it is made, by whom and for what wages. Can the contemporary, neo-liberal, international economy, which distributes the good things of life so unevenly, be defended? This is an uncomplicated question that invites an unqualified 'no', so perhaps it should be rephrased to allow for a more nuanced position – is the current world economy reformable so that it could deliver a more just world? Or are there practical alternatives to current arrangements that would deliver higher levels of social justice? Here the answers are indeed less clear-cut.

The first thing that has to be said is that it is already the case that the neo-liberal 'Washington Consensus' that governed IMF conditionality and World Bank loans in the early 1990s, and required of poor countries that they prioritize low inflation, end price controls, cut government spending and open themselves to the world economy, is widely regarded as having failed even within the community of IMF/World Bank/US Treasury officials who created it in the first place. It is now generally recognized that there have been very few 'success stories' for the Washington Consensus and plenty of examples of increased suffering for ordinary people, when cuts in government spending were usually targeted on the poor, and the ending of price controls on basic foodstuffs added to the misery. Figures such as Joseph Stiglitz, until 1999 Chief Economist at the World Bank, and Ravi Kanbur, until his resignation in 2000 the Editor-to-be of the *World Development Report 2000*, have acknowledged that this is so and moved towards developing a post-Washington Consensus (Stiglitz, 1998). Such a new consensus is, of course, unlikely to satisfy the critics of globalization, but it does indicate a greater degree of flexibility than the IMF and World Bank are usually credited with. Even so, the reforms will not get to the heart of the matter – it is not so much the details of the policies advocated by the Washington institutions that the protestors object to, but rather the assumptions that underlie these policies. What are these assumptions, and can they actually be defended?

The first premise of neo-liberalism is that there is no substitute for the market economy. Liberals have, of course, always believed this, but the collapse of communism in the 1980s has given this position wider credibility; if there is one clear lesson to be learnt from the Soviet experiment it is that once the early stages of industrialization have been gone through, the command economy cannot be made to work – and even at the early stages, five-year plans and the like require unacceptable levels of state coercion. The range of variables which need to be kept in play for a modern complex planned economy to work is simply too large to be modelled even using the most advanced computers – and this is so even without taking into consideration issues such as consumer choice (Nove, 1983 and 1991). Different kinds of market economy are available, but some kind of market is a necessity; since the emergence of industrial society, the most persistent opponents of liberal capitalism from left and right have argued that it is both possible and desirable to replace the impersonal forces of the market by conscious human control – they were wrong, and this error has enormous significance for the evolution of human society and the prospects for revolution. Richard Rorty captures this significance very crisply when he remarks that '[if] you still long for total revolution, for the Radical Other on a world historical scale, the events of 1989 show that you are out of luck' (Rorty, 1998, p. 229). This is not quite right; a revolution based on the socialization of poverty, the kind of primitive communism created by Pol Pot in his mercifully brief reign in Cambodia, is still possible – but this is not the kind of Radical Other that progressive thinkers have sought for the last two hundred years.

The second assumption of neo-liberal thought, and liberalism in general, is that free trade will benefit the poor – this is perhaps the most important bone of contention between those on different sides of the barricades at Seattle and Genoa. The central point is that poor countries, precisely because they are poor, by definition have lower labour costs; if they can combine this feature with reasonable levels of education and political stability then, left to its own devices, the international division of labour will work to channel capital in their direction and, in the medium-to-long run, this will work to equalize wages and general levels of development. The result will be to transfer some kinds of production from the rich world to the poorer world; metal-bashing workers in the advanced industrial world will have to retrain and it may be difficult for them to find work. It is easy to see why trade unions in the North will resist this trend, but what is very difficult to understand is why those who claim to have the interests of the South at heart will support them in their resistance. Southern governments also find this difficult to understand, which is why they are so deeply suspicious of the anti-globalization movement, who seem so adept at finding reasons why measures that would benefit the South are, really, undesirable. The ethical case against agricultural protection by the North is even more clear-cut; again, it is easy to see why heavily subsidized European farmers might want to exclude competition from the South, less easy to see why this should be regarded as a progressive position.

In so far as they have a coherent position, the opponents of free trade object to the fact that it will lead to production for the world market in Southern countries rather than production oriented towards local needs – the argument is that the poor in these countries would benefit more from a successful subsistence economy than they would from a trading economy. In the short run this might well be true, but the longer-term result of such a subsistence economy would be to deny the peoples of the South access to the kind of living standards that their Northern counterparts take for granted – if the peoples of the South are themselves prepared to forgo these living standards, then they have a right to do so, but it is much less clear that Northern well-wishers (or comparatively well-off Southern elites) should be allowed to take this decision on their behalf. The debate over the value to the poor of an open economy is closely related to the third basic assumption of current neo-liberal thought, which is that the basic problem of the less-developed countries is a lack of development capital and that such capital can only flow to these countries in sufficient quantities via private capital markets. Aid budgets are dwarfed by the amounts of money that private corporations and banks have at their disposal, and would be even in the unlikely event that there was sufficient political support in the North for them to be multiplied tenfold. The only way that the South will get access to the development capital it needs is via global private capital markets, and this fact has important implications in a number of areas. It suggests that pressure should be put on global firms to change the kind of investments they make rather than to prevent them from operating in the South at all. It also suggests that any solution to the 'debt crisis' in the least-developed countries that involves a write-off of debt must be drawn up in such a way that it does not act as a disincentive to future private lending.

If some of the most basic assumptions of neo-liberalism seem to be broadly right, ought not the programme to be endorsed as a whole? The problem is that while the model set out above may well be correct in its essentials, current political realities make it difficult for the poor to gain the theoretical benefits that it promises. It is difficult to persuade the poor of the benefits of free trade while the rich are protectionist; even though the theoretical argument in favour of open markets is still valid in such circumstances, the political rhetoric of 'fair trade' and counter-protectionism is very powerful. More to the point, a great deal of the difficulty with the neo-liberal model lies in the weakness of state structures in many parts of the South; for example, the kind of political stability needed to attract investment simply does not exist in much of sub-Saharan Africa, likewise the necessary educational and technical skills. Moreover, strong states are needed not just to attract capital but to ensure that the terms under which it is invested are as favourable to the poor as possible – here it is not so much the strength of the state that is important, but the integrity of elites, their willingness or unwillingness to be bought off by global firms.

There is a more general point here – market economies everywhere and always require strong, relatively incorruptible state authorities if they are to form the economic basis for a just society. Free trade and open markets are a recipe for continual change and upheaval, and strong states are needed to manage this process and to ensure that the losers are protected from its consequences – that their living standards are maintained in the short run and that they have the opportunity to retrain and find different kinds of work in the longer run. The adherents of contemporary neo-liberalism tend too readily to forget this requirement, but an international aid policy genuinely oriented to the poor would be one that promoted responsible, capable and democratic political authorities in poor countries, backed up by active civil societies. To its credit, Britain's Department for International Development has attempted to reorient much of the aid it disburses along these lines; this is 'democracy promotion' in a full sense, rather than the formal notion of spreading democratic institutions usually understood by that term (DFID, n.d.; M. Cox et al., 2000).

   The posited need for strong state authorities takes the argument back to the themes of this book, but, before leaving behind neo-liberalism, some other caveats need to be made to the general support offered above for the key elements of the neo-liberal model. Most important, the fact that markets and private capital are essential features of the model tells us rather less than most adherents of neo-liberalism assume it does. There are lots of ways of organizing a market economy, from the social-democratic approaches of classic Scandinavian politics, via the successful social market of post-1945 (West) Germany, to such neo-liberal models as contemporary New Zealand. Similarly, there are different ways of organizing private enterprises, from the classic multinational corporation to the producer co-operatives that in countries such as Denmark have competed successfully in world markets. Moreover, the case for private enterprise in general has proved quite compatible with the public ownership of basic utilities in a great many successful capitalist economies. In short, there are genuine choices to be made here, even if the choice of a fully socialized economy is currently off the menu.

   A second caveat is summarized by the term 'currently' in the last sentence. The dismal failure of the regimes of really existing socialism suggests that, for the moment, there is no alternative to some kind of market-based economy, but tells us much less about the longer-term trajectory of the system. A socialism based on global wealth rather than the socialization of poverty may, one day, become a practical possibility – and such was, of course, the basis for Marx's writing a century and a half ago. Marx himself and the early Marxists were always clear that they were not producing an emotional, moralizing, romantic critique of capitalism focusing on the sins of the latter and based on nostalgia for a simpler, purer rural past; they would have been horrified at the turning against progress so characteristic of the contemporary anti-globalization movement. Of course, faith in the future of scientific socialism was easier when science itself was less suspect and when the environmental problems that would come with economic growth were not understood – but one suspects that thinkers true to the spirit of Marx would embrace globalization and look to 'science' to solve the problems its successes have created.

## Sovereignty, Rights and Justice in a Post-Westphalian Global Politics

If strong state authorities are the solution to a great many of the ills of globalization, does this not constitute an endorsement of Westphalian norms, of the rights of states in a sovereignty-based system? No, because the sovereign state is not a synonym for the strong state. The possession of an effective administration and bureaucracy, the ability to shape events in the public interest and to shield one's people from the worst consequences of uncontrolled market forces, is only contingently related to the legal status of being sovereign. Obviously, if one state is effectively under the control of another its ability to perform these functions will be severely impaired – but this says nothing about situations in which sovereignty is pooled and shared. It is certainly arguable that the various individual countries that make up the European Union are far more effective, far stronger, as a result of their membership of a body which undoubtedly involves the loss of sovereignty than they would be if they were to try to preserve their sovereignty and act in the world independently of each other – and it is notice-able that, for example, most British 'Eurosceptics' tacitly acknowledge that this is so, by their plans to become part of another wider grouping as members of the North American Free Trade Area, or at least, as super-loyal American allies.

Equally, the strong state is not necessarily a threat to the rights of the individual. Again, the European example is instructive; the European Convention on Human Rights certainly limits what states can do, thus interfering with their sovereignty, but it is by no means clear that they are prevented from acting in the interests of their peoples thereby. The kind of effective state administration that is needed to manage the impact of globalization ought not to be considered hampered by measures that defend the rights of the individual – just to the contrary, the best justification for a strong state is precisely that it can protect the rights of the individual. However, lest this all seem a little too good to be true, it is clear that strong and effective state administrations do have an impact on the relationship between the universal and the particular, between the interests of particular communities and the interests of humanity as a whole. Neo-liberalism asserts that, ultimately, these interests are identical, but that is in the very long run, and, as Lord Keynes famously remarked, in the long run we are all dead. In the meantime, in the here and now, there is a clear problem; the changes that accom-pany globalization are painful and one of the things that effective states can, and do, do is to try to ensure that this pain is borne by someone other than their own citizens. Comparatively well-organized states whose governments are responsive to the imme-diate needs of their peoples – and who want to be re-elected – will resist painful steps if they can, even when, in the longer run, their peoples have an interest in the goals that such steps are oriented towards. It is ultimately for this reason that successive American administrations have been unwilling to tackle the issue of the environment effectively, although, of course, the lobbying activities of US energy companies has reinforced this unwillingness. Here we can return to Strange's diagnosis of Westfailure. The Westphalian sovereignty system legitimates this kind of self-interestedness, and hampers the development of inter-governmental mechanisms to cope with problems of environmental degradation. Strange perhaps underestimates the extent to which states are capable, given sufficient will, of developing projects to protect their own citizens from the immediate impact of globalization, but she is surely right to argue that, under current conditions, the capacity of states to co-operate to solve collective problems is massively sub-optimal.

The theorists of global democracy [ . . . ] wish to push beyond Westphalia by develop-ing global institutions that are democratically based and capable of overriding the legal autonomy of the states whose short-run conception of their own interests stands in the way of the development of solutions to the global problems identified by Strange (Held, 1995; Archibugi and Held, 1995; Archibugi et al., 1998). [ . . . ] [T]he problem with this position is that there is a degree of circularity to the case in its favour – a sense that the world constitutes a community is required before a global democracy could be effective, yet such a sense is unlikely to emerge in the absence of some kind of global democracy. Contemporary liberal democracies emerged from pre-democratic state structures; by analogy, global democracy would require the existence of a global state-structure that could be democratized. Most commentators have assumed that the emergence of such a world empire is both implausible and undesirable. However, some of the more interesting theorists of globalization contest this judgement; the title of Michael Hardt and Antonio Negri's recent book, *Empire*, conveys their sense that the world is being reshaped by globalization into an empire, albeit of a different kind from past examples. Their belief in the possibility of a genuine global democracy rests on this characterization (Hardt and Negri, 2000).

This is, however, a judgement that applies in the long run, and we must live in the here and now – apart from anything else, we have no way of knowing how long the long run will be. An astute Roman of the age of Claudian emperors might well have expressed doubts as to the long-term sustainability of Roman rule, but it would be two to three hundred years before his descendants noticed that the long term was about to become the short term. Today's international order is certainly based on the very tense, uneasy, unstable and frequently counter-productive co-existence and interaction of territorially based political units on the one hand, and increasingly deterritorialized economic and social systems on the other. There is no doubt but that this leads to the kind of impasses identified by Strange – and perhaps justifies describing the current order as a failure – but there is no reason to think that a new order which will resolve the tension is likely to emerge in the near future. Some write of our age as an 'interregnum', a period between two orders, the old state-centric system and a new, global, political order. The frame of reference here is quasi-Marxist, the underlying thought being that one social formation has exhausted its possibilities but still has the resources to delay the emergence of its successor (M. Cox et al., 2000). Perhaps so, but this is no help to us in setting a timescale for the emergence of the new order. It may be implausible that the Westphalia System will survive the twenty-first century, but then implausibility attaches to any prediction one might make about the course of events over the next hundred years. Intelligent science-fiction writers are probably a better guide to the future than either Westphalian or post-Westphalian international political theorists.

[ . . . ]

## References

Archibugi, D. and Held, D. (eds) (1995) *Cosmopolitan Democracy*. Cambridge: Polity.

Archibugi, D., Held, D. and Kühler, M. (eds) (1998) *Re-imagining Political Community: Studies in Cosmopolitan Democracy*. Cambridge: Polity.

Bové, J., Dufour, F. and de Casparis, A. (2001) *The World is Not for Sale*. London: Verso.

Brown, C. (1999) Susan Strange: A Critical Appreciation. *Review of International Studies*, 25: 531–5.

Cox, M., Ikenberry, J. and Inoguchi, T. (eds) (2000) *American Democracy Promotion: Impulses, Strategies and Impacts*. New York: Oxford University Press.

DFID (Department for International Development) (n.d.) *Making Government Work for Poor People*. www.dfid.gov.uk.

Frank, T. (2001) *One Market Under God*. London: Secker and Warburg.

Giddens, A. (1999) *The Runaway World*. Cambridge: Polity.

Giddens, A. (2000) *The Third Way and its Critics*. Cambridge: Polity.

Hardt, M. and Negri, A. (2000) *Empire*. Cambridge, MA: Harvard University Press.

Harvey, N. (1998) *The Chiapas Rebellion*. Durham, NC: Duke University Press.

Held, D. (1995) *Democracy and the Global Order*. Cambridge: Polity.

Hertz, N. (2001) *The Silent Takeover*. London: Heinemann.

Klein, N. (2001) *No Logo*. London: Flamingo.

'Marcos, Subcomandante' et al. (2001) *Our Word is Our Weapon*. London: Serpent's Tail.

Monbiot, G. (2000) *Captive State*. Basingstoke: Macmillan.

Nove, A. (1983) *The Economics of Feasible Socialism*. London: Allen and Unwin.

Nove, A. (1991) *The Economics of Feasible Socialism Revisited*. London: Unwin Hyman.

Rorty, R. (1998) The End of Leninism, Havel, and Social Hope. In *Truth and Progress: Philosophical Papers Vol. 3*, Cambridge: Cambridge University Press.

Stiglitz, J. (1998) *More Instruments and Broader Goals: Moving towards the Post-Washington Consensus*. Helsinki: UN University.

Strange, S. (1994) Wake up Krasner! The World *has* Changed. *Review of International Political Economy*, 1: 209–19.

Strange, S. (1998) Globaloney. *Review of International Political Economy*, 5, 704–11.

Strange, S. (1999) The Westfailure System. *Review of International Studies*, 25: 345–54.

Van der Pijl, K. (1998) *Transnational Classes and International Relations*. London: Routledge.

# 50

# Beyond the States System?

## *Hedley Bull*

If an alternative form of universal political order were to emerge that did not merely constitute a change from one phase or condition of the states system to another, but led beyond the states system, it would have to involve the demise of one or another of the latter's essential attributes: sovereign states, interaction among them, such that they form a system; and a degree of acceptance of common rules and institutions, in respect of which they form a society.

## A System But Not a Society

It is conceivable that a form of universal political organisation might arise which would possess the first and the second of these attributes but not the third. We may imagine, that is to say, that there might exist a plurality of sovereign states, forming a system, which did not, however, constitute an international society. Such a state of affairs would represent the demise of *the* states system, which [ ... ] is an international society as well as an international system. There would be states, and interaction among them on a global basis, but the element of acceptance of common interests or values, and, on the basis of them, of common rules and institutions, would have disappeared. There would be communications and negotiations among these states, but no commitment to a network of diplomatic institutions; agreements, but no acceptance of a structure of international legal obligation; violent encounters among them that were limited by the capacity of the belligerents to make war, but not by their will to observe restraints as to when, how and by whom it was conducted; balances of power that arose fortuitously, but not balances that were the product of conscious attempts to preserve them; powers that were greater than others, but no agreed conception of a great power in the sense of a power with special rights and duties.

Whether or not the states system, at some point in the future, has ceased to be an international society, it might well be difficult to determine. There may be acceptance of common rules and institutions by some states, but not by others: how many states have to have contracted out of international society before we can say that it has ceased to exist? Some rules and institutions may continue to find acceptance, but others not: which rules and institutions are essential? Acceptance of rules and institutions may be difficult to determine: does it lie in verbal assent to these rules, in behaviour that conforms strictly to them, or in willingness to defer to them even while evading them? Granted these difficulties [ ... ] there is ample historical precedent for an international system that is not an international society [ ... ].

An international system that is not an international society might nevertheless contain some elements of order. Particular states might be able to achieve a degree of domestic order, despite the absence of rules and institutions in their relations with one another. Some degree of international order might also be sustained by fortuitous balances of power or relationships of mutual nuclear deterrence, by great power spheres of preponderance unilaterally imposed, by limitations in war that were the consequence of self-restraint or limitations of capacity. But an international system of this kind would be disorderly in the extreme, and would in fact exemplify the Hobbesian state of nature.

## States But Not a System

It is also conceivable that a form of universal political organisation might emerge which possessed the first of the essential attributes that have been mentioned but not the second. We may imagine that there are still sovereign states, but that they are not in contact or interaction with each other, or at all events do not interact sufficiently to cause them to behave as component parts of a system. States might be linked with each other so as to form systems of states in particular regions, but there would not be any global system of states. Throughout the world as a whole there might be mutual awareness among states, and even contact and interaction on a limited scale, but it would no longer be the case that states in all parts of the world were a vital factor in one another's calculations.

It might be difficult to determine how much decline in the global interaction of states would have to have taken place before we could say that they had ceased to form a system. If there is a high degree of interaction throughout the world at the economic and social levels, but not at the strategic level, can we say that there is a global system? Does a global states system cease to exist merely because there are some societies that are excluded from it? Even today in the jungles of Brazil or in the highlands of Papua/New Guinea there are societies scarcely touched by what we nevertheless call the global states system.

Once again, there is ample historical precedent for an alternative to the states system of this kind; [ ... ] it was not before the nineteenth century that there arose any states system that was global in dimension. Does such an alternative represent a superior path to world order?

It has often been maintained that it does. A series of isolated or semi-isolated states or other kinds of community might each achieve a tolerable form of social order within its own confines, and a form of world order would exist that was simply the sum of the order that derived from each of these communities. At the same time the classic sources of disorder that arise in a situation of interaction between states would be avoided because interaction itself would be avoided or kept to a minimum.

This was the substance of Rousseau's vision of a world of small self-sufficient states, each achieving order within its own confines through the operation of the general will of its community, and achieving order in their relations with one another by minimising contact.[1] It also entered into the prescription that Washington laid down for the United States in his Farewell Address: 'The great rule of conduct for us in regard to foreign relations is, in extending our commercial relations, to have with them as little *political* connection as possible.'[2] This for Washington was a maxim only for the United

States, which was in a position of actual physical isolation from the powers that might threaten her. Cobden later transformed it into a general prescription for all states in his dictum: 'As little intercourse as possible betwixt the governments, as much connection as possible between the nations of the world.'[3]

Cobden believed in non-intervention in the most rigid and absolute sense. He opposed intervention in international conflicts as well as civil ones; for ideological causes (such as liberalism and nationalism on the European continent) of which he approved, as well as for causes of which he disapproved (such as the interventionism of the Holy Alliance); and for reasons of national interest such as the preservation of the balance of power or the protection of commerce. He rejected the distinctions John Stuart Mill drew between intervention in the affairs of civilised countries and intervention in a barbarian country, and between intervention as such and intervention to uphold the principle of non-intervention against a power that had violated it.[4] He even opposed the attempt to influence the affairs of another country by moral suasion, and declined to sanction the formation of any organisation in England for the purpose of interfering in another country, such as the organisations formed to agitate against slavery in the United States. However, in Cobden's vision the promotion of the maximum systematic interaction at the economic and social levels was just as important as the promotion of minimum interaction at the strategic and political levels. Assuming as he did the desirability of universal pursuit by governments of *laissez-faire* policies in relation to the economy, he was able to imagine that the strategic and political isolation of states from one another might coexist with their economic interdependence.[5]

A form of universal political organisation based on the absolute or relative isolation of communities from one another, supposing it to be a possible development, would have certain drawbacks. If systematic interaction among states has in the past involved certain costs (international disorder, the subjection of the weak to the strong, the exploitation by the rich of the poor), so also has it brought certain gains (assistance to the weak and the poor by the strong and the rich, the international division of labour, the intellectual enrichment of countries by each other). The prescription of universal isolationism, even in the limited form Cobden gave it of political and strategic non-interventionism, implies that the opportunities arising from human interaction on a global scale will be lost, as well as that the dangers to which it gives rise will be avoided.

## World Government

It is conceivable also that a form of universal political organisation might arise lacking the first of the above essential attributes, namely sovereign states. One way in which this might occur is through the emergence of a world government.

We may imagine that a world government would come about by conquest, as the result of what John Strachey has called a 'knock-out tournament' among the great powers, and in this case it would be a universal empire based upon the domination of the conquering power;[6] or we may imagine that it would arise as the consequence of a social contract among states, and thus that it would be a universal republic or cosmopolis founded upon some form of consent or consensus. In the latter case it may be imagined that a world government would arise suddenly, perhaps as the result of a crash programme induced by some catastrophe such as global war or ecological breakdown (as envisaged by a succession of futurologists from Kant to Herman Kahn), or it may be thought of as arising gradually, perhaps through accretion of the powers of the United Nations. It may be seen as coming about as the result of a direct, frontal assault on the political task of bringing states to agree to relinquish their sovereignty, or, as on some 'functionalist' theories, it may be seen as the indirect result of inroads made on the sovereignty of states in non-political areas.

There has never been a government of the world, but there has often been a government supreme over much of what for those subjected to it was the known world. Throughout the history of the modern states system there has been an undercurrent of awareness of the alternative of a universal government, and of argument on behalf of it: either in the form of the backward-looking doctrine calling for a return to Roman unity, or in the form of a forward-looking doctrine that sees a world state as the consequence of inevitable progress. In the twentieth century there has been a revival of world government doctrine in response to the two World Wars.

The classical argument for world government is that order among states is best established by the same means whereby it is established among individual men within the state, that is by a supreme authority. This argument most commonly relates to the goal of minimum order, and especially the avoidance of war, which is said to be an inevitable consequence of the states system. But it is also sometimes advanced in relation to goals of optimum order; it is often argued today, for example, that a world government could best achieve the goal of economic justice for all individual men, or the goal of sound management of the human environment.

The classical argument against world government has been that, while it may achieve order, it is destructive of liberty or freedom: it infringes the liberties of states and nations (as argued by the ideologists of the successful grand alliances that fought against universal monarchy); and also checks the liberties of individuals who, if the world government is tyrannical, cannot seek political asylum under an alternative government.

The case for world government may thus appear to rest on an assumed priority of order over international or human justice or liberty. It may be argued, however, that the states system affords a better prospect than world government of achieving the goal of order also [ ... ].

## A New Mediaevalism

It is also conceivable that sovereign states might disappear and be replaced not by a world government but by a modern and secular equivalent of the kind of universal political organisation that existed in Western Christendom in the Middle Ages. In that system no ruler or state was sovereign in the sense of being supreme over a given territory and a given segment of the Christian population; each had to share authority with vassals beneath, and with the Pope and (in Germany and Italy) the Holy Roman Emperor above. The universal political order of Western Christendom represents an alternative to the system of states which does not yet embody universal government.

All authority in mediaeval Christendom was thought to derive ultimately from God and the political system was basically theocratic. It might therefore seem fanciful to contemplate a return to the mediaeval model, but it is not fanciful to imagine that there might develop a modern and secular counterpart of it that embodies its central characteristic: a system of overlapping authority and multiple loyalty.

It is familiar that sovereign states today share the stage of world politics with 'other actors' just as in mediaeval times the state had to share the stage with 'other associations' (to use the mediaevalists' phrase). If modern states were to come to share their authority over their citizens, and their ability to command their loyalties, on the one hand with regional and world authorities, and on the other hand with sub-state or sub-national authorities, to such an extent that the concept of sovereignty ceased to be applicable, then a neo-mediaeval form of universal political order might be said to have emerged.

We might imagine, for example, that the government of the United Kingdom had to share its authority on the one hand with authorities in Scotland, Wales, Wessex and elsewhere, and on the other hand with a European authority in Brussels and world authorities in New York and Geneva, to such an extent that the notion of its supremacy over the territory and people of the United Kingdom had no force. We might imagine that the authorities in Scotland and Wales, as well as those in Brussels, New York and Geneva, enjoyed standing as actors in world politics, recognised as having rights and duties in world law, conducting negotiations and perhaps able to command armed forces. We might imagine that the political loyalties of the inhabitants of, say, Glasgow, were so uncertain as between the authorities in Edinburgh, London, Brussels and New York that the government of the United Kingdom could not be assumed to enjoy any kind of primacy over the others, such as it possesses now. If such a state of affairs prevailed all over the globe, this is what we may call, for want of a better term, a neo-mediaeval order.

The case for regarding this form of universal political organisation as representing a superior path to world order to that embodied in the states system would be that it promises to avoid the classic dangers of the system of sovereign states by a structure of overlapping authorities and criss-crossing loyalties that hold all peoples together in a universal society, while at the same time avoiding the concentration of power inherent in a world government. The case for doubting whether the neo-mediaeval model is superior is that there is no assurance that it would prove more orderly than the states system, rather than less. It is conceivable that a universal society of this kind might be constructed that would provide a firm basis for the realisation of elementary goals of social life. But if it were anything like the precedent of Western Christendom, it would contain more ubiquitous and continuous violence and insecurity than does the modern states system.

## Non-historical Alternatives

We must finally note the possibility that an alternative will develop to the states system which, unlike the four that have just been considered, does not conform to any previous pattern of universal political organisation.

Of course, any future form of universal political organisation will be different from previous historical experience, in the sense that it will have certain features that are unique and will not exactly resemble any previous system. My point is not this trivial one but the more serious one that a universal political system may develop which does not resemble any of the four historically derived alternatives even in broad comparison. The basic terms in which we now consider the question of universal political organisation could be altered decisively by the progress of technology, or equally by its decay or retrogression, by revolutions in moral and political, or in scientific and philosophical ideas, or by military or economic or ecological catastrophes, foreseeable and unforeseeable.

I do not propose to speculate as to what these non-historical alternatives might be. It is clearly not possible to confine the varieties of possible future forms within any finite list of possible political systems, and for this reason one cannot take seriously attempts to spell out the laws of transformation of one kind of universal political system to another. It is not possible, by definition, to foresee political forms that are not foreseeable, and attempts to define non-historical political forms are found in fact to depend upon appeals to historical experience. But our view of possible alternatives to the states system should take into account the limitations of our own imagination and our own inability to transcend past experience.

## Notes

1   See 'Rousseau on war and peace', in Stanley Hoffmann, *The State of War: Essays in the Theory and Practice of International Politics* (London: Pall Mall Press, 1965).
2   This is quoted by Richard Cobden at the beginning of 'England, Ireland and America': see *The Political Writings of Richard Cobden* (London: Cassell, 1886), p. 3.
3   Ibid., p. 216.
4   John Stuart Mill, 'A few words on non-intervention', in *Dissertations and Discussions*, vol. 3 (London: Longmans, Green, 1867).
5   See, especially, Cobden, 'England, Ireland and America' and 'Russia, 1836', in *Political Writings*.
6   John Strachey, *On the Prevention of War* (London: Macmillan, 1962).

# Index

accountability: democratic 38–9, 40, 173–4,
    371, 373, 467, 533
  in financial markets 386
  of government networks 108, 191–2,
    193–6, 201, 207, 233, 470–1, 478–81,
    483, 563
  of INGOs 108, 468
  and legitimacy 9, 163, 194, 195
  personal 516
  and regionalization 301
  and transnational democracy 485–6, 501,
    503–4, 509–10, 527, 563
Acheson, Dean 148
Ackerman, Bruce 515
'action at a distance', globalization as 3, 39,
    67, 73 n.1, 273
activism, global 487
Adler, E. 181
advertising, global 242–3
Africa, Sub-Saharan: and democracy 10
  and development 11, 291, 313, 433
  and inequalities 430, 436, 444, 446
  and regionalism 364
  and trade 313–14, 315–16, 424
agreements, regulatory 191
agriculture: and government policies 352–3,
    445
  protection 364, 373, 495, 571
Ahmed, Akbar 243, 244–5
Alesina, Alberto and Perotti, Roberto 388
Almond, Gabriel 533
Alston, Philip 193, 195, 196–7, 199,
    203 n.14
anarchy, and Hobbes' dilemma 122–3,
    149–50, 151, 153–4, 157–8
Anderson, Benedict 285 n.2
anti-globalization 41, 111, 269, 272, 440–6,
    447, 451, 487–8, 564–75
  protests 4, 82, 495, 564
APEC see Asia-Pacific Economic
    Cooperation

Aron, Raymond 106, 107, 472 n.2
Ashworth, H., Allison, G. and Redcliffe,
    N. 459
Asia-Pacific Economic Cooperation (APEC)
    76, 140, 220
  and regionalization 12, 20, 124, 213–14,
    314
Association of Southeast Asian Nations
    (ASEAN) 12, 20, 76, 290, 360, 361
authoritarianism, state 122–3, 148–50, 156,
    157, 205, 207, 562
authority, political: multiple spheres 125,
    224–32
  of nation-state 122, 123, 127–33, 151,
    162–4, 560
  non-state 130–2, 133
autonomy: individual 487, 503, 514–16, 524,
    559–60
  of nation-states 11, 13, 34–5, 64, 204, 302,
    560
  of national economies 23, 24, 28, 312,
    335–46, 370, 384, 385, 387–97, 560, 574

Bank for International Settlements 344, 470,
    494
banks: and derivatives market 344–5
  multinational 26, 207, 466
  regulation 71, 190–1, 341, 470
  and reserve requirements 356–7
Barry, Brian 568
Bauman, Z. 92, 97 n.3
Beck, U. 142
Beijing Conference on Women 460–1, 472,
    487, 498, 527
Bell, Daniel 60–1, 66 n.1
belle époque, and international economy 4, 7,
    19–21, 23, 24–5, 52, 100–1, 300
bilateralism 81, 109, 155, 364, 466, 469
'black hole syndrome' 365
Blair, Tony 328
Bodin, Jean 151

boundaries: cultural meaning 236, 242–3
  as porous 3, 124, 189, 208, 223, 226–7, 303,
    306, 370
  *see also* territory
Bové, José, Dufour, François and de
    Casparis, Anna 568
Braudel, F. 6, 311
✓ Bretton Woods system 22, 30, 100, 201, 335,
    391, 477
  and embedded liberalism 387–8, 389
  failure of 374, 490
Britain: and European Union 141
  and financial openness 344
  as hegemon 100
  and inequalities 434–5, 437
  and tax reform 405–6
broadcasting, direct by satellite (DBS) 254
Brown, Chris 487–8, 504, 564–75
Buchanan, Pat 353, 495
Bull, Hedley 152, 214–15, 488, 577–82
Burnheim, J. 502
Bush, George 147, 196, 206, 327, 367
Bush, George W. 174
Buzan, Barry 367

Cable, Vincent 349
Cairo Conference on Population Control
    472, 487, 527
capital markets (international): and exit
    threats 13, 27, 385–6, 388–91, 393, 410
  globalization 4, 26, 35, 77, 300, 311–12,
    335, 437, 542
  growth 65, 208
  inequalities in 82, 108, 324, 426, 466–7
  integration in 24, 340–6, 370, 386, 388–92,
    397
  liberalization 478, 542
  offshore 374
  openness in 343–4, 373, 395, 572
  regulation 37, 189–202
  US 112, 113
  and welfare states 28
  *see also* securities markets
capital mobility: and capital flight 27, 375,
    395–6, 404, 426, 466
  and decline of social corporatism 409–12,
    415–16
  and foreign investment 99, 101, 103, 208,
    324
  and global production 21–2, 182, 390–2,
    571–2
  increase in 21, 35, 208

  as measure of financial integration 19, 29,
    274, 342–3, 561
  and national economies 13, 116, 139, 180,
    301, 338, 354–5, 374, 384–5
  nineteenth-century 381
  and taxation levels 375–6, 381, 385,
    388–90, 393–5, 396, 403–9, 415
  and welfare regimes 13, 302, 381, 388–9,
    403–16
capitalism: consolidation 1, 5
  contradictions of 372
  and cultural identity 269
  defence 569–73
  and democracy 370–2, 508, 510
  'disorganized' 104
  global 19, 21, 25–6, 53, 62, 93, 299–300,
    477, 487
  and global inequalities 108, 109, 138, 371
  as global network 136, 137–8, 272
  and information technology 1, 80, 137, 145
  informational 25, 308, 311–30, 421, 430–7
  and myth of globalization 5, 6, 7, 21
  and nation-states 11, 27, 89, 95, 135–6,
    137–42, 145, 370–6, 565
  as new global order 53, 116–19, 147
  opposition to 565–8
  post-industrial 25, 117
  restructuring 326–30, 455
  'turbo' 21, 25
  varieties 23, 573
Cardoso, Fernando Henrique 327, 328
Castells, Manuel: and global economy 299,
    300
  and global inequality 421, 430
  and identity 270, 271
  and informational capitalism 308, 311–30,
    421, 430–7
  and 'network society' 87
CENTO, as hegemonic regionalism 360
change: and realist view of states 106,
    213–14
  and technology 7, 130–1
Chayes, Abram and Antonia 189, 193, 200
child labour 380, 431, 452, 549, 567
China: and appropriation of media 256–7
  and capitalism 138
  and economic control 355
  and foreign investment 318, 324, 351
  and globalization 326, 327, 447–51, 453
  and inequalities 425, 433, 436, 440–6, 447,
    452
  and media 256–7

and NGOs 207
and revival of the *qipau* 275–6
as threat to US dominance 113–14
and trade 314, 315–16, 326, 448
CIS (Commonwealth of Independent States):
and inequalities 424–5, 435–6
and regionalism 364, 365
citizenship: global 243, 287–96, 544–5
multiple 522
national 110, 138, 182
civil society: and citizen networks 487, 560–2
global 18, 27, 33, 36, 38, 108, 135, 142–3,
145, 157, 204–5, 230, 559–63
and the military 185–6
regional 361, 362
and security 183–4
and the state 8–14, 32, 82, 121–5, 127–8,
140, 152, 217, 560
transnational 11, 16, 468, 487, 496, 501,
504–6, 509, 527
*see also* INGOs
civilization, early world civilizations 55–6
Clark, Ian 123, 177–86
Clinton, William Jefferson (Bill) 190, 219,
326, 327
Cobden, Richard 579
Cold War: and Asian states 129
and economic integration 350
and peace dividend 548
and redistribution of power 11, 124, 147–8,
154, 157, 204, 491
and regional cooperation 362–3, 366–7
and security 181, 223, 365
colonialism: and investment 335, 339
and sovereignty 9, 152
and territorialism 89, 116
Commission on Global Governance 494, 496,
497, 499, 501
communication 17–18, 40, 52, 65, 80, 81–2,
246–57, 483
access to 76, 255
asymmetrical flows 254–5
commercial model 236
emergence 247–51
and global culture 279, 287, 525
and global economy 311, 342, 370, 465
and interaction capacity 16, 71
and international news agencies 247,
248–50, 254
and national cultures 16, 235, 236, 239, 270
and patterns of reception 255–7
and redistribution of power 204–5

and regulation of spectrum space 247,
250–1
by satellite 253–4, 255
by telegraph and cable 14, 17, 80, 101, 130,
247–8, 249, 253–4, 354
and terrorism 110
and trade 101, 247
as uneven 52, 252–5, 313, 425, 428
*see also* information technology; media;
space–time compression
communism *see* socialism
communitarianism 33, 36, 484, 506
communities: epistemic 220
of fate 11, 15, 17, 32, 484; overlapping 174,
287, 485, 505, 509, 519, 522–5
imagined 15, 109–10, 279, 509
of will 56
competition: and 'creative chaos' 300
global 19, 20–1, 26, 28, 301, 375, 385,
542–3
and inequalities 29–30, 38, 108, 426
and USA 147
complexity, increased 79, 81–3, 122–3, 149,
153–6, 223, 227, 305
compliance, and global governance 225,
227–9, 230, 469, 470, 472, 507
Comte, Auguste 287
conglomerates, financial 345
Connolly, W. E. 502
consent 9, 517, 579
conservatism, and globalization 2
constitutionalism 150–1, 157, 169, 370
consumerism 141, 266, 287, 330
contract, social, and security 177, 186
core and periphery
and division of labour 29, 304, 421
in regional blocs 20, 30
in world-system theory 62
corporations, multinational *see* corporations,
transnational
corporations, transnational 467
and banking 26, 207
definition 306–7
and economic integration 350, 425
and economic power 62–3, 566
and foreign direct investment 103, 131,
317–18, 568, 572
and global economy 20–1, 24, 26, 62–3,
98–9, 105, 305, 455
and global institutions 158
and global production chains 24, 300,
306–8, 317–20, 322

corporations, transnational (*cont.*)
  and internationalization of production
    21–2, 80, 317–18
  and manufacturing 335–6
  and media 16, 17–18, 236, 242, 252–4,
    260–8, 261–3
  and mobility of production 21–2, 386,
    389–90, 393, 456, 465
  as multinational 102–3, 105, 141, 299, 319
  and the nation-state 37, 62–3, 131–2,
    207–8, 227, 319, 374, 423
  origins 57
  and public governance 102–4
corporatism, social 388, 403, 409–12, 415–16
corruption 231, 329, 487, 553–5, 572
cosmopolitanism 42, 237, 239, 243, 279,
  284–5
  and civil society 561
  cultural 525–6
  and democracy 485, 486, 502–4, 506, 544–7
  economic 524–5
  evidence for 289–94
  future prospects 294–6
  and global governance 287–96, 484–5,
    503–4, 514–27
  globalist views 483–4, 485, 502–4
  institutionalization 521–6
  legal 522–3
  and the nation-state 485, 486, 520–1
  political 523–4
  principles 515–21
Council of Europe, and human rights 169
Cox, R. W. 180, 214–15
Crawford, B. 180–1, 182–3
Crawford, J. and Marks, S. 163
credit markets: access to 363, 554–5
  and interest rates 356
  and international relations 132, 228, 542,
    565
  state control 413, 565
crime: globalized 208, 370, 427, 433
  war crimes 165–7, 173, 493, 543
culture, global 17–18, 237, 244–5, 278–85, 287
culture, national 4, 14–18, 63, 98, 235–7
  and 'Americanization' 108, 110, 113, 241,
    265–6
  and conflict 240–1, 257, 274–5, 284, 349
  and 'culture areas' 284–5
  and 'ethno-history' 281–2, 283, 284–5
  and global communication 235, 236, 525
  and global mass culture 16, 38, 275
  globalist views 17–18, 34, 235, 269–70

  and hybridity 18, 240, 241, 242–4, 275,
    525–6
  and identity 236–7, 242, 269–76, 427
  protection 263–4
  and regionalization 362
  sceptical views 14–16, 37, 110, 235, 269–76
  and vernacular mobilization 282–4

Dahl, Robert 485–6, 501, 508, 510, 530–9
debt: private 467
  public 78–9, 392, 395–6, 466, 554, 572
decision-making: and democracy 485, 504–5,
    509–10, 517–18, 531–2
  impacts 70–1, 79
  shared 218, 422, 452, 483, 560
decolonization, and the nation-state 9–10,
  138
deficit, political 483, 501, 530
deindustrialization, in developed states 22,
  26, 29, 65, 139
delegation, and democracy 531, 532
democracy: and capitalist economy 370–2,
  508
  cosmopolitan 485, 486, 502–4, 506, 544–7
  deliberative 485, 504–6
  and globalization 363, 562, 574–5
  and human rights 168–9, 172
  and liberal-internationalism 500–1, 503
  liberal/representative 10, 107, 108, 123,
    150, 163–4, 327, 467, 505, 510, 531
  and the public good 32–3, 534–5
  radical pluralist 501–2
  sceptical views 485–6, 506–10, 530–9,
    542–7
  transnational 485, 500–10, 530–9
  *see also* accountability
Deng Xiaoping 275–6
derivatives market 344–5, 389
deterritorialization: globalization as 52, 85–8,
  117, 308, 575
  and identity 273–5
Deudney, D. 183–4
development assistance, official (ODA) 548
Dicken, Peter 299–300, 303–9
dimensions of globalization 62–5, 75–7, 81,
  112–13
  organizational 71–2, 72
  spatio-temporal 68, 69–73, 85
distance *see* space–time
distancing, symbolic 256–7
division of labour, international 79, 100, 155,
  313–14, 455–6

in core and periphery 29, 304, 421
  globalist views 26, 38, 64–5, 299–300,
    303–4, 421, 448, 571–2
  intra-firm 320
  sceptical views 22, 30, 300
Dollar, David and Kraay, Aart 422, 442, 443,
    447–54
Dryzek, J. S. 504, 505, 512 n.27
Dylan, Bob 487, 564

East Asia: and democracy 10
  economic crisis (1997–8) 201, 268, 426,
    542, 565; and G7 governments 31; global
    effects 24, 78–9, 113, 291, 325, 357, 424,
    437, 470; and IMF 78, 470, 479; recovery
    437
  and economic growth 11, 25, 29, 140, 147,
    424, 477, 480–1
  and foreign investment 25
  and international trade 338
  and location of production 22
  and strong states 23, 129, 140–1
East Asian Economic Caucus (EAEC) 362,
    364
Eastern Europe: and civil society 559, 560
  and democracy 10
  and European Union 315
  and inequalities 424–5, 435–6
  and nationalism 244, 274
  as transition economies 26, 327, 467, 479
Economic Security Council 494–5
economy, global 5, 6, 19–28, 98, 299–302
  'borderless' 24, 467
  and capitalism 62–3, 138–42
  defence 570–1
  definition 311
  globalist views 24–8, 299–300, 303–9,
    311–30
  governance 22–3, 26–7, 30–1, 79, 99,
    102–4, 189, 215–16, 477–81, 494–6
  and inequalities 28–32, 70, 76, 107–8, 175,
    325, 353, 379–83, 448–54
  and international economy 1–5, 99, 101–4,
    300, 304–5
  as knowledge-based 78, 312, 320–2
  and national economies 19–23, 35, 65, 98,
    101–2, 112, 227, 349–58, 384–97, 494–6
  and national elites 26, 53, 328–9
  and political economy 299, 326–30, 368,
    370–6, 455
  post-industrial 25, 117
  regionalized 314–15

regulation 30, 109, 138, 145, 155, 175,
    189–202, 311, 465, 470–1
  sceptical views 299, 300–2, 335–46,
    349–58, 384–97
  segmentation 324–5
  and triadization 5, 20, 25, 99
  and USA 112–14, 147, 354–7
  and world economy 62, 311
  see also globalization, economic
economy, international 98–105, 407, 542
  and credit 132, 228
  and globalized economy 1–5, 99, 101–4,
    300, 304
  and inter-national economy 99, 100–1,
    104–5, 215
economy, national: and capital flight 375,
    395–6, 404
  and capital mobility 13, 116, 139, 180, 301,
    338, 354–5, 374, 384–5, 572
  and globalized economy 19–23, 98, 101–2,
    208, 227, 335–46, 384–97, 424, 494–6
  and inter-national economy 99, 100–1,
    300
  and Keynesianism 10, 65, 139, 353–4, 368,
    373–4, 376 n.1, 387–8, 389, 413–14
  management 109, 125
  and supply-side policies 10, 35, 412,
    414–15
  see also macro-economic policies;
    openness; sovereignty, state, and
    economy
effectiveness of global governance 191, 225,
    232
Eichengreen, B. and Irwin, D. A. 340
Elias, Norbert 559, 560
elites: and corruption 329, 553–5, 572
  and cosmopolitanism 289, 506, 547
  and economic globalization 26, 53, 313,
    328–9, 566
  and foreign policy 486, 533, 535, 536,
    537–8
  and global governance 501, 546–7
  in government networks 191–2, 193–6,
    216–17
  and information technology 204–5
  and mobility 239, 322–3, 425
  and national culture 14–15, 237, 279,
    281–2, 283–4
  and pressure groups 142, 174
  and sovereignty 149
Empire, global order as 53, 116–19, 574–5
Engels, Friedrich 108, 373

environment: degradation 6, 142, 287, 427,
    455, 488, 523
  and environmental globalism 76, 80, 81,
    112–13, 352, 370, 567
  and environmental movement 18, 487
  in international law 170–2, 173, 195
  and the nation-state 565–6, 574
  protection 109, 143, 198, 206–7, 209, 211,
    289, 424, 467–8
  and sustainability 424
ethic, global 30, 33–7, 424
ethnicity 143, 145
  and culture 281–2, 283–5
  and identity 181, 182, 211, 274–5, 349
  and nationalism 283–4, 289, 493
Europe: and early globalization 56–9
  see also European Union; triadization
European Union (EU)
  and accountability 194–5
  and anti-militarism 144
  Convention on Human Rights 168–9, 173,
    574
  and economic governance 102, 494–5
  and economic integration 102, 153, 214, 287–8
  and foreign investment 351
  as Fortress Europe 362, 364, 465
  and GATT 141
  and governance 27, 124, 213–15, 217–18,
    221, 228, 230
  and identity 110, 294
  and internal market 375–6
  and legitimacy 296
  and monetary union 289, 355, 391–2, 414, 533
  and multilateralism 27, 153
  and nationalism 288
  and neoliberalism 328
  and new medievalism 488
  and production chains 307
  and regionalization 20, 68, 141, 301,
    314–15, 326, 361–4
  and shared sovereignty 12, 23, 141, 154–5,
    210–11, 526, 573–4
  and 'social dimension' 359, 527
  and social exclusion 431–2
  and transnational democracy 506, 507,
    509–10, 531–2, 535–7, 543
  and WTO 22
Evans, Peter 226, 233 n.1
exchange rates: fixed 335, 354–5, 373, 374,
    387–8, 389–92, 397, 414
  floating 342, 346, 391–2, 397
  and globalization of markets 208, 312, 341

exclusion, social 29, 325, 421, 430–3, 436–7,
    518
expenditure, government: and market
    integration 28, 384, 393–5, 397
  and taxation 407–8
exports see trade
extensity of global flows 67–8, 69, 71, 77, 80,
    138, 235, 342

Falk, Richard 365, 501, 519
fetishism, spatial 52, 96
fiscal policy 299, 354, 357–8, 380, 391, 413–16
  constraints on 109, 139–40, 312, 392, 394,
    396
Fischer, Stan 480
Ford Foundation 494–5, 499
foreign policy: and democracy 486, 533–7
  and disaggregated state 190
  and poverty 548
  realist 107, 109
  unilateralist 52, 111, 112, 178, 491, 578–9
'fragmegration' 125, 223–4, 226–8, 230–3, 366
Freedman, L. 179–80, 185
freedom, economic, and social order 359–68
Friedman, Thomas 78, 82, 106–8, 110
Fukuyama, F. 214, 327, 561
fundamentalism, religious 244

G3, and triadization 99, 221
G7 governments: and governance of global
    economy 5, 22, 27, 31, 138, 140, 494
  and manufacturing share 324–5
G22 201
Gandhi, Mahatma 427
Garrett, Geoffrey 302, 384–97, 405, 415
Gates, Bill 21
GATT 138, 140–1, 375, 380, 494, 562
  and developing countries 453, 468–9
  Uruguay Round 82, 155, 241, 315, 469, 548
  and US interests 112
Gellner, Ernest 281
Genoa, G8 summit 487, 527, 564, 567, 571
genocide 165–6, 224, 550
geography, social: and deterritorialization 52,
    85–8, 90, 117
  and methodological territorialism 88–90,
    94, 226–7
  and situation 18, 453–4, 525
geopolitics: and centrality of states 1, 53, 63,
    121–2, 137, 507
  changes in 10–11
  and global inequalities 28, 524

'hard' 135–6, 141, 144, 145, 196
'soft' 136, 141, 143, 145, 192, 194, 196
Gereffi, G. and Korzeniewicz, M. 307
Germany, and capital mobility 413, 414
Giddens, Anthony 51, 60–5, 92, 96, 177, 273, 287, 568
Gilpin, Robert 300–1, 349–58
Global Environmental Authority 211
globalism: contemporary thickening 77–83
    economic 76–7, 78–9, 81, 138–42
    environmental 76, 80, 81, 112–13, 352, 370, 427, 488, 567
    and interdependence 51–2, 75–83, 100, 112
    military 76–7, 79–80, 81–2, 112–13
    and phases of globalization 7
    social 77, 81, 112, 113
    and USA 112
globalist theories 2, 39, 487
    and democracy 531–2
    and financial deregulation 37, 236, 565
    and global economy 24–8, 299–300, 303–9, 311–30
    and global governance 41, 485, 514–27, 564–75
    and global inequalities 28–30, 38, 63, 447–54, 566
    and nation-states 11–14, 27, 121–4, 127–33, 145, 287, 305–7, 483–4, 562
    and national culture 17–18, 34, 235
    and the political good 33–7, 483–4
    and structural change in social organization 6, 7
    and taxation 302
    and transnational democracy 500–10
    and world order 483–4
globality 52, 85–8
    and identity 270
    and territoriality 90
globalization: benefits of 57–9, 108, 569–73
    challenges of 39–42
    complexity of 242–3
    conceptualizations 51, 52, 67–73, 84–90
    contradictions 1, 106–11
    cultural 6, 17–18, 34, 65, 108, 110
    definitions 3–4, 51, 67–8, 246
    economic 19–28, 77, 299–302;
        consequences 352–3, 403–16; as limited 335–46, 350–2; and macroeconomic policy 353–8; as myth 4–6, 52, 98–105; see also capital markets; capital mobility; economy, global; internationalization; market, global; neoliberalism
    of globalization 232
    historical forms 7, 51, 55–9, 69–73, 77–8, 84, 335, 381–2, 423
    as ideology 52
    limits 1, 53, 58, 108, 335–46, 350–2, 477–81
    and modernity 7, 51, 60–5, 88, 92, 215, 236–7, 271–3
    normative considerations 32–7, 483–8
    and political power 58, 108, 139–40, 189, 386–92
    reactions to 42, 509–10
    and regionalization see regionalization
    and social corporatism 410–12
    and social democracy 28, 196, 301, 388
    and social power 6, 8, 51, 95
    as spatial transformation 51, 52, 60, 85
    as supraterritoriality 52, 85–8, 89, 94, 273–5
    and terrorism 110
    understanding 3–8, 51–3
    see also dimensions of globalization; integration; interaction, global; internationalization; power; territory
globalization theory: competing views 2, 61–2, 565
    emergence 1–2
    and globalization as cause and outcome 52, 92–4, 95–6
    and international theory 94–7
    see also globalist theories; scepticism
Gold Standard 100, 208, 338, 340, 341–2, 343, 345–6, 350, 373, 381
Gonzalez, Felipe 327, 328
good, political: globalist views 33–7, 483–4, 524
    sceptical views 32–3, 37, 484
Gould, Stephen 430
governance, global 11, 42, 109, 124–5, 189–202
    and compliance 225, 227–9, 230, 469, 470, 472, 507
    and cosmopolitanism 287–96, 484–5, 503–4, 514–27
    deliberative model 486, 504–6
    disaggregated 224
    economic 22–3, 26–7, 30–1, 53, 79, 99, 102–4, 215–16
    failure of 422, 477–81
    'hub-and-spoke' 53, 112–14, 124, 218–19
    and inequality 423–5, 429, 467, 486, 562
    and leadership 228–9

as multilayered 12, 27, 35–6, 38, 41,
    217–18, 219, 228, 230–1, 518–19, 545
and nation-state 189–202, 484–5, 488
in new global order 124–5, 223–33, 463–72
and pre-governance 220
prospects and problems 484–5, 489–99
regional 27, 124–5, 172, 213–21
sceptical views 484–5, 489–99, 542–7
and sovereignty 11, 53, 61, 109, 116, 121,
    162–75, 198–9, 231, 467
and transgovernmentalism 124, 189–202
see also institutions, global
government, world 488, 545, 579–80; see also
    governance, global
Gramsci, A. 366
Greenspan, Alan 79
growth, economic: in East Asia 140, 147,
    424, 477, 481
and environmental degradation 565–6, 573
and global markets 23, 374, 416, 422, 477
and inequality 388, 423, 433, 436, 444–6,
    447–52, 551–2, 561–3
and international relations 63, 133
and social stability 10, 385, 388, 428
sustainable 481
and trade 23, 444–6, 447–8, 450–4, 466,
    477, 561, 571
Guehenno, J.-M. 177
Guibernau, M. 181

Haas, Peter 220
Habermas, Jürgen 486, 542–7
Halliday, Fred 484, 489–99
Hardt, Michael and Negri, Antonio 53,
    116–19, 574–5
Harvey, David 87, 215
Hayek, Friedrich von 327, 371, 372
health: expenditures 480
improvements in 434
and insecurity 426–7
'hegemonic stability thesis' 5–6, 40–1, 213,
    229, 367–8, 464, 490–1, 507–8
hegemonism: and decolonization 10
and regionalization 366–7
see also USA, as hegemon
Heidegger, Martin 87
Held, David 123–4, 162–75, 287, 485, 502–3,
    509, 514–27
and McGrew, Anthony 1–42
and McGrew, Anthony et al. 51, 67–73, 77,
    315
Hertz, Noreena 564, 568

Herz, John M. 150, 179
Hettne, Björn 301, 359–68
hierarchy, and international order 31, 229,
    463–72
Higgott, Richard 220
Hinsley, F. H. 151, 159 n.19
Hirst, Paul and Thompson, Grahame 52,
    98–105, 215, 288, 300, 335–46, 508
HIV/AIDS, spread 76, 287, 321, 426–7, 480
Hobbes, Thomas 32, 122–3, 148–50, 151, 156,
    157–8
Hobsbawm, E. 303
Hoffmann, Stanley 1, 53, 106–11, 181, 472 n.2
Holsti, K. J. 177
home-working 456–7
Hoogvelt, A. 20, 93
Huber, E. and Stephens, J. D. 410, 412, 414
human rights 19, 123, 164, 423–4
and active agency 516, 519, 524
and global polity 486, 544
and individual worth 515–16
and poverty 549
protection 36, 167–9, 172–3, 174, 179, 195,
    524, 574
and responsibilities 516–17
violations 166–7, 196–7, 200, 427, 487
Hutchings, K. 502, 504
hybridity, cultural 18, 240, 241, 242–4, 525–6

identity: cosmopolitan 287–96
cultural 236–7, 242, 269–76, 427; as
    collective treasure 269–70; and
    deterritorialization 273–5; and
    institutional modernity 271–2, 274; as
    power 270–1
ethnic 181, 182, 211, 274–5, 349
global 42, 135, 143, 237, 243, 279–81
hybrid 18, 117, 125, 211, 275, 525–6
multiple 228, 271, 291
national, and cultural globalization 17–18,
    37, 106, 110, 288; definition 289; and
    global governance 287, 290–4; and
    nationalism 14–16, 33, 38, 42, 125, 244,
    561; and political identity 16, 33–4, 36,
    38, 41, 110; and regional identity 61; and
    security 181; and shared experiences
    279–81, 289; and territorialism 89–90,
    273–5
regional 61, 211, 288, 360
identity politics 17, 121, 135, 143, 145, 182,
    274, 349
IMF see International Monetary Fund

imperialism: and communications 248
  cultural 265, 269, 273, 278
  of economic internationalization 30–1, 38, 85
  European 58, 77, 116–17
  and expansion of capitalism 5, 6
  and global inequalities 28
  of globalized capitalism 53, 116–19
  US 53, 85, 112, 117–18
India: and globalization 326, 327, 428, 447, 449–51, 453
  and inequalities 435–6, 440–6, 450–1
  and regionalization 363, 364
  and trade 315–16
individual, and the state 165, 483–4, 498–9
Indonesia, and East Asian crisis 78, 437, 479
industrialism, global 65, 139, 142, 182, 335
inequality 30–2, 38, 40–1, 325, 353, 421–2
  in capital markets 82, 108, 324, 426, 466–7
  and capitalism 63, 109, 138, 371
  in communication and information 76, 250, 255, 421, 430–7
  and distributional impacts 41, 70, 109, 207–8, 380–1, 384, 430–1, 465–8, 550–2
  of gender 422, 455–61
  and global justice 486, 548–56
  globalist views 28, 29–30, 38, 447–54, 561–3, 566
  of income 371, 433–7, 440–5, 448–9, 451–2, 467, 548–9
  increase in 423–4, 435–6, 440–6, 447, 465–6, 524
  and international law 174–5
  intranational 26, 29–30, 325, 382, 425, 434–7, 441–3, 566
  and neoliberalism 28–30, 421, 562, 566
  and polarization 431, 434, 436–7
  sceptical views 28, 30–2, 38, 109, 384–97, 486
  and social stability 379–81, 384–97, 428
  in trade 313
  and world order 463–72
  see also poverty
inflation, and financial markets 391, 414
information, international flows 250, 308, 311–12
information technology: and capitalism 1, 80, 137, 145, 311–30, 421, 430–1
  costs 131–2
  and democracy 107
  and government networks 191, 193, 201–2
  and inequality 441, 444, 446

and interdependence 7, 52, 65, 79–80, 112, 227
and national cultures 16, 40, 235
and redistribution of power 124, 130–1, 145, 204–6, 208
social impact 253–4, 256–7, 428, 560
and trade 101
see also communication
infrastructures: and extensity and intensity of global connectedness 3, 51, 71, 235, 342
  government provision 370, 384–5, 388, 487–8
  and trade 313
  see also communication; information technology
Inglehart, Ronald 291–3
INGOs: and accountability 194–5, 207
  and environmental globalism 80, 142
  and global governance 467–8, 489, 496–7, 546, 559
  and global politics 12, 41, 108, 230
  and government networks 191, 194–6, 201, 206–7, 423, 561–2
  and human rights 168
  impact propensity of global flows 67–8, 69–71, 79, 83, 145, 253–4, 465–8
  increase in 82, 191, 205
  and minority group rights 169, 196
  and redistribution of power 204, 205–6, 209, 211–12, 428
institutionalism, liberal 501
institutionalization of global networks see networks, global
institutions, global 2, 71, 79–80, 109–10, 123, 157
  and citizen networks 560–1
  and civil society 501, 510, 560
  and cosmopolitanism 237, 290, 484
  and democracy 530–9, 574–5
  failure 422, 477–81
  and global governance 27, 79, 109, 121, 489–98, 509–10
  and government networks 197–9, 201–2
  hybrid 197, 211, 214, 226
  and inequality 463, 464–72
  and nation-states 153, 209–10, 485
  and policy-making role 27, 218, 467
  see also International Monetary Fund; United Nations; World Bank; World Trade Organization
insurance, social, see protection, social; welfare state

integration: and authority of states 127–33
  and development 29, 314, 441, 444, 447–54
  in financial markets 24, 274, 340–6, 386,
    388–92, 397
  and fragmentation 181, 204, 223–4, 226–8,
    230–3, 366
  and gender inequalities 422, 455–61
  and inequality 421, 424–5, 440–1, 444, 447–54
  and law of one price 351
  and macroeconomic policy 393–5, 403–16
  nineteenth-century 1, 19–20, 98, 299,
    304–5, 350, 373, 381, 425
  perverse 433
  and poverty reduction 422, 448
  regional 102, 214, 216, 362–8, 376, 466, 494
  sceptical view 299, 335–46
  and social disintegration 379–83, 384–97,
    403
  and trade 313–14, 315, 336, 444–5
  as uneven 305, 306–8, 313–14, 337–40,
    350, 421, 455, 465, 562
  see also economy, global; European
    Union; Organization for Economic
    Cooperation and Development
intensity of global flows 3, 67–8, 69, 71, 77,
    78, 80–3, 145, 236
interaction, global 7, 84, 122, 136, 145, 246,
    578
  increase in 3–4
  and inter-national economy 100
  interaction capacity 16, 71
  modes of 72
  velocity 52, 67–8, 69, 79–80, 82, 139, 235, 312
interconnectedness: and cosmopolitanism
    485, 523, 525–6
  and global civil society 487, 559–60
  historical forms 69–73
  impact 67–8, 79, 83, 122, 145, 253–4, 465–8
  increasing 1, 3–4, 11–13, 38, 67
  and infrastructures 71, 312
  intensity 40, 67–8, 69, 71, 77, 78, 80–3,
    145, 169–70, 236, 246, 305
  and international economy 100–1, 311, 455
interdependence: accelerating 1, 3, 65, 67, 73
    n.1, 190, 224–5
  compared with globalism 51–2, 75–83
  complex 1, 81–3, 122–3, 149, 153–6, 157,
    225, 287, 467
  globalist views 25, 29
  and globalization 75, 84, 100, 101–2,
    112–14, 246, 494–5, 579
  regional 20, 25

sceptical views 21–3
  and science and technology 320–2
  and security 178
  as temporary 5–6
interest rates 190, 312, 354–6, 374–5, 384–5,
    392, 394, 396–7
  convergence 24, 341, 342
intergovernmentalism 38, 143, 216–17, 218,
    483–4, 510
International Monetary Fund (IMF): and
    accountability 108, 191, 194, 233, 470–1,
    472, 478, 563
  and civil society 210
  and East Asian crisis 78, 470, 479
  failure 477–80
  and geopolitical interests 174
  and global capitalism 27, 30–1, 138, 327–8,
    570
  and global governance 494
  and inequality 422, 457
  and production chains 307
  and structural adjustment 5, 30, 174
  and USA 112, 194
international non-governmental
    organizations see INGOs
international political economy (IPE): and
    gender inequality 455–61
  and 'hegemonic stability thesis' 5–6, 213,
    229, 367–8, 464, 490–1, 507–8
  and 'new medievalism' 199, 214–16, 488
international relations: and centrality of the
    state 9, 53, 106, 123, 189, 217
  and credit markets 132, 228, 542, 565
  and democracy 500–1
  and global political economy 455
  and inequality 463–72
  realist views 5–6, 95, 96, 127–8, 133,
    148–51, 464, 490, 565
  and security 179
  and state sovereignty 122–3, 147–58, 162,
    189, 200
  and supraterritoriality 87–8, 94
  and terrorism 106
  theories 61, 62, 94–7, 216, 217
International Telecommunication Union
    (ITU) 211, 251
internationalism: and age cohort 42, 237,
    290, 293–4, 295–6, 497–8
  and transgovernmentalism 197, 198, 199,
    201–2
  and transnational democracy 485, 500–1,
    503, 510

internationalization 38, 68
  of business 21, 335–6
  and centrality of the state 121, 189, 218
  and developing countries 22
  of financial systems 335–46, 565
  globalization as 5, 84, 88, 303, 305
  and imperialism 30–1, 38, 85
  and national economies 20, 32, 98, 302,
    410, 414–15
  of political authority 27
  of production 21–2, 317–18, 335, 388–9
  and security of states 178
  and taxation 404–5, 408–9
  as temporary 5–6
  as uneven 52, 252–5, 305, 308–9, 421
  see also economy, international
Internet: access to 76, 206, 229, 239, 425, 428
  and globalized science 320–1
  impact 17, 80, 114, 423
  and new communities 204
  US importance 76, 114
intervention: in economy 103, 371, 373, 375,
    384–97, 409, 414–15, 524
  international 81, 152, 157, 179, 209, 231,
    302, 343, 365, 491–3, 543, 579
  intra-state 139–40
  regional 107, 361
investment, and savings 342–3, 345, 372
investment, foreign: and bilateralism 109
  and capital flight 395–6, 404
  colonial 335, 339
  in developing economies 25, 99, 351, 424,
    446, 447–8, 450–4, 568, 572
  growth 208, 311, 317
  historic 78–9, 373
  by OECD countries 25, 317, 324, 425
  and social corporatism 411–12
  and taxation 406–7
  and transnational corporations 103, 131,
    317–18, 568, 572
Irwin, Douglas 382
Islam: and cultural globalization 244–5, 256
  and Moslem world 55–6, 76
isolationism 36, 108, 578–9

Jameson, F. 8, 215
Japan: and anti-militarism 144
  and economic growth 433, 444
  and inequalities 435
  and monetary policy 357
  and multinational companies 103, 318
  and openness 344, 381, 444

and regional governance 220, 364
  as strong state 129, 140, 147, 316, 326
  see also triadization
Jefferson, Thomas 118
justice, international criminal 109, 111, 166,
    200, 523, 544
justice, social 108, 359, 483, 486–7, 510,
    548–56, 566

Kaiser, Karl 195
Kaldor, Mary 178, 274–5, 487, 559–63
Kant, Immanuel 40, 485, 544, 546, 578
Kapstein, Ethan 383, 385
Katzenstein, Peter 387
Keohane, Robert O. 122–3, 147–58, 501
Keohane, Robert O. and Nye, Joseph S. Jr.
    51–2, 73 n.3, 75–83, 217
Keynes, John Maynard 368, 478, 574
Kissinger, Henry 106
Klein, Naomi 564, 568, 570
Krasner, Stephen D. 151
Krugman, Paul 308
Kuttner, Robert 191
Kymlicka, W. 506
Kyoto Summit and Protocol on the
    Environment 171, 174, 228, 472

labour: bargaining power 103–4, 116, 371,
    374–5, 379–80, 388, 410–12
  individualization 431
labour market: global 158, 379–80
  and inequality 322–4, 425, 426, 431
  and migration 336–7, 338–9, 351–2, 381–2,
    448, 454, 495–6
  as open 103
  and over-exploitation 431
Lam, Ricky and Wantechekon, Leonard 557
    n.22
Lash, S. and Urry, J. 104
Latin America: debt crises 392
  and democracy 10
  and development 11, 25, 29, 291, 426, 430,
    436
  and election monitoring 210
  and foreign investment 318
  and IMF 479
  and inequalities 268, 434–7, 444
  and trade 314, 315–16
law, international: and cosmopolitanism 503,
    514, 521–3, 527
  and the environment 170–2, 173, 195
  and global governance 11, 121, 162–75, 190

law, international: and cosmopolitanism (*cont.*)
   and government networks 200
   and human rights 18, 167–9, 172–3, 174,
     195, 524
   origins 9
   and rules of warfare 164–5, 167, 173
   and sovereignty 162–75, 189
   and war crimes 165–7, 173, 543
legitimacy: and accountability 9, 11, 163, 194,
   195
   challenges to 13–14, 34, 38, 122, 123, 128,
     137, 327
   and democracy 169, 172, 327, 371–2, 373,
     509, 546
   and global institutions 174, 296, 470, 486,
     526, 539, 544, 545
   and security 184
liberalism: and constitutional government
   150–1
   embedded 374, 386–97
   and globalization 2
   and internationalism 201, 500–1, 503
liberalization, globalization as 84, 88, 116,
    138–40, 155, 311, 327, 444, 542
Lindblom, C. 501
Lindert, Peter and Williamson, Jeffrey 451
lingua franca, and global culture 3, 114, 284,
   321
Linklater, A. 509
loans, international, short-term 344–5
localization: and cosmopolitanism 520
   and democracy 508, 518
   and 'fragmegration' 223–4
   and globalization 6, 51, 60–1, 67–8, 103,
    145, 231–2, 255–6, 270–1, 311, 465
   of production 308–9, 311, 376
   and radical democratic pluralism 501–2
   *see also* territory
Locke, John 32, 151, 546
Luard, Evan 159 n.14

Maastricht Treaty 153, 289, 326, 328, 363,
   380, 413, 527, 536
McChesney, Robert 236, 260–8
McCrone, David and Surridge, Paula
   294–5
McGrew, Anthony 485, 500–10
Mckenzie, R. and Lee, D. 404
MacKinder, A. 1
McLuhan, Marshall 61, 239
McNamara, K. R. 414
McNeill, W. H. 55, 56

macro-economic policies 10, 327–8
   and capital mobility 135, 342–3, 386–95,
    403–16, 466
   constraints on 299, 384, 385–6, 542–3
   effectiveness 139–40, 353–8, 403–16, 444,
    451
   Keynesian 10, 65, 139, 353–4, 368, 373–4,
    387–8, 389, 413–14
   monetarist 414
Maddison, A. 433
Madison, James 151
majoritarianism 507, 562–3
Mann, Michael 122, 135–45, 177, 288
market, global 5, 20, 23, 26, 28–9, 239, 287, 300
   and communications 101
   indivisibility of authority in 127, 133
   and inequality 423–4
   and international relations 132
   and the nation-state 122, 128, 132, 299,
    302, 327, 486, 565
   regulation 30, 99, 102, 104, 109, 175, 307,
    444, 478, 542
   and security 124
   and social stability 379–81, 384–97
market, social 359, 573
Marx, Karl 1, 52, 93, 94, 96, 108, 287, 373, 573
Marxism: and capitalism 5, 566–7, 573
   and global inequalities 30
   and theories of the state 217
Massey, Doreen 241–2, 244
Mathews, Jessica 124–5, 204–12
Mayall, J. 509
media: asymmetrical flows 254–5
   and deregulation of ownership 236, 260–5
   and domestic protection 263–4, 570
   and localized reception 236, 255–7, 270–1
   and national cultures 239, 242, 270, 526
   transnational 16, 17–18, 51, 65, 110,
    246–57, 260–8
   *see also* communication
medievalism, 'new' 199, 214–16, 488, 577–82
Memoranda of Understanding (MOUs) 191,
   200, 203 n.16
MERCOSUR 20, 27, 314–15, 494
Mexico: economic crisis (1994–5) 325, 357,
   467, 470, 542
   and inequalities 435, 436, 441
   and trade 450
migration: and freedom of movement 101,
    338–9, 373, 448, 454, 495
   and global labour market 336–7, 338–9,
    351–2, 381–2, 495–6

globalized 24, 139, 223, 239–40, 242–3, 323–4, 370
    late nineteenth-century 351, 373, 381–2
    and security issues 182
Milanovic, Branko 442, 443
military order: expenditure on 548
    and multilateralism 12–13
    and post-militarism 144
    and revolution in military affairs 185
    world 64, 76–7, 79–80, 81–2, 483
Mill, John Stuart 287, 327, 546, 579
Mills, C. Wright 94
minority groups, rights 128–9, 167, 169, 196, 517
MNCs see corporations, transnational
mobility: of capital see capital mobility
    of commodities 239
    of people see migration
Modelski, George 51, 55–9
modernity: in classical social theory 1, 92, 96
    and globalization 7, 51, 60–5, 88, 92, 215, 236–7, 244–5
    and identity 271–3, 274
    and reflexivity 60, 64, 65, 232
Monbiot, George 564
monetary policy 354–7, 374–5, 412–16
    constraints on 109, 312, 389, 390–2, 397, 415
Montesquieu, Charles de Secondat, Baron de 151
Moravcsik, A. 398 n.29
Morgenthau, Hans J. 63, 107, 151
multilateralism: economic 22, 26–7, 38, 315, 380, 423
    and environmental protection 170–2, 173, 467–8
    as hierarchical 31, 463, 469
    and human rights regime 167–9
    political 41, 153–5
    and regionalism 359–68
    and rules of warfare 164–5, 167, 173
    and security 178, 186
Murdoch, Rupert 264
music industry, ownership 266, 267

nation-state: Asian 129
    and capitalism 11, 27, 89, 95, 135–6, 137–42, 145, 270–6, 565
    centrality of 53, 63–4, 106, 121–2, 124, 154, 189, 204, 212, 218, 299
    and civil society 8–14, 121–5, 140, 152, 204–5, 217, 560
    and cosmopolitan polity 485, 521–2

    and democracy 485–6, 506, 508, 509, 517–18, 530–1
    disaggregated 124, 189–202, 217–18
    effects of globalization 8–14, 27, 34, 38, 116, 135–45, 299, 349–58, 403–16, 494–6, 560
    as ethically bounded political community 32–3, 506, 544–5
    ethnic 143, 145, 211, 349, 467, 493
    formation and rule 8–11, 163, 279
    and global inequalities 32, 175
    and global markets 122, 128, 132, 299, 302, 327, 486, 565
    globalist views 11–14, 27, 121–4, 127–33, 145, 287, 305–7, 483–4, 562
    and international order 9–11, 116–19, 121–3, 157–8
    and international relations 61, 62, 123
    and local nationalisms 60–1
    and modernity 64
    modest 137
    and multinational state 289
    and national culture 14–16, 17, 63
    and national interest 109, 121, 143, 148, 150, 152, 153, 190, 208, 574
    and neoliberal economics 11, 27–8, 195, 196, 227, 299, 327–8
    and political economy of globalization 326–30, 370–6
    and the political good 32–7
    recognition 10, 133, 493
    and redistribution of power 124–5, 139–40, 189–90
    sceptical views 8–11, 38, 63–4, 89, 121, 123, 287–8, 349–58, 359–68, 403–16
    and 'society of states' 9–10, 38, 110, 162, 463, 507, 577
    strengthening 58
    strong 23, 129, 140, 147, 180, 199, 220, 316, 326, 573–5
    threats to 122, 135–45
    and transnational corporations 62–3, 131–2, 207–8, 227, 319, 423
    'world-state' 61, 110
    see also authority, political; economy, national; legitimacy; security; sovereignty; territory
nationalism: civic 289
    cultural 15–16, 17, 38, 42, 124, 212, 244, 281–2, 288
    economic 125, 212, 494–6, 561
    ethnic 283–4, 289, 349, 498

nationalism: civic (*cont.*)
  'extended' 360, 368
  local 60–1
  political 17, 42, 281
nationalization, and globalization 68
NATO (North Atlantic Treaty Organization) 31, 81
  and public opinion 288
  and role in Yugoslavia 490, 492, 493, 548
  and US leadership 147
Nau, Henry 203 n.14
Negri, Antonio 569
neo-functionalism, and regional governance 216–17, 218
neo-mercantilism 359, 367–8
neoliberalism: critique of 572–3
  defence of 570–2, 574
  and gender inequalities 422, 455–61
  and global inequalities 28–30, 421, 430–7, 562, 566
  and globalization 84, 88, 116, 138–40, 405, 501, 526, 560–1
  and media ownership 263–4, 268
  and myth of globalization 5, 21, 27–8, 52
  and the nation-state 11, 27–8, 195, 196, 199, 227, 299, 327–8, 384, 412–16, 499
networks: citizen 228, 487, 560–2
  global: density 78–9, 112, 145, 235, 329–30; emergence 6, 247–51; extensity 67–8, 69, 71, 77, 80, 92–3, 122, 124–5, 136, 138, 143, 169–70, 227, 235; and global capitalism 136, 137–8; hub and spoke model 112–14; institutionalization 79–80, 109–10, 121, 123, 157–8, 229–30, 232; of labour 323–4; and security 178, 180–1, threats to 144
  government: accountability 191–2, 193–6, 201, 207, 233, 470–1, 478–81, 483, 563; advantages 199–200; and global governance 189–202; and international institutions 192, 197–9, 201–2; and legislation 195, 200; and minimalist global agenda 192, 196–7
  INGO 205–7
  inter-national 136, 137, 139, 141, 143, 145, 215
  local 136, 137, 138–9, 145
  regional 220
  transnational 11, 123–4, 136, 138–9, 141, 143–5, 155, 156, 217
  *see also* production
news agencies, international 247, 248–50, 254

NGOs *see* INGOs
NICs: and anti-globalization 567
  and division of labour 26, 65, 304
  and economic growth 424, 430
  and exports 26, 313–14, 457, 477
  and foreign direct investment 25, 99, 351, 424, 446, 447–8, 450–4, 568, 572
NIEs *see* NICs
Nixon, Richard M. 491
Norris, Pippa 42, 237, 287–96
North American Free Trade Agreement (NAFTA) 290, 494
  and economic deregulation 327, 465, 527
  and economic integration 102, 141
  and governance 125, 213–14
  and government networks 198
  and 'hub-and-spoke' governance 52, 125, 218–19
  and labour market 339
  and NGOs 206
  and production chains 307, 386
  and regionalization 20, 147, 314–15, 362
  and USA 219, 469, 533, 537
North, Douglass C. and Thomas, Robert Paul 151, 159 n.17
North–South *see* inequality; Third World
North–South Summits 472
nuclear weapons, and state security 179, 184–5
Nussbaum, M. C. 515–16
Nye, Joseph S. Jr. 53, 112–14

Ohmae, K. 103, 287, 308
O'Neill, O. 37
openness 24, 337–40, 344, 355–8, 380–1, 571–2
  and economic growth 23, 29, 444–6, 447–8, 450–2, 466
  in financial markets 343–4, 373, 395, 572
  and hegemonic stability 366
  in labour markets 103
  and taxation 381, 385, 387, 388, 395, 405, 408–9
  and welfare protection 301–2, 385, 386–9, 397
order, global 483–8
  and capitalism 53, 116–19, 147
  as Empire 53, 116–19, 574–5
  globalist views 483
  and governance 125, 223–33, 463–72
  and inequality 463–5
  and the nation-state 9–11, 121–3, 157–8, 577–8
  and the political good 33–7

order, social, and economic freedom 359–68
Organization of American States (OAS)
    209–10
Organization for Economic Cooperation and
    Development (OECD): and 'collective
    saving' 345
  and complex interdependence 155, 156
  and deindustrialization 22, 26, 29
  and direct foreign investment 25, 317, 324,
    425
  and economic integration 20, 25, 30, 384,
    392, 396, 421, 494
  and global trade 324, 425
  and government expenditure 393–4
  and inequalities 425, 428, 433, 435
  and multinationals 318
  and regulation 197, 202 n.4, 543
  and science and technology 320
  and services trade 22, 314
  and taxation 406, 407
  and welfare regimes 302
Organization for Security and Cooperation
    in Europe (OSCE) 169, 209
  Parliamentary Assembly 195
organizations, international, and global
    politics 11–12, 41
  see also INGOs
organizations, transgovernmental regulatory
    (TROs) 190–2
Orwell, George 266

Patomaki, H. 502, 504
Payne, A. J. and Gamble, A. M. 213–14
Payne, Anthony 124, 213–21
Perot, Ross 353, 386
Picciotto, Sol 193–4
Pinochet, Augusto 200
pluralism: framed 520
  radical democratic 485, 501–2
Pogge, Thomas W. 486–7, 518, 548–56, 568
Polanyi, K. 366, 367–8, 375, 386, 562
politics: and authority of the state 122, 123,
    127–9
  comparative studies 216–17
  and complex interdependence 81–3, 122–3,
    153–6, 157
  disillusionment with 127
  and economic globalization 299, 386–92
  and ethnicity 143, 145, 211, 274–5, 349
  global 11–14, 27, 39–40, 52
  of identity 135, 143, 145, 182, 274, 349
  political cleavages 561–3

and zones of conflict and of peace 149,
    156–7, 509
  see also deficit, political; globalization;
    nation-state
Pontusson, J. and Swenson, P. 410
Porter, Michael 308
post-globalization, and 11 September attacks
    1, 53, 106–11
post-industrialization: and capitalism 25, 117
  and cosmopolitanism 291–3
postmodernity: and global culture 278, 291–3
  and globalization 88, 117, 145, 215
poverty: absolute/extreme 421, 431, 436,
    441–2, 445, 449, 548–9
  and effects of globalization 29–31, 40,
    58–9, 196–7, 291, 431, 571–2
  and global institutions 479
  increasing 421–2, 425, 436–7, 440–6, 459
  reduction 29, 422, 423–4, 447–54, 486–7,
    548–56
  see also inequality
power: and civil society 8–14, 32, 82, 121–5,
    127–9
  and cosmopolitanism 520
  economic 175, 299, 409–10, 425, 472, 478;
    and communications 246, 248, 253;
    realist view 106, 107; and transnational
    corporations 62–3; of USA 112–14, 147
  and Hobbes's dilemma 122–3, 148–50,
    464
  and international sovereignty 164, 167–72,
    173–5, 464
  military 104, 112–13, 147; realist view 106,
    107; and sovereignty 64; see also
    globalism, military
  in modern state 9, 11, 40, 124–5, 130–1,
    199, 204–12, 486
  'soft' 112, 192, 194, 196
  structural inequalities 174–5, 501
  symbolic 246–57
  transformations 26, 39, 51, 58, 67, 71–2, 95,
    108, 139–40, 189–90, 483
pressure groups 41, 142, 219, 371
production: globalization 21–2, 299–300,
    303–9, 311, 385–6, 388–92
  and individualization of labour 431
  informational 320–2
  as localized 308–9, 311, 376
  and production chains and networks 7, 24,
    26, 300, 306–8, 317–20, 322, 323–4
  and trade 336, 337–40
  see also division of labour, international

profit: and ethics 424
  and government intervention 371–2, 406, 408
property rights 151, 384, 388, 450, 542
  intellectual 198, 315, 318, 453, 465, 469, 562
protection, social 23, 28, 29–30, 106, 301–2,
    375, 379–83, 403–16
protectionism: in *belle époque* 24, 100
  and free trade 138, 289, 314, 316, 373, 387,
    448, 487, 567, 572
  in media 241, 263–4
  regional 362, 364, 368, 495
  and welfare issues 382–3

Rawls, John 441, 551–2, 555
realism: and anarchy 149–50, 153, 506
  and centrality of states 106
  in foreign policy 107, 109
  and global inequalities 31
  and 'hegemonic stability thesis' 213, 229,
    490–1, 507–8
  and international relations 5–6, 95, 96,
    127–8, 133, 148–51, 464, 565
  and national security 122, 183–4
  and state sovereignty 148–9
  and transnational democracy 507–8
regimes, international 12, 22, 41, 167–70, 200,
    226
region, definitions 360
regionalization 5, 6, 12, 68, 90, 121
  and 'black hole syndrome' 365
  and developing countries 22, 466
  dimensions 362–3
  dynamics 363–5
  and globalization 24–5, 38, 125, 299–301,
    314–16, 339–40, 353
  and governance 27, 125, 172, 213–21
  hegemonic versus autonomous 360, 363
  and hegemonism 366–7
  levels of complexity 360–2
  market-led 220
  'new' 359–68, 466
  and 'new medievalism' 214–16
  and regional identity 61, 211, 288, 360
  and security 181, 361, 362–3, 364–5
  and triadization 20–1, 25, 300
  universalistic 360
regulation: banking 71, 190–1, 341, 470
  economic 30, 99, 102, 104, 109, 138, 145,
    155, 175, 301, 307, 311
  financial 37, 189–202, 236, 426, 470–1, 565
  global *see* governance, global
  and inequality 465–6

in media 236, 260
  and the nation-state 483
  social 143
  of trade 19, 211, 228, 375, 468–9
  *see also* law, international
Reich, Robert 319, 386
Reinicke, Wolfgang H. 226–7
relations, social: extensiveness of networks
    67–8, 69, 71, 77, 92–3, 122–3, 124–5, 136,
    138, 169–70, 235
  transformation 3, 51, 52, 60–1, 67–8
religion: and early globalization 55–6, 76, 77
  and identity 244–5
republicanism, global civic 485, 502, 503
resources, international resources privilege
    554–5
restructuring, economic: and global
    inequalities 30, 430, 455–8, 461, 467,
    479, 554, 566, 570
  and post-industrialization 25
Rhodes, R. A. W. 215
Rio de Janeiro, Earth Summit and
    Declaration 171–2, 206–7, 472, 487, 527
'risk society' 135, 142
Risse-Kappen, T. 217, 218
Robins, Kevin 235–6, 239–45
Rodrik, Dani 233 n.1, 301–2, 379–83, 387,
    388–9, 390, 395, 405, 417 n.11
Rorty, Richard 571
Rosenau, James 125, 215–16, 223–33
Rosenberg, Justin 52, 92–7
Rousseau, Jean-Jacques 578
Rubin, Robert 480
Ruggie, J. G. 87, 179, 186, 215, 387, 388
Rushdie, Salman 16, 87, 241, 243, 526
Russia: financial crisis 78, 315, 325, 357, 470
  and globalization 327–8, 329
  and inequalities 435–6, 441, 446
  *see also* Soviet Union

Sachs, Jeffrey 321
Saint-Simon, Claude Henri de Rouvray 1
Sandel, M. 503
Sassen, S. 542, 547 n.2
satellite communication 253–4, 255
savings, and investment 342–3, 345, 372
scepticism 2, 39
  and cosmopolitanism 287–96, 485, 506
  and financial integration 299, 335–46
  and global economy 299, 300–2, 335–46,
    349–58, 384–97
  and global governance 484–5, 489–99

and global inequalities 28, 30–2, 38, 107–8, 109, 384–97
and globalization as cause and outcome 52, 92–7
and myth of globalization 4–6, 52, 98–105
and the nation-state 8–11, 38, 63–4, 89, 121, 123, 287–8, 349–58, 359–68, 403–16
and national culture 14–16, 37, 110, 235
and persistence of national economies 19–23, 299
and the political good 32–3, 37, 484
and the security state 177–86
and taxation 302
and transnational democracy 485–6, 506–10, 530–9, 542–7
and world order 483
Scharpf, Fritz 301, 370–6
Schattschneider, E. F. 70
Schmitter, Philippe 532
Scholte, Jan Aart 52, 84–90, 94, 96
Schroeder, Gerhard 328
science, selective globalization 320–2
SEATO, as hegemonic regionalism 360
Seattle, protests against WTO 82, 232, 487, 527, 552, 564, 571
securities markets 200, 202, 211, 341–2, 343–5, 356
security 10, 106, 157, 287, 471, 543, 568
and ethno-national conflict 284, 349
and global inequality 28, 41, 424, 426–8
and globalized crime 208, 427
internationalization 12–13, 178
and privatization 180, 183
regional 181, 361, 362–3, 364–5
and security communities 81, 157, 179, 362
and the security state 123, 177–86
and territory 123, 178, 179–80, 184
self-determination 164, 167, 172, 175, 370, 464, 493, 509
Sen, Amartya 557 n.17
11 September terrorist attacks 1, 4, 23, 52, 53, 106, 113
services, trade in 22, 312–13, 314, 315–16, 318, 469
sex tourism 457–8
Shapiro, I. 500
Shapiro, Michael 243
Shaw, Martin 144, 184–6
Short, Clare 569
Slaughter, Anne-Marie 124, 189–202
Smith, Adam 79, 130, 133, 303, 327, 403–4, 448
Smith, Anthony D. 15, 16, 237, 244, 278–85, 287–8
social democracy: and effects of economic globalization 28, 196, 301–2, 388, 403–16, 566–7
and globalism 29–30, 568
and local democracy 508
and national capitalisms 21, 573
social movements, transnational 18, 34, 36, 41, 135, 143, 527
and global civil society 487, 559–63
and identity 236, 270
social theory: classical 52, 92–4, 96
and international relations 127, 131–2
socialism: collapse 1, 7, 11, 24, 31, 138, 147, 274, 371, 571
and globalization 2, 31, 561, 566–7, 573
society: global 53, 109, 145, 152, 179, 463, 577–8
'network' 87, 432–3, 435
'world society' 51, 542–7
solidarity: ethnic 107
global 423, 455, 544–7, 550
national 28–9, 486
regional 110, 154
social, threats to 29–30
Sørenson, George 153, 179
Soros, George 21, 328
South Asian Association for Regional Cooperation (SAARC) 361, 364
South Korea: development 29, 129, 319, 446, 552
and financial crisis 78, 467
and inequalities 433, 435, 437, 444
sovereignty, cosmopolitan 521–2
sovereignty, liberal international 123–4, 164–75, 514, 520, 524
achievements 172–3
assessment 173–5
and environmental protection 170–2, 173
and human rights 167–9, 172–3, 174
and rules of warfare 164–5, 167, 173
and war crimes 165–7, 173, 493
sovereignty, popular 32, 509
sovereignty, state 9, 11, 27–8, 63, 83, 137
challenges to 13, 22–3, 38, 39, 110, 121, 124, 133, 135, 326, 467, 486
classic theory 162–4, 172
and complex interdependence 122–3, 149, 153–6
and constitutionalism 150–1, 157
disaggregated 200

sovereignty, state (*cont.*)
  economic 299, 301–2, 327–8, 349, 495
  and economy 208
  and global governance 11, 53, 61, 109, 116, 121, 189, 198–9, 231, 484
  and global sovereignty 53, 116–19
  as institution 148–9, 150–4
  and international law 162–75, 189
  and international relations 122–3, 147–58, 162, 189, 200
  and new medievalism 577–82
  realist view 148–9
  and reflexivity 64, 232
  shared 11–12, 23, 141, 154–5, 204, 210–11, 287, 526, 573–4
  and territory 64, 179, 180, 189, 204, 215, 223, 370, 520
  and transnational terrorism 107, 111, 370
  and Westphalian states system 9, 61, 89, 94–5, 96, 151–2, 156, 204, 216, 365, 464, 565–6, 573–5
Soviet Union: and military technology 183, 185
  and spread of capitalism 138, 147
  *see also* Russia
space–time, in classical social theory 92–4, 95–6
space–time compression 3–4, 67–8, 69–73, 76, 227, 423, 455
  and communication 3, 73 n.1, 82–3, 85–7, 92–3, 95–6, 223, 246
stability: economic 405, 466–7, 470, 478, 481
  social 30, 379–83, 384–97, 444
stakeholding, and democracy 505–6, 510, 518
state *see* nation-state
states system: end of 565–6, 575
  and international relations 94–5, 96, 151–2
  and new medievalism 199, 214–16, 488, 577–82
  and sovereignty 9, 61, 89, 151–2, 156, 204, 216, 365, 464, 565–6, 573–5
  and world government 488
Steans, Jill 422, 455–61
Steinmo, S. 404
Stiglitz, Joseph 78, 422, 477–81, 570
Stockholm Conference on the Environment 264, 470
Stopford, J. M. and Strange, S. 131, 307
Strachey, John 579
Strange, Susan 122, 127–33, 201, 203 n.34, 357, 565–6, 568, 574–5
stratification, global 71, 72, 138

structural adjustment programmes (SAPs) 5, 30, 174, 479, 570
subsidiarity 198, 518
Sun Yat-sen 276
supraterritoriality, globalization as 52, 85–8, 89, 94, 179
sustainability 424, 481
Swank, Duane 302, 395, 403–16

Tanzi, Vito 404
taxation: and location of production 389–90, 543
  and mobility of capital 13, 375–6, 381, 384–5, 388–90, 393–5, 396, 403–9, 415
  reforms 405–8
  regional and global 525
  and welfare state 28, 302, 387, 388
technology: and development 441, 444, 446
  military 130–1, 178, 180–1, 183, 185
  selective globalization 320–2, 324–5, 465–6
  *see also* information technology
territorialism, methodological 88–90, 94, 226–7
territory: and democracy 502, 503, 505, 506, 508, 517
  effects of globalization 7–8
  and globalization as supraterritoriality 52, 85–8, 89, 94, 179
  and localization of production 308–9, 311, 376
  and nation-state 9, 11, 32–3, 39, 63–4, 90, 116–17, 121, 137
  and national security 124, 178, 179–80, 184
  and sovereignty 64, 179, 180, 189, 204, 215, 223, 370, 520
  *see also* boundaries; localization
terrorism, transnational 107, 110–11, 214, 370, 467
  11 September attacks 1, 4, 23, 52, 53, 106, 113
Third World: and communication conglomerates 253
  differentiation 29
  and information and communication flows 250, 255
  marginalization 29, 30, 99, 300, 315–16, 466
  and multinationals 318
  and nation-states 180
  and regionalization 364
  *see also* inequality
Thompson, John B. 236, 246–57
Thucydides 148

TNCs *see* corporations, transnational
Tomlinson, John 236–7, 269–76
trade: and early globalization 57
  and economic growth 23, 444–6, 447–8,
    450–4, 466, 477, 561, 571
  'fair' 380
  and Fortress Europe 362, 364, 465
  growth and transformation in 312–14, 324,
    335, 351, 373
  and inter-national economy 100
  and international integration 84, 336, 380,
    384, 444–5
  intra-firm 316, 317–18
  regionalized 213, 312, 314–15, 466, 495
  regulation 19, 211, 228, 375, 468–9
  role in globalization 138, 141, 154–5,
    303–4, 311
  *see also* services, trade in
trade unions 456, 561
  and anti-globalization 41, 567, 571
  and macro-economic policy 393–5, 409–10,
    411–12
transgovernmentalism 124, 189–202
triadization 5, 20–1, 25, 38, 99, 174–5, 300
trilateralism, northern 138–9
TROs, and government networks 190–2

uncertainty, and globalism 79, 223, 224–5,
  291, 384, 389–90, 397
unemployment: and economic growth 29,
  426, 445, 478, 479
  long-term 432
  and macro-economic policy 403, 412, 414,
    415
UNESCO, and information flows 250
unilateralism, US 52, 111, 112, 229
United Nations Development Programme 477
  Human Development Reports 323, 421,
    423–9, 434, 436, 473 n.15, 508, 549
United Nations (UN): and accountability
  194, 563
  Charter 173, 493
  Decade for Women 458–61
  and election monitoring 210
  General Assembly 133, 169, 209, 472, 490,
    543
  Human Development Index 433–4
  and human rights 167–8, 205, 423, 543
  International Covenant on Civil and
    Political Rights 168–9
  and international intervention 209–10,
    491–3, 543

International Labour Organization 168,
  431, 436, 510, 556 n.6
  and legitimacy 296, 526, 544
  and minority group rights 169
  and natural resources 170–1
  peace-keeping role 491–3, 498, 543
  powers 109, 110
  and regulation 197, 228
  Security Council 121, 168, 209, 471, 472,
    490–1, 492, 543–4
  and transnational democracy 543
  Universal Declaration of Human Rights
    167–8, 423, 543, 544, 557 n.23
  *see also* governance, global
universalization, globalization as 84–5, 88,
  138, 142, 145, 423
USA: and bilateralism 155, 364, 469
  and Cold War 147–8, 185, 491
  and creation of globalization 53, 85, 108,
    112–14, 148, 326
  and cultural hegemony 108, 110, 113, 241,
    254–5, 265–6, 270
  and direct foreign investment 317, 318,
    345, 351
  and economic regulation 109–10, 194, 197,
    354–7
  and environmental issues 206, 566, 574
  and free trade 315, 351
  and global governance 22, 31, 53, 109–10,
    117–19, 201–2, 208, 228–9, 469, 471, 491
  as hegemon 112, 152, 201, 229, 315, 326,
    363, 366–8, 464, 470, 478, 491, 542
  inequalities in 382, 431, 432, 434
  and the Internet 114
  and media 254–5, 260–3
  and national economy 140, 141–2, 147–8,
    327, 430
  and national interest 109, 143, 148, 173–4,
    326, 574
  and 'New World Order' 464
  and regional governance 219
  and sovereignty 149, 151
  state structure 219
  as superpower 140, 144, 147, 180
  and taxation 396, 406–7
  and unilateralism 52, 111, 112, 229, 469,
    578–9
  and war against terrorism 111
  and WTO 495, 510, 567
  *see also* North American Free Trade
    Agreement; 11 September terrorist
    attacks; triadization

values, global 497–8, 509, 514–15
Väyrynen, Raimo 226
velocity of global flows 52, 67–8, 69, 79–80,
    82, 139, 235, 312
violence: state 9–10, 63, 64, 124, 137, 166,
    183–6, 507, 560
    transnationalization 12–13, 178
    see also terrorism, transnational; war

Wade, R. 140, 421
Walker, Rob 95, 502
Wallerstein, Immanuel 61–2, 311
Wallerstein, M. and Przeworski, A. 404
Waltz, Kenneth N. 148, 154, 160 n.33
Walzer, M. 509
war: civil 81, 107, 152, 157, 428, 464
    and effects of technological change 130–1,
        178
    and globalization 107, 110
    and Hobbes's dilemma 122–3, 149–50,
        156
    and identity politics 274
    and post-militarism 144
    privatization 183
    reluctance of states to engage in 177
    and rules of warfare 164–5, 167, 173
    war crimes 165–7, 173, 493, 543
Washington Consensus 5, 414, 446, 478, 480,
    570
Washington, George 578–9
Waters, Malcolm 94
weapons: of mass destruction (WMD) 106,
    107, 113, 144, 179, 184–5
    regulations on use 165
Weber, Max 52, 94, 96, 108, 282
welfare state: early 373–4
    economic effects 387–8
    effects of capital mobility 13, 301–2,
        375–6, 381, 388–9, 403–16
    effects of globalization 23, 28, 135, 196,
        299, 327, 353, 561, 566
    and social exclusion 432
    and trade 380–1, 387
    see also social democracy
Wendt, Alexander 153
westernization, globalization as 85, 269–70,
    272

Westphalia Treaties (1648): and society of
    states 9–10, 39, 162
    see also medievalism; states system
Wight, Martin 149, 151–2, 159 n.25
Williamson, Jeffrey 382
Wilson, Woodrow 500
Winchester, Simon 240
Wolf, Martin 421–2
women, role 455–61, 489, 498
Woods, Ngaire 422, 463–72
World Bank: and accountability 108, 191,
    194, 210, 233
    failure 477–8, 479, 480
    and global bonds 345
    and global capital 5, 27, 30–1, 138, 327, 570
    and inequality 422, 436, 440, 441, 443–5
    and the nation-state 199, 210, 494
    and structural adjustment 5, 30, 174
    and USA 112, 194
World Economic Forum 233
World Intellectual Property Organisation 198
World Trade Organization (WTO): and
    accountability 108, 195, 233, 510, 563
    and free trade 101, 138, 315, 376, 380,
        445–6, 565
    and geopolitical interests 174
    and global capital 27, 195
    and inequality 422, 423, 453, 479–80, 562
    and nation-states 264, 423, 445–6, 494, 509
    and production chains 307
    protests against 82, 232, 487, 495, 564, 567,
        571
    and regional bodies 22
    and regulation 19, 211, 228, 375, 469
World Values Surveys 42, 290–4
world-system theory 1, 2, 61–2
Wriston, Walter 208
WTO see World Trade Organization

Yergin, Daniel and Stanislaw, Joseph 349
Yugoslavia: and ethnic conflict 227, 244, 274,
    365, 464, 498
    and international intervention 107, 490,
        492–3, 548
    and war crimes 166

Zacher, Mark 223

Learning Resources
Centre